Model
Subdivision Regulations

Planning and Law

Model Subdivision Regulations

Planning and Law

A Complete Ordinance and Annotated Guide to
Planning Practice and Legal Requirements

Robert H. Freilich
and
Michael M. Shultz

PLANNERS PRESS
AMERICAN PLANNING ASSOCIATION
Chicago, Illinois   Washington, D.C.

Second edition

Copyright 1995 by the American Planning Association
1313 E. 60th St., Chicago, IL 60637
ISBN (paperback edition): 0-918286-87-5
ISBN (hardbound edition): 0-918286-88-3
Library of Congress Catalog Number 93-71516

First edition published as *Model Subdivision Regulations: Text and Commentary*,
© 1975 by the American Society of Planning Officials.

Contents

About the Authors

Robert H. Freilich, AICP, is a partner in the law and planning firm of Freilich, Leitner & Carlisle (Kansas City, Missouri) and Freilich, Kaufman, Fox & Sohagi (Los Angeles, California). The firm represents more than 80 major cities, counties, and states nationwide in every aspect of land use planning, regulation, and litigation.

Professor Freilich is professor of law at the University of Missouri-Kansas City School of Law. He was visiting professor of law at the Harvard Law School during the 1984-85 academic year, and at the London School of Economics and Reading University, England, for the 1974-75 academic year.

Professor Freilich is a graduate of the University of Chicago (A.B.) and holds the LL.B. degree from Yale Law School, and LL.M. and J.S.D. degrees from Columbia University School of Law as John Jay Fellow. Professor Freilich is Editor of *The Urban Lawyer*, the national quarterly journal on urban law of the American Bar Association, Section of Urban, State and Local Government Law. He is the chair-elect of the Planning and Law Division of the American Planning Association; director of the Annual Planning and Zoning Institute; and vice chairman of the advisory board of the Municipal Legal Studies Center of the Southwestern Legal Foundation. He is also chairman of the Publications Committee of the National Institute of Municipal Law Officers/State and Local Law Center, a member of the advisory board of the *Land Use and Environment Law Review*, the board of directors of the Rocky Mountain Land Use Institute, and the American College of Real Estate Lawyers.

Professor Freilich is the author of "Cases and Materials on Land Use" (West 1994) with Callies and Roberts; "State and Local Government Debt Financing" (Callaghan 1993) (with Gelfand, Editor); "Takings After Lucas: Growth Management, Planning and Regulation Implementation Will Work Better Than Before," in *After Lucas: Land Use Regulation and the Taking of Property Without Compensation* (ABA 1993, David Callies, Editor) with Garvin; "Transportation Congestion and Growth Management: Comprehensive Approaches to Resolving America's Major Quality of Life Crisis" (*Loyola Law Review* 1991) with White; "Municipal Strategies For Imposing Valid Development Exactions: Responding to *Nollan* (*Zoning & Planning Law Report* 1987) with Morgan; "Public-Private Partnerships in Joint Development: The Legal and Financial Anatomy of Large-Scale Urban Development Projects" (*Municipal Finance Journal* 1986) with Nichols; "Solving

The Taking Equation" (15 *Urban Lawyer* 1983); "The Sword and Shield: Section 1983 Liability of State and Local Government of the Civil Rights Act" (American Bar Association 1983) with Carlisle; "The Land Use Awakening—Zoning Law in the 70's" (American Bar Association 1981) with Stuhler; and "Model Regulations for Land Subdivision" (American Planning Association 1976) with Levi.

In July 1984, Federal Judge Scott O. Wright of the United States District Court for the Western District of Missouri appointed Professor Freilich to serve as special master in *United States of America v. Conservation Chemical Company*, one of the largest and most complex environmental hazardous waste cases in the country.

Professor Freilich was the counsel in *Golden v. Planning Board of the Town of Ramapo* in the New York Court of Appeals and U.S. Supreme Court, the leading case establishing the constitutionality of growth management in the United States.

He has appeared as appellate counsel in more than 100 land use and municipal cases in state and federal courts of appeal and supreme court, and has been an expert planning and law witness in many of the nation's most complex land use litigation matters.

Professor Freilich has been at the forefront of zoning and subdivision law, development of growth management plans of state and local governments, and financing of infrastructure and public-private development law. The following is a sampling of the more than 80 counties, cities, and states represented by Professor Freilich:

- Pierce, Snohomish, and Thurston counties, Washington, on development of countywide planning policies.
- King County (Seattle), Washington, and Lexington-Fayette County, Kentucky, on preservation of river valleys and agricultural lands.
- Metropolitan Seattle—consultant on transportation corridors, rail transit, and economic development corridors.
- Metropolitan Council, Minneapolis-St. Paul—principal consultant on establishment and update of development framework.
- State of Hawaii—consultant on revision of state land use system; consultant, Maui, Hawaii, and Honolulu counties.
- Hilton Head and Kaiawah islands, South Carolina, on preparation of growth management, transportation congestion management, and wetlands protection ordinances.
- State of New Jersey, principal consultant for the state development and redevelopment plan.
- State of California, principal consultant on the Governor's Growth Management Strategy.
- State of Florida, principal consultant on development of state transportation corridors and joint development legislation.

- Montgomery County, Maryland, transportation congestion management program and arterial highway impact fees.
- Houston, Richardson, Arlington, Plano, and Fort Worth, Texas, on capital facility impact fees.
- Dallas (Texas) Area Rapid Transit (DART) on financing and joint development program for station sites, and Dallas-Fort Worth on regional airport joint development plan.
- Bloomington, Minnesota, public-private development of Mall of America.
- Los Angeles, California, citywide transportation corridor and node system for development permit allocation system.
- Orange, Palm Beach, Sarasota, Monroe (Florida Keys), and Escambia counties, Florida; Gainesville, Hall, Columbus, Fulton and DeKalb counties, Georgia, on growth management, impact fees, concurrency, and adequate public facilities.
- San Diego, Oceanside, Riverside, and Ventura County, California, on growth management, impact fees, and intergovernmental cooperation.

Professor Freilich is a frequent speaker at the national meetings of the American Bar Association, American Law Institute, American Planning Association, the National Institute of Municipal Law Officers, and the National Association of Counties. He is often invited to appear before individual city, county, regional, and state organizations.

Michael M. Shultz is an attorney in Fort Collins, Colorado, specializing in land use law. Until recently, he was city attorney for the City of Loveland, Colorado. He was an associate professor of law at the University of Missouri-Kansas City School of Law and director of the school's master's in urban legal studies program. Professor Shultz taught courses in land use planning, state and local government, law and finance, property, and civil rights litigation. Professor Shultz has written and spoken extensively on the subject of subdivision control law. His primary research has focused on the problem of premature and antiquated subdivisions and the development of techniques for the readjustment of previously platted lands. Among Professor Shultz's publications are *The Premature Subdivision of Land in Colorado*, a monograph published by the Lincoln Institute of Land Policy; "Subdivision Improvement Agreements and Guarantees: A Primer," published by Washington University's School of Law; and "The Failure of Subdivision Control in the Western United States: A Blueprint for Local Government Action," published by the University of Utah College of Law.

The authors wish to thank Elizabeth Garvin, Associate, Freilich, Leitner & Carlisle, for her invaluable assistance in producing the second edition of *Model Subdivision Regulations*.

Foreword to Second Edition

Since the advent of the first publication of these regulations, major changes have occurred in the field of land use regulation. Many of these developments were chronicled a decade ago by Freilich & Stuhler in "The Land Use Awakening: Zoning Law in the 70's" (American Bar Association, 1981) relating to the advent of growth management, state and regional land use planning, exclusionary zoning, flexible zoning (TDRs, impact and performance zoning), environmental protection, historic preservation, the "taking" issue, civil rights liability, regional general welfare, as well as procedural reforms in standing, the quasi-judicial categorization of individual rezonings (Fasano Rule), and the development of model codes. All of these new developments, completely updated to 1994, have been integrated into this completely revised edition.

Major changes in the law of subdivision regulation have occurred in other crucial areas, primarily in the area of financing capital facilities generated by new development. See Callies, Freilich & Roberts, *Cases and Materials on Land Use* (West Publishing Co. 1994) (Chapter III—Hard Choices: Financing Infrastructure Through New Development). The decline of fiscal solvency of the federal government during the 1980s, accompanied by massive increases in the deficiencies of our existing capital facility infrastructure (see *Hard Choices, Summary Report of the National Infrastructure Study Prepared for the Joint Economic Committee of the Congress* (1984) and *Report of National Council on Public Works Improvements* (1987)), has occasioned dramatic new strategies and is the focus of the Clinton administration policies on infrastructure and environment. State and local governments have been required to halt the subsidization of growth at the urban fringe, increasingly to adopt user fees and impact fees to finance new growth-related facilities, while utilizing the general fund only to pay for services, operation, maintenance, and upgrading of deficient facilities serving existing development. The full extent of local government utilization of the spectrum of development regulatory charges—from facility benefit assessments, "supplementary" two-tier utility rates to impact fees—is fully explored in this new edition with a complete set of new capital financing provisions. It also includes all the significant judicial decisions of federal and state courts after the United States Supreme Court decision in *Lucas v. South Carolina Coastal Council* in 1992, together with an analysis of emerging new state statutes in the field.

The increasingly difficult problem of providing for affordable housing is highlighted in this new edition through new regulations and analysis of "linkage" fees, housing trust funds, and bonus/incentive regulatory provisions. Developer problems with the vesting of development rights (see Shultz, *Vested Property Rights in Colorado: The Legislature Rushes in Where . . .*, 66 Denver U.L. Rev. 1 (1988)) has been fully explored and new regulations developed, including analysis of the emerging statutes authorizing "development agreements," "vesting tentative maps," and "deemed approved" restrictions.

This book fully explores developer remedies, vastly expanded by the U.S. Supreme Court decision in *First English Evangelical Church v. County of Los Angeles* (1987), authorizing monetary compensation for regulatory takings, together with expansion of rights in areas of procedural and substantive due process.

On the public side of the ledger, this edition documents fully the continued growth and vitality of growth management systems since Professor Freilich's successful development and advocacy of the "Ramapo Plan" in *Golden v. Planning Board of the Town of Ramapo* (N.Y. Court of Appeals and U.S. Supreme Court) in 1972, establishing the constitutionality of timing and sequencing controls. The section on the utilization of adequate public facility and concurrency provisions is completely new, with exhaustive commentary on the advancement of growth management techniques.

Extensive analysis and updating of the regulations and commentary was undertaken in the broad area of assurance for completion and maintenance of improvements, particularly improvement agreements and guarantees. (*See*, Shultz and Kelly, *Subdivision Improvement Requirements and Guarantees: A Primer*, 28 J. Urb. Contemp. L. 3 (1985)) Finally, there is a new look at the old problem of dealing with the antiquated and premature subdivision in urban infill areas and rural fringe areas that prevents proper development of the community.

The authors believe that, as we enter the midpoint of the '90s, the use of these regulations will stimulate the effective implementation of modern planning goals, objectives, and strategies to deal with the nation's mounting crises in urban and existing neighborhood decline, environmental protection, energy shortfall, agricultural land loss, loss of viable economic development, and housing affordability. What the nation lacks is not the techniques and knowledge to solve our problems, but the state, regional, and local political will to apply the knowledge that we have, learning to adjust competing interests through effective dispute resolution and developing consensus around goals.

We are indebted to so many people that proper appreciation may not be afforded. To our wives for their constant support and encouragement; to the American Planning Association for its continued backing of the project and understanding in the light of inevitable delays—particularly to Frank So, Marya Morris, and Rodney Cobb for allowing much of this material to be presented and tested at APA conferences and institutes; to Professor Freilich's partners and associates who were so helpful in reviewing and preparing material for the project—particularly Martin Leitner, Terry Morgan, Mike Fry, and Mark White; to law clerks and student research assistants Sally Connet, David Boushek, Samantha Masters, and Carolyn Poulin; to Diana Hughes, H. Francy Smith, and Florence Severns for their outstanding and tireless secretarial assistance, without which this project would never have been completed. Special thanks go to Professors David Callies, Bruce Kramer, Eric Strauss, Tom Roberts, and David Gelfand for their help in discussion of critical materials. Additionally, our thanks and appreciation go to the Southwestern Legal Foundation Municipal Legal Studies Center and France McCoy; the University of Wisconsin and Phil Bennett; and Frank Schnidman, of the FAU/FIA Joint Center for Environmental and Urban Problems. Lastly, to Professor Freilich's former author, Peter S. Levi, who contributed so much to this entire endeavor in the first edition.

Robert H. Freilich
Michael M. Shultz
Spring 1995
Kansas City, Missouri

Excerpts from Foreword to First Edition (1974)

These Model Regulations for the Control of Land Subdivision are intended for use by municipalities and counties across the nation. They represent the result of a decade or more of work on model subdivision regulations in New York and Missouri, including the extensive handling of hundreds of subdivision plats both for municipalities and private developers, and each provision is the careful composite of relevant court decisions on subdivision regulation, practical experience, and pertinent standards for design and improvement published by national planning, engineering, landscape engineering, recreation, park, and other professional associations. Each textual provision is carefully documented and annotated and, in the belief of the authors, represents the soundest form of regulation which is likely to be upheld by the courts. The provisions are carefully keyed to the provisions of the Standard City Planning Enabling Act (SEPA), which has been widely adopted by most states as the form of its enabling act. Each attorney, engineer, planner, subdivider, or municipal official is advised to review carefully his or her own state's enabling act and interpretive judicial decisions for any provisions unique to that state, but, in general, these Regulations will prove useful under all state statutes. The Models have also been geared to operate as a municipal "special development" ordinance under the American Law Institute's *A Model Land Development Code* § 2-203, and meet the requirements of the *Code*. A special appendix has been provided which explains the treatment of subdivision regulation under the proposed *Model Land Development Code* should any state adopt the *Code* or its substantial equivalent in the near future.

A second feature of these regulations reflects the possibility of use of the regulations by large and small municipalities, including rural as well as urban locations. Provisions have been included for major and minor subdivision approval which will allow for the handling of both complex and simple land subdivision and splits. Similarly, provisions allow for variations in the type of administration which cities can use including: performance bonding or requirements for provision of improvements in lieu of bonding; optional provisions for "sectionalizing," "model homes," "sketch plat approval," and "preliminary subdivision approval," in addition to final approval; alternatives for mandatory dedications and money in lieu of land (including the *Associated Home Builders v. City of Walnut Creek* standards); and alternatives for street design, curbing, sewerage, or off-site drainage, depending on the size of the community, its urban or rural character, and the relationship to community planning. Wherever possible, references to other national model subdivision regulations (such as the 1952 HHFA regulations) are included to allow the municipality diversity in its selection of standards. It is most important, however, for each adopting authority to recognize that the uniqueness of these regulations lies in the uniformity and consistency of provisions from beginning to end. The adoption of alternative provisions should be weighed carefully to ensure that definitions, administration, and standards are in conformance and consistent with the other provisions. As far as the authors can determine, the regulations exhaustively treat all subjects concerning subdivision, including resubdivision, criminal and civil penalties, offers of dedication, variances, authority and purposes, definition of subdivision, evasion of loopholes in definitions, nonresidential subdivision, construction plans, escrows and completion, and building permits and certificates of occupancy, and the relationship of their issuance to subdivision activity.

We wish to make very clear, however, that this text is not a treatise on subdivision regulations. We do not purport to cover all cases in the field, and indeed such an effort would have obscured the basic text of the regulations themselves; rather, we have selected materials to highlight the purposes of the regulations. Beyond that, we refer any reader to the basic treatises on the subject. If we have omitted any areas of concern, it is not for lack of an exhaustive review of the practical experiences of the authors, the literature on the subject, and the relevant statutes and court decisions.

A further element in this text is the inclusion of forms for use by the planning commission, administrative staff, and counsel, which comprehensively cover the subject matter of the regulations and which should simplify, enormously, the task of administering the regulations. These forms include comprehensive checklists and should ensure that no procedural or substantive area of subdivision regulation will be overlooked.

The regulations, in an earlier form, were published in Volume 36 of the *Missouri Law Review*, Winter 1971, and gratitude is expressed to the *Law Review* for permission to reprint parts thereof. Substantial revision and updating of authority has been performed.

We hope that these regulations will be useful to the American people in bringing under control the processes of land utilization in America in accordance with more rational planning to preserve our priceless ecological resources.

Robert H. Freilich
Peter S. Levi
April 15, 1974
Kansas City, Missouri

The History of Subdivision Regulations

FOUR PERIODS OF CHANGING DEVELOPMENT

A new subdivision of land is not an isolated experience involving only the buyer and seller. The pattern of a subdivision becomes the pattern of a community, which in turn may influence the character of an entire city.[1] If growth is to be orderly and rational, control over land development must be exercised.

In the early part of this century, the line of urbanization moved westward, and land speculation represented a global fever.[2] Uncontrolled subdivision of land left many communities without adequate streets, water mains, or sewers. Governments often extended their facilities to many more people than the facilities were designed to serve. Urban areas became characterized by "sprawl," disorderly, chaotic growth, followed by depressed economic values.[3]

Today, subdivision regulations are a tool for fashioning development in defined ways and by prescribed methods, regulating the use of private land in the public interest.[4] But prior to 1928, the purpose behind subdivision regulations was to provide a more efficient method for selling land, permitting a seller to record a plat of land by dividing it into blocks and lots, laid out and sequentially numbered. During this first period of subdivision regulation, plats or maps of a subdivision showed the location of individual lots, public areas, and streets, and were recorded in the office of the county clerk or recorder of deeds. Sales of land could then be made by reference to this recorded plat, rather than by a more cumbersome description in metes and bounds. The platting of land reduced costs and prevented conflicting deeds. Uniformity was established in survey methods and boundary and monument descriptions.[5] Real property taxes became easier to assess and collect.

1

A second period of subdivision regulation commenced in 1928 when it was recognized officially that subdivision regulation could be used to control urban development, particularly through requirements for on-site subdivision improvements. The Standard City Planning Enabling Act (SPEA), published by the Department of Commerce, was offered in that year as a partial answer to the problems created by land speculation and premature subdivision. The SPEA shifted the concept of subdivision regulation away from a procedure exclusively for recording land to one providing a means to implement a comprehensive community plan. Emphasis on requiring internal improvements for the subdivision was added to the convenient method for transferring lots by plat reference. The new enabling act included provisions dealing with the "arrangement of streets in relation to other existing or planned streets and to the master plan, for adequate and convenient open spaces of traffic, utilities, access of fire fighting apparatus, recreation, light, and air, and for avoidance of congestion of population, including minimum width and area of lots."[6] Following state adoption of enabling acts patterned on the SPEA, decisions from state courts across the country indicated acceptance of the use of subdivision regulations as a substantive land use control device.[7]

The SPEA, however, did not gain uniform acceptance in state legislatures. In this area of land use regulation, states have tended to go their separate ways, adopting varied legislation representing each state's attempt to balance private property rights with the public's interest in regulating new development.[8]

This second period of subdivision regulation continued through World War II and was marked by the passage of state subdivision enabling acts influenced by the SPEA, "designed to enact comprehensive regulatory standards which would facilitate orderly future growth along preconceived lines; in short, a planned community growth."[9] Legislation of this period reveals the change in emphasis of subdivision regulation from merely a recording device designed "to provide a method for filing maps officially so that future conveyancing instruments refer to a parcel of real estate by lot numbers . . . and to set forth sound engineering standards for maps so filed so as to avoid surveying errors,"[10] to a tool to shape the growth of the entire community, but primarily emphasizing on-site subdivision improvements.[11]

After World War II, the concern in subdivision regulation shifted into a third phase. Communities felt the increasing demand that subdivision activity, particularly in the suburbs, was placing on inadequate municipal facilities and services located away from the site of the subdivision. Concern focused on the needs of new subdivision residents for public open space, parks and recreation facilities and adequate streets bordering the subdivision. Governments added new provisions to their subdivision regulations concerning the mandatory dedication of roads, parks, school sites, and open space.[12] New devices for collecting money in lieu of land dedication also were added to state acts and local regulations to develop schools and parks in the vicinity of the subdivision; the courts generally upheld these provisions.[13]

The new regulations, however, were hardly adequate to stem the tide of sprawl that typified urban America. Major governmental reports in the late 1960s and early 1970s emphasized the need to control urban sprawl as the number one priority in land use planning. The problems attendant to sprawl are numerous: wasteful and inefficient use of the land coupled with increased utility and municipal capital, maintenance and service costs, rising tax rates, environmental degradation, poor quality of services, and racial and socioeconomic exclusion.[14] The National Commission on Urban Problems (the Douglas Commission) was directed by the President to study the problems that urban areas were facing. The commission surveyed the problems of suburban development, urban sprawl, and premature subdivision. After two years of deliberation, five volumes of testimony, and 19 separate technical reports, the commission recommended to the President and Congress:

> At the metropolitan scale, the present techniques of development guidance have not effectively controlled the timing and location of development. Under traditional zoning, jurisdictions are theoretically called upon to determine in advance the sites needed for various types of development. . . . In doing so, however, they have continued to rely on techniques which were never designed as timing devices and which do not function well in controlling timing. The attempt to use large lot zoning, for example, to control timing has all too often resulted in scattered development on large lots, prematurely establishing the character of much later development—the very effect sought to be avoided. *New types of controls are needed if the basic metropolitan scale problems are to be solved.*[15]

In response to the increasing call for control of urban sprawl, new subdivision regulation techniques began to emerge that went far beyond regulating the design of the subdivision and its immediate impact on the community. Communities denied subdivision approval where development could cause serious off-site flooding, environmental degradation, or worsen the problem of inadequate off-site municipal facilities, such as roads and sewers.[16]

Ultimately, in the landmark decision of *Golden v. Planning Board of the Town of Ramapo*, the New York high court upheld the constitutionality of timing and sequential controls of residential subdivision activity for the life of a comprehensive plan (18 years).[17] This marked the emergence of growth management, a fourth phase of subdivision regulation in the 1970s. This new phase resulted in a linking of the police power controls of zoning with environmental and subdivision regulations to assure that development did not impose unreasonable negative impacts on the community.[18]

In the fourth period of subdivision regulation, subdivision controls were related to the external environment and the community's comprehensive plan.

Subdivision regulations were allowed to help pace the development of the community.[19]

The subdivision of land did not, however, present problems only for urban areas. The premature subdivision of land that plagued the eastern United States during the first period of subdivision development has also struck the Sunbelt states and many of the Rocky Mountain states.[20] The federal Office of Interstate Land Sales Registration (OILSR), which administers the registration requirements of the Interstate Land Sales Full Disclosure Act,[21] reported that more than nine million undeveloped lots were registered for sale or lease since the inception of the act. The vast majority of those lots are in a handful of states. Specifically, 61 percent of all subdivisions registered with the OILSR are found in five states, while 77 percent are located in 10 states.[22] Large scale lot-sale subdivisions, those with 1,000 or more acres, are similarly concentrated. For example, 17 counties in the United States have between 5 and 15 percent of their land area devoted to large lot-sale subdivisions. The majority of these counties are in Florida, Texas, California, Arizona, New Mexico, and Colorado.[23]

Not every subdivision registered with the OILSR, however, is a premature subdivision—one created before any immediately foreseeable need for building activity. For example, Rio Rancho, New Mexico, has three new homes completed every day and 216 new residents every month.[24] It also is true, however, that there is little building activity in many of the registered subdivisions. One subdivision near El Paso, Texas, contains over 85,000 acres and has been subdivided into 150,000 lots.[25] Less than 800 of those lots contain homes, leaving more than 99 percent of the subdivision undeveloped.[26]

The most fundamental consequence of the premature subdivision of land is the premature commitment of the land to residential development. Premature subdivision reserves a tract of real property for residences before any need for building exists. Thus, the location, layout, and density of the subdivision is established long before any substantial building occurs. By the time that a need to build exists, the subdivision may be obsolete because the design standards used at the time of platting are no longer considered appropriate.[27] Premature subdivision also contributes to environmental degradation. Even when there is no building within a subdivision, the clearing and grading of land may have substantial impact on the natural environment, contributing to erosion and drainage problems.[28] Environmental consequences increase dramatically when building occurs. Often, premature subdivisions lack central water and wastewater treatment systems. Individual lot purchasers must drill wells and install septic tanks or other individual sewage disposal systems. These systems may pollute wells within the subdivision and contribute to pollution of neighboring streams and lakes.

During the fourth phase of subdivision regulation, many local governments adopted provisions that brought unregulated subdivision activity to a halt.[29] As a result, the challenge for these governments now is to deal with subdivisions created before substantive regulations were in place.[30] Some local governments have failed, however, to deal with premature subdivision,[31] and they undoubtedly will have to confront the problems at some point in the future.

Planning commissions and legislative bodies have assumed the responsibility for protecting the public and future owners and occupants of property in a subdivision by imposing reasonable conditions on development.[32] These conditions are designed to mitigate the impact of development on the entire community as well as to assure quality development within the subdivision itself. As early as 1952, a subdivision application was denied on the grounds that no adequate water supply was provided for the residents.[33]

Today, several other conditions are considered before subdivision approval is granted. A prime example is imposing restrictions to control development in areas where replacing natural vegetation—which would normally absorb rain runoff—with artificial concrete, asphalt, and steel construction would lead to increased flooding problems. Planning boards have been given authority under some statutes to require "that the land shown on such plats be of such a character that it can be used safely for building purposes without danger to health or peril from fire, flood, or other menace."[34] This should help prevent the alteration of natural streams by residential and commercial building, which would lead to increased flooding damage from smaller amounts of rainfall.

Courts also have upheld the denial of subdivision approval when off-site roads leading to the subdivision site are inadequate in surface and width to handle the volume of traffic that would be generated by the proposed subdivision.[35] This is a new extension of the requirement that the subdivision's internal roads must be adequate and provide appropriate access to the lots.[36]

The potential for water pollution in off-site areas furnishes another justification for establishing stringent subdivision regulations. The New York Court of Appeals has held that the threat of pollution to local wells and to a community's entire water basin warranted the enactment of a zoning ordinance increasing lot sizes. That reduced the number of septic tanks, thereby decreasing the likelihood that effluent from the subdivision would seep into the community's water sources.[37] Similarly, to protect navigable waters from deterioration or degradation due to uncontrolled shoreland development, the Wisconsin Supreme Court upheld as constitutional and nonconfiscatory an ordinance preventing development that would alter the natural character of land within 1,000 feet of a navigable lake and within 300 feet of a navigable river. The court held that the public trust duty of the state to protect waters for navigation, as well as for fishing, recreation, and scenic beauty, justified the stringent development control.[38] The requirement that a developer contribute toward improvement of an off-site drainage basin was upheld by the New Jersey Supreme Court under a municipality's implied authority to require off-site improvements in the protection of the public interest.[39]

CURRENT REFINEMENTS

Whether subdivision control law has entered a fifth phase remains to be seen. To a great extent, most case law and statutory developments in the field have refined existing practices or doctrines. Still, one can point to several trends in land use control law generally, and subdivision control law in particular. The first important trend is to condition land use approvals, including subdivision approval, on the availability of adequate public services and facilities. Although local governments often have considered the impact that approval of a land use application would have on community services and facilities,[40] the better approach is to require local governments to make an affirmative finding that there are adequate community services and facilities.

A related trend is to impose a wide variety of impact fees on developers who create a need for or benefit from community services and facilities. The concept of making development pay its own way now goes beyond the mere dedication of parkland and school sites. It includes contribution to the cost of providing all publicly produced benefits—roads, police and fire services, medical services, water and sewer services, libraries, and more.[41]

A third trend in land use control law is to require consistency between specific land use decisions and the comprehensive or master plan for the community.[42] The consistency doctrine is not new by any means, but it increasingly is receiving judicial and statutory recognition. Even when consistency is not required as a per se rule, it may be persuasive when considering the reasonability of the government's action.

A fourth trend emerging in land use control law is the recognition that many land use decisions lack the characteristics of legislative action and are better characterized as administrative or quasi-judicial actions.[43] Given the real character of many land use approval processes, including subdivision control, the courts have held that applicants for approval and neighbors of land that is the subject of a land use application have procedural due process rights.[44] Moreover, the courts will apply a stricter standard of review when a decision-making process is characterized as other than legislative.[45]

There also is an increasing emphasis on public-private joint ventures in real estate development.[46] Rather than government acting only as a regulator of development, it becomes involved in the development process, permitting the development of public facilities in conjunction with the commercial or residential structures being constructed. These joint ventures often result when the government is interested in acquiring property for a public use and the property owner proposes a project that will benefit both the government and the owner.[47]

The final trend that can be identified is a move to simplify the presently complex and time-consuming land use approval process.[48] Developers often must obtain discretionary approvals from federal, state, and local officials and may even need approval from a regional planning body. At the local government level, the developer may need to obtain a variety of approvals and permits.[49] This process takes time, is costly, and may often doom worthwhile projects. Related to this procedural complexity is the difficulty that a developer may have in demonstrating a vested right to finish a project once it has been commenced. Case law and state statutes appear to be developing sympathy for the property owner.[50]

None of these trends presently stands out as a major facet of land use control law that would allow one to identify a fifth phase of subdivision regulation. Each is important, however, and persons in the field should recognize these movements because they will have an impact on the manner in which the public and private sectors will operate in the foreseeable future.

This brief review of the history of subdivision regulation reveals the evolution of subdivision controls from a convenient mapping method to a complete process of community planning and protection. Subdivision development does more than create lots for sale or development, it establishes a virtually permanent pattern of community growth and leaves a legacy for future generations. Subdivision controls must be up to the challenge presented by the subdivision process.

GOALS AND PURPOSES OF THE MODEL REGULATIONS

The Model Regulations developed here and in the commentary will demonstrate how subdivision regulations can accomplish a community's goals and objectives. The general purpose here is to identify the problems concerning subdivision regulations nationally and to suggest various solutions to these problems based on existing legislation. The Model Subdivision Regulations include traditional components of subdivision control, but they also include provisions designed to reflect developments in the law. Thus, there are dramatic changes from the original model drafted by Freilich and Levi. For the most part, these changes represent the evolution in land use control law generally. Moreover, no model ordinance is meant to be static. A model must keep abreast of state of art changes and incorporate those changes likely to be upheld by the courts, but be cautious in incorporating those changes that may create liability for the local government.

It must be emphasized that the Model is drafted without reference to any specific state statute. It always is necessary for local governments that lack home rule authority to identify statutory authority—whether express or implied—for the adoption of specific control techniques. Although the model is drafted with a municipal government in mind, the regulations are equally suitable for adoption by county governments.

The text following each article of the Model explores the rationale for various control techniques. This rationale often is based on a general view of existing statutory authority, case law, increasingly complex federal constitutional requirements,[51] and the need to reconcile the competing interests of property owners who wish to develop their properties with the interests of other members of the community who will be impacted by that development. The text identifies changes from the original model and explains the reason for the change. One should not be misled into believing, however, that there is one set of control techniques optimally suited for all governments. Often, the decision to choose one technique over another is somewhat arbitrary. What is important is that the control techniques embodied in the subdivision regulation ordinance be consistent with one another and that there is some underlying logic that can justify the selection of one technique or procedure.

Finally, despite the obvious assumption of this book that subdivision controls carry the heaviest load in regulating the development of land, these controls are only one of many regulatory schemes imposed on real estate development. As a consequence, subdivision controls must be consistent and work with other land controls. When possible, control schemes should be merged so that the number of discrete land use approval processes can be reduced. Indeed, it has been suggested that local governments adopt a unified development ordinance. Although there is merit to providing "one stop shopping" for developers, most local governments continue to enforce separate subdivision, zoning, building/ housing, and health regulations. Consequently, the model is based on the premise that subdivision control is a relatively discrete component of a government's overall system of development controls.

NOTES

1. N. WILLIAMS, JR., AMERICAN LAND PLANNING LAW 156.01 (1985).

2. Land speculation often resulted in economically depressing situations. One of the more famous personalities to fall victim to the rainbow of land speculation was Charles Dickens. In the 1840s, Dickens succumbed to the economic temptations of Cairo City, Illinois, located at the junction of the Mississippi and Ohio Rivers. He invested more than he could afford, not knowing that the prime land was generally submerged most of the year. His realization and bitterness prompted the novel MARTIN CHUZZLEWIT, which reflected Dickens's temperament following his visit to the United States in 1842. Dickens's comment following this trip is a summation of the results of premature land speculations: "A dismal swamp on which the half-built houses rot away; cleared here and there for the space of a few yards, and teeming with rank unwholesome vegetation, in whose baleful shade the wretched wanderers who are tempted hither, droop and die, and lay their bones; the hateful Mississippi circling and eddying before it, and off upon its southern course, a shiny monster hideous to behold; a hotbed of disease, an ugly sepulchre, a grave uncheered by any gleam of promise; a place without one single quality, in earth or air or water, to commend it, such is this dismal Cairo." *See* E. RACHLIS & J. MARQUSEE, THE LANDLORDS 37-40 (1973).

3. Speculation brought orators of unusual distinction to the American scene. One of the most exotic stories is about El Camino Real, a street 219 feet wide to accommodate 20 lanes, yet only one-half mile long, leading to the storied city of Boca Raton, Florida. High pressure sales (by orators no less famous than William Jennings Bryan) resulted in skyrocketing prices of the lots until the bottom dropped out during the infamous Florida land bust of the 1920s. The gimmick was "vision"—"Can you imagine a city not being there?"—and the result was pathos. *See* A. JOHNSTON, THE LEGENDARY MIZNERS

235, 238, 242, 272, 274, 276-7 (1953). The Interstate Land Sales Full Disclosure Act of 1968, 15 U.S.C. 1702 (1968), now requires that interstate sale of unimproved lots in subdivisions of 25 or more units be registered with the U.S. Secretary of Housing and Urban Development and a detailed "report" of the land be made available to prospective purchasers of lots.

Other federal acts offering consumer protection in real estate transactions involving subdivision lot sales are: The Truth in Lending Act, 15 U.S.C.A. §§ 1601 *et seq.* (including Regulation Z, 12 C.F.R. §§ 226 *et seq.*, the administrative guidelines for the act); The Federal Trade Commission Act, 15 U.S.C.A. §§ 41 *et seq.* (under the act the FTC, upon complaint and hearing, may issue a cease and desist order to a land subdivider misrepresenting the product); and The Postal Reorganization Act, 39 U.S.C.A. § 3005 (providing for criminal prosecutions of persons conducting schemes or devices for obtaining money or property through the mails by use of false or fraudulent pretenses, representations, or promises). *See* CALLIES & FREILICH, CASES AND MATERIALS ON LAND USE, 402 (West 1986 & Supp. 1988). Similarly, states have enacted Blue Sky laws made applicable to land subdivision sales (Florida Realty Inc. v. Kirkpatrick, 509 S.W.2d 114 (Mo. Sup. 1974); have adopted the Uniform Consumer Credit Code (UCCC) providing disclosure protections and penalties UCCC § 5-203(1)(a); and there remains common law judicial protection through the erosion of the doctrine of caveat emptor by use of judicial theories of fraud, express and implied warranty, negligence, and strict liability to provide injunctive relief or compensation for the unwary home buyer. (*See, e.g.*, Foxcroft Townhome Owners Ass'n v. Hoffman Rossner Corp., 435 N.E.2d 210 (Ill. App. 1982); Crowder v. Vandendeale, 564 S.W.2d 879 (Mo. 1978).)

4. Marx v. Zoning Board of Appeals, 137 A.D.2d 333, 529 N.Y.S.2d 330 (App. Div. 2d Dept. 1988) "Subdivision control is aimed at protecting the community from an uneconomical development of land and assuring persons living in the area where the subdivision is sought that there will be adequate streets, sewers, water supply and other essential services."

5. *See* Gates, *History of Public Land Development*, 3 AMERICAN LAW OF PROPERTY 12.102 (A. Casner ed. 1952).

6. Standard City Planning Enabling Act 14 (1928) (hereinafter cited as "SPEA"). At this point a caveat should be mentioned. Just as the zoning requirement contained in the Standard Zoning Enabling Act (hereinafter cited as "SZEA") that zoning "be in accordance with a comprehensive plan" was never at first interpreted under these enabling acts to require that a master plan precede adoption of a zoning ordinance (Haar, *In Accordance With a Comprehensive Plan*, 68 HARV. L. REV. 1154 (1954)), it was generally held that a master plan is not required in order to adopt valid subdivision regulations. Nelson, *The Master Plan and Subdivision Control*, 16 ME. L. REV. 107 (1964).

Nevertheless, denial of subdivision approval may be based upon failure to comply with provisions of an adopted master plan. *See* Board of County Comm'rs v. Gaster, 401 A.2d 666 (Md. 1979) (although the subdivision plat met all zoning requirements, the county legislative body could properly disapprove the application because it failed to comply with the master plan's density provision and its projected impact on roads and school districts); Save Centennial Valley Ass'n v. Schultz, 284 N.W.2d 452 (S.D. 1979) (the approval of a subdivision in an agricultural area was ruled void by the court because the commission, in approving it, disregarded the clear interest of the comprehensive plan).

7. Typical of this was a 1938 decision of the New Jersey Supreme Court: "[I]t is essential to adequate planning that there be provision for future community needs reasonably to be anticipated. We are surrounded with the problems of planless growth. The baneful consequences of haphazard development are everywhere apparent, there are evils affecting the health, safety, and prosperity of our citizens that are well-nigh unsurmountable because of the prohibitive corrective cost. To challenge the power to give proper direction to community growth and development in the particulars mentioned is to deny the vitality of a principle that has brought men together in organized society for their mutual advantage. A sound economy to advance the selective in local affairs is the primary aim of local government." Mansfield & Swett, Inc. v. West Orange, 198 A. 225, 229 (N.J. 1938).

8. Note, *Analysis of Subdivision Control Legislation*," 28 IND. L.J. 544 (1952); M. ANDERSON & B. ROSWIG, PLANNING, ZONING, & SUBDIVISION: A SUMMARY OF STATUTORY LAW IN THE FIFTY STATES, 228 (1966) (Standard City Planning Enabling Act is reprinted in Appendix A). Two other model acts of the same vintage—Bassett & Williams's Municipal Planning Enabling Act

and Bettman's Municipal Subdivision Act—are reprinted in Bassett. BASSETT, WILLIAMS, BETTMAN & WHITTEN, MODEL LAWS FOR PLANNING CITIES, COUNTIES, AND STATES (1935).

9. Lake Intervale Homes, Inc. v. Parsippany-Troy Hills, 147 A.2d 28, 35 (N.J. 1958).

10. *Id.* at 33.

11. *See* Brous v. Smith, 106 N.E.2d 503 (N.Y. 1952) the leading case for establishing the validity of *on-site* requirements that a road giving access to the proposed structures be "suitably improved" before a building permit may be issued. Four problems with "on-site" regulations must be carefully addressed however:

(a) The requirements must be related to the health, safety, and general welfare of the subdivision itself. Unreasonable requirements external to needs created by the subdivision will be found to be unlawful action. Parks v. Watson, 716 F.2d 646 (9th Cir. 1983) (refusal of a city to vacate a street unless the developer dedicates wholly extraneous geothermal wells); New Jersey Builders Assn. v. Bernards Township, 511 A.2d 740 (N.J. Super. 1985) (relationship between the development and the need for improvements must be clear, direct, and substantial).

(b) The requirements must be expressly contained in the regulations. Southern Coop. Dev. Fund v. Driggers, 696 F.2d 1347 (11th Cir. 1983) (improper to deny plat approval on grounds not explicit in the subdivision regulations).

(c) "Oversized facilities" built by a developer should allow for proper equitable redistribution to other sharing developments through reimbursement techniques. *See* D. HAGMAN & D. MISCYNSKI, WINDFALLS FOR WIPEOUTS (1978).

(d) Excessive on-site requirements should be scrutinized to avoid unnecessary inflation of housing costs. *See* R. BURCHELL & D. LISTOKIN, THE IMPACT OF LOCAL GOVERNMENT REGULATIONS ON HOUSING COSTS, AMERICA'S HOUSING PROSPECTS AND PROBLEMS (Rutgers University, Center for Urban Policy Research, 1980); LISTOKIN & WALKER, THE SUBDIVISION AND SITE PLAN HANDBOOK ORDINANCE (Rutgers University Center For Urban Policy Research, 1989).

12. *See* Heyman & Gilhool, *The Constitutionality of Imposing Increased Community Costs on New Suburban Residents Through Subdivision Exactions*, 73 YALE L.J. 1119, 1121 (1964); Ayres v. City of Los Angeles, 338 P.2d 498 (Cal. 1949) (dedication of perimeter streets bordering subdivision); Rosen v. Village of Downers Grove, 167 N.E.2d 230 (Ill. 1960) (dedication of public

school site). Kamhi v. Yorktown, 547 N.E.2d 346 (N.Y. 1989); River Birch Assoc. v. Raleigh, 388 S.E.2d 538 (N.C. 1990); Nunziato v. Planning Bd. of Edgewater, 541 A.2d 1105 (N.J. Super. 1988); Sudarsky v. City of New York, 779 F. Supp. 287 (S.D.N.Y. 1991).

13. Coulter v. City of Rawlins, 662 P.2d 888 (Wyo. 1983); Krughoff v. City of Naperville, 354 N.E.2d 480 (Ill. App. Ct. 1976); City of College Station v. Turtle Rock Corp., 680 S.W.2d 802 (Tex. 1984); Black v. City of Waukesha, 371 N.W.2d 389 (Wis. Ct. App. 1985). Jenad, Inc. v. Village of Scarsdale, 218 N.E.2d 673 (N.Y. 1966); Associated Home Builders v. Walnut Creek, Inc., 484 P.2d 606 (Cal. 1971). *See generally*, Smith, *From Subdivision Improvement Requirements to Community Benefit Assessments and Linkage Payments: A Brief History of Land Development Exactions*, 50 L. & CONTEMP. PROBS. 5, 14 (Winter 1987).

14. *See* National Commission on Urban Problems (Douglas Commission), "Alternatives to Urban Sprawl," at 45, Research Report No. 15 (1968); New York State Planning Law Revision Study Document No. 4 (Feb. 1970) (see proposed Land Use and Development Planning Law 2-106, Feb. 1970); American Law Institute, "A Model Land Development Code," Tent. Draft No. 1 2-101, 2-201, 2-206, (1970); F. Bair, *Toward a Regulatory System for Use, Development, Occupancy, and Construction* (Planning Advisory Service Report No. 243) (1969).

15. National Commission on Urban Problems (Douglas Commission), "Building the American City," 245 (1968) (emphasis added).

16. Eschette v. City of New Orleans, 245 So.2d 383 (La. 1971) (drainage); Pearson Kent Corp. v. Bear, 271 N.E.2d 218 (N.Y. 1971) (inadequate off-site roads); Salamar Builders, Inc. v. Tuttle, 29 N.Y.2d 221, 275 N.E.2d 585 (1971) (environmental protection of off-site water resources); Rouse/Chamberlain, Inc. v. Board of Supervisors, 504 A.2d 375 (Pa. Commw. Ct. 1986) (ecological considerations); Canter v. Planning Bd., 390 N.E.2d 1128 (Mass. App. Ct. 1979) (streets and stormwater drainage); Hrenchuk v. Planning Bd., 397 N.E.2d 1292 (Mass. App. Ct. 1979) (inadequate street access); North Landers Corp. v. Planning Bd., 400 N.E.2d 273 (Mass. App. Ct. 1980) (inadequate off-site roads); Wright Dev., Inc. v. City of Wellsville, 608 P.2d 232 (Utah 1980) (water mains); Land County v. Oregon Bldgs. Inc., 606 P.2d 676 (Ore. Ct. App. 1980) (sidewalks); Garipay v. Town of Hanover, 351 A.2d 64 (N.H. 1976) (inadequate access via

off-site roads); Just v. Marinette County, 201 N.W.2d 761 (Wis. 1972) (shoreland zoning). *See generally* N. WILLIAMS, AMERICAN LAND PLANNING LAW 156.04-156.05 (1985).

17. Golden v. Planning Bd. of Town of Ramapo, 285 N.E.2d 291 (N.Y. 1972).

18. Freilich, *Golden v. Town of Ramapo, Establishing a New Dimension in American Planning Law*, 4 URB. LAW. ix (Summer 1972). *See also* L. BURROWS, GROWTH MANAGEMENT: ISSUES, TECHNIQUES, & POLICY IMPLICATIONS, 59 (1978). Prevention of deterioration or over-burdening of the infrastructure is the primary rationale for the use of sequential timing as a legitimate exercise of the police power. Contractors & Builders' Ass'n v. City of Dunedin, 329 So.2d 314 (Fla. 1976); Coulter v. City of Rawlins, 662 P.2d 888 (Wyo. 1983); Hollywood, Inc. v. Broward County, 431 So.2d 606 (Fla. Dist. Ct. App. 1983).

19. In Golden v. Planning Bd. of Town of Ramapo, 285 N.E.2d 291 (N.Y. 1972), a zoning ordinance was upheld whereby developers would not be permitted to subdivide and develop their land for periods of up to 18 years until the town completed scheduled capital improvements necessary to assure the adequacy of public facilities for subdivision residents. The court held that if a comprehensive plan is reasonable and not exclusionary, there is no reason why it should not be time-related. *See also* Diversified Properties, Inc. v. Town of Hopkinton Planning Bd., 480 A.2d 194 (N.H. 1984); *but see* Robinson v. City of Boulder, 547 P.2d 228 (Colo. 1976) (en banc) (authorizing timing controls through subdivision regulation but not through extraterritorial utility extension). *See generally* CALLIES, FREILICH & ROBERTS, CASES AND MATERIALS ON LAND USE (West 1994).

20. Many of the states experiencing the greatest population increases from 1970 to 1980 were in the western United States. For example, Colorado's population increased 30.7 percent, Wyoming's 41.6 percent, Arizona's 53.1 percent and Nevada's 83.5 percent. *See* R. ELLICKSON & H. TARLOCK, LAND-USE CONTROLS figure 1-2, at 8 (1981).

21. 15 U.S.C. § 1704 (1982).

22. Consequently, unless the developer is eligible for an exemption, *see* 15 U.S.C. § 1702 (1982), it must satisfy complex and comprehensive registration and disclosure requirements. Specifically, it is unlawful for a developer to sell or lease a lot in a subdivision unless a statement of record is in effect, thereby registering the land

with HUD and the purchaser or lessee has received a property report. *Id.* at 1703(a); 24 C.F.R. § 1700.1 (1987). Failure to comply with the property report requirement enables the purchaser or lessee to revoke the contract within two years from the date of signing. 15 U.S.C. § 1703(c) (1982). While the statute appears to require two separate documents—a statement of record and property report, the regulations have made the property report a part of the statement of record, thereby combining the two documents. 24 C.F.R. § 1710.100(a) (1987). For the information that a developer must include in the statement of record and property report, *see id.* at 1705; 24 C.F.R. §§ 1710.20, .101-.219 (1987). *See also* P. BARRON, FEDERAL REGULATION OF REAL ESTATE, para. 3.02[5], at 3-24 to 3-25 (rev. ed. 1980). For the procedure for filing a statement of record or amendments, *see* 15 U.S.C. 1706 (1982); 24 C.F.R. 1710.20, .23 (1987). *See also* Barron, para. 3.02[5][c], at 3-25 to 3-28. For a discussion of the two-year rescission remedy, *see* Peretz, *Rescission Under the Interstate Land Sales Full Disclosure Act*, 58 FLA. B.J. 297 (1984).

23. Stroud, *The Magnitude of Large Lot-Sales Subdivisions in the United States*, 3 THE PLATTED LANDS PRESS: A JOURNAL OF LAND READJUSTMENT STUDIES 1, 2 (Jan. 1986). As Stroud notes, "[i]f all HUD listings are included, the total exceeds 19,000 interstate land sales operations in the United States with over 700 subdivisions exceeding 1,000 acres in size." *Id.*

24. Carrier, "Boomtown Rises from Desert Scam," The Denver Post, Mar. 22, 1987, at 1-A. Rio Rancho, which is located near Albuquerque, has a population of 25,000 residents and is the fastest growing city in New Mexico. *Id.* Originally a 91,000-acre subdivision, Rio Rancho residents voted to incorporate in 1981. *Id.* at 16-A. At that time over 75,000 lots had been sold. *Id.* The city, however, encompasses only 20,000 acres; consequently, more than "40,000 people still own 50,000 acres of essentially useless land" outside the city limits. *Id.* at 1-A.

25. *Id.* at 3.

26. *Id.* at 2.

27. Under the antifraud provisions of the Interstate Land Sales Full Disclosure Act, a developer or agent may not represent that the developer will provide roads, sewers, water, gas, electric service, or recreational amenities without stipulating in the contract for the provision of these amenities. 15 U.S.C. § 1703(2)(d). In addition, the statute prohibits the use of the property report for any promotional purposes before the effective date of the statement of record and then requires the use of the property report in its entirety. *Id.* at 1707(b). *See also* 24 C.F.R. § 1715.20 (1987) (sets forth list of promotional activities that constitute an unlawful sales practice); *id.* at 1715.25 (sets forth advertising representations that are regarded as misleading unless developer provides specific safeguards to guarantee the accuracy of the representation); *id.* at 1715.50 (requires the display of a disclaimer statement on all written material in connection with the sale of a lot for which a statement of record is in effect); *id.* at 1710.9, .12, .13 (requires contracts to contain safeguard provisions in order for the sale or lease of a lot in a subdivision to be exempt from the entire act or from the act's registration and disclosure paragraphs). For a discussion of unlawful and misleading sales practices, *see* Barron, *supra* note 22, para. 3.02[7] at 3-31 to 3-32.

28. The belief that economic salvation for an area will result from development is unrealistic. Residential development, under traditional revenue raising schemes, simply does not pay for the full cost of services provided to the new development. *See* Bird, *Environmental and Economic Impact of Rapid Growth on a Rural Area: Palm Coast*, 2 ENVTL. AFFAIRS 154, 157-58 (1972). For environmental impact of subdivision *see* Godorov v. Board of Comm'rs, 475 A.2d 964 (Pa. Commw. Ct. 1984).

29. Jordan v. Village of Menomenee Falls, 317 N.W.2d 442 (Wis. 1966) (dedication of land or fee-in-lieu for recreational purposes upheld); Norsco Enters. v. City of Fremont, 126 Cal. Rptr. 659 (Cal. Ct. App. 1976) (park fees as a condition of condo conversion upheld).

30. *See generally*, M. SHULTZ & J. GROY, THE PREMATURE SUBDIVISION OF LAND IN COLORADO (Lincoln Institute of Land Policy 1986).

31. The local government committee of the Colorado Bar Association is in the process of drafting state laws to address the problem of premature subdivision. Premäture subdivisions have been called the "sleeping giant" of Florida's growth management problems. Schnidman, *Resolving Platted Lands Problems: The Florida Experience*," 1 LAND ASSEMBLY & DEVELOPMENT 27 (1987).

32. Noble v. Chairman of Menahem Township, 219 A.2d 335, 340 (N.J. Super. Ct. App. Div. 1966); City of College Station v. Turtle Rock Corp., 680 S.W.2d 802 (Tex. 1984).

33. Shorb v. Barkley, 240 P.2d 337 (Cal. Dist. Ct. App. 1952).

34. Kessler v. Town of Shelter Island Planning Bd., 338 N.Y.S. 2d 778, 780 (App. Div. 1972). *See also* Durant v. Town of Dunbarton, 430 A.2d 140 (N.H. 1981); E. Grossman & Sons, Inc. v. Rocha, 272 A.2d 496 (R.I. 1977).

35. Diversified Properties, Inc. v. Town of Hopkinton Planning Bd., 480 A.2d 194 (N.H. 1984); Pearson Kent Corp. v. Bear, 271 N.E.2d 218 (N.Y. 1971); Smith v. Township Comm., 244 A.2d 145 (N.J. Super. Ct. App. Div. 1968); Isabelle v. Town of Newbury, 321 A.2d 570 (N.H. 1974); Traymore Assoc. v. Board of Supervisors, 357 A.2d 729 (Pa. Commw. Ct. 1976).

36. New Jersey Builders Ass'n v. Mayor, 511 A.2d 740 (N.J. Super. Ct. Law Div. 1985) (township's off-tract improvement ordinance would have been valid had a "clear, direct and substantial" relationship between the development and improvement been shown).

37. Salamar Builders, Inc. v. Tuttle, 275 N.E.2d 585 (N.Y. 1971).

38. Just v. Marinette County, 201 N.W.2d 761 (Wis. 1972); Salem v. Kenosha County, 204 N.W.2d 467 (Wis. 1973).

39. Divan Builders, Inc. v. Planning Bd., 334 A.2d 30 (N.J. 1975).

40. Ehrenberg v. City of Concord, 421 A.2d 128 (N.H. 1980); Szeles-Natale, Inc. v. Board of Comm'rs, 368 A.2d 1336 (Pa. Commw. Ct. 1977); Durant v. Town of Dunbarton, 430 A.2d 140 (N.H. 1981); Lake Intervale Homes, Inc. v. Township of Parsippany-Troy Hills, 147 A.2d 28 (N.J. 1958).

41. Banberry Dev. Corp. v. South Jordan City, 631 P.2d 899 (Utah 1981); Board of Education v. Surety Developers, Inc., 347 N.E.2d 149 (Ill. 1975); J.W. Jones Co. v. City of San Diego, 203 Cal. Rptr. 580 (Ct. App. 1984). *See* Freilich & Morgan, *Municipal Strategies for Imposing Valid Development Exactions: Responding to Nollan*, 10 ZONING & PLAN. L. REP. 169 (Dec. 1987).

42. Lampton v. Pinaire, 610 S.W. 2d 915 (Ky. Ct. App. 1981); J.W. Jones Co. v. City of San Diego, 203 Cal. Rptr. 580 (Ct. App. 1984).

43. Coffey v. Maryland Nat'l Capital Park & Planning Comm'n, 441 A.2d 1041 (Md. App. 1982); Board of County Comm'rs v. Gaster, 401 A.2d 666 (Md. App. 1979).

44. Ehrenberg v. City of Concord, 421 A.2d 128 (N.H. 1980); Bienz v. City of Dayton, 566 P.2d 904 (Ore. Ct. App. 1977); Patenaude v. Town of Meredith, 392 A.2d 582 (N.H. 1978); Southern Coop. Dev. Fund v. Driggers, 696 F.2d 1347 (11th Cir. 1983).

45. Weeks Restaurant Corp. v. City of Dover, 404 A.2d 294 (N.H. 1979); In re Great Waters of America, Inc., 435 A.2d 956 (Vt. 1981).

46. Miller v. City of Port Angeles, 691 P.2d 229 (Wash. Ct. App. 1984); Fasano v. Washington County Comm'n, 507 P.2d 23 (Ore. 1973).

47. *See* Freilich & Nichols, *Public-Private Partnership in Joint Development: The Legal and Financial Anatomy of Large Scale Urban Development Projects,* 7 Mun. Fin. J. 1 (Winter 1986); Freilich & Chinn, *Transportation Corridors: Shaping and Financing Urbanization Through Integration of Eminent Domain, Zoning and Growth Management Techniques,* 55 UMKC L. Rev. 153 (1987).

48. *See* Listokin & Walker, The Subdivision and Site Plan Handbook (Center for Urban Policy Research, Rutgers 1989).

49. In re Belgrade Shores, Inc., 371 A.2d 413 (Me. 1977) (environmental board permit); Hale v. First Nat'l Bank of Mt. Prospect, 372 N.E. 2d 959 (Ill. App. Ct. 1978) (approval of zoning board of appeals).

50. Howard County v. JJM, Inc., 482 A.2d 908 (Md. App. 1984); Norco Constr., Inc. v. King County, 649 P.2d 103 (Wash. 1982). State law in Pennsylvania grants the developer a vested right to develop his property according to an approved development plan, irrespective of any intervening zoning regulation. Pa. Stat. Ann. tit. 53, 10508(4) (Purdon Supp. 1987).

51. *See* Lucas v. South Carolina Coastal Council, 112 S. Ct. 2886 (1992); Yee v. City of Escondido, 112 S. Ct. 1522, 118 L. Ed. 2d 153 (1992); Nollan v. California Coastal Comm'n, 483 U.S. 825, 107 S. Ct. 3141, 97 L. Ed. 2d 677 (1987).

1

General Provisions

1.1 **Title.** These regulations shall officially be known, cited, and referred to as the Subdivision Regulations of _____ (name of municipality) (hereinafter "these regulations").

1.2 **Policy**

1. It is declared to be the policy of the municipality to consider the subdivision of land and the subsequent development of the subdivided plat as subject to the control of the municipality pursuant to the official master plan of the municipality for the orderly, planned, efficient, and economical development of the municipality.

2. Land to be subdivided shall be of such character that it can be used safely for building purposes without danger to health or peril from fire, flood, or other menace, and land shall not be subdivided until adequate public facilities and improvements exist and proper provision has been made for drainage, water, sewerage, and capital improvements such as schools, parks, recreational facilities, transportation facilities, and improvements.

3. The existing and proposed public improvements shall conform to and be properly related to the proposals shown in the Master Plan, Official Map, and the capital budget and program of the municipality, and it is intended that these regulations shall supplement and facilitate the enforcement of the provisions and standards contained in building and housing codes, zoning ordinances, the Master Plan, Official Map and land use plan, and the capital budget and program of the municipality.

4. Land that has been subdivided prior to the effective date of these regulations should, whenever possible, be brought within the scope of these regulations to further the purposes of regulation(s) identified in Section 1.3.

1.3   Purposes. These regulations are adopted for the following purposes:

1. To protect and provide for the public health, safety, and general welfare of the municipality.
2. To guide the future growth and development of the municipality in accordance with the Master Plan.
3. To provide for adequate light, air, and privacy, to secure safety from fire, flood, and other danger, and to prevent overcrowding of the land and undue congestion of population.
4. To protect the character and the social and economic stability of all parts of the municipality and to encourage the orderly and beneficial development of the community through appropriate growth management techniques assuring the timing and sequencing of development, promotion of infill development in existing neighborhoods and non-residential areas with adequate public facilities, to assure proper urban form and open space separation of urban areas, to protect environmentally critical areas and areas premature for urban development.
5. To protect and conserve the value of land throughout the municipality and the value of buildings and improvements upon the land, and to minimize the conflicts among the uses of land and buildings.
6. To guide public and private policy and action in order to provide adequate and efficient transportation, water, sewerage, schools, parks, playgrounds, recreation, and other public requirements and facilities.
7. To provide the most beneficial relationship between the uses of land and buildings and the circulation of traffic throughout the municipality, having particular regard to the avoidance of congestion in the streets and highways and the pedestrian traffic movements appropriate to the various uses of land and buildings, and to provide for the proper location and width of streets and building lines.
8. To establish reasonable standards of design and procedures for subdivisions and resubdivisions in order to further the orderly layout and use of land, and to ensure proper legal descriptions and monumenting of subdivided land.
9. To ensure that public facilities and services are available concurrent with development and will have a sufficient capacity to serve the proposed subdivision and that the community will be required to bear no more than its fair share of the cost of providing the facilities and services through requiring the developer to pay fees, furnish

land, or establish mitigation measures to ensure that the development provides its fair share of capital facilities needs generated by the development.

10. To prevent the pollution of air, streams, and ponds; to assure the adequacy of drainage facilities; to safeguard the water table, and to encourage the wise use and management of natural resources throughout the municipality in order to preserve the integrity, stability, and beauty of the community and the value of the land.

11. To preserve the natural beauty and topography of the municipality and to ensure appropriate development with regard to these natural features.

12. To provide for open spaces through the most efficient design and layout of the land, including the use of average density in providing for minimum width and area of lots, while preserving the density of development as established in the zoning ordinance of the municipality.

13. To ensure that land is subdivided only when subdivision is necessary to provide for uses of land for which market demand exists and which are in the public interest.

14. To remedy the problems associated with inappropriately subdivided lands, including premature subdivision, excess subdivision, partial or incomplete subdivision, scattered and low-grade subdivision.

1.4 Authority. The Planning Commission of _____ (name of municipality) (hereinafter "Planning Commission") is vested with the authority to review, approve, conditionally approve and disapprove applications for the subdivision of land, including sketch, preliminary, and final plats. The Planning Commission may grant variances from these regulations pursuant to the provisions of Section 1.12.

1.5 Jurisdiction

1. These regulations apply to all subdivision of land, as defined in Section 2.2 (_____), located within the corporate limits of the municipality or outside the corporate limits as provided by law.

2. No land may be subdivided through the use of any legal description other than with reference to a plat approved by the Planning Commission in accordance with these regulations.

3. The Planning Commission also shall have the authority to review and approve, conditionally approve or disapprove the sale, lease, or development of lands subdivided prior to or following the effective date of these regulations as follows:

   a. The plat of the subdivided land was recorded without the prior approval of the Planning Commission or the Governing Body whether or not prior approval was required at the time the land was subdivided and the plat contains contiguous lots in common ownership where one or more of the lots are undeveloped, whether the lots are owned by the original subdivider or an immediate or remote grantee from the original subdivider;

b. The plat of the subdivided land has been of record for more than five (5) years, was not approved after _____ (the effective date of these regulations) and contains contiguous lots in common ownership where one or more of the contiguous lots are undeveloped, whether the lots are owned by the original subdivider or an immediate or remote grantee from the original subdivider;

c. The plat has been of record for more than five (5) years, was approved after _____ (the effective date of these regulations) and contains contiguous lots in common ownership where one or more of the contiguous lots is undeveloped and one or more is nonconforming under the zoning ordinance, whether the lots are owned by the original subdivider or an immediate or remote grantee from the original subdivider;

d. The original subdivider or his successor failed to complete subdivision improvement requirements pursuant to a subdivision improvement agreement entered into when the plat for the subdivided land was approved and the plat contains contiguous lots in common ownership where one or more of the contiguous lots is undeveloped, whether the lots are owned by the original subdivider or an immediate or remote grantee from the original subdivider; except that this Section 1.5(3)(d) shall not apply if the municipality has obtained possession of sufficient funds from security provided by the subdivider with which to complete construction of improvements in the subdivision.

e. Whenever the jurisdiction of the Planning Commission extends to one of the situations described in Section 1.5 (3)(a)-(d), only the sale, lease, transfer, or development of an undeveloped lot or lots contiguous to a lot or lots in common ownership shall be subject to these regulations.

4. No land described in this Section 1.5 shall be subdivided or sold, leased, transferred or developed until each of the following conditions has occurred in accordance with these regulations:

a. The subdivider or his agent has submitted a conforming sketch plat of the subdivision to the Administrative Assistant for the Planning Commission; and

b. The subdivider or his agent has obtained approval of the sketch plat, a preliminary plat when required, and a final plat from the Planning Commission or the Governing Body; and

    c. The subdivider or his agent files the approved plats with the Clerk and Recorder for _____ (the county in which the municipality is located).

  5. No building permit or certificate of occupancy shall be issued for any parcel or plat of land created by subdivision after the effective date of, and not in substantial conformity with, the provisions of these subdivision regulations, and no excavation of land or construction of any public or private improvements shall take place or be commenced except in conformity with these regulations.

1.6   **Enactment.** In order that land may be subdivided in accordance with these purposes and policies, these subdivision regulations are hereby adopted and made effective as of _____ (the effective date of these regulations). All applications for subdivision approval, including final plats, pending on the effective date of these regulations shall be reviewed under these regulations except that these regulations will not apply if preliminary plat approval was obtained prior to the effective date of these regulations and the subdivider has constructed subdivision improvements prior to submission of the final plat as required by the municipality unless the Planning Commission determines on the record that application of these regulations is necessary to avoid a substantial risk of injury to public health, safety, and general welfare.

1.7   **Interpretation, Conflict, and Separability**

  1. *Interpretation.* In their interpretation and application, the provisions of these regulations shall be held to be the minimum requirements for the promotion of the public health, safety, and general welfare. These regulations shall be construed broadly to promote the purposes for which they are adopted.

    a. *Public Provisions.* These regulations are not intended to interfere with, abrogate, or annul any other ordinance, rule or regulation, statute, or other provision of law except as provided in these regulations. Where any provision of these regulations imposes restrictions different from those imposed by any other provision of these regulations or any other ordinance, rule or regulation, or other provision of law, the provision which is more restrictive or imposes higher standards shall control.

    b. *Private Provisions.* These regulations are not intended to abrogate any easement, covenant or any other private agreement or restriction, provided that where the provisions of these regulations are more restrictive or impose higher standards or regulations than such easement, covenant, or other private agreement or restriction, the requirements of these regulations shall govern. Where the provisions of the easement, covenant, or private agreement or restriction impose duties and obligations more restrictive or standards that are higher than the requirements of these regulations, or the determinations of the Planning Commission or the Governing Body in approving a subdivision or in enforcing these regulations, and the private provisions are not inconsistent with these regulations or the determinations made under these regulations, then the private provisions shall be operative and supplemental to these regulations and the determinations made under the regulations.

3. *Separability.* If any part or provision of these regulations or the application of these regulations to any person or circumstances is adjudged invalid by any court of competent jurisdiction, the judgment shall be confined in its operation to the part, provision, or application directly involved in the controversy in which the judgment shall be rendered and it shall not affect or impair the validity of the remainder of these regulations or the application of them to other persons or circumstances. The Governing Body hereby declares that it would have enacted the remainder of these regulations even without any such part, provision, or application which is judged to be invalid.

1.8   **Saving Provision.** These regulations shall not be construed as abating any action now pending under, or by virtue of, prior existing subdivision regulations, or as discontinuing, abating, modifying, or altering any penalty accruing or about to accrue, or as affecting the liability of any person, firm, or corporation, or as waiving any right of the municipality under any section or provision existing at the time of adoption of these regulations, or as vacating or annulling any rights obtained by any person, firm, or corporation by lawful action of the municipality except as shall be expressly provided for in these regulations.

1.9   **Reservations and Repeals.** Upon the adoption of these regulations according to law, the Subdivision Regulations of _____(name of municipality) adopted _____ (date of enactment), as amended, are hereby repealed, except as to those sections expressly retained in these regulations.

1.10 **Amendments.** For the purpose of protecting the public health, safety, and general welfare, the Planning Commission may from time to time propose amendments to these regulations which shall then be approved or disapproved by the Governing Body at a public meeting following public notice.

1.11 Public Purpose. Regulation of the subdivision of land and the attachment of reasonable conditions to land subdivision is an exercise of valid police power delegated by the state to this municipality. The developer has the duty of compliance with reasonable conditions laid down by the Planning Commission for design, dedication, improvement, and restrictive use of the land to conform to the physical and economic development of the municipality and to the health, safety, and general welfare of the future lot owners in the subdivision and of the community at large.

1.12 Variances, Exceptions, and Waiver of Conditions

1. *General.* Where the Planning Commission finds that extraordinary hardships or practical difficulties may result from strict compliance with these regulations and/or the purposes of these regulations may be served to a greater extent by an alternative proposal, it may approve variances, exceptions, and waiver of conditions to these subdivision regulations so that substantial justice may be done and the public interest secured, provided that the variance, exception, or waiver conditions shall not have the effect of nullifying the intent and purpose of these regulations; and further provided the Planning Commission shall not approve variances, exceptions, and waiver of conditions unless it shall make findings based upon the evidence presented to it in each specific case that:
    a. The granting of the variance, exception, or waiver of conditions will not be detrimental to the public safety, health, or welfare or injurious to other property;
    b. The conditions upon which the request is based are unique to the property for which the relief is sought and are not applicable generally to other property;
    c. Because of the particular physical surroundings, shape, or topographical conditions of the specific property involved, a particular hardship to the owner would result, as distinguished from a mere inconvenience, if the strict letter of these regulations is carried out;
    d. The relief sought will not in any manner vary the provisions of the Zoning Ordinance, Master Plan, or Official Map, except that those documents may be amended in the manner prescribed by law.
2. *Conditions.* In approving variances, exceptions, or waivers of conditions, the Planning Commission may require such conditions as will, in its judgment, secure substantially the purposes described in Section 1.3.
3. *Procedures.* A petition for a variance, exception, or waiver of conditions shall be submitted in writing by the subdivider at the time when the preliminary plat is filed for the consideration of the Planning Commission. The petition shall state fully the grounds for the application and all of the facts relied upon by the petitioner.

1.13 Enforcement, Violations, and Penalties

1. *General*
   a. It shall be the duty of the Administrative Assistant to the Planning Commission to enforce these requirements and to bring to the attention of the Municipal Prosecuting Attorney or his designated agent any violations of these regulations.
   b. No owner, or agent of the owner, of any parcel of the land located in a proposed subdivision shall transfer or sell any part of the parcel before a final plat of the subdivision has been approved by the Planning Commission in accordance with the provisions of the regulations and filed with the Clerk and Recorder of _____ (county in which municipality is located).
   c. The subdivision of any lot or any parcel of land by the use of metes and bounds description for the purpose of sale, transfer, lease, or development is prohibited.
   d. No building permit shall be issued for the construction of any building or structure located on a lot or plat subdivided or sold in violation of the provisions of these regulations, nor shall the municipality have any obligation to issue certificates of occupancy or to extend utility services to any parcel created in violation of these regulations.
2. *Violations and Penalties.* Any person who violates any of these regulations shall be subject to a fine of not more than $_____, or imprisonment for a term not exceeding _____, or both, such fine and imprisonment pursuant to the provisions of Section_____ of the _____ statutes of the State of _____.
3. *Civil Enforcement.* Appropriate actions and proceedings may be taken in law or in equity to prevent any violation of these regulations, to prevent unlawful construction, to recover damages, to restrain, correct, or abate a violation and to prevent illegal occupancy of a building structure or premises. These remedies shall be in addition to the penalties described above.

COMMENTARY ON ARTICLE 1

Authority

The starting point for the adoption of any local regulatory ordinance is determining whether the local government possesses the necessary authority to adopt the ordinance.[1] Local governments possess no inherent power to regulate subdivision development and, lacking a state enabling statute, local regulation is void.[2] Even when enabling legislation exists, local authority is limited to the extent permitted by state law.[3] Although differences may exist in the political nature of cities and counties,[4] both governmental units possess only such powers delegated to them by the state legislature and those that are necessarily implied.[5] In addition, when a local government attempts to regulate subdivision development, it must enact its regulations pursuant to the proper state law and in the manner prescribed by that law.[6] Thus, a local government may not enact planning regulations to accomplish zoning purposes because state enabling statutes limit the purposes for which planning regulations can be used.[7]

When state statutes prescribe a procedure by which local governments exercise their power,[8] generally the local governments are not free to deviate from that procedure.[9] Thus, if state law permits the local government to accept a bond in lieu of completing subdivision improvements, the government may not require a cash escrow.[10] Likewise, if the law requires that the developer complete improvements or tender a performance bond prior to final plat approval, the local government cannot agree with the developer that it will install the improvements and assess the costs against the lots in the subdivision.[11] Finally, if state law permits the local government to require the developer to improve and dedicate a road within the subdivision, the government cannot require the developer to reserve a right-of-way for future use as a road.[12]

A local government possesses more than express statutory power—it also possesses powers that are necessarily implied to permit the government to accomplish the purposes of the state legislation. The courts vary in the breadth that they give to the notion of "necessarily implied" powers. Jurisdictions that continue to follow Dillon's Rule[13] construe local powers narrowly,[14] while other jurisdictions liberally construe municipal authority.[15] Thus, courts have upheld the authority to require a nonstatutory bond when the requirement assisted the developer in qualifying for government guaranteed financing.[16] Courts also have permitted local governments to require a cash deposit in addition to the statutorily required bond,[17] to require a maintenance bond guaranteeing against defects in the improvements,[18] and to require the payment of inspection fees.[19] Flexible regulations are helpful to the local government and the developer because subdivision regulations can be related more effectively to the needs of the particular type of development. Courts have upheld a system of classifying developments as being within the power of the local government to provide reasonable regulations for development.[20]

The authority for local government to impose various land use regulations may be found in a number of places. First, and most obviously, state enabling statutes often mandate that local governments exercise subdivision control authority.[21] Second, a state may have a general enabling statute that authorizes local government to exercise land use control powers.[22] Third, more general statutes that authorize regulation of matters of local importance, such as roads and streets, may be the basis for certain land use controls.[23] Fourth, local authority to operate municipal utilities may sustain certain land use regulations, including limitations on the extension of utilities as a growth control measure and connection fees.[24] Finally, a local government may have the necessary authority to adopt land use regulations pursuant to a general delegation of power to local governments to enact all laws necessary to protect public health, safety, welfare, and general morals.[25]

Home rule governments are in a different position than statutory governments—those that derive their powers from specific state statutes. In some states, a constitutional or statutory provision may authorize local governments to organize themselves under a charter form of government.[26] There are two basic views on home rule authority: first, that the provision authorizing home rule is a grant of authority and that local powers must be found within the terms of the grant and, second, that the provision acts only as a limit on local power and that local governments possess all powers that the state legislature lawfully may delegate to them.[27] Normally, home rule or charter governments possess greater authority to regulate land use than statutory governments.[28]

The Model Regulations often contain provisions that are not expressly authorized by most state subdivision control enabling legislation. Indeed, it is possible that some state courts would hold that certain provisions of the Model are not even impliedly authorized by state law. Still, one purpose of the Model is to suggest innovative methods for improving local subdivision control authority, and it must be kept in mind that not all of these methods may be upheld under the various state laws.

In addition to the limitations imposed by state law, a local government's power is limited by its own ordinances and regulations.[29] Local governments must base any decision to approve or disapprove a subdivision or to require certain improvements on factors that can be found in the local regulations,[30] and the reviewing authority cannot rely on facts not in the record when rendering its decision.[31]

Policy and Purposes

The statement of the policy and purposes behind subdivision regulations is extremely important.[32] If a court can appreciate the justification for local subdivision controls, it will be more willing to infer the necessary authority from the relevant statutes. Sections 1.2 and 1.3 of the Model indicate the underlying policy goals and the specific purposes for which the regulations are adopted. These purposes serve as a yardstick for the developer and the reviewing agency. Without these general guidelines and more precise standards found throughout the Model Regulations, a court could hold that a planning commission would be acting arbitrarily in denying approval of a plat.[33]

In states that are strict adherents to Dillon's Rule, the purposes and the standards of subdivision regulations will be narrowly construed.[34] In this respect it is important to distinguish older cases interpreting the old map acts from decisions decided after the Standard City Planning Enabling Act (SPEA) was prepared. An example of this is an 1890 Missouri case that established the principle that the power of a planning commission or other reviewing agency dealing with subdivision regulations is derived from the state enabling act and any condition for approval may be imposed only if it is authorized by the statute.[35] These early cases should be closely scrutinized before reliance is placed on such a strict statement of law. These cases were generally decided before modern concepts of planning and power to regulate for health, safety, and general welfare were introduced.[36]

A classic California case represents the more appropriate view that subdivision regulation is an exercise of the police power rather than an effort merely to regulate map or plat specifications.[37] In that case, the subdivider contended that the conditions imposed were not expressly provided for in the statute. The California Supreme Court held that conditions not expressly provided for, but which are not inconsistent with the statute and are reasonably required by the subdivision, are lawful. While many state courts have been rigid followers of Dillon's Rule, restricting the scope of local legislative initiative, a decision such as *Ayres* is consistent with the modern trend of decisions.

Subdivision control, therefore, becomes a tool of overall community planning, intended to avert community blight and deterioration by requiring that development proceed in a carefully specified way that is consistent with public health, safety, and welfare.[38]

Purposes

Because statutes that authorize municipal planning commissions to impose subdivision controls frequently do not articulate the purpose of control,[39] it is extremely important to articulate these purposes in the subdivision regulations and apprise the court that the purposes are in accord with the statutory objective of regulation. Section 1.3 of the Model Regulations (Purposes) delineates many objectives common to zoning ordinances, but identifies other objectives as well: the planning of new streets, utilities and improvements; the platting of new neighborhoods; the preservation of open space for essential public needs; the promotion of land values; the preservation of the environment; the assurance of adequate public services and facilities; and protection of the community from unnecessary costs that will result from imperfect development.[40]

The relationship to the master plan, official map, and capital budget should be expressed so as to afford the great latitude of reasonableness that adherence to planning will afford.[41] A local government should not view subdivision regulation as an isolated tool;[42] rather, the regulations must be integrated into a comprehensive scheme of land use controls. Zoning regulations and subdivision regulations should be compared and inconsistencies between the two must be resolved.[43] Duplication of specific regulations in zoning and subdivision control ordinances should be avoided.

In addition, subdivision regulations should be consistent with the local master plan.[44] A lesser deference may be due the Official Map of the jurisdiction.[45] If the master plan and zoning ordinance permit high-density residential development in an area, it will be difficult for the government to deny a subdivision application on the grounds of inappropriate use or excessive density.[46]

Section 1.4 of the Model Regulations vests the power and authority to review, approve, conditionally approve, or disapprove a subdivision application in the local planning commission. In some jurisdictions, the legislative body of a community cannot adopt plans or regulations governing subdivisions if there is a duly elected planning commission.[47] Some courts have held that the existence of a planning commission is a prerequisite for the adoption of subdivision regulations.[48]

The pattern of most subdivision enabling statutes is to vest such authority in the planning board.[49] Title 11, § 14 of SPEA provides for the adoption of subdivision regulations by a planning commission, and for planning commission review of subdivision applications. The Model Regulations assume, however, that the local governing body will adopt subdivision regulations, which are then implemented by the planning commission. The decision to vest final authority in the planning commission, with presumed expertise in land use matters, versus the governing body that may be more accountable to the public, is a difficult one. The Model Regulations take the middle ground. They allow the planning commission to review and to approve or disapprove subdivision applications, but they permit appeals to the governing body, which may override the planning commission's actions.[50]

Jurisdiction

The regulations in 1.5 extend the jurisdiction of the planning commission to all subdivisions located within the corporate limits of the municipality.[51] No plats can be approved within these boundaries unless first submitted to the commission. Provision is made in the SPEA for jurisdiction in Title 11, § 12. Where a municipality has been given extraterritorial jurisdiction over subdivisions, the power is normally based upon the assumption that the municipality is affected by development around it and that, under circumstances of normal growth, the municipality will eventually annex the area and should not be burdened by inadequate utilities, streets, and plat layouts.[52] The constitutionality of extraterritorial subdivision powers has been clearly established.[53]

Other methods for controlling extraterritorial growth, apart from direct subdivision control, are zoning, utility extension, and annexation. In recent years municipalities have been given the power to zone extraterritorially.[54] Even where that power is lacking, the law of standing[55] in zoning cases has been relaxed to permit extensive intervention by municipalities into zoning and planning decisions of other municipalities.[56] The courts have also begun to read regional requirements into the enabling act phrase "in accordance with a comprehensive plan."[57] The effect of this requirement is to force land use decision makers to evaluate regional impacts when making specific land use decisions. For example, a city might challenge a county zoning decision for failing to take into account the impact that the zoning approval would have on the city. Of course, most state enabling statutes for subdivision control do not require that subdivision approvals be in accordance with a comprehensive plan.

Municipalities can exert considerable extraterritorial control over development by the extension or nonextension of municipal utility services.[58] In its earlier form, the law required that a municipality, once serving an extraterritorial area, could not refuse to extend its services to other potential customers.[59] However, present law is beginning to recognize that a municipality can be compelled to extend its services only if it has held out the prospect of services by providing them to other developers in the same general area[60]— and even then it may shift the capital costs to the developer[61] or even charge higher rates.[62]

A municipality need not be overly concerned with extraterritorial control if the county or counties in which it is located have substantive subdivision controls.[63] A number of states have mandated that counties establish planning commissions and adopt subdivision regulations.[64] In addition, local governments may enter into intergovernmental agreements that can harmonize the land use controls of the various jurisdictions. These cooperative agreements can prevent developers from playing one local government against another.[65]

One important feature of the jurisdictional provision in the Model Regulations is the inclusion of already subdivided land within the scope of the regulations. Too often, subdivision regulations operate only prospectively. Yet, there is no reason why local governments cannot regulate land that already is platted. Section 1.5(3) of the Model Regulations divides platted lands into three categories: (1) lands platted without approval of a planning commission or governing body; (2) lands platted more than five years and before the effective date of the Model Regulations; and (3) lands platted for more than five years and after the adoption of the Model Regulations. In each case, it is the intent of the Model Regulations to bring within the scope of review any contiguous, undeveloped lots in common ownership, whether the lots are owned by the original subdivider or an immediate or remote grantee from the original subdivider, including a foreclosing lender.

The purpose of section 1.5(3) is to cause contiguous, undeveloped lots in common ownership to obtain contemporary plat approval. Thus, the Model Regulations assume the plat approval should have a "shelf life" of five years. If after five years, the subdividers or some other person owns contiguous, undeveloped lots, the owner will have to obtain subdivision approval under regulations then existing.

Most importantly, section 1.5(3) permits a local government to deal with prematurely platted lands. In many jurisdictions, subdividers platted land long before the need for development.[66] Unless an owner has acquired a vested right to develop the contiguous lots, the local government probably has the power to require already platted lands to be replatted under current regulations.[67] A few courts have held, however, that developers may acquire vested rights upon submission of a conforming subdivision application.[68]

Conflicts, Saving Provision, Reservations, and Repeals

The Model Regulations are not intended to interfere with, annul, or abrogate any existing ordinance, rule, regulation, or statute.[69] If the Model Regulations are enacted at a time when other regulations affecting development are in effect, those regulations with the higher standards or which are more restrictive will control.[70] Except as they replace existing subdivision regulations, adoption of the Model Regulations cannot cause a lowering of existing standards—their impact can be only to strengthen present control.

Section 1.7(2)(a)-(b) provides that adoption of the Model Regulations does not abrogate any valid enforceable easement, covenant, or other private agreement or restriction.[71] However, where the subdivision regulations are more restrictive, they clearly govern.[72]

Section 1.8 is the "saving" provision. This section provides that the regulations will not abate any action pending under preexisting subdivision regulations. Rights of both private parties and the municipality that are established prior to the enactment of the Model Regulations will not be impaired.

As noted previously, the Model Regulations may be enacted to complement existing land use regulations and, in the event of inconsistency, the regulations containing the strictest provision or highest standard will prevail. The Model Regulations are intended, however, to supersede existing subdivision regulations. If the Model Regulations need to be changed, an amendment procedure is provided in section 1.10. Unlike zoning law in some states, it should not be necessary to show that the amendment is necessitated by changed conditions or to correct a mistake.[73] As is the case when adopting any ordinance, the amendment must fall within the purview of the police power by promoting the health, safety, and welfare of the community. In order to allow for citizen participation in the amendment process, any proposed changes in the adopted regulations must be preceded by public hearings.[74]

Public Purpose

Section 1.11 of the Model Regulations is designed to grant to municipalities the power to impose conditions on subdivision development as a valid exercise of the police power. In some earlier cases the imposition of conditions was permitted on the ground that the subdivision of land is a "privilege" extended to the landowner.[75] The courts in these cases reasoned that such conditions could not be unconstitutional because the landowner could refuse to plat and could sell his land as unplatted real estate.[76]

The current theory that supports subdivision regulation is that the imposition of reasonable conditions on the subdivision of land is a proper exercise of the police power and reasonably related to the protection of the general health, safety, and welfare of the community.[77] Only a minority of states still suggest that a municipality must find wording in a state enabling statute in order to impose a reasonable condition.[78] These cases largely are a reflection of the early map acts which were not viewed as an important land use control tool. To be valid, a municipality must adopt valid subdivision regulations that contain reasonably specific criteria for imposing conditions.[79] The restrictions placed upon development also must be reasonable.[80]

In the absence of a statute, demands such as a required payment to be used for educational purposes may be beyond the scope of the police power delegated to municipalities under the subdivision control enabling statute.[81] On the other hand, a court may infer the power to impose certain fees or requirements on the subdivision of land even though a state statute does not expressly authorize the fee or requirement.[82] This must be distinguished from the statutory requirement that once the municipality has approved a preliminary development plan that it cannot add new conditions when the plan is submitted for final approval.[83]

Variances, Exceptions and Waiver of Conditions

If an extraordinary hardship or a practical difficulty would arise from strict compliance with the regulations, section 1.12 authorizes the planning commission to grant variances, exceptions, or waivers of conditions.[84] A provision for permitting such relief from subdivision regulations to "relieve practical difficulties or unnecessary hardship" has been held to give a subdivision ordinance flexibility to support a plenary power to vary.[85] The standard has been held sufficient to avoid an unconstitutional delegation of authority to vary a dedication requirement.[86] An application for relief will be denied, however, if an owner requests it merely for his own convenience, such as when the land is not usable due to error or poor assumptions on the owner's part.[87]

The courts have not always approved of delegating to an administrative agency the power to waive a statutory requirement without standards sufficient to channel the discretion of the agency and provide a basis for judicial relief, similar to that of a variance.[88] Thus a planning board may refuse to approve a waiver of conditions in the regulations when the only supporting evidence is that compliance would add significantly to development costs.[89] Where state law permits a planning board to waive improvements not required by the public interest, it cannot waive completion of improvements or the posting of a bond, which the public interest requires.[90]

Enforcement

A person who violates the provisions of the Model Regulations will be subject to possible fine and/or imprisonment. In addition to the penalties found in section 1.13(2), section 4.7 permits the withholding or revocation of building permits and certificates of occupancy if a subdivider violates certain consumer protection laws. The Model Regulations also provide that a person who violates the regulations is subject to the penalty imposed by any applicable statute. Most existing statutes provide for fines and possible imprisonment for an illegal sale of a lot. Yet, there are a number of alternative remedies:

1. The municipality may set aside the sale;
2. The private purchaser may be denied administrative relief (issuance of building permits or certificates of occupancy);
3. The statute may make the sale illegal and void;
4. Title may be made voidable—thus, only the vendee could void the sale;
5. The municipality can request injunctive relief.[91]

The duty of enforcement lies with the administrative assistant to the planning commission, who must notify the prosecuting attorney of any violations.

The owner of a subdivision may not transfer or sell any lot before the planning commission has granted subdivision approval. This requirement helps to ensure that land is developed according to proper standards. Lawyers are unlikely to give opinion letters to buyers, sellers, or lenders affirming the propriety of a transaction if it would violate local subdivision regulations. Similarly, a title company should be reluctant to insure title for an illegally created parcel.

Nonetheless, attempts to evade subdivision regulations are quite common. Transfers of land to cotenants, lot splits and minor subdivisions are among the most common devices for evasion.[92] A classic example of evasion occurs when a parcel of land is conveyed to several persons in joint tenancy. The joint tenants then "suffer" the creation of parcels through a partition action, with the referee establishing an elaborate scheme for roads, easements, etc., in the partition order. Such a scheme was voided.[93]

The case law is not entirely clear regarding the rights of "innocent" purchasers in an illegal subdivision. One case has held that the government could not compel purchasers to comply with subdivision regulations before it issued them a building permit.[94] A later case, however, held that although the city could not deny building permits to persons in an illegal subdivision, it could impose reasonable conditions on the issuance of the permits and thereby accomplish the same purposes as subdivision regulation.[95] Presumably, local regulations regarding the issuance of building permits would have to specify the conditions that must be met before the government will issue the permit.[96]

Governmental Liability

In the subdivision approval process, the municipality itself may incur certain liability. A question exists, however, whether a municipality can be subject to liability for the negligent approval of a subdivision. Discretionary functions of a governmental nature generally cannot form the basis for liability in tort.[97] Similarly, a court may find that a local government does not owe a duty to specific persons as a part of its land use control activities.[98] If a municipality contracts for an improvement, adopts a plan, and supervises construction, liability might be imposed.[99] As the subdivision becomes more integrated into the community, the municipality's failure to perform its duties could lead to tort liability.[100]

NOTES

1. Board of Supervisors v. Machnick, 410 S.E.2d 607 (Va. 1991); Butzgy v. Glastonbury, 523 A.2d 1258 (Conn. 1987); Lake County v. Truett, 758 S.W.2d 529 (Tenn. App. 1988) (the regulations themselves must be duly adopted); Landquest, Inc. v. Planning Board of Hoosick, 539 N.Y.S.2d 666 (A.D., 3rd Dept. 1989); Board of Supervisors v. Tohickon Creek Associates, 553 A.2d 492 (Pa. Commw. 1989); Urban v. Planning Board of Manasquan, 569 A.2d 275 (N.J. Super. 1990).

2. *See* Bella Vista Ranches, Inc. v. City of Sierra Vista, 613 P.2d 302, 303 (Ariz. Ct. App. 1980); El Dorado at Santa Fe, Inc. v. Board of County Comm'rs, 551 P.2d 1360, 1367 (N.M. 1976).

3. Transamerica Title Ins. Co. v. Cochise County, 548 P.2d 416, 421 (Ariz. Ct. App. 1976) (county was without power to regulate division of land into parcels of more than 35 acres); State v. Vusserm, 767 P.2d 858 (Mont. 1988) (county may not narrow statutory definition of "occasional sales" which are exempted from subdivision regulations; Landquest, Inc. v. Planning Board of Hoosick, 538 N.Y.S.2d 666 (A.D. 3rd Dept. 1989) (Planning Board limited to review plat if land is not more than 20 percent developed).

4. Counties act in two capacities: (1) as a local government unit acting as a state agent in carrying out state delegated functions at the local level; and (2) as a local government exercising comprehensive local government powers. *See* D. MANDELKER, LAND USE LAW § 4.31 (1988).

5. *See* New Jersey Shore Builders Ass'n v. Township of Marlboro, 591 A.2d 950 (N.J. Super. 1991); El Dorado at Santa Fe, Inc. v. Board of County Comm'rs, 551 P.2d 1360, 1364 (N.M. 1976) (referring to counties).

6. *See* Lemm Dev. Corp. v. Bartlett, 580 A.2d 1082 (N.H. 1990); Anderson v. Pima County, 558 P.2d 981, 983 (Ariz. Ct. App. 1976) (county could not enact security methods for subdivision improvements as an interim zoning measure without strict compliance with state law); Magnolia Dev. Co. v. Coles, 89 A.2d 664, 667 (N.J. 1952) (city could regulate subdivisions only by adopting regulations according to mandate of state law, including notice and hearing).

7. Southwick Inc. v. Lacey, 795 P.2d 712 (Wash. App. 1990); Kaufman & Gold Constr. Co. v. Planning & Zoning Comm'n, 298 S.E.2d 148, 153-57 (W. Va. 1982); Singer v. Davenport, 264 S.E.2d 637, 640-42 (W. Va. 1980).

8. Batch v. Chapel Hill, 376 N.E.2d 22 (N.C. 1989) review granted, 324 N.C. 543 (1989) (because of the similar issues involved in subdivision applications and zoning variance applications, rules applicable to the latter become quasi-judicial, are logically extended to proceedings on subdivision approval); Thornbury Township Board of Supervisors v. W.D.C. Inc., 546 A.2d 74 (Pa. 1988) (a board of supervisors determining whether to approve subdivision plan is acting in a quasi-judicial (adjudicative) rather than legislative capacity); Allied Realty, Ltd. v. Upper Saddle River, 534 A.2d 1019 (N.J. 1987), *cert. denied*, 540 A.2d 1284 (N.J. 1988) (board reviewing application for subdivision must afford landowner opportunity to show that circumstances have changed since previous resolution denying approval).

9. Century 21 Properties, Inc. v. Tigard, 783 P.2d 13 (Ore. App. 1989), *review denied*, 787

P.2d 888 (Or. 1990); El Dorado at Santa Fe, Inc. v. Board of County Comm'rs, 551 P.2d 1360, 1364 (N.M. 1976).

10. LaSalle Nat'l Bank v. Village of Brookfield, 420 N.E.2d 819, 821-22 (Ill. App. Ct. 1981); King v. Perkasie Borough Zoning Hearing Board, 551 A.2d 354 (Pa. Commw. 1989) (a municipality lacks power to require a subdivider to construct streets in an adjoining municipality).

11. Friends of the Pine Bush v. Planning Bd., 450 N.Y.S.2d 966, 968 (App. Div. 1982); Kode Harbor Dev. Associates v. County of Atlantic, 533 A.2d 858 (N.J. 1989) (where jurisdiction of a county planning board is based solely on the effect of a plan upon drainage, the board cannot impose requirements relating to an off-site county road unrelated to drainage).

12. Brazer v. Borough of Mountainside, 262 A.2d 857, 865 (N.J. 1970); *see also* Eyde Constr. Co. v. Charter Township of Meridian, 386 N.W.2d 687 (Mich. 1986) (developer can compel township to remove conditions from preliminary plat approval for dedication of recreation lands where State Subdivision Control Act grants no express or implied authority).

13. *See* Freilich & Schwach, *Authority of State and Local Governments to Issue Debt: Sources and Limitations,* in Gelfand STATE & LOCAL GOVERNMENT DEBT FINANCING 1:02 (1991); R. ELLICKSON & A. TARLOCK, LAND USE CONTROLS: CASES AND MATERIALS 36-37 (1981) (discussing the doctrine that narrowly construes local government powers and is named for its advocate, Judge Dillon). *See also* D. MANDELKER, D. NETSCH & P. SALSICH, STATE AND LOCAL GOVERNMENT IN A FEDERAL SYSTEM 83-89 (2d ed. 1983) (discussing Dillon's Rule).

14. *See* New Jersey Builders Ass'n v. Mayor of Bernards Township, 528 A.2d 555 (1987) ("the plain meaning and obvious legislative intent was to limit municipal authority only to require impact fees for improvements, the need for which arose as a *direct consequence* of the particular subdivision or development under review"); Hylton Enters. v. Board of Supervisors, 258 S.E.2d 577, 581 (Va. 1979) (finding no power to require off-site road improvements); Projects American Corp. v. Hilliard, 711 S.W.2d 386 (Tex. App.—Tyler 1986).

15. *See* El Shear v. Planning Bd., 592 A.2d 240 (N.J. Super. 1991); K & P, Inc. v. Plaiston, 575 A.2d 804 (N.H. 1990); Savonich v. Township of Lawrence, 219 A.2d 902, 906 (N.J. Super. Ct. Law Div. 1966) (applying the New Jersey Con-

stitution); Board of Police Comm'rs v. White, 370 A.2d 1070 (1976) (from statutory duty to bargain with employees it can be inferred that city may enter into contract for binding arbitration); Associated Home Builders v. City of Walnut Creek, 484 P.2d 606 (1971), *appeal dismissed,* 404 U.S. 878 (establishing a "reasonable relationship" test instead of a "specifically and uniquely attributable" test for subdivision dedication and exaction.

16. Genesee County Bd. of Road Comm'rs v. North American Dev. Co., 119 N.W.2d 593, 597 (Mich. 1963).

17. Savonich v. Township of Lawrence, 219 A.2d 902, 906 (N.J. Super. Ct. Law Div. 1966).

18. Legion Manor, Inc. v. Municipal Council, 231 A.2d 201, 204 (N.J. 1967).

19. Economy Enters. v. Township Comm'n, 250 A.2d 139, 142 (N.J. Super. Ct. App. Div. 1969) (holding, however, the requirement in this case invalid for lack of standards); Key West v. R.L.J.S. Corp., 537 So.2d 641 (Fla. App. Dist. 3, 1989) (developmental fees may be imposed upon a developer after building permits have been issued notwithstanding that they can no longer be passed on to purchasers of the unit).

20. Delight, Inc. v. Baltimore County, 624 F.2d 12, 14-15 (4th Cir. 1980).

21. *See, e.g.,* CAL. GOV'T CODE § 66411; *see generally* CALLIES, FREILICH & ROBERTS, CASES AND MATERIALS ON LAND USE, ch. 3 (West 1994); Mandelker, *supra* note 4, at § 9.03.

22. *See, e.g.,* Local Government Land Use Control Enabling Act, COLO. REV. STAT. §§ 29-20-101 to -107 (1986). *But see* Pennobscot, Inc. v. Board of County Comm'rs of Pitkin County, 642 P.2d 915 (Colo. 1982) (limiting scope of the land use control enabling act). *See also* Beaver Meadows v. Board of County Comm'rs, 709 P.2d 928 (Colo. 1985) (reviewing variety of land use enabling legislation and upholding off-site road improvement requirement as condition to planned unit development approval).

23. *See, e.g.,* Bethlehem Evangelical Lutheran Church v. City of Lakewood, 626 P.2d 668 (Colo. 1981) (finding that local authority to "facilitate adequate provisions for transportation, water, sewage, schools, parks and other public requirements" sustained street improvement and land dedication requirements as condition to issuance of building permit); similarly off-site street improvements may be required providing there is a rational nexus to the needs generated by the subdivision, Frisella v. Farmington, 550 A.2d 102 (N.H. 1988); Lee

County v. New Testament Baptist Church, 507 So.2d 626 (Fla. App. Dist. 2, 1987).

24. Dateline Builders, Inc. v. Santa Rosa, 194 Cal. Rptr. 258 (1983) (upholding refusal to extend sewer connections to a subdivision that constituted leapfrog development inconsistent with city and county general plan); Unity Venture v. Lake County, 631 F. Supp 181 (N.D. Ill. 1986) (development denied sewer extension unless annexation to adjoining village was applied for); First American Federal Savings & Loan Assoc. v. Royall, 334 S.E.2d 792 (N.C. App. 1985) (withholding approval pending completion of water line); *but see* Robinson v. City of Boulder, 547 P.2d 228 (Col. 1976).

25. *See* C. SANDS & M. LIBONATI, LOCAL GOVERNMENT LAW § 13.06, at 13-29 (1982) ("The trend of decision is to give effect to general welfare and similar broad grants of power subject only to the limitations of reasonableness and constitutionality"); *see* Marx v. Zoning Bd. of Appeals, 529 N.Y.S.2d 330 (App. Div. 2nd Dep't 1988) ("subdivision control is aimed at protecting the community from uneconomical development of land and assuring persons living in the area where the subdivision is sought that there will be adequate streets, sewers, water supply and other essential services").

26. *See id.* at § 13.03.

27. *Id.* at 13-9. For an example of a constitutional home rule provision that delegates all lawful authority to charter governments, see Mo. Const. art. VI, § 19(a): "Any city which adopts or has adopted a charter for its own government, shall have all powers which the general assembly of the state of Missouri has authority to confer upon any city, provided such powers are consistent with the constitution of this state and are not limited or denied either by the charter so adopted or by statute. Such a city shall, in addition to its home rule powers, have all powers conferred by law." *See generally* Sandalow, *The Limits of Municipal Power Under Home Rule: A Role For the Courts*, 48 MINN. L. REV. 643 (1964).

28. *See, e.g.*, Moore v. City of Boulder, 484 P.2d 134, 136-37 (Colo. Ct. App. 1971). *See also* Cherry Hills Farms, Inc. v. City of Cherry Hills Village, 670 P.2d 777 (Colo. 1983); J.W. Jones Companies v. City of San Diego, 203 Cal. Rptr. 580 (Ct. App. 1984) (both discussing authority of local governments to impose fees or taxes on new development).

29. Urban v. Planning Bd., 592 A.2d 240 (N.J. 1991); Akin v. South Middletown Township Zoning Hearing Bd., 547 A.2d 883 (Pa. Commw. 1988); Butzgy v. Glastonbury, 523 A.2d 1258 (1987) (in passing on plans for a proposed subdivision, a planning commission is bound by its own regulations); Central Metairie Civic Assoc. v. Jefferson Parish Council, 484 So.2d 706 (La. App. 5th Cir. 1986) *cert. denied* 486 So.2d 751 (La. 1986) (once the planning commission has exercised its authority in drafting regulations pertaining to subdivision development, it is bound by those regulations and "shall administer" them. It exceeds its authority in denying approval of the preliminary plat on considerations other than the minimum standards set forth in the subdivision ordinance); Lake County v. Truett, 758 S.W.2d 529 (Tenn App. 1988) (the regulations must be duly adopted).

30. Canter v. Planning Bd., 347 N.E.2d 691, 693 (Mass. App. Ct. 1976) (local government could not refuse to approve subdivision because of access and traffic problems when local ordinances did not include these factors as a basis for decision); Reed v. Planning Comm'n, 544 A.2d 1213 (Conn. 1988) (either the enabling statute or local ordinance must specifically list all of the standards the commission can apply in reviewing subdivision plats); Richardson v. Little Rock Planning Comm'n, 747 S.W.2d 116 (Ark. 1988) (when a subdivision meets minimum standards to which a preliminary plat must conform, it is arbitrary as a matter of law to deny approval of a plat that meets those standards). *But see* Grant's Farm v. Town of Kitteny, 554 A.2d 799 (1989) (an enabling act could authorize the planning board to deny plat approval if the board determined that the subdivision would cause traffic congestion or pose a danger to the shoreland).

31. Kaufman & Gold Constr. Co. v. Planning & Zoning Comm'n, 298 S.E.2d 148, 155-56 (W. Va. 1982).

32. Note that board goals and objectives, such as statements relating to adequate public facilities and uneconomical development, will assist the court in balancing the regulations' enhancement of the health, safety, and general welfare versus the detriment to the landowner. Thus, the strong statement in Marx v. Zoning Bd. of Appeals, 529 N.Y.S.2d 330 (2d Dep't 1988) ("subdivision control is *aimed* at protecting the community . . .").

33. Southern Co-op Dev. Fund v. Driggers, 696 F.2d 1347, 1352 (11th Cir. 1983) (a reviewing unit cannot impose ad hoc conditions even if its intention is to carry out the purpose of the subdivision regulations). Knutson v. State of Indiana, 157 N.E.2d 469 (Ind. 1959). *Accord* Columbia Corp. v. Town Bd. of Pacific, 286 N.W.2d 130 (Wis. 1979).

34. *See* Frug, *The City as a Legal Concept*, 93 HARV. L. REV. 1059, 1100 (1980) (discussing the original basis for Dillon's Rule, which was to limit the "intermingling of the public and the private sectors"). A number of recent decisions have rejected Dillon's Rule in a number of contexts. *See, e.g.*, State v. Hutchinson, 624 P.2d 1116, 1118 (Utah 1980) (rejecting Dillon's Rule as "archaic, unrealistic, and unresponsive to the current needs of both state and local governments and [as] effectively nullif[ying] the legislative grant of general police power to the counties"); United Business Com'n v. San Diego, 154 Cal. Rptr. 263 (1979) (municipalities' power as broad as that of legislature, provided such powers do not conflict with state laws).

35. State *ex rel.* Strother v. Chase, 42 Mo. App. 342 (1890). It should be noted that the *Strother* case was handed down at a time when, as the court stated, only two conditions were imposed by an 1887 statute on plat approval: a map correctly showing the streets and an indication of the dimensions and numbers of the lots. Other cases have strictly construed plat approval in such narrow fashion: State *ex rel.* Lewis v. City Council of Minneapolis, 168 N.W. 188 (Minn. 1918), holding that a city could not require grading under a statute referring only to direction and width of streets; Magnolia Dev. Co. v. Coles, 89 A.2d 664 (N.J. 1952), holding that, in the absence of enabling authority, there was no power to require sidewalks, curbs, or gutters; *In re* Lake Secor Dev. Co., 252 N.Y.S. 809 (N.Y. Sup. Ct. 1931) holding that under a statute referring only to streets, light, and air, there could be no requirement for installation of water systems. *Accord* Briar West, Inc. v. City of Lincoln, 291 N.W.2d 730 (Neb. 1980).

36. While modern theory of subdivision control rests primarily upon the police power, the earlier cases relied on the concept that a developer has no common law right to the unimpeded development of land. Initial efforts of municipalities to regulate subdivision focused on imposing conditions and exactions on developers in exchange for recording a subdivision plat under the old map acts. The imposition of these conditions was justified on grounds that recording a subdivision plat map was a *privilege* that brought a benefit to the developer. *See* Ridgefield Land Co. v. City of Detroit, 217 N.W.

58 (Mich. 1928) (owner of land subdivision voluntarily dedicates sufficient land for streets in return for the privilege and advantage of having the plat recorded). Under the privilege theory, the law gives the developer no right to have it recorded. Newton v. American Surety Co., 148 S.W. 311 (Ark. 1941). Although a developer benefitted by recording a plat, the privilege rationale for imposing exactions gave way when platting became a regulatory requirement and cities and courts relied on the theory that subdivision regulations were a reasonable means of protecting the health, safety, and general welfare. But the concept of privilege still survives. *See* Trent Meredith, Inc. v. City of Oxford, 170 Ca. Rptr. 685 689 (Ct. App. 1981) (a facilities fee in lieu of land for school financing is valid as a levy upon the "privilege" of developing. *See* CALLIES, FREILICH & ROBERTS, CASES & MATERIALS ON LAND USE 154 (West 1994).

37. Ayres v. City Council, 207 P.2d 1 (Cal. 1949). *See also* Beaver Meadows v. Board of County Comm'rs, 709 P.2d 928 (Colo. 1985).

38. Coffey v. Maryland-Nat'l Capital Park & Planning Comm'n, 441 A.2d 1041 (Md. Ct. Spec. App. 1982); Divan Builders, Inc. v. Planning Bd., 334 A.2d 30 (N.J. 1975); Lewis v. Livingston Tp., 173 A.2d 391 (N.J. 1961). "Farsighted developers were and are aware of these dangers. But many subdivisions are constructed without regard to the convenience or well-being of the resulting community and in course of time sink inevitably into the status of a slum; the poor location of new subdivisions `where street systems and housing were not conformed to topography' is listed as the `first slum-inducing factors.'" (K. FORD, SLUMS AND HOUSING 444 [1936])." C. HAAR, LAND USE PLANNING 346 (2d ed. 1971).

39. R. ANDERSON, AMERICAN LAW OF ZONING, 25.03, at 275 (3d ed. 1968).

40. *See generally* Reps, *Control of Land Subdivision by Municipal Planning Boards*, 40 CORNELL L.Q. 258 (1955); Storke & Spears, *Subdivision Financing*, 28 ROCKY MT. L. REV. 549 (1956); Shultz & Kelley, *Subdivision Improvement Requirements and Guarantees: A Primer*, 28 J. URB. L. & CONTEMP. PROBS. 1 (1985).

41. Golden v. Planning Bd. of Town of Ramapo, 334 N.Y.S.2d 138, 285 N.E.2d 291 (1972), *appeal dismissed*, 409 U.S. 1003 (1972), where the court placed great weight on the relationship of planning and the restrictions placed on private land by subdivision controls; Board of County

Comm'rs v. Gaster, 401 A.2d 666 (Md. App. 1979). *See also* COUNCIL ON ENVIRONMENTAL QUALITY, THE TAKING ISSUE 290 (1973):

The importance of a sound factual presentation is apparent in the urban context as well. The Township of Ramapo, on the outskirts of the New York metropolitan area, successfully defended a growth control ordinance before New York's highest court with success due in no small part to a thorough presentation of their case. . . . The town was able to present a vast array of planning data in their defense. In its statement of the facts in Golden v. Planning Board of the Town of Ramapo, the Court of Appeals pointed to the Town Master Plan, whose "preparation included a four volume study of the existing land uses, public facilities, transportation, industry and commerce, housing needs and project populations trends. . . . Additional sewer district and drainage studies were undertaken which culminated in the adoption of a capital budget. . . ." *Golden,* 285 N.E.2d at 294.

Thus not only could the town rely upon a large number of formal municipal actions, adoption of a master plan, a capital budget, zoning and subdivision regulations and the like, but they could also document each with thorough and detailed planning studies. This impressive detail allowed the court to open its consideration of legal issues on the premises that: "The undisputed effect of these integrated efforts in land use planning and development is to provide an overall program of orderly growth and adequate facilities through a sequential development policy commensurate with progressing availability and capacity of public facilities." The court could at the outset of its discussion of the taking issue, term the program reasonable, "both in its inception and its implementation." *See also* J.W. Jones Companies v. City of San Diego, 203 Cal. Rptr. 580 (Cal. App. 1984). For a complete description of the Ramapo plan developed by and defended in the courts by Professor Freilich, *see* CALLIES, FREILICH & ROBERTS, CASES AND MATERIALS ON LAND USE, 572-589 (West 1994).

42. Mansfield & Swett v. Town of West Orange, 198 A. 225 (N.J. 1938) (". . . it is essential to adequate planning that there be provision for future community needs reasonably to be anticipated").

43. Annison v. Hoover, 517 S.2d 420 (La. App. 1st Cir. 1987) (the property will be governed by the more stringent or restrictive of the local zoning regulations or subdivision building restrictions). Tuckner v. May, 419 N.W.2d 836 (Minn. App. 1988) (minimum lot size restrictions).

44. SAVE Centennial Valley Ass'n v. Schultz, 284 N.W.2d 452 (S.D. 1979) (the approval of a subdivision in an agricultural area was ruled void by the court because the commission, in approving it, disregarded the clear intent of the comprehensive plan). Board of County Comm'rs v. Gaster, 401 A.2d 666 (Md. App. 1979) (although subdivision met all zoning requirements, the application was properly disapproved because it failed to comply with the master plan's density provision and because of its detrimental impact on roads and school facilities).

45. *See* Nigro v. Planning Bd., 584 A.2d 1350 (N.J. 1991) (the Supreme Court of New Jersey held that an "official map" deserved substantial but not absolute deference when reviewing a subdivision application).

46. *See, e.g.,* Kaufman & Gold Constr. Co. v. Planning & Zoning Comm'n, 298 S.E.2d 148, 153-57 (W. Va. 1982).

47. Gates Mills Inv. Co. v. Parks, 266 N.E.2d 552 (Ohio 1971).

48. Rahway v. Raritan Homes, Inc., 91 A.2d 409 (N.J. Super. Ct. App. Div. 1952).

49. M. ANDERSON & B. ROSWIG, PLANNING, ZONING, SUBDIVISION: A SUMMARY OF STATUTORY LAW IN THE 50 STATES 228 (1966). *See* CONN. GEN. STAT. § 8-25 (West 1971); SPEA Title 1 § 2. The Bassett Model placed the power in the municipal legislative body, *e.g.,* New Jersey plats can be reviewed by the governing body or Planning Board, but the governing body adopts the subdivision regulations. N.J. STAT. ANN. § 40:55 D-25 (Supp. 1987) *See also* N.Y. Village Law § 7-728 (McKinney 1973). *But see* Quillen v. Aspen Planning & Zoning Comm'n, 697 P.2d 406 (Colo. 1985); Wright Dev. Inc. v. City of Wellsville, 608 P.2d 232 (Utah 1980).

50. *See* § 3.8 of the Model Regulation.

51. The text of the Model Regulations does not provide for examples of "extra-territorial" control by a municipality outside of its corporate boundaries. A municipality does not generally have any inherent authority to exercise police powers outside of its boundaries. Such powers, however, can be conferred by statute, since a state has plenary authority to delegate its power. *See* D. HAGMAN & J. JUERGENSMEYER, URBAN PLANNING AND LAND DEVELOPMENT CONTROL LAW § 5.9 at 149 (2d ed. 1986); Gomillion v.

Lightfoot, 364 U.S. 339 (1960); Hunter v. Pittsburgh, 207 U.S. 161 (1907). More than half of the states have provided for extraterritorial subdivision approval by statute. F. Sengstock, Extraterritorial Powers in the Metropolitan Area 66-69 (1962). Jurisdiction is often extended up to five miles beyond the city limits as provided in the Standard Planning Enabling Act §§ 6, 2. Bettman's Municipal Subdivision Regulation Act § 1 recommended a three-mile limit. *See* Bassett, Williams, Bettman & Whitten, Model Laws for Planning Cities, Counties and States 84 (1935); Rice v. Oshkosh, 435 N.W.2d 252 (Wis. 1989) (although a city has extraterritorial jurisdiction over subdivisions within three miles off its boundary, it lacks authority where the land is located within a town that has specific power to require improvements).

52. Village of Lake Bluff v. Jacobson, 454 N.E.2d 734 (Ill. App. Ct. 1983); D. Hagman & J. Juergensmeyer, Urban Planning and Land Development Control Law 150-151 (2d ed. 1986). Melli & DeVoy, *Extraterritorial Planning and Urban Growth*, 1959 Wis. L. Rev. 55.

53. Hunt v. City of Tuscaloosa, __ U.S.__ (19__); Petterson v. City of Naperville, 137 N.E.2d 371 (Ill. 1956); Village of Lake Bluff v. Jacobson, 454 N.E.2d 734 (Ill. App. Ct. 1983). The extraterritorial power is divided by statute in a number of ways. Rather than give exclusive jurisdiction to the city, the county may also be required to approve plats, particularly where the county has its own subdivision regulations. Under other statutes, the county approves but must seek the advice of the city. Under yet other statutes, extraterritorial power of the city is limited to major aspects of the subdivision, such as street location. *See generally* D. Hagman & J. Juergensmeyer, Urban Planning and Land Development Control Law (2d ed. 1986); N. Williams, American Land Planning Laws § 156.03 (1985).

54. Schlientz v. City of North Platte, 110 N.W.2d 58 (Neb. 1961); Walworth Co. v. City of Elkhorn, 133 N.W.2d 257 (Wis. 1956). The power may not be unlimited and may have to be shared with the surrounding county, *cf.* American Sign Corp. v. Fowler, 276 S.W.2d 651 (Ky. 1955) (limited to a "reasonable" area). *See* State v. Heck, 817 P.2d 247 (N.M. App. 1991) ("Where land is located in the extraterritorial zone within the platting jurisdiction of both [the county and the city,] both governmental entities exercise concurrent jurisdiction" and "approval of a subdivision plat must be secured from both.") Where

a subdivision straddles two municipalities each has authority over the application. Dotterer v. Zoning Hearing Board, 488 A.2d 1023 (Pa. Commw. 1991); Rice v. Oshkosh, 435 N.W.2d 252 (Wis. 1989).

55. Ayer, *The Primitive Law of Standing in Land Use Disputes: Some Notes From a Dark Continent*, 55 Iowa L. Rev. 344, 346-347 (1969). *See also* Students Challenging Regulatory Agency Procedures v. United States, 414 U.S. 1035 (1973); Sierra Club v. Morton, 405 U.S. 727 (1972) (both concerning standing in environmental litigation).

56. Stocks v. City of Irvine, 170 Cal. Rptr. 724 (Cal. App. 1981); Hope, Inc. v. County of DuPage, 738 F.2d 797 (7th Cir. 1984); Wis. Stat. Ann. § 236.12(2)(b) - (3), 236.13(1)(c) (West 1987), for instance, allows county planning commission jurisdiction in incorporated areas. *See* Township of River Vale v. Town of Orangetown, 403 F.2d 684 (2d. Cir. 1968); Allen v. Coffel, 488 S.W.2d 671 (Mo. App. 1972); Borough of Cresskill v. Borough of Dumont, 104 A.2d 441 (N.J. 1954); Borough of Roselle Park v. Township of Union, 272 A.2d 762 (N.J. Super. 1970); Reynolds v. Waukesha County Park & Planning Comm'n, 324 N.W.2d 897 (Wis. Ct. App. 1982). *See generally* R. Anderson, American Law of Zoning 5.17, 5.26 (3d ed. 1986). For extensive analysis of this area *see* Freilich & Bass, *Exclusionary Zoning: Suggested Litigation Approaches*, 3 Urb. Law. 344 (1971).

57. Appeal of M.A. Kravitz, 460 A.2d 1075 (Pa. 1983); Associated Homes Builders v. Livermore, 567 P.2d 473 (Ca. 1976); City of Del Mar v. City of San Diego, 183 Cal. Rptr. (4th Dist. 1982); Berenson v. Town of New Castle, 341 N.E.2d 236 (N.Y. 1975); SVAE v. Town of Bothell, 576 P.2d 401 (Wash. 1978); Southern Burlington County N.A.A.C.P. v. Mt. Laurel Township, 456 A.2d 390 (N.J. 1983); McDermott v. Village of Calverton Park, 454 S.W.2d 577 (Mo. 1970); Fanale v. Borough of Hasbrouck Heights, 139 A.2d 749 (N.J. 1958); Borough of Cresskill v. Borough of Dumont, 104 A.2d 441 (N.J. 1954); In re Kit-Mar Builders, 268 A.2d 765 (Pa. 1970); In re Girsch, 263 A.2d 395 (Pa. 1970).

58. *See generally* Freilich & Ragsdale, *Timing and Sequential Controls—The Essential Basis for Effective Regional Planning: An Analysis of the New Directors for Land Use Control in the Minneapolis-St. Paul Metropolitan Region*, 58 Minn. L. Rev. 1009 (1974); Morgan & Shonkwiler, *Urban Development and Statewide Planning: Challenges of the 1980's*, 61 Ore. L . Rev. 351 (1982); Dateline

Builders v. City of Santa Rosa, 194 Cal. Rptr. 258 (1983).

59. Del Marva Enter. v. Dover, 282 A.2d 601 (Del. 1971); Robinson v. City of Boulder, 547 P.2d 228 (Colo. 1976); Reid Dev. Corp. v. Parsippany-Troy Hills Tp., 89 A.2d 667 (N.J. 1952). *But see* City of Corbin v. Kentucky Utils. Co., 447 S.W.2d 356 (Ky. 1969).

60. Dateline Builders, Inc. v. City of Santa Rosa, 196 Cal. Rptr. 258 (Ct. App. 1983); Annot., "Right to Compel Municipality to Extend Its Water System," 48 A.L.R.2d 1222 (1956); Rose v. Plymouth Township, 173 P.2d 285 (Utah 1946) (insufficient facilities); Swanson v. Marvin Mun. Water Dist., 128 Cal. Rptr. 485 (Cal. App. 1976) (shortage of water capacities) and Capture Realty Corp. v. Board of Adjustment, 313 A.2d 624 (N.J. 1973) (environmental concerns).

61. Divan Builders, Inc. v. Planning Bd., 334 A.2d 30 (N.J. 1975) (concept of conditioning plat approval on payment of a fee to construct off-site drainage facilities was upheld); Crownhill Homes, Inc. v. City of San Antonio, 433 S.W.2d 448 (Tex. 1958); Banberry Dev. Corp. v. South Jordan City, 631 P.2d 899 (Utah 1981) (water connection fee as a condition of plat approval upheld).

62. Meglino v. Township Comm., 510 A.2d 1134 (N.J. 1986); Town of Terrell Hills v. City of San Antonio, 318 S.W.2d 85 (Tex. 1958). Usually, utility extension and district formations are used to allow for subdivision and urbanization. Occasionally such districts may be formed to manage the rate of growth. Wilson v. Hidden Valley Water Dist., 63 Cal. Rptr. 889 (Cal. App. 1967).

63. Rice v. Oshkosh, 435 N.W.2d 252 (Wis. 1989) (A city may not exercise its extraterritorial jurisdiction within three miles of its boundaries where the land is located within another jurisdiction that has specific power to regulate the subdivision).

64. *See, e.g.*, COLO. REV. STAT. §§ 30-28-103, 30-28-133 (1986); *compare* Pickle v. Board of County Comm'rs, 764 P.2d 262 (Wyo. 1988).

65. *See* ADVISORY COMM. ON INTERGOVERNMENTAL RELATIONS, A HANDBOOK FOR INTERLOCAL AGREEMENTS AND CONTRACTS 2-3 (1967). *See generally* 1 SANDS & LIBONATI, LOCAL GOVERNMENT LAW Ch. 6 (1987); Hall & Wallack, *Intergovernmental Cooperation and the Transfer of Powers*, 1981 U. ILL. L. REV. 775; City of Oakland v. Williams, 103 P.2d 168 (1940); State *ex rel.* Grimes County Taxpayers Ass'n v. Texas Mun. Power Agency, 565 S.W.2d 258 (1978); Frank v. City of Cody, 572 P.2d 1106 (1977); Where a parcel straddles two jurisdictions, each jurisdiction has authority over the application for subdivision approval, Dotterer v. Zoning Hearing Bd., 588 A.2d 1023 (Pa. Commw. 1991).

66. *See, e.g.*, Stroud, *The Magnitude of Large Lot-Sale Subdivisions in the United States*, 3 THE PLATTED LANDS PRESS 1, 2 (Jan. 1986); *Antiquated Subdivisions: Beyond Lot Mergers and Vested Rights*, conf. proceedings, Lincoln Institute of Land Policy, Cambridge, Mass. (1984) (examining California). M. Shultz & J. Groy, *The Premature Subdivision of Land in Colorado*, Lincoln Institute of Land Policy, Cambridge, Mass., Monograph #86-10 (1986) (examining Colorado).

67. *See, e.g.*, Sherman-Colonial Realty Corp. v. Goldsmith, 230 A.2d 568, 572 (Conn. 1967); Toothaker v. Planning Bd. of Billerica, 193 N.E.2d 582, 584 (Mass. 1963).

68. See Littlefield v. Inhabitants of Town of Lyman, 447 A.2d 1231, 1233 (Me. 1982) (holding that property owner obtained vested right upon submission of application for subdivision approval when the application has been considered by the government); *see also* TEX REV. STAT., Art. 4413 (301), sections 7.001 *et seq.* (1987) (the approval of an application for subdivision approval shall be considered solely on the basis of requirements or ordinances in effect at the time the application was filed).

69. *See* D. HAGMAN & J. JUERGENSMEYER, URBAN PLANNING AND LAND DEVELOPMENT CONTROL LAW, 251 (2d ed. 1986): "In order to develop it is generally necessary to comply with both subdivision and zoning ordinances"; Oakland Court v. York Township, 339 N.W.2d 873 (Mich. Ct. App. 1983) (even absent specific requirement in the subdivision regulations for compliance with the zoning ordinance, such compliance is implied); *cf.* Day v. City of Los Angeles, 11 Cal. Rptr. 325 (Cal. App. 1961).

70. Landry Estates, Inc. v. Jones, 67 Misc.2d 354, 324 N.Y.S.2d 255 (1971) (environmental regulations). Even if an approved subdivision exists and a zoning ordinance is subsequently passed preventing the lots being used as subdivided, the subdivider has no vested right to develop the subdivision. Lake Intervale Homes, Inc. v. Parsippany-Troy Hills Tp., 147 A.2d 28 (N.J. 1958); York Township Zoning Bd. of Adjustment v. Brown, 182 A.2d 706 (Pa. 1962), Mayor and City Council of Baltimore v. Crane, 352 A.2d 786 (Md. 1976), unless a statute exists granting the subdivider such vested right for a specific period of time. Hilton Acres v. Klein, 174 A.2d 465 (N.J. 1961). *See, e.g.*, CAL. GOV'T

CODE § 66498.1 (West Supp. 1987); MASS. GEN. LAWS ANN. ch. 40A, § 6 (West Supp. 1987); PA. STAT. ANN. tit. 53, § 10508(4) (Purdon Supp. 1986); WASH. REV. CODE ANN. §§ 58.17.170 (Supp. 1987). *See generally* Witt, *Vested Rights in Land Uses—A View from the Practitioner's Perspective,* 21 REAL PROP., PROB. & TRUST J. 317 (1986).

71. Fuller v. Hill Properties, Inc., 259 So.2d 398 (La. Ct. App. 1972); Western Land Co. v. Trusbulaski, 495 P.2d 624 (Nev. 1972). An ordinance that permits less restrictive uses than those to which property is limited by a covenant in a deed is usually held not to impair the efficacy of the latter, 4 A. RATHKOPF, THE LAW OF ZONING AND PLANNING § 74-1 (1972 & Supp. 1982); Martin v. Mayor and Aldermen of Annapolis, 214 A.2d 800, 806 (Md. 1965); Clintwood Inc. v. Adams, 287 N.Y.S.2d 235 (App. Div. 1968). An attempt to override a lawful enforceable private covenant may result in a finding of inverse condemnation, Burger v. City of St. Paul, 64 N.W.2d 73 (Minn. 1954); Berger, *Conflicts Between Zoning Ordinances and Restrictive Covenants,* 43 NEB. L. REV. 449 (1964). *But see,* Hendlin v. Fairmount Constr. Co., 72 A.2d 541 (N.J. Super. Ct. App. Div. 1950). But a private restrictive covenant that violates public policy or offends constitutional provisions on racial discrimination will be voided regardless of its more restrictive effect, Sullivan v. Little Hunting Park, Inc., 396 U.S. 229 (1969) (violation of 42 U.S.C. § 1981, 1982); Barrows v. Jackson, 346 U.S. 249 (1953); Smedley, *A Comparative Analysis of Title VIII and Section 1982,* 22 VAND. L. REV. 459 (1969). In one instance, where the owner uses a reverter clause to enforce a racial bias that requires the property to be returned to the original owner or his heirs in lieu of enforcement of a covenant, the Supreme Court has enforced the racial restrictions on the grounds that the reverter occurs automatically without interference of the state and the enforcement of donative intent is a fundamental aspect of the law. Evans v. Abney, 396 U.S. 435 (1970); Charlotte Park & Recreation Comm'n v. Barringer, 88 S.E.2d 114 (N.C. 1955), *cert. denied sub nom.* Leeper v. Charlotte Park & Recreation Comm'n, 350 U.S. 983 (1956).

72. LaSalle Nat'l Bank v. Village of Palatine, 236 N.E.2d 1 (Ill. App. Ct. 1968); City of Richlawn v. McMakin, 230 S.W.2d 902 (Ky. 1950). Rathkopf in his treatise states: "The absurdity of a claim that a zoning restriction which is fully operative against land theretofore wholly free from any restriction, is ineffective against land burdened with a private restriction, is obvious." A. RATHKOPF, THE LAW OF ZONING AND PLANNING § 74-4 (1972 & Supp. 1982).

73. *See, e.g.,* Miller v. City of Albuquerque, 554 P.2d 665, 668 (N.M. 1976). *But see* Roseta v. County of Washington, 458 P.2d 405 (1969) (rejecting the change—mistake doctrine).

74. For an excellent analysis of the need for public hearings in planning decision making, see Plager, *Participatory Democracy and the Public Hearing: A Functional Approach,* 21 ADMIN. L. REV. 153 (1969).

75. Newton v. American Sec. Co., 148 S.W.2d 311 (Ark. 1941); Ridgefield Land Co. v. Detroit, 217 N.W. 58 (Mich. 1928).

76. J. BEUSCHER & R. WRIGHT, LAND USE 279 (1969); Shultz & Kelley, *Subdivision Improvement Requirements and Guarantees: A Primer,* 28 WASH. U.J. URB. & CONTEMP. L. 1, 32 n. 151 (1985). The privilege theory has largely fallen into disfavor, Pavelka, *Subdivision Exactions: A Review of Judicial Standards,* 25 WASH. U.J. URB. & CONTEMP. L. 269, 283 (1983), but is still used by some courts to justify subdivision exactions, Lampton v. Pinaire, 610 S.W.2d 915 (Ky. Ct. App. 1981).

77. Wald Corp. v. Metropolitan Dade County, 338 So.2d 863 (Fla. Dist. Ct. App. 1976); Mansfield & Swett, Inc. v. City of West Orange, 198 A. 225 (N.J. 1938); Brous v. Smith, 106 N.E.2d 503 (N.Y. 1952); Swinney v. City of San Antonio, 483 S.W.2d 556 (Tex. Civ. App. 1971); Banberry Dev. Corp. v. South Jordan City, 631 P.2d 899 (Utah 1981); Ayres v. City Council of Los Angeles, 207 P.2d 1 (Cal. 1949).

78. *See* Annotation, "Validity and Construction of Regulations as to Subdivision Maps or Plats," 11 A.L.R.2d 524, 535 (1950); Tuxedo Homes v. Green, 63 So.2d 812 (Ala. 1953). A case illustrating the minority position is Hylton Enter. v. Board of Supervisors, 258 S.E.2d 577 (Va. 1979).

79. Southern Coop. Dev. Fund v. Driggers, 696 F.2d 1347 (11th Cir. 1983) (denial of plat approval must be based on precise standards in the subdivision regulations); Beaver Meadows v. Board of County Comm'rs, 709 P.2d 928 (Colo. 1985) (imposition of road improvement as condition of planned unit development approval was invalid when not specifically authorized by state statutes and local regulations, despite general authorizations and policies); State *ex rel.* Jackson & Morris, Inc. v. Smuczynski, 102 N.E.2d 168 (Ill. App. Ct. 1951) (village having failed to adopt a subdivision ordinance for its guidance as required by statute, must approve plat as a "ministerial" act); Rahway v. Raritan Homes, Inc., 91 A.2d 409 (N.J. Super. Ct. App. Div. 1952) (no power to regulate subdividing until city complied with state statute requiring appointment of planning board and adoption of subdivision ordinance regulations).

80. Salamar Builders, Inc. v. Tuttle, 325 N.Y.S.2d (N.Y. 1971); Harbor Farms, Inc. v. Nassau Co. Planning Comm'n, 334 N.Y.S.2d 412 (App. Div. 1972) (planning commission can consider environmental impact of a subdivision); Miller v. City of Port Angeles, 691 P.2d 229 (Wash. Ct. App. 1984).

81. West Park Ave., Inc. v. Ocean Township, 224 A.2d 1 (N.J. 1967). *See also* Southern Coop. Dev. Fund v. Driggers, 696 F.2d 1347, 1351 (11th Cir. 1983) (planning commission has no authority to impose ad hoc requirements not in the subdivision regulations).

82. *See, e.g.,* Legion Manor, Inc. v. Municipal Council, 231 A.2d 201 (N.J. 1967).

83. Board of Supervisors v. West Chestnut Realty Corp., 532 A.2d 942 (Pa. Commw. 1987). Similarly a preliminary approval may not be denied on the basis of standards applicable only to final approval of a subdivision plan. Cherry Valley Assoc. v. Stroud Township Bd. of Supervisors, 554 A.2d 149 (Pa. Commw. 1989).

84. The power to vary the application of subdivision regulations is usually vested in the planning commission, R. ANDERSON, AMERICAN LAW OF ZONING, § 23.29 (3d ed. 1968). Arrigo v. Planning Bd. of Franklin, 429 N.E.2d 355 (Mass. App. 1981). Generally a provision for waiver or variance reserves to the planning board the right to make a case-by-case determination of what is proper for a given subdivision and only upon application by the developer. Canter v. Planning Bd. of Westborough, 390 N.E.2d 1128 (Mass. App. 1979). If the statute permits, the variance may be heard by the zoning board of adjustment. N.Y. Gen. City Law § 36 (McKinney 1968); Fisher v. Dame, 433 A.2d 366 (Me. 1981); *In re* Blum, 158 N.Y.S.2d 772 (App. Div. 1956). Absent a provision granting the board of adjustment authority to grant variances or exceptions, such a board is without power in subdivision matters. Noonan v. Zoning Bd. of Review, 159 A.2d 606 (R.I. 1960). Moreover the granting of a variance by a board of adjustment does not mandate plat approval by the planning board. Panariello v. Demetri, 472 N.Y.S.2d 17 (App. Div. 2nd Dept, 1984) and the zoning board of appeals may not authorize issuance of a build-

ing permit where the planning board has exclusive jurisdiction to release certain conditions. Planning Board of Easton v. Koenig, 429 N.E.2d 81 Mass. App. 1981). For general statutory provisions granting variance authority to planning commissions, *see* N.Y. Gen. City Law § 33:

[The] Planning Board may waive, subject to appropriate conditions and guarantees, for such period as it may determine, the provision of any or all such improvements as in its judgment of the special circumstances of a particular plat or plats are not requisite in the interests of the public health, safety, and general welfare.

See also OHIO REV. CODE ANN. § 711.10 (1976). *See generally* D. HAGMAN & J. JUERGENSMEYER, URBAN PLANNING & LAND DEVELOPMENT CONTROL LAWS, § 7.6 (2d ed. 1986).

85. Arrigo v. Planning Bd. of Franklin, 429 N.E. 2d 355 (Mass. App. 1981); Blevens v. Manchester, 170 A.2d 121 (N.H. 1961).

86. Southern Pac. Co. v. Los Angeles, 51 Cal. Rptr. 197 (Cal. App.), *appeal dismissed,* 385 U.S. 647 (1966); Smith v. Morris Township, 244 A.2d 145 (N.J. Super. Ct. App. Div. 1968); Blevens v. Manchester, 170 A.2d 121 (N.H. 1961).

87. Randolph Hills, Inc. v. Montgomery County Council, 285 A.2d 620 (Md. Ct. Spec. App. 1972); Leveille v. Sander, 328 N.Y.S.2d 342 (App. Div. 1972); Battles v. Board of Adjustment & Appeals, 711 S.W.2d 297 (Tex. Ct. App. 1986).

88. Lyman v. Planning Bd. of City of Winchester, 224 N.E. 2d 493 (Mass. 1967). Thus, where a planning board has authority to waive conditions it may not do so without making findings supported by evidence. Smith v. Township Comm. of Morris, 244 A.2d 145 (N.J. Super. 1968). Any such waiver should be explicit and not left to implication. Lakes Envtl. Ass'n v. Town of Naples, 486 A.2d 91 (Me. 1984). Most courts have determined that action upon a request for such a waiver should be supported by findings of fact sufficient to support judicial review. Amato v. Randolph Township Planning Bd., 457 A.2d 1188 (N.J. Super, 1982); Town of Hinsdale v. Emerson, 453 A.2d 1249 (N.H. 1982), *but see* Arrigo v. Planning Bd. of Franklin, 429 N.E.2d 355 (Mass. App. 1981); Windsor v. Planning Bd., 531 N.E. 2nd 272 (Mass. App. 1988). Where state law grants authority to planning commissions to exempt subdivision submittal in certain specified instances in which the purposes of the subdivision platting statute would not require plat approval—but subject to application to the commission for a waiver—a municipal regulation automatically exempting certain subdivisions was held to conflict with the state statutory scheme. Kenai Peninsula Borough v. Kenai Peninsula Bd. of Realtors, Inc., 652 P.2d 471 (Alaska 1982).

89. Garden State Homes, Inc. v. Heusner, 400 N.Y.S.2d 598 (App. Div. 3d Dep't. 1977).

90. Friends of the Pine Bush v. Planning Bd. of Albany, 450 N.Y.S.2d 966 (App. Div. 3d Dept., 1982) aff'd. 452 N.E.2d 1252; Hart Realty Co. v. Wright Township Bd. of Supervisors, 457 A.2d 240 (Pa. Commw. 1982) (abuse of discretion to waive installation of capped sewers after sewer authority determined not to extend the trunk line to serve the subdivision; Wheatley v. Planning Bd., 388 N.E.2d 315 (Mass. App. 1979).

91. Clemons v. City of Los Angeles, 222 P.2d 439 (Cal. 1950); Bonner Properties, Inc. v. Planning Bd. of Franklin Township, 449 A.2d 1350 (N.J. Super. Ct. Law Div. 1982) (civil action to set aside conveyances made prior to final subdivision approval); J.D. Land Corp. v. Allen, 277 A.2d 404 (N.J. Super. Ct. App. Div. 1971) (withholding of certificate of occupancy); Town of Nags Head v. Tillett, 315 S.E. 2d 740 (N.C. Ct. App. 1984) (town cannot declare void a conveyance that has already occurred, but can deny building permits); O.T. Seal v. Polehn, 628 P.2d 746 (Ore. Ct. App. 1981) (sales made in violation of subdivision regulations should be voidable, not void); State v. Fowler, 525 P.2d 1061 (Ore. Ct. App. 1974) (real estate agent liable for selling lots in violation of subdivision regulations); State ex rel. Craven v. City of Tacoma, 385 P.2d 372 (Wash. 1963); D. HAGMAN & J. JUERGENSMEYER, URBAN PLANNING & LAND DEVELOPMENT CONTROL LAW 261-62 (2d ed. 1986).

92. Adams v. Village of Westhampton Beach, 336 N.Y.S.2d 662 (Sup. Ct. 1972); Gerard v. San Juan City, 715 P.2d 149 (Wash. Ct. App. 1986); Kates v. City of Seattle, 723 P.2d 493 (Wash. Ct. App. 1986); *see* D. HAGMAN & J. JUERGENSMEYER, URBAN PLANNING LAND DEVELOPMENT CONTROL LAW 197-98 (2d ed. 1986).

93. Pratt v. Adams, 40 Cal. Rptr. 505 (Ct. App. 1964). *See also* Bright v. Board of Supervisors, 135 Cal. Rptr. 758 (Cal. App. 1977) (conveyance to joint tenants and subsequent partition was held to be a subdivision and subject to the subdivision regulations).

94. Munns v. Stenman, 314 P.2d 67, 73 (Cal. App. 1957).

95. Keizer v. Adams, 471 P.2d 983, 986 (Cal. 1970).

96. *Cf.* Slagle Constr. Co. v. County of Contra Costa, 136 Cal. Rptr. 748 (Cal. App. 1977) (government conditioned issuance of building permit on underground installation of utility lines).

97. Kulpinski v. City of Tarpon Springs, 473 So.2d 813 (Fla. Dist. Ct. App. 1985) (in an action against the city for negligent approval of a plat, the court didn't rule on the city's liability, but held the developer liable); Visidor Corp. v. Cliffside Park, 225 A.2d 105 (N.J. 1966); Panepinto v. Edmart, Inc., 323 A.2d 533 (N.J. Super. Ct. App. Div. 1974); Brenner v. Township of Jackson, 228 A.2d 721 (N.J. Super. Ct. App. Div. 1967); Foley v. Hamilton, 659 S.W.2d 356 (1983) (city has governmental immunity for tort liability for negligent approval of plat); City of Round Rock v. Smith, 687 S.W.2d 300 (Tex. 1985) (in an action for negligent subdivision approval, the approval is a governmental rather than a discretionary action, and the city is therefore protected by governmental immunity).

98. See, e.g., Breiner v. C & P Home Builders, Inc., 536 F.2d 27 (3d Cir. 1976) (concerning government failure regarding drainage system for subdivision).

99. Kulpinski v. City of Tarpon Springs, 473 So.2d 813 (Fla. Dist. Ct. App. 1985); Lovett v. Borough of Keyport, 42 A.2d 199 (N.J. Super Ct. App. Div. 1945); Newman v. Ocean Township, 21 A.2d 841 (N.J. Super. Ct. App. Div. 1941).

100. Rodrigues v. Hawaii, 472 P.2d 509 (Haw. 1970); Eschette v. City of New Orleans, 245 So.2d 383 (La. 1971).

Definitions[1]

2.1 Usage.

1. For the purpose of these regulations, certain numbers, abbreviations, terms, and words shall be used, interpreted, and defined as set forth in this Article 6.
2. Unless the context clearly indicates to the contrary, words used in the present tense include the future tense and words used in the plural include the singular.

2.2 Words and Terms Defined.

1. *Adequate Public Facilities.* Facilities determined to be capable of supporting and servicing the physical area and designated intensity of the proposed subdivision as determined by the Governing Body based upon specific levels of service.
2. *Administrative Assistant to the Planning Commission.* The officer appointed by the Governing Body to administer these regulations and to assist administratively other Boards and Commissions. If no such officer is appointed, the Building and Zoning Inspector shall serve also as Administrative Assistant.
3. *Affordable Housing.* Housing that is affordable to very low-income, low-income, or moderate-income persons as defined by the Department of Housing and Urban Development regulation for the municipality and is maintained for occupancy exclusively for such very low-income, low-income, or moderate-income person(s) for a period of not less than thirty (30) years through the use of a covenant or deed restriction, a development agreement, or by

transferring an interest to a state or municipal housing agency or nonprofit housing organization.

4. *Affordable Unit.* A designated unit of affordable housing which is sold or rented to a household of very low, low, or moderate income.

5. *Alley.* A public or private right-of-way primarily designed to serve as secondary access to the side or rear of those properties whose principal frontage is on some other street.

6. *Annual Net Income.* Net income as defined in _____ [insert appropriate state or local code section here].

7. *Applicant.* The owner of land proposed to be subdivided or its representative who shall have express written authority to act on behalf of the owner. Consent shall be required from the legal owner of the premises.

8. *Area of Benefit.* An area of land which is designated by the Planning Commission as receiving benefits from or creating the need for the construction, acquisition, or improvement of a Public Facilities Project.

9. *Area-related Facility.* A capital improvement which is designated in the capital improvements program as serving new development and which is not a site-related facility. Area-related facility may include land dedication or construction of an oversized capital improvement, whether located offsite, or within or on the perimeter of the development site.

10. *Assessment District.* See *Public Facility Service Area*.

11. *Average Density.* See *Cluster Zoning*.

12. *Base Price.* 2.5 times the median income for a family of four persons for _____ [insert appropriate geographic designation here] on the date on which a housing unit is sold.

13. *Base Rent.* Thirty percent (30%) of the median income for the _____[insert appropriate geographic designation here].

14. *Block.* A tract of land bounded by streets, or by a combination of streets and public parks, cemeteries, railroad rights-of-way, shorelines of waterways, or boundary lines of municipalities.

15. *Bond.* Any form of a surety bond in an amount and form satisfactory to the Governing Body. All bonds shall be approved by the Governing Body whenever a bond is required by these regulations.

16. *Buffer.* See External Buffer

17. *Building.* Any structure built for the support, shelter, or enclosure of persons, animals, chattels, or movable property of any kind.

18. *Building and Zoning Inspector.* The person designated by the local government to enforce the Zoning Ordinance. If no Administrative Assistant to the Planning Commission is appointed to administer these regulations, the Building and Zoning Inspector shall administer these regulations.

19. *Capital Improvement.* A public facility with a life expectancy of three or more years, to be owned and operated by or on behalf of the local government.

20. *Capital Improvements Program.* A plan setting forth, by category of public facilities, those capital improvements and that portion of their costs which are attributable to serving new development within designated service areas for such public facilities over a period of specified years (10-20). Capital improvements program may refer either to the plan for a particular service area or to the aggregation of capital improvements and the associated costs programmed for all service areas for a particular category of public facilities.

21. *Central Sewerage System.* A community sewer system including collection and treatment facilities established by the developer to serve a new subdivision in an outlying area.

22. *Central Water System.* A private water company formed by a developer to serve new subdivision in an outlying area. It includes water treatment and distribution facilities.

23. *Certify.* Whenever these regulations require that an agency or official certify the existence of some fact or circumstance, the municipality by administrative rule may require that such certification be made in any manner, oral or written, which provides reasonable assurance of the accuracy of the certification.

24. *Cluster Zoning.* A technique which allows lots to be reduced in size and buildings sited closer together provided the total development density does not exceed that which could be constructed on the site under conventional zoning and the remaining land is utilized for open space or public purposes.

25. *Collector Roads.* A road intended to move traffic from local roads to secondary arterials. A collector road serves a neighborhood or large subdivision and should be designed so that no residential properties face onto it.

26. *Common Ownership.* Ownership by the same person, corporation, firm, entity, partnership, or unincorporated association; or ownership by different corporations, firms, partnerships, entities, or unincorporated associations, in which a stockbroker, partner, or associate, or a member of his family owns an interest in each corporation, firm, partnership, entity, or unincorporated association.

27. *Community Improvement District.* See *Public Facility Service Area.*

28. *Concurrency.* Requirement that development applications demonstrate that adequate public facilities be available at prescribed levels of service concurrent with the impact or occupancy of development units.

29. *Condominium.* A unit available for sale in fee simple contained in a multi-occupancy project subject to covenants and restrictions placing control over the common facilities in an elected board.

30. *Construction of Housing by a Sponsor.* Construction of housing units by an entity which includes the sponsor as a partner or joint venture, provided that the sponsor has general liability for the obligations of such entity. Construction of housing shall include rehabilitation of substandard, deteriorated units which:
    a. Are unsafe, unsanitary, or a danger to the health, safety, or welfare of an occupant;
    b. Have a rehabilitation cost in excess of $20,000 per unit; and
    c. Have been occupied continuously for three years prior to commencement of construction to rehabilitate the units, except for those units owned and operated by a government agency or a nonprofit organization.

31. *Construction Plan.* The maps or drawings accompanying a subdivision plat and showing the specific location and design of improvements to be installed in the subdivision in accordance with the requirements of the Planning Commission as a condition of the approval of the plat.

32. *Contiguous.* Lots are contiguous when at least one boundary line of one lot touches a boundary line or lines of another lot.

33. *Cooperative.* An entire project which is under the common ownership of a Board of Directors with units leased and stock sold to individual cooperators.

34. *Credit.* The amount of the reduction of an impact fee or fees, payments or charges for the same type of capital improvement for which the fee has been charged.

35. *Cul-de-Sac.* A local street with only one outlet that terminates in a vehicular turnaround and having an appropriate terminal for the safe and convenient reversal of traffic movement.

36. *Design Criteria.* Standards that set forth specific improvement requirements.

37. *Designated Unit.* A housing unit identified and reported to Administrative Assistant by the sponsor of an office development project subject to Section 5.13 of these Regulations as a unit that shall be affordable to households of low or moderate income for 20 years.

38. *Developer.* The owner of land proposed to be subdivided or its representative who is responsible for any undertaking that requires review and/or approval under these regulations. See *Subdivider.*

39. *Development Agreement.* Agreement between the Governing Body and developer through which the Governing Body agrees to vest development use or intensity or refrain from interfering with sub-

sequent phases of development through new legislation in exchange for the provision of public facilities or amenities by the developer in excess of those required under current community regulations.

40. *Easement.* Authorization by a property owner for another to use the owner's property for a specified purpose.
41. *Equivalent Dwelling Units.* See *Service Unit.*
42. *Escrow.* A deposit of cash with the local government or escrow agent to secure the promise to perform some act.
43. *Exactions.* Requirement of development to dedicate or pay for all or a portion of land or costs of public facilities as a condition of development approval.
44. *Expenditure.* A sum of money paid out in return for some benefit or to fulfill some obligation. The term includes binding contractual commitments whether by development agreement or otherwise to make future expenditures as well as any other substantial change in position.
45. *External Buffer.* A naturally vegetated area or vegetated area along the exterior boundaries of an entire development processed in accordance with a multiphase or phased subdivision application which is landscaped and maintained as open space in order to eliminate or minimize conflicts between such development and adjacent land uses.
46. *Fair Share.* A properly balanced and well-ordered plan to meet the housing needs of the community and the region.
47. *Final Subdivision Plat.* The map of a subdivision to be recorded after approval by the Planning Commission and any accompanying material as described in these regulations.
48. *Flexible Zoning.* Zoning which permits uses of land and density of buildings and structures different from those which are allowed as of right within the zoning district in which the land is situated. Flexible zoning applications shall include, but not be limited to, all special permits and special uses, planned unit developments, group housing projects, community unit projects, and average density or density zoning projects.
49. *Frontage.* That side of a lot abutting on a street or way and ordinarily regarded as the front of the lot; but it shall not be considered as the ordinary side of a corner lot.
50. *Frontage Street.* Any street to be constructed by the developer or any existing street where development shall take place on both sides.
51. *Governing Body.* The body of the local government having the power to adopt ordinances.
52. *Grade.* The slope of a road, street, or other public way specified in percentage terms.

53. *Health Department and Health Officer.* The agency and person designated by the Governing Body to administer the health regulations of the local government.
54. *Health, Safety, or General Welfare.* The purpose for which municipalities may adopt and enforce land use regulations for the prevention of harm or promotion of public benefit to the community; commonly referred to as police power.
55. *High Density.* Those residential zoning districts in which the density is equal to or greater than one dwelling unit per 10,000 square feet.
56. *Highway, Limited Access.* A freeway or expressway providing a trafficway for through traffic, in respect to which owners or occupants of abutting property on lands and other persons have no legal right to access to or from the same, except at such points and in such manner as may be determined by the public authority having jurisdiction over the trafficway.
57. *Homeowners Association.* See *Property Owners Association.*
58. *Household.* Any person or persons who reside or intend to reside in the same housing unit.
59. *Household of Low Income.* A household composed of one or more persons with a combined annual net income for all adult members which does not exceed the qualifying limit for a lower-income family of a size equivalent to the number of persons residing in such household, as set forth for the _____ [insert appropriate state or local code section here].
60. *Household of Moderate Income.* A household composed of one or more persons with a combined annual net income for all adult members which does not exceed the qualifying limit for a median-income family of a size equivalent to the number of persons residing in such household _____ [insert appropriate state or local code section here].
61. *Housing Unit* or *Unit.* A dwelling unit as defined in _____ [insert appropriate state or local code section here].
62. *Impact Fee.* A fee imposed on new development by the local government pursuant to this article in order to mitigate the impacts on community facilities created by the demand for capital improvements by the new development. Impact fees do not include the dedication of rights-of-way or easements for such facilities, or the construction of such improvements. Impact fees also do not include [describe here fees exempt by statute or falling outside definition].
63. *Improvements.* See *Lot Improvement* or *Public Improvement.*
64. *Individual Sewage Disposal System.* A septic tank, seepage tile sewage disposal system, or any other approved sewage treatment device.

65. *Infill Development.* Development designed to occupy scattered or vacant parcels of land which remain after the majority of development has occurred in an area.

66. *Landscaping.* Acting with the purpose of meeting specific criteria regarding uses of outside space, including ground cover, buffers, and shade trees.

67. *Linkage.* A program that requires developers constructing nonresidential structures to either construct affordable housing units or pay money in lieu of construction into a designated fund to provide housing for the future employees of the site.

68. *Local Government.* The municipality of _____.

69. *Local Government Attorney.* The licensed attorney designated by the Governing Body to furnish legal assistance for the administration of these regulations.

70. *Local Government Engineer.* The licensed engineer designated by the Governing Body to furnish engineering assistance for the administration of these regulations.

71. *Local Road.* A road whose sole function is to provide access to abutting properties and to other roads from individual properties and to provide right-of-way beneath it for sewer, water, and storm drainage pipes.

72. *Lot.* A tract, plot, or portion of a subdivision or other parcel of land intended as a unit for the purpose, whether immediate or future, of transfer of ownership, or possession, or for building development.

73. *Lot, Corner.* A lot situated at the intersection of two (2) streets, the interior angle of such intersection not exceeding 135 degrees.

74. *Lot Improvement.* Any building, structure, place, work of art, or other object situated on a lot.

75. *Low Density.* Those residential zoning districts in which the density is equal to or less than one dwelling unit per 40,000 square feet.

76. *Major Subdivision.* All subdivisions not classified as minor subdivisions, including but not limited to subdivisions of four (4) or more lots, or any size subdivision requiring any new street or extension of the local government facilities or the creation of any public improvements.

77. *Market Value.* The fair market value of a designated unit at the time such value is determined by the Administrative Assistant.

78. *Master Plan.* A comprehensive plan for development of the local government prepared and adopted by the Planning Commission, pursuant to State law, and including any part of such plan separately adopted and any amendment to such plan, or parts thereof.

79. *Master Preliminary Plat.* That portion of a preliminary plat submitted in connection with a multiphase or phased subdivision application

which provides the information and graphics meeting the requirements of this ordinance for the purpose of implementing an integrated development scheme for all phases of the proposed subdivision.

80. *Medium Density.* Those residential zoning districts in which the density is between 10,000 and 40,000 square feet per dwelling unit.

81. *Metropolitan or Regional Planning Commission and Metropolitan or Regional Council of Governments.* The agency performing A-95 review of all federal grant-in-aid projects that are required to be reviewed by regional and state planning boards to ensure the projects conform to regional and state needs; the planning agency established to carry on regional or metropolitan comprehensive planning.

82. *Minor Subdivision.* Any subdivision containing not more than three (3) lots fronting on an existing street, not involving any new street or road, or the extension of municipal facilities or the creation of any public improvements, and not adversely affecting the remainder of the parcel or adjoining property, and not in conflict with any provision or portion of the Master Plan, Official Map, Zoning Ordinance, or these regulations.

83. *Model Home.* A dwelling unit used initially for display purposes which typifies the type of units that will be constructed in the subdivision and which will not be permanently occupied during its use as a model.

84. *Money in Lieu of Land.* Payment of money into a municipally earmarked fund to provide for acquisition of facilities off-site in place of dedicating land or providing such facility on site.

85. *Municipality.* See *Local Government.*

86. *Neighborhood Park and Recreation Improvement Fund.* A special fund established by the Governing Body to retain monies contributed by developers in accordance with the "money in lieu of land" provisions of these regulations.

87. *New Development.* A project involving the construction, reconstruction, redevelopment, conversion, structural alteration, relocation, or enlargement of any structure; or any use or extension of land; any of which has the effect of increasing the requirements for capital improvements, measured by number of service units to be generated by such activity, and which requires either the approval of a plat pursuant to the City's subdivision regulations, the issuance of a building permit, or connection to the City's water or sanitary sewer system.

88. *Nonresidential Subdivision.* A subdivision whose intended use is other than residential, such as commercial or industrial.

89. *Notice of Noncompliance.* A notice issued by the Administrative Assistant to the Planning Commission informing the applicant for

approval of a major subdivision that the sketch plat is not in compliance with these regulations and that the applicant may not apply for preliminary plat approval.

90. *Notice to Proceed.* A notice issued by the Administrative Assistant to the Planning Commission informing the applicant for approval of a major subdivision that the sketch plat is in compliance with these regulations and that the applicant may proceed to apply for preliminary plat approval.

91. *Offset.* The amount of the reduction of an impact fee designed to fairly reflect the value of area-related facilities or other oversized facilities, pursuant to rules herein established or administrative guidelines, provided by a developer pursuant to the local government's subdivision or zoning regulations or requirements.

92. *Off-Site.* Any premises not located within the area of the property to be subdivided, whether or not in the common ownership of the applicant for subdivision approval.

93. *Office Development Project.* Any new construction, addition, extension, conversion, or enlargement, or combination thereof, of an existing structure which includes any gross square feet of office space.

94. *Office Use.* Space within a structure or portion thereof intended or primarily suitable for occupancy by persons or entities which perform, provide for their own benefit, or provide to others at that location, services including but not limited to the following: professional, banking, insurance, management, consulting, technical, sales, and design; or the office functions of manufacturing and warehousing businesses, but excluding retail uses; repair; any business characterized by the physical transfer of tangible goods to customers on the premises; wholesale shipping, receiving, and storage; and design showcases or any other space intended and primarily suitable for display of goods. This definition shall include all uses encompassed within the meaning of _____ [insert appropriate state or local code section here].

95. *Official Map.* The map established by the Governing Body pursuant to law showing the streets, highways, parks, drainage systems and setback lines laid out, adopted, and established by law, and any amendments or additions to adopted by the Governing Body resulting from the approval of subdivision plats by the Planning Commission and the subsequent filing of approved plats.

96. *Official Master Plan.* See *Master Plan*.

97. *Ordinance.* Any legislative action, however denominated, of a local government which has the force of law, including any amendment or repeal of any ordinance.

98. *Owned Unit.* A designated unit which is a condominium, stock cooperative, or community apartment.

99. *Owner.* The record owners of the fee or a vendee in possession, including any person, group of persons, firm or firms, corporation or corporations, or any other legal entity having legal title to or sufficient proprietary interest in the land sought to be subdivided under the definition of *Same Ownership.*

100. *Performance Criteria.* Regulation of development based on open space ratio, impervious surface ratio, density, and floor area ratio.

101. *Perimeter Street.* Any existing street to which the parcel of land to be subdivided abuts on only one (1) side.

102. *Person.* Any individual or group of individuals, or any corporation, general or limited partnership, joint venture, unincorporated association, or governmental or quasi-governmental entity.

103. *Phased Subdivision Application.* An application for subdivision approval submitted pursuant to a Master Preliminary Plat, or at the option of the subdivider, pursuant to a specific plan in which the applicant proposes to immediately subdivide the property but will develop in one or more individual phase(s) over a period of time. A phased subdivision application may include an application for approval of, or conversion to, horizontal or vertical condominiums, nonresidential development projects, planned unit developments, mixed-use projects, and residential developments.

104. *Planned Unit Development (PUD).* A development constructed on a tract of minimum size under single ownership planned and developed as an integral unit and consisting of a combination of residential and/or nonresidential uses on the land.

105. *Planning Commission.* The local government's Planning Commission established in accordance with law.

106. *Police Power.* Inherent, delegated, or authorized legislative power for purposes of regulation to secure health, safety, and general welfare.

107. *Preliminary Plat.* The preliminary drawing or drawings, described in these regulations, indicating the proposed manner or layout of the subdivision to be submitted to the Planning Commission for approval.

108. *Primary Arterial.* A road intended to move through traffic to and from major attractors such as central business districts, regional shopping centers, colleges and/or universities, military installations, major industrial areas, and similar traffic generators within the governmental unit; and/or as a route for traffic between communities or large areas and/or which carries high volumes of traffic.

109. *Property Owners Association.* An association or organization, whether or not incorporated, which operates under and pursuant to recorded

covenants or deed restrictions, through which each owner of a portion of a subdivision—be it a lot, parcel site, unit plot, condominium, or any other interest—is automatically a member as a condition of ownership and each such member is subject to a charge or assessment for a pro-rated share of expense of the association which may become a lien against the lot, parcel, unit, condominium, or other interest of the member.

110. *Public Facility* means [separately identify categories of public facilities and the types of improvements for which an impact fee will be charged for each such category under this article]. Public facility excludes those improvements that are site-related facilities.

111. *Public Facility Impact Fee.* An impact fee to be imposed and collected for [identify category of public facility and define for each category for which a fee is to be charged].

112. *Public Facility Improvements Program* [identify improvements program to correspond to public facilities for which an impact fee will be charged]. The adopted plan, as may be amended from time to time, which identifies the public facilities and their costs for each public facility benefit area or subarea, which serve new development for a period not to exceed ten (10) years, which are to be financed in whole or in part through the imposition of public facilities fees pursuant to this article.

113. *Public Facilities Project.* Any and all public improvements the need for which is directly or indirectly generated by development, including but not limited to the following:

a. Water mains, pipes, conduits, tunnels, hydrants, and other necessary works and appliances for providing water service.

b. Lines, conduits, and other necessary works and appliances for providing electric power service.

c. Mains, pipes, and other necessary works and appliances for providing gas service.

d. Poles, posts, wires, pipes, conduits, lamps, and other necessary works and appliances for lighting purposes.

e. Sidewalks, crosswalks, steps, safety zones, platforms, seats, statuary, fountains, culverts, bridges, curbs, gutters, tunnels, subways or viaducts, parks and parkways, recreation areas, including all structures, buildings, and other facilities necessary to make parks and parkways and recreation areas useful for the purposes for which intended.

f. Sanitary sewers or instrumentalities of sanitation, together with the necessary outlets, cesspools, manholes, catch basins, flush tanks, septic tanks, disposal plants, connecting sewers, ditches, drains, conduits, tunnels, channels, or other appurtenances.

g. Drains, tunnels, sewers, conduits, culverts and channels for drainage purposes; with necessary outlets, cesspools, manholes, catch basins, flush tanks, septic tanks, disposal plants, connecting sewers, ditches, drains, conduits, channels, and appurtenances.

h. Pipes, hydrants, and appliances for fire protection.

i. Breakwaters, levees, bulkheads, groins and walls of rock, or other material to protect the streets, places, public ways, and other property from overflow by water, or to prevent beach erosion or to promote accretion to beaches.

j. Retaining walls, embankments, buildings, and any other structures or facilities necessary or suitable in connection with any of the work mentioned in this section.

k. Compaction of land, change of grade or contours, construction of caissons, retaining walls, drains, and other structures suitable for the purpose of stabilizing land.

l. Works, systems, or facilities for the transportation of people, including rolling stock and other equipment appurtenant thereto.

m. All other work auxiliary to that described in subparagraph 12 which may be required to carry out that work, including terminal and intermediate stations, structures, platforms, or other facilities which may be necessary for the loading of people into and unloading of people from such transportation facilities.

n. The grading or regrading, the paving or repaving, the planking or replanking, the macadamizing or remacadamizing, the graveling or regraveling, and the oiling or reoiling of streets.

o. Acquisition, construction, improvement, and equipping of temporary and permanent school buildings.

p. Acquisition, construction, improvement, and equipping of fire stations.

q. Acquisition, construction, improvement, and equipping of police stations.

r. Acquisition, construction, and installation of traffic signs, signals, lights, and lighting.

s. Public works maintenance facilities.

t. All other work auxiliary to any of the above which may be required to carry out that work including, but not limited to, the maintenance of Public Facilities Projects and administrative, engineering, architectural, and legal work performed in connection with establishing, implementing, and monitoring Public Facilities Projects.

u. Acquisition of any and all property, easements, and rights-of-way which may be required to carry out the purposes of the project.

114. *Public Facility Service Area.* The service area for [identify category of public facility and define for each category for which a fee is to be charged].

115. *Public Hearing.* An adjudicatory proceeding held by the Planning Commission preceded by published notice and actual notice to certain persons and at which certain persons, including the applicant, may call witnesses and introduce evidence for the purpose of demonstrating that plat approval should or should not be granted. Witnesses shall be sworn and subject to cross-examination. The rules of civil procedure binding on the courts shall not, however, bind the Planning Commission.

116. *Public Improvement.* Any drainage ditch, roadway, parkway, sidewalk, pedestrianway, tree, lawn, off-street parking area, lot improvement, or other facility for which the local government may ultimately assume the responsibility for maintenance and operation, or which may effect an improvement for which local government responsibility is established.

117. *Public Meeting.* A meeting of the Planning Commission or Governing Body preceded by notice, open to the public and at which the public may, at the discretion of the body holding the public meeting, be heard.

118. *Recoupment.* The imposition of an impact fee to reimburse the local government for capital improvements previously oversized to serve new development.

119. *Regional Planning Commission and Regional Council of Governments.* See *Metropolitan or Regional Planning Commission.*

120. *Registered Engineer.* An engineer properly licensed and registered in the State.

121. *Registered Land Surveyor.* A land surveyor properly licensed and registered in the State.

122. *Rental Unit.* A designated unit which is not a condominium, stock cooperative, or community apartment.

123. *Resubdivision.* Any change in a map of an approved or recorded subdivision plat that affects any street layout on the map or area reserved thereon for public use or any lot line, or that affects any map or plan legally recorded prior to the adoption of any regulations controlling subdivisions.

124. *Retail Use.* Space within any structure or portion thereof intended or primarily suitable for occupancy by persons or entities which supply commodities to customers on the premises including, but not limited to, stores, shops, restaurants, bars, eating and drinking businesses, and the uses defined in _____ [insert appropriate state or local code section here], and also including all space accessory to such retail use.

125. **Right-of-Way.** A strip of land occupied or intended to be occupied by a street, crosswalk, railroad, road, electric transmission line, oil or gas pipeline, water main, sanitary or storm sewer main, shade trees, or for any other special use. The usage of the term "right-of-way" for land platting purposes shall mean that every right-of-way hereafter established and shown on a final plat is to be separate and distinct from the lots or parcels adjoining such right-of-way and not included within the dimensions or areas of such lots or parcels. Rights-of-way intended for streets, crosswalks, water mains, sanitary sewers, storm drains, shade trees, or any other use involving maintenance by a public agency shall be dedicated to public use by the maker of the plat on which such right-of-way is established.

126. **Road, Classification.** For the purpose of providing for the development of the streets, highways, roads and rights-of-way in the governmental unit, and for their future improvement, reconstruction, realignment, and necessary widening, including provision for curbs and sidewalks, each existing street, highway, road, and right-of-way, and those located on approved and filed plats, have been designated on the Official Map of the local government and classified therein. The classification of each street, highway, road, and right-of-way is based upon its location in the respective zoning districts of the local government and its present and estimated future traffic volume and its relative importance and function as specified in the Master Plan of the local government. The required improvements shall be measured as set forth for each street classification on the Official Map.

127. **Road, Dead-End.** A road or a portion of a road with only one (1) vehicular-traffic outlet.

128. **Road Right-of-Way Width.** The distance between property lines measured at right angles to the center line of the street.

129. **Sale or Lease.** Any immediate or future transfer of ownership, or any possessory interest in land, including contract of sale, lease, devise, intestate succession, or other transfer of an interest in a subdivision or part thereof, whether by metes and bounds or lot and block description.

130. **Screening.** Either (a) a strip at least ten (10) feet wide of densely planted (or having equivalent natural growth) shrubs or trees at least four (4) feet high at the time of planting, of a type that will form a year-round dense screen at least six (6) feet high; or (b) an opaque wall or barrier or uniformly painted fence at least six (6) feet high.

131. **Secondary Arterial.** A road intended to collect and distribute traffic in a manner similar to primary arterials, except that these roads service

minor traffic-generating areas such as community commercial areas, primary and secondary educational facilities, hospitals, major recreational areas, churches, and offices and are designed to carry traffic from collector streets to the system of primary arterials.

132. *Security.* The letter of credit or cash escrow provided by the applicant to secure its promises in the subdivision improvement agreement.

133. *Service Area.* The area for a particular category of public facilities within the jurisdiction of the local government and within which impact fees for capital improvements will be collected for new development occurring within such area and within which fees so collected will be expended for those types of improvements for that category of public facility identified in the public facility improvements program. Service areas may be subdivided into subareas for purposes of assuring that impact fees collected and expended therein reasonably benefit new development within such areas.

134. *Service Unit.* Either [identify, collectively, each service unit for each category of public facility for which an impact fee is to be charged], which is the standardized measure of consumption, use, or generation attributable to a new unit of development for that category of public facility and which is set forth in the impact fee schedules for that category of public facility.

135. *Setback.* The distance between a building and the street line nearest to the building.

136. *Shade Tree.* A tree in a public place, street, special easement, or right-of-way adjoining a street as provided in these regulations.

137. *Site-related facility.* An improvement or facility which is for the primary use or benefit of a new development and/or which is for the primary purpose of safe and adequate provision of [identify categories of public facilities for which an impact fee is to be charged] to serve the new development, and which is not included in the capital improvements program and for which the developer or property owner is solely responsible under subdivision or other applicable regulations.

138. *Sketch Plat.* A sketch preparatory to the preliminary plat (or final plat in the case of minor subdivisions) to enable the subdivider to save time and expense in reaching general agreement with the Planning Commission as to the form of the plat and the objectives of these regulations.

139. *Specific Plan.* A document encompassing a specific geographic area of the local government which is prepared for the purpose of specifically implementing the local government comprehensive plan by (1) refining the policies of the comprehensive plan to a specific geographic area; (2) containing specific recommendation as to the detailed policies and regulations applicable to a focused development scheme. The

specific plan shall consist of goals, objectives and policies; requirements for capital improvements; the level of service required for public
facilities; physical and environmental conditions; housing and land
use characteristics of the area; and maps, diagrams, and other appropriate materials showing existing and future conditions.

140. *Sponsor.* An applicant seeking approval for construction of an office
development project subject to Section 5.13 of these Regulations, such
applicant's successors and assigns, and/or any entity which controls
or is under common control with such applicant.

141. *Street.* See *Road.*

142. *Structure.* Anything constructed or erected.

143. *Subdivide.* The act or process of creating a subdivision.

144. *Subdivider.* Any person who (1) having an interest in land, causes it,
directly or indirectly, to be divided into a subdivision or who (2)
directly or indirectly, sells, leases, or develops, or offers to sell, lease,
or develop, or advertises to sell, lease, or develop, any interest, lot,
parcel site, unit, or plat in a subdivision, or, who (3) engages directly
or through an agent in the business of selling, leasing, developing, or
offering for sale, lease, or development a subdivision or any interest,
lot, parcel site, unit, or plat in a subdivision, and who (4) is directly or
indirectly controlled by, or under direct or indirect common control
with any of the foregoing.

145. *Subdivision.* Any land, vacant or improved, which is divided or
proposed to be divided into two (2) or more lots, parcels, sites, units,
plots, condominiums, tracts, or interests for the purpose of offer, sale,
lease, or development whether immediate or future, either on the
installment plan or upon any and all other plans, terms, and conditions. Subdivision includes the division or development of residen-
tially and nonresidentially zoned land, whether by deed, metes and
bounds description, devise, intestacy, lease, map, plat, or other recorded instrument. Subdivision includes resubdivision and condominium creation or conversion.

146. *Subdivision Agent.* Any person who represents, or acts for or on behalf
of, a subdivider or developer, in selling, leasing, or developing, or
offering to sell, lease, or develop any interest, lot, parcel, unit, site, or
plat in a subdivision, except an attorney-at-law whose representation
of another person consists solely of rendering legal services.

147. *Subdivision Improvement Agreement.* A contract entered into by the
applicant and the Planning Commission on behalf of the municipality
by which the applicant promises to complete the required public
improvements within the subdivision within a specified time period
following final subdivision plat approval.

148. *Subdivision, Major.* See *Major Subdivision*
149. *Subdivision, Minor.* See *Minor Subdivision*
150. *Subdivision Plat.* The final map or drawing, described in these regulations, on which the subdivider's plan of subdivision is presented to the Planning Commission for approval and which, if approved, may be submitted to the County Clerk or Recorder of Deeds for filing.
151. *Temporary Improvement.* Improvements built and maintained by a subdivider during construction of the subdivision and prior to release of the performance bond.
152. *Tract.* A lot. The term "tract" is used interchangeably with the term "lot," particularly in the context or subdivision, where a "tract" is subdivided into several lots, parcels, sites, units, plots, condominiums, tracts, or interests.
153. *Transfer of Development Rights.* The conveyance of development rights by deed, easement, or other legal instrument, authorized by ordinance or regulation, to another parcel of land and the recording of that conveyance.
154. *Use to Use Relationship.* Focusing on the unique aspects of established, newly developed and redeveloping neighborhoods, and commercial/industrial areas in order to achieve improved compatibility and fit of infill development projects and at the same time assist in the preservation and conservation of stable existing neighborhoods and commercial areas.
155. *Vested Rights.* Right to initiate or continue the establishment of a use which will be contrary to a restriction or regulation coming into effect when the project associated with the use is completed.

1. Additional material appropriate to specific local jurisdictions should be considered for insertion into these definitions.

COMMENTARY ON ARTICLE 2

The definitional section of the regulations, like many other parts of the Model Regulations, is intended to provide specificity in areas where ambiguity would lead to confusion and the opportunity to evade the requirements.* All generic

* Many sources were drawn upon for the creation of these definitions. In addition to the first edition of the Model Subdivision Regulations, credit must be given to: LISTOKIN & WALKER, THE SUBDIVISION AND SITE PLAN HANDBOOK, Center for Urban Policy Research (Rutgers, 1989); MANDELKER, LAND USE LAW (2d ed. 1988); RATHKOPF, THE LAW OF ZONING AND PLANNING (4th ed. 1986); KENDIG, PERFORMANCE ZONING, American Planning Association (1980); ROHAN, ZONING AND LAND USE CONTROLS (1988); Burrows, ed., A SURVEY OF ZONING DEFINITIONS, American Planning Association (1989); BROUGH, A UNIFIED DEVELOPMENT ORDINANCE, American Planning Association (1985).

and technical terms are precisely defined so that easy reference can be made to the usage in the regulations.

The failure to include an adequate and comprehensive set of definitions in any statute or ordinance can only lead to uncertainty in the long run—both for the community and the developer. It is unusual, to say the least, that the drafters of the SPEA thought that it was unnecessary to define statutory terms.[1] Terms that are vague and lack clear definition may lead a court to declare a provision in a land use ordinance invalid. The imprecision may be either in the enabling statute itself or in the subdivision regulations.[2]

Subdivision approval of cooperative and condominium units is a case in point. A distinction must be made between the conversion of a multifamily apartment building to a cooperative or condominium, and the initial construction of such units. If the municipality defines the construction of all multiple-family buildings as a subdivision (whether conventional, cooperative, or condominium), it is clearly permissible to regulate under the subdivision regulations.[3] Most states permit treating a condominium project as a subdivision even where traditional landlord-rental projects are exempted.[4]

Where, however, a conventional landlord-owned apartment building was not treated as a subdivision, conversion to a condominium or cooperative might not be subject to subdivision approval or zoning restriction.[5] Similarly, if a conventional landlord apartment building were subject to tentative subdivision map approval, the city could not subject the property to additional conditions upon a proposed conversion to condominium form of ownership.[6] Courts have invalidated subdivision regulations as being too vague when they required that a subdivision have "adequate" access,[7] or mandated "harmonious" development,[8] or permitted parallel streets in cases of "unusual" topography.[9] In each case, specific definitions could have saved the regulations at issue.

Similarly, a planning commission must be careful to make definitions and standards broadly inclusive in order to avoid judicial determinations that its actions are ultra vires in denying subdivision approval based upon considerations other than the minimum standards set forth in the subdivision ordinance.[10]

Because the Regulations contained here are a model, several terms have been defined generally to be consistent with the provisions of the Standard City Planning Enabling Act, but those terms may have to be defined further for a particular statute or local need. For example, the term "governing body" has been applied to the body that has appropriate legislative powers. Depending on the jurisdiction, this may be a city council, town board, village board of trustees, county court, county commission, county legislature, or other incorporated political subdivision. Each adopting jurisdiction will have to review carefully the provisions of the Model and make necessary adjustments. Similarly, the language of the Model uses the term "local government" in place of municipality. This is the language used by the

American Law Institute's Model Land Development Code and is a substitution for the language of the SPEA.[11] The language of the Model also uses terms such as "local government attorney" and "governmental engineer" in place of municipal attorney or county engineer. These terms will have to be adjusted to local needs. With appropriate adjustments, the Model may be adopted by municipalities, townships, and county governments.

The definition of subdivision will vary from state to state in the various enabling acts.[12] The definitions differ mainly in relation to the number of smaller parcels that must be created to constitute a subdivision and to whether the division of the tract must include a new street.[13] The broad definition adopted in the Model Regulations will eliminate most of the problems of subdivision evasion and is readily acceptable to the courts.[14] Most of the modern enabling statutes that include a definition of "subdivision" have been construed to authorize each governmental authority to define the term.[15] The government may not, however, regulate subdivisions that are not within the statutory definition.[16] The Model Regulations provide, in line with all statutory authority, that a violation of the regulations by subdividing without planning commission approval is subject to criminal and civil sanction.[17] Violation includes evasion of subdivision regulations through court actions for the partition of land.[18]

NOTES

1. *See* SPEA, Appendix B, General Statement; Some Details, Definitions: "A few definitions, only those felt to be absolutely necessary, have been included. The terms used in the act are so commonly understood that definitions are unnecessary. *Definitions are generally a source of danger; they give to words a restricted meaning*" (emphasis added). Thus, the courts have generally held that the term "plat" itself is a word of art in the planning profession and refers to any subdivision map that is required to be submitted for approval. Richards v. Abbottsford Homeowners Ass'n, 809 S.W.2d 193 (Tenn. App. 1990). *But see* "Regulations which restrict the use of land must be drafted with special care in the selection of language and meticulous attention to the definition of terms. Absent such careful draftsmanship, the objectives of a zoning ordinance may be lost in the process of construction." R. ANDERSON, AMERICAN LAW OF ZONING § 18.01 at 213 (3d ed. 1986). *See also* Reps & Smith, *Control of Urban Land Subdivision*, 14 SYRACUSE L. REV. 405 (1963).

2. The failure to define "subdivision" as "division or partition into lots, parcels, sites, (see Art. 2.2 (81)) *units*, plots or interests for purpose of offer, sale, lease or *development*" can often lead to difficulty. Thus, *compare* York v. Cragin, 541 A.2d 932 (Me. 1988) (pursuant to a statute which defined "subdivision" only as "division of a tract or parcel of land into 3 or more *lots*," the construction of a building divided into apartments (i.e., "units") does not constitute a subdivision) or Botti v. Russell, 580 N.Y.S.2d 505 (1992) (nor does the merger of one-half of a lot to one parcel and the other half to a second parcel constitute a subdivision) *with* Orrin Dressler, Inc. v. Burr Ridge, 527 N.E.2d. 1063 (Ill. App. 2d Dist. 1988) (the division of two lots into four lots was subject to the subdivision statute where lot lines will change by the division). *But see*, Lucas v. North Texas Mun. Water Dist., 723 S.W.2d 811 (Tex. App. 1986) (where definition of subdivision includes act of partition itself, i.e., development, without regard to a transfer of ownership, then a subdivision of land includes development and where a water district set aside and planned to fence a 75-acre tract to be developed, the district "subdivided" its property), with Persons v. City of Fort Worth,

790 S.W.2d 865 (Tex. App. Ft. Worth 1990) (the acts of the city in enlarging the zoo and including the enlarged area within the zoo fence do not constitute a partition or subdivision so as to require platting).

3. Maplewood Village Tenants Ass'n v. Maplewood Village, 282 A.2d 428 (N.J. 1971) (planning controls, including the requirement of subdivision approval, could not be employed by a municipality against only condominium construction since it is *use* rather than *form of ownership* that is the proper concern of subdivision and zoning regulation. A municipality may impose subdivision controls only if it imposes the same controls on conventional landlord-owned apartment buildings). A California court recently held that a local government may adopt supplementary development and design standards pursuant to the Subdivision Map Act covering condominium conversions that reasonably relate to purposes of the act. Soderling v. City of Santa Monica, 191 Cal. Rptr. 140 (Ct. App. 1983). *See also* Shelter Creek Dev. Corp. v. City of Oxnard, 669 P.2d 948 (Cal. 1983). *But see* York v. Cragin, 541 A.2d 932 (Me. 1988) (the construction of a building divided into apartments, or the alteration of a building to accommodate family units does not constitute a subdivision under a statute defining a subdivision as a "division of a tract or parcel of land into 3 or more lots").

4. Norsco Enter. v. City of Fremont, 54 Cal. App. 3d 488, 126 Cal. Rptr. 659 (1976) (condominium projects may be treated as a subdivision); Minnesota Uniform Condominium Act, 1980 New Laws, ch. 582; N.H. Rev. Stat. Ann. 36.1 VIII; Colo. Rev. Stat. 30-28-101 (condominium development included); N.Y. Real Prop. Law § 339f(2) overriding Gerber v. Town of Clarkstown, 78 Misc.2d 221, 356 N.Y.S.2d 926 (1974) and Kaufman & Broad Houses of Long Island, Inc. v. Albertson, 73 Misc.2d 84, 341 N.Y.S.2d 321 (1972). *But see* West Va. 1980 New Laws H.B. 788, p. 21; and Rhode Island 1982 New Laws, ch. 329, p. 1111 (construction of condominiums not subject to subdivision approval).

5. *See* Note, *The Condominium Conversion Problem: Causes and Solutions*, 1980 Duke L.J. 306; Note, The Validity of Ordinances Limiting Condominium Conversion; Catham Realty Corp. v. Town of Southhampton, 468 N.Y.S.2d 36 (A.D. 2d Dept. 1983); Griffin Dev. Co. v. City of Oxnard, 152 Cal. App. 3d 846, 199 Cal. Rptr. 739 (1984).

6. El Patio v. Permanent Rent Control Bd. of City of Santa Monica, 110 Cal. App. 3d 915, 168 Cal. Rptr. 276 (1980).

7. North Landers Corp. v. Planning Bd., 400 N.E.2d 273 (Mass. App. 1980).

8. Kaufman & Gold Constr. Co. v. Planning & Zoning Comm'n, 298 S.E.2d 148 (W. Va. 1982).

9. Sonn v. Planning Comm'n, 374 A.2d 159 (Conn. 1976).

10. Reed v. Planning & Zoning Comm'n, 544 A.2d 1213 (Conn. 1988); Richardson v. Little Rock Planning Comm'n, 747 S.W.2d 116 (Ark. 1988); Central Metairie Civic Assoc. v. Jefferson Parish Council, 484 So.2d 706 (La. App. 5th Cir. 1986) *cert. denied* 486 So.2d 751 (La. 1986).

11. Section 12 of the SPEA grants subdivision jurisdiction to "municipalities" and, with the exception of extraterritorial jurisdiction granted to municipalities, limits such jurisdiction to the "corporate" limits of the municipality. The American Law Institute, *Model Land Development Code*, Tentative Draft No. 1, § 1.101 (1968) grants all power to "local governments," which include counties, cities, towns, and villages. The obvious addition is the county, which has been authorized in many states to control land subdivision in unincorporated land. *See generally*, Reps and Smith, *Control of Urban Land Subdivision*, 14 Syracuse L. Rev. 405 (1963). The term "local government" then is more inclusive and appropriate than "municipality," and we have gone along with the ALI usage. *See also* D. Mandelker, Land Use Law, 120 (2d ed. 1988).

12. *See* commentary on Article 3 for a detailed analysis of the meaning of subdivision.

13. Sugarman v. Lewis, 488 A.2d 709 (R.I. 1985) ("subdivision" is the division of land in such a way so as to require the provision of a new street). State v. Emmich, 580 P.2d 570 (Ore. Ct. App. 1978) ("subdivision" is the division of land into four or more lots). *See also* R. Anderson, American Law of Zoning, § 18.15, at 302 (1986).

14. Adams v. Incorporated Village of Westhampton Beach, 336 N.Y.S. 2d 662 (App. Div. 2nd Dept. 1972). In 1979 Rhode Island amended its laws to delete the provision that *any* division of land requiring the provision of new streets was a subdivision. *See also* Sugarman v. Lewis, 488 A.2d 709 (R.I. 1985).

15. Board of Supervisors v. Georgetown Land Co., 131 S.E.2d 290 (Va. 1963). *See generally* Callies, Freilich & Roberts, Cases and Materials on Land Use (West 1994). The "objectives" of subdivision control may be included as a definition. One example was recently cited by a court:

"Subdivision control is aimed at protecting the community from an uneconomical development of land and assuring person living in the area where the subdivision is sought that there will be adequate streets, sewers, water supply and other essential services," Marx v. Zoning Bd. of Appeals, 529 N.Y.S.2d 330 (2d Dept. 1988).

16. *See* Pennobscott, Inc. v. Board of County Comm'rs, 642 P.2d 915 (Colo. 1982); Lemm Development Corp. v. Bartlett, 580 A.2d 1082 (N.H. 1990) (a planning board cannot use its power to regulate the subdivision of land that has already been improved and subdivided).

17. *See e.g.*, State v. Baker, 618 P.2d 997 (Ore. Ct. App. 1980) (violation of state subdivision laws is a felony); State v. Fowler, 525 P.2d 1061 (Ore. Ct. App. 1974) (statute prohibiting sale of unsubdivided land does not limit liability to property owner, but extends liability to real estate agent). *See generally* Schultz & Kelley, *Subdivision Improvement Requirements and Guarantees: A Primer*, 28 WASH. U.J. URB. & CONTEMP. L. 1 (1985); M. ANDERSON & B. ROSWIG, PLANNING, ZONING, SUBDIVISIONS: A SUMMARY OF STATUTORY LAW IN THE 50 STATES 228, Chart No. 13 (1966).

18. *See* Cassidy v. Ginter, Inc., 296 A.2d 293 (Pa. 1972), where 12 property owners commenced a partition action for the purpose of circumventing the subdivision regulations of the county, and the court held that the action was a violation of state and local subdivision laws. *See also* Pratt v. Adams, 40 Cal. Rptr. 505 (Ct. App. 1964); Bright v. Board of Supervisors, 135 Cal. Rptr. 758 (Ct. App. 1977).

3

Subdivision Application Procedure and Approval Process

3.1 General Procedure.

1. *Classification of Subdivisions.* Before any land is subdivided the owner of the property proposed to be subdivided, or his authorized agent, shall apply for and secure approval of the proposed subdivision in accordance with the following procedures, which include two (2) principal steps for a minor subdivision and three (3) principal steps for a major subdivision:
   a. *Minor Subdivision.*
      i. Sketch Plat
      ii. Final Subdivision Plat
   b. *Major Subdivision.*
      i. Sketch Plat
      ii. Preliminary Plat
      iii. Final Subdivision Plat

2. *Official Submission Dates.* For the purpose of these regulations, for both major and minor subdivisions, the date of the meeting of the Planning Commission at which the public meeting or hearing on approval of a sketch, preliminary or final subdivision plat, including any adjourned date thereof, is closed, shall constitute the Official Submission Date of the plat on which the statutory period required for formal approval, conditional approval or disapproval of the sketch, preliminary or final subdivision plat shall commence to run.

3. *Coordination of Flexible Zoning Application with Subdivision Approval.*

    a. It is the intent of these regulations that subdivision review be carried out simultaneously with the review of flexible zoning applications under the Zoning Ordinance. The plans required for flexible zoning applications shall be submitted in a form to satisfy the requirements of the subdivision regulations.

    b. *General Requirement.* Whenever the Zoning Ordinance authorizes flexible zoning applications which permit uses of land and density of buildings and structures different from those which are allowed as of right within the zoning district in which the land is situated, and the application entails the division of the land, vacant or improved, into two (2) or more lots, parcels, sites, units, plots, or interests for the purpose of offer, sale, lease, or development, either on the installment plan or upon any or all other plans, terms, or conditions, including resubdivision, whether residential or nonresidential, subdivision approval by the Planning Commission shall be required in addition to all other procedures and approvals required in the Zoning Ordinance, whether or not applicable zoning procedures also require Planning Commission approval, review or recommendation. Flexible zoning applications shall include, but not be limited to, all special permits and special uses, planned unit developments, group housing projects, community unit projects, average density or density zoning projects, and shall apply to all such applications, whether before the Governing Body, Board of Zoning Adjustment, Planning Commission, Building and Zoning Inspector, or other official or agency of the local government.

    c. *Procedure to Be Followed:*

        i. Sketch Plat and Preliminary Plat Approval Required. Whenever a flexible zoning application is submitted which involves a subdivision of land as set forth in Section 3.1(3)(b) of these regulations, the application shall be submitted first to the Governing Body, Board, Commission, Agency, or Official authorized to accept the application under the Zoning Ordinance. The application shall be made on the forms required for a sketch plat as set forth in Section 3.2 of these regulations and shall include all information required of a sketch plat application as set forth in Sections 3.2 and 8.1. The Governing Body, Board, Commission, Agency, or Official shall then refer the application to the Planning Commission for sketch plat and, when required, preliminary plat approval. The Planning Commission shall also, when applicable under the provisions of the Zoning Ordinance, make such reviews of use, density, and bulk standards as are required under the flexible zoning regulation.

ii. Referral Back for Zoning Approval. After completing its review the Planning Commission shall refer the sketch plat and preliminary plat (when required) with its decision of approval, conditional approval, or disapproval, together with such recommendations and reviews of use, density, and bulk standards as it was required to make under the flexible zoning regulation of the Zoning Ordinance, to the Governing Body, Board, Commission, Agency, or Official authorized under the Zoning Ordinance to approve the application. Application shall then be made to the Planning Commission for final plat approval. No building permits or certificates of occupancy shall be issued for the project until the zoning application has been finally approved and the final subdivision plat is recorded with the Clerk and Recorder's Office for _____ (the county in which the municipality is located).

d. *Resubdivisions of Flexible Zoning Developments.*

i. A flexible zoning development or land use plan may be subdivided or resubdivided for purposes of sale or lease after the project plan has been finally approved and development completed or partially completed.

ii. If the subdivision or resubdivision of a flexible zoning development will create a new lot line, the applicant shall make application to the Planning Commission for the approval of the subdivision or resubdivision. The Planning Commission shall approve the subdivision only if an amended zoning application also is approved for the flexible development plan, by the Governing Body, Board, Commission, Agency, or Official having jurisdiction under the Zoning Ordinance, for all provisions governing use, density, and bulk standards.

3.2 Sketch Plat.

1. *Discussion of Requirements.* Before preparing the sketch plat for a subdivision, the applicant shall schedule an appointment and meet with the Administrative Assistant to the Planning Commission to discuss the procedure for approval of a subdivision plat and the requirements as to general layout of streets and for reservations of land, street improvements, drainage, sewerage, fire protection, and similar matters, as well as the availability of existing services, includ-

ing schools. The Administrative Assistant shall also advise the applicant, when appropriate, to discuss the proposed subdivision with
those officials who must eventually approve those aspects of the
subdivision plat coming within their jurisdiction.

2. *Application Procedure and Requirements.* Prior to subdividing land
   and after meeting with the Administrative Assistant, the owner of the
   land, or his authorized agent, shall file an application for approval of
   a sketch plat with the Planning Commission. The application shall:
   a. Be made on forms available at the office of the Administrative
      Assistant to the Planning Commission;
   b. Include all contiguous holdings of the owner including land in
      "common ownership" as defined in these regulations, with an
      indication of the portion which is proposed to be subdivided,
      accompanied by an affidavit of ownership, which shall include the
      dates the respective holdings of land were acquired, together with
      the book and page where each conveyance to the present owner is
      recorded in the Clerk and Recorder's Office. The affidavit shall
      advise as to the legal owner of the property, the contract owner of
      the property, the date the contract of sale was executed, and, if any
      corporations are involved, a complete list of all directors, officers,
      and stockholders of each corporation owning more than five per-
      cent (5%) of any class of stock;
   c. Be accompanied by minimum of seven (7) copies of the sketch plat
      as described in these regulations and complying in all respects with
      these regulations;
   d. Be presented to the Administrative Assistant to the Planning Com-
      mission in duplicate;
   e. Be accompanied by a fee of _____ Dollars ($_____) per lot (sug-
      gested: $10/lot); also
   f. The application shall include an address and telephone number of
      an agent located within the territory of the local government who
      shall be authorized to receive all notices required by these regula-
      tions.

3. *Classification and Approval Procedure.* The Administrative Assistant
   shall determine whether the sketch plat constitutes a minor or major
   subdivision and notify the applicant of the classification within twenty
   (20) days from the date that the sketch plat is submitted to the
   Administrative Assistant.
   a. *Minor Subdivision.* If the sketch plat constitutes a minor subdivi-
      sion, the Administrative Assistant shall place the matter on the next
      available regular meeting agenda of the Planning Commission for
      formal approval, disapproval or conditional approval of the sketch

plat following a public hearing. The Commission shall provide notice and hold public hearing on the sketch plat in the same manner required for preliminary plats in Section 3.3 (2). The Planning Commission shall approve, conditionally approve, or disapprove the sketch plat within thirty (30) days from the Official Submission Date. Subsequent to an approval or conditional approval by the Planning Commission, the applicant may proceed directly to the filing of an application for approval of a final subdivision plat as provided in these regulations. If the sketch plat of a minor subdivision is disapproved by the Planning Commission, the applicant may appeal to the governing body as provided in Section 3.8. The applicant shall have one (1) year from the date that the sketch plat is approved by the Planning Commission (or Governing Body upon appeal) to submit a final subdivision plat, after which time a new sketch plat must be submitted for approval.

b. *Major Subdivision.*

   i. Notice to Proceed.

     If the sketch plat constitutes a major subdivision, the Administrative Assistant shall issue a Notice to Proceed only if the sketch plat complies with all applicable laws governing the subdivision of land. The Notice to Proceed shall include, as appropriate, recommended changes in the sketch plat to be incorporated into the preliminary plat to assist the applicant in obtaining preliminary plat approval from the Planning Commission. If the Administrative Assistant determines that the sketch plat does not comply with all applicable laws governing the subdivision of land and the applicant refuses to modify the sketch plat, the Administrative Assistant shall issue a Notice of Noncompliance. The Administrative Assistant shall issue either the Notice to Proceed or the Notice of Noncompliance not later than twenty (20) days after the date on which the sketch plat was submitted to the Administrative Assistant. After receipt of a Notice to Proceed, the applicant must first file an application for approval of a preliminary plat, as provided in these regulations, before filing for final subdivision plat approval.

   ii. Referral of Sketch Plat.

     If the Administrative Assistant issues a Notice to Proceed, the Administrative Assistant shall transmit the sketch plat for review to appropriate officials or agencies of the local government, adjoining counties or municipalities, school and special districts, and other official bodies as it deems necessary or as mandated by law, including any review required by metropolitan, regional, or state bodies under applicable state or federal law. The Administrative Assistant shall request that all officials and agencies to whom a request for review has been made, submit their report to the Administrative Assistant within thirty (30) days after receipt of the request. The Administrative Assistant will consider all the reports submitted by the officials and agencies concerning the sketch plat and shall submit a report to the Planning Commission upon the applicant's submission of a preliminary plat.

3.3   **Preliminary Plat.** No sooner than thirty (30) days and no later than 120 days after the date of the Notice to Proceed, the applicant may apply for preliminary plat approval. If the applicant fails to apply for preliminary plat approval within the 120-day period, a new sketch plat must be submitted.

1.   *Application Procedure and Requirements.* Based on the Notice to Proceed, the applicant shall file in duplicate with the Administrative Assistant an application for approval of a preliminary plat if it elects to proceed. The preliminary plat shall conform substantially with the sketch plat submitted by the applicant and which formed the basis for the Notice to Proceed. The application shall:

   a.   Be made on forms available at the office of the Administrative Assistant to the Planning Commission together with a fee of _____ Dollars ($_____) per lot (suggested: $10/lot).

   b.   Include all land which the applicant proposes to subdivide and all land immediately adjacent extending one hundred (100) feet from the subject property, or of that directly opposite the subject property, extending one hundred (100) feet from the street frontage of opposite land, with the names of owners as shown in the Assessor's files. This information may be shown on a separate current Tax Map reproduction from the Assessor's Office showing the subdivision superimposed on the Tax Map.

   c.   Be accompanied by a minimum of ten (10) copies of the preliminary plat as described in these regulations.

   d.   Be accompanied by a minimum of three (3) copies of construction plans as described in these regulations.

   e.   Comply in all respects with the sketch plat.

   f.   Be presented to the Administrative Assistant to the Planning Commission at least four (4) weeks prior to a regular meeting of the Commission.

2.   *Public Hearing.* Upon receipt of a formal application for preliminary plat approval and all accompanying material, the Administrative

Assistant to the Planning Commission shall call a public hearing for the next scheduled meeting of the Planning Commission to be held at least four (4) weeks after the date of the application. The Administrative Assistant shall submit a notice for publication in one (1) newspaper of general circulation to be published at least fifteen (15) days prior to the public hearing and mail notices to all property owners, as specified in Section 3.3 (1) (b), and shall maintain file copies of the plat and construction plans when appropriate for public review prior to the hearing. The Administrative Assistant to the Planning Commission shall furnish four (4) posters to the applicant to be posted by the applicant on the four (4) closest public roads in visible locations surrounding the proposed subdivision property at least ten (10) days prior to the public hearing. At the time of the public hearing, the applicant shall submit an affidavit stating that the applicant has placed four (4) posters provided to him by the Administrative Assistant to the Planning Commission on the four (4) closest public roads in visible locations surrounding the proposed subdivision property.

3. ***Preliminary Approval.*** After the Planning Commission has reviewed the preliminary plat and construction plans, the report of the Administrative Assistant, any municipal recommendations and testimony and exhibits submitted at the public hearing, the applicant shall be advised of any required changes and/or additions. The Commission shall approve, conditionally approve, or disapprove the preliminary plat within thirty (30) days from the Official Submission Date. One (1) copy of the proposed preliminary plat shall be returned to the developer with the date of approval, conditional approval, or disapproval and the reasons therefore accompanying the plat. Before the Commission approves a preliminary plat showing park reservation or land for other local government use that is proposed to be dedicated to the local government, the Commission shall obtain approval of the park or land reservation from the Governing Body. If the Planning Commission disapproves the proposed subdivision, the applicant may execute an appeal in the manner prescribed in Section 3.8.

4. ***Standards for Approval of Preliminary Plats.*** No preliminary plat of a proposed subdivision shall be approved by the Planning Commission unless the applicant proves by clear and convincing evidence that:
   a. Definite provision has been made for a water supply system that is sufficient in terms of quantity, dependability, and quality to provide an appropriate supply of water for the type of subdivision proposed;
   b. If a public sewage system is proposed, adequate provision has been made for such a system and, if other methods of sewage disposal

are proposed, that such systems will comply with federal, state, and local laws and regulations;

c. All areas of the proposed subdivision which may involve soil or topographical conditions presenting hazards or requiring special precautions have been identified by the subdivider and that the proposed uses of these areas are compatible with such conditions;

d. The subdivider has the financial ability to complete the proposed subdivision in accordance with all applicable federal, state, and local laws and regulations;

e. There is not other available subdivided land in the jurisdiction of the municipality that would be suitable for the applicant's proposed uses of the subdivision;

f. The proposed subdivision will not result in the scattered subdivision of land that leaves undeveloped parcels of land lacking urban services between developed parcels;

g. The subdivider has taken every effort to mitigate the impact of the proposed subdivision on public health, safety, and welfare.

The Planning Commission is authorized to disapprove the preliminary plat even though the land proposed for subdivision is zoned for the use to which the proposed subdivision will be put and the proposed use is consistent with the Master Plan.

5. *Public Improvements.* The Planning Commission may require that all public improvements be installed and dedicated prior to the signing of the final subdivision plat by the Chairman of the Planning Commission. If the Planning Commission does not require that all public improvements be installed and dedicated prior to signing of the final subdivision plat by the Chairman of the Planning Commission, the Planning Commission shall require that the applicant execute a subdivision improvement agreement and provide security for the agreement as provided in Section 4.1 (2). The Planning Commission shall require the applicant to indicate on the plat all roads and public improvements to be dedicated, all special districts for water, fire, and utility improvements which shall be required to be established or extended, and any other special requirements deemed necessary by the Planning Commission in order to conform the subdivision plat to the Official Map and the Master Plan of the local government.

6. *Effective Period of Preliminary Plat Approval.* The approval of a preliminary plat shall be effective for a period of one (1) year from the date that the preliminary plat is approved by the Planning Commission or the Governing Body, at the end of which time the applicant must have submitted a final subdivision plat for approval. If a subdivision plat is not submitted for final approval within the one (1) year period, the

preliminary approval shall be null and void, and the applicant shall be required to submit a new plat for sketch plat review subject to the then existing zoning restrictions and subdivision regulations.

7. ***Zoning and Subdivision Regulations.*** Every preliminary plat shall conform to existing zoning regulations and subdivision regulations applicable at the time that the proposed preliminary is submitted for the approval of the Planning Commission unless the Planning Commission or Governing Body has taken official action toward amending the applicable zoning and subdivision regulations and the applicant has reason to know of that action.

8. ***Grading of Site Prior to Final Approval.*** Subsequent to preliminary approval the developer may apply for a topsoil and excavation permit from the Planning Commission or such other agency or person as the Governing Body shall direct, and upon receipt of the permit may commence construction to the grades and elevations required by the approved preliminary plat.

9. ***Model Homes.*** For the purpose of allowing the early construction of model homes in a subdivision, the Planning Commission in its sole discretion may permit a portion of a major subdivision involving no more than two (2) lots to be created in accordance with the procedures for minor subdivisions, provided the portion derives access from an existing city, township, county, or state highway, and provided no future road or other improvement is anticipated where the lots are proposed. The subdivision plat for the "minor" portion shall be submitted to the Planning Commission simultaneously with the preliminary plat for the entire major subdivision. Subsequent to preliminary approval, the model homes may be constructed, subject to such additional requirements as the Planning Commission may require.

3.4 **Amendments to Preliminary Plat.** At any time after preliminary plat approval and before submission of a final plat, the applicant may request of the Administrative Assistant that an amendment be made in the approval or conditional approval of the preliminary plat. Under regulations established by the Planning Commission, the Administrative Assistant may agree to proposed amendments that are deemed to be minor. If the proposed amendment is major, the Planning Commission shall hold a public hearing on the proposed major amendment in accordance with the same requirements for preliminary plat approval found in Section 3.2 (2). Any public hearing on a proposed major amendment shall be limited to whether the proposed major amendment should or should not be approved. The Commission shall approve or disapprove any proposed major amendment and may make any modifications in the terms and conditions of preliminary plat approval reasonably related to the proposed amendment. If the applicant is unwilling to accept the proposed major amendment under the terms and conditions required by the Commission, the applicant may withdraw the proposed major amendment. A major amendment shall include, but is not limited to, any amendment that results in or has the effect of decreasing open space in the subdivision by ten percent (10%) or more or increasing density in the subdivision by ten percent (10%) or more shall be a major amendment. An applicant may not propose more than two (2) amendments—whether major or minor—to any preliminary plat. The Commission shall render a decision on the proposed major amendment within thirty (30) days after the meeting at which the public hearing was held, including any adjourned session, was closed.

3.5   Final Subdivision Plat.

1. *Application Procedure and Requirements.* Following the approval of the sketch plat in the case of a minor subdivision, or of the preliminary plat in the case of a major subdivision, the applicant, if he wishes to proceed with the subdivision, shall file with the Planning Commission an application for final approval of a subdivision plat. The application shall:

   a. Be made on forms available at the Office of the Administrative Assistant to the Planning Commission, together with a fee of _____ Dollars ($_____) for reproduction of plans (suggested: $12/lot).

   b. Include the entire subdivision, or section thereof, which derives access from an existing state, county, or local government highway.

   c. Be accompanied by a minimum of ten (10) copies of the subdivision plat and the construction plans, as described in these regulations.

   d. Comply in all respects with the sketch plat or preliminary plat, as approved, whichever is applicable, depending upon the classification of the subdivision.

   e. Be presented to the Administrative Assistant to the Planning Commission at least four (4) weeks prior to a regular meeting of the Commission in order that a public meeting may be scheduled and the required fifteen (15) days public notice and personal notice to the owners listed in Section 3.5 (1)(h) may be given. The notice shall advise the public that the final plat and all conforming documents have been received by the Planning Commission and may be reviewed by members of the public who may then submit written comments to the Commission concerning whether final approval should be granted. The notice shall include a deadline for receipt of comments and shall include the date of the public meeting at which final plat approval will be considered.

f. Be accompanied by all formal irrevocable offers of dedication to the public of all streets, local government uses, utilities, parks, and easements, in a form approved by the Local Government Attorney; and the subdivision plat shall be marked with a notation indicating the formal offers of dedication as follows:

The owner, or his representative, hereby irrevocably offers for dedication to the local government all the streets, local government uses, easements, parks, and required utilities shown on the subdivision plat and construction plans in accordance with an irrevocable offer of dedication dated _____, and recorded in the Clerk and Recorder's Office for _____(county in which municipality is located).

By_____

(Owner or Representative)

Date_____

The applicant shall deliver a full covenant and warranty deed to all dedicated lands and improvements in proper form for recording, together with a title policy for the local government in the sum *not less* than ten thousand dollars ($10,000), which sum shall be determined by the Local Government Attorney before signing of the final subdivision plat.

g. Be accompanied by the subdivision improvement agreement and security, if required, in a form satisfactory to the Local Government Attorney and in an amount established by the Planning Commission upon recommendation of the Local Government Engineer and shall include a provision that the subdivider shall comply with all the terms of the resolution of final subdivision plat approval as determined by the Planning Commission and shall include, but not be limited to, the performance of all required subdivision and off-site improvements, and that all improvements and land included in the irrevocable offer of dedication shall be dedicated to the local government free and clear of all liens and encumbrances on the premises.

h. Be accompanied by stamped No. 10 envelopes addressed to each owner of property immediately adjacent extending one hundred (100) feet from the subject property, or of that directly opposite the subject property extending one hundred (100) feet from the street frontage of the opposite property owners as are correct within the knowledge of the applicant as shown on the latest tax assessment roll along with printed notices that those property owners may review the final plat documents and submit written comments to the Planning Commission on whether the final approval should be granted.

i.   Be accompanied by an inspection fee in an amount to be determined on the basis of the provisions of these regulations and by written assurance from the public utility companies and improvement districts that necessary utilities will be installed and proof that the applicant has submitted petitions in writing for the creation or extension of any improvement districts as required by the Planning Commission upon preliminary plat approval. The applicant shall also pay a _____ dollar ($_____) fee (suggested: $50.00 for each street sign shown in the construction plans, which street signs shall be installed by the local government.

2. *Endorsement of Health Authorities.* The final subdivision plat shall be properly endorsed by the Health Department or Health Officer with respect to all sewer and water facilities and that same comply with all rules, regulations, and requirements of local government, regional, state, and federal authorities.

3. *Notice of Public Meeting.* Upon receipt of formal application and all accompanying material, the Administrative Assistant to the Planning Commission shall call a public meeting for the next scheduled meeting of the Planning Commission to be held at least four (4) weeks after the date of the application. The Administrative Assistant shall submit a notice for publication in one (1) newspaper of general circulation to be published at least fifteen (15) days prior to the public meeting and mail notices to all property owners, as specified in Section 3.5 (1)(h), and shall maintain file copies of the plat and construction plans for public review prior to the meeting. The Administrative Assistant to the Planning Commission shall furnish four (4) posters to the applicant to be posted by the applicant on the four (4) closest public roads in visible locations surrounding the proposed subdivision property at least ten (10) days prior to the public meeting. All notices shall advise that the final plat for the subdivision and related documents are on file with the Planning Commission and may be reviewed by members of the public who may then submit written comment on whether final plat approval should be granted. The notices shall include a deadline for receipt of comments and shall include the date, time and place of the public meeting at which final plat approval will be considered.

4. *Public Meeting and Determination.* At the public meeting, the applicant shall furnish an affidavit as to placement of posters required by

Section 3.3(2). After the public meeting, the Planning Commission shall, within thirty (30) days from the Official Submission Date for the final subdivision plat, approve or disapprove the subdivision application by resolution which shall set forth in detail any reasons for disapproval. One copy of the final subdivision plat shall be returned to the applicant with the date of approval or disapproval noted on the plat, and, if the plat is disapproved, the reasons for disapproval accompanying the plat.

5. *Appeal in the Event of Disapproval.* If the Planning Commission disapproves the final plat, the applicant may appeal to the Governing Body in the manner prescribed in Section 3.8.

6. *Submission and Review.* Subsequent to the resolution of the Planning Commission, three (3) paper copies of the construction plans, and one (1) copy of the original of the subdivision plat on tracing cloth, and/or reproduction mylar, and two (2) copies of the subdivision plat on sepia paper and two (2) copies of the subdivision plat on paper shall be submitted to the Administrative Assistant for final review. A check payable to the County Clerk and Recorder in the amount of the current filing fee shall be provided. No final approval shall be endorsed on the plat until a review has indicated that all requirements of the resolution have been met.

3.6 Vested Rights and Development Agreements.

1. *Effect of Approval.* Except as otherwise provided in this Section 3.6, no vested rights shall accrue to the owner or developer of any subdivision by reason of preliminary or final plat approval until the actual signing of the final plat by the Chairman of the Planning Commission.

2. *Effect of Recordation.* Except as otherwise provided in this Section 3.6, no vested rights shall accrue to the owner or developer of any subdivision by virtue of the recordation of a final plat.

3. *Applicable Laws.* To obtain final plat approval, the applicant shall be in compliance with all federal and state laws applicable at the time that the final plat is considered for approval by the Planning Commission. The applicant also shall be in compliance with all local laws and regulations applicable at the time that the preliminary plat was submitted to the Planning Commission in accordance with Section 3.3(7) (or, if a minor subdivision, at the time the sketch plat was submitted to the Administrative Assistant to the Planning Commission), except that the applicant shall comply with those local laws and regulations in effect at the time that the final plat is considered for approval by the Commission if the Planning Commission makes a determination on the record that compliance with any of those local laws and regulations

is reasonably necessary to protect public health and safety. If the Planning Commission required the applicant to complete public improvements in the subdivision prior to final plat approval, and the improvements have, in fact, been completed, the applicant may be required to comply with local laws and regulations in effect at the time that the final plat is considered for approval only if the Planning Commission makes a finding on the record that such compliance is necessary to prevent a substantial risk of injury to public health, safety and general welfare.

4. **Development Agreements.** The municipality may, but under no circumstances is it required to, enter into a Development Agreement:

   a. *General.* The Development Agreement shall constitute a binding contract between the subdivider of the proposed subdivision and the municipality (the "parties") and shall contain those terms and conditions agreed to by the parties and those required by this Section 3.6(4). The Local Government Attorney or designee is authorized to negotiate Development Agreements on behalf of the municipality.

   b. *Covenants.* Any covenant by the municipality contained in the Development Agreement to refrain from exercising any legislative, quasi-legislative, quasi-judicial or other discretionary power, including rezoning or the adoption of any rule or regulation that would affect the proposed subdivision, shall be limited to a period of five (5) years. The covenant shall also contain a proviso that the municipality may, without incurring any liability, engage in action that otherwise would constitute a breach of the covenant if it makes a determination on the record that the action is necessary to avoid a substantial risk of injury to public health, safety, and general welfare. The covenant shall contain the additional proviso that the municipality may, without incurring any liability, engage in action that otherwise would constitute a breach of the covenant if the action is required by federal or state law.

   c. *Third Party Rights.* Except as otherwise expressly provided in the Development Agreement, the Development Agreement shall create no rights enforceable by any party who/which is not a party to the Development Agreement.

   d. *Limitation on Liability.* The Development Agreement shall contain a clause that any breach of the Development Agreement by the municipality shall give rise only to damages under state contract law and shall not give rise to any liability for violation of the fifth and fourteenth amendments of the U.S. Constitution or similar state constitutional provisions.

    e. *Developer's Compliance.* The Development Agreement shall include a clause that the government's duties under the Agreement are expressly conditioned upon the subdivider's substantial compliance with each and every term, condition, provision, and covenant of the Agreement, all applicable federal, state and local laws and regulations, and its obligations under the subdivision improvement agreement.

    f. *Adoption.* The Development Agreement shall be adopted by the governing body pursuant to applicable state and local laws and shall be recorded in the Clerk and Recorder's Office of _____(county in which municipality is located).

    g. *Incorporation as Matter of Law.* All clauses, covenants, and provisos required by these regulations to be included in a Development Agreement shall be incorporated into the Development Agreement as a matter of law without respect to the intent of the parties.

3.7 Signing and Recordation of Subdivision Plat.

1. *Signing of Plat.*
   a. When a subdivision improvement agreement and security are required, the Chairman of the Planning Commission and the Administrative Assistant to the Planning Commission shall endorse approval on the final plat after the agreement and security have been approved by the Planning Commission, and all the conditions of the resolution pertaining to the final plat have been satisfied.
   b. When installation of improvements is required prior to recordation of the final plat, the Chairman of the Planning Commission and Administrative Assistant to the Planning Commission shall endorse approval on the final plat after all conditions of the resolution have been satisfied and all improvements satisfactorily completed. There shall be written evidence that the required public facilities have been installed in a manner satisfactory to the local government as shown by a certificate signed by the Local Government Engineer and Local Government Attorney stating that the necessary dedication of public lands and improvements has been accomplished.

2. *Recordation of Plat.*
   a. The Chairman and Administrative Assistant will sign the tracing cloth or reproducible mylar original of the final subdivision plat and two (2) sepia prints of the final subdivision plat. The sepia prints will be returned to the applicant's engineer.
   b. It shall be the responsibility of the Administrative Assistant to the Planning Commission to file the final plat with the County

Clerk and Recorder's Office within ten (10) days of the date of signature. Simultaneously with the filing of the final plat, the Administrative Assistant to the Planning Commission shall record the agreement of dedication together with such legal documents as shall be required to be recorded by the Local Government Attorney.

3. *Sectionalizing Major Subdivision Plats.* Prior to granting final approval of a major subdivision plat, the Planning Commission may permit the plat to be divided into two or more sections and may impose such conditions upon the filing of the sections as it may deem necessary to assure the orderly development of the plat. The Planning Commission may require that the subdivision improvement agreement and security be in such amount as is commensurate with the section or sections of the plat to be filed and may defer the remaining amount of the security until the remaining sections of the plat are offered for filing. The developer may also file irrevocable offers to dedicate streets and public improvements in the sections offered to be filed and defer filing offers of dedication for the remaining sections until those sections, subject to any conditions imposed by the Planning Commission, shall be granted concurrently with final approval of the plat. If sectionalizing is approved, the entire approved subdivision plat including all sections shall be filed within ninety (90) days after the date of final approval with the local government Clerk's Office and such sections as have been authorized by the Planning Commission shall be filed with the County Clerk and Recorder's Office. Such sections must contain at least ten percent (10%) of the total number of lots contained in the approved plat. The approval of all remaining sections not filed with the Clerk and Recorder's Office shall automatically expire unless such sections have been approved for filing by the Planning Commission, all fees paid, all instruments and offers of dedication submitted and subdivision improvement agreements, security and performance bonds, if any, approved and actually filed with the Clerk and Recorder's Office within three (3) years of the date of final subdivision approval of the subdivision plat.

3.8   Appeals to Governing Body. The applicant for subdivision approval may appeal the disapproval of any sketch, preliminary, or final subdivision plat by the Planning Commission by filing a Notice of Appeal with the governing body, with a copy to the Planning Commission, no later than ten (10) days after the date on which the Planning Commission notifies the applicant that it has disapproved the sketch, preliminary, or final subdivision plat. The Notice of Appeal shall set forth in clear and concise fashion the basis for the appeal. The appeal shall be considered at the next regularly scheduled public meeting of the Governing Body, at which time it may affirm or reverse the decision of the Planning Commission. The Governing Body may reverse the decision of the Planning Commission only by a unanimous vote of the members of the governing body present at the meeting. On appeal, the applicant shall be allowed to make a presentation to the Governing Body under such terms, conditions and procedures as established by the Governing Body. The Governing Body shall render a decision affirming or reversing the Planning Commission no later than forty-five (45) days after the date on which the Notice of Appeal is filed. If the Governing Body reverses the Planning Commission, the applicant may proceed to submit a preliminary or final plat as is appropriate under the conditions for approval agreed to by the governing body.

3.9 Time Periods for Action. Whenever these regulations establish a time period for action by the Governing Body, Planning Commission, Administrative Assistant to the Planning Commission, or any other person or entity and the action is not taken within the time period, the applicant shall have a right to file an action in mandamus to compel action. In addition, the municipality shall be liable to the applicant in the sum of $500 for each and every day that the municipality fails to act following the expiration of the time period. The government's duty to act is not dependent on the applicant's substantial compliance with all applicable application and approval procedures.

3.10 Suspension and Invalidation of Final Plat. If the municipality suspends final plat approval for any subdivision plat under these regulations, it shall record a document with the Clerk and Recorder's Office for _____(name of county in which municipality is located) declaring that final approval for the subdivision is suspended and that the further sale, lease, or development of property within the subdivision is prohibited except that this prohibition shall not apply to persons or parties who have acquired property from the subdivider unless the person or party acquiring property meets the definition of "common ownership" in Section 2.2(26). If any court of competent jurisdiction invalidates final plat approval for any subdivision, the municipality shall record a document with the Clerk and Recorder's Office for _____(county in which municipality is located) declaring that the final plat for the subdivision is no longer valid and that further subdivision activity is prohibited.

COMMENTARY ON ARTICLE 3

The application and review procedure outlined in Article 3 involves a two-step process for minor subdivisions and a three-step process for major subdivisions. The procedures are designed to achieve maximum coordination between the developer and the planning commission with the least amount of administrative delay.[1] As the developer proceeds from initial pre-application conference with the administrative assistant [§ 2.2(2)] and the submission of the sketch plat, to the more detailed tentative and final plats, an agreement is reached on the overall concept and best design for the subdivision and the conditions necessary to mitigate the impact of the development on the community. This methodology assures the developer that there is always one official (administrative assistant) with whom all papers shall be filed and information received about the progress of the application,[2] especially when the application must be reviewed by numerous departments of the municipality and outside federal, state, regional, and local officials and governments.[3] This prevents undue expense to the developer and delays in review by agencies outside of the planning department and planning commission.[4]

In the last few years, there has been much emphasis on improving the efficiency of land use approval processes.[5] Poorly drafted subdivision regulations waste valuable resources—both time and money—for the public and private sectors. Poorly drafted regulations include those that lack cohesive organization and precise language; those that create unduly complicated and cumbersome approval procedures; and those that have been amended without any thought of integrating the amendments into the existing process. Subdivision regulations, like any regulatory scheme, must be reviewed periodically to ensure that substantive provisions are not obsolete and to conform the written regulations with the actual application review process. The Model Regulations attempt to strike a proper balance between the need for the careful analysis of subdivision applications and the need for regulatory efficiency.[6]

In section 3.1(1), the Model Regulations require that the application for subdivision approval be made by either the owner of the land proposed to be subdivided or the landowner's authorized agent. The definition of ownership in section 2.2(99) requires that the applicant have *legal title* or a sufficient proprietary interest in the land sought to be subdivided. The forms in Appendix C require that the record owner of the property be disclosed. If the owner is a nonresident, a local agent capable of receiving notices and service of process must be indicated on the application. These provisions will help eliminate later problems of personal jurisdiction in litigation.[7] The requirement of legal ownership prevents contract purchasers of the land from making applications. Contract purchasers are considered by the courts as only equitable owners of the property[8] and the contracts are usually made contingent on zoning and subdivision approval. Without approval, the contract is not executed and the application by the contract buyer is often speculative. It is prudent to have the application made or joined by the legal owner so as to be bound by the plat approval. The propriety of the requirements that the application must be made by the legal owner or appropriate agent (who may be the contract purchaser) has been upheld by the courts.[9]

THE APPLICATION PROCESS

The recommended procedure for subdivision plat approval may be summarized briefly.[10] The developer meets with the administrative assistant to discuss the proposed development. This mandatory meeting is for the basic purpose of informing the applicant of current subdivision approval procedures. The administrative assistant indicates the procedures that will be required and directs the developer to contact the other governmental agencies concerned with the development. The developer then submits an application for sketch plat [3.2(2)] to the administrative assistant. This is more efficient than submission to the planning commission as provided for in the Housing and Home Finance Authority's *Suggested Land Subdivision Regulations*.[11]

The sketch plat lays out the approximate location of existing features and planned construction and provides ownership information. The administrative assistant classifies the subdivision as either major (four or more lots and a new street) or minor (less than four lots and no new street) at this time. If it is a minor subdivision, preliminary plat review is not necessary. The administrative assistant then schedules a public hearing before the planning commission on the proposed subdivision. If the proposed subdivision sketch plat is approved or conditionally approved, the applicant may proceed directly to the filing of a final plat.

The "major-minor" classification of subdivisions is an important development appearing in recent statutory amendments and in the national literature.[12] In the Model Regulations, a major subdivision requires a three-stage procedure (sketch, preliminary, and final plat), whereas a minor subdivision requires only two steps (sketch plat directly to final plat approval). Many statutes or subdivision regulations of localities define subdivision as being the division of land into more than two parcels.[13] Other statutes or local ordinances may exempt from municipal review subdivisions that do not involve the creation of new streets or public improvements.[14] Presumably the purpose of these regulations is to exempt from subdivision review the simple lot split that creates no need for public improvements and the subdivision of large parcels of agricultural or rural land. This has the theoretically beneficial purpose of protecting the farmer from onerous bureaucratic regulations and excluding minor divisions of land because of the relatively small impact they are perceived to make on patterns of land development. However, it avoids the only appropriate criteria of measuring developmental impact in determining subdivision classification and constitutes an evasion of the goals and objectives of subdivision regulation.[15] Such provisions establish enormous areas for avoidance and legal trouble for subsequent purchasers of lots divided without subdivision approval.[16]

The alternative of "major" and "minor" subdivision classification meets the needs that subdivision regulation was designed to fulfill but lessens the rigors of plat approval for smaller subdivisions or agricultural and rural lot splits. For maximum effectiveness, a "tight" definition of subdivision is preferable; however, the classification into major or minor accommodates the differences in detail necessitated by complex versus simple subdivisions.[17]

THE PROBLEMS WITH EXEMPTION

Exempting large parcels from subdivision control in urban counties negates many of the theories behind the need for subdivision regulations, such as creating new streets, shaping the future of municipal utility services, parks, and open spaces, and having a recorded system of plats on file. Colorado, for example, has experienced a proliferation of 35- and 40-acre mini-ranches because county regulations, by statute, exempt any lot of 35 acres or more. If the legislative purpose is to remove such subdivisions from the rigors of plat approval, the major-minor method suggested in the Model would seem more appropriate. Major subdivisions contain four or more lots and/or a major improvement or new street. Minor subdivisions contain less than four lots and no major improvement or new street. The distinction permits minor subdivisions to go through an abbreviated review process; however, the plat is still reviewed and properly recorded.[18]

A key to the process of closing off all loopholes is to require that any subdivision of land, whether by deed or otherwise, and for whatever purpose, must be reviewed. Section 2.2 (145) of the Model Regulations defines a subdivision as:

> Any land, vacant or improved, which is divided into two (2) or more lots, parcels (a) sites, units, plots, or interests for the purpose of sale, lease (b) or development, either on the installment plan or upon any and all other plans, terms and conditions, including resubdivision (c). Subdivision includes the division or development of residentially and nonresidentially (d) zoned land, whether by deed, metes and bounds description, devise (e), intestacy, map, plat, or other recorded instrument.[19]

A definition that exempts a tract of land from subdivision approval based on the number of lots or that creates other loopholes will lessen the ability of the local government to regulate development by allowing a developer to build two or three houses at a time without subdivision approval or to create legal building lots without planning commission review.[20] By requiring every division of land to be reviewed, the municipal or county assessor and the recorder of deeds can immediately detect lot splits by deed or otherwise and report this to the attorney and building inspector (or administrative assistant). Section 1.13(1)(b) of the Model prohibits any transfer of land without subdivision approval.

In the event of an illegal transfer, section 1.13(1)(d) provides that no building permit may be issued.[21] This may seem a harsh result for an innocent purchaser of the lot, but there is no way for a municipal regulation to declare that the title to the land is void. Under the SPEA, a local government may provide for criminal sanctions, fines, or injunctive relief.[22] The purchaser of the illegal lot may then seek a rescission of the contract and damages from the seller and the municipality may enjoin further illegal subdivision activity.[23]

If state law requires that certain divisions of land be exempt from subdivision control, the local government should consider two possibilities. First, the exemption should not be self-executing. The subdivider should be required to prove entitlement to the exemption to the satisfaction of the government.[24] Second, the government should establish exemption criteria to ensure that exemptions are being used legitimately and not for the purpose of avoiding subdivision regulations.[25] If state law provides an exemption for the granting of a security interest, the exemption criteria could determine if the interest was granted to secure a bona fide debt or whether the parties intended to accomplish a "friendly foreclosure."[26]

FLEXIBLE ZONING

Local governments must be prepared to integrate subdivision regulations with the handling of flexible zoning procedures, such as planned unit developments, cluster zoning, floating zones, and group housing projects.[27] The Model Land Development Code, Appendix B, would authorize an integrated single subdivision and zoning land development code.[28] The Model Regulations, section 3.1(3), provide for complete subdivision review and approval whenever a flexible development plan being approved under zoning also meets the definition of subdivision. These provisions help to ensure planning commission participation in the review process.[29] The body that creates the master plan and has the comprehensive view of the community and its needs ought to be a principal actor in the development review process.

OVERVIEW OF THE APPROVAL PROCESS

The approval process for major developments, whether subdivisions, site plans, cluster developments, or planned unit developments (PUD), is essentially the same throughout the country. In general, plans for a proposed development are scrutinized by the appropriate board or commission in two or three distinct steps, each step representing a progression with respect to the information required for project approval. A model subdivision and site plan handbook, originally circulated as a model ordinance in 1987 for the New Jersey Department of Community Affairs and published by David Listokin and Carole Walker of the Center for Urban Policy Research at Rutgers University,[30] expressly adopts the three-step approval process set out in our 1976 *Model Subdivision Regulations*,[31] as well as several other leading sources and authorities in the field.[32]

The three steps in this process [§ 3.1(1)] are: (1) sketch plat or concept plan approval; (2) preliminary plat approval; and (3) final plat approval. The Model Regulations utilize only a two-step process for minor subdivision approval [§ 3.2(3)(a)]. In many states, a preapplication conference occurs [§ 3.2(1)] at which the developer and planning officials discuss the merits of the proposal and the application process.[33] To facilitate better understanding of these approval procedures, an outline of these three steps in further detail follows.

The sketch plat approval process and preapplication conference provides an opportunity for the applicant to present its basic concept to local planning officials and hear their input, suggestions, and concerns. Listokin and Walker explain that such initial procedures are:

> A mechanism designed to permit the developer of a large-scale project to go before the planning board with the description, but not full engineering details of the project, and secure formal approval of basic development parameters such as the total number of residential units and nonresidential square footage. Once having secured such approval, the developer proceeds with full engineering plans to be considered at the *preliminary* subdivision and *site plan* review stages.[34]

The sketch plat lays out the approximate location of existing features and planned construction and provides ownership information. Because of the vague description of the development, in most states the approval of the sketch plat has little binding force on either the developer or the local government. However, the developer is given the opportunity to learn of municipal suggestions that can be incorporated into the formal preliminary plan application without incurring significant expenditures.

The second stage, the preliminary plan or preliminary plat application, involves an examination of the proposal in much greater detail than at the sketch plat stage. This stage determines whether the project will be approved, and if so, the conditions that must be met. Preliminary plan approval is the key discretionary decision-making point in the approval process. Subsequent final approval is merely ministerial, as will be described below.[35] The applicant is required to submit detailed information on all aspects of the development, including street layout, preservation of natural site features, and recreational and parking facilities, to assure that the decision makers and all parties interested in the project have the opportunity to review all significant facets of the project.[36]

At this stage of the approval process, the governing body is compelled to evaluate the proposal in light of its effect on the general health, safety, and welfare of the community. Although the standards applied to the proposal are statutorily predetermined, the board has broad discretion to approve, approve conditionally, or deny the proposal.[37]

Given the important task before the governing body, it is absolutely essential that it have a complete picture of the proposed development and all available data before it passes judgment on a preliminary plat or site plan. Thus, it is incumbent upon a developer to submit all required documents before seeking preliminary approval.[38] If a governing body approves an application without adhering to the procedural requirements, then the board has denied the application's opponents procedural due process.[39] The courts well understand the need for preliminary applications.[40]

Unlike preliminary plan approval, local government has little discretion in approving final plan applications. Courts generally consider final plan or final plat approval to be a ministerial act.[41]

To obtain final approval, a developer need only demonstrate that it has met all the conditions the governing body attached to its preliminary approval; prepare the necessary maps, plats, and documents; post a performance bond; and perform other minor acts. Thus, after preliminary approval, the developer should be confident that final approval is simply a formality, and should proceed with full knowledge of certain approval if all conditions are met. The governing body cannot attach new conditions to final approval, nor can it deny final approval for reasons not presented during preliminary approval. Similarly, the developer cannot submit a final plan that substantially differs from the preliminary plan, except to meet conditions imposed on the approval of the preliminary plan.[42]

This description of the three steps of plan approval makes it clear that preliminary approval is easily the most crucial step of the three. It is at this phase of the process that the governing body exercises its discretion to prevent the development from disturbing the general welfare of the community.

At the concept plan phase, the development is too vaguely described for the governing body to interpose concrete conditions or objections. On the other hand, it is too late for the board to raise new issues and objections during the final approval process. In sum, the best (and statutorily envisioned) opportunity a local government has to avoid irreparable consequences is at the preliminary plan stage. It is, therefore, vital that the governing body fully appreciate exactly what it is approving when it votes on a preliminary plan.

MINOR SUBDIVISIONS

If the administrative assistant determines that the subdivision is minor, a public hearing is scheduled before the planning commission on approval of the sketch plat. If the planning commission approves or conditionally approves the subdivision sketch plat, preliminary plat approval is not required and the applicant may proceed directly to the final plat approval stage.[43] It is important to note that even though an expedited process is used for the minor subdivision, it is subject to the same substantive requirements as a major subdivision. If the planning commission disapproves the sketch plat, the applicant may appeal to the legislature pursuant to Section 3.8 of the Regulations.

The advantages of this procedure are obvious. First, only a few subdivisions should qualify for minor subdivision status. The less significant impacts of a minor subdivision should generally minimize the need for extensive review of the proposal. The local government must take care, however, that developers are not using the process to avoid the more substantial procedures for major subdivisions.[44] The planning commission always is free to seek outside advice on the proposal for a minor subdivision. The minor subdivision process simply is an expedient way to handle small-scale subdivisions that will have minimal impacts on the community. Of course, many small subdivisions collectively will have at least as great an impact as one large subdivision. Thus, review is necessary and the applicant should be required to mitigate impacts and to pay appropriate fees.

MAJOR SUBDIVISIONS

Sketch Plat and Referral to Interested Agencies

If the administrative assistant determines that the proposed subdivision is major and in substantial compliance with local law, the assistant will issue a Notice to Proceed.[45] A Notice of Noncompliance issues if the proposed subdivision is not in substantial compliance with local law and the applicant refuses to modify the sketch plat.[46] Upon receipt of the Notice to Proceed, the applicant may file a preliminary plat within 30 to 120 days from the date of the Notice to Proceed.[47] The administrative assistant also refers the sketch plat to a number of agencies for review and comment. It is important, therefore, to make sure that the sketch plat is sufficiently specific to permit a meaningful review.[48] In view of planning commission approval of the subdivision, it is wise to refer the sketch plat to the governing body for comment on the proposed subdivision.

The procedure of referring the sketch plat for review differs from the practice of referring the preliminary plat for review. Often, the planning commission may conditionally approve a preliminary plat dependent on the views and recommendations of referral agencies. The Model Regulations procedure is designed to put the subdivider on notice at the time of preliminary plat review of the conditions that other agencies believe are necessary if the planning commission is to approve the preliminary plat.

Submission of the plat to other agencies and officials [§ 3.2(b)(ii)], such as school boards, metropolitan, regional, and state agencies, and health boards for review of health, fire, water, and regional planning objectives, encourages and promotes community development in the manner best designed for public goals and objectives.[49] Indeed, submission to regional and state agencies is now required in a number of circumstances.[50] Foremost is the metropolitan and regional review for all projects, including housing developments, subsidized or insured by the federal government. These review requirements, originally created for metropolitan areas by statute,[51] were extended under the Office of Management and Budget Circular A-95 (Title IV of the Intergovernmental Cooperation Act of 1968), which provided for review of applications for federal financial assistance by state, regional, and metropolitan clearinghouses.[52] The A-95 review program has been replaced by a review program at the state level, which provides for coordinated review by state and local officials of proposed projects requesting federal financial assistance.[53]

A number of state laws also require that a subdivision application be referred for extensive environmental review by state, regional, or federal authorities. The Council on Environmental Quality published a major text outlining nine new innovative land-use regulatory systems, which range from the San Francisco Bay and Conservation Commission, the Lake Tahoe Regional Planning Agency (Nevada-California), and the Massachusetts and Wisconsin Wetland and Shoreland Protection Programs to the Maine and Vermont Environmental and Site Location Laws.[54] All of these systems radically affect the subdivision approval process by requiring approvals on the questions of environmental impact, pollution, governmental services, highway congestion, and conformance with local and state plans. The American Law Institute's *Model Land Development Code* identifies many areas of critical state and regional concern that require extraordinary review of certain subdivisions,[55] but these provisions have not effectively made their way into state law.[56]

Alternatives to the ALI model code provisions have been implemented on both state and regional levels. States have essentially recalled some of the powers delegated to local governments by zoning and planning enabling legislation in order to exercise a variety of state and regional land use controls at the state level.[57] Hawaii was the first state to adopt a statewide land use classification and regulation system in 1961. With relatively few changes, it is still in place today.[58]

Florida utilized a substitute, the Environmental Land and Water Management Act, for the ALI model code state and regional provisions. While this act dealt with developments of regional impact (DRIs), problems remained with standards for siting unwanted developments such as landfills and power generating facilities.[59]

Vermont's approach to state land use management and regulation represents an amalgam of the Hawaii and Florida systems. Act 250 was passed almost entirely in response to a ski tourism boom that led to intense and relatively large-scale development pressure in fragile environmental areas. As in Florida and Hawaii, there was a direct attempt to tie the permit process to comprehensive planning.[60]

Oregon, arguably the most plan-oriented of those states with state land use controls, is also one of the few that has tried to guide rather than merely authorize planning and local zoning. The courts in Oregon have been supportive of the state goals, strict in conformance requirements, and watchful that the Land Conservation and Development Commission not overstep its bounds.[61] Recently a number of these state programs have been enhanced and an entire group of new states joined the list (Florida, 1985; New Jersey, 1986; Maine, 1988; Vermont, 1988; Rhode Island, 1988; and Georgia, 1989). Others considering adopting statewide land use systems are California, Massachusetts, and South Carolina.[62]

Regional, as opposed to statewide, land use controls—which partially or entirely supersede local zoning and other land use controls—spring from the same source of power. Regional controls, however, tend to focus on a particular resource rather than on truly statewide conservation and development problems. The Adirondack Park Agency Act was passed for the purposes of administering and enforcing a planning process to answer concerns at the regional, state, and local levels.[63] While the Adirondack Act concerned itself with intrastate problems, the Tahoe Regional Planning Compact was an interstate agreement between Nevada and California. Unfortunately, the states are generally at odds over the pace and intensity of development that should be permitted in the Tahoe region.[64] A final example of regulation on a regional level is the Pinelands Protection Act, developed in connection with the National Parks and Recreation Act. These two acts were designed to "combine limited public acquisition with land use controls developed and implemented through a cooperative program involving Federal, State and local governments as well as concerned private groups and individuals."[65]

The primary factor behind state or regional review of local land use applications is the fear that local officials will not take into account the greater-than-local effects of their decision to approve and deny land use applications. Many local governments increasingly are relying on fiscal impact analysis in evaluating land use applications. This analysis cannot take into account regional environmental impacts of an approved land use application or the regional socioeconomic impacts of a denial of low-income residential subdivision. Some commentators have flatly condemned the implementation of land use controls by local governments.[66]

Even if enabling acts do not expressly provide for such outside review and approval, it has been upheld in some jurisdictions pursuant to the purpose of "securing adequate provision for water, sewerage, drainage, and other requirements."[67] Review by external authorities usually is not mandatory unless expressly authorized by statute; thus, the planning commission has the discretion as to which agencies to seek out for review.[68] The Model Regulations [§ 3.2(b)(ii)] maintain this discretion but require transmittal for review by adjoining local governments and otherwise where mandated by state law. When the planning commission has sent out a sketch plat or preliminary plat for review, it may not deny subdivision approval on the grounds that a dispute has arisen between two external agencies over which one will provide needed services.[69]

The most difficult issue with referral agencies is the delay that their review may cause. Many state and regional agencies are poorly prepared to respond to every application for subdivision approval. As a result, a state may provide that referral agencies have a specific time period within which to respond. If they do not respond in a timely fashion, their favorable response is deemed to have been given.[70] Referral does little good unless proposals for subdivision are actually reviewed. The best approach is to use state and regional referral agencies only for subdivisions that exceed certain size limitations or have other characteristics that make them suitable for outside review.

It should be clear from all of the above that the approval of a subdivision is becoming more and more complicated.[71] It is highly recommended that the developer have both a planner and an attorney advising him in all steps of the subdivision approval process.[72] In addition, the planning commission must be guided by the legal advice of the local government attorney's office throughout all stages of the subdivision process.

Preliminary Plat Approval

The application procedure and requirements for preliminary plat approval are set forth in Section 3.3(1).[73] The intermediate step of submission of a preliminary plat usually is a local innovation authorized by ordinance but not specifically mentioned in state enabling legislation,[74] except in a few states.[75] The Standard City Planning Enabling Act provides: "The regulations or practice of the commission may provide for a tentative approval of the plat previous to such installation; but any such tentative approval shall be revocable and shall not be entered on the plat."[76]

The administrative assistant must prepare a report for the planning commission incorporating the responses of referral agencies. The commission then holds a public hearing on the preliminary plat. To protect the developer, within 30 days after the close of the hearing (the Official Submission Date), the planning commission must render its decision.[77] This complies with the rule in a few courts that whether or not tentative approval is specifically made a part of the statutory procedure for review, the statutory period within which the planning commission must make a decision runs from preliminary rather than from final approval.[78] The purpose of preliminary plat approval is to enable the planning commission to review all substantive aspects of the subdivision without forcing the developer to prepare a final set of plat maps which will then be expensive to change. After preliminary approval, the developer should be confident that final approval is simply a ministerial act so long as there is compliance with any conditions imposed at preliminary approval.[79]

It is important that a public hearing be held at the preliminary approval stage, even if the statute requires a public hearing only at final approval. The statutory public hearing or meeting at final approval will normally be a formality because of the extensive investment of the time and energy by all parties concerned. Without a public hearing, adjoining property owners, concerned citizens, and other municipalities or regional agencies may not be given an opportunity to inform the planning commission about conditions of which the commission is unaware.

The SPEA states: "Before the adoption of the plan or any such part, amendment, extension or addition the commission shall hold at least one public hearing thereon."[80] Unfortunately, however, the enabling acts in many states make no provision for a public hearing.[81] This is a serious omission; where the enabling statute does not specifically provide for a hearing, some courts may refuse to read in a hearing requirement.[82] Some provision, such as Section 3.3(2) should, at the minimum, give the planning commission the discretionary power to hold a hearing. Such hearing requirements can be justified under the authority of the planning commission to adopt rules for the transaction of business, which they are permitted to do. Section 3.3(2) of the Model Regulations also provides for certified mail notices and suitable posting to assure public awareness of the application for preliminary plat review. A number of state courts have expressly or impliedly held that plat approval is quasi-judicial in nature.[83] Thus, in these states, notice to interested persons and an opportunity to be heard may be constitutionally required.[84] Because preliminary plat approval establishes the basis for final subdivision plat approval, its denial, approval, or conditional approval should be subject to judicial review.[85]

The current Model Regulations include two new provisions respecting preliminary plat approval. The first expressly provides specific standards that the planning commission must consider when deciding whether to approve a preliminary plat.[86] The applicant for subdivision approval has the obligation to demonstrate by clear and convincing evidence at the public hearing that: (1) there is adequate provision for water; (2) there is adequate provision for sewage disposal; (3) all necessary precautions have been taken to deal with topographic conditions and geologic hazards; (4) the developer has the financial ability to complete the proposed development; (5) there is not other suitable land in the community that already has been subdivided; (6) the proposed subdivision of land will not contribute to scattered development; and (7) every effort has been taken to mitigate the impact of the proposed subdivision on the community.[87]

Requirements four and five may be controversial. Both are designed to avoid the evils that result from a failed development project and from excessive subdivision. The excessive subdivision of land has long been recognized as a cause for many problems that may plague a local government.[88] Section 3.3(4) permits the planning commission to deny subdivision approval even if the subject land is properly zoned for its intended use and the use is consistent with the comprehensive or master plan. This provision is contrary to the law in some states that specific land use decisions must be consistent with the comprehensive plan.[89]

The second new provision with respect to preliminary plats expressly permits amendments to the preliminary plat following its approval.[90] Often a developer comes to final plat approval with substantial changes from the preliminary plat as approved. The developer may argue that the changes became necessary as the project progressed. The local government must then decide if the final plat substantially conforms to the preliminary plat as approved despite these changes.[91] Section 3.4 permits amendments to be approved administratively so long as they do not materially change the nature or scope of the subdivision as reviewed and approved. In addition, the developer is limited in the number of minor amendments that may be sought by the thresholds that trigger major amendment review.

Multi-Phased Projects (Phased Development Review Process)

The subdivision approval process becomes much more complicated when a proposed development will be built in phases over an extended period of time and/or involve multiple parties in the process.[92] Especially difficult are the arrangements for on and offsite improvements to assure the adequate public facility standards of the regulations.[93] These complexities have been heightened where a state has mandated a "concurrency management" requirement upon local government prohibiting the issuance of development permits or approvals unless existing or programmed public facilities and services are available at the levels of service adopted in the comprehensive plan.[94] Local governments may also use the powers of the standard planning and zoning enabling acts[95] to adopt adequate public facility requirements.[96] Montgomery County, Maryland, enforces its adequate public facilities ordinance at the preliminary subdivision stage.[97] The City of San Diego recently considered an ordinance that establishes an annualizing phasing limit tying development approval to the capacity at adopted levels of service of existing transportation facilities and new facilities included in a 20-year CIP.[98]

Where a concurrency requirement exists, large-scale projects must be phased in such a manner that the necessary facilities are in place when the impact of the development occurs.[99] Consequently, if the demand for public facilities or services needed to accommodate a subsequent development phase increases following the issuance of a development permit for a prior phase in the approval process—or if public facilities or services included in the concurrency determination are not constructed as scheduled in the CIP—subdivision approval may have to be delayed for future phases pending the achievement of the adopted levels of service.[100] Accordingly, it is desirable to implement a policy for early vesting to provide certainty in the development approval process while protecting the municipality's ability to track the available capacity of public facilities and services.

The phased development review process incorporated into the model regulations integrates all of the basic discretionary project review into a single process (including plan amendment, rezoning, subdivision, and site plan review) and identifies flexible time limits for the development of subsequent project phases. The major tool for implementation is the use of a *master preliminary plat*. The master preliminary plat allows early review of the project and an award of vested rights and favorable development procedures to the developer in exchange for the provision of public benefits and the implementation of quality design.

The master preliminary plat ties together the initial stage of subdivision approval (which contains the preliminary plat for the first subdivision phase) and the future subdivision phases into a single document that forms the basis for development exactions, environmental mitigation, roadway access, and community design. Detailed platting procedures are required only for the initial development phase, with only general development parameters delineated for subsequent development phases.

From the developer's perspective, one of the more troublesome aspects of phased development proposals is the probability that land development regulations will change before the development proceeds to final approval and construction. When development regulations change while the project is proceeding through the approval process, significant expenses may be incurred to comply with new and unanticipated regulatory requirements. These unexpected requirements can significantly raise the cost of development to the consumer and result in diminished profitability to the developer. To avoid this problem, the master preliminary plat process allows a governmental entity to guarantee that, under appropriate circumstances, uses and intensities will be vested for a time certain. As part of the regulatory process, the developer should be required to provide certain corresponding benefits to the municipality in the form of, for example, affordable housing, contributions to public facilities above what would otherwise be required, infill development, environmental protection, or open space provision.

In order to ensure the continued viability of multi-phased development proposals and to protect the ability of developers to attract financing for developments with lengthy build-out periods, master preliminary plats should be accompanied by development agreements.

Vested Rights/Development Agreements

Section 3.6 deals with rights that accrue upon preliminary plat approval. The section makes clear that a developer should expect only those rights expressly provided for in the regulations. The applicant is protected against changes in local laws and regulations following the submission of the preliminary plat to the planning commission. Thus, the Model Regulations adopt the minority view that development rights, at least those resulting from subdivision approval, vest upon submission of the subdivision plat.[101] This rule protects the applicant from changes in the law that are made in direct response to the applicant's proposal.[102] The applicant must, however, be in compliance with all applicable federal and state laws at the time the final plat is considered for approval.[103] Moreover, the local government can subject the subdivision to rules and regulations adopted after submission of the preliminary plat if it is necessary to do so to protect public health and safety and the planning commission makes a finding on the record to that effect.[104] If the planning commission required the applicant to complete subdivision improvements as a condition precedent to final plat, and the improvements were completed, the subdivision could be subjected to rules and regulations adopted after submission of the preliminary plat only if compliance is necessary to "prevent a substantial risk of injury to public health, safety, and general welfare."[105]

This vested rights provision is designed to strike a balance between private expectations regarding development and the public's interest in regulating land use. A prospective applicant should be able to review existing land use regulations and then determine whether subdivision approval should be sought at that time. The vesting upon application rule provides the certainty that real estate development requires. The government, on the other hand, may impose newly adopted or amended regulations on the applicant following submission of the preliminary plat so long as it makes a finding on the record that public health and safety justify imposition of new or different regulations. A court should not readily hold that the applicant has a vested right to develop the subdivision free from the new or amended regulations because the applicant knows from the outset that the government may impose new or amended regulations to protect public health and safety.[106]

The Model Regulations further provide for development agreements.[107] A development agreement is a contract between a local government unit and a private holder of development rights.[108] The principal purpose of such an agreement is to specify the land use regulations that will apply to the relevant property during the term of the agreement.[109] In return for agreement on the regulations, the developer will provide certain guarantees concerning improvements, exactions, and other charges to be dedicated or paid to the local government over the life of the agreement.[110] Development agreements can provide a great deal of certainty to both the developer and the local government, particularly when implemented in conjunction with a multiphase development project.[111]

The concept of the development agreement emerged from the need of land developers to be certain that the government would not adopt restrictive land use regulations. The vested rights doctrine, described earlier in this chapter, did not generally protect the developer who had not yet received land use approvals for phases of the development to be undertaken at a later date. These later phases were subject to the majority rule that subdivision plats filed before enactment of a specific subdivision law are subject to the new law unless substantial construction had occurred.[112] Yet many multiphase developments are platted and constructed over many years. Consequently, development agreements were created.

The ability of the local government unit to enter into a development agreement, like other local government powers, is authorized by the state legislature. To date, nine states expressly authorize local governments to enter into development agreements.[113] Aside from *specific* statutory authorization, local governments in other states may also possess the authority to enter into development agreements based upon home rule authority or other statutes reasonably inferring such power.[114]

Given that a local governmental unit possesses the authority to enter into a development agreement, there are still certain limits as to what each party may demand from the other. The city may request that the developer provide public improvements onsite as well as offsite, either of which may be greater than the developer's proportionate share.[115] The city may also request the developer to provide mixed uses or affordable housing.[116] The city may request that the developer participate in agricultural land preservation[117] or utilize transfer of development rights provisions.[118]

The development agreement, in order to vest density and uses under existing regulations, should require attainment of one or more critical public policies:[119]

1. Advancement and not mere conformity to the adopted comprehensive plan, capital improvements program, financing strategies and implementing zoning, subdivision, environmental, and related ordinances.

2. Advancement of critical goals, objectives, policies, and strategies of the community.

3. Contributions of infrastructure both onsite and offsite in excess of those merely required by existing regulations.

4. Provision for joint public-private development that provides revenue enhancement for the municipality.

5. Provision of affordable housing and other critical socially needed treatment or social facilities, including child care.

6. Protection of open space, environmentally sensitive lands, natural habitats, historic and archeological resources, regional or statewide facilities, in excess of what can be required under existing regulations.

7. Utilization of flexible and innovative techniques, including transfer of development rights; land acquisition funding; solar, light, energy,

noise, and avigation easements; advanced design, mixed use, new town, and heightened performance standards.

Determination of vested rights is a critical component of the agreement. Vested rights, as discussed previously, are the rights of the developer to complete the project under existing regulations.[120] A right vests when a development is shielded from changes in zoning, regulations, or exaction demands made by any and all local government permit-granting entities.[121] Vesting allows the developer to proceed, confident that the investment and anticipated return will not be jeopardized by future government regulatory action.

Developers of multiphase projects in particular stand to lose a judicial determination of vested rights. In reviewing vested rights claims, courts have looked at a number of factors, including: consideration of whether there has been a government act formally authorizing a course of conduct or development; whether the developer has acted in good faith and incurred substantial expenses and obligations; and whether the obligations incurred have been so substantial that it would be unfair or inequitable to eliminate the rights the developer has relied upon.[122] In most cases, the test for governmental action upon which reliance would be justified is the issuance of a building permit.[123]

With a multiphased project, however, the issuance of a building permit is often the last step in a protracted process and considerable resources may be expended prior to this point.[124] Thus, a developer's reliance on the government's approval of the first phase of a project did not vest any right to undertake, let alone complete, the subsequent phases.[125] As a result of this limitation on the vested rights doctrine, local governments agreed to refrain from interfering with the development of subsequent phases by rezoning the subject project in exchange for additional consideration from the developer. As development agreements have evolved, they now may contain numerous promises by both the developer and the local government.[126]

Aside from the issue of statutory authority, the most important legal barrier to the enforcement of a development agreement is the "reserved powers doctrine."[127] This doctrine, at its most basic, prohibits the government from contracting away its inherent governmental powers;[128] the government may not promise to exercise or refrain from exercising the police power—the power to protect and promote public health, safety, and welfare.[129]

Development agreements can be defended against reserved power challenges, because development agreements constitute a present reasonable exercise of the police power and therefore no reserved power is being bargained away.[130] Benefits resulting from development agreements that arguably serve the public welfare include: the settling of vested rights problems and the corresponding incentive for private investment; the ability of local government to develop better comprehensive plans through more flexible, individualized regulation decisions; and the benefits to consumers resulting from a more efficient development approval process.[131] Further consideration must be given to protections against reserved power challenges written into the states' existing development agreement statutes.[132] Between the potential benefits and the built-in protections, the public welfare is not threatened but actually enhanced using development agreements.[133] Some courts have avoided the reserved powers question altogether by taking a wider view and upholding agreements that were limited in time and rationally related to a legitimate state interest.[134]

Of greater concern to local governments considering the use of development agreements now and in the near future are the recent land use regulation decisions from the United States Supreme Court. Even with their contractual characteristics, development agreements have been properly identified in the literature as a "novel packaging of regulatory requirements"[135] or the "most sophisticated form of exaction."[136] As such, development agreements must be analyzed against existing law relevant to such regulation, specifically the case of *Nollan v. California Coastal Commission.*[137]

Nollan dealt with a transaction in which the granting of an easement by the landowner was made a condition to attain a reconstruction permit on a beach house. In holding that the situation constituted a taking, the Supreme Court analyzed the nexus between the condition and the original purpose of the building restriction.[138] The Court failed to find any connection between the required easement and the purported purpose of the exaction, and stated that "unless the permit condition serves the same governmental purpose as the development ban, the building restriction is not a valid regulation of land but an 'out-and-out plan of extortion.'"[139]

Accepting that developing agreements are a "voluntary exaction" subject to the *Nollan* standard,[140] a development condition must pass a three-part test to be valid: (1) the municipality must be able to justify a complete prohibition of a proposed use; (2) such prohibition must not constitute a taking; and (3) the condition must substantially advance the purpose of the regulation.[141]

It is the third prong that will most affect development agreements.[142] The analysis is focused on whether the proposed exaction advances the applicable land use regulation. Consequently, great care must be taken in the negotiation of the development agreement to ensure that conditions relate to the impacts of the proposed development and that the conditions further the goals of the existing land use regulation concerning which modification is desired by the developer.

The Model Regulations do not generally limit the promises that either the developer or government may make to one other.[143] The regulations do, however, limit the time period of the agreement to five years and require that certain provisions be included for the protection of the local government.[144] In the agreement, the developer must agree to limit any claim predicated on the government breach of the agreement to state law contract claims and not allege constitutional violations. A reviewing court should consider this waiver to be knowing and voluntary on the developer's part because the development agreement is not a necessary part of any land use approval and execution of the agreement is not a condition precedent to the right of the developer to commence development.[145]

It is especially important to condition the government's obligations under the development agreement on the developer's compliance with all laws—federal, state, and local. Local law includes the developer's compliance with any conditions imposed on the land use approval that are related to the execution of the development agreement.

Because a developer will be prohibited by most subdivision regulations and statutes from obtaining any building permits until the final plat is recorded, the Model Regulations permit the interim grading of the development site (upon receipt of a top-soil and excavation permit from the planning commission)[146] and the construction of two model homes[147] as a separate minor subdivision.

FINAL APPROVAL

Final subdivision approval rests in the hands of the planning commission under the SPEA,[148] but in a few states, the local legislative body exercises final authority on the planning commission's recommendation.[149] The Model Regulations prescribe that the application for final plat approval must be made to the administrative assistant on specific forms with 10 copies of the plat and detailed construction plans.[150] In addition, the applicant must show compliance with all conditions of preliminary approval (such as the petitioning for the formation of special lighting, water, or sewer districts); submission of the appropriate lot, plan, and inspection fees (bond amount); the fee for street signs; an executed subdivision improvement agreement and letter of credit as required; all irrevocable offers of dedications and escrow deeds for all easements and public areas (see Model Regulations § 3.5(1)(f); and that envelopes have been furnished for notifying adjoining property owners. This fixed method of submission is important, for the period in which the government must approve or disapprove the final plat begins to run only from the time of a valid submission[151] to the appropriate government official.[152]

The Model Regulations do not require a public hearing on the final subdivision plat. Rather, the local government publishes notice that the final plat has been submitted and is available for review and solicits comments on whether approval should be granted.[153] This notice and comment process should be consistent with federal procedural due process requirements.[154]

The Model Regulations provide that the final determination on plat approval shall be made within 30 days after the close of the public meeting on final approval. This procedure follows from the legal principle that the planning commission has the presumptive power in its regulations to determine the submission date of the application. Second, in submitting the application for final approval, the applicant has the power to extend the time for decision by agreement between the planning commission and the developer.[155] The agreement of the developer to extend the period for the issuance of the decision on final plat approval is significant because in many states the planning commission must act within 30 to 60 days[156] or there is a presumption of approval or a right of the subdivider to record without planning commission approval.[157]

The Model Regulations do not adopt the so-called "deemed approved" process. Instead, the regulations expressly provide that the applicant may file an action in mandamus to compel the planning commission to act.[158] In addition, the municipality is liable to the applicant for $500 for each day that the decision is delayed.[159] The government's duty to act is not dependent on the applicant's substantial compliance with final plat submission requirements.[160] If the applicant has not complied with those requirements, then the planning commission should simply deny final plat approval. It should be noted that the planning commission must also render a decision on the preliminary plat within 30 days of the official submission date—the date on which the public hearing on the preliminary plat closes.[161] If the work load of the local government makes this time period unrealistic, the government should extend the period. The government must, however, render judgment within a reasonable period of time.[162] It can be argued that state laws that require plat approval within a certain period of time apply only to final plat approval and not to preliminary plat approval.[163]

A few states require that the planning commission's decision be in writing.[164] This logical requirement is set forth in the Model Regulations, § 3.5(4). This is extremely useful in those states where an appeal from the planning commission goes to the legislative body prior to judicial review,[165] More importantly, a fully documented decision should be sent to the developer to give notice that any statutory appeal period has commenced with the filing of the decision.

RECORDATION

The recordation of the final plat follows final approval. Because of the importance attached to the ministerial act of recordation of a plat, the Model Regulations recommend that the administrative assistant be charged with that duty.[166] If any conditions were attached to final plat approval, largely dealing with technical corrections, the final plat should not be signed or recorded unless the conditions are satisfied.

Not all subdivisions should be recorded in one plat at one time. Where there is a proposed major development that lends itself to staged development because of size, financing, or lack of adequate governmental services, the Model Regulations empower the planning commission to permit sectionalized development over a period of time if proper dedications are made and adequate security is offered.[167] This procedure will protect the developer from changes in subdivision regulations that may be made prior to final approval of its entire plat, such as road widths, paving specifications, and drainage requirements.[168] Without a provision for sectionalized development, however, the developer will not be protected against subsequent changes in the zoning regulations.[169] In order to obtain this protection, the developer would have to file the final approval of the entire subdivision within the normal one-year period.

In addition, if a court invalidates final plat approval following a legal challenge, the government should record a document in the real property records setting forth the invalidation.[170] This should ensure that lots within a subdivision that no longer legally exists are not sold or developed.

APPEAL FROM FINAL DECISION

The Model Regulations permit the applicant for subdivision approval to appeal certain adverse decisions by the planning commission—most importantly, the denial of sketch, preliminary, or final plat approval.[171] The appeal must be taken within 10 days from the date of the denial by filing a notice of appeal that sets forth the basis of the appeal.[172] The applicant/appellant has a right to appear before the legislative body, but the regulations do not require a public hearing on the appeal. The legislative body's decision on the appeal must be rendered within 45 days from the date that the notice of appeal is filed.[173] The Model Regulations do not provide for appeals to the legislative body when the planning commission approves or conditionally approves a plat. If the legislative body reverses a denial of plat approval, however, it may impose conditions on the approval.[174]

FEES

The fees required as part of the subdivision approval process are another important part of ensuring sound community growth without burdening already financially strapped local governments. The developer should bear the cost of review under the theory that its development proposal has created the need for review. The fees should be set to cover the reasonable costs of inspection, processing, and review that will be incurred by the planning commission and its employees.[175] The fees charged to subdividers may not be used for revenue purposes for the community.[176] In a few cases, fees have been struck down where not specifically authorized by statute,[177] but the fact that all enabling statutes authorize a planning commission to adopt its rules and procedures should constitute adequate authorization.[178]

The Model Regulations authorize the local government to suspend final plat approval as a method of enforcing any obligations that the subdivider owes to the government, including the construction of public improvements.[179] The government files a document giving public notice of suspension of approval in the real property records. This suspension of final approval may, in certain circumstances, be a powerful tool in causing the completion of public improvements by the developer or a successor in interest, including a foreclosing lender. The power to suspend final plat approval should be reasonably inferred from state enabling statutes.

Municipalities should also consider drafting a development agreement. As a preliminary note, it must be stressed that it is difficult to set forth a model outside the context of a particular transaction. Substantive elements will vary from project to project, and negotiations based on the parties' particular interests will likely result in substitute language. As a practical matter, a development agreement is like any agreement between parties with disparate interests. Parties seeking a degree of certainty in a transaction are well-advised to fully and completely set forth their bases, intentions, understandings, and expectations within the terms of their agreement. This will lessen the likelihood of misunderstanding and allow the performance of all parties to be measured.

Some of the more important provisions of a development agreement warrant comment. Reciting the parties' intent allows the city to demonstrate that its actions are an exercise of police powers, as opposed to contracting them away. Further, reciting the parties' intent shows that the property owner's obligations under the agreement are related to needs generated by his project. The attachment of council findings also demonstrates the council's exercise of power within its general authority over the city's land use scheme. The inclusion of definitions and attachment of exhibits goes to the goal of fully and completely stating the parties' agreement, and will aid in any construction that becomes necessary.

The heart of a development agreement establishes the city's existing rules, regulations, and official policies governing all aspects of use as those applicable to the project. This provides property owners the certainty they desire, which was the impetus for the utilization of development agreements.

The city needs to retain flexibility in carrying out its function and obligation to govern the development of the community. This flexibility may entail substituting or adding rules, regulations, and policies when conditions so warrant. By reserving the authority to respond to changing conditions, the city is able to support a position that it is currently exercising and will be able in the future to continue exercising its authority over the subject property. Reservation of the authority to respond to change also shows that the city has not contracted away its police powers. While property owners would ideally like to "freeze" all land use regulations based on the execution of a development agreement, such an agreement would not likely survive a legal challenge in many jurisdictions.

Thus, the city's retained flexibility serves to bring the transaction into compliance with applicable law.

The remaining sections and provisions should further state the parties' expectations and set forth the structure for their relations. Certain optional provisions, such as requiring arbitration of disputes or the maintaining of insurance, should be considered in some situations. From the perspective of a property owner, a city's development agreement may be inadequate as far as city assurances to mitigate disincentives to the project and to agree to the development of all phases of a project. Such assurances should be the subject of negotiation.

The advantage of development agreements and reason for their existence is certainty. Completeness and detail are essential to certainty, and only the parties can see to their needs in this regard.

NOTES

1. For a detailed outline of the developer's procedural steps in the processing of a subdivision from the purchase of raw land until the sale of the lots to individual purchasers, *see* Kaiser & Weiss, *Local Public Policy and the Residential Development Policy*, 32 LAW AND CONTEMP. PROBS. 232 (1967). The process is somewhat more involved and complicated for large subdivisions or new communities, but the techniques and processes are similar. *See generally* E. EICHLER & M. KAPLAN, THE COMMUNITY BUILDERS (1970). *See also* U.S. DEPARTMENT OF HOUSING AND URBAN DEVELOPMENT, REDUCING THE DEVELOPMENT COSTS OF HOUSING ACTIONS FOR STATE AND LOCAL GOVERNMENTS (1979).

2. The administrative assistant can also be titled "a permit expeditor or ombudsman." *See* U.S. DEPARTMENT OF HOUSING AND URBAN DEVELOPMENT, STREAMLINING LOCAL REGULATIONS, A HANDBOOK FOR REDUCING HOUSING AND DEVELOPMENT COSTS, May 1983, No. 11 at 36: "In some communities, one staff person, known as a permit expeditor or ombudsman, guides development applications through the review process and serves as the developer's prime contact person. The ombudsman can assist in the preparation of the application and serve as a go-between during the review and approval stages."

3. *See* U.S. DEPARTMENT OF HOUSING AND URBAN DEVELOPMENT, STREAMLINING LOCAL REGULATIONS, A HANDBOOK FOR REDUCING HOUSING AND DEVELOPMENT COSTS, May 1983, No. 11 at 36: "One-Stop Permit Processing." Aside from the written materials and forms, the application *procedures* themselves can be structured to assist rather

than deter the developer. One-step permit processing is a procedural reform that has become a popular technique implemented in a variety of ways:

- Reshuffling offices to locate all permit functions in one geographic area
- Establishing a central information center where staff members provide materials and explain procedures to developers
- Assigning to one department or office the primary responsibility for accepting and processing all applications and maintaining files. This central department coordinates all reviews, schedules hearings, and serves as the sole contact for the developer
- The staff review phase of the development approval process can be smoothed through the following techniques: the use of permit expediters and joint review committees, contracting out site plan reviews, using deadlines, and fast-tracking processing.

4. *See* U.S. DEPARTMENT OF HOUSING AND URBAN DEVELOPMENT, REDUCING THE DEVELOPMENT COSTS OF HOUSING: ACTIONS FOR STATE AND LOCAL GOVERNMENTS (1979): "Administrative simplification can substantially reduce the time required, coordinate the requisite analyses and thereby reduce upward pressure of permit approvals on housing prices." p. 164; BOSSELMAN, FEURER & SIEMON, THE PERMIT EXPLOSION: COORDINATING THE PROLIFERATION, The Urban Land Institute (1976); Longhini, *How Three Cities Fared in One-Step Permitting*, 31 PLANNING 44 (Oct. 1978); SEIDEL, HOUSING COSTS AND GOVERNMENTAL REGULATIONS: CONFRONTING THE REGULATORY MAZE, Rutgers

Center for Urban Policy Research (1978) (Chapter Seven: The Effect of Subdivision Regulations on Housing Costs).

5. J. VRANICKER, W. SANDERS & D. MOSENA, STREAMLINING LAND USE REGULATION (1980); *Thirteen Perspectives on Regulatory Simplification*, Urban Land Institute Research Report No. 29 (1979); U.S. DEPARTMENT OF HOUSING AND URBAN DEVELOPMENT, STREAMLINING LOCAL REGULATIONS, A HANDBOOK FOR REDUCING HOUSING AND DEVELOPMENT COSTS, May 1983, No. 11.

6. *See* Bosselman, *Time and the Regulatory Process: Recent Decisions*, 1 LAND USE INSTITUTE PLANNING, REGULATION, LITIGATION, EMINENT DOMAIN, AND COMPENSATION 1 (ALI-ABA Course of Study Materials, 1986).

7. In Mullane v. Central Hanover Bank & Trust Co., 339 U.S. 306 (1950), service on the owner of record at the last known address of record is required to obtain personal service for an in personam judgment. Service on a designated agent is considered personal service. For litigation over notice requirements, *see* Folsom Rd. Civic Ass'n v. Parish of St. Tammany, 425 So.2d 1318 (La. Ct. App. 1983); Board of Comm'rs v. Quaker Constr. Co., 441 A.2d 801 (Pa. Commw. Ct. 1982); Korkuch v. Planning Bd. of Eastham, 526 N.E.2d 1301 (Mass. App. 1988); Allied Realty Ltd. v. Upper Saddle River, 534 A.2d 1019 (N.J. Super. 1987) (it is incumbent upon the reviewing agency to afford the developer notice and the opportunity to be heard to show that circumstances have changed since a previous resolution denying subdivision approval).

8. Clay v. Landreth, 45 S.E.2d 875 (Va. 1948); Arko Enter. v. Wood, 185 So.2d 734 (Fla. Dist. Ct. App. 1966); J.C. Penney Co. v. Koff, 345 So.2d 732 (Fla. Dist. Ct. App. 1977); SMITH & BOYER, SURVEY OF THE LAW OF PROPERTY 254 (2d ed. 1971).

9. *See* Halverson v. City of Bellevue, 704 P.2d 1232 (Wash. Ct. App. 1985) (where city was on notice of an adverse possessor of pending subdivision, it was error to approve the subdivision on application by someone whose claim to title was not clear); Fullam v. Kronman, 275 N.Y.S.2d 44 (Sup. Ct. 1966), *aff'd*, 298 N.Y.S.2d 865 (App. Div. 1970), *aff'd*, 257 N.E.2d 57 (1970) (application by contract vendee is not proper and planning board need not act).

10. Numerous task forces and studies have examined subdivision plat approval procedures in detail. *See* LISTOKIN & WALKER, THE SUBDIVISION AND SITE PLAN HANDBOOK at 176, 177, Rutgers Center for Urban Policy Research (1989); NATIONAL LEAGUE OF CITIES, STREAMLINING YOUR LO-CAL DEVELOPMENT PROCESS, Tech. Bull. 10 (1981); VRANICAR, SANDERS & MOSENA, STREAMLINING LAND USE REGULATIONS, A GUIDEBOOK FOR LOCAL GOVERNMENTS, (Nov. 1980); So, *Regulatory Simplification: Can the Local Administrative Process Be Improved*, in Annette Kolis (ed.), THIRTEEN PERSPECTIVES ON REGULATORY SIMPLIFICATION, The Urban Land Institute, Research Report No. 29 (1979); Longhini, *Streamlined Permitting Procedures*, PAS REVIEW 1 (1978).

11. HOUSING & HOME FINANCE AUTHORITY, SUGGESTED LAND SUBDIVISION REGULATIONS § II(A) (1950). These regulations were suggested as models for communities in order to accommodate insured FHA subdivision projects. The model is out of date today and fails to reflect many of the new concepts in subdivision regulation such as dedication of land, money in lieu of land, and off-site factors as related to subdivision approval.

12. *See* Listokin & Walker, *supra* note 10 at 178-179:

Classify development by level of significance (i.e. "minor" versus "major"). Such a strategy separates projects with minor impacts and processes them through an abbreviated approval routine.

The model subdivision ordinances referred to in this study incorporate similar recommendations to improve processing. Freilich and Levi classify development as either major or minor and provide accelerated review and abbreviated submission requirements for the latter. (FREILICH & LEVI, MODEL SUBDIVISION REGULATIONS (1975), Section 2.1.)

The Indiana Model County Subdivision Regulations incorporate similar provisions (PATTERSON, MODEL COUNTY SUBDIVISION REGULATIONS, Publication H-83-4, July 1983). The Oregon Model Land Development Ordinance classifies development into three "types" depending on "how minimal their effect is on others (OREGON BUREAU OF GOVERNMENT RESEARCH AND SERVICE, PROCEDURE FOR MAKING LAND DEVELOPMENT DECISIONS—A SUPPLEMENT TO THE MODEL LAND DEVELOPMENT ORDINANCE, Feb. 1983).

13. *See e.g.*, WIS. STAT. ANN. 236.45(2)(a) (West 1987) (five or more parcels is a subdivision and subject to the subdivision regulations, but a city that has a planning agency may provide for more restrictive regulations); CAL. BUS. & PROF. CODE ANN. 11000 (West 1987) (a division of five or more lots is a subdivision). The Massachusetts statutes, MASS. GEN. LAWS ANN. Ch. 41, 81(L) (West 1979), provide that a division of land of two or more lots is subject to the subdivision regulations, unless the division fronts on an existing way. Retting v. Planning Bd., 126 N.E.2d 104 (Mass. 1955). A Pennsylvania definition invokes subdivision controls only where there is a division of a tract into three or more lots. Appeal of Valicente, 184 A.2d 263 (Pa. 1962). *See generally* HAGMAN & JUERGENSMEYER, URBAN PLANNING & LAND DEVELOPMENT CONTROL LAWS 7 (2d ed. 1986).

14. Sugarman v. Lewis, 488 A.2d 709 (R.I. 1985); Taylor v. Marshall, 376 A.2d 712 (R.I. 1977); Dube v. Senter, 219 A.2d 456 (N.H. 1966); Cherry Hills Village v. Shafroth, 349 P.2d 368 (Colo. 1960).

15. Village of Lake Bluff v. Jacobson, 454 N.E.2d 734 (Ill. Ct. App. 1983) (developmental impact is the criterion that should be used when determining when the subdivision regulations should be applied); Green v. Bourbon County Joint Planning Comm'n, 637 S.W.2d 626 (Ky. 1982) (exemption of large, presumably agricultural lots was invalid for circumvention of subdivision regulations). *See generally* Hagman & Juergensmeyer, *supra* note 13, at 7.5.

16. *See* Burden, *Missoula County Subdivision Inventory Report*, 14 MONTANA ENVIRONMENTAL INFORMATION CENTER (1980), Montana study that demonstrates the problems with exemptions from subdivision control. Although Montana is by no means a highly urbanized state, it has experienced substantial subdivision activity as part of the phenomenon of marketing recreational or second home subdivisions throughout the United States. In a six-year period, from 1973-1979, 169 subdivision plats were recorded in Missoula County, an area experiencing heavy development pressure. At the same time, more than 2,000 certificates of survey were recorded. The certificate of survey process is a perfunctory review mechanism for subdivisions that do not fall within the full review requirements of Montana's subdivision control law. The 2,246 certificates of survey effectively subdivided more than 38,000 acres of land. Indeed, it is estimated that more than 70 percent of all divisions of land in Montana use one or more of the exemptions found in that state's subdivision control law.

17. CALLIES & FREILICH, CASES AND MATERIALS ON LAND USE, Subdivision Controls at 333 (West 1986, Supp. 1988); Graves v. Bloomfield Planning Bd., 235 A.2d 51 (N.J. Super. 1967); Donovan v. City of New Brunswick, 141 A.2d 134 (N.J. Super. 1958). The New Jersey statute found in N.J. STAT. ANN. § 40:55 D-5 specifically excludes from minor subdivisions a planned development, any new street, and the extension of any off-tract improvement. Under New Jersey law a municipality may, if it wishes, subject even minor subdivisions to the complete requirements of "major" subdivisions. *Cf.* Noble v. Chairman and Township Comm. of Mendham, 219 A.2d 335 (N.J. Super.), *aff'd* 223 A.2d 497 (N.J. Sup. Ct., 1966). *See also* WASH. REV. CODE § 58.17.020; 5 ZIEGLER, RATHKOPF'S THE LAW OF ZONING AND PLANNING, Subdivisions: Authority 64.03 (1989).

18. This same distinction is sometimes recognized by statute, N.J. STAT. ANN. 40:55, D-25 (West Supp. 1987), but has been used with great success in municipal regulations, notably Fairlawn, New Jersey; Charlotte, North Carolina; and Ramapo, New York. *See* Graves v. Bloomfield Planning Bd., 235 A.2d 51 (N.J. Super. Ct. Law Div. 1967); Noble v. Township Comm., 219 A.2d 335 (N.J. Super. Ct. App. Div. 1966); Stoker v. Town of Irvington, 177 A.2d 61 (N.J. Super. Ct. Law Div. 1961). Several courts have held a minor subdivision regulation to be unconstitutional as not germane to subdivision control and traffic planning, and for being an unreasonable restraint on alienation, Kass v. Lewin, 104 So.2d 572 (Fla. 1958). *Accord* Green v. Bourbon City Joint Planning Comm'n, 637 S.W.2d 626 (Ky. 1982).

19. This definition eliminates the following problems: (a) division into lots does not include division into parcels, since the former implies "building lots," Bloom v. Planning Bd., 191 N.E.2d 684 (Mass. 1963); Wall v. Ayrshire Corp., 352 S.W.2d 496 (Tex. Civ. App. 1961); Goldstein v. Planning Bd., 144 A.2d 724 (N.J. Super. Ct. App. Div. 1958); (b) leases may be excluded (i.e., trailer parks), Higdon v. Campbell County Fiscal Court, 374 S.W.2d 511 (Ky. 1964); (c) resubdivision may be excluded unless specifically defined, Vinyard v. St. Louis County, 399 S.W.2d 99 (Mo. 1966); this also eliminates "checkerboarding," *see* Note, *Substandard Lots and the Exception Clause—"Checkerboarding" As a Means of Circumvention*, 16 SYRACUSE L. REV. 612 (1965); (d) nonresidential subdivisions may be exempted from subdivision control, Clark v. Sunset Hills Memorial Park, 273 P.2d 645 (Wash. 1954); Green v. Bourbon City Joint Planning Comm'n, 637 S.W.2d 626 (Ky. 1982) (agricultural exemption); (e) Metzdorf v. Borough of Rumson, 170 A.2d 249 (N.J. Super. Ct. App. Div. 1961) (testamentary (devise) or interfamily divisions of property may be excluded), Kiska v.

Skrensky, 138 A.2d 523 (Conn. 1958); (f) Mount Laurel Township v. Barbieri, 376 A.2d 541 (N.J. Super. 1977) (subdivision effected through "contrived" partition action is invalid); and (g) Gerard v. San Juan County, 715 P.2d 149 (Wash. App. 1986) (a related sequence of conveyances and subdivisions constructed so as to use short plat exemptions to create an 18-parcel-long platting was held to be an illegal effort to circumvent the purposes of the platting ordinance.)

20. *See* Jack Homes, Inc. v. Baldwin, 241 N.Y.S.2d 487 (Sup. Ct. 1963).

21. Town of Nags Head v. Tillett, 315 S.E.2d 740 (N.C. Ct. App. 1984) (town can deny building permits for violation of subdivision regulations). *But see* State *ex rel.* Craven v. City of Tacoma, 385 P.2d 372 (Wash. 1963) (withholding of a building permit has sometimes been invalidated in absence of statutory authority). *See generally* Hagman & Juergensmeyer, *supra* note 13, at 7.7.

22. "Whoever . . . transfers or sells or agrees to sell or negotiates to sell . . . before such plat has been approved by the planning commission . . . shall forfeit and pay a penalty of $100.00 for each lot sold. The municipal corporation may enjoin such transfer or sale or agreement by action for injunction brought in any court of equity jurisdiction or may recover said penalty by a civil action in any court of competent jurisdiction." Standard City Planning Enabling Act 16; *see also* Lake County v. Truett, 758 S.W.2d 529 (Tenn. App. 1988) (evidence that a developer violated planning commission regulations in selling subdivision lots without approval supports the issuance of an injunction to prohibit developer from further sale of lots); Johnson v. Hinds County, 524 So.2d 947 (Miss. 1988) (county successfully obtained an injunction and declaratory judgment against a developer and landowners with respect to an illegally subdivided development). For a general discussion of injunctive relief, *see* SHONKWILER & MORGAN, LAND USE LITIGATION (West 1986, Supp. 1988).

23. Ogan v. Ellison, 682 P.2d 760 (Ore. 1984) (purchasers of unplatted property have a cause of action against the vendors of the property for fraud and breach of contract). *See also* Keizer v. Adams, 471 P.2d 983 (Cal. 1970); Howland v. Acting Superintendent of Bldgs., 102 N.E.2d 423 (Mass. 1951); Clemons v. City of Los Angeles, 222 P.2d 439 (Cal. 1950). *See generally* Note, *Prevention of Subdivision Control Evasion in Indiana,* 40 IND. L.J. 445 (1965).

24. *See* Commentary Chapter 1 regarding variances, exceptions, and waiver of conditions.

25. Gerard v. San Juan County, 715 P.2d 149 (Wash. App. 1986) (a related sequence of conveyances and subdivisions constructed so as to use short plat exemptions to create an 18-parcel-long subdivision was held to be an illegal effort to circumvent the purposes of the platting ordinance).

26. *See* Commentary Chapter 1 regarding variances, exceptions, and waiver of conditions; *see also* Friends of the Pine Bush v. Planning Bd. of Albany, 450 N.Y.S.2d 966 (App. Div. 3d Department, 1982), *aff'd* 452 N.E.2d 1252.

27. Miller v. Forty West Builders, 489 A.2d 76 (Md. Ct. Spec. App. 1985) (cluster zones); Bonner Properties v. Planning Bd. 449 A.2d 1350 (N.J. Super. Ct. Law Div. 1982) (subdivision regulations do apply to planned unit developments even if no division of land is contemplated); City of Urbana v. City of Champaign County, 389 N.E.2d 1185 (Ill. 1975) (subdivision regulations do not apply to planned unit developments where no division of land is contemplated). *See generally* URBAN LAND INSTITUTE, LEGAL ASPECTS OF PLANNED UNIT DEVELOPMENT (Tech. Bull. No. 52, 1965); Lloyd, *Symposium of Planned Unit Development,* 114 U. PA. L. REV. 3 (1965).

28. The Model Land Development Code (American Law Institute, A Model Land Development Code, 1976) suggested the integration of zoning and subdivision ordinances and regulations into a single, integrated land "development ordinance," HAGMAN & JUERGENSMEYER, URBAN PLANNING AND LAND DEVELOPMENT CONTROL LAWS, 3.5 (West, 1986); ROHAN, ZONING AND LAND USE CONTROLS, 33.02[1] (Matthew Bender, 1990); FREILICH, AWAKENING THE SLEEPING GIANT: NEW TRENDS AND DEVELOPMENTS IN ENVIRONMENTAL AND LAND USE CONTROLS, 1974 Institute on Planning, Zoning and Eminent Domain 1, 16-18 (S.W. Legal Foundation, Matthew Bender): "when completed, the American Law Institute's Model Land Development Code will be a significant contribution toward modernizing existing planning and zoning statutes, regulations and practices. . . . One of its major improvements over existing law is the requirement that both zoning and subdivision regulations be combined in a single "development ordinance." No state has mandated such an integration and it presently is a practice that is voluntarily growing in a small number of jurisdictions. *See* FLA. STAT. ANN. § 163.3161 *et seq.* and WASH. ANN. § 35A.63.061 (for cities), in which both states have

substantially revised the planning and land use control statutes but have not required integrated subdivision and zoning codes.

29. The broadest purpose of subdivision controls is to guide community development and to implement a comprehensive plan for community development. Coffey v. Maryland-National Capital Park & Planning Comm'n, 441 A.2d 1041 (Md. 1982); Lake Interwole Homes, Inc. v. Parsippany Troy Hills, 147 A.2d 28 (N.J. 1958) (to facilitate sound and orderly future municipal growth along preconceived lines, in short a planned community growth); Marx v. Zoning Bd. of Appeals, 529 N.Y.S.2d 330 (App. iv. 2d Department, 1988) (subdivision control is aimed at protecting the community from improper development of land).

30. D. Listokin & C. Walker, *supra* note 10; D. LISTOKIN AND C. BAKER, MODEL SUBDIVISION AND SITE PLAN ORDINANCE, (Rutgers Center for Urban Policy Research, 1987).

31. R. FREILICH & P. LEVI, MODEL SUBDIVISION REGULATIONS: TEXT AND COMMENTARY, 33-43 (American Society of Planning Officials, 1975).

32. Listokin & Walker, *supra* note 10, at xvi, citing the following authorities: FREILICH & LEVI, MODEL SUBDIVISION REGULATIONS: TEXT AND COMMENTARY (American Society of Planning Officials, 1975); BROUGH, A UNIFIED DEVELOPMENT ORDINANCE (American Planning Association, 1985); URBAN LAND INSTITUTE, NATIONAL ASSOCIATION OF HOME BUILDERS AND AMERICAN SOCIETY OF CIVIL ENGINEERS, RESIDENTIAL STREETS: OBJECTIVES, PRINCIPLES AND DESIGN CONSIDERATIONS (Urban Land Institute, 1976); NATIONAL ASSOCIATION OF HOME BUILDERS, SUBDIVISION REGULATION HANDBOOK: NAHB LAND DEVELOPMENT SERIES (National Association of Home Builders, 1978); INSTITUTE OF TRANSPORTATION ENGINEERS, RECOMMENDED GUIDELINES FOR SUBDIVISION STREETS (Institute of Transportation Engineers, 1984).

33. Hagman & Juergensmeyer, *supra* note 13, at 7.6; YEARWOOD, LAND SUBDIVISION REGULATION, 216-17 (Praeger, 1971). Alternatives to the ALI Model Code provisions have been implemented on both state and regional levels. In order to exercise a variety of state and regional land use controls themselves, states essentially took back some of the powers delegated to their local governments through zoning and planning enabling legislation. *See* CALLIES & FREILICH, CASES AND MATERIALS ON LAND USE, Chap. 9 (West 1986 & Supp. 1988). Hawaii was the first state to adopt a statewide land use classification and regulation system in 1961. With relatively few

changes, it is still in place today. Neighborhood Bd. v. State Land Use Comm'n, 629 P.2d 1097 (Hawaii 1982); BOSSELMAN & CALLIES, THE QUIET REVOLUTION IN LAND CONTROL (1971); CALLIES, REGULATING PARADISE: LAND USE CONTROLS IN HAWAII (1984). Florida attempted to substitute the Environmental Land and Water Management Act for the ALI Model Code. While the act dealt effectively with developments of regional impact (DRIs), there were difficulties with the tough problem of siting unwanted developments such as landfills and power generating facilities. *See* Askew v. Cross Key Waterways, 372 So.2d 913 (Fla. 1978); Graham v. Estuary Properties, Inc., 399 So.2d 1374 (Fla. 1981); Pelham, *Regulating Developments of Regional Impact: Florida and the Model Development Code*, 29 U. FLA. L. REV. 789 (1977); Dafter Township v. Reid, 345 N.W.2d 689 (Mich. App. 1983) (state may issue construction permit for a landfill in the face of local government opposition). Vermont's approach to state land use management and regulation represents an amalgam of the Hawaii and Florida systems. Act 250 was passed almost entirely in response to a ski tourism boom which led to intense and relatively large-scale development pressure in relatively fragile environmental areas. As in Florida and Hawaii, there was a direct attempt to tie the permit process to comprehensive planning. *See* Committee to Save the Bishop's House v. Medical Centers of Vermont, 400 A.2d 1015 (Vt. 1979); BOSSELMAN & CALLIES, THE QUIET REVOLUTION IN LAND USE CONTROL, Chap. 2 (Council on Environmental Quality, 1972). Oregon, arguably the most plan-oriented of those states that have adopted state land use controls, is also one of the only states that tried to mandate, rather than permit, local zoning. The courts in Oregon have been supportive of the goals, strict in conformance requirements, and careful not to let the Land Conservation and Development Commission overstep its bounds. *See* Haviland v. Land Conserv. & Dev. Comm'n, 609 P.2d 423 (Ore. App. 1980); Fasano v. Board of County Comm'rs, 507 P.2d 23 (Ore. 1973); LEONARD, MANAGING OREGON'S GROWTH: THE POLITICS OF DEVELOPMENT PLANNING (1983). Regional, as opposed to statewide, land use controls that partially or entirely supersede local zoning and other land use controls spring from the same source of power. Regional controls, however, tend to focus on a particular resource rather than on truly statewide conservation and development problems. The Adirondack Park Agency Act was passed for the purposes of administering and enforcing a planning process to recognize the concerns at the regional, state, and local levels. *See* Horizon Adirondack Corp. v. State, 388 N.Y.S. 2d 235 (1976); LIROFF AND DAVIS, PROTECTING OPEN SPACE: LAND USE CONTROL IN THE ADIRONDACK PARK (1981). While the Adirondack Act concerned itself with intrastate problems, the Tahoe Regional Planning Compact was an interstate agreement between Nevada and California. Unfortunately, the states are generally at odds over the pace and intensity of development that should be permitted in the Tahoe region. *See* California Tahoe Regional Planning Agency v. Harrah's Corp., 509 F. Supp. 753 (D. Nev. 1981); CALLIES, FREILICH & ROBERTS, CASES AND MATERIALS ON LAND USE, ch. 8 (West 1994). A final example of regulation on a regional level is the Pinelands Protection Act, which was developed in connection with the National Parks and Recreation Act. These two acts were designed to "combine limited public acquisition with land use controls developed and implemented through a cooperative program involving Federal, State and local governments as well as concerned private groups and individuals." CALLIES & FREILICH, CASES AND MATERIALS ON LAND USE, Chap. 9 (West 1986 & Supp. 1988). *See* Orleans Builders & Developers v. Byrne, 453 A.2d 200 (N.J. App. Div. 1982); Note, *New Jersey's Pinelands Plan and the Taking Question*, 7 COL. J. ENVR. L. 227 (1982).

34. Listokin & Walker, *supra* note 10, at 18 (emphasis supplied).

35. Board of Supervisors v. West Chestnut Realty Corp., 532 A.2d 942 (Pa. Commw. 1987) (A municipality that has approved a preliminary development plan cannot add new conditions when the plan is submitted for final approval. Similarly, the developer cannot change the plan except to meet conditions of the preliminary approval); Youngblood v. Board of Supervisors, 556 P.2d 556 (Cal. 1978) ("approval of the final map thus becomes a ministerial act once the appropriate officials certify that it is in substantial compliance with the previously approved tentative map.")

36. Several courts have recognized that this step is the most important of the three. *See* Commonwealth Properties, Inc. v. Washington County, 582 P.2d 1384, 1389 (Or. App. 1978); Boutet v. Planning Bd., 253 A.2d 53, 56 (Me. 1969). In Youngblood v. Board of Supervisors, 22 Cal.3d 644, 655 (1979), the California Supreme Court explained: "[T]he date when the tentative map comes before the gov-

erning body for approval is the crucial date when that body should decide whether to permit the proposed subdivision. Once the tentative map is approved, the developer often must expend substantial sums to comply with the conditions attached to that approval. . . . Consequently it is only fair to the developer and to the public interest to require the governing body to render its discretionary decision whether and upon what conditions to approve the proposed subdivision when it acts on the tentative map."

37. Durant v. Town of Dunbarton, 430 A.2d 140, 142-43 (N.H. 1981); Floyd v. County Council, 461 A.2d 76, 82 (Md. 1983); Woodson Lumber Co. v. City of College Station, 752 S.W.2d 744 (Tex. Ct. App. 1988); Wiggers v. County of Skagit, 596 P.2d 1345, 1350 (Wash. 1979); Shoptaugh v. Board of County Comm'rs, 543 P.2d 524, 528 (Colo. App. 1975); Mobil America, Inc. v. Sandoval County Comm'n, 518 P.2d 774 (N.M. 1974). In Messer v. Town of Chapel Hill, 297 S.E.2d 632 (N.C. App. 1982), the court ruled that Chapel Hill could deny a subdivision plat that met all of the statutory requirements because the developer refused to locate the required open space where the city considered it to be more useful. While the governing body can by no means be arbitrary in its decision, it is clear that the board must have adequate discretion to protect the general welfare of the citizenry.

38. *See* Tuscarora Forests v. Fermanagh Bd. of Supervisors, 471 A.2d 137 (Pa. Commw. 1984); Kensington Rd. Ltd. v. Planning Bd. of Bronxville, 480 N.Y.S.2d 369 (App. Div. 2d Dept, 1984).

39. City of Tuscaloosa v. Brian, 505 So.2d 330 (Ala. 1987)

40. *See* Rockway v. Stefani, 543 P.2d 1089, 1093 (Ore. App. 1975) (quoting Frankland v. City of Lake Oswego, 517 P.2d 1042, 1048, 1051 (Ore. 1973): "Obviously, in order to guarantee a well conceived and well designed planned unit development, the planning authorities must have the necessary plans and information from the developer before making a decision. . . . First it gives the planning authorities and the City Council full knowledge of what they are asked to approve before they grant a zone change. Secondly, it gives any opponent complete information about the project. It serves no worthwhile purpose for an ordinance to allow a full public hearing on a proposed planned unit development and zone change if the facts are not available. There is nothing to debate. Neither the opponents nor the proponents would know the issues, and the governing body charged with making a decision would be doing so in a vacuum."

41. Bienz v. City of Dayton, 566 P.2d 904 (Ore. 1977); Reynolds v. City Council of Longmont, 680 P.2d 1350 (Colo. App. 1984); Youngblood v. Board of Supervisors, 556 P.2d 556 (Cal. 1978).

42. Board of Supervisors v. West Chestnut Realty, 531 A.2d 942 (Pa. Commw. 1987).

43. Model Regulations § 3.2(3)(a). The final plat must be submitted within one year from the date that the sketch plat was approved.

44. Gerard v. San Juan County, 715 P.2d 149 (Wash. 1986) (purchasers of 165 acres who sought to subdivide their land through a series of conveyances structured to take advantage of exemptions from prior county approval under the county's short plat ordinance circumvented the requirements of the subdivision regulations that properly defined the subdivision as a long plat requiring prior approval of county before subdivision); *see also* on strict control of evasion generally, Orrin Dressler, Inc. v. Burr Ridge, 527 N.E.2d 106 (Ill. App. 1988); Corcovan v. Planning Bd. of Sudbury, 530 N.E.2d 357 (Mass. 1988).

45. Model Regulations at § 3.2(3)(b)(i).

46. *Id.*

47. *Id.* at § 3.3.

48. *Id.* at § 3.2(3)(b)(ii).

49. In Moore v. City of Lawrence, 654 P.2d 445 (Kan. 1982), the requirement of health department review was upheld. *See also* Independence Park, Inc. v. Board of Health, 530 N.E.2d 1235 (1988). *See generally*, ROHAN, ZONING AND LAND USE CONTROLS 45.02(2) (1986).

50. Eversdyk v. Wyoming City Council, 421 N.W.2d 574 (Mich. App. 1988) (referral to Michigan Department of Natural Resources after tentative approval granted by city council); Secretary of Health & Mental Hygiene v. Crowder, 405 A.2d 279 (Md. App. 1979) (septic percolation tests); Ocean Acres, Inc. v. State Dept. of Envtl. Protection, 403 A.2d 967 (N.J. Super. 1979), *cert. denied*, 407 A.2d 1226 (1979); South Cent. Coast Regional Comm'n v. Charles A. Pratt Constr. Co., 180 Cal. App. Rptr. (Cal. App. 5th Dist., 1982); Graham v. Estuary Properties, Inc., 399 So.2d 1374 (Fla. 1981) (mandatory referral of sensitive ecological wetlands to Southwest Florida Regional Planning Council for developments of regional impact).

51. Demonstration Cities and Metropolitan Development Act of 1966, 204, Pub. L. No. 89-754, 80 Stat. 1255 (1966).

52. Brussat, *Realizing the Potentials of A-95*, PLANNING (1971); the reviews, which were advisory only, sought to identify the relationship of the development project to area comprehensive plans. Heyman, *Legal Assaults on Land use Regulations*, 5 URB. LAW. 17 (1973).

53. 45 C.F.R. 1233 (1988). The review system that replaced the A-95 program became effective in 1983. It allows each state, at its discretion, to establish its own process for review and comment on proposed federally financed projects. A state is not required to establish a state process.

54. Bosselman & Callies, *supra* note 33. *See also* Los Virgenes Homeowners Fed'n v. Los Angeles County, 233 Cal. Rptr. 18 (Cal. Ct. App. 1986) (certification of environmental impact report as a condition of approval of a conditional use permit was supported by substantial evidence); *In re* McDonald's Corp., 505 A.2d 1202 (Vt. 1985) (court upheld requirement that developments of a certain size comply with state environmental laws); Goodman v. Board of Comm'rs, 411 A.2d 838 (Pa. Commw. Ct. 1980) (approval of nonresidential subdivisions can properly depend on state and federal environmental legislation).

55. AMERICAN LAW INSTITUTE, A MODEL LAND DEVELOPMENT CODE art. 7-8 (1976). In 7-401 to 7-405, the state planning agency is also empowered to define *large-scale development* that is likely to present issues of state or regional significance and to subject such development to special review similar to the processes applicable to development of special state or regional benefit.

56. CALLIES, FREILICH & ROBERTS, CASES AND MATERIALS ON LAND USE, ch. 3 (West 1994).

57. *See id.* at ch. 8.

58. Neighborhood Bd. v. State Land Use Comm'n, 629 P.2d 1097 (Hawaii 1982); BOSSELMAN & CALLIES, THE QUIET REVOLUTION IN LAND CONTROL (1971); Callies, REGULATING PARADISE: LAND USE CONTROLS IN HAWAII (1984).

59. *See* Askew v. Cross Key Waterways, 372 So.2d 913 (Fla. 1978); Graham v. Estuary Properties, 399 So.2d 1374 (Fla. 1981); Pelham, *Regulating Developments of Regional Impact: Florida and the Model Development Code*, 29 U. FLA. L. REV. 789 (1977); Dafter Township v. Reid, 345 N.W.2d 689 (Mich. App. 1983) (state may issue construction permit for a landfill in the face of local government opposition).

60. *See* Committee to Save the Bishop's House v. Medical Centers of Vermont, 400 A.2d 1015 (Vt. 1979); BOSSELMAN AND CALLIES, THE QUIET REVOLUTION IN LAND USE CONTROL, Ch. 2 (1971).

61. *See* Haviland v. Land Conserv. & Dev. Comm'n, 609 P.2d 423 (1980); Fasano v. Board of County Comm'rs, 507 P.2d 23 (Ore. 1973); LEONARD, MANAGING OREGON'S GROWTH: THE POLITICS OF DEVELOPMENT PLANNING (1983).

62. DeGrove, *Growth Management and Governance, The Second Wave of State Actions,* 32, in UNDERSTANDING GROWTH MANAGEMENT, CRITICAL ISSUES AND A RESEARCH AGENDA, (Urban Land Institute, 1989).

63. *See* Horizon Adirondack Corp. v. State, 388 N.Y.S.2d 235 (1976); LIROFF AND DAVID, PROTECTING OPEN SPACE: LAND USE CONTROL IN THE ADIRONDACK PARK (1981).

64. *See* California Tahoe Reg. Plan. Agenda v. Harrah's Corp., 509 F. Supp. 753 (1981); Callies, Freilich & Roberts, *supra* note 56, at ch. 9.

65. Callies, Freilich & Roberts, *supra* note 56, at ch. 9. *See* Orleans Builders & Developers v. Byrne, 453 A.2d 200 (N.J. App. Div. 1982); Note, *New Jersey's Pinelands Plan and the Taking Question,* 7 COL. J. ENVR. L. 227 (1982).

66. *See, e.g.,* Delogu, *The Misuse of Land Use Control Powers Must End: Suggestions for Legislative and Judicial Responses,* 32 ME. L. REV. 29 (1980); Ellickson, *Alternatives to Zoning: Covenants, Nuisance Rules, and Fines as Land Use Controls,* 41 U. CHI. L. REV. 681 (1973).

67. *See* Independence Park v. Board of Health, 530 N.E.2d 1235 (1988) (court upheld conditions placed on subdivision plat by Board of Health requiring municipal sewer line hookup that would otherwise have been inapplicable to developer); State Dept. of Health v. Framat Realty, 407 So.2d 238 (Fla. Dist. Ct. App. 1981) (to protect the public health by the safe disposal of sewage); Castle Estates, Inc. v. Park & Planning Bd., 182 N.E.2d 540 (Mass. 1962) (to prevent engineering traffic hazards); Mifford v. City of Tulare, 228 P.2d 847 (Cal. Ct. App. 1951) (to prevent pollution from sewer and water systems).

68. Tehan v. Scrivani, 468 N.Y.S.2d 402 (App. Div. 1983) (where legitimate environmental concerns exist, city should take advantage of optional coordinated review by sister agencies); Rosen v. Village of Downers Grove, 167 N.E.2d 230 (Ill. 1960) (review requested by board of education, but held not mandatory unless required by statute).

69. Residential Estates, Inc. v. Ziemba, 329 N.Y.S.2d 590 (Sup. Ct. 1971), *aff'd,* 330 N.Y.S.2d 778 (App. Div. 1972).

70. *See, e.g.,* COLO. REV. STAT. § 30-28-136(1) (1986).

71. Kessler, *The Development Agreement & Its Use in Resolving Large-Scale, Multi-Party Development Problems: A Look at the Tool and Suggestions for Its Application,* 1 J. LAND USE & ENVTL. L. 451, 451 (1985). *See also* Shultz & Kelley, *Subdivision Improvement Requirements and Guarantees: A Primer,* 28 J. URB. & CONTEMP. L. 3, 33-64 (1985).

72. *See* Flynn, *Practical Problems of a Subdivider's Counsel In Creating a Subdivision,* 58 ILL. B.J. 110 (1969).

73. A similar procedure is found in the Housing & Home Finance Authority's model, *supra* note 11, at II(b).

74. 4 R. ANDERSON, AMERICAN LAW OF ZONING § 25.13 (1986).

75. ILL. ANN. STAT. Chapter 24, § 11-12-8 (Smith-Hurd Supp. 1987); N.J. STAT. ANN. § 40, § 55 D-25 (West Supp. 1987). A few states have incorporated the practice as a necessary procedural requirement. *See* Roland Lavoie Constr. Co. v. Building Inspector of Ludlow, 191 N.E.2d 697 (Mass. 1963); Harris v. Planning Comm'n, 193 A.2d 499 (Conn. 1963).

76. Standard City Planning Enabling Act 14 (U.S. Dept. of Commerce, 1928) (hereinafter cited as SPEA.)

77. Model Regulations § 3.3(3).

78. Appeal of Sterner's Mill Assocs., 430 A.2d 371 (Pa. Commw. Ct. 1981); State *ex rel.* Wollett v. Oestreicher, 121 N.E.2d 454 (Ohio 1953). The provision also may protect a developer, adjoining owners, or community groups where the law states that the time within which a subdivision approval or disapproval may be challenged begins with the preliminary plat approval. Nelson v. South Brunswick Planning Bd., 201 A.2d 741 (N.J. Super. Ct. App. Div. 1964).

79. The grounds for the decision on the preliminary plat is the standard by which the planning authority later acts to grant or deny approval of the final plat. Commonwealth Properties v. Washington County, 582 P.2d 1384 (Ore. Ct. App. 1978). *See* Board of Supervisors v. West Chestnut Realty Corp., 532 A.2d 942 (1987). *See also* Greenlawn Memorial Park v. Town of Neenah Bd. of Supervisors, 71 N.W.2d 403 (Wis. 1955); Tippecanoe Area Plan Comm'n v. Sheffield Developers, 394 N.E.2d 176 (Ind. Ct. App. 1979). *But see* Cherry Valley Assoc. v.

Stroud Township Bd. of Supervisors, 554 A.2d 149 (Pa. Commw. 1989); Quillen v. Aspen Planning and Zoning Comm'n, 697 P.2d 406 (Colo. Ct. App. 1984). Because final plat approval is often viewed as ministerial, only a public meeting, rather than a public hearing, should be required at that time.

80. SPEA, *supra* note 76, at 8.

81. Section 15 of the SPEA, *supra* note 76, requires that a public hearing be held on subdivision approval, notice of which must be given by publication and by mail to adjacent property owners. At least 16 jurisdictions have adopted the same or similar requirements. ALA. CODE § 11-52-32 (1975); ARK. STAT. ANN. § 19-2830 (1980); IND. CODE ANN. § 18-7-5-48 (Burns Supp. 1987); LA. REV. STAT. ANN. § 33.113 (1951); MASS. GEN. LAWS ANN. ch. 41, § 81T (West 1979); MICH. COMP. LAWS § 125.45 (1979); MONT. CODE ANN. § 11-3843 (Supp. 1977); N.J. STAT. ANN. § 40:55 (D-25) (West Supp. 1987); N.Y. TOWN LAW § 282 (McKinney 1987); N.Y. VILLAGE LAW § 7-740 (1973); N.D. CENT. CODE § 40-48-21 (1983); OKLA. STAT. ANN. tit. 19, § 863.9 (West 1962); R.I. GEN. LAWS § 45-23-9 (1980); TENN. CODE ANN. § 13-4-304 (1980); WASH. REV. CODE §§ 58.17.010-58.17.050 (Supp. 1987).

82. Edwards Engineering Corp. v. Davies, 471 A.2d 119 (Pa. Commw. Ct. 1984) (board was not obligated to conduct public hearings on subdivision plans). *Accord* Feldman v. Star Homes, Inc., 84 A.2d 903 (Md. 1951). *But see* Scarsdale Meadows, Inc. v. Smith, 249 N.Y.S.2d 229 (Ct. App. Div. 1964) (the planning board cannot refuse to grant a hearing).

83. Thornbury Township Bd. of Supervisors v. W.W.D., Inc., 546 A.2d 744 (1968); Mutton Hill Estates, Inc. v. Town of Oakland, 468 A.2d 989 (Me. 1983); Hill v. County Ct., 601 P.2d 905 (Ore. Ct. App. 1979); Horn v. County of Ventura, 596 P.2d 1134 (Cal. 1979); Wes Linn Land Co. v. Board of County Comm'rs, 583 P.2d 1159 (Ore. Ct. App. 1978); Bienz v. City of Dayton, 566 P.2d 904 (1977).

84. *See, e.g.,* Horn, 596 P.2d at 721-22 (subdivision approval is adjudicatory in nature, and therefore those affected by such land use decisions were constitutionally entitled to notice and opportunity to be heard prior to the final decision). *See* Selinger v. City of Redlands, 216 Cal. App. 3d 259, 264 Cal. Rptr. 499 (1989) (building moratorium did not toll application of Permit Streamlining Act (P.S.A.) but court denied relief on the grounds that P.S.A. is unconstitutional under Horn. Disagrees with holding of

Palmer v. Ojai, 178 Cal. App. 3d 280, 223 Cal. Rptr. 542 (1988).

85. Board of Comm'rs v. Quaker Constr. Co., 441 A.2d 801 (Pa. Commw. Ct. 1982); Nelson v. South Brunswick Planning Bd., 201 A.2d 741 (N.J. Super. Ct. App. Div. 1964); Castle Estates, Inc. v. Park & Planning Bd., 182 N.E.2d 540 (Mass. 1962); Lakeshore Dev. Corp. v. Plan Comm'n, 107 N.W.2d 590 (Wis. 1961). *But see* Paul Livoli, Inc. v. Planning Bd. of Marlborough, 197 N.E.2d 785 (Mass. 1964).

86. Model Regulations § 3.3(4).

87. In Dunkin' Donuts of New Jersey v. Township of North Brunswick Planning Bd., 475 A.2d 71 (N.J. App. Div. 1984), the defendant planning board's denial of plaintiff's application for site approval was based solely upon the anticipated detrimental impact of the proposed use on off-site traffic flow congestion and safety. *See also* Daviau v. Planning Comm'n of Putnam, 387 A.2d 562 (Conn. 1978) (access street narrower than required by regulations especially where the subdivider does not own or have an easement in the land requiring the improvement); Colborne v. Corrales, 739 P.2d 972 (N.M. 1987); Garipay v. Town of Hanover, 351 A.2d 64 (N.H. 1976) (offsite roads inadequate to handle the traffic generated by the subdivision); Grant's Farm v. Town of Kitteny, 554 A.2d 799 (Me. 1989) (an enabling act could authorize the denial of plat approval if the planning board determined that the subdivision would cause traffic congestion or pose a danger to shoreland); Fleckinger v. Jefferson Parish Council, 510 So.2d 429 (La. App. 5th Cir. 1987) (when an area is unique it is not unreasonable for the council to conclude that it is in the best interest of the general welfare to preserve the beauty and integrity of these unique sections by refraining from subdividing).

88. *See* CORNICK, PREMATURE SUBDIVISION AND ITS CONSEQUENCES (1938); BASSETT, ZONING (1936).

89. *See, e.g.,* Board of County Comm'rs v. Gaster, 401 A.2d 666 (Md. Ct. Spec. App. 1979) (MD. ANN. CODE art. 66B, §§ 5.01-5.08 [1988] requires enactment of subdivision regulations that implement the master plan, therefore the city can properly reject subdivision plat not in compliance with the master plan). *Accord* Coffey v. Maryland National Capital Park & Planning Comm'n, 441 A.2d 1041 (Md. Ct. Spec. App. 1982). Some state statutes require zoning ordinances and subdivision regulations to be consistent with the comprehensive plan. *See, e.g.,* ARIZ. REV. STAT. ANN. 9-461, §§ 9-461.05(A), 9-

461.08, 9-462.01(E) (1977), interpreted by Haines v. City of Phoenix, 727 P.2d 339 (Ariz. Ct. App. 1986); CAL. GOV'T CODE § 66474(a), (b) (West 1983).

90. Model Regulations § 3.4.

91. Board of Supervisors v. West Chestnut Realty Corp., 532 A.2d 942 (1987) (developer cannot change plan unless the purpose is to meet the initial approval conditions); Commonwealth Properties v. Washington County, 582 P.2d 1384 (Ore. Ct. App. 1978) (once tentative approval of a subdivision plat is given, zoning authority is held to its own terms in final action).

92. The development of multiphased projects is fraught with complexities and uncertainties in the areas of marketing, financing, design, and time. Kessler, *The Development Agreement and Its Use in Resolving Large Scale, Multi-Party Development Problems: A Look at the Tool and Suggestions for Its Application,* 1 J. LAND USE & ENVT. L. 451 (1985); Flynn, *Practical Problems of a Subdivider's Counsel in Creating a Subdivision,* 58 ILL. B. J. 110 (1969).

93. Shultz & Kelley, *supra* note 71, at 33-64.

94. *See* Freilich & White, *Transportation Congestion and Growth Management: Comprehensive Approaches to Resolving America's Major Quality of Life Crisis,* 24 LOYOLA L.A.L. REV. 915, 941 (1991) at note 139, citing the following enabling legislation: MD. ANN. CODE art. 66B, § 10.01 (1988) (authorizing enactment of ordinances requiring planning, staging, or provision of adequate public facilities); N.H. REV. STAT. ANN. §§ 674.21-.22 (1986 & Supp. 1990) (authorizing timing and sequencing provisions where city has enacted a CIP); FLA. STAT. ANN. § 163.3202(2)(g) (West 1990) (mandating local governments to adopt adequate public facility requirements assuring availability concurrent with the impacts of development as measured by adopted Plan LOS standards; Washington has recently adopted legislation requiring concurrency management within urban growth area boundaries, RGW § 36.70A.110(3) (1990).

95. Standard Zoning Enabling Act (U.S. Dept. of Commerce Tent. Draft No. 1, 1968) reprinted in 5 R. ANDERSON, AMERICAN LAW OF ZONING 3D 3201 at 4-9 (1986).

96. See the leading case of Golden v. Planning Bd. of Town of Ramapo, 285 N.E.2d 291 (N.Y. 1972), *appeal dismissed,* 409 U.S. 1003 (1972); Donohoe Constr. Co. v. Montgomery County Council, 567 F.2d 603 (4th Cir. 1977); and Swanson v. Marin Mun. Water Dist., 128 Cal. Rptr. 485 (Cal. App. 1976).

97. Montgomery County, Md. Code Ch. 50, § 50-35(K) (1973). The county employs a two-tiered review system. First, LOS standards are assigned within policy areas. A staging ceiling is established for the policy area based on the carrying capacity of existing transportation facilities and those scheduled in the county and state CIPs. A special ceiling allocation is established for affordable housing. Second, Local Area Transportation Review is applied where: (1) the project is above a certain threshold size; (2) the project is near a congested intersection; or (3) the policy area is within five percent of the staging ceiling. This level of review is required because some projects could otherwise satisfy policy area review while causing local congestion. For a discussion of the Montgomery County APFO, *see* D. GODSCHALK, CONSTITUTIONAL ISSUES OF GROWTH MANAGEMENT, 309-27 (rev. ed. 1979); Porter, *Montgomery County's Growth Fracas,* URB. LAND, June 1982, at 34; Tierney, *Maryland's Growing Pains: The Need for State Regulation,* 16 U. BALT. L. REV. 201, 226-27 (1987).

98. City of San Diego, Emergency Transportation Congestion Management and Development Phasing Ordinance of 1990 (July 5, 1990, prepared by Freilich, Stone, Leitner & Carlisle, Kansas City, Missouri, and Los Angeles).

99. FLA. STAT. ANN. § 163.3202(2); § 163.3177(10)(h).

100. Some leeway can be granted allowing local governments to issue development permits where the necessary facilities do not currently exist but are planned for construction in the CIP within three years. Florida Administrative Code § 9J-5.0055(2) (for roads or transit facilities).

101. In many states the developer need comply only with subdivision regulations in place at the time of preliminary *approval.* Shultz & Kelley, *supra* note 71, at 37. The regulations do, however, reserve to the government the authority to alter the regulations applicable to the subdivision to protect public health and safety. Model Regulations § 3.6(3). *Compare* Dwyer v. McTygue, 519 N.Y.S.2d 630 (1987) (approval of subdivision plat does not vest landowner permanent right to proceed consistently with the approval unless landowner proceeds within a reasonable time to develop the land).

102. The developer will be subject to regulations pending at the time the preliminary plat is submitted if the developer has reason to know of their pendency. For a detailed analysis of the whole subject of vested rights and changes in zoning and land use regulations, *see* Freilich, *Interim Development Controls: Essential Tools for Implementing Flexible Planning and Zoning,* 49 J. Urb. L. 65 (1971); Rhodes, Hauser & DeMeo, *Vested Rights: Establishing Predictability in a Changing Regulatory System,* 13 Stetson L. Rev. 1 (1983); Heeter, *Zoning Estoppel: Application of the Principles of Equitable Estoppel and Vested Rights to Zoning Disputes,* 5 Urb. L. Ann. 63 (1971). Without the provisions of § 3.6 of the model regulations, the general rule is that zoning changes can affect a plat even after approval, recordation, and issuance of building permits, until substantial work is performed on the development site. Ardolino v. Borough of Florham Park Bd. of Adjustment, 130 A.2d 847 (N.J. 1957). *Accord* B.B.& C. Constr. v. Benzinger Township, 437 A.2d 101 (Pa. Commw. Ct. 1981). The planning commission, of course, cannot generally hold up approval of a subdivision until a revised zoning ordinance becomes effective. Wallkill Manor, Ltd. v. Coulter, 337 N.Y.S.2d 366 (App. Div. 1972), *aff'd,* 305 N.E. 2d 494 (1973); Norco Constr., Inc. v. King County, 627 P.2d 988 (Wash. Ct. App. 1981); but if a valid interim development ordinance is in effect or the zoning ordinance proposal is actually up for hearing, administrative delay may be valid. *See* Russian Hill Improvement Ass'n v. Board of Permit Appeals, 423 P.2d 824 (Cal. 1967); A.J. Aberman, Inc. v. City of New Kensington, 105 A.2d 586 (Pa. 1954); E. McQuillin, The Law of Municipal Corporations 25.157 at 499 (3d ed. & Supp. 1987).

103. Whether real property rights are "vested" so as to prevent a local government from altering those rights to conform to subsequently enacted legislation is a question generally addressed under two theoretically distinct doctrines—vested rights and equitable estoppel. While theoretically distinct, the two doctrines are frequently used interchangeably. *See* DeStefano v. City of Charleston, 403 S.E.2d 648 (S.C. 1991). Under a vested rights analysis, the focus is upon the *landowner's right* to proceed notwithstanding a change in development regulations. Under an estoppel analysis, the focus is upon the *municipality's conduct* and the extent to which the landowner has relied upon that conduct. D. Callies & R. Freilich, Cases and Materials on Land Use 197 (1986). Three elements are generally required to invoke estoppel: (1) the property owner must lack both the knowledge and the means of knowledge of the truth of the facts in question, (2) there must be reliance on the conduct of the government unit, and (3) the

relying party must have incurred expenses or obligations as a result of the reliance so as to constitute a prejudicial change in position. The Florida Companies v. Orange County, 411 So.2d 1008 (Fla. 5th Dist. Ct. App. 1982). The DeStefano decision may show the difficulty in establishing reliance on governmental conduct, the hardest of the three tests to meet. In DeStefano, the developer replatted a previously approved 40-lot subdivision, adding 12 lots and eliminating a drainage easement, which the developer and deputy city engineer no longer believed was necessary. The plat was erroneously recorded by the deputy city engineer. When the city subsequently downzoned the property and refused to issue building permits the developer sued and claimed estoppel. The South Carolina Supreme Court held that the error or mistake of an agent or officer of the local government cannot give rise to estoppel. *See also* Cunningham & Kremer, *Vested Rights, Estoppel and the Land Development Process,* 29 Hasting L.J. 625 (1978).

104. Model Regulations § 3.6(3).

105. *Id.*

106. *In re* Appeal by Mark-Garner Assocs., Inc., 413 A.2d 1142, 1144-46 (Pa. Commw. Ct. 1980) (no basis for reliance beyond the three-year statutory limit for vested rights); Lampton v. Pinaire, 610 S.W.2d 915, 921-22 (Ky. Ct. App. 1981) (replat is subject to new, stricter subdivision requirements). *See generally* E. McQuillin, *supra* note 102, at § 25.155; R. Anderson, American Law of Zoning § 6.23 (3d ed. 1986).

107. Model Regulations § 3.

108. D. Callies & M. Grant, *Paying for Growth and Planning Gain: An Anglo-American Comparison of Development Conditions, Impact Fees and Development Agreements,* 23 Urb. Law. 221 (1991).

109. *Id.*

110. *Id.*

111. Although usually considered in the context of a trade-off involving land use conditions and exaction obligations balanced against provision of municipal services and a regulatory freeze, development agreements have been used to facilitate agricultural land preservation to compensate for lost tax revenues, to foster community development, and to bolster available low- and moderate-income housing supplies. Wegner, *Moving Toward the Bargaining Table: Contract Zoning, Development Agreements, and the Theoretical Foundations of Government Land Use Deals,* 65 N.C. L. Rev. 956, 994-95 (1987); Holliman, *Development Agreements and Vested Rights in California,* 13 Urb. Law. 44 (1981); Kramer, *Development Agreements,*

To What Extent Are They Enforceable? 10 REAL ESTATE L.J. 29 (1981).

112. *See* Dawe v. City of Scottsdale, 581 P.2d 1136, 1137 (Ariz. 1978).

113. Taub, *Development Agreements*, 42 LAND USE L. & ZON. DIG. 3 (Oct. 1990); ARIZ. REV. STAT. ANN. 1 § 9-500.05 (1990); CAL. GOV'T CODE §§ 65864-65869.5 (1990); COLO. REV. STAT. §§ 24-68-101—24-68-106 (199); FLA. STAT. §§ 163.3220—163.3243 (1989); HAWAII REV. STAT. § 46-121—46-132 (1988); LA. REV. STAT. ANN. § 33.4780.21—4780.33 (West 1990); MINN. STAT. 462.358 (Subd. 3C (West 1990); NEV. REV. STAT. §§ 278.0201—278.0207 (1990); and N.J. REV. STAT. § 40:55D-45.2. *See generally* Fulton, *Building and Bargaining in California*, 4 CAL. LAW. 36 (No. 12, 1984). *See also* Hagman, *Estoppel and Vesting in the Age of Multi-Land Use Permits*, 11 SW. U.L. REV. 545, 489-90 (1979).

114. *See* Taub, *supra* note 113; Callies, Freilich & Roberts, *supra* note 56.

115. This provides clear advantage to the local governmental unit over impact fees because impact fees are usually limited to only the proportionate share of off-site improvements. *See, e.g.,* CAL. GOV'T CODE § 65865-2 (West).

116. S. Mark White, *Affordable Housing: Proactive and Reactive Planning Strategies* 53, Planners Advisory Service Report No. 441 (American Planning Association, 1992).

117. Delucchi v. County of Santa Cruz, 179 Cal. App. 3d 814, 225 Cal. Rptr. 43 (land conservation contract designed to preserve land in coastal zone for agricultural and compatible uses).

118. Transfer of development rights (TDRs) are essential tools for preservation of open space, agricultural lands, historic structures, and environmentally sensitive lands. The use of TDRs permits total regulation of the protected resource without a finding of a taking because development rights are granted to the property, which can be sold for value, thus creating a compensatory regulation. The concept has been upheld against taking and substantive due process, but state statutory and constitutional authority must be carefully considered. Only two cases to date have restricted the concept—one based on statutory procedure requiring TDRs to be incorporated within zoning, the other (Arizona) rejecting the concept as a substitute for taking compensation. *See* Penn Cent. Transp. Co. v. City of New York, 438 U.S. 104 (1978) (historic preservation TDR prevents taking); City of Hollywood v. Hollywood, 432 So.2d 1332

(Fla. 1983) (preservation of beachfront TDR prevents taking); Freilich & Senville, *Takings, TDRs and Environmental Preservation: Fairness and the Hollywood North Beach Case*, 35 LAND USE L. & ZON. DIG. 4 (Sept. 1983); West Montgomery County Citizens Ass'n v. Maryland National Capital Park & Planning Comm'n, 309 Md. 183, 522 A.2d 1328 (1987) (an off-site TDR scheme held ultra vires when implemented through comprehensive plan—but may be instituted through zoning); Barancik v. County of Marin, 872 F.2d 834 (9th Cir. 1989) (upheld county's TDR regulations against substantive due process challenge); Corrigan v. City of Scottsdale, 720 P.2d 528, 540 (Ariz. App. 1985), *affirmed in part, vacated in part*, 720 P.2d 513 (Ariz. 1986) (transfer of density credits not just compensation for property taken by eminent domain under Arizona Constitution, which requires compensation for takings in form of money damages); Glisson v. Alachua County, 558 So.2d 1030 (Fla. App. 1990), *review denied*, 570 So.2d 1304 (Fla. 1990) (availability of TDRs prevented determination that landowners were deprived of all economically viable use).

119. *See* Model Agreement § 101-4, Criteria for Entering into Development Agreements.

120. Sigg, *California's Development Agreement Statute*, 15 SW. U.L. REV. 695, 696 (1985).

121. *Id.*

122. SIEMON & LARSEN WITH PORTER, VESTED RIGHTS: BALANCING PUBLIC AND PRIVATE DEVELOPMENT EXPECTATIONS, 6-7 (Urban Land Institute, 1982).

123. *Id.* at 24.

124. *Id.*

125. *See* Dawe v. City of Scottsdale, 581 P.2d 1136, 1137 (Ariz. 1978); Lake Intervale Homes, Inc. v. Township of Parsippany-Troy Hills, 147 A.2d 28, 37 (N.J. 1958). *See generally* Shultz & Kelley, *supra* note 71, at 74-75.

126. Model Regulations § 3; Callies, Statutory Development Agreements: Analysis, Checklist and Model Agreement (1987) (unpublished manuscript).

127. *See, e.g.,* Kramer, *Development Agreements: To What Extent Are They Enforceable?* 10 REAL EST. L.J. 29 (1981); Fry, *Modern Development: Vested Rights or Development Agreements*, 55 UMKC L. REV. 483 (1987); Wegner, *supra* note 111 at 965.

128. *See, e.g.,* Attman/Glazer P.B. Co. v. Mayor and Aldermen of Annapolis, 314 Md. 675, 552 A.2d 1277 (1989) (city attempts to "settle" the appeal of a zoning appeal by attempting to bind itself to a future zoning and conditional use decision).

129. Coleman v. Bossier City, 291 So.2d 410 (La. Ct. App. 1974) (contract by city in which city had taken over water and sewage facilities constructed by developers and promised to repay developers one-half of the cost of construction of such facilities was void).

130. Holliman, *Development Agreement and Vested Rights in California*, 13 Urb. Law. 44, 53 (1981).

131. Crew, Development Agreements After Nollan v. California Coastal Commission, 107 S. Ct. 3141 (1987), p.10, n.33 (unpublished manuscript).

132. For instance, the various statutes incorporate provisions limiting the duration of regulatory freezes (Fla. Stat. Ann. § 163.3229); providing periodic review for good faith compliance (Cal. Gov't Code § 65865.1); providing for the application of new, nonconflicting regulations to the property (Cal. Gov't Code § 65866); and providing for modification or suspension to comply with state or federal law (Cal. Gov't Code § 65869.5); or for interruption of the development if it becomes perilous to the public (Haw. Rev. Stat. § 46-127).

133. Also weighing in favor of development agreements, and countering the reserved powers questions, is the constitutional contracts clause, U.S. Const. art. I, section 10, which prohibits a state from passing laws impairing the obligation of contracts, including public contracts. Recognizing that the police power is not infinite, the contracts clause, in summary, allows impairment of an existing contract by passage of police power regulations only if the exercise of the police power is reasonable and necessary to serve an important public purpose, with heightened judicial scrutiny applied where a state impairs its own contractual obligations. *See* Fry, *Modern Development: Vested Rights or Development Agreements*, 51 UMKC L. Rev. 483, 498-500, citing United States Trust Co. v. New Jersey, 431 U.S. 1 (1976).

134. Briarcliffe West Townhouse Owners' Ass'n v. Wiseman Constr. Co., 454 N.E.2d 363 (Ill. App. Ct. 1983) (homeowners' association was third-party beneficiary of subdivision improvement agreement).

135. Wegner, *supra* note 111, at 1000.

136. Crew, *supra* note 131, at 9.

137. 483 U.S. 825 (1987).

138. *Id.* at 836.

139. *Id.*

140. Crew, *supra* note 131, at 26.

141. *Id.* at 17-18.

142. *Id.* at 29-34.

143. Model Regulations § 3.6(4)(a) ("terms and conditions agreed to by the parties").

144. *Id.* at § 3.6(4)(b).

145. Waiver of rights.

146. Model Regulations § 3.3(8).

147. *Id.* at § 3.3(9).

148. *See* SPEA, *supra* note 76, at 15.

149. *See* Mo. Ann. Stat. §§ 89.420, 89.444 (Vernon 1986). Each person is advised to check the appropriate state statute for the formal provision. *See also* Wright Dev. Inc. v. City of Wellsville, 608 P.2d 232 (Utah 1980). *See generally* E. Yokely, Law of Subdivisions 52 at 219 (2d ed. 1981).

150. Model Regulations § 3.5(1); Appendix B.

151. Treat v. Town Planning & Zoning Comm'n, 143 A.2d 448 (Conn. 1958); Gorton v. Silver Lake Township, 494 A.2d 26 (Pa. Commw. Ct. 1985) (planning commission's failure to act within the 90-day time limit imposed by law was not deemed to be approval, as the application was massively deficient).

152. Schonberg v. Fargo Planning Comm'n, 110 N.W.2d 830 (N.D. 1961).

153. Model Regulations § 3.5(3).

154. Case denying two hearings.

155. State *ex rel.* James L. Callan, Inc. v. Barg, 89 N.W.2d 267 (Wis. 1958); Metropolitan Homes, Inc. v. Town Plan & Zoning Comm'n, 202 A.2d 241 (Conn. 1964). *Compare* Rouse/Chamberlin, Inc. v. Board of Supervisors, 504 A.2d 375 (Pa. Commw. 1986).

156. Bensalem Township v. Blank, 539 A.2d 948 (Pa. Commw. Ct. 1988) (90 days after the regular meeting of the reviewing agency); Norco Constr., Inc. v. King City, 649 P.2d 103 (Wash. 1982) (90 days after preliminary application); Stoner v. Planning Bd., 266 N.E.2d 891 (Mass. 1971) (60 days after final approval). *But see* C&D Partnership v. City of Gahanna, 474 N.E.2d 303 (Ohio 1984) (council delay beyond the 30-day time limit in order to investigate serious flooding problems on the development site was proper). *See also* Paladac Realty Trust v. Rockland Planning Comm'n, 541 A.2d 919 (Me. 1988) (if ordinance does not specify time frame, hearing must be held within a reasonable time).

157. 3 R. Anderson, American Law of Zoning 28.04 (3d ed. 1986). The subdivider may have to bring an action to enforce this right. A mandamus proceeding is used to compel the issuance of a certificate of approval, and the planning

commission cannot raise the merits of the application. *See* DiStefano v. Miller, 497 N.Y.S.2d 433 (App. Div. 1986) (applicant was entitled to approval regardless of the fact that the plat was inconsistent with zoning regulations); Wallberg v. Planning Bd. of Pound Ridge, 495 N.Y.S.2d 731 (App. Div. 2d Dept 1985); Corse v. Ridley, 36 Pa. D. & C.3d 302 (1983); Appeal of Buchsbaum, 540 A.2d 1389 (Pa. Commw. 1988); Larrivee v. Timmons, 525 A.2d 1037 (Me. 1987). *See* Savage v. Town of Rye, 415 A.2d 873 (N.H. 1980) (held that when planning board failed to approve the plat within the required 90 days, subdivider could record without the board's written endorsement). Sandlin v. Goldstein, 87 So.2d 861 (Ala. 1956); Rothey Bros. v. Elizabeth Township, 112 A.2d 87 (Pa. 1955). Automatic approval may be waived in some instances. *See* Dune Assoc., Inc. v. Anderson, 500 N.Y.S.2d 741 (A.D.2d. 1986) (valid approval moratorium in place); Anastasio v. Planning Bd. of West Orange, 507 A.2d 1194 (1986) *certif. denied*, 526 A.2d 136 (delays resulting from litigation were not unreasonable). *But see* Pateman v. Marra, 138 Misc.2d 807, 525 N.Y.S.2d 533 (1988) (running of approval time not tolled by moratorium).

158. Model Regulations § 3.9. Mandamus is an extraordinary equitable remedy, the purpose of which is to enforce the performance of a clear and positive duty. It will issue only to command performance of a duty, and does not give or define a right that one does not already have. The party who seeks performance has the burden to prove his legal right to the performance. M&L Homes, Inc. v. Zoning & Planning Comm'n, 445 A.2d 591, 597-98 (1982); Hillis Homes, Inc. v. Snohomish County, 647 P.2d 43, 47 (1982).

159. Model Regulations § 3.9.

160. *Id.*

161. Model Regulations § 3.3(3).

162. The unreasonable lapse of time can prove to be "unconstitutionally detrimental to a developer harmed by this action." Norco Constr., Inc. v. King County, 649 P.2d 103, 107 (Wash. 1982) (en banc). A governmental entity must act within a reasonable time frame, and cannot exercise its police power "so lethargically as to effectively confiscate private property." Schoeller v. Board of County Comm'rs, 568 P.2d 869 (Wyo. 1977). For a thorough review of governmental delaying tactics see Delogu, *The Misuse of Land Use Control Powers Must End: Suggestions For Legislative & Judicial Responses*, 32 Me. L. Rev. 29 (1980).

163. This was expressly decided in Fishman v. Arnzen, 275 N.Y.S.2d 669 (Sup. Ct. 1966) (a planning board does not have to hold a hearing within 30 days of submission if the plat is not in final form; the subdivider is not entitled to a certificate of approval).

164. Conn. Gen. Stat. Ann. § 8-26 (West 1971); N.Y. Town Law § 276 (McKinney 1987); N.J. Stat. Ann. § 40:55 (D-25) (West Supp. 1987). "[F]indings of fact would be required even in the absence of statutory duty in order to facilitate judicial review, ensure careful administrative deliberations, assist the parties in preparing for review, and restrain agencies within the bounds of their instruction." Kenai Peninsula Borough v. Ryherd, 628 P.2d 557 (Alaska 1981). *See* Model Regulations § 3.5(4).

165. Caine v. City of Lakewood, 187 N.E.2d 594 (Ohio Ct. App. 1963); Levesque v. Inhabitants of Town of Eliot, 448 A.2d 876 (Me. 1982). *See* Model Regulations § 3.8.

166. *Id.* at § 3.5(4). In Colorado, for example, the subdivider has 30 days within which to challenge the denial of final plat approval. Colo. R. Civ. P. 106(a)(4).

167. *See also* SPEA, *supra* note 76, at 10: "In general, the commission shall have such powers as may be necessary to enable it to fulfill its functions, promote municipal planning, or carry out the purposes of this act."

168. Model Regulations § 3.7(3).

169. Pennyton Homes v. Planning Bd., 197 A.2d 870 (N.J. 1964); Levin v. Livingston Township, 173 A.2d 391 (N.J. 1961); Hilton Acres v. Klein, 174 A.2d 465 (N.J. 1961).

170. Model Regulations § 3.10.

171. Model Regulations § 3.7(2)(a).

172. *Id.* at § 3.8.

173. *Id.*

174. *Id.*

175. *Id.*

176. American Society of Planning Officials, *Subdivision Fees Revisited* 4 (Information Report No. 202, Sept. 1965), which states the reasons underlying this practice as follows: "Experience suggests, however, that in many communities fees are substantially lower than costs. In those communities, the public at large pays a cost that could be passed on the developer. It is not clear why the developer should not be required to assume this cost, just as he must (in many communities) assume the costs for streets, sewers, and building inspections incident to his development.... Inspection fees, based on actual cost, should be charged in addition." *See also* Merrelli v. City of St. Clair Shores, 96 N.W.2d 144 (Mich. 1959).

177. Teter v. Clark County, 704 P.2d 1171 (Wash. 1985); S & P Enterprises v. City of Memphis, 672 S.W.2d 213 (Tenn. Ct. App. 1983); Haugen v. Gleason, 359 P.2d 108 (Ore. 1961). The fee should be scrutinized for reasonableness; an excessive fee will be stricken as an illegal tax. West Park Ave., Inc. v. Ocean Township, 224 A.2d 1 (N.J. 1967).

178. Gordon v. Village of Wayne, 121 N.W.2d 823 (Mich. 1963). Similarly, where a statute, CONN. GEN. STAT. § 8-26 (West 1971), provides for specified fees for subdivision applications *and inspections of subdivision* improvements, the exaction of additional sums based upon the cost of improvements is ultra vires. Avonside, Inc. v. Zoning and Planning Comm'n, 215 A.2d 409 (Conn. 1965).

179. In the leading case in this area, Telimar Homes, Inc. v. Miller, 218 N.Y.S.2d 175 (App. Div. 1961), despite the use of a statutory procedure for sectionalizing, the court held that changes involving sidewalks, curbs, and other *subdivision* requirements would be upheld for the sections not filed with the county clerk. Curiously, the court refused to apply new *zoning* regulations for larger lot sizes since it was clear that the drainage and roads were designed for all four sections and therefore the developer had a vested right to a nonconforming use as to the entire tract. The tract was divided into four sections, the map for the first section was approved, and the plat filed with the county clerk; the map for the remaining sections was filed with the local government clerk, as per statute. *See also* Appeal by Mark-Garner Assoc., Inc., 413 A.2d 1142 (Pa. Commw. Ct. 1980).

4

Assurance for Completion and Maintenance of Improvements

4.1 Improvements and Subdivision Improvement Agreement.

1. *Completion of Improvements.* Before the final subdivision plat is signed by the Chairman of the Planning Commission, all applicants shall be required to complete, in accordance with the Planning Commission's decision and to the satisfaction of the Local Government Engineer, all the street, sanitary and other public improvements, including lot improvements on the individual lots of the subdivision, as required in these regulations, specified in the final subdivision plat and as approved by the Planning Commission, and to dedicate those public improvements to the local government, free and clear of all liens and encumbrances on the dedicated property and public improvements.

2. *Subdivision Improvement Agreement and Guarantee.*
   a. *Agreement.* The Planning Commission in its sole discretion may waive the requirement that the applicant complete and dedicate all public improvements prior to approval of the final subdivision plat and, as an alternative, permit the applicant to enter into a subdivision improvement agreement by which the subdivider covenants to complete all required public improvements no later than two (2) years following the date on which the Chairman of the Planning Commission signs the final subdivision plat. The applicant shall

covenant to maintain each required public improvement for a period of one (1) year following the acceptance by the governing body of the dedication of that completed public improvement and also shall warrant that all required public improvements will be free from defect for a period of two (2) years following the acceptance by the governing body of the dedication of the last completed public improvement. The subdivision improvement agreement shall contain such other terms and conditions agreed to by the applicant and the Planning Commission.

b. *Covenants to Run.* The subdivision improvement agreement shall provide that the covenants contained in the agreement shall run with the land and bind all successors, heirs, and assignees of the subdivider. The subdivision improvement agreement will be adopted by the Planning Commission, and when necessary, the governing body, pursuant to applicable state and local laws and shall be recorded in the Clerk and Recorder's Office of _____ (county in which municipality is located).

c. *Security.* Whenever the Planning Commission permits an applicant to enter into a subdivision improvement agreement, it shall require the applicant to provide a letter of credit or cash escrow as security for the promises contained in the subdivision improvement agreement. Either security shall be in an amount equal to one hundred twenty percent (120%) of the estimated cost of completion of the required public improvements, including lot improvements. The issuer of the letter of credit or the escrow agent, as applicable, shall be acceptable to the Planning Commission.

    i. Letter of Credit. If the applicant posts a letter of credit as security for its promises contained in the subdivision improvement agreement, the credit shall (1) be irrevocable; (2) be for a term sufficient to cover the completion, maintenance and warranty periods in Section 4.1(2)(a); and (3) require only that the government present the credit with a sight draft and an affidavit signed by the Local Government Attorney attesting to the municipality's right to draw funds under the credit.

    ii. Cash Escrow. If the applicant posts a cash escrow as security for its promises contained in the subdivision improvement agreement, the escrow instructions shall provide: (1) that the subdivider will have no right to a return of any of the funds except as provided in section 4.2 (2)(b); and (2) that the escrow agent shall have a legal duty to deliver the funds to the municipality whenever the Local Government Attorney presents an affidavit to the agent attesting to the municipality's right to receive funds whether or not the subdivider protests that right.

If and when the municipality accepts the offer of dedication for the last completed required public improvement, the municipality shall execute a waiver of its right to receive all but twenty-five percent (25%) of the funds represented by the letter of credit or cash escrow if the subdivider is not in breach of the subdivision improvement agreement. The residual funds shall be security for the subdivider's covenant to maintain the required public improvements and its warranty that the improvements are free from defect.

3. *Temporary Improvement.* The applicant shall build and pay for all costs of temporary improvements required by the Planning Commission and shall maintain those temporary improvements for the period specified by the Planning Commission. Prior to construction of any temporary facility or improvement, the developer shall file with the local government a separate subdivision improvement agreement and a letter of credit or cash escrow in an appropriate amount for temporary facilities, which agreement and credit or escrow shall ensure that the temporary facilities will be properly constructed, maintained, and removed.

4. *Costs of Improvements.* All required improvements shall be made by the developer, at its expense, without reimbursement by the local government or any improvement district except that, as may be allowed under state law, the developer may form or cause to be formed a special district or districts to construct and finance the construction of required public improvements excluding lot improvements on individual lots. If the subdivider does form or cause to be formed a special district for the purposes identified in this section, the government shall not release the subdivider from its obligations under any subdivision improvement agreement nor shall the government release any security, in whole or in part, until the special district has sold bonds or otherwise certifies to the municipality that it has an absolute right to raise revenues sufficient to construct, maintain, and warrant the quality of the required public improvements.

5. *Governmental Units.* Governmental units to which these contract and security provisions apply may file, in lieu of the contract and security, a certified resolution or ordinance from officers or agencies authorized to act in their behalf, agreeing to comply with the provisions of this Article.

6. *Failure to Complete Improvement.* For subdivisions for which no subdivision improvement agreement has been executed and no security has been posted, if the improvements are not completed within the

period specified by the Planning Commission in the resolution approving the plat, the sketch plat or preliminary plat approval shall be deemed to have expired. In those cases where a subdivision improvement agreement has been executed and security has been posted and required public improvements have not been installed within the terms of the agreement, the local government may then: (1) declare the agreement to be in default and require that all the improvements be installed regardless of the extent of the building development at the time the agreement is declared to be in default; (2) suspend final subdivision plat approval until the improvements are completed and record a document to that effect for the purpose of public notice; (3) obtain funds under the security and complete improvements itself or through a third party; (4) assign its right to receive funds under the security to any third party, including a subsequent owner of the subdivision for which improvements were not constructed, in whole or in part, in exchange for that subsequent owner's promise to complete improvements in the subdivision; (5) exercise any other rights available under the law.

7. *Acceptance of Dedication Offers.* Acceptance of formal offers of dedication of streets, public areas, easements, and parks shall be by ordinance of the governing body. The approval of a subdivision plat by the Planning Commission, whether sketch, preliminary or final, shall not be deemed to constitute or imply the acceptance by the municipality of any street, easement, or park shown on plat. The Planning Commission may require the plat to be endorsed with appropriate notes to this effect.

4.2   Inspection of Improvements.

1. *General Procedure and Fees.* The Planning Commission shall provide for inspection of required improvements during construction and ensure their satisfactory completion. The applicant shall pay to the municipality an inspection fee based on the estimated cost of inspection, and where the improvements are completed prior to final plat approval, the subdivision plat shall not be signed by the Chairman of the Planning Commission unless the inspection fee has been paid at the time of application. These fees shall be due and payable upon demand of the municipality and no building permits or certificates of occupancy shall be issued until all fees are paid. If the Local Government Engineer finds upon inspection that any one or more of the required improvements have not been constructed in accordance with the municipality's construction standards and specifications, the applicant shall be responsible for properly completing the improvements.

2. *Release or Reduction of Security.*
   a. *Certificate of Satisfactory Completion.* The governing body will not accept dedication of required improvements, nor release nor reduce the amount of any security posted by the subdivider until the Local Government Engineer has submitted a certificate stating that all required improvements have been satisfactorily completed and until (1) the applicant's engineer or surveyor has certified to the Local Government Engineer, through submission of a detailed "as-built" survey plat of the subdivision, indicating location, dimensions, materials, and other information required by the Planning Commission or Local Government Engineer, that the layout of the line and grade of all public improvements is in accordance with construction plans for the subdivision, and (2) a title insurance policy has been furnished to and approved by the Local Government Attorney indicating that the improvements have been completed, are ready for dedication to the local government, and are free and clear of any and all liens and encumbrances. Upon such approval and recommendation by the Planning Commission, Local Government Engineer, and Local Government Attorney, the governing body shall thereafter accept the improvements for dedication in accordance with the established procedure.
   b. *Reduction of Escrowed Funds and Security.* If the security posted by the subdivider was a cash escrow, the amount of that escrow shall be reduced upon actual acceptance of the dedication of public improvements and then only to the ratio that the cost of the public improvement for which dedication was accepted bears to the total cost of public improvements for the subdivision. In no event shall a cash escrow be reduced below twenty-five per cent (25%) of the principal amount. Funds held in the escrow account shall not be released to the subdivider, in whole or in part, except upon express written instructions of the local government attorney. At the end of the maintenance and warranty periods, all escrowed funds, if any, shall be released to the subdivider. If the security provided by the subdivider was a letter of credit, the Local Government Attorney shall execute waivers of the municipality's right to draw funds under the credit upon actual acceptance of the dedication of public improvements and then only to the ratio that the cost of the public improvement for which dedication was accepted bears to the total cost of public improvements for the subdivision. In no event shall waivers be executed that would reduce the security below twenty-five percent (25%) of its original amount.

4.3 Escrow Deposits for Lot Improvements.

1. *Acceptance of Escrow Funds.* Whenever, by reason of the season of the year, any lot improvements required by the subdivision regulations cannot be performed, the Building and Zoning Inspector may issue a certificate of occupancy, provided there is no danger to health, safety, or general welfare upon accepting a cash escrow deposit in an amount to be determined by the Local Government Engineer for the cost of the lot improvements. The subdivision improvement agreement and security covering the lot improvements shall remain in full force and effect.

2. *Procedures on Escrow Fund.* All required improvements for which escrow monies have been accepted by the Building and Zoning Inspector at the time of issuance of a certificate of occupancy shall be installed by the subdivider within a period of nine (9) months from the date of deposit and issuance of the certificate of occupancy. If the improvements have not been properly installed at the end of the time period, the Building and Zoning Inspector shall give two (2) weeks written notice to the developer requiring it to install the improvements, and if they are not then installed properly, the Building and Zoning Inspector may request the governing body to proceed to contract out the work for the installation of the necessary improvements in a sum not to exceed the amount of the escrow deposit. At the time of the issuance of the certificate of occupancy for which escrow monies are being deposited with the Building and Zoning Inspector, the developer shall obtain and file with the Building and Zoning Inspector prior to obtaining the certificate of occupancy a notarized statement from the purchaser or purchasers of the premises authorizing the Building and Zoning Inspector to install the improvements at the end of the nine-month period if the improvements have not been duly installed by the subdivider.

4.4 Maintenance of Improvements.

The developer shall be required to maintain all required public improvements on the individual subdivided lots and provide for snow removal on streets and sidewalks, if required by the Planning Commission, until acceptance of the improvements by the governing body. If there are any certificates of occupancy on a street not dedicated to the local government, the local government may on twelve (12) hours notice plow the street or effect emergency repairs and charge those costs to the developer. Following the acceptance of the dedication of any public improvement by the local government, the government may, in its sole discretion require the subdivider to maintain the improvement for a period of one (1) year from the date of acceptance.

4.5 Deferral or Waiver of Required Improvements.

1. The Planning Commission may defer or waive at the time of final approval, subject to appropriate conditions, the provision of any or all public improvements as, in its judgment, are not requisite in the interests of the public health, safety, and general welfare, or which are inappropriate because of the inadequacy or inexistence of connecting facilities. Any determination to defer or waive the provision of any public improvement must be made on the record and the reasons for the deferral or waiver also shall be expressly made on the record.

2. Whenever it is deemed necessary by the Planning Commission to defer the construction of any improvement required under these regulations because of incompatible grades, future planning, inadequate or nonexistent connecting facilities, or for other reasons, the subdivider shall pay his share of the costs of the future improvements to the local government prior to signing of the final subdivision plat by the Chairman of the Planning Commission, or the developer may execute a separate subdivision improvement agreement secured by a letter of credit guaranteeing completion of the deferred improvements upon demand of the local government.

4.6 Issuance of Building Permits and Certificates of Occupancy.

1. When a subdivision improvement agreement and security have been required for a subdivision, no certificate of occupancy for any building in the subdivision shall be issued prior to the completion of the required public improvements and the acceptance of the dedication of those improvements by the local government, as required in the Planning Commission's approval of the final subdivision plat.

2. The extent of street improvement shall be adequate for vehicular access by the prospective occupant(s) and by police and fire equipment prior to the issuance of an occupancy permit. The developer shall, at the time of the offer of dedication, submit monies in escrow to the local government in a sum determined by the Local Government Engineer for the necessary final improvement of the street.

3. No building permit shall be issued for the final ten percent (10%) of lots in a subdivision, or if ten percent (10%) be less than two (2), for the final two (2) lots of a subdivision, until all public improvements required by the Planning Commission for the subdivision have been fully completed and the local government has accepted the developer's offer(s) to dedicate the improvements.

4.7 Consumer Protection Legislation and Conflicts of Interest Statutes.

1. No building permit or certificate of occupancy shall be granted or issued if a developer or its authorized agent has violated any federal, state or local law pertaining to (1) consumer protection; or (2) real estate land sales, promotion, or practices; or (3) any applicable conflicts-of-interest legislation with respect to the lot or parcel of land which is the subject of the permit or certificate until a court of competent jurisdiction so orders.

2. With respect to any lot or parcel of land described in the immediately preceding section, if a building permit or certificate of occupancy has been granted or issued, it may be revoked by the municipality until a court of competent jurisdiction orders otherwise, provided that in no event shall the rights of intervening innocent third parties in possession of a certificate of occupancy be prejudiced by any such revocation.

3. Any violation of a federal, state, or local consumer protection law, including, but not limited to: Postal Reorganization Act of 1970; the Federal Trade Commission Act of 1970; Interstate Land Sales Full Disclosure Act; the Truth in Lending Act; the Uniform Commercial Credit Code; state "Blue Sky" laws; state subdivision disclosure acts, or any conflicts of interest statute, law, or ordinance shall be deemed a violation of these regulations and subject to all of the penalties and proceedings as set forth in Section 1.13.

COMMENTARY ON ARTICLE 4

INTRODUCTION

The planning commission has the authority to require the subdivider to install all of the required public improvements before a subdivision plat is finally approved and recorded.[1] Requiring improvements to be completed before plat approval often causes long delays and expense to a developer who can neither sell lots nor begin the construction of homes until the plat is recorded.[2] Final subdivision plat approval may be granted prior to completion of improvements if the subdivider guarantees to complete the improvements,[3] which takes the form of requiring the subdivider to post some type of security for its promise to complete improvements following final plat approval.[4]

Article 4 of the Model Regulations retains the planning commission's discretion to require the subdivider to complete public improvements prior to final plat approval.[5] If the planning commission opts to have the subdivider bond the improvements in lieu of completion, it should require the developer to enter into a subdivision improvement agreement in which the developer agrees to provide a surety bond, letter of credit, or cash escrow as security.[6] Improvements generally include sidewalks, gutters, roads, drainage facilities, water and sewage systems, landscaping, utilities, fire protection facilities, and street signs. The number and types of subdivision improvements that a local government can require a developer to complete must have a reasonable relationship to capital improvement program requirements and the requirement must be included in the subdivision regulations themselves.[7] Most recently, local governments have also required developers to undertake or pay for off-site improvement,[8] pay for the cost of extending off-site utilities,[9] or provide easements to accommodate off-site use.[10] The developer must design improvements according to standards and specifications referenced in the subdivision regulations, and these improvements may be required from the regulation themselves or pursuant to standards of coordinate state and local agencies.[11] Some jurisdictions permit variances from required improvements when the requirements will result in extreme hardship to the developer, the variance will not threaten the public interest, and the variance will not result in a waiver of statutory requirements of performance guarantees.[12]

Acceptable security methods vary by jurisdiction, with the most common requirement being a corporate surety bond "or other adequate security."[13] Where the subdivision is subject to approval by a number of agencies, the developer may be required to post several bonds.[14] Most jurisdictions, however, permit a consolidated bond for all of the required improvements. The usual term of the bond or security agreement is two years from the date of final plat approval.[15] If, after two years, the developer fails to complete the improvements, the local government may declare a default unless the parties have extended the term of the bond or agreement.[16] "Other adequate security" includes cash or property escrows, letters of credit, or commitments of funds by lenders.[17] The government may use a phased overall preliminary approval process by which the developer obtains final approval and records only those portions of the subdivision plat for which improvements are required immediately.[18]

The local government should base the amount of the bond or other security on a cost estimate of the required improvements and may predicate that figure on the developer's estimates after review by the planning authority.[19] Some jurisdictions provide for a margin of error by requiring that the bond or security be equal to 120 percent of the projected cost of improvements.[20] As the developer completes improvements, the amount of the bond or security should be reduced, usually to a fixed number of lots or a minimum of 10 percent of the security.[21]

The local government may also require a maintenance bond to ensure that the improvements are sound and to pay for any maintenance costs for a limited time after the local government accepts the improvements.[22] Most governments require the developer to pay administrative fees to offset the cost of inspecting improvements during construction and installation of the improvements and prior to acceptance.[23] After the developer notifies the government that improvements are complete, the improvements will be inspected and, if acceptable to the local government, the security will be released.[24]

Regardless of the form chosen to secure completion of subdivision improvements, the local government must perform a supervisory function to assure itself that the developer has constructed and completed the improvements in compliance with applicable regulations and specifications. The local government and the planning commission might consider requiring both a performance bond and a payment bond. The former insures only that the work has been completed. There is no assurance that all labor and material costs have been paid for. Under most state statutes, such persons may file a mechanic's lien on the improvement and, if the local government accepts the dedication of the improvement, it may find itself liable for such payment in the event of developer insolvency.[25]

The local government may avoid this prior to final plat approval by obtaining and recording an offer of irrevocable dedication with a title search to ensure that there are no prior liens. A provision in the bond that requires dedication of the improvements after construction free and clear of all liens and encumbrances makes it a payment bond as well as a performance bond. Without such a provision, a court may refuse to extend the bond to include a guarantee of all labor and material furnished.[26] This supervisory function usually constitutes a three-step process that includes inspection, approval, and acceptance of the improvements.[27]

When all or part of the improvements are completed or substantially completed, the developer may notify the local government engineer and request an inspection.[28] The engineer then performs a site inspection and prepares a detailed report.[29] Ordinarily, the inspection must be made within a specified time after the request is submitted.[30]

The engineer's report indicates whether the improvements are approved, partially approved, or rejected and can be used for several purposes. If the engineer rejects any of the improvements, the report should set out the reasons for rejection and the steps necessary to gain approval. Additionally, the report serves to notify the surety, lender, or escrow agent that all or a portion of the improvements have been accepted, thus permitting the partial release of the bond or escrowed funds, or the disbursement of set-aside funds. Generally, neither the approval itself nor the release or partial release of security constitutes an acceptance of dedication.[31]

Finally, the engineer forwards a copy of the report to the local government agency charged with accepting dedication of the completed improvements.[32] A failure to follow these steps may result in automatic approval.[33] Acceptance of dedication constitutes the final step in the supervisory process and results in the transfer of title from the developer to the local government unit.[34]

Ordinarily, acceptance is accomplished by ordinance, but it also may result from the local government's exercise of dominion and control over the improvements.[35] State law may require the local government to accept each part of the improvements as they are completed.[36] The significance of the acceptance of dedication is that it results in the transfer of ownership of the improvements. After the date of acceptance, the burden of maintaining and repairing the improvements falls upon the local government unless the developer has agreed to perform these functions.[37]

TYPES OF SECURITY

Most state enabling acts permit the use of a variety of security devices and each form of security presents its own particular set of advantages and disadvantages that the local government should consider in light of the overall purposes of subdivision regulation.

Surety Bond

The corporate surety bond is undoubtedly the most widely authorized and utilized security device under existing law for assuring the completion of required subdivision improvements.[38] On its face, the bond is a deceptively simple instrument. It includes a joint and several promise by the developer, as principal, and the surety company, as obligor, to pay a specified penal sum to the local government unit, as obligee.[39] If the developer performs all of the obligations of its underlying agreement with the obligee, the bond becomes null and void.[40]

A surety bond is always a three-party instrument.[41] The developer has paid a fee to a corporate surety in consideration for the surety's promise to guarantee the completion of the improvements for the benefit of the local government.[42]

Unlike insurance, the surety underwrites relatively few bonds. Thus, the surety must be assured that the developer has both the technical and the financial capacity to perform all obligations to the local government.[43] The bond premium is a function of the risk of loss with respect to each individual developer and each particular project, in contrast to insurance, which spreads its risk over the entire portfolio through the underwriting of multiple policies.[44] As a result of heavy losses sustained in the recent past, corporate sureties increasingly have become reluctant to underwrite bonds guaranteeing subdivision improvements. As a result, only the largest, most credit-worthy developers can obtain surety bonds.[45]

Accordingly, a surety will be willing to bond a particular project only if a variety of other inducements in addition to the premium are included. These inducements usually take the form of collateral and promises by various individuals, companies, and lenders to indemnify the surety in the event that it is required to pay on the bond. It is universally required that in addition to the developer itself, all general partners or major shareholders and their spouses also will be required to indemnify the surety. In addition, the development lender occasionally may be asked either to lend the collateral funds or to issue its letter of credit securing the bonding company.[46]

The surety bond, when available at all, may be prohibitively expensive. Even when the cost is within acceptable limits, the bond imposes a heavy cost burden on the project,[47] especially when the lender is asked to lend additional funds or to provide a letter of credit for the benefit of the surety. The additional security will result in higher costs to the developer, which must be paid in addition to the bond premium.[48] When the lender is willing to extend the additional security, it legitimately may be asked why that security cannot be directed to the benefit of the local government unit rather than to the surety, thus eliminating the bond and saving the cost of the premium.[49]

In the event of the developer's default, the local government will call for the surety's performance of the obligation under the bond. Depending upon the language of the bond, the surety will have a number of options.[50] If the project is close to completion, the surety might advance necessary funds directly to the defaulting developer. Sureties rarely invoke this option because the funds advanced do not directly reduce the stated bond amount or the surety's potential liability on the bonds.[51]

Nevertheless this may reduce the surety's ultimate liability to the extent that the developer actually uses the funds to complete the required improvements. Thus, when the surety has had a long-standing relationship with the developer and the default is not the result of bad faith,[52] the surety's best interests may dictate financing the defaulting developer or hiring another contractor to complete the work.[53]

The surety's options suffer from one common and significant deficiency. If the surety chooses to undertake the actual completion of the improvements, either by financing the developer or by hiring a new contractor, liability may be incurred as a principal for completion of the required improvements. Thus, the local government may hold the surety to full performance of the defaulted developer's outstanding obligations without regard to the penal sum of the bond.[54] To eliminate the potential risk of liability beyond the face amount of the bond, the surety may attempt to induce the local government unit to complete the improvements for a fixed amount by way of a settlement agreement.[55]

Primarily because of the substantial risk of excess liability that may result if the surety undertakes to complete the improvements for the defaulting developer, sureties most often will elect to rest on the bond and prepare to pay damages up to the stated amount.[56] Unfortunately, this election usually will generate major litigation.[57]

The local governmental unit will succeed in its suit against the surety if it can establish five elements: (1) it had authority to exact improvements from the developer;[58] (2) the developer agreed to complete the improvements;[59] (3) the local government had authority to require the developer to secure a bond;[60] (4) the developer failed to complete the improvements;[61] and (5) the local government was damaged in a reasonably consequential and ascertainable amount.[62]

The surety may interpose a number of defenses based on the above elements or other affirmative defenses: (1) the cause of action has not yet accrued;[63] (2) the limitation period has expired;[64] (3) the government's action is barred for want of prosecution;[65] (4) the surety is discharged because of modification of the underlying agreement;[66] (5) the local government failed to perform a condition precedent to the surety's obligation;[67] (6) the government has accepted the improvements, either expressly,[68] impliedly,[69] or by operation of law;[70] and (7) the bond payment provision constitutes an unenforceable penalty.[71]

Cash Escrow

In its simplest form, the cash escrow consists of the developer's deposit with an escrow agent of a specified sum of money, usually the estimated cost of the required improvements. If the improvements are completed by the developer and accepted by the government, the agent releases the escrowed funds to the developer. If, however, the developer fails to complete the improvements as required, the agent releases the funds to the government.[72] The basic cash escrow may be as onerous to the developer as if it were required to construct all of the improvements in advance of any sales,[73] because it results in that portion of the project being double-funded since the work still must be paid for as it progresses.[74] Accordingly, parties have adopted various adaptations in an attempt to alleviate some of the more burdensome aspects of cash escrows.

The first variation consists of periodic releases of portions of the escrowed funds as the project progresses.[75] To that extent, the project will be double-funded at least in an amount equal to the amount of each release.[76] Nevertheless, provided that the government acts with all due dispatch in inspecting, approving, and accepting completed improvements, and in ordering the release of funds, the amount of the double-funding may be limited.[77]

The government must take care that it does not permit the release of too great a portion of the escrowed funds. This is particularly important when the total deposit is less than the value of all improvements, when the cost of labor and material is escalating rapidly, or when the value of the improvements is underestimated at the outset. In the event of the developer's default, the government may find itself with an escrow fund that is insufficient to cover the cost of completing the required improvement and yet be unable to withhold building permits and/or certificates of occupancy.[78]

Cash deposits ordinarily constitute part of the proceeds of the development loan.[79] Accordingly, in a second variation, the lender itself may be induced to segregate or set aside funds from the loan proceeds in an amount sufficient to complete the required improvements. The lender should issue a set-aside letter to the local government agreeing to segregate funds and to disburse these funds only after the developer has completed the improvements and the government has approved and accepted them.[80] The lender's premature release of funds prior to the government's approval of the release may result in the lender's liability to the government in the event of the developer's default.[81]

Despite the deficiencies of the set-aside method of securing the completion of required improvements, this method actually may be structured to the lender's advantage. The lender may rely on state statutes requiring that the government inspect completed improvements and approve or disapprove the release of set-aside funds within a reasonable time after the developer's request.[82] This tends to increase cash flow to the project and minimizes the double-funding overlap problem.[83]

Finally, the lender may retain the option to complete the required improvements if the developer defaults.[84] Although this can entail the expenditure of funds in excess of the set-aside amount, it may be justified as an effort to enhance the value and marketability of the collateral.

Personal and Real Property Escrow

Personal and real property escrow is structured in much the same way as a cash escrow. If the developer defaults, the local government gains access to the personal and real property and can sell the property to raise the funds necessary to complete the required improvements. Among the various types of property that the government can escrow are stocks and bonds, personal property such as the developer's equipment, and the developer's real property.[85]

The property escrow involves some major drawbacks. Valuation of real property, equipment, and personal property is uncertain at best.[86] Serious problems also arise with the small or undercapitalized developer who uses the land to finance the project from the original owner, the development lender, and the contractor for the development's public improvements.[87] Release of lots may be required, which often leaves the poorest lots left as the basis for the government's security.

Letter of Credit

Most local governments also have the authority to accept letters of credit as security.[88] Although letters of credit offer significant advantages over other security devices, they are not widely used except for the standby letter of credit.[89] In any letter of credit transaction, three separate and distinct relationships exist. First, there is the underlying subdivision improvement agreement between the developer and the local government. Second, there is the agreement between the developer and a bank for the issuance of the credit. Finally, there is the agreement or undertaking of the bank to pay the amount of the credit to the local government upon the satisfaction of certain conditions.[90]

In recent years, the letter of credit has been used in a guarantee or standby role to reduce the risk of nonperformance of a wide array of contractual obligations. In this context, the standby letter of credit differs significantly from the commercial letter of credit because the credit is intended to be presented for payment only if the developer under the underlying agreement fails to perform its obligation.[91]

The usefulness of the standby letter of credit stems from its most important and unique characteristic: the undertaking of the bank is absolutely independent of the underlying agreement between the developer and the local government.[92] As a result, the beneficiary of the credit, the local government, is entitled to collect on the credit prior to pursuing its claim against the developer and irrespective of the local government's ability to demonstrate the existence of a default or compensable injury.[93] The standby letter of credit provides a number of advantages over the surety bond and other forms of security. If the credit is to be effective as a security device, however, it is essential that it be clearly understood, its terms adequately outlined in the underlying agreement, and, ultimately, that it be carefully drafted and closely monitored.

Upon the developer's default on his obligation to complete subdivision improvements, the local government's primary objective is to collect on the credit. Collection ordinarily is a simple procedure requiring only that the local government present its draft or demand together with documentation in compliance with the terms of the credit.[94] Neither the Uniform Commercial Code (U.C.C.) nor the Uniform Customs and Practice (U.C.P.) permits an assignment of the right to draw under a letter of credit unless the credit is expressly designated as assignable or transferable.[95]

This restriction is doubly important in the case of a standby credit, where documentation is generally limited to an affidavit certifying the existence of the developer's default.[96] Thus, a prudent developer ordinarily would insist that his standby credit not be assignable, since his only protection against an unwarranted draw is the good faith of the local government and the accuracy of its affidavit.[97]

In most circumstances the local government will have no need to assign proceeds of the letter of credit. If the local government elects, after the developer's default, to complete improvements itself, the local government itself will draw on the credit and retain the proceeds prior to disbursement as the work progresses. The right to assign proceeds is important only when an unsuccessful project is taken over by a subsequent developer. The local government may then find it desirable to assign the proceeds of the credit to the subsequent developer as an incentive to undertake to complete the improvements in a timely manner.[98]

As a security device, a revocable letter of credit is worthless because the bank may revoke it at any time prior to payment, perhaps even after the local government has presented its draft. Thus, the underlying subdivision improvement agreement should expressly require delivery of an irrevocable letter of credit. Moreover, in view of the presumed revocability under the U.C.P., the credit itself should clearly state that it is irrevocable.[99]

The second and most common way that a credit can be terminated prior to payment is by expiration. Since subdivision improvement agreements typically provide that the required improvements be installed, inspected, and approved within a definite period of time, the credit usually recites a specific expiration date that coincides with or follows shortly after the completion date designated in the underlying agreement.[100] Time is of the essence in letter of credit transactions, and the expiration date will be strictly enforced.[101]

As a security device, the standby letter of credit offers a number of advantages over other forms of security. Because the credit represents the independent obligation of the issuer, the local government has the benefit of the substituted credit of the issuer, presumably a lending institution with financial resources far in excess of those of the developer.[102] To some extent, then, the local government need not rely so heavily on the creditworthiness of the developer. By requiring that the credit be issued by a financial institution, the local government shifts some of the burden of assessing the developer's creditworthiness from itself to the issuer. Moreover a standby letter of credit is generally much less expensive and easier to obtain than a surety bond.[103] Ordinarily, the developer is a customer of the issuing bank, and the issuing bank often is the lender of the development loan. Because the developer/bank relationship already exists, the bank's cost of issuing the credit is minimal.[104]

The standby credit also is advantageous because it provides liquidity for the local government's claim for damages in the event of the developer's default.[105] Upon presentation of its draft, along with any required supporting documentation, the local government can convert its claim against the developer into cash, thereby providing the necessary funds to complete the improvements. Because of the independent nature of the bank's obligation, the bank will be obligated to honor the credit irrespective of any claims or defenses that the developer may have in connection with the underlying agreement.[106]

The standby credit is a particularly useful device for shifting the burden of litigating the underlying issues without the benefit of the contested funds.[107] Assume, for example, that the developer had given his unsecured promise to construct $1 million worth of required improvements and then failed to construct any improvements at all. Upon default, the local government would have a cause of action against the developer for breach of promise. During the months or years it may take for the lawsuit to wind its way through the courts, the developer (or his successor) would have the use of the $1 million that should have been used to construct the improvements. The local government would be able to complete the improvements itself only at public expense. By agreeing to provide a letter of credit, the developer has implicitly agreed that the local government may call upon the funds even before it is required to prove that the developer is in default.[108] Thus, the local government has the use of those funds during the time it takes to sort out all the disputes connected with the underlying subdivision improvement agreement. This increases its bargaining strength during settlement negotiations.[109]

CASE LAW CONCERNING SUBDIVISION IMPROVEMENT AGREEMENTS AND GUARANTEES

The government may be required to complete improvements at its own expense if the developer fails to complete the project and security is not obtained. One court has held that a local government is not free to complete improvements and assess the costs to lot owners when state law requires completion of improvements or a bond before final approval.[110]

When the local government fails to obtain a bond to secure performance by the developer or obtains an inadequate bond, residents in the subdivision may be able to force the government to construct or complete the improvements.[111] The government may not assess the costs of improvements against lot owners where they would be paying for the improvements twice—once through the purchase of the home and second to repay the government.[112]

Although no cases exist in which citizens successfully have required a local government to exercise its rights against a developer or surety after a default, one case does report that citizens successfully forced a local government to complete improvements after a default by a bonded developer.[113]

When the government accepts a bond or other security to guarantee the completion of subdivision improvements, the government may declare a default at the end of the specified period if the improvements are not completed[114] or are otherwise defective.[115] It is not necessary that the developer and the government enter into an underlying written contract before the duty of the surety will arise because, on the basis of the bond, the courts will find an implied in fact contract.[116] If the developer has abandoned the project and cannot under any circumstances complete improvements within the permitted time, the government may declare an anticipatory breach.[117]

A preliminary plat approval places no obligation upon the developer to complete the development or any required improvements. The duty to complete improvements ordinarily arises with final approval.[118] The requirement, however, that the developer commence activities before the duty to complete improvements arises is not a condition implied in law.[119] Rather, the duty is implied in fact, based on the agreement of the parties, or is express, based on state laws or local ordinances.[120]

The local government need not complete improvements before it commences an action on a bond or other security, since the purpose of the bond or other security arrangement is to protect the government from completing improvements at its own expense.[121] The government should not be forced to spend general revenues or incur indebtedness prior to bringing an action on the security agreement.[122]

Generally, the courts hold that the bond securing completion of subdivision improvements is in the nature of an indemnification bond; it is not a penal bond that will permit the government to claim the entire bond proceeds irrespective of the costs of completion.[123] The measure of the government's damages constitutes the reasonable cost of completing the improvements itself or through a third party.[124] If no development has taken place, the developer may be able to assert that the government has no need to complete improvements for a nonexistent subdivision.[125] Occasionally, the agreement with the developer,[126] the local ordinance, or state law limits the obligation to complete improvements to a degree commensurate with actual development.[127]

Unless the parties agree otherwise, the liability of the developer is not limited to the amount of the bond, a result based either on state statutory law[128] or common law.[129] The bond secures only the developer's promise to complete improvements and, if the developer is solvent, the government can collect the full amount of damages after breach. On the other hand, the government is limited to the face amount of the bond if it brings an action on the bond.[130] The government, however, may pursue its rights against either the principal or the surety because the principal always remains liable on the bond.[131]

Subdivision improvement guarantees have several purposes: protection of the community at large from the cost of completing subdivision improvements, protection of homebuyers in the subdivision from incomplete or inadequate improvements, and protection of neighbors of the subdivision that may be injured if improvements are incomplete or inadequate. A fourth group that often seeks protection from subdivision improvement guarantees includes contractors, subcontractors, suppliers, and laborers that work on the subdivision. Generally, only the government may maintain a cause of action on an improvement guarantee. A number of courts, however, have permitted the government to assign either its cause of action or any proceeds that it might collect under the guarantee to a third party when the third party completes subdivision improvements.

A third-party suit on the subdivision improvement guarantee is predicated on the theory that the local government and developer intended the guarantee to benefit the third party. Consequently, the third party should be entitled to sue as a third-party beneficiary. Lot owners and homeowners in the subdivision retain the strongest argument for bringing suit as intended beneficiaries of the improvement guarantee. Despite rhetoric that may give lot owners and homeowners encouragement,[132] nearly all courts have held that consumers in a subdivision may not maintain an action as third-party beneficiaries of a subdivision improvement guarantee.[133] A lot owner's inability to maintain a cause of action on a bond applies even though the bond states that it is for the purpose of protecting consumers in the subdivision; the courts hold that the government acts beyond its statutory authority when it attempts to create a cause of action in third parties.[134]

The courts' reasoning is not always clear in these cases. In *City of University City ex rel. Mackey v. Frank Miceli & Son Realty & Building Co.*,[135] the Missouri Supreme Court based its decision on the fact that third parties had no right under a performance bond[136] when, in fact, the actual reason for denying recovery was that the nature of the injury fell outside the scope of the bond.[137] In *Fleck v. National Property Management*, the Utah Supreme Court determined that the injury suffered by the plaintiff was not foreseeable and, therefore, denied recovery.[138]

In *Town of Ogden v. Earl R. Howarth & Sons, Inc.*,[139] a New York trial court granted a right of action to a lot owner as a third-party beneficiary of a contract between the developer and the local government. The court reasoned that the lot owner could be brought within the class of persons that would receive a "special benefit" from the contract. The court took notice "of the all too often evidenced difficulty of purchasers of homes in exacting fair compliance with building contracts by builder-vendors."[140]

Laborers, materialmen, and subcontractors have fared no better in attempting to collect under a subdivision improvement guarantee. These parties have no right of action as third-party beneficiaries of a performance bond[141] or a combined performance and payment bond when the major purpose of the bond is to secure performance.[142] Courts also have held that subcontractors are not entitled to collect under a letter of credit[143] or a cash escrow agreement.[144] The fact that the guarantee may contain language implying that third parties have a cause of action provides no help because the courts either construe the language narrowly[145] or hold that the government's action creating the right constitutes an ultra vires act.[146]

When a local government receives a cash escrow from a subdivider and the government rejects the subdivision proposal, one court has held that a judgment creditor can attach the subdivider's funds.[147] That result may mean that a local government should exercise extreme care when it returns any cash or a security deposit to a developer if a third party has attached the cash or security.[148]

One of the strongest cases for permitting third parties to recover under a bond or other security occurs when the third party has completed subdivision improvements after the developer's default. The situation differs from a third-party beneficiary's claim because the third party acquires the cause of action held by the government. *Morro Palisades Co. v. Hartfort Accident & Indemnity Co.*[149] is a leading case often cited for the proposition that a third party cannot recover under an assignment of the government's cause of action following the developer's default. In *Morro*, however, the evidence revealed that the third party had never actually completed the improvements and that it never intended to do so.[150] The court recited the general rule that the performance bond runs in favor of the government and any action on the bond must be brought in the name of the government.[151]

Two courts confronted by an assignment of the government's cause of action have upheld the assignments and distinguished *Morro*.[152] In both cases, the courts stressed the fact that the government made the assignments to fulfill the purposes of the performance bond—completion of subdivision improvements.[153]

To avoid the problem of failure to bring suit in the name of the government, several courts have considered whether a government may assign any proceeds that it obtains in exchange for the assignee's completion of the improvements. The courts are split on the authority of the government to make such an assignment.[154] On the one hand, one can argue that if the government can complete performance by employing a third party to construct the improvements, it should be able to assign bond proceeds to that party.[155] On the other hand, courts may perceive that the assignee, who usually has taken over completion of the development after a foreclosure or accepted a deed in lieu of foreclosure, should be required to complete the improvements or post bond just as any other developer must do.[156] When the purchaser of the development replats the property, denial of the assignment may be proper;[157] but, if the purchaser merely does what the original developer was obligated to do, it should be able to receive the bond proceeds.[158]

A similar problem occurs when a subsequent developer completes improvements that were the obligation of the first developer and then intervenes in the government's action against the developer. In *Commonwealth ex rel. Pennsylvania Securities Commission v. Reliance Development Corp.*,[159] the Pennsylvania Superior Court held that the subsequent developer was entitled to recover from the cash escrow to recoup the cost of completing improvements that had been its predecessor's obligation. In *Hellam Township v. DiCicco*,[160] the court faced a similar situation only two years later, but in *DiCicco* it was unclear whether the subsequent developer would complete the improvements.[161] Thus, the court held that the surety could not reopen a confessed judgment on the ground that the township would be unjustly enriched if the subsequent developer completed the improvements.[162] In fact, the court hinted that the surety might be unable to reopen the judgment even if the subsequent developer who had been obligated to complete the improvements would not be unjustly enriched.[163]

DEDICATION OF IMPROVEMENTS

Section 4.1 of the Model Regulations requires the subdivider to dedicate streets, easements, parks, and other public use areas, as well as public improvements, to the government. Section 3.5(1)(f) requires the developer to attach to its application for final approval *an irrevocable offer of dedication* of all streets, municipal uses, utilities, parks, and easements, with the dedication to be recorded in the recorder of deeds office. The final plat is also to be marked with such a notation. Escrow deeds to all such lands are required to be delivered to the local government with a title policy showing clear title. These procedures are vital for the protection of the local government and should be complied with strictly.

Due to the stringencies of the common law rule on the dedication of land, a local government should require an irrevocable offer to dedicate land that permits a subsequent acceptance by the local government while the offer remains open.[164] Statutory dedication, on the other hand, usually provides that the recording of a plat makes the dedication effective without acceptance by the local government[165] or inferred by slight acts.[166] Because the local government does not want to receive such lands or to be immediately responsible for the provision of services to or maintenance of dedicated lands or improvements until the developer has completed construction of public improvements, the Model Regulations require that the governing body must accept an offer to dedicate by legislative act.[167] Dedication prior to construction of the improvements may require that the local government place the public improvement project out for competitive bid and that it act as the financial agent in the process.[168] The government should require an express offer of dedication because, even though an offer to dedicate is usually inferred under a common law dedication where the plat shows streets and public places,[169] it may be dangerous to rely on such an inference because the law requires an *intent* to dedicate.[170]

Therefore the Model Regulations require both an express offer of dedication and delivery of a warranty deed in escrow to establish the offer beyond question.[171] The offer of dedication must be made irrevocable, present, and continuing[172] because an offer of dedication, unless irrevocable, may be revoked at any time prior to acceptance by the local government.[173] The Model also provides that the offer of dedication can be accepted only by the local government's governing body.[174] The planning commission's approval of the subdivision plat does not constitute or imply acceptance[175] and the plat should be endorsed with appropriate notes to this effect. The clearest evidence of acceptance of the dedication should be a resolution or ordinance of the governing body.[176]

Recordation of the irrevocable offer of dedication will prevent the rights of third parties from intervening as innocent purchasers for value without notice of the dedication offer.[177] A title policy is required with the application for final approval to assure that title is clear in the developer.[178] The title company should deliver a preliminary report at time of delivery of the deed and a final policy with an updated search at the time of the governing body's acceptance. The title search will reveal whether there are any mechanic's liens or other unacceptable encumbrances on the property prior to acceptance. The subdivision improvement agreement should address this problem and provide the government with a remedy if the developer cannot convey clear title. In some states, a mechanic's lien may attach to land even though it is filed after the sale by the developing owner (or transfer to the local government); therefore, it is incumbent on the local government attorney to insist on affidavits and releases from all contractors and subcontractors of the developer before recommending acceptance of the offer to dedicate.

The Model Regulations require the delivery of deeds into escrow.[179] This is an important protective device for the local government. In the event of subsequent transfers of the subdivided property, the escrow deed can be recorded upon the government's acceptance and will be valid in view of the recorded irrevocable offer of dedication. It also protects against the disappearance of the original owner at the time of acceptance, death, or legal disability to transfer land. Upon the condition of the local government's acceptance of the offer of dedication being satisfied, the deed is deemed to have been delivered at the time of its first delivery to the local government.[180] A delivery of the deed to the local government as escrowee is generally permissible,[181] but if the common law in the applicable state forbids the government, which is the grantee, from acting as the escrow agent,[182] the title company can serve that function.

FEDERAL LAW RELATING TO SUBDIVISION IMPROVEMENTS

The federal government has enacted a variety of consumer protection laws designed to assist the purchaser of lots in a subdivision.[183] [184] The Federal Securities Act of 1933 was the model upon which the Interstate Land Sales Full Disclosure Act was patterned.[185] Under the Securities Act, full disclosure of all material facts relating to a public offering of securities must be made to all prospective purchasers. Because the Securities Act is designed to protect purchasers of securities, its application to subdivision purchasers is limited to land sales classified as either on "investment contract" or some form of third-party profit-making device.[186]

While the term "investment contract" is undefined by the Securities Act, the U.S. Supreme Court has defined it as ". . . a contract, transaction or scheme whereby a person invests his money in a common enterprise *and is led to expect profits solely from the efforts of the promoter or third party.*"[187] A land developer is not subject to the securities laws merely by agreeing to perform minimal managerial functions. Rather, the test is "essential managerial efforts which affect the failure or success of the enterprise."[188]

The best known federal consumer protection legislation relating to real estate subdivision is the Interstate Land Sales Full Disclosure Act.[189] In the Full Disclosure Act, Congress reflected the view that a comprehensive statutory scheme was needed to protect consumers who purchased real estate sold in interstate markets.[190] The regulations implementing the Full Disclosure Act are located at 24 C.F.R. 1700.1-.100 (1987). The Full Disclosure Act was enacted as part of the Housing and Urban Development Act of 1968,[191] to combat the widespread fraud that existed in the land sales industry in the early 1960s.[192]

The Full Disclosure Act applies to "any land which is located in any state or in a foreign country, which is divided or is proposed to be divided into fifty or more lots, whether contiguous or not, for the purpose of sale or lease as part of a common promotional plan."[193] Section 1703(a)(1) requires anyone[194] who uses an instrument of interstate commerce to sell, lease, advertise, or offer for sale or lease lots in a subdivision either (1) to register the land with the Department of Housing and Urban Development (HUD) and furnish the purchaser or lessee an extensive property report prior to execution of any contract, or (2) to fit within one of the statute's exemptions.[195]

The Full Disclosure Act provides for two series of exemptions. The first series provides exemption from the entire act.[196] For example, the Full Disclosure Act does not apply to subdivisions containing fewer than 50 lots or to the sale or lease of lots to any person who acquires the lots for the purpose of engaging in the business of constructing residential, commercial, or industrial buildings or for the purpose of resale or lease of the lots to persons engaged in that business.[197]

The second series provides exemptions from the Full Disclosure Act's registration and disclosure provisions, but not from the antifraud provisions.[198] The registration and disclosure requirements do not apply to the following: (1) the sale of lots in a subdivision containing fewer than 50 lots; (2) the sale of lots if, beginning with the first sale in the subdivision, no more than 12 lots are sold or leased in the subsequent 12-month period and, thereafter, in any subsequent 12-month period, the sale or lease of the first 12 lots remains exempt as long as no more than 12 lots were sold or leased in each prior 12-month period; (3) the sale of lots in a subdivision consisting of noncontiguous parts if each noncontiguous part contains not more than 20 lots and if the purchaser or lessee (or spouse) has made a prior personal, on-the-lot inspection; (4) the sale or lease of lots in a subdivision in which each lot is at least 20 acres; (5) the sale or lease of lots in a subdivision if the lots are restricted to single-family residences and if a municipal or county government specifies minimum standards for the development of the subdivision and the subdivision meets those standards; (6) the sale or lease of lots in a subdivision if the developer is engaged in an intrastate sales or leasing operation, the purchaser or lessee (or spouse) has made a personal, on-the-lot inspection, the lot is free and clear of liens, encumbrances, and adverse claims and the contract contains several specific provisions; and (7) the sale and lease of lots in a subdivision containing fewer than 300 lots if the purchaser's or lessee's principal residence is within the same standard metropolitan statistical area, the lot is free and clear of liens, the purchaser or lessee (or spouse) has made a personal, on-the-lot inspection, and the developer provides certain assurances.[199]

Neither series of exemptions is applicable when the method of sale, lease, or other disposition of land is adopted for the purpose of evading the Full

Disclosure Act.[200] The eligibility for the exemptions, however, is self-executing, which means that a developer is not required to obtain HUD approval to take advantage of the exemption.[201] The developer, however, may request an advisory opinion from the Secretary of HUD as to whether an offering qualifies for an exemption.[202] In addition, the HUD secretary may issue a no action letter when the sale or lease of lots is subject to the registration and disclosure requirements, but the particular circumstances of the sale do not justify the need for affirmative action to enforce the act to protect public interest or prospective purchasers.[203] The issuance of a no action letter, however, does not affect any of the purchaser's rights under the act and it will not limit future action by the secretary if it is later decided that affirmative action is necessary to protect public interest or prospective purchasers.[204] If the developer elects to take any exemption, it is responsible for maintaining records to demonstrate that it has met the exemption requirement.[205]

In addition to the statutory exemptions outlined above, the Full Disclosure Act expressly authorizes the HUD secretary to exempt from the act

> any subdivisions or any lots in a subdivision, if he finds that the enforcement of the . . . [act] with respect to such subdivision or lots is not necessary in the public interest and for the protection of purchasers by reason of the small amount involved or the limited character of the public offering.[206]

Pursuant to this authority, the secretary has exempted the following transactions: (1) the sale of lots for less than $100 each; (2) the sale of lots to a bona fide land sales business; and (3) the sale of a lot to a person who owns an improved contiguous lot.[207]

In addition to the Full Disclosure Act, many states have statutes that regulate the sale of in-state and/or out-of-state land,[208] and have executed agreements with the Office of Interstate Land Sales Regulation (OILSR) to coordinate the registration requirements under the federal and state laws.[209] The Full Disclosure Act also provides that the HUD secretary may certify a state for equivalency under the federal registration program.[210] HUD has certified five states—Arizona, California, Florida, Georgia, and Minnesota.[211] The effect of certification is that a developer which complies with a certified state's law does not have to file a statement of record with HUD but only a copy of the state's disclosure report.[212] In order to certify a state, "a determination must be made that the state has either disclosure requirements or substantive requirements, or a combination of the two for 'in-state' subdivisions, and administers them so as to offer purchasers equivalent protection in those matters for which the federal law requires disclosure."[213]

The Full Disclosure Act required HUD to establish a program of interstate land sales registrations.[214] Consequently, unless the developer is eligible for an exemption, it must satisfy complex and comprehensive registration and disclosure requirements. Specifically, it is unlawful for a developer to sell or lease a lot in a subdivision unless a statement of record is in effect, thereby registering the land with HUD, and the purchaser or lessee has received a property report.[215] Failure to comply with the property report requirement enables the purchaser or lessee to revoke the contract within two years from the date of signing.[216] While the statute appears to require two separate documents, a statement of record and a property report, the regulations have made the property report a part of the statement of record, thereby combining the two documents.[217] In furtherance of its responsibilities, HUD created the Office of Interstate Land Sales Registration.[218]

The Full Disclosure Act also contains antifraud provisions that prohibit unlawful and misleading sales practices and that require certain consumer protection terms in contracts between developers and buyers or lessees. Under the antifraud provisions, a developer or agent may not represent that the developer will provide roads, sewers, water, gas, electric service, or recreational amenities without stipulating in the contract for the provision of these amenities.[219] In addition, the statute prohibits the use of the property report for any promotional purposes before the effective date of the statement of record and then requires the use of the property report in its entirety.[220]

The impact of the Full Disclosure Act remains somewhat limited. "The developer can still sell land under water if he discloses it."[221] Disclosure acts impose only a duty of disclosure, not a duty to cure the defects relating to the land once the disclosure requirements have been met.[222]

STATE STATUTORY AND JUDICIAL LAW

Virtually every state has enacted its own "Blue Sky" securities laws.[223] In construing these laws, the states are not required to adhere to the federal tests and in fact some have not, opting to afford increased protection.[224] The purchaser of out-of-state land is now far more protected than in the past.[225] Eight states classify out-of-state subdivision offerings as securities.[226] In addition to classifying foreign real estate as a security, some of the better regulations will provide that there be onsite inspection by the appropriate commission, and further, that performance bonds be put up to ensure that the necessary amenities are provided.[227]

A state Blue Sky law regulates the sale of securities in order to protect the public from deceptive or fraudulent practices. The states have generally construed certain real estate transactions to be a security, when, as in the federal law, there exists an overall scheme or plan in which money is invested with the expectation that the investor will receive a return on the investment from the effort provided by a third party or promoter. In interpreting whether a transaction is a security, the courts look through form to substance and consider the facts and circumstances surrounding the transaction to ascertain the true intent of the parties. Blue

Sky laws usually fall into four classifications: (1) violations amounting to security fraud (no licensing or qualifying by meeting minimum standards exist under this type of Blue Sky law);[228] (2) statutes concerned with the licensing of dealers but not providing specific requirements for the security;[229] (3) minimum requirements for the security involved;[230] and (4) combinations of (2) and (3) above.[231]

The states have also entered the field of consumer protection involving the disclosure of credit terms. The most notable example of state action is the Uniform Consumer Credit Code (UCCC or the U-triple C]. Like the Truth in Lending Act,[232] it covers real estate transactions involving the extension of credit and offers a right of rescission in the credit sale of an interest in land. The borrower must be purchasing primarily for personal, family, household, or agricultural purposes. Should the creditor violate the disclosure provisions of the UCCC, liability is created to the buyer for twice the amount of the credit service or loan finance charge plus reasonable attorney fees. The liability cannot be less than $100 or more than $1,000.[233]

Finally, the judicial doctrine of caveat emptor[234] has been slowly eroded away by the states through the use of judicial theories of fraud, express and implied warranty, negligence, and strict liability to provide injunctive relief or compensation for the unwary home purchaser.[235] The implied warranty of habitability has been extended and applied both to the newly constructed house (the residence itself), water wells, septic tanks, and other improvements immediately supporting the residences,[236] but it must constitute a serious defect affecting a vital living element of the home.[237] The warranty is usually limited to the first purchaser even if the second purchaser is a city.[238]

Section 4.7 of the Model Regulations attempts to integrate local subdivision regulation with federal and state consumer protection laws. Because Article 4 concerns assurances that the subdivider will create a quality subdivision, it is appropriate for the local government to insist that the subdivider be in compliance with consumer protection laws before final plat approval is granted and that the subdivider stay in compliance with those laws as a condition precedent to the issuance of building permits or certificates of occupancy. On the other hand, the government should be careful not to interfere with the issuance of permits or certificates unless a violation of law is proved. Otherwise, the subdivider may successfully sue the government for violating its constitutional rights.[239]

NOTES

1. *See*, CALLIES & FREILICH, CASES AND MATERIALS ON LAND USE, Chap. 4D "Requirements for Internal Subdivision Improvements," (West 1986, Supp. 1991). *See also* Brous v. Smith, 106 N.E.2d 503 (N.Y. 1952) (on-site improvements); Divan Builders, Inc. v. Planning Bd. of Wayne Township, 334 A.2d 30 (N.J. 1975); Ghen v. Piasecki, 410 A.2d 708 (N.J. Super. App. Div. 1980); CPW Investments #2 v. Troy, 401 N.W.2d 864 (Mich. App. 1986); Majers v. Shining Mountains, 750 P.2d 449 (Mont. 1988).

2. A number of states have passed "deemed approved" statutes that require applications for approval of a subdivision plat within specified periods of time to avoid the hardship of long delay and expense. *See* PA. STAT. § 10508(3), N.Y. TOWN LAW § 274-a(2). Even in the absence of a "deemed approved" statute, the hearing and decision must be held and rendered within a "reasonable" period of time. Paladac Realty Trust v. Rockland Planning Comm., 541 A.2d 919 (Me. 1988). These statutes will not be applied where the delay was caused by a valid interim development ordinance pending general plan amendment which imposed a moratorium on plat approvals. Dune Assoc., Inc. v. Anderson, 500 N.Y.S. 2d 741 (A.D. 2d Dept. 1986); *but see* Turnpike Woods, Inc. v. Town of Stony Point, 514 N.E.2d 380 (N.Y. 1987). (The New York Court of Appeals held that the portion of the local law which purported to suspend under an emergency moratorium, for six months, a town planning board's duty to act on an application for a subdivision's final plat approval was ineffective to supersede the state's town law which required that the planning board act within 45 days.)

3. L. Kendig, *Performance Guarantees*, LAND USE L. & ZONING DIG. 4 (Feb. 1983).

4. *See* Friends of the Pine Bush v. Planning Bd. of the City of Albany, 450 N.Y.S. 2d 966 (A.D.3d, 1982) (where the improvements are not installed by the developer prior to final approval, the planning commission has no discretion to waive the requirement of posting a performance bond).

5. Model Regulations, § 4.1(1). Compare N.Y. TOWN LAW § 277 (McKinney 1990); N.J. STAT. ANN. § 40A:5-16 (West 1967). Section 14 of the Standard City Planning Enabling Act ("SPEA") (U.S. Dept. of Commerce, 1928) provides: "In lieu of such improvements and utilities prior to the final approval of the plat, the commission may accept a bond with surety to secure to the municipality the actual construction and installation of such improvements . . ."

6. Marks and Masters Constr. v. Western Casualty & Surety, 684 S.W.2d 863 (Mo. Ct. App. 1984); Board of Supervisors v. Ecology One, 245 S.E.2d 425 (Va. 1978); McKenzie v. Arthur McIntosh & Co., 200 N.E.2d 138 (Ill. App. Ct. 1964); Pennyton Homes, Inc. v. Planning Bd., 197 A.2d 870 (N.J. Super. 1964); Ragghianti v. Sherwin, 16 Cal. Rptr. 583 (Cal. App. 1961); University City *ex rel.* Mackey v. Frank Miceli and Sons Realty and Bldg. Co., 347 S.W.2d 131 (Mo. 1961); City of Buena Park v. Boyar, 8 Cal. Rptr. 674 (Cal. App. 1960); Town of Stoneham v. Savelo, 170 N.E.2d 417 (Mass. 1960); Enola v. Wendt, 333 P.2d 498

(Cal. App. 1959); Morro Palisades Co. v. Hartford Accident & Indem. Co., 340 P.2d 628 (Cal. 1959); County of Los Angeles v. Margulis, 44 P.2d 608 (Cal. App. 1935). *See generally* Shultz & Kelley, *Subdivision Improvement Requirements and Guarantees: A Primer*, 28 J. URB. & CONTEMP. LAW 1 (1985); L. Kendig, *Performance Guarantees*, LAND USE L. & ZONING DIG. 4 (Feb. 1983); B. Rogal, *Subdivision Improvement Guarantees* (Planning Advisory Service Report No. 298, 1974); LAUTNER, SUBDIVISION REGULATIONS: AN ANALYSIS OF LAND SUBDIVISION CONTROL PRACTICES (Public Administration Service, 1941).

American Society of Planning Officials, *Performance Bonds For the Installation of Subdivision Improvements* 24 (Planning Advisory Service Report No. 48, March 1958):

> The bonds are most easily obtained in those localities where the market for new lots is good and are most easily obtained by developers whose credit is high and whose experience is good. Difficulty in getting performance bonds is in direct proportion to the risk involved, either because of the uncertainty of the market or the poor credit or lack of experience of the developer. The performance bond does serve a useful purpose in reducing the cost of land development, where there is the sensible requirement that subdivided land must be improved. The bond serves to lessen cost of tied-up capital, but it can only do this if the city exerts every effort to expedite subdivision approval and to release security promptly.

7. In order to constrain local government action and prevent an unconstitutional delegation of power, reasonable relational standards should exist for determining what improvements the local government can require. In the absence of standards it is improper to deny plat approval on grounds not explicit in the subdivision regulations. Southern Cooperative Development Fund v. Driggers, 696 F.2d 1347 (11th Cir. 1983). Similarly, unreasonable or unrelated requirements may be found to result in unconstitutional action, Parks v. Watson, 716 F.2d 646 (9th Cir. 1983) (unreasonable), McKain v. Toledo City Planning Comm'n, 270 N.E.2d 370 (Ohio App. 1971) (unrelated). Occasionally, state statutes specify the improvements that local governments can require. *See, e.g.*, MONT. CODE ANN. § 76-3-501 (1983) (lists numerous types of requirements that local government may require). In other instances, the state grants broad authority to the local government. *See, e.g.*, NEV. REV. STAT. § 278.462.2 (1983) (local government may require such improvements as are "reasonably necessary"). Most often the local government must infer the list of permissible improvements from the purposes of the state statute. *See, e.g.,* N.M. Stat. Ann. § 3-19-6.B(4) (1978); Wash. Rev. Code Ann. § 58.17.110 (1983).

8. The term "off-site improvement" is used in two different ways, off the subdivision site or off the lots in the subdivision. For purposes of this article, off-site improvements refer to those improvements not within the physical boundaries of the subdivision. *See id.*; Note, *Subdivision Exactions: A Review of Judicial Standards,* 25 Wash. U.J. Urb. & Contemp. L. 269, 276-77 (1983). The model incorporates a provision to reimburse the developer for off-site improvements with excess capacity over the actual need for facilities generated by the subdivision. *See, e.g.,* Summit County, Utah, Development Code ch. 13.5(13) (1982) (requiring easements for local public utilities).

9. Several local governments have adopted provisions to reimburse the developer for off-site improvements that others will use or for excess capacity improvements, such as a water main. *See* Provo, Utah, Subdivision Regulations § 15.18.040 (1978). *See* Callies & Freilich, Cases and Materials on Land Use, Chap. 4, "Internal Subdivision Improvements" at 347 (West 1986):

> A particular problem is created by the need for oversized facilities to handle future growth. If a development is the first to develop within a planning area, drainage or sewerage basin, it may be required to provide larger sized facility or excess capacity to handle the future development in the area. Without providing for equitable distribution of improvement costs one developer will sustain a "wipeout" while later developers will accrue a "windfall." *See* D. Hagman & D. Miscynski, Windfalls For Wipeouts (1978). A major issue in recent years deals with excessive regulatory costs associated with various stages of development, i.e., zoning growth controls, building codes, subdivision requirements and title costs. For an interesting article, *see* Burchell & Listokin, The Impact of Local Government Regulations on Housing Costs and Potential Avenues for State Meliorative Measures in America's Housing: Prospects and Problems, (Rutgers University Center for Urban Policy Research, 1980). Off-site improvements may be required if the subdivision regulations authorize denial of subdivision approval because of lack of adequate public facilities to serve the subdivision. Nollan v. California Coastal Comm'n, 483 U.S. 825 (1987); Garipay v. Town of Hanover, 351 A.2d 64 (N.H. 1976); Pearson Kent Corp. v. Bear, 271 N.E.2d 218 (N.Y. 1971); Village Square No. 1, Inc. v. Crow-Frederick Retail Ltd. Partner-

ship, 551 A.2d 471 (Md. 1989) (an ordinance which requires the party desiring off-site public facilities to pay the cost of extending them does not deny equal protection despite the fact that other adjoining property owners may benefit without cost).

10. Colborne v. Corrales, 739 P.2d 972 (N.M. 1987). But the off-site requirements must be explicit in the ordinances, Reed v. Planning & Zoning Comm'n, 544 A.2d 1213 (Conn. 1988) and reasonably related, Unlimited v. Kitsap County, 750 P.2d 651 (Wash. 1988).

11. Friel v. Triangle Oil Co., 542 A.2d 863 (Md. 1988) (planning commission could properly rely on opinions of state agencies with regard to matters peculiarly within their competence). Independence Park, Inc. v. Board of Health, 530 N.E.2d 1235 (Mass. 1988).

12. In Friends of the Pine Bush v. Planning Bd. of the City of Albany, 450 N.Y.S. 2d 966 (A.D.3d, 1982) the court held that while certain improvements may be waived if not necessary to the public health, safety, or welfare, the remainder must be installed prior to final approval or bonded pursuant to statute. No waiver or variance for the statutory requirement of performance guarantees is permissible.

13. *See, e.g.,* N.Y. General City Law § 33 (1982) (authorizing a performance bond sufficient to cover the full cost of improvements required by the planning commission); Ariz. Rev. Stat. Ann. §-9-463.01.C.8 (1983) (requiring the posting of "performance bonds, assurances or such other security as may be appropriate"); or deposit of funds in an escrow account has been deemed within the authority of the Subdivision Control Act. CPW Investments #2 v. Troy, 401 N.W.2d 864 (Mich. App. 1986).

14. *See, e.g.,* Ore. Rev. Stat. § 92.090(4)(b), (5)(b) (1983) (requiring a bond for water improvement and a bond for sewerage improvement). *See also* Seidel, *Housing Costs & Government Regulations* 21 (1978) (Maryland developer required to obtain four bonds).

15. Tuckerman v. Dassler, 121 N.Y.S. 2d 205 (N.Y. Sup. 1953).

16. For an extensive analysis of the rationale needed to declare a default versus extending the agreement, *see* L. Kendig, *Performance Guarantees,* Land Use L. & Zoning Dig. 4 (Feb. 1983).

17. *See, e.g.,* Colo. Rev. Stat. § 30-28-101(11) (1973) (listing variety of assurance methods); N.M. Stat. Ann. § 3-19-6.C (1978) (listing three methods to assure completion of improvements including installation by the government and an assessment of lots).

18. *See* Thornton, Colo., Code 62-13.A (1983); Seidel, *supra* note 14 at 136; the performance bond must be requested before the final plat is approved. McKenzie v. Arthur T. McIntosh & Co., 200 N.E.2d 138 (Ill. App. 1964) (there can be no retroactive opening of a plat to require a performance bond once a plat has been approved).

19. *See, e.g.*, Wasatch County, Utah, Development Code 92 (bond amount determined by the board of county commissioners based on the developer's estimated cost of construction).

20. *Id.* (110 percent); Summit County, Utah, Development Code ch. 13.4(7)(3) (1982) (120 percent).

21. *See, e.g.*, Colo. Rev. Stat. § 30-28-137(1) (1973).

22. *See* Freilich and Levi, *Model Regulations for the Control of Land Subdivision*, 36 Mo. L. Rev. 1, 17-18 (1973). As an alternative to a bond, the local government may retain a percentage of the security after completion of improvements to guard against defects in workmanship. *See* Summit County, Utah, Development Code ch. 13.4(7)(3) (1982) (retaining 10 percent of the land or escrow as security). Maintenance bonds have been upheld as an extension of the requirement of guaranteeing performance. Legion Manor, Inc. v. Township of Wayne, 231 A.2d 201 (N.J. 1967) (approving a maintenance bond equal to 10 percent of the performance bond for all defects in materials and workmanship appearing within three years).

23. *See* Summit County, Utah, Development Code ch. 13.10 (1982) (authorizing reasonable fees). Fees must bear a reasonable relationship to the cost of administration and inspection.

24. *See, e.g.*, Teton County, Wyo., Comprehensive Plan and Implementation Program ch. IV, 4 (1980) (requiring release of security within seven days of inspection if improvements meet standards).

25. Tanner Companies v. Insurance Marketing Servs., Inc., 154 Ariz. 442, 743 P.2d 951 (App. 1987). Subcontractor was not required to file lien in order to recover for its services in improving streets under bond, where applicable ordinance provided that bond could not be released until all claims by laborers and materialmen were paid and thus practical effect of bond and ordinance was to guarantee payment to subcontractor after improvements had been accepted by county.

26. W.S. Dickey Clay Mfg. Co. v. Ferguson Inv. Co., 388 P.2d 300 (Okla. 1963).

27. Rogal, *supra* note 6, at 11.

28. *See, e.g.*, Township of Barnegat v. DCA of N.J., Inc., 437 A.2d 909, 910 (N.J. Super. Ct. App. Div. 1981); Mertz v. Lakatos, 381 A.2d 497, 499 (Pa. Commw. Ct. 1978).

29. The municipality ordinarily will charge an inspection fee of 1 percent to 2 percent of the estimated value of the improvements. *See* Contractors and Builders Ass'n of Pinellas County v. City of Dunedin, 329 So.2d 314 (Fla. 1976) (authorizing administrative charges to cover the reasonable cost of administration or enforcement as being valid regulatory purpose so long as not "greatly in excess of the costs of regulation."). Broward County v. Janis Development Corp., 311 So.2d 371 (Fla. App. 1975) The area of administrative fees is controversial. As noted in Dunedin, reasonable fees imposed for examination and inspection of completion of improvements are properly chargeable to the developer as a valid exercise of the police power. Economy Enterprises Inc. v. Township Comm. of Manalapan, 250 A.2d 139 (N.J. App. 1969). The test is not an exact balance and a reasonable excess will not operate to invalidate the ordinance. Prudential Co-op Realty Co. v. City of Youngstown, 160 N.E. 695 (Ohio 1928); but see National Realty Corp. v. City of Virginia Beach, 163 S.E.2d 154 (Va. 1968) (unauthorized without express statute).

30. *E.g.*, Township of Barnegat v. DCA of N.J., Inc., 437 A.2d 909, 910 (N.J. Super. Ct. App. Div. 1981) (inspection and report must be made within 65 days); Mertz v. Lakatos, 381 A.2d 497, 499 (Pa. Commw. Ct. 1978) (inspection and report must be made within 40 days).

31. A subdivider who has made an offer of dedication and has sold lots in the subdivision to which the dedication is related cannot withdraw the offer, notwithstanding that the municipality has not yet accepted the offer. Foreal Homes, Inc. v. Muttontown, 512 N.Y.S. 2d 899 (App. Div. 2d Dept. 1987).

32. *See e.g.*, Home Builders League of S. Jersey, Inc. v. Township of Evesham, 440 A.2d 1361, 1363 (N.J. Super. Ct. App. Div. 1981).

33. *See e.g.*, Mertz v. Lakatos, 381 A.2d 497, 500 (Pa. Commw. Ct. 1978).

34. The municipality must exercise a second type of "inspection" right to ensure that it is receiving clear title to all dedicated improvements. *See* Rogal, *supra* note 6, at 11.

35. Home Builders League of S. Jersey, Inc. v. Township of Evesham, 440 A.2d 1361, 1363 (N.J. Super. Ct. App. Div. 1981).

36. *See, e.g.,* County of Kern v. Edgemont Dev. Corp., 35 Cal. Rptr. 629, 631 (Cal. App. 1963) (specifying four requirements for partial acceptance) (if the improvements are unrelated or easily separable, the municipality may be unable to refuse a requested partial acceptance). Toll Bros. I Inc. v. Greenwich, 582 A.2d 1276 (N.J. Super 1990) (the local government may not compel the developer to complete the improvements but must allow for the posting of a proper performance bond or surety at the developer's option); Highfield II, Inc. v. Upper St. Clair, 560 A.2d 294 (Pa. Commw. 1989) (a performance bond, however, may be required in lieu of completing improvements).

37. However, the prior removal of snow and the repair of potholes on a road offered for dedication does not constitute an acceptance of the dedication. Dwyer v. McTygue, 519 N.Y.S. 2d 630 (N.Y. 1987). New Jersey Shore Bldrs. Assoc. v. Township of Marlboro, 591 A.2d 959 (N.J. Super. 1991) (a bond cannot be required for facilities that will not be dedicated to the local government, but will be turned over to a private utility).

38. Seidel, *supra* note 14, at 136 (citing Center for Urban Policy Research, Survey of Municipalities (1976)).

39. Gorton, "Surety Bonds," in HANDBOOK OF CONSTRUCTION MANAGEMENT AND ORGANIZATION 86 (Frein ed. 1980).

40. Gorton, *supra* note 39, at 86.

41. CONNERS, CALIFORNIA SURETY AND FIDELITY BOND PRACTICE § 1.4 (1969).

42. Gorton, *supra* note 39, at 83.

43. Gorton, *supra* note 39, at 83, 87.

44. Conners, *supra* note 41, at § 1.4.

45. *See* R. HARRIS, CONSTRUCTION AND DEVELOPMENT FINANCING 2-15 (1982); M. MADISON & J. DWYER, THE LAW OF REAL ESTATE FINANCING 9.11 (1981); Rogal, *supra* note 6, at 1, 3; Seidel, *supra* note 14, at 135.

46. Harris, *supra* note 45, at 2-15.

47. Rogal, *supra* note 6, at 6. When the developer can obtain surety bonds only at an exorbitant cost, the municipality's insistence upon their use may effectively eliminate the small developer from the development process. *Id.* at 3. *See also* Gorton, *supra* note 39, at 84 (surety companies to assume the burden of weeding out unworthy and irresponsible bidders). In a broader sense, the cost of the surety bond constitutes part of the overall cost of subdivision regulation. While the municipality has an obvious interest in securing the completion of qual-ity subdivision improvement, the added cost of regulation, nevertheless, may have the effect of excluding those in low to moderate income brackets from the housing market. *See* S. Seidel, *supra* note 14, at 125. Some commentators, however, argue that strict bonding requirements should be used as a direct tool to upgrade the quality of land planning and development. McPherson, *An Underused Form of Land Use Control—Subdivision Improvement Bond Requirements,* 45 PA. B.A.Q. 461, 476-77 (1974); Yearwood, *Performance Bonding for Subdivision Improvements,* 46 J. URB. L. 67, 68 (1968).

48. Harris, *supra* note 45, at 2-15.

49. *Id.*; Seidel, *supra* note 14, at 135.

50. In general, suretyship contracts should be construed according to ordinary contract principles rather than construed strictly against the surety as in the case of an insurance contract. Conners, *supra* note 41, at § 1.5.

51. *Id.* at 12.9; Gorton, *supra* note 39, at 91.

52. Although some defaults result from theft or diversion of progress payments, the major factors that contribute to developer failures are cost overruns, unanticipated delays attributable to poor weather conditions, labor or material shortages, economic downturns, and poor sales. *See* Gorton, *supra* note 39, at 85. *See also* Harris, *supra* note 45, at 6-5 and 6-7 (discussing signs indicating impending default).

53. Financing the defaulting developer may be favorable to the surety if the default is the result of a temporary problem, the project is nearly complete, the developer probably can work through the situation, and penalties may be saved. Conners, *supra* note 41, at § 12.10. Similarly, through hiring another contractor the risk may be spread to two additional parties, the new contractor and the contractor's surety. Conners, *supra* note 41, at § 12.6.

54. Caron v. Andrew, 284 P.2d 544, 549-50 (Cal. App. 1955) (surety remained responsible for performance of its assumed obligation when the surety assumed contractor's obligations); Copeland Sand & Gravel v. Insurance Co. of N. Am. 596 P.2d 623, 625 (Ore. Ct. App. 1979) (surety liable for damages flowing from its breach where it under took to complete the principal's obligations), *rev'd,* 607 P.2d 718 (1980).

55. Conners, *supra* note 41, at § 12.7. Ordinarily, the municipality uses the settlement funds to hire its own contractor to complete the improvements. *See id.* In some circumstances, however, the municipality may be able to utilize its own maintenance or construction crews. The surety should pay the municipality a fixed amount necessary to complete the improvements in exchange for a general release of liability and without releasing the developer's liability to the surety.

56. Conners, *supra* note 41, at § 3.8. Although denoted as a penalty, courts ordinarily hold that the face amount of the bond is the limit of the surety's liability rather than a forfeiture amount. *Id.* at § 2.3. *See, e.g.,* Board of Supervisors v. Ecology One, Inc., 245 S.E.2d 425, 430 (Va. 1978) (nothing in the bond, statute, or ordinance indicated an intent to create a forfeiture bond). *See also* City of Rye v. Public Serv. Mut. Ins. Co., 315 N.E.2d 458, 459 (1974) (without statutory authority, the agreement providing for forfeiture is unenforceable).

57. In addition to protecting the right of reimbursement, the surety also will be inclined to litigate the issue of damages. *See* General Ins. Co. of Am. v. City of Colorado Springs, 638 P.2d 752, 759 (Colo. 1981).

58. *See, e.g.,* Bella Vista Ranches, Inc. v. City of Sierra Vista, 613 P.2d 302, 303 (Ariz. Ct. App. 1980) (city lacked authority to regulate subdivisions in absence of an enabling statute); Anderson v. Pima County, 558 P.2d 981, 983 (Ariz. Ct. App. 1976) (in absence of an enabling statute, county lacked authority to require security for completion of improvements); Wood Bros. Homes v. City of Colorado Springs, 568 P.2d 487, 490-91 (Colo. 1977) (requirement that the developer bear the entire cost of an off-site improvement exceeded the authority granted by ordinance); Hylton Enterprises v. Board of Supervisors, 258 S.E.2d 577, 581 (Va. 1979) (neither statute nor ordinance granted the county express or implied authority to require improvements to public highways abutting subdivision).

59. *See, e.g.,* Fireman's Fund Indem. Co. v. County of Sacramento, 3 Cal. Rptr. 607, 608 (Cal. App. 1960) (county's acceptance of subdivision map and bond created a contract to complete improvements required by statute); Indian River County v. Vero Beach Dev. Inc., 201 So.2d 922, 924 (Fla. Dist. Ct. App. 1967) (agreement to make improvements includes implied agreement to comply with specifications required in subdivision regulations); Township of Hampden v. Tenny, 379 A.2d 635, 638 (Pa. Commw. Ct. 1977) (agreement to include improvements as a condition of subdivision approval implies agreement to complete improvements or to reimburse township for costs of completion).

60. *See, e.g.,* Pacific County v. Sherwood Pacific, Inc., 567 P.2d 642, 647 (Wash. Ct. App. 1977) (authority to require completion bond necessarily implied from statutory powers expressly granted to county). *See* Genesee County Bd. of Road Comm'rs v. North Am. Dev. Co., 119 N.W.2d 593, 597 (Mich. 1963) (when developer voluntarily agreed to make nonrequired off-site improvements in exchange for the board's assurances to the FHA, the bond securing the developer's performance was enforceable on contract theory). *But see* Anderson v. Pima County, 558 P.2d 981, 983 (Ariz. Ct. App. 1976) (county lacked authority to require bonds or other security in absence of an enabling act).

61. Generally, completion includes the municipality's approval and acceptance of dedication. When no building activity has begun, however, the courts may bar the municipality from collecting on the bond. Town of New Windsor v. Inbro Dev. Corp., 448 N.Y.S.2d 99, 100 (Sup. Ct. 1982); *cf.* County of Yuba v. Central Valley Nat'l Bank, 97 Cal. Rptr. 369, 371-72 (Cal. App. 1971) (recovery on letter of credit barred when the developer commenced no activity). *But see* Colorado Nat'l Bank v. Board of County Comm'rs, 634 P.2d 32, 38 (Colo. 1981) (court permitted recovery on letter of credit even though the developer commenced no activity).

62. When the purpose of the bond is to secure completion of required improvements, the usual measure of damages is the cost of completion. General Ins. Co. of Am. v. City of Colorado Springs, 638 P.2d 752, 758-59 (Colo. 1981); Board of Supervisors v. Ecology One, Inc., 245 S.E. 2d 425, 429-30 (Va. 1978); Pacific County v. Sherwood Pac., Inc., 567 P.2d 642, 648-49 (Wash. Ct. App. 1977).

63. *See* City of Norman v. Liddell, 596 P.2d 879 (Okla. 1979). In *Liddell,* the ordinance required the city to initiate a suit to recover for non-completion "prior to the expiration of the bond." *Id.* at 881. The developer had agreed to complete all improvements within two years, and the bond's expiration date was the last day of the two-year period. The court held, however, that the developer would not have been in breach prior to the expiration of the full two-year period, and, therefore, the cause of action could not arise until that time had elapsed. *Id.* *See also* Sherwood Forest No. 2 Corp. v. City of Norman, 632 P.2d 368, 369-70 (Okla. 1980) (construing same ordinance). But see Board of Supervisors v. Ecology One, Inc., 245 S.E.2d 425, 428 (Va. 1978) (county permitted to maintain action prior to the completion date when evidence indicated that the developer had abandoned the contract).

64. *See, e.g.*, City of New Orleans v. Mark C. Smith & Sons, Inc., 339 So.2d 321, 322 (La. 1976) (applying a five-year limitation period for actions on contract rather than the shorter limitation period pertaining to "public works" contracts).

65. *See, e.g.*, City of Los Angeles v. Gleneagle Dev. Co., 133 Cal. Rptr. 212, 225 (Cal. App. 1976) (dismissing an action against the surety for want of prosecution).

66. Pacific County v. Sherwood Pac., Inc., 567 P.2d 642, 649-50 (Wash. Ct. App. 1977) (modification of specifications and extension of time for performance did not discharge surety when the bond secured completion "to the satisfaction of the County Road Engineer," within a specified time unless "extended at the option of the County Road Engineer").

67. City of Medford v. Fellsmere Realty Co., 187 N.E.2d 849, 852 (Mass. 1963).

68. County of Kern v. Edgemont Dev. Corp., 35 Cal. Rptr. 629, 631 (Cal. App. 1963) (developer obligated to maintain improvements after completion, inspection, and approval by the county when the developer failed to apply for partial acceptance).

69. Anne Arundel County v. Lichtenberg, 283 A.2d 782, 787 (Md. 1971) (county's recordation of deeds does not waive the requirement of formal written acceptance); Home Builders League of S. Jersey, Inc. v. Township of Evesham, 440 A.2d 1361, 1363 (N.J. Super. Ct. App. Div. 1981) (township's release of bond was not an exercise of dominion and control resulting in acceptance of dedication).

70. *Compare* Mertz v. Lakatos, 381 A.2d 497, 500 (Pa. Commw. Ct. 1978) (township's failure to approve or disapprove within the statutory period resulted in deemed approval and release of liability) *with* Township of Barnegat v. DCA of N.J., Inc., 437 A.2d 909, 912 (N.J. Sup. Ct. App. Div. 1981) (when the township failed to approve or disapprove within the statutory period, deemed approval would not result unless improvements were in fact substantially complete at the time of notice of completion).

71. City of Rye v. Public Serv. Mut. Ins. Co., 315 N.E.2d 458, 459, (N.Y. 1974).

72. Rogal, *supra* note 6, at 6-7.

73. Seidel, *supra* note 14, at 135.

74. Harris, *supra* note 45, at 2-18.

75. *See id.* Seidel, *supra* note 14, at 135. K.

Hovanian at Lawrenceville, Inc. v. Lawrence Township, 560 A.2d 1297 (N.J. Super. 1988) (where the local government engineer has certified that 70 percent of the improvements have been completed, the township attorney may not refuse to release the appropriate portion of the bond insuring completion).

76. Harris, *supra* note 45, at 2-18.

77. Seidel, *supra* note 14, at 136. The results of one survey indicate that most municipalities release bonds or escrowed funds within 65 days of completion. *Id.* at 156 n.32.

78. If the escrow fund proves insufficient to cover the cost of completion, the municipality may not be able to withhold building permits or certificates of occupancy in an attempt to force completion. *Cf.* Key Fed. Sav. & Loan Ass'n v. Anne Arundel County, 460 A.2d 86, 91-92 (Md. 1983) (when the county exacted completion bond as condition of plat approval, it could not subsequently withhold building permits or occupancy certificates pending completion); Incorporated Village of Northport v. Guardian Fed. Sav. & Loan Ass'n, 384 N.Y.S.2d 923, 926 (Sup. Ct. 1976) (village could not withhold a certificate of occupancy after accepting a bond as security for completion of the required improvements).

79. Harris, *supra* note 45, at 2-18. Weingarten v. Lewisboro, 144 Misc.2d 849 (N.Y. Sup. Ct. 1989).

80. Madison & Dwyer, *supra* note 45, at 9-11. Pocono Township v. Hall, 561 A.2d 53 (Pa. Commw. 1989) (a developer is liable on a bond to improve a road whether or not dedication had been accepted or offered).

81. The loan documents should specify that any funds subsequently paid to the municipality because of a shortage in the set-aside fund will be added to the developer's original loan amount. *See* Madison & Dwyer, *supra* note 45, at § 9-12.

82. *Id.* at § 9-11. See Township of Barnegat v. DCA of N.J., Inc., 437 A.2d 909, 910 (N.J. Super. Ct. App. Div. 1981); Mertz v. Lakotos, 381 A.2d 497, 499-500 (Pa. Commw. Ct. 1978).

83. Harris, *supra* note 45, at 2-18.

84. Madison & Dwyer, *supra* note 45, at 9-11. Oak Shores Property Owners Ass'n v. Noble County Bd. of Comm'rs, 564 N.E.2d 319 (Ind. App. 1990) (approving a performance bond does not obligate the county to complete the roads at the county's expense where the cost exceeds the bond).

85. Rogal, *supra* note 6, at 7.

86. In one recent survey, approximately 9 percent of the responding municipalities indi-

cated that the property escrow was an acceptable form of security. *See* Seidel, *supra* note 14, at 136 (citing Center for Urban Policy Research, *Survey of Municipalities* (1976)). Apparently, the acceptance of stocks and bonds by these municipalities for use in the property escrow is fairly common. Rogal, *supra* note 6, at 7. The potentially wide fluctuations in value of most marketable securities, however, tend to make them unsuitable as an effective source of sufficient funds to enable the municipality to complete improvements upon the developer's default. *See* Seidel, *supra* note 14, at 135.

87. Harris, *supra* note 45, at 2-19. Rogal, *supra* note 6, at 7.

88. Although the corporate surety bond is by far the most widely permitted security device, *see* Seidel, *supra* note 14, at 136 (citing Center for Urban Policy Research, Survey of Municipalities (1976)), most state enabling legislation permits the use of bonds, assurances, "or other adequate security." *See* Shultz & Kelley, *supra* note 6, at 40. *See generally, . . . Or Other Adequate Security: Using, Structuring and Managing the Standby Letter of Credit to Ensure the Completion of Subdivision Improvements,* 19 URB. LAW. 39 (1987).

89. *See generally* J. DOLAN, THE LAW OF LETTERS OF CREDIT, § 3.02-.06 (1984). Recently there has been a growing interest in standby letters of credit. *See, e.g.,* Leon, *Letter of Credit: A Primer,* 45 MD. L. REV. 432 (1986); Mueller, *Letters of Credit: A New Tool of Trade for the Real Estate Attorney,* 38 BAYLOR L. REV. 109 (1986).

90. *See* Shultz & Kelley, *Subdivision Improvement Agreements that Limit the Developer's Exposure to Liability,* 2 PRAC. REAL EST. LAW. 39, 40-41 (1986). For an excellent judicial summary of basic letter of credit law, *see* Colorado Nat'l Bank v. Board of County Comm'rs, 634 P.2d 32 (Colo. 1981).

91. Dolan, *supra* note 89, at § 1.04; Pastor v. National Republic Bank, 390 N.E.2d 894, 897 (Ill. 1979).

92. *See, e.g.,* Philadelphia Gear Corp. v. Central Bank, 717 F.2d 230, 235 (5th Cir. 1983); Voest-Alpine Int'l Corp. v. Chase Manhattan Bank, 707 F.2d 680, 682 (2d Cir. 1983). *See* U.C.C. § 5-114(1), 2A U.L.A. 259 (1977); Uniform Customs and Practice for Documentary Credits (U.C.P.), art. 3 (1983 revision).

93. "An issuer must honor a draft or demand for payment which complies with the terms of the relevant credit regardless of whether the goods or documents conform to the underlying contract for sale or other contract between the customer and the beneficiary." U.C.C. § 5-114(1), 2A U.L.A. 259 (1977).

94. U.C.C. § 5-114(1), 2A U.L.A. 259 (1977).

95. U.C.C. § 5-116(1), 2A U.L.A. 274 (1977). Note that the U.C.P. is somewhat more restrictive than the U.C.C. in that it requires that the credit be expressly designated as "transferable." U.C.P. art. 54(b) (1983 revision). "Terms such as 'divisible,' 'fractionable,' 'assignable,' and 'transmissible' add nothing to the meaning of the terms 'transferable' and shall not be used." *Id.* The U.C.P. appears to permit amendments to the credit, however, without the consent of the developer. U.C.P. art. 10(d); AMF Head Sports Wear Inc. v. Ray Scott's All-American Sports Club, Inc., 448 F.Supp. 222 (D. Ariz. 1978).

96. Assignability of the right to draw under a letter of credit might be important to the local government where a change in jurisdiction over the project is anticipated, for example, due to merger, annexation, disannexation, and the like. *See* Pastor v. Nat'l Rep. Bank, 26 U.C.C. Rep. Serv. 988, 992-93 (Ill. 1979).

97. Presumably, the developer can also take some comfort in the knowledge that any judgment against the local government for wrongful presentation will probably be collectible. A developer party may obtain injunctive relief against the bank to prevent the bank from honoring a fraudulent presentment. *See* U.S.S. § 5-114(2)(b), 2A U.L.A. 259 (1977); Dynamics Corp. of Am. v. Citizens & Southern Nat'l Bank, 356 F. Supp. 991, 998-999 (N.D. Ga. 1973); Intraworld Indus. v. Girard Trust Bank, 336 A.2d 316, 323-25 (Pa. 1975). However, the injunction will not issue based on the mere allegation that there was no underlying breach of the agreement between the account party and the beneficiary. A clever developer may sue for injunctive relief against the local government to prevent it from making a presentment. Steinmeyer v. Warner Consol. Corp., 116 Cal. Rptr. 57, 60 (Cal. App. 1974).

98. *See* Shultz & Kelley, *A Model Subdivision Improvement Agreement and Guarantee: Beyond Empty Promises and Broken Hearts,* J. AM. PLAN. A. (1987).

99. U.C.P. art. 7(c) (1983 revision); *cf.* Conoco, Inc. v. Norwest Bank Mason City, N.A., 767 F.2d 470 (8th Cir. 1985) (holding that letter of credit incorporating U.C.P. and providing that credit "will remain in force" was irrevocable credit.

100. All credits subject to the U.C.P. must bear an expiration date. U.C.P. art. 46(a) (1983 revision). The subdivision improvement agreement may also provide that if all required improvements are completed in accordance with the agreement, the letter of credit will be surrendered by the beneficiary or canceled prior to its expiration date.

101. Consolidated Aluminum Corp. v. Bank of Virginia, 704 F.2d 136, 138 (4th Cir. 1983); Cypress Bank v. Southwestern Bell Tel. Co., 610 S.W.2d 185, 187 (Tex. Civ. App. 1980).

102. A letter of credit backed only by a contingent promissory note is not a "deposit" insured by the FDIC. Federal Deposit Ins. Corp. v. Philadelphia Gear Corp., 106 S.Ct. 1981, 1932 (1986). Thus, in view of the frequency of bank and savings and loan failures in recent years, the local government must consider the financial strength of the issuer as well as that of the developer.

103. Sureties generally employ a two-step analysis when qualifying a developer. The first step includes an assessment of the developer's net quick worth. The second focuses on the developer's track record in the industry. *See* Gorton, *supra* note 39, at 87-90. As a result of the strict qualifying process, only the most creditworthy developers are able to obtain surety bonds. *See* Harris, *supra* note 45, at 2-15. Letters of credit, on the other hand, appear to be readily obtainable without regard to the developer's experience in the industry. While a variety of factors may be considered by the bank in determining its fee for issuing the credit, a fee equal to 1 to 2 percent of the amount of the credit is not uncommon.

104. Dolan, *supra* note 89, at § 3.07[3].

105. *Id.* at § 3.07[1].

106. U.C.C. § 5-114(1), 2A U.L.A. 259 (1977); Summit Ins. Co. v. Central Nat'l Bank, 624 S.W.2d 222, 225 (Tex. Ct. App. 1981); Lumbermans Acceptance Co. v. Security Pac. Nat'l Bank, 150 Cal. Rptr. 69 (Cal. App. 1978).

107. ITEK Corp. v. First Nat'l Bank, 730 F.2d 19, 24 (1st Cir. 1984); *see* KMW Int'l v. Chase Manhattan Bank, N.A., 606 F.2d 10, 15 (2d Cir. 1979).

108. *See* U.C.C. § 5-114(1) and comment 1, 2A U.L.A. 259-61 (1977). If the credit is properly drafted, the most that will be required regarding the substantive issue of default is the written statement of an appropriate official certifying that a default exists.

109. Shultz & Kelley, *Subdivision Improvement Guarantees: A Primer*, 28 J. Urb. & Contemp. L. 1 (1985); Gorton, "Surety Bonds" in Handbook of Constructive Management and Organization 86 (J. Frein ed. 1980).

110. Friends of the Pine Bush v. Planning Bd. of the City of Albany, 450 N.Y. S.2d 966, 968 (A.D. 3rd 1982). Although the result in this case is correct, it is curious because the holding reverses the traditional model of government provision of services in favor of developer-provided services. While most cases question whether the government can require the developer to make improvements, *Pine Bush* holds that the government cannot do this in the case of a new subdivision.

111. *See* Safford v. Board of Comm'rs, 387 A.2d 177, 182 (Pa. Commw. Ct. 1978); Kennedy v. Lehman Township, 459 A.2d 921, 922 (Pa. Commw. Ct. 1983).

112. The *Safford* court stressed that the local government was required to complete improvements "at its own expense." 387 A.2d at 180. The city likely would have a cause of action against the developer if the city obligated the developer to construct improvements without requiring the developer to obtain a bond. The developer, however, may be judgment-proof. Although it appears reasonable to permit the government to assess costs against property in the subdivision if it is assumed that lot owners did not already pay for improvements, it is likely that the developer incorporated the estimated cost of improvements into the selling price of lots or homes and then failed to construct improvements. If the government is permitted to assess property owners for its cost of construction, they will have paid for the improvements twice.

As an alternative to suing the government to force it to complete improvements, one plaintiff sought to collect under her title insurance policy when local officials refused to issue a building permit because the developer failed to complete improvements in the subdivision. Hocking v. Title Ins. & Trust Co., 234 P.2d 625, 626 (Cal. 1951). Unfortunately for the plaintiff, the court found that the developer's failure did not affect the marketability of the plaintiff's title. *Id.* at 629.

113. Norton v. First Fed. Sav., 624 P.2d 854, 855-56 (Ariz. 1981). *See also* Gordon v. Robinson Homes, Inc., 174 N.E.2d 381, 384 (Mass. 1961) (suggesting that lot owners mandamus the local government to enforce their rights). The local government will have the option of completing the improvements where the cost will exceed the amount of the bond. Oak Shores Property Owners Ass'n v. Noble County Bd. of Comm'rs, 564 N.E.2d 319 (Ind. App. 1990).

114. *See* Sherwood Forest No. 2 Corp. v. City of Norman, 632 P.2d 368, 370 (Okla. 1980) (cause of action accrues on the expiration of the two-year period in the bond); City of Norman v. Liddell, 596 P.2d 879, 882 (Okla. 1979) (action may be brought on expiration of the two-year period set for completion).

115. *See* Town of Brookfield v. Greenridge, Inc., 418 A.2d 907, 911 (Conn. 1979) (implied obligation to construct improvements according to industry standards). *Town of Brookfield* also demonstrates that the bond constitutes a sufficient basis for the surety's obligation and no express contract for completion of improvements is required to create the surety's duty to pay on default. *Id.* at 909. Moreover, a bond will incorporate the minimum requirements reflected in the local subdivision regulations and the courts will charge the surety with knowledge of these regulations. *See* Indian River County v. Vero Beach Dev., Inc., 201 So.2d 922, 924 (Fla. Dist. Ct. App. 1967); City of Medina v. Holdridge, 346 N.E.2d 339, 342 (Ohio 1970).

116. *See* Fireman's Fund Indem. Co. v. County of Sacramento, 3 Cal. Rptr. 607, 608 (Cal. App. 1960).

117. Board of Supervisors v. Ecology One, Inc., 245 S.E.2d 425, 427 (Va. 1978).

118. Two courts have held that *commencement of developer* after recording of the plat is a condition precedent to the developer's duty to complete improvements. County of Yuba v. Central Valley National Bank, Inc., 97 Cal. Rptr. 369 (Cal. App. 1971) (the court found an implied condition in the letter of credit issued by the bank that development had to commence before the bank's liability could arise); Town of New Windsor v. Inbro Development Corp., 448 N.Y.S. 2d 99 (A.D., 1982) (commencement of development was a prerequisite to the obligation to complete improvements based on the language of the local ordinance). *Id.* at 99. The local ordinance, following state law, provided that the government could collect bond proceeds on the developer's default only to the extent that the developer had begun construction in the development project. *Id.* at 99. Although the court speaks of a condition precedent, the issue actually is one of a lack of damages. *See also* Commonwealth v. Reliance Dev. Corp., 392 A.2d 792, 793 (Pa. Super. Ct. 1978) (the developer was obligated to construct improvements only as it developed and sold lots; therefore when the developer defaulted, he was obligated only for improvements required by the one lot that he had sold).

119. Colorado Nat'l Bank v. Board of County Comm'rs, 634 P.2d 32, 36-39 (Colo. 1981) (mere failure of the developer to construct improvements triggered the banks obligation under the letter of credit).

120. *See* Fireman's Fund Idem. Co. v. County of Sacramento, 3 Cal. Rptr. 607, 608-09 (Cal. App. 1960). In *Fireman's Fund,* although the parties stipulated that the developer had done no work in the subdivision, the surety was liable for the developer's default. County of Yuba v. Central Valley Nat'l Bank, 97 Cal. Rptr. 369 (Cal. App. 1971), makes no reference to *Fireman's Fund.* In General Ins. Co. of Am. v. City of Colorado Springs, 638 P.2d 752 (Colo. 1981), the Colorado Supreme Court distinguished *County of Yuba,* noting that in *General Insurance* the parties to the bond "did not condition their obligation on the development of any land adjacent to the street extensions." *Id.* at 758-59 n.7. The court continued: "[The parties] intended to secure to the city the construction and installation of the street extensions up to the amount of the bond, irrespective of the commencement of actual construction of road improvements or partial completion thereof." *Id.*

121. *See* Los Angeles County v. Margulis, 44 P.2d 608, 609 (Cal. App. 1935); General Ins. Co. of Am. v. City of Colorado Springs, 638 P.2d 752, 759 (Colo. 1981); Pacific County v. Sherwood Pac., Inc., 567 P.2d 642, 648 (Wash. Ct. App. 1977).

122. If the government does borrow funds to complete improvements, the surety remains liable to the government because the government's damages did not disappear when it borrowed funds. Although this liability appears to be obvious, in City of Ames v. Schill Builders, Inc., 274 N.W.2d 708, 712 (Iowa 1979), a surety attempted to avoid its obligation because the city borrowed funds to complete improvements. *See also* City of Sacramento v. Trans Pac. Indus., 159 Cal. Rptr. 514, 518 (Cal. App. 1979) (holding that the city's damages continued even though a subsequent developer completed improvements in exchange for an assignment of proceeds obtained in the city's action against the surety).

123. *See* General Ins. Co. of Am. v. City of Colorado Springs, 638 P.2d 752, 758 (Colo. 1981); Board of Supervisors v. Ecology One, Inc., 245 S.E.2d 425, 430 (Va. 1978); Pacific County v. Sherwood Pac., Inc., 567 P.2d 642, 648 (Wash. Ct. App. 1977); *but see* Genessee County Bd. of Road Comm'rs v. North Am. Dev. Co., 119 N.W.2d

593, 597-98 (Mich. 1963), where the court did uphold the bond amount as liquidated damages, permitting the government to collect the face amount of the bond. Most courts will require the government to refund excess funds after completing the improvements unless the government establishes that the amount of the funds constituted a settlement of the government's claim against the developer and surety. *See* M. Zerman Realty & Bldg. Corp. v. Borough of Westwood, 319 A.2d 441, 442 (N.J. 1974). Although the courts construe performance bonds to constitute indemnification bonds, local governments constitutionally may require a penal bond so long as the requirement is rationally related to the purposes of the statute. *See* City of Rye v. Public Serv. Mut. Ins. Co., 315 N.E.2d 458 (N.Y. 1974) (stating in dictum that the court would uphold a contractor's penal bond if permitted by statute).

124. Los Angeles County v. Margulis, 44 P.2d 608, 609 (Cal. App. 1935); General Ins. Co. of Am. v. City of Colorado Springs, 638 P.2d 752, 759 (Colo. 1981); Town of Brookfield v. Greenridge, Inc., 418 A.2d 907, 913 (Conn. 1979); Pacific County v. Sherwood Pac., Inc., 567 P.2d 642, 648 (Wash. Ct. App. 1977).

125. *See* County of Yuba v. Central Valley Nat'l Bank, 97 Cal. Rptr. 369, 371-72 (Cal. App. 1971) (holding that commencement of development is a condition precedent to the developer's duty to complete improvements).

126. *See* Commonwealth *ex rel.* Pennsylvania Sec. Comm'n v. Reliance Dev. Corp., 392 A.2d 792, 793 (Pa. Super. Ct. 1978) (the agreement with the developer required the developer to complete improvements only when it developed and sold lots).

127. *See* Town of New Windsor v. Inbro Dev. Corp., 448 N.Y.S.2d 99 (Sup. Ct. 1982). In *Town of New Windsor*, state law limited collection of bond proceeds to an amount necessary to complete improvements to an extent commensurate with building development. *Id.* New York Village Law also limits the expenditures of the government to the amount of the bond to avoid placing the burden for completing improvements on the local citizenry. *See* Village of Warwick v. Republics Ins. Co., 488 N.Y.S.2d 589, 592 (Sup. Ct. 1980).

128. *See* Safford v. Board of Comm'rs, 387 A.2d 177, 182 (Pa. Commw. Ct. 1978) (the local ordinance specifically provided that the developer would be liable for the cost of completion if it exceeded the amount of the bond).

129. *See* Town of Brookfield v. Greenridge, Inc., 418 A.2d 907, 912-13 (Conn. 1979) (the court explained that the government's claim was in two counts, one on the bond and one on the developer's agreement to construct improvements). *See also* City of Bellefontaine Neighbors v. J.J. Kelley Realty & Bldg. Co., 460 S.W.2d 298, 300 (Mo. Ct. App. 1970) (the city's complaint was in two counts, one on the contract with the developer and one on the bond).

130. *See* Board of Supervisors v. Ecology One, Inc., 245 S.E.2d 425, 429 (Va. 1978) (holding that a recovery on the bond is limited to the amount of the bond). Because the bond is only security for the developer's promise to perform, no reason exists why the bond should limit recovery on his promise. The government should be able to collect the cost of completion unless it has agreed that the amount of the bond is liquidated damages. *See* Town of Stoneham v. Savelo, 170 N.E.2d 417, 419 (Mass. 1960) (reasonable cost of completion is the measure of damages). In practice, the bond may act as the limit of the government's recovery because the defaulting developer is judgment proof. Between co-principals on a bond, the owner of the property will have primary liability in the case of default. *See* Dick Kelchner Excavating, Inc. v. Gene Zimmerman, Inc., 264 N.E.2d 918, 923 (Ohio 1970) (co-principal who is owner of the property must indemnify the other principal who is the contractor).

131. Dick Kelcher Excavating, Inc. v. Gene Zimmerman, Inc., 264 N.E.2d 918, 922 (Ohio 1970).

132. *See, e.g.,* Brous v. Smith, 106 N.E.2d 503, 506, (N.Y. 1952) (subdivision regulations benefit the consumer in the subdivision and the community at large). *See also* Transamerica Title Ins. Co. v. Cochise County, 548 P.2d 416, 420 (Ariz. Ct. App. 1976) (purpose of subdivision regulations "is to ensure that consumers who purchase lots in residential developments are provided with adequate streets, utilities, drainage, and generally pleasant, healthy, and livable surroundings"). *But see* Norton v. First Fed. Sav., 624 P.2d 854, 857 (Ariz. 1981) (a general purpose for a statute did not create a specific legal right in a group of persons the statute was designed to protect).

133. *See, e.g.,* Norton v. First Fed. Sav., 624 P.2d 854, 858 (Ariz. 1981) (lot owners were not third-party beneficiaries of the performance bond or contract to post the performance bond); Gordon v. Robinson Homes, Inc., 174

N.E.2d 381, 382-83 (Mass. 1961); City of University City *ex rel.* Machey v. Frank Miceli & Sons Realty & Bldg. Co., 347 S.W.2d 131, 134-35 (Mo. 1961); Fleck v. National Property Management, 590 P.2d 1254, 1256 (Utah 1979) (Hall, J., concurring).

134. *See* Gordon v. Robinson Homes, Inc., 174 N.E.2d 381, 382 (Mass. 1961). Although the bond recited that it was for the use and benefit of persons that may purchase lots in the subdivision, the court held that the lot owner could not maintain an action because the local planning authority was the primary authority for enforcing subdivision regulations. *Id.* at 383. Thus, the local government acted beyond its statutory authority when it attempted to create a specific right in lot owners. *Id.* at 382. The rule enunciated in *Gordon Homes* is both bad policy and bad law. While subdivision improvement requirements and guarantees are designed to protect the community from being saddled with the cost of completing improvements, they also serve to protect consumers. It should be within the implied power of the local government to create a right in consumers to enforce the guarantee. *Gordon Homes* does suggest that lot owners may have a right to compel the government to exercise its right. *Id.* at 384.

135. 347 S.W.2d 131 (Mo. 1961).

136. *Id.* at 134.

137. *Id.* The court stated that the "contract, ordinance and bond are not reasonably subject to the construction that they were intended for the protection of adjoining property owners," when the actual issue before the court was whether the parties intended the bond to indemnify lot owners from injury occasioned by failure to complete the improvements.

138. 590 P.2d 1254, 1255-56 (Utah 1979) (Hall, J., concurring). In *Fleck*, the plaintiffs were purchasers of lots subject to a prior lien. *Id.* at 1255. The subdivider had covenanted to complete improvements in the subdivision and obtained a performance bond to secure completion. Eventually, the prior lienholder foreclosed its lien and the plaintiffs lost the property at the foreclosure. Plaintiffs asserted that the developer had failed to complete improvements as promised, thereby diminishing the value of the lots and making it impractical for them to purchase at the foreclosure sale. Justice Hall, concurring, asserted that the lot owners were not third-party beneficiaries irrespective of whether the injury that they suffered was foreseeable. He noted that the local ordinance that set forth the

bond requirement had as its main purpose "the objective of protecting the public by assuring that before the county takes responsibility for the maintenance of streets and other facilities that the required improvements have been completed so as not to burden the public with the added expense." *Id.* at 1256-57.

To declare that the government alone is vested with a right on an improvement guarantee is conclusory and the courts have not adequately explained the basis for this result. One concern is that third parties can deplete the guarantee before the money can be used to complete the improvements. If the purpose for which third parties can use the money, however, is limited to completing improvements, it would not matter who compelled the developer or surety to complete the improvements. Of course, a lot owner should not be permitted to collect under a guarantee if the money is not aside for improvements. *See* Berman v. Aetna Casualty & Sur. Co., 115 Cal. Rptr. 566, 568 (Cal. App. 1974) (the court stated in dictum that a lot owner that had completed improvements would have a right to intervene in a suit brought by the government to recoup the costs of completion).

139. 294 N.Y.S.2d 430, 433 (Sup. Ct. 1968).

140. *Id. Howarth* is limited to a contract between the developer and the city and does not address the issue of a third party right of action under a performance guarantee. Nevertheless, the case is significant because it contrasts the normal rule against a third party right of action on a government contract with the situation of the developer-government-homebuyer. The court noted that the class of persons that could sue as third-party beneficiaries would be limited and damages would be relatively minor. Thus, the court forthrightly addressed the policy considerations of its decision. *See also* Berman v. Aetna Casualty & Sur. Co., 115 Cal. Rptr. 566 (Cal. App. 1974). The court suggested that a lot owner that had completed improvements could intervene in a suit brought by the local government to recoup the costs of completion and to avoid a windfall to the government. *Id.* at 568. The court's suggestion, however, constitutes dictum because the court held that the plaintiff's suit was barred on res judicata grounds. *Id.* at 568. Apparently, the trial court in an earlier action had held that Berman could not intervene and he failed to appeal. *See id.* at 912, 115 Cal. Rptr. at 568.

141. Evola v. Wendt Constr. Co., 338 P.2d 498, 501 (Cal. App. 1959). *See also* J.I. Newton Co.

v. Martin Dev. Co., 193 So. 2d 464, 465 (Fla. Dist. Ct. App. 1967) (subcontractors are not entitled to reimbursement from defaulting contractor's performance bond).

142. Scales-Douwes Corp. v. Paulaura Realty Corp., 249 N.E.2d 760, 761 (N.Y. 1969) (holding that the paramount purpose of the subdivision improvement bond was to secure performance and not guarantee payment to suppliers).

143. Schmidt-Tiago Constr. Co. v. City of Colorado Springs, 633 P.2d 533, 534 (Colo. Ct. App. 1981).

144. Tom Morello Constr. Co. v. Bridgeport Fed. Sav. & Loan Ass'n, 421 A.2d 747, 751 (Pa. Super. Ct. 1980) (holding that the escrow agent was entitled to make payments to the developer rather than to the contractor).

145. Weber v. Pacific Indemn. Co., 22 Cal. Rptr. 366, 369 (Cal. App. 1962).

146. W.S. Dickey Clay Mfg. Co. v. Ferguson Inv. Co., 388 P.2d 300, 304 (Okla. 1963) (holding that the planning authority had no power to require a condition in the performance bond that contractors, subcontractors, materialmen, and laborers should be paid). Local governments, in fact, do have an incentive to ensure that all work on the improvements is paid for so that it does not accept the improvements subject to any liens or encumbrances. At least one court has suggested that the lienor can enforce its rights against the local government after it assumes control of the improvements. *See* Scales-Douwes Corp. v. Paulaura Realty Corp., 249 N.E.2d 760, 761 (N.Y. 1969).

The rule against a third party right of recovery sometimes leads to harsh results. *See* Ragghianti v. Sherwin, 16 Cal. Rptr. 583, 587 (Cal. App. 1961). The rather complicated facts in *Ragghianti* arose when a housing contractor who was constructing homes in a subdivision failed to pay a street contractor. The title insurance company paid the street contractor's claim and subsequently brought an action against the owner of the property, who had posted a performance bond with the local government. The owner, believing that he was liable to the third party under the bond, paid the claim and then sought reimbursement from the housing contractor. The court held that third parties had no claim under the bond and further held that Ragghianti's payment was voluntary and, therefore, denied him a right to reimbursement from the defendant housing contractor. *Id.* at 587.

147. Cammarano v. Borough of Allendale, 167 A.2d 431, 432 (N.J. Super. 1961).

148. A local government should use an escrow agent so that it does not bear the risk of returning the deposit to the wrong person. Although the government can resort to interpleader, it will find itself in a lawsuit not of its own making. In fact, to constitute a true escrow, a third party would be required to hold funds or other collateral securing performance.

149. 340 P.2d 628 (Cal. 1959) (en banc).

150. *Id.* at 628.

151. *Id.* at 631. *See also* Village of Warwick v. Republic Ins. Co., 428 N.Y.S.2d 589, 593 (Sup. Ct. 1980) (the court in dictum stated that an assignment of the government's right would be ineffective).

152. County of Will v. Woodhill Enters., Inc., 274 N.E.2d 476, 481-82 (Ill. App. Ct. 1971); Clearwater Assocs. v. F.H. Bridge & Son, Contractors, 365 A.2d 200, 202 (N.J. Super. Ct. App. Div. 1976).

153. For example, in *Clearwater Associates*, the assignee who was a 50 percent owner of the development property "expressly undertook to complete the improvements" and the improvements in fact, were completed at the time the assignee commenced the suit. 365 A.2d at 203.

154. *Compare* City of Sacramento v. Trans Pacific Indus., Inc., 159 Cal. Rptr. 514, 520 (Cal. App. 1979) (upholding assignment) and Board of Supervisors v. Ecology One, Inc., 245 S.E.2d 425, 429 (Va. 1978) (upholding assignment) *with* City of Ames v. Schill Builders, Inc., 292 N.W.2d 678, 682 (Iowa 1980) (invalidating assignment) and Village of Warwick v. Republic Ins. Co., 428 N.Y.S.2d 589, 592 (Sup. Ct. 1980) (invalidating assignment).

155. *See, e.g.,* Board of Supervisors v. Ecology One, Inc., 245 S.E.2d 425, 429 (Va. 1978) ("The assignment . . . was for the purpose of obtaining performance guaranteed by the bond . . . [Since the work was performed], we perceive no reason for finding that the assignment was invalid").

156. Village of Warwick v. Republic Ins. Co., 428 N.Y.S.2d 589, 593 (Sup. Ct. 1950) ("Having become the owners of a parcel of real property, the bank found it . . . in its interest to subdivide the property . . . the bank, like any other developer, either had to install improvements required . . . or post security . . .").

157. City of Ames v. Schill Builders, Inc., 292 N.W.2d 678, 681 (Iowa 1980) (holding that the mortgagee that accepted a deed in lieu of foreclosure and then replatted property thus became a developer and was not entitled to an assignment of bond proceeds). In an earlier case, the Iowa Supreme Court upheld an arrangement by which the mortgagee had lent the city funds in exchange for an assignment of bond proceeds. City of Ames v. Schill Builders, Inc., 274 N.W.2d 708, 712 (Iowa 1979). When the case came before the court the second time, the facts had changed. The mortgagee who had become the owner of the property replatted a portion of the development and agreed to complete the improvements in exchange for an assignment of bond proceeds. The court held that this arrangement was invalid. 292 N.W.2d at 680-81.

158. *See* City of Sacramento v. Trans. Pac. Indus., Inc., 159 Cal. Rptr. 514, 518 (Cal. App. 1979). The court reasoned that a purchaser of lots in a financially troubled subdivision could take an assignment of bond proceeds in exchange for completion of the improvements. The court stated: "When [the] City entered into the agreement with Watkins . . . [the] City's damages did not magically disappear. Watkins did not promise to construct the improvements as a gift; he extracted consideration from the City in the form of [the] City's conditional promise to repay him if it prevailed in its action against defendants." *Id.* The court distinguished *Morro* on the grounds that the city had not alienated a "chose-in-action . . . it merely promised to pay Watkins for his work if it was successful in the lawsuit." *Id.* at 520.

159. 392 A.2d 792, 795 (Pa. Super. Ct. 1978). The facts in *Reliance* are indicative of development problems. The original developer became insolvent after selling only one lot in the subdivision. The property was sold at a sheriff's sale and the developer went into receivership. The receiver brought an action to recover the cash escrow put up by the developer. The local government interpleaded the purchaser who had completed the improvements, and the trial court held for the government. *Id.* at 793. On appeal, the government, which had disavowed any claim to the money, failed to file a brief in support of itself. *Id.* at 794. The appellate court determined that the purchaser of the property was entitled to reimbursement, but only for improvements that were the obligation of the original developer. *Id.* at 795. Because the original developer was obligated only to complete improvements for lots that were sold, the purchaser's recovery was minimal. *Id.* at 795.

160. 429 A.2d 1183 (Pa. Super. Ct. 1981).

161. *Id.* at 1185.

162. *Id.* at 1186.

163. *Id.* at 1185-86.

164. Village of S. Holland v. Korzen, 357 N.E.2d 1302 (Ill. App. Ct. 1976); 3 R. ANDERSON, AMERICAN LAW OF ZONING § 19.26 at 446 (3d ed. 1986).

165. Morrow v. Richardson, 128 S.W.2d 560 (Ky. 1939); Collins v. Zander, 61 So.2d 897 (La. Ct. App. 1952); Maddox v. Katzman, 332 N.W.2d 347 (Iowa Ct. App. 1982).

166. Shoreline Builders Co. v. Park Ridge, 209 N.E.2d 878 (Ill. App. Ct. 1965); Shields v. Harris County, 248 S.W.2d 510 (Tex. 1952); Needham v. Winthrop Harbor, 163 N.E. 468 (Ill. 1928); Kelroy v. Clear Lake, 5 N.W.2d 12 (Iowa 1942); Hughes v. Town of Mexico Beach, 455 S.W.2d 566 (Fla. Dist. Ct. App. 1984).

167. Model Regulations § 4.1(7).

168. Safford v. Board of Commissioners, 387 A.2d 177 (Pa. Commw. Ct. 1978) (where the borough approved and recorded the plat without guarantees for public improvements, it is responsible for construction of such improvements, but may then seek recovery of costs from subdivider). *Accord* Cox v. Utah Mortgage & Loan Corp., 716 P.2d 783 (Utah 1986).

169. Whippoorwill Crest Co. v. Stratford, 141 A.2d 241 (Conn. 1958); Highway Holding Co. v. Yara Engineering Corp., 123 A.2d 511 (N.J. 1956); Maxwell v. Booth, 73 N.W.2d 177 (Neb. 1955); Hughes v. Town of Mexico Beach, 455 So.2d 566 (Fla. Dist. Ct. App. 1984).

170. Coffin v. Old Orchard Dev. Corp., 186 A.2d 966 (Pa. 1962); Reiman v. Kale, 403 N.E.2d 1275 (Ill. App. Ct. 1980); Arkansas County v. Reif, 532 S.W.2d 131 (Tex. Ct. App. 1975).

171. Fortson Investing Co. v. Oklahoma City, 66 P.2d 96 (Okla. 1937); Coffin v. Old Orchard Dev. Corp., 186 A.2d 966 (Pa. 1962).

172. *See* Appendix C for the form of the irrevocable offer of dedication. An agreement to dedicate in the future is not an offer to dedicate. Young v. Jewish Welfare Federation, 371 S.W.2d 767 (Tex. 1963).

173. Payne v. Godwin, 133 S.E. 481 (Va. 1926); Phillips Petroleum Co. v. Eckroat, 46 P.2d 464 (Okla. 1935); Levine v. Young, 104 N.Y.S.2d 1004 (1951); Foster v. Atwater, 38 S.E.2d 316 (N.C. 1946).

174. Model Regulations § 4.1(7).

175. This is consonant with the common law rule. Board of County Comm'rs v. F.A. Sebring Realty, 63 So.2d 256 (Fla. 1953); Chattaway v. New London, 51 A.2d 917 (Conn. 1947).

176. O'Brien v. Chicago, 105 N.E.2d 917 (Ill. App. Ct. 1952) (resolution of acceptance); Saucelli

v. Hempstead, 143 N.Y.S.2d 889 (1954) (resolution by legislative body); Cucchiara v. Robinson, 34 So.2d 84 (La. Ct. App. 1948) (ordinance of acceptance); Easter v. Mullins, 289 S.E.2d 462, 465 (W. Va. 1982) (no dedication to public use arises by the subdivision and recording of a plat unless the public authority expressly or by clear implication accepts the dedication).

177. SMITH-BOYER, SURVEY OF THE LAW OF PROPERTY, 326 n.15 (1971).

178. Model Regulations § 4.2(2)(a).

179. Model Regulations § 3.5(1)(f). Malone v. West Marlborough Township Bd. of Supervisors, 603 A.2d 708 (Pa. Commw. 1992) (a developer has standing to apply for approval of a subdivision plat only if he or she demonstrates ownership of the subject property at the time of the board vote); Batchelder v. Planning Bd., 575 N.E.2d 366 (Mass. App. 1991) (trustee's claim of adverse possession was not sufficient to satisfy planning board's owner of record requirements, and the board may not waive record title requirements where surety from actual owner is required for installation of municipal facilities).

180. BURBY, REAL PROPERTY 303 (3rd ed. 1965); 4 H. TIFFANY, REAL PROPERTY 722 (ed. 1940).

181. Burby, *supra* note 180, at 304; Chillemi v. Chillemi, 78 A.2d 750 (Md. 1951); Lerner Shops of N. Carolina, Inc. v. Rosenthal, 34 S.E.2d 206 (N.C. 1945). This is the modern rule. The attorney should check the rule applicable to his or her state.

182. The majority common law rule forbids a conditional escrow delivery to the grantee itself. Tiffany, *supra* note 180, at 217; Sweeney v. Sweeney, 11 A.2d 806 (Conn. 1940).

183. The doctrine of caveat emptor has been slowly eroded away by the states through judicial use of theories of fraud, express and implied warranty, negligence, and strict liability to provide injunctive relief or compensation. *See* Foxcroft Townhome Owners Ass'n v. Hoffman Rosner Corp., 435 N.E.2d 210 (Ill. App. 1982); Crowder v. Vandendeale, 564 S.W.2d 879 (Mo. 1978); Wright v. Creative Corp., 498 (P.2d 1179 (Colo. App. 1972); Patitucci v. Drelich, 379 A.2d 297 (N.J. Super. L. 1977); Connor v. Great Western Savings & Loan Ass'n, 447 P.2d 609 (Cal. 1968); and Rogers v. Seyphers, 161 S.E.2d 81 (S.C. 1968).

184. The Federal Trade Commission Act, 15 U.S.C.A. §§ 41 *et. seq.* (cease and desist order to an advertiser misrepresenting a product—including sales of lots in land subdivisions); the Postal Reorganization Act, 39 U.S.C.A. § 3005 (providing for criminal prosecution of persons convicted of conducting a scheme or device for obtaining money or property through the mails by use of false pretenses, representations or promises—which has application in subdivision lot sales); the Truth in Lending Act, 15 U.S.C.A. §§ 1601 *et. seq.* and Regulation Z, 12 C.F.R. §§ 226 *et. seq.*, the administrative equivalent of the act, offers consumer protection in real estate transactions involving subdivision lot sales (Adema v. Great Northern Development Co., 374 F. Supp. 318 (N.D. Ga. 1973); the Federal Securities Act of 1933, 15 U.S.C.A. §§ 77a *et. seq.* (full disclosure of all material facts relating to a public offering of securities must be made to all prospective purchasers); and the Interstate Land Sales Full Disclosure Act (registration and disclosure requirements for subdivisions where lots are sold in interstate commerce).

185. Schenker v. United States, 529 F.2d 96 (9th Cir.), *cert. denied,* 429 U.S. 818 (1976). In Securities Act cases "specific intent" to violate the law is not a required element of "mere registration requirements." United States v. Murdock, 290 U.S. 389 (1933); see also Bryan v. Amrep Corp., 429 F. Supp. 313 (S.D.N.Y. 1977) (specific intent not required under Interstate Land Sales Act).

186. *See* CALLIES & FREILICH, CASES AND MATERIALS ON LAND USE, notes on federal statutes and disclosures at pp. 400-402 (West 1986, 1991 Supp.).

187. Securities Exchange Commission v. W.J. Howey Co., 328 U.S. 293, 298 (U.S. 1946). In David v. Rio Rancho Estate, Inc., 401 F. Supp. 1045 (S.D.N.Y. 1975) the plaintiff claimed that subdivision land was offered as an investment. In rejecting the claim the court held that the promotional materials when fairly read emphasized the residential aspect of the development more than investment potential.

188. SEC v. Glenn W. Turner Enterprises, 474 F.2d 476, 482 (9th Cir. 1973). In Happy Investment Group v. Lakeworld Properties, 396 F. Supp. 175 (N.D.Cal. 1975) the issue of whether two lots sold to plaintiff in a recreational subdivision were federal securities was answered in the negative. Applying the rules of *Howey* and *Glenn Turner,* the court found that no investment contract existed since title passed to the plaintiff and defendants did not retain "essential managerial control."

189. 15 U.S.C. §§ 1701-1720 (1982); *see* United States v. Dacus, 634 F.2d 441 (9th Cir. 1980) for a complete description of the act and upholding the constitutionality of the regulation provisions.

190. *See* P. BARRON, FEDERAL REGULATION OF REAL ESTATE (rev. ed. 1980) for a discussion concerning the initial adoption of the act. *See also* Coffey & Welch, *Federal Regulations of Land Sales: Full Disclosure Comes Down to Earth*, 21 CASE W. RES. L. REV. 5 (1969); Girard, *Consumer Protection—Land Sales*, 56 WOMEN LAW. J. 12 (1970); Morris, *The Interstate Land Sales Full Disclosure Act: Analysis and Evaluation*, 24 S. CAR. L. REV. 331 (1972); Comment *Applying the Interstate Land Full Disclosure Act*, 51 ORE. L. REV. 381 (1972); Comment *The Interstate Land Sales Full Disclosure Act*, 21 RUTGERS L. REV. 714 (1967); Krechter, *Federal Regulation of Interstate Land Sales*, 4 REAL PROP. PROB. & TR. J. 327 (1969).

191. P.L. 90-448, § 1, 82 Stat. 476.

192. H.R. Rep. No. 154, 96th Cong., 1st Sess. 16, *reprinted in* 1979 U.S. CODE CONG. & ADMIN. NEWS 2317. *See* Pierce v. Apple Valley, Inc., 597 F. Supp. 1480 (S.D. Ohio 1984) (purpose of the act is to ensure full disclosure to consumers prior to purchasing or leasing a subdivision lot and to prohibit and punish fraud in the land sales industry). *See generally* Heffler, *The Interstate Land Sales Act: A Little Condominium May Be a 'Lot'* 1 PROB. AND PROP. 17, 17 (March/April 1987) ("Congress enacted the Act in 1968 in response to fraud on unsophisticated individuals committed by unscrupulous promoters"); the Interstate Land Sales Act was patterned after the Federal Securities Act of 1933, 15 U.S.C.A. §§ 77a *et. seq.* (under the Securities Act, full disclosure of all material facts relating to a public offering of securities must be made to all prospective purchasers).

193. 15 U.S.C. § 1701(3) (1982); 24 C.F.R. § 1710.1 (1987).

194. The provisions of the act apply to "any developer or agent." 15 U.S.C.A. §§ 1703(a). Lenders who only finance the purchase of subdivision lots are not covered by the statute. Adema v. Great Northern Dev. Co., 374 F. Supp. 318 (N.D. Ga. 1973).

195. 15 U.S.C. § 1703(a)(1) (1982); 24 C.F.R. § 1710.3 (197). *See* Romanus v. American Triad Land Co., 675 S.W.2d 122 (Mo. Ct. App. 1984) (sale took place when parties initialed the contract and developer violated the act by failing to furnish property report at that time). In addition to self-executing statutory exemptions, Mosher v. Southridge Associates, 552 F. Supp. 1226 (W.D. Pa. 1982) the Secretary of HUD has discretionary power to grant additional exemptions under 15 U.S.C.A. § 1702(c).

196. 15 U.S.C. § 1702 (1982); 24 C.F.R. § 1710.5 (1987).

197. 15 U.S.C. § 1702(a)(1) & (7) (1982); 24 C.F.R. § 1710.5(a) & (g) (1987).

198. 15 U.S.C. § 1702(b) (1982); 24 C.F.R. § 1710.6-.14 (1987).

199. 15 U.S.C. § 1702(b)(1)-(5), (7)-(8) (1982), 24 C.F.R. § 1710.6-.10, .12-.13 (1987). For discussions of the two series of exemptions, *see* Barron, *supra* note 190, ¶ 3.02[4], at 3-7 to 3-21; Malloy, *The Interstate Land Sales Full Disclosure Act: Its Requirements, Consequences, and Implications for Persons Participating in Real Estate Development*, 24 B.C.L. REV. 1186 (1983).

200. 15 U.S.C. § 1702 (1982); 24 C.F.R. § 1710.4(a) (1987).

201. 24 C.F.R. § 1710.4(d).

202. *Id.* § 1710.17.

203. *Id.* § 1710.18(a).

204. *Id.* § 1710.18(c).

205. *Id.*

206. 15 U.S.C. § 1702(c) (1982).

207. 24 C.F.R. § 1710.14(a)(1), (3), (4) (1987). *See generally* Barron, *supra* note 190, at 3.02[4][d], at 3-21 to 3-23 (provides detailed summary of the regulatory exemptions).

208. *See, e.g.,* ARIZ. REV. STAT. ANN. § 32-2181 (1983); CAL. BUS. & PROF. CODE §§ 10237-38.8, 11000-11200 (West 1983); ORE. REV. STAT. §§ 92.305-.990 (1983).

209. For an excellent summary of the statutes, regulations, and policies of the 50 states dealing with land sales registration requirements, *see* THE DIGEST OF STATE LAND SALES REGULATIONS (Bloch & Ingersoll eds. 1981).

210. 15 U.S.C. § 1708(a) (1982). *See also* 24 C.F.R. §§ 1710.500-.599 (1987) (establishes criteria and procedures for certifying state land sales and land development standards programs).

211. *1987 HUD Report to the Congress,* Interstate Land Sales Registration Program 10 (March 1986).

212. 15 U.S.C. § 1708(b) (1982).

213. 1987 HUD Report, *supra* note 211.

214. 15 U.S.C. § 1704 (1982).

215. *Id.* § 1703(a); 24 C.F.R. § 1700.1 (1987).

216. 15 U.S.C. § 1703(c) (1982).

217. 24 C.F.R. § 1710.100(a) (1987). For the information that a developer must include in the statement of record and property report, *see id.* § 1705; 24 C.F.R. §§ 1710.20, .101-.219 (1987). *See also* Barron, *supra* note 190, ¶ 3.02[5], at 3-24 to 3-25. For the procedure for filing a statement of record or amendments, *see* 15 U.S.C. § 1706 (1982); 24 C.F.R. § 1710.20, .23 (1987). *See also*

Barron, *supra* note 190, ¶ 3.02[5][c], at 3-25 to 3-28. For a discussion of the two-year rescission remedy, *see* Peretz, *Rescission Under the Interstate Land Sales Full Disclosure Act*, 58 FLA. B.J. 297 (1984).

218. 24 C.F.R. § 1700.15 (1987).

219. 15 U.S.C. § 1703(2)(d).

220. *Id.* § 1707(b). *See also* 24 C.F.R. § 1715.20 (1987) (sets forth list of promotional activities that constitute an unlawful sales practice); *id.* § 1715.25 (sets forth advertising representations that are regarded as misleading unless the developer provides specific safeguards to guarantee the accuracy of the representation); *id.* § 1715.50 (requires the display of a disclaimer statement on all written material in connection with the sale of a lot for which a statement of record is in effect); *id.* §§ 1710.9, .12, .13 (requires contracts to contain safeguard provisions in order for the sale or lease of a lot in a subdivision to be exempt from the entire act or from the act's registration and disclosure paragraphs). For a discussion of unlawful and misleading sales practices, *see* Barron, *supra* note 190, ¶ 3.02[7], at 3-31 to 3-32.

221. "HUD Acts to Curb Land Sales Fraud," New York Times Sept. 6, 1973, at 3, col. 1. *See also* Coffey & Welch, *supra* note 190, at 51. HUD has enacted new regulations to prevent developers from avoiding the disclosure provision of the act. The property report regulation must be stamped with a clear warning in red print, "Purchaser should read this document before signing anything." Documents waiving a 48-hour-revocation right must be separate, the developer must make a certified disclosure of his financial condition and the timetable for promised improvements, and advertising must conform to the property report and not be misleading. 2 C.F.R. § 226 (1987).

222. However, the information that is required to be disclosed to prospective purchasers is for their benefit; therefore any omission or untrue statements will trigger liability. Hester v. Hidden Valley Lakes, Inc., 495 F. Supp. 48 (N.D. Miss. 1980).

223. For an excellent summary of the statutes, regulations, and policies of the 50 states relating to land sales registration requirements, *see* THE DIGEST OF STATE LAND SALES REGULATIONS (Bloch & Ingersoll eds. 1981).

224. Commissioner v. Hawaii Market Center, Inc., 485 P.2d 105 (Hawaii 1971); Florida Realty, Inc. v. Kirkpatrick, 509 S.W.2d 114 (Mo. 1974).

225. D.M. Parks in the introduction to THE GREAT LAND HUSTLE 168 (1972) (between 1969 and 1972 the number of states that have some form of land sales controls reached 35 but the laws tended to be weakest in states where land hustlers are most active, such as Florida).

226. California, Georgia, Kansas, Maine, Minnesota, Missouri, Tennessee, Vermont, and West Virginia.

227. *See, e.g.*, CAL. ANN. BUS. & PROF. CODE §§ 11000 *et. seq.* If a state in which the land is located has minimal subdivision or other type of regulation to ensure that the land is properly developed and adequate amenities provided, mere disclosure under a securities law is of little help to the purchaser who will later find no roads, sewers, or utilities.

228. *See* ARIZ. REV. STAT. §§ 44-1801 to 44-2037, MINN. STAT. ANN. §§ 83.01 *et. seq.*, and NEB. REV. STAT. §§ 81-1101 *et. seq.*; *see also* L. LOSS AND E. COWETT, BLUE SKY LAW 19 (1958).

229. COLO. REV. STAT. §§ 11-51-101 *et. seq.*

230. ME. REV. STAT. ANN. §§ 751-891; TENN. CODE ANN. §§ 48-2-101 *et. seq.*

231. CALLIES & FREILICH, CASES AND MATERIALS ON LAND USE, ch. 4, at 404 (1986, 1991 Supp.); Smith, *State "Blue Sky" Laws and the Federal Securities Act*, 34 MICH. L. REV. 1135 (1936).

232. 15 U.S.C.A. §§ 1601 *et. seq.* and Regulation Z, 12 C.F.R. §§ 226 *et. seq.*

233. U.C.C.C. § 5-203(1)(a).

234. McDonald v. Mianecki, 398 A.2d 1283 (N.J. 1979) (contains useful language regarding the death of "caveat emptor"—buyer beware common law doctrines—and particularly describes the need for courts and legislatures to equate real estate law with personal property emerging doctrines).

235. *See* CLARK & SMITH, THE LAW OF PRODUCT WARRANTIES (Warren, Gorham & Lamont 1991 Supp.); Foxcroft Townhome Owners Ass'n v. Hoffman Rosner Corp., 435 N.E.2d 210 (Ill. App. 1982); Crowder v. Vandendeale, 564 S.W.2d 879 (Mo. 1978); Patitucci v. Drelich, 379 A.2d 297 (N.J. Super 1977); Wright v. Creative Corp., 498 P.2d 1179 (Colo. App. 1972); Conner v. Great Western Sav. & Loan Ass'n, 447 P.2d 609 (Cal. 1968); Rogers v. Scyphers, 161 S.E.2d 81 (S.C. 1968).

236. McDonald v. Mianecki, 398 A.2d 1283 (N.J. 1979) (the implied warranty of habitability applies to a builder who constructed plaintiff's new home and to the well which yielded unpotable water); Conklin v. Hurley, 428 So.2d 654 (Fla. 1983) (applies to residence itself, water well, septic tanks, and other improvements immediately supporting the residence, but not to a remote collapsed seawall).

237. Avonscher v. Mandora, 484 A.2d 675 (N.J. 1984) (doesn't apply to home improvement contractor who built patio to existing home).

238. Redarowicz v. Ohlendorf, 441 N.E.2d 324 (Ill. 1982); Nastri v. Wood Bros. Homes, 690 P.2d 158 (Ariz. Ct. App. 1984); Chubb Group of Insurance Cos. v. C.F. Murphy & Assocs, 656 S.W.2d 766 (Mo. Ct. App. 1983).

239. Littlefield v. City of Afton, 785 F.2d 596 (8th Cir. 1986).

Requirements for Improvements, Reservations, and Design

5.1 General Improvements.

1. *Conformance to Applicable Rules and Regulations.* In addition to the requirements established in these regulations, all subdivision plats shall comply with the following laws, rules, and regulations:
   a. All applicable statutory provisions.
   b. The local government zoning ordinance, building and housing codes, and all other applicable laws of the appropriate jurisdictions.
   c. The Official Master Plan, Official Map, Public Utilities Plan, and Capital Improvements Program of the local government, including all streets, drainage systems, and parks shown on the Official Map or Master Plan as adopted.
   d. The special requirements of these regulations and any rules of the Health Department and/or appropriate state or substate agencies.
   e. The rules of the State Highway Department if the subdivision or any lot contained therein abuts a state highway or connecting street.
   f. The standards and regulations adopted by the Local Government Engineer and all boards, commissions, agencies, and officials of the Local Government.
   g. All pertinent standards contained within the planning guides published by the applicable regional or metropolitan planning commission or Metropolitan Council of Governments.
   h. Plat approval may be withheld if a subdivision is not in conformity with the above laws, regulations, guidelines, and policies

as well as the purposes of these regulations established in Section 1.3 of these regulations.

2. ***Adequate Public Facilities.*** No preliminary plat shall be approved unless the Planning Commission determines that public facilities will be adequate to support and service the area of the proposed subdivision. The applicant shall, at the request of the Planning Commission, submit sufficient information and data on the proposed subdivision to demonstrate the expected impact on and use of public facilities by possible uses of said subdivision. Public facilities and services to be examined for adequacy will include roads and public transportation facilities, sewerage, and water service. (Note, some jurisdictions will also allow adequacy requirements for schools, police stations, fire houses, and health clinics.)

   a. Periodically the Governing Body will establish by resolution, after public hearing, guidelines for the determination of the adequacy of public facilities and services. To provide the basis for the guidelines, the Planning Commission must prepare an analysis of current growth and the amount of additional growth that can be accommodated by future public facilities and services. The Planning Commission must also recommend any changes in preliminary plat approval criteria it finds appropriate in the light of its experience in administering these regulations.

   b. The applicant for a preliminary plat must, at the request of the Planning Commission, submit sufficient information and data on the proposed subdivision to demonstrate the expected impact on and use of public facilities and services by possible uses of said subdivision.

   c. *Comprehensive Master Plan Consistency Required.* Proposed public improvements shall conform to and be properly related to the Local Government's comprehensive plan and all applicable capital improvements plans.

   d. *Water.* All habitable buildings and buildable lots shall be connected to a public water system capable of providing water for health and emergency purposes, including adequate fire protection.

   e. *Wastewater.* All habitable buildings and buildable lots shall be served by an approved means of wastewater collection and treatment.

   f. *Stormwater Management.* Drainage improvements shall accommodate potential runoff from the entire upstream drainage area and shall be designed to prevent increases in downstream flooding. The Local Government may require the use of control methods such as retention or detention, and/or the construction of offsite drainage improvements to mitigate the impacts of the proposed developments.

g. *Roads.* Proposed roads shall provide a safe, convenient, and functional system for vehicular, pedestrian, and bicycle circulation; shall be properly related to the comprehensive plan; and shall be appropriate for the particular traffic characteristics of each proposed development.

h. *Extension Policies.* All public improvements and required easements shall be extended through the parcel on which new development is proposed. Streets, water lines, wastewater systems, drainage facilities, electric lines, and telecommunications lines shall be constructed through new development to promote the logical extension of public infrastructure. The Local Government may require the applicant of a subdivision to extend offsite improvements to reach the subdivision or oversize required public facilities to serve anticipated future development as a condition of plat approval.

3. ***Self-Imposed Restrictions.*** If the owner places restrictions on any of the land contained in the subdivision greater than those required by the Zoning Ordinance or these regulations, such restrictions or reference to those restrictions may be required to be indicated on the subdivision plat, or the Planning Commission may require that restrictive covenants be recorded with the County Recorder of Deeds in a form to be approved by the Local Government Attorney. When allowed by law, the subdivider shall grant to the local government the right to enforce the restrictive covenants.

4. ***Plats Straddling Municipal Boundaries.*** Whenever access to the subdivision is required across land in another local government, the Planning Commission may request assurance from the Local Government Attorney that access is legally established, and from the Local Government Engineer that the access road is adequately improved, or that a guarantee has been duly executed and is sufficient in amount to assure the construction of the access road. In general, lot lines should be laid out so as not to cross municipal boundary lines.

5. ***Monuments.*** The applicant shall place permanent reference monuments in the subdivision as required in these regulations and as approved by a Registered Land Surveyor.

a. Monuments shall be located on street right-of-way lines, at street intersections, angle points of curve and block corners. They shall be spaced so as to be within sight of each other, the sight lines being contained wholly within the street limits.

b. The external boundaries of a subdivision shall be monumented in the field by monuments of stone or concrete, not less than thirty (30) inches in length, not less than four (4) inches square or five (5) inches in diameter, and marked on top with a cross, brass plug, iron rod, or other durable material securely embedded; or by iron rods or pipes at least thirty (30) inches long and two (2) inches in diameter. These monuments shall be placed not more than 1,400 feet apart in any straight line and at all corners, at each end of all curves, at the point where a curve changes its radius, at all angle points in any line, and at all angle points along the meander line, those points to be not less than twenty (20) feet back from the bank of any river or stream, except that when such corners or points fall within a street, or proposed future street, the monuments shall be placed in the side line of the street.

c.   All internal boundaries and those corners and points not referred to in the preceding paragraph shall be monumented in the field by like monuments as described above. These monuments shall be placed at all block corners, at each end of all curves, at a point where a river changes its radius, and at all angle points in any line.

d.   The lines of lots that extend to rivers or streams shall be monumented in the field by iron pipes at least thirty (30) inches long and seven-eighths (7/8) inch in diameter or by round or square iron bars at least thirty (30) inches long. These monuments shall be placed at the point of intersection of the river or stream lot line, with a meander line established not less than twenty (20) feet back from the bank of the river or stream.

e.   All monuments required by these regulations shall be set flush with the ground and planted in such a manner that they will not be removed by frost.

f.   All monuments shall be properly set in the ground and approved by a Registered Land Surveyor prior to the time the Planning Commission recommends approval of the final plat.

6.   ***Character of the Land.*** Land that the Planning Commission finds to be unsuitable for subdivision or development due to flooding, improper drainage, steep slopes, rock formations, adverse earth formations or topography, utility easements, or other features that will reasonably be harmful to the safety, health, and general welfare of the present or future inhabitants of the subdivision and/or its surrounding areas, shall not be subdivided or developed unless adequate methods are formulated by the developer and approved by the Planning Commission, upon recommendation of the Local Government Engineer, to solve the problems created by the unsuitable land conditions. Such land shall be set aside for uses as shall not involve any danger to public health, safety, and welfare.

7. *Subdivision Name.* The proposed name of the subdivision shall not duplicate, or too closely approximate phonetically, the name of any other subdivision in the area covered by these regulations. The Planning Commission shall have final authority to designate the name of the subdivision, which shall be determined at sketch plat approval.

5.2 Lot Improvements.

1. *Lot Arrangement.* The lot arrangement shall be such that there will be no foreseeable difficulties, for reasons of topography or other conditions, in securing building permits to build on all lots in compliance with the Zoning Ordinance and Health Regulations and in providing driveway access to buildings on the lots from an approved street.

2. *Lot Dimensions.* Lot dimensions shall comply with the minimum standards of the Zoning Ordinance. Where lots are more than double the minimum required area for the zoning district, the Planning Commission may require that those lots be arranged so as to allow further subdivision and the opening of future streets where they would be necessary to serve potential lots, all in compliance with the Zoning Ordinance and these regulations. In general, side lot lines shall be at right angles to street lines (or radial to curving street lines) unless a variation from this rule will give a better street or lot plan. Dimensions of corner lots shall be large enough to allow for erection of buildings, observing the minimum front-yard setback from both streets. Depth and width of properties reserved or laid out for business, commercial, or industrial purposes shall be adequate to provide for the off-street parking and loading facilities required for the type of use and development contemplated, as established in the Zoning Ordinance.

3. *Lot Orientation.* The lot line common to the street right-of-way shall be the front line. All lots shall face the front line and a similar line across the street. Wherever feasible, lots shall be arranged so that the rear line does not abut the side line of an adjacent lot.

4. *Double Frontage Lots and Access to Lots.*
   a. *Double Frontage Lots.* Double frontage and reversed frontage lots shall be avoided except where necessary to provide separation of residential development from traffic arterials or to overcome specific disadvantages of topography and orientation.
   b. *Access from Major and Secondary Arterials.* Lots shall not, in general, derive access exclusively from a major or secondary street. Where driveway access from a major or secondary street may be necessary for several adjoining lots, the Planning Commission may require that such lots be served by a combined access drive in order to limit possible traffic hazards on the street. Where possible, driveways

should be designed and arranged so as to avoid requiring vehicles to back into traffic on major and secondary arterials.

5. *Soil Preservation, Grading, and Seeding.*

   a. *Soil Preservation and Final Grading.* No certificate of occupancy shall be issued until final grading has been completed in accordance with the approved final subdivision plat and the lot precovered with soil with an average depth of at least six (6) inches which shall contain no particles more than two (2) inches in diameter over the entire area of the lot, except that portion covered by buildings or included in streets, or where the grade has not been changed or natural vegetation seriously damaged. Topsoil shall not be removed from residential lots or used as spoil, but shall be redistributed so as to provide at least six (6) inches of cover on the lots and at least four (4) inches of cover between the sidewalks and curbs, and shall be stabilized by seeding or planting.

   b. *Lot Drainage.* Lots shall be laid out so as to provide positive drainage away from all buildings, and individual lot drainage shall be coordinated with the general storm drainage pattern for the area. Drainage shall be designed so as to avoid concentration of storm drainage water from each lot to adjacent lots.

   c. *Lawn-Grass Seed and Sod.* (Seeding and sod requirements should, of course, reflect local conditions.) Lawn-grass seed shall be sown at not less than four (4) pounds to each one-thousand (1,000) square feet of land area. In the spring, the seed shall be sown between March 15 and May 15; and in the fall, the seed shall be sown between August 15 and September 30. The seed shall consist of a maximum of ten percent (10%) rye grass by weight and minimum of ninety percent (90%) of permanent bluegrass and/or fescue grass by weight. All seed shall have been tested for germination within one (1) year of the date of seeding, and the date of testing shall be on the label containing the seed analysis. All lots shall be seeded from the roadside edge of the unpaved right-of-way back to a distance of twenty-five (25) feet behind the principal residence on the lot. No certificate of occupancy shall be issued until respreading of soil and seeding of lawn has been completed; except that between October 1 and March 15, and between May 15 and August 15, the applicant shall submit an agreement in writing signed by the developer and the property owner, with a copy to the Building and Zoning Inspector, that respreading of soil and seeding of lawn will be done during the immediate following planting season as set forth in this selection, and leave a cash escrow for performance in an amount determined by the Building and Zoning Inspector. Sod may be used to comply with any requirement of seeding set forth herein.

6. *Debris and Waste.* No cut trees, timber, debris, earth, rocks, stones, soil, junk, rubbish, or other waste materials of any kind shall be buried in any land, or left or deposited on any lot or street at the time of the issuance of a certificate of occupancy, and removal of those items and materials shall be required prior to issuance of any certificate of occupancy on a subdivision. No items and materials as described in the preceding sentence shall be left or deposited in any area of the subdivision at the time of expiration of any subdivision improvement agreement or dedication of public improvements, whichever is sooner.

7. *Waterbodies and Watercourses.* If a tract being subdivided contains a water body, or portion thereof, lot lines shall be so drawn as to distribute the entire ownership of the water body among the fees of adjacent lots. The Planning Commission may approve an alternative plan whereby the ownership of and responsibility for safe maintenance of the water body is so placed that it will not become a local government responsibility. No more than twenty-five percent (25%) of the minimum area of a lot required under the Zoning Ordinance may be satisfied by land that is under water. Where a watercourse separates the buildable area of a lot from the street by which it has access, provisions shall be made for installation of a culvert or other structure, of design approved by the Local Government Engineer.

8. *Subdivision Improvement Agreement and Security to Include Lot Improvement.* The applicant shall enter into a separate subdivision improvement agreement secured by a letter of credit or cash escrow to guarantee completion of all lot improvement requirements including, but not limited to, soil preservation, final grading, lot drainage, lawngrass seeding, removal of debris and waste, fencing, and all other lot improvements required by the Planning Commission. Whether or not a certificate of occupancy has been issued, the local government may enforce the provisions of the subdivision improvement agreement where the provisions of this section or any other applicable law, ordinance, or regulation have not been met.

5.3 Roads.

1. *General Requirements.*
   a. *Frontage on Improved Roads.* No subdivision shall be approved unless the area to be subdivided shall have frontage on and access from an existing street on the Official Map, or if there is no Official Map, unless such street is:

      i. An existing state, county, or township highway; or

      ii. A street shown upon a plat approved by the Planning Commission and recorded in the County Recorder of Deeds' office. Such street or highway must be suitably improved as required by the highway rules, regulations, specifications, or orders, or be secured by a performance bond required under these subdivision regulations, with the width and right-of-way required by these subdivision regulations or the Official Map Plan.

Wherever the area to be subdivided is to utilize existing road frontage, the road shall be suitably improved as provided above.

b. [Optional] *Level of Service.* No development shall be approved if such development, at full occupancy, will result in or increase traffic on an arterial or collector so that the street does not function at a level of service of C or better as described in section ___. The applicant may propose and construct approved traffic mitigation measures to provide adequate roadway capacity for the proposed development. The applicant for any development projected to generate more than 1,000 vehicle trip ends per day shall submit a traffic impact analysis.

c. *Grading and Improvement Plan.* Roads shall be graded and improved and conform to the local government construction standards and specifications and shall be approved as to design and specifications by the Local Government Engineer, in accordance with the construction plans required to be submitted prior to final plat approval.

d. *Classification.* All roads shall be classified as either [insert road types, e.g., major arterial, minor arterial, collector, or local]. In classifying roads, the Local Government shall consider projected traffic demands after 20 years of development.

e. *Topography and Arrangement.*

      i. Roads shall be related appropriately to the topography. Local roads shall be curved wherever possible to avoid conformity of lot appearance. All streets shall be arranged so as to obtain as many building sites as possible at, or above, the grades of the streets. Grades of streets shall conform as closely as possible to the original topography. A combination of steep grades and curves shall be avoided. Specific standards are contained in the design standards of these regulations.

      ii. All streets shall be properly integrated with the existing and proposed system of thoroughfares and dedicated rights-of-way as established on the Official Map and/or Master Plan.

      iii. All thoroughfares shall be properly related to special traffic generators such as industries, business districts, schools, churches, and shopping centers; to population densities; and to the pattern of existing and proposed land uses.

iv. Minor or local streets shall be laid out to conform as much as possible to the topography to discourage use by through traffic, to permit efficient drainage and utility systems, and to require the minimum number of streets necessary to provide convenient and safe access to property.

v. The rigid rectangular gridiron street pattern need not necessarily be adhered to, and the use of curvilinear streets, cul-de-sacs, or U-shaped streets shall be encouraged where such use will result in a more desirable layout.

vi. Proposed streets shall be extended to the boundary lines of the tract to be subdivided, unless prevented by topography or other physical conditions, or unless in the opinion of the Planning Commission such extension is not necessary or desirable for the coordination of the layout of the subdivision with the existing layout or the most advantageous future development of adjacent tracks.

vii. In business and industrial developments, the streets and other accessways shall be planned in connection with the grouping of buildings, location of rail facilities, and the provision of alleys, truck loading and maneuvering areas, and walks and parking areas so as to minimize conflict of movement between the various types of traffic, including pedestrian.

f. *Blocks.*

i. Blocks shall have sufficient width to provide for two (2) tiers of lots of appropriate depths. Exceptions to this prescribed block width shall be permitted in blocks adjacent to major streets, railroads, or waterways.

ii. The lengths, widths, and shapes of blocks shall be such as are appropriate for the locality and the type of development contemplated, but block lengths in residential areas shall not exceed two thousand two hundred (2,200) feet or twelve (12) times the minimum lot width required in the zoning district, nor be less than four hundred (400) feet in length. Wherever practicable, blocks along major arterials and collector streets shall be not less than one thousand (1,000) feet in length.

iii. In long blocks the Planning Commission may require the reservation of an easement through the block to accommodate utilities, drainage facilities, or pedestrian traffic.

iv. Pedestrianways or crosswalks, not less than ten (10) feet wide, may be required by the Planning Commission through the center of blocks more than eight hundred (800) feet long where deemed essential to provide circulation or access to schools, playgrounds, shopping centers, transportation, or other community facilities. Blocks designed for industrial uses shall be of such length and width as may be determined suitable by the Planning Commission for prospective use.

g. *Access to Primary Arterials.* Where a subdivision borders on or contains an existing or proposed primary arterial, the Planning Commission may require that access to such streets be limited by one of the following means:

   i. The subdivision of lots so as to back onto the primary arterial and front onto a parallel local street; no access shall be provided from the primary arterial, and screening shall be provided in a strip of land along the rear property line of such lots.

   ii. A series of cul-de-sacs, U-shaped streets, or short loops entered from and designed generally at right angles to such a parallel street, with the rear lines of their terminal lots backing onto the primary arterial.

   iii. A marginal access or service road (separated from the primary arterial by a planning or grass strip and having access at suitable points).

h. *Road Names.* The sketch plat as submitted shall not indicate any names for proposed streets. The Planning Commission shall name all roads upon recommendation of the Administrative Assistant at the time of preliminary approval. The Administrative Assistant shall consult the local postmaster prior to rendering its recommendation to the Planning Commission. Names shall be sufficiently different in sound and spelling from other road names in the municipality so as not to cause confusion. A road which is (or is planned as) a continuation of an existing road shall bear the same name.

i. *Road Regulatory Signs.* The applicant shall deposit with the local government at the time of final subdivision approval the sum of fifty dollars ($50) for each road sign required by the Local Government Engineer at all road intersections. The Local Government shall install all road signs before issuance of certificates of occupancy for any residence on the streets approved. Street name signs are to placed at all intersections within or abutting the subdivision, the type and location of which to be approved by the Local Government Engineer.

j. *Street Lights.* Installation of street lights shall be required in accordance with design and specification standards approved by the Local Government Engineer.

k. *Reserve Strips.* The creation of reserve strips shall not be permitted adjacent to a proposed street in such a manner as to deny access from adjacent property to the street.

l. *Construction of Roads and Dead-End Roads.*

   i. Construction of Roads.

   The arrangement of streets shall provide for the continuation of principal streets between adjacent properties when the continuation is necessary for convenient movement of traffic, effective fire protection, for efficient provision of utilities, and where the continuation is in accordance with the Local Government traffic plan. If the adjacent property is undeveloped and the street must temporarily be a dead-end street, the right-of-way shall be extended to the property line. A temporary T- or L-shaped turnabout shall be provided on all temporary dead-end streets, with the notation on the subdivision plat that land outside the normal street right-of-way shall revert to abuttors whenever the street is continued. The Planning Commission may limit the length of temporary dead-end streets in accordance with the design standards of these regulations.

   ii. Dead-End Roads (Permanent).

   Where a road does not extend beyond the boundary of the subdivision and its continuation is not required by the Planning Commission for access to adjoining property, its terminus shall normally not be nearer to such boundary than fifty (50) feet. However, the Planning Commission may require the reservation of an appropriate easement to accommodate drainage facilities, pedestrian traffic, or utilities. A cul-de-sac turnaround shall be provided at the end of a permanent dead-end street in accordance with Local Government construction standards and specifications. For greater convenience to traffic and more effective police and fire protection, permanent dead-end streets shall, in general, be limited in length in accordance with the design standards of these regulations.

2. **Design Standards.**

   a. *General.* In order to provide for roads of suitable location, width, and improvement to accommodate prospective traffic and afford satisfactory access to police, firefighting, snow removal, sanitation, and road-maintenance equipment, and to coordinate roads so as to compose a convenient system and avoid undue hardships to adjoining properties, the following design standards for roads are hereby required (Road classification may be indicated on the Master Plan or Official Map; otherwise, it shall be determined by the Planning Commission. Guidelines for classification are available from many local professional engineering associations, such as local chapters of the American Public Works Association, or from national organizations such as the American Association of State Highway and Transportation Officials.)

b. *Road Surfacing and Improvements.* After sewer and water utilities have been installed by the developer, the developer shall construct curbs and gutters and shall surface or cause to be surfaced roadways to the widths prescribed in these regulations. All surfacing shall be of a character as is suitable for the expected traffic and in harmony with similar improvements in the surrounding areas. Types of pavement shall be as determined by the Local Government Engineer. Adequate provision shall be made for culverts, drains, and bridges. All road pavement, shoulders, drainage improvements and structures, curbs, turnarounds, and sidewalks shall conform to all construction standards and specifications adopted by the Planning Commission, Local Government Engineer, or Governing Body and shall be incorporated into the construction plans required to be submitted by the developer for plat approval.

c. *Excess Right-of-Way.* Right-of-way widths in excess of the standards designated in these regulations shall be required whenever, due to topography, additional width is necessary to provide adequate earth slopes. Such slopes shall not be in excess of three-to-one.

d. *Railroads and Limited Access Highways.* Railroad rights-of-way and limited access highways where so located as to affect the subdivision of adjoining lands shall be treated as follows:

i. In residential districts a buffer strip at least 25 feet in depth in addition to the normal depth of the lot required in the district shall be provided adjacent to the railroad right-of-way or limited access highway. This strip shall be part of the platted lots and shall be designated on the plat: "This strip is reserved for screening. The placement of structure on this land is prohibited."

ii. In districts zoned for business, commercial, or industrial uses the nearest street extending parallel or approximately parallel to the railroad right-of-way shall, wherever practicable, be at a sufficient distance from the railroad right-of-way to ensure suitable depth for commercial or industrial sites.

iii. When streets parallel to the railroad right-of-way intersect a street which crosses the railroad right-of-way at grade, they shall, to the extent practicable, be at a distance of at least 150 feet from the railroad right-of-way. Such distance shall be determined with due consideration of the minimum distance required for future separation of grades by means of appropriate approach gradients.

e. *Intersections.*

    i. Streets shall be laid out so as to intersect as nearly as possible at right angles. A proposed intersection of two (2) new streets at an angle of less than seventy-five (75) degrees shall not be acceptable. An oblique street should be curved approaching an intersection and should be approximately at right angles for at least one hundred (100) feet therefrom. Not more than two (2) streets shall intersect at any one point unless specifically approved by the Planning Commission.

    ii. Proposed new intersections along one side of an existing street shall, wherever practicable, coincide with any existing intersections on the opposite side of such street. Street jogs with center-line offsets of less than 150 feet shall not be permitted, except where the intersected street has separated dual drives without median breaks at either intersection. Where streets intersect major streets, their alignment shall be continuous. Intersection of major streets shall be at least eight hundred (800) feet apart.

    iii. Minimum curb radius at the intersection of two (2) local streets shall be at least twenty (20) feet; and minimum curb radius at an intersection involving a collector street shall be at least twenty-five (25) feet. Alley intersections and abrupt changes in alignment within a block shall have the corners cut off in accordance with standard engineering practice to permit safe vehicular movement.

    iv. Intersections shall be designed with a flat grade wherever practical. In hilly or rolling areas, at the approach to an intersection, a leveling area shall be provided having not greater than a two percent (2%) rate at a distance of sixty (60) feet, measured from the nearest right-of-way line of the intersecting street.

    v. Where any street intersection will involve earth banks or existing vegetation inside any lot corner that would create a traffic hazard by limiting visibility, the developer shall cut such ground and/or vegetation (including trees) in connection with the grading of the public right-of-way to the extent deemed necessary to provide an adequate sight distance.

vi. The cross-slopes on all streets, including intersections, shall be three percent (3%) or less.

   f. *Bridges.* Bridges of primary benefit to the applicant, as determined by the Planning Commission, shall be constructed at the full expense of the applicant without reimbursement from the Local Government. The sharing expense for the construction of bridges not of primary benefit to the applicant as determined by the Planning Commission, will be fixed by special agreement between the Governing Body and the applicant. The cost of bridges that do not solely benefit the developer shall be charged to the developer pro rata based on the percentage obtained by dividing the service area of the bridge into the area of the land being developed by the subdivider.

3. **Road Dedications and Reservations.**

   a. *New Perimeter Streets.* Street systems in new subdivisions shall be laid out so as to eliminate or avoid new perimeter half-streets. Where an existing half-street is adjacent to a new subdivision, the other half of the street shall be improved and dedicated by the subdivider. The Planning Commission may authorize a new perimeter street where the subdivider improves and dedicates the entire required street right-of-way width within its own subdivision boundaries.

   b. *Widening and Realignment of Existing Roads.* Where a subdivision borders an existing narrow road or when the Master Plan, Official Map, or zoning setback regulations indicate plans for realignment or widening a road that would require use of some of the land in the subdivision, the applicant shall be required to improve and dedicate at its expense those areas for widening or realignment of those roads. Frontage roads and streets as described above shall be improved and dedicated by the applicant at its own expense to the full width as required by these subdivision regulations when the applicant's development activities contribute to the need for the road expansion. Land reserved for any road purposes may not be counted in satisfying yard or area requirements of the Zoning Ordinance whether the land is to be dedicated to the municipality in fee simple or an easement is granted to the Local Government.

5.4   Drainage and Storm Sewers.

1. *General Requirements.* The Planning Commission shall not recommend for approval any plat of subdivision that does not make adequate provision for storm and flood water runoff channels or basins. The storm water drainage system shall be separate and independent of

any sanitary sewer system. Storm sewers, where required, shall be designed by the Rational Method, or other methods as approved by the Planning Commission, and a copy of design computations shall be submitted along with plans. Inlets shall be provided so that surface water is not carried across or around any intersection, nor for a distance of more than 600 feet in the gutter. When calculations indicate that curb capacities are exceeded at a point, no further allowance shall be made for flow beyond that point, and basins shall be used to intercept flow at that point. Surface water drainage patterns shall be shown for each and every lot and block.

2. *Nature of Storm Water Facilities.*

   a. *Location.* The applicant may be required by the Planning Commission to carry away by pipe or open ditch any spring or surface water that may exist either previously to, or as a result of the subdivision. Such drainage facilities shall be located in the road right-of-way where feasible, or in perpetual unobstructed easements of appropriate width, and shall be constructed in accordance with the construction standards and specifications.

   b. *Accessibility to Public Storm Sewers.*

      i. Where a public storm sewer is accessible, the applicant shall install storm sewer facilities, or if no outlets are within a reasonable distance, adequate provision shall be made for the disposal of storm waters, subject to the specifications of the Local Government Engineer. However, in subdivisions containing lots less than 15,000 square feet in area and in business and industrial districts, underground storm sewer systems shall be constructed throughout the subdivisions and be conducted to an approved out-fall. Inspection of facilities shall be conducted by the Local Government Engineer.

      ii. If a connection to a public storm sewer will be provided eventually, as determined by the Local Government Engineer and the Planning Commission, the developer shall make arrangements for future storm water disposal by a public utility system at the time the plat receives final approval. Provision for such connection shall be incorporated by inclusion in the subdivision improvement agreement required for the subdivision plat.

   c. *Accommodation of Upstream Drainage Areas.* A culvert or other drainage facility shall in each case be large enough to accommodate potential runoff from its entire upstream drainage area, whether inside or outside the subdivision. The Local Government Engineer shall determine the necessary size of the facility, based on the provisions of the construction standards and specifications assuming conditions of maximum potential watershed development permitted by the Zoning Ordinance.

d. *Effect on Downstream Drainage Areas.* The Local Government Engineer shall also study the effect of each subdivision on existing downstream drainage facilities outside the area of the subdivision. Local government drainage studies together with such other studies as shall be appropriate, shall serve as a guide to needed improvements. Where it is anticipated that the additional runoff incident to the development of the subdivision will overload an existing downstream drainage facility, the Planning Commission may withhold approval of the subdivision until provision has been made for the expansion of the existing downstream drainage facility. No subdivision shall be approved unless adequate drainage will be provided to an adequate drainage watercourse or facility.

e. *Areas of Poor Drainage.* Whenever a plat is submitted for an area that is subject to flooding, the Planning Commission may approve such subdivision provided that the applicant fills the affected area of the subdivision to an elevation sufficient to place the elevation of streets and lots at a minimum of twelve (12) inches above the elevation of the one hundred (100) year floodplain, as determined by the Local Government Engineer. The plat of the subdivision shall provide for an overflow zone along the bank of any stream or watercourse, in a width that shall be sufficient in times of high water to contain or move the water, and no fill shall be placed in the overflow zone nor shall any structure be erected or placed in the overflow zone. The boundaries of the overflow zone shall be subject to approval by the Local Government Engineer. The Planning Commission may deny subdivision approval for areas of extremely poor drainage.

f. *Floodplain Areas.* The Planning Commission may, when it deems it necessary for the health, safety, or welfare of the present and future population of the area and necessary to the conservation of water, drainage, and sanitary facilities, prohibit the subdivision of any portion of the property that lies within the floodplain of any stream or drainage course. These floodplain areas shall be preserved from any and all destruction or damage resulting from clearing, grading, or dumping of earth, waste material, or stumps, except at the discretion of the Planning Commission.

3. *Dedication of Drainage Easements.*

a. *General Requirements.* When a subdivision is traversed by a watercourse, drainageway, channel, or stream, there shall be provided a storm water easement or drainage right-of-way conforming substantially to the lines of such watercourse, and of such width and construction as will be adequate for the purpose. Wherever possible, it is desirable that the drainage be maintained by an open channel with landscaped banks and adequate width for maximum potential volume of flow.

b. *Drainage Easements.*

 i. Where topography or other conditions are such as to make impractical the inclusion of drainage facilities within road rights-of-way, perpetual, unobstructed easements at least fifteen (15) feet in width for drainage facilities shall be provided across property outside the road lines and with satisfactory access to the road. Easements shall be indicated on the plat. Drainage easements shall extend from the road to a natural watercourse or to other drainage facilities.

 ii. When a proposed drainage system will carry water across private land outside the subdivision, appropriate drainage rights must be secured and indicated on the plat.

 iii. The applicant shall dedicate, either in fee or by a drainage or conservation easement, land on both sides of existing watercourses to a distance to be determined by the Planning Commission.

 iv. Low-lying lands along watercourses subject to flooding or overflowing during storm periods, whether or not included in areas for dedication, shall be preserved and retained in their natural state as drainage ways. Such land or lands subject to periodic flooding shall not be computed in determining the number of lots to be utilized for average density procedures nor for computing the area requirement of any lot.

5.5 Water Facilities.

1. *General Requirements.*

 a. When a public water main is not accessible, the developer shall take necessary action to extend or create a water-supply district for the purpose of providing a water-supply system capable of providing for domestic water use and fire protection.

 b. When a public water main is accessible, the developer shall install adequate water facilities (including fire hydrants) subject to the specifications of state or local authorities. All water mains shall be at least six (6) inches in diameter.

 c. Water main extensions shall be approved by the officially designated agency of the state or local government.

    d. The location of all fire hydrants, all water supply improvements, and the boundary lines of proposed districts, indicating all improvements proposed to be served, shall be shown on the preliminary plat, and the cost of installing same shall be borne by the developer and included in the subdivision improvement agreement and security to be furnished by the developer.

2. *Individual Wells and Central Water Systems.*

    a. In zoning districts with a density of one unit per acre or less and when a public water system is not available in the discretion of the Planning Commission, individual wells may be used or a central water system provided in a manner so that an adequate supply of potable water will be available to every lot in the subdivision. Water samples shall be submitted to the Health Department for its approval, and individual wells and central water systems shall be approved by the appropriate health authorities. Approvals shall be submitted to the Planning Commission prior to final subdivision plat approval.

    b. If the Planning Commission requires that a connection to a public water main be eventually provided as a condition to approval of an individual well or central water system, the applicant shall make arrangements prior to receiving final plat approval for future water service. Performance or cash bonds may be required to ensure compliance.

3. *Fire Hydrants.* Fire hydrants shall be required for all subdivisions except those coming under Section 5.5(2). Fire hydrants shall be located no more than 1,000 feet apart and within 500 feet of any structure and shall be approved by the applicable fire protection unit. To eliminate future street openings, all underground utilities for fire hydrants, together with the fire hydrants themselves, and all other supply improvements shall be installed before any final paving of a street shown on the subdivision plat.

5.6 Sewerage Facilities.

1. *General Requirements.* The applicant shall install sanitary sewer facilities in a manner prescribed by the local government construction standards and specifications. All plans shall be designed and approved in accordance with the rules, regulations, and standards of the Local Government Engineer, Health Department, and other appropriate agency. Necessary action shall be taken by the applicant to extend or create a sanitary sewer district for the purpose of providing sewerage facilities to the subdivision when no district exists for the land to be subdivided.

2. ***High-Density Residential and Nonresidential Districts.*** Sanitary sewerage facilities shall connect with public sanitary sewerage systems. Sewers shall be installed to serve each lot and to grades and sizes required by approving officials and agencies. No individual disposal system or treatment plants (private or group disposal systems) shall be permitted. Sanitary sewerage facilities (including the installation of laterals in the right-of-way) shall be subject to the specifications, rules, regulations, and guidelines of the Health Officer, Local Government Engineer, and appropriate state agency.

3. ***Low- and Medium-Density Residential Districts.*** Sanitary sewerage systems shall be constructed as follows:

   a. When a public sanitary sewerage system is reasonably accessible, the applicant shall connect with same and provide sewers accessible to each lot in the subdivision.

   b. When public sanitary sewerage systems are not reasonably accessible but will become available within a reasonable time (not to exceed fifteen [15] years), the applicant may choose one of the following alternatives:

      i. Central sewerage system with the maintenance cost to be assessed against each property benefited. Where plans for future public sanitary sewerage systems exist, the applicant shall install the sewer lines, laterals, and mains to be in permanent conformance with such plans and ready for connection to such public sewer mains; or

      ii. Individual disposal systems, provided the applicant shall install sanitary sewer lines, laterals, and mains from the street curb to a point in the subdivision boundary where a future connection with the public sewer main shall be made. Sewer lines shall be laid from the house to the street line, and a connection shall be available in the home to connect from the individual disposal system to the sewer system when the public sewers become available. Such sewer systems shall be capped until ready for use and shall conform to all plans for installation of the public sewer system, where such exist, and shall be ready for connection to such public sewer main.

   c. When sanitary sewer systems are not reasonably accessible and will not become available for a period in excess of fifteen (15) years, the applicant may install sewerage systems as follows:

      i. Medium-Density Residential Districts. Only a central sewerage system may be constructed. No individual disposal system will be permitted. Where plans exist for a public sewer system to be built, for a period in excess of fifteen (15) years, the applicant shall install all sewer lines, laterals, and mains to be in permanent conformance with such plans and ready for connection to such public sewer main.

ii. Low-Density Residential District. Individual disposal systems or central sewerage systems shall be used.

4. *Mandatory Connection to Public Sewer System.* If a public sanitary sewer is accessible and a sanitary sewer is placed in a street or alley abutting upon property, the owner of the property shall be required to connect to the sewer for the purpose of disposing of waste, and it shall be unlawful for any such owner or occupant to maintain upon any such property an individual sewage disposal system.

5. *Individual Disposal System Requirements.* If public sewer facilities are not available and individual disposal systems are proposed, minimum lot areas shall conform to the requirements of the Zoning Ordinance and percolation tests and test holes shall be made as directed by the local government Health Officer and the results submitted to the Health Department. The individual disposal system, including the size of the septic tanks and size of the tile fields or other secondary treatment device, shall also be approved by the Health Officer.

6. *Design Criteria for Sanitary Sewers.*
   a. *General Guidelines.* These design criteria are not intended to cover extraordinary situations. Deviations will be allowed and may be required in those instances when considered justified by the Local Government Engineer.
   b. *Design Factors.* Sanitary sewer systems should be designed for the ultimate tributary population. Due consideration should be given to current zoning regulations and approved planning and zoning reports where applicable. Sewer capacities should be adequate to handle the anticipated maximum hourly quantity of sewage and industrial waste together with an adequate allowance for infiltration and other extraneous flow. The unit design flows presented below should be adequate in each case for the particular type of development indicated. Sewers shall be designed for the total tributary area using the following criteria:

One- and Two-Family Dwellings	.02 cubic feet per second (c.f.s.)/ acre
Apartments	
One and Two Story	.02 c.f.s./acre
Three through Six Story	.03 c.f.s./acre

Commercial

Small Stores, Offices, and Miscellaneous Business	.02 c.f.s./acre
Shopping Centers	.02 c.f.s./acre
High Rise	As directed by Local Gov. Eng.
Industrial	As directed by Local Gov. Eng.

These design factors shall apply to watersheds of 300 acres or less. Design factors for watersheds larger than 300 acres and smaller than 1,000 acres shall be computed on the basis of a linear decrease from the applicable design factor for an area of 300 acres to a design factor of .01 c.f.s./acre for an area of 1,000 acres unless otherwise directed by the Local Government Engineer. Design factors for watersheds larger than 1,000 acres shall be .01 c.f.s./acre unless otherwise directed by the Local Government Engineer.

c. *Maximum Size.* The diameter of sewers proposed shall not exceed the diameter of the existing or proposed outlet, whichever is applicable, unless otherwise approved by the Local Government Engineer.

d. *Minimum Size.* No public sewer shall be less than eight (8) inches in diameter.

e. *Minimum Slope.* All sewers shall be designed to give mean velocities when flowing full of not less than 2.7 feet per second. All velocity and flow calculations shall be based on the Manning Formula using an N value of 0.013. The design slopes shall be evenly divisible by four (4). The slopes shall be minimum for the size indicated. Exceptions to these minimum slopes shall be made at the upper end of lateral sewers serving under thirty (30) houses. Sewers at the upper end shall have a minimum slope of 0.76 percent. When lateral sewers serve less than ten (10) houses, the minimum slope shall be not less than one (1) percent. (See table below.)

MINIMUM SLOPES FOR SEWER SIZE INDICATED	
Sewer Size (inches)	Minimum Slope (feet per 100 feet)
8	0.60
10	0.44
12	0.36
15	0.28
18	0.24
21	0.20
24	0.16

f. *Alignment.* All sewers shall be laid with straight alignment between manholes, unless otherwise directed or approved by the Local Government Engineer.

g. *Manhole Location.* Manholes shall be installed at the end of each line; at all changes in grade, size, or alignment; at all intersections; and at distances not greater than 400 feet for sewers 15 inches and smaller, and 500 feet for sewers 18 inches in diameter and larger.

h. *Manholes.* The difference in elevation between any incoming sewer and the manhole invert shall not exceed 12 inches except where required to match crowns. The use of drop manholes will require approval by the Local Government Engineer. The minimum inside diameter of the manholes shall conform to those specified by the Local Government Engineer. Inside drop manholes will require special considerations; however, in no case shall the minimum clear distance be less than that indicated above. When a smaller sewer joins a larger one, the crown of the smaller sewer shall not be lower than that of the larger one. The minimum drop through manholes shall be 0.2 feet.

i. *Sewerage Locations.* Sanitary sewers shall be located within street or alley rights-of-way unless topography dictates otherwise. When located in easements on private property, access shall be to all manholes. A manhole shall be provided at each street or alley crossing. End lines shall be extended to provide access from street or alley right-of-way when possible. Imposed loading shall be considered in all locations. Not less than six (6) feet of cover shall be provided over the top of pipe in street and alley rights-of-way or three (3) feet in all other areas.

j. *Cleanouts and Lampholes.* Cleanouts and lampholes will not be permitted.

k. *Water Supply Interconnections.* There shall be no physical connection between a public or private potable water supply system and a sewer which will permit the passage of any sewage or polluted water into the potable supply. Sewers shall be kept removed from water supply wells or other water supply sources and structures.

l. *Relation of Sewers to Water Mains.* A minimum horizontal distance of ten (10) feet shall be maintained between parallel water and sewer lines. At points where sewers cross water mains, the sewer shall be constructed of cast iron pipe or encased in concrete for a distance of ten (10) feet in each direction from the crossing, measured perpendicular to the water line. This will not be required when the water main is at least two (2) feet above the sewer.

5.7   Sidewalks.

1. *Required Improvements.*
   a. Sidewalks shall be included within the dedicated nonpavement right-of-way of all roads shown in [indicate section].
   b. Concrete curbs are required for all roads when sidewalks are required by these regulations or when required in the discretion of the Planning Commission.
   c. Sidewalks shall be improved as required in Section 5.3(2)(b) of these regulations. A median strip of grassed or landscaped areas at least two (2) feet wide shall separate all sidewalks from adjacent curbs.
2. *Pedestrian Accesses.* The Planning Commission may require, in order to facilitate pedestrian access from the roads to schools, parks, playgrounds, or other nearby roads, perpetual unobstructed easements at least twenty (20) feet in width. Easements shall be indicated on the plat.

5.8   Utilities.

1. *Location.* All utility facilities, including but not limited to gas, electric power, telephone, and CATV cables, shall be located underground throughout the subdivision. Whenever existing utility facilities are located above ground, except when existing on public roads and rights-of-way, they shall be removed and placed underground. All utility facilities existing and proposed throughout the subdivision shall be shown on the preliminary plat. Underground service connections to the street property line of each platted lot shall be installed at the subdivider's expense. At the discretion of the Planning Commission, the requirement for service connections to each lot may be waived in the case of adjoining lots to be retained in single ownership and intended to be developed for the same primary use.
2. *Easements.*
   a. Easements centered on rear lot lines shall be provided for utilities (private and municipal) and such easements shall be at least ten (10) feet wide. Proper coordination shall be established between the subdivider and the applicable utility companies for the establishment of utility easements established in adjoining properties.
   b. When topographical or other conditions are such as to make impractical the inclusion of utilities within the rear lot lines, perpetual unobstructed easements at least ten (10) feet in width shall be provided along side lot lines with satisfactory access to the road or rear lot lines. Easements shall be indicated on the plat.

5.9   Public Uses.

1. *Parks, Playgrounds, and Recreation Areas.*

   a. *Recreation Standards.* The Planning Commission shall require that land be reserved for parks and playgrounds or other recreation purposes in locations designated on the Master Plan or otherwise where such reservations would be appropriate. Each reservation shall be of suitable size, dimension, topography, and general character and shall have adequate road access for the particular purposes envisioned by the Planning Commission. The area shall be shown and marked on the plat, "Reserved for Park and/or Recreation Purposes." When recreation areas are required, the Planning Commission shall determine the number of acres to be reserved from the following table, which has been prepared on the basis of providing three (3) acres of recreation area for every one hundred (100) dwelling units. The Planning Commission may refer such proposed reservations to the local government official or department in charge of parks and recreation for recommendation. The developer shall dedicate all such recreation areas to the local government as a condition of final subdivision plat approval.

      i. Table of Recreation Requirements.

Single-Family Lots Size of Lot	Percentage of Total Land in Subdivision to be Reserved for Recreation Purposes
80,000 sq.ft. & greater	1.5%
50,000 sq.ft.	2.5%
40,000 sq.ft.	3.0%
35,000 sq.ft.	3.5%
25,000 sq.ft.	5.0%
15,000 sq.ft	8.0%

      ii. Multifamily and High-Density Residential. The Planning Commission shall determine the acreage for reservation based on the number of dwelling units per acre to occupy the site as permitted by the Zoning Ordinance.

   b. *Minimum Size of Park and Playground Reservations.* In general, land reserved for recreation purposes shall have an area of at least four (4) acres. When the percentages from the Table of Recreation Requirements would create less than four (4) acres, the Commission may require that the recreation area be located at a suitable place on the edge of the subdivision so that additional land may be added at such time as the adjacent land is subdivided. In no case shall an area of less than two (2) acres be reserved for recreation purposes if it will be impractical or impossible to secure additional lands in order to increase its area. Where recreation land in any subdivision is not reserved, or the land reserved is less than the percentage in Section 5.9(1)(a), the provisions of Section 5.9(1)(d) shall be applicable.

c. *Recreation Sites.* Land reserved for recreation purposes shall be of a character and location suitable for use as a playground, playfield, or for other recreation purposes, and shall be relatively level and dry; and shall be improved by the developer to the standards required by the Planning Commission, which improvements shall be included in the subdivision improvement agreement and security. A recreation site shall have a total frontage on one (1) or more streets of at least two hundred (200) feet, and no other dimension of the site shall be less than two hundred (200) feet, and no other dimension of the site shall be less than two hundred (200) feet in depth. The Planning Commission may refer any subdivision proposed to contain a dedicated park to the local government or department in charge of parks and recreation for a recommendation. All land to be reserved for dedication to the local government for park purposes shall have prior approval of the Governing Body and shall be shown marked on the plat, "Reserved for Park and/or Recreation Purposes."

d. *Alternative Procedure: Money in Lieu of Land.* Where, with respect to a particular subdivision, the reservation of land required pursuant to this section does not equal the percentage of total land required to be reserved in Section 5.9(1)(a), the Planning Commission shall require, prior to final approval of the subdivision plat, that the applicant deposit with the Governing Body a cash payment in lieu of land reservation. Such deposit shall be placed in a Neighborhood Park and Recreation Improvement Fund to be established by the Governing Body. The deposit shall be used by the local government for improvement of a neighborhood park, playground, or recreation area including the acquisition of property. The deposit must be used for facilities that actually will be available to and benefit the persons in the subdivision for which payment was made and be located in the general neighborhood of subdivision. The Planning Commission shall determine the amount to be deposited, based on the following formula: two hundred dollars ($200) multiplied by the number of times that the total area of the subdivision is divisible by the required minimum lot size of the zoning district in which it is located, less a credit for the amount of land actually reserved for recreation purposes, if any, as the land reserved bears in proportion to the land required for reservation in Section 5.9(1)(a), but not including any lands reserved through density zoning.

e. *Applicability to Land Utilizing Average Density.* Any subdivision plat in which the principle of average density of flexible zoning has been utilized shall not be exempt from the provisions of its section, except as to such portion of land which is actually dedicated to the local government for park and recreation purposes. If no further area, other than the area to be reserved through averaging, is required by the Planning Commission, the full fee shall be paid as required in Section 5.9(1)(d). If further land is required for reservation, apart from that reserved by averaging, credit shall be given as provided by Section 5.9(1)(d).

f. *Other Recreation Reservations.* The provisions of this section are minimum standards. None of the paragraphs above shall be construed as prohibiting a developer from reserving other land for recreation purposes in addition to the requirements of this section.

2. **Other Public Uses.**

a. *Plat to Provide for Public Uses.* Except when a applicant utilizes planned unit development or density zoning in which land is set aside by the developer as required by the provision of the Zoning Ordinance, whenever a tract to be subdivided includes a school, recreation uses [in excess of the requirements of Section 5.9(1)], or other public use as indicated on the Master Plan or any portion thereof, the space shall be suitably incorporated by the applicant into its sketch plat. After proper determination of its necessity by the Planning Commission and the appropriate local government official or other public agency involved in the acquisition and use of each such site and a determination has been made to acquire the site by the public agency, the site shall be suitably incorporated by the applicant into the preliminary and final plats.

b. *Referral to Public Body.* The Planning Commission shall refer the sketch plat to the public body concerned with acquisition for its consideration and report. The Planning Commission may propose alternate areas for such acquisition and shall allow the public body or agency 30 days for reply. The agency's recommendation, if affirmative, shall include a map showing the boundaries and area of the parcel to be acquired and an estimate of the time required to complete the acquisition.

    c. *Notice to Property Owner.* Upon a receipt of an affirmative report, the Planning Commission shall notify the property owner and shall designate on the preliminary and final plats that area proposed to be acquired by the public body.

    d. *Duration of Land Reservation.* The acquisition of land reserved by a public agency on the final plat shall be initiated within twelve (12) months of notification, in writing, from the owner that he intends to develop the land. Such letter of intent shall be accompanied by a sketch plat of the proposed development and a tentative schedule of construction. Failure on the part of the public agency to initiate acquisition within the prescribed 12 months shall result in the removal of the "reserved" designation from the property involved and the freeing of the property for development in accordance with these regulations.

5.10 Preservation of Natural Features and Amenities.

1. *General.* Existing features that would add value to residential development or to the local government as a whole, such as trees, as herein defined, watercourses and falls, beaches, historic spots, and similar irreplaceable assets, shall be preserved in the design of the subdivision. No trees shall be removed from any subdivision nor any change of grade of the land effected until approval of the preliminary plat has been granted. All trees on the plat required to be retained shall be preserved, and all trees where required shall be welled and protected against change of grade. The sketch plat shall show the number and location of existing trees as required by these regulations and shall further indicate all those marked for retention and the location of all proposed shade trees required along the street side of each lot as required by these regulations.

2. *Shade Trees Planted by Developer.*

    a. As a requirement of subdivision approval the applicant shall plant shade trees on the property of the subdivision. Such trees are to be planted within five (5) feet of the right-of-way of the road or roads within and abutting the subdivision, or, at the discretion of the Planning Commission, within the right-of-way of such roads. One (1) tree shall be planted for every forty (40) feet of frontage along each road unless the Planning Commission, upon recommendation of the Local Government Engineer, shall grant a waiver. The waiver shall be granted only if there are trees growing along the right-of-way or on the abutting property which, in the opinion of the Planning Commission, comply with these regulations.

b. New trees to be provided pursuant to these regulations shall be approved by the Local Government Engineer and shall be planted in accordance with the regulations of the Local Government Engineer. The trees shall have a minimum trunk diameter (measured twelve [12] inches above ground level) of not less than two (2) inches. Only Oak, Honey Locust, Hard Maples, Ginkgo, or other long-lived shade trees, acceptable to the Local Government Engineer and to the Planning Commission, shall be planted.

3. *Shade Tree Easement and Dedication.* The preliminary plat and final plat shall reserve an easement authorizing the local government to plant shade trees within five (5) feet of the required right-of-way of the local government. No street shall be accepted for dedication until the Local Government Engineer shall inform the Planning Commission and the Governing Body that compliance, where necessary, has been made with these regulations.

5.11 Nonresidential Subdivisions.

1. *General.* If a proposed subdivision includes land that is zoned for commercial or industrial purposes, the layout of the subdivision with respect to the land shall make provision as the Planning Commission may require. A nonresidential subdivision shall also be subject to all the requirements of site plan approval set forth in the Zoning Ordinance. Site plan approval and nonresidential subdivision plat approval may proceed simultaneously at the discretion of the Planning Commission. A nonresidential subdivision shall be subject to all the requirements of these regulations, as well as such additional standards required by the Planning Commission, and shall conform to the proposed land use and standards established in the Master Plan, Official Map, and Zoning Ordinance.

2. *Standards.* In addition to the principles and standards in these regulations, which are appropriate to the planning of all subdivisions, the applicant shall demonstrate to the satisfaction of the Commission that the street, parcel, and block pattern proposed is specifically adapted to the uses anticipated and takes into account other uses in the vicinity. The following principles and standards shall be observed:

   a. Proposed industrial parcels shall be suitable in area and dimensions to the types of industrial development anticipated.

   b. Street rights-of-way and pavement shall be adequate to accommodate the type and volume of traffic anticipated to be generated thereupon.

   c. Special requirements may be imposed by the local government with respect to street, curb, gutter, and sidewalk design and construction.

    d. Special requirements may be imposed by the local government with respect to the installation of public utilities, including water, sewer, and storm water drainage.

    e. Every effort shall be made to protect adjacent residential areas from potential nuisance from a proposed commercial or industrial subdivision, including the provision of extra depth in parcels backing up on existing or potential residential development and provisions for a permanently landscaped buffer strip when necessary.

    f. Streets carrying nonresidential traffic, especially truck traffic, shall not normally be extended to the boundaries of adjacent existing or potential areas.

COMMENTARY ON ARTICLE 5

ENABLING LEGISLATION AND GENERAL REQUIREMENTS

Those sections of subdivision regulations that impose conditions on development and design standards may very well be the most important aspect of the subdivision control process. The right to require installation and construction of improvements prior to approval of a plat is premised on two considerations: (1) protecting the health, safety, and welfare of the occupants of the homes to be constructed within the subdivision and neighbors of the subdivision, and (2) reducing the financial burden on hard-pressed municipalities by requiring the developer to make the initial installation of capital improvements reasonably required by development, after which the local government assumes responsibility for maintenance and repair.[1]

There are three types of requirements on which subdivision approval is conditioned. First, a prohibition against any subdivision activity in areas where street access, soil, subsoil, or flooding conditions would create dangers to health or safety if development were allowed.[2] Second, the proposed subdivision should be consistent with the comprehensive plan for the area.[3] This includes requirements for reservation of space within the subdivision for planned parks, schools, public roads, and other improvements. Third, the subdivision should be designed in a manner that avoids overburdening area facilities—facilities that often are located outside the subdivision itself.[4] The authority to deny development approval on multiple grounds based on inadequate public facilities and open space is well established.[5]

Enabling legislation generally sets the parameters within which requirements may be imposed by a local government. The Standard Planning Enabling Act[6] defined these parameters as follows:

Such regulations may provide for the proper arrangement of streets in relation to other existing or planned streets and to the master plan for adequate and convenient open spaces, for traffic, utilities, access of fire-fighting apparatus, recreation, light and air, and for the avoidance of congestion of population, including the minimum width and area of lots.[7]

The American Law Institute's *Model Land Development Code* (ALI Code) provides even greater authority. The control of land subdivision is exercised as part of a comprehensive set of development regulations and not under a separate procedure.[8] In granting a special development permit, the land development agency may attach special conditions to the approval of the subdivision.[9] These conditions may concern any matter subject to regulation under the ALI Code, including means for:

- Minimizing any adverse impact of the development upon other land, including the hours of use and operation and the type and intensity of activities that may be conducted;[10]
- Controlling the sequence of development, including when it must be commenced and completed;
- Controlling the duration of use of development and the time within which any structure must be removed;
- Assuring that the development is maintained properly in the future;
- Designating the exact location and nature of development; and
- Establishing more detailed records by submission of drawings, maps, plats, or specifications.

EFFECT OF SUBDIVISION REGULATION REQUIREMENTS UPON LOW- AND MODERATE-INCOME HOUSING

Before examining the type of design standards and the public improvement requirements that the government may impose on the subdivision of land, it is important to consider the potentially exclusionary impacts of these requirements. Subdivision regulations that demand various physical improvements for proper development amenities often evoke the criticism that the cost of housing to the purchaser is unnecessarily increased and that the provision of low- and moderate-income housing is thereby impeded.[11] Such criticism may be circumspect because any additional cost can be amortized over the lengthy period of the mortgage (often up to 40 years under FHA-insured or subsidized programs) and in actuality will represent a small fractional part of the monthly payment. Moreover, recent studies have shown that growth management regulations, impact fees, and site development costs are not passed on to the consumer of the housing as much as they are passed back to the owner of the land and actually help to reduce the land-cost component of the housing package,[12] encourage production of low-cost housing,[13] and do not dampen development or drive it to other communities.[14] The alternative is a subdivision improperly designed and constructed, with the municipality responsible for furnishing sidewalks, curbs, street extensions, drainage, sewers, and other improvements that were omitted by the developer. The homeowner or tenant will have the burden of paying for these expenses through property taxes or special assessments. Instead of amortizing this cost over a long-term mortgage, payment will usually have to be made over a shorter period of time, substantially raising monthly housing costs. This alternative technique for providing and financing public improvements probably will increase, rather than lessen, the exclusionary impact of subdivision controls.[15]

In addition, there are important policy and legal considerations which recognize that low- and moderate-income families should not be deprived of decent housing. Nor should distinctions be made between low- and moderate-income housing on the one hand and middle-income on the other when it comes to design standards and the public improvements available to the subdivision.[16] Rather than deprive the poor of quality housing by the elimination of design standards and public improvement requirements, subsidies could be made available to families who cannot afford decent housing at market prices. Distinctions in the quality of low- to moderate-income housing, prevalent in the past, have been a major cause of the existence and spread of slums, impacted areas, and social disorder.[17]

New approaches are called for in dealing with the community's need for low- and moderate-income housing in light of the financial burden involved.[18] One approach suggests that low- and moderate-income housing be exempt from local zoning if subject to objective state or federal standards.[19] An alternative approach would grant a preferred status to certain land uses commonly subject to exclusionary zoning practices, so that the burden is cast upon the municipality to justify its police power or zoning regulation.[20] Legislation[21] authorizing a state board of zoning appeals to override municipal zoning regulations and to issue comprehensive permits to a specified class of developers for construction of low- and moderate-income housing has been held constitutionally valid.[22] Connecticut has recently passed legislation similar to that of Massachusetts. However, the denial or conditional approval of a proposed affordable housing project is appealed to a special judicial panel.[23] The Connecticut legislation combines the Massachusetts approach with the judicial remedies established by the New Jersey Supreme Court.[24]

A more recent innovation, adopted at the local rather than state level of government, is the so-called linkage program.[25] A linkage program requires a developer to mitigate the impact of certain developments, usually large-scale office projects, on the community by requiring the developer to construct or finance low-income housing.[26] The linkage concept is similar to impact fees, dedications, and money in lieu of land for parks and recreation. The rational nexus standard of *Nollan v. California Coastal Commission*, 483 U.S. 825 (1987), justifies requiring the provider of jobs to pay for the housing facilities needed because of the employment created. The local government must be careful, however, to comply fully with the rational nexus standards of *Nollan* and its state and federal court progeny.[27] The underlying assumption is that the development of a large-scale office project creates jobs, which in turn create a need for low-income housing that the market cannot satisfy. Thus, rather than having the community bear the cost of providing this housing, the burden is cast on the developer. Because of the economic impact of linkage on new development, it is doubtful that it will be adopted on a widespread basis.[28] Moreover, the linkage program may be based on assumptions about the impact of commercial development that cannot be sustained on close examination.[29]

SUBDIVISION DESIGN AND LOT LAYOUT

Section 5.1(1) sets out general provisions relating to all proposed subdivisions. These provisions require coordination of subdivision design standards with the zoning ordinance map and text, the land use plan element, other elements of the comprehensive plan, the major street plan, and other state or regional planning guides.[30] These planning tools will be of inestimable value in obtaining the subdivider's cooperation in providing park and school sites, in tying the interior and exterior street patterns to arterial highway plans, and in promoting development that conforms with long-range community and regional goals.[31]

Careful attention should be given to the topography of the subdivision to assure that development does not occur in environmentally critical or hazardous areas.[32] The subdivision design should reflect certain basic elements of sound development:[33]

- Preservation of the character of the land.
- Economy of construction.
- Inclusion of special facilities.
- Variation in design.
- Privacy and sociability.
- Individual lot sizes that are practicable and desirable.

Lot layout should be governed by three requirements: (1) a buildable site on each lot, (2) grading and drainage of each lot, and (3) coordination of sizes of lots with requirements for community infrastructure.[34]

Before examining specific design standards and subdivision improvement requirements, it will be helpful to examine the law concerning the specificity of regulations. Unambiguous standards for imposing subdivision improvement requirements serve two purposes. First, the standards place the developer on notice as to governmental requirements to secure approval of the subdivision. Second, standards constrain official action, limiting the opportunity for arbitrary and discriminatory decision making. Thus, the courts generally have held that subdivision regulations must set reasonable standards to restrain the discretion of decision makers and must be reasonably definite so that property owners may know in advance what is required of them.[35] General standards are permissible if they can be applied to concrete fact situations and are sufficient to limit discretion.[36]

Stating the test for sufficient standards is easier than applying it to actual situations. Courts have invalidated subdivision regulations as being too vague when they required that a subdivision have adequate access,[37] or mandated "harmonious development,"[38] or permitted parallel streets in cases of "unusual topography,"[39] or simply failed to place the developer on adequate notice that the government would impose water and drainage requirements.[40] On the other hand, the courts have upheld a state law requiring "sufficient and adequate roads," a "well-planned" development and "sufficient information" to be sub-mitted to the planning authority,[41] as well as a local ordinance where the planning authority "might" require extra-wide streets and bituminous concrete berms.[42]

Several sections of the Model Regulations address requirements for internal improvements of the subdivision. Section 5.3(2)(d) addresses the need for screening and buffering residential lots that abut a dedicated roadway or an alley or service road. Screens are used to provide adequate privacy and protec-tion, as well as for their aesthetic qualities. Screening between two lots lessens the transmission of noise, dust, and glare. Even minimal screening can provide an impression of separation of spaces, and more extensive screening can shield entirely one use from the visual assault of an adjacent use. Screening establishes a greater sense of privacy from visual or physical intrusion, the degree of privacy varying with the intensity of the screening. Screening and buffering should be flexible to allow for variation depending upon the nature of the adjoining uses.

Section 5.3 deals with requirements for adequate roads.[43] A subdivision must have access to an existing or planned major road. All lots within a subdivision and part of lot splits shall have at least one boundary adjacent to a public street or road, except that private streets may be permitted as part of a planned unit development.[44] Fronting homes on existing arterial highways leads to service and safety problems of considerable dimension and should be avoided. Streets should be related to existing major street plans or official maps or, where none exists, to existing arteries.[45] The number of intersections along major streets should be held to a minimum, and double frontage lots should be avoided as well as street jogs of less than 150 feet. Blocks should be of a width sufficient to hold two tiers of building lots.[46] It is important that a complete and comprehen-sive street naming and numbering system be followed.[47] The final authority for this function has been left with the planning commission. A continuation of an existing street should bear the existing name, and new streets should be given names that are different from other streets in the community and reflect interesting historical, topographical, or cultural features.[48]

Adequate streets and highways bear an important relationship to newly developed subdivisions. As early as 1949, a developer was required to dedicate the portion of the perimeter highway that was related to the needs of the subdivision.[49] The rationale for such dedication has been aptly stated:

> In a time of emergency, such as sickness, accident, fire, or other catastrophe, . . . a road over which automobiles and fire apparatus can travel safely must always be available, otherwise great suffering, property damage, and even loss of life may result. . . . Unimproved or defective roads can cause a complete breakdown of services in a community. The state has a legitimate and real interest in requiring that the means of access to the new construction be properly improved and sufficient for the purpose.[50]

A planning commission has been held to have the power to deny residential or commercial subdivision approval or zoning where the proposed project would create danger by burdening inadequate approaches to the development with increased traffic into and out of the proposed subdivision.[51] The New York Court of Appeals in *Pearson-Kent Corp. v. Bear* concluded that the county planning commission could look beyond the internal requirements of the proposed plat itself and consider, among other things, the safety and general welfare of the entire county.[52] Unreasonable dedication requirements, however, may be found to result in a taking of private property. For example, dedication requirements may be invalid if: (1) the city has taken no steps to provide the roads shown on the master plan, but required the subdivider to dedicate the land needed for the street's extension;[53] (2) the widening requirement involved a main thoroughfare 700 feet from, and totally unrelated to, the proposed subdivision;[54] (3) the dedication required title and improvement to a road fronting the subdivision but far in excess of the needs "reasonably" generated by the subdivision;[55] (4) the city attempted to single out an individual user from all others by applying subdivision dedication requirements to a single tract of land involving a church's application for a permit to improve church property;[56] and (5) a denial of plat approval for failure to provide for extension of a street through the parcel as proposed in the city's general plan was viewed as going beyond mere planning and was used as a tool to thwart plaintiff's development.[57] A provision for granting variances from strict dedication requirements in cases of hardship is useful in sustaining specific constitutionality.[58]

One problem that local governments may encounter results from requiring a subdivider to reserve land within the subdivision for future road development. This required reservation will be illegal if the government causes the subdivider to be denied the beneficial use of its land for an unreasonable period of time.[59] This is true especially if the government intends to acquire the reserved land by eminent domain.[60]

The standards established for the construction of roads and improvements must be related specifically to area densities authorized in the zoning ordinance.

Higher density developments generate greater loads on public facilities and streets that are necessary to service present and future residents, and should provide a pro rata share of public improvements. The size of the improvement is determined by the existing population and by the projected population densities of the area as determined by planning studies.[61] Based on these factors, the impact of existing development on the need for facilities and services can be determined.

A particular problem is created by the need for "oversized facilities" to handle future growth. If a particular subdivision is the first to develop within a planning area, or drainage or sewerage basin, the government may want the development to provide a larger-sized improvement or an excess capacity facility to handle the future development in the area. Many times the first development, lying at the foot of a drainage basin or close to major roads, must provide five-foot culverts or arterial roads, while developments farther away need only 12-inch culverts or local roads.[62] If a method for providing for the equitable distribution of improvement costs is not established, one developer will sustain a "wipeout" while the other will accrue a "windfall."[63] One solution for this apparent inequity is to establish an improvement district that will reimburse the developer for "excess" improvements or utilize an "excess capacity" sharing arrangement among developers.[64] Without utilization of special district assessment or reimbursement provisions, due process requires that offsite, excess improvement or dedication requirements be reasonably related to the needs created by the proposed subdivision.[65]

DRAINAGE AND STORM SEWER REQUIREMENTS

Drainage and storm sewers are among the most critical public improvements within a subdivision.[66] In most areas of the country, subdivisions should be required to provide storm and flood-water runoff channels or basins independent of the sanitary sewer system.[67] Drainage facilities should be located in road rights-of-way or other unobstructed easements. The size of storm sewers should not be based solely on present needs, but rather on the contemplated density of the drainage basin. The plat must take into account upstream and downstream drainage obstructions, with appropriate provisions for drainage easements if a subdivision traverses a watercourse.[68]

A city must be careful to assure adequate review of subdivision plats for drainage facilities. Several courts have ruled that homeowners had stated a cause of action in maintaining that a city was negligent in approving a subdivision plat that overtaxed the drainage system of the city so as to cause flood damage.[69]

State and local government units have made considerable use of floodplain zoning and subdivision regulation to restrict the nature and intensity of development within both stream channels and floodplains.[70] Within the channel, such regulation prevents impediments to navigation and the stream's carrying capacity. It also clearly relates to the protection of health, safety, and welfare that may be threatened by flooding. The regulation of land-use development adjacent to watercourses may also result in more attractive open space and areas of scenic and recreational value.

Most standard enabling acts do not specifically mention the control of flooding as a purpose for subdivision control, but courts have been willing to imply this power.[71] Many legislatures have now added flood control as a purpose for zoning and subdivision legislation or have adopted other special enabling legislation.[72] The constitutionality of government regulation of development in the floodplain seems clear,[73] except on the outer edges of floodplain zones where the danger is less and the courts may tend to see the government's real purpose as obtaining public open space at private expense.[74]

Many local governments now have the power to control development in or around wetlands, swamps, shorelands, and other water-related, environmentally critical areas.[75] Because the objectives and methods of wetland regulation are unique, such controls may require special legislative authorization.[76] There has been a liberal tendency in the courts toward holding wetland regulation valid.[77] This may be due in part to the ascending importance of ecological objectives. These objectives may be so important that development that changes or threatens to change the natural character of the land may even be prohibited without compensation.[78] Occasionally courts have held that wetland regulation goes beyond the scope of the police power and becomes a device for producing public benefit rather than for protecting against public harm.[79]

In addition to subdivision regulations, the use of environmental impact statements, either accomplished indirectly through performance standards in zoning ordinances[80] or through local environmental impact ordinance provisions,[81] can regulate subdivision drainage and storm run-off systems. Local governments cannot afford to rely on the environmental impact statement required under the National Environmental Protection Act (NEPA),[82] as its coverage includes only federally related actions, and, thus, does not affect the majority of subdivisions.[83]

Following Congress's lead, however, a number of states have enacted a variety of relatively stringent environmental protection statutes.[84] The California Environmental Quality Act (CEQA),[85] patterned after NEPA, provides a broad statement of environmental policy, coupled with an environmental impact statement (EIS) requirement. CEQA is a major contribution to the field because its EIS requirement reaches not only direct state actions but local regulatory activities such as the issuance of permits, licenses, certificates, and subdivision approvals.[86] Other states may expressly require an environmental assessment during the subdivision approval process.[87]

Environmental regulation, an EIS requirement, has also reached the local level. Bowie, Maryland, was one of the country's first municipalities to pass an ordinance establishing the circumstances under which an EIS is necessary and the procedures for preparing and filing the EIS.[88] The significance of determining the threat to the environment through such statements or other adequate procedures should not be ignored. The planning commission must be prepared for conflicts between an EIS requirement and any "deemed approved" time limits in the approval process. Jurisdictions that have been faced with this issue have generally held up the approval in favor of a full environmental audit, finding the applications incomplete without the EIS.[89]

SANITARY SEWER SYSTEMS

The requirements set out in the Model Regulations for sewerage facilities are an example of requirements geared toward future development as well as present development. In areas where public sanitary systems are not available but will become so within a reasonable time (15 years), the subdivider may put in either a central sewerage system or an individual disposal system; but in either event, the subdivider is required to put in "capped sewers."[90] Capped sewers are simply unused laterals installed and ready for use when the time comes to provide public sewers to the subdivision. The advantages of such a system are numerous.[91] For the homeowner, the cost of sewers will be included in the mortgage cost and amortized. Several advantages appear for the municipalities as well. Extension of the sewer facilities can be geared to the city's capital improvements program. The requirement for capped sewers thus becomes an effective and potent tool of "development timing," encouraging more orderly growth as new subdivisions connect with existing sewer lines. The burdens in the form of increased costs falling on the developer are offset by cheaper raw land costs resulting from greater land-use density. The requirements set out in the Model Regulations may be adjusted for smaller communities with lesser needs.

A short-term moratorium can be utilized in areas lacking adequate sewer and water facilities to prevent development.[92] Local governments also have imposed moratoria on the issuance of building permits to ensure that critical water supplies will not be exhausted and that the utilization of water will proceed in accordance with sound planning.[93] Generally, a municipal authority is under a duty imposed by the equal protection clause,[94] and possibly a common law duty, to provide sewer or water facilities to those willing to tender the going rate.[95] Furthermore, the courts have held that an environmental moratorium must be kept temporary, within the limits of necessity, and must not be an attempt to place a general community burden on the individual.[96] The present state of the law permits a temporary restraint for a general environmental problem if the community is using good faith efforts to rectify the problem.[97]

The Federal Water Pollution Prevention and Control Act[98] now requires states to establish strict controls on and standards for water quality for *intrastate* as well as *interstate* waters. When the states fail to comply, the head of the Environmental Protection Agency is authorized to take over the program.[99] In addition, the federal Environmental Protection Agency regulates water quality through a permit system, in coordination with existing state programs.[100]

BIKEWAYS AND PEDESTRIAN WAYS

A bikeway may be defined as a pathway designed to be used by bikers. Although ideally bikeways are separated from streets and sidewalks, they can take one of the following forms: (1) *bicycle paths* designed specifically to satisfy the physical requirements of bicycling; (2) *bicycle lanes* at the edge of streets reserved and marked for the exclusive use of bicycles; and (3) *shared or bicycle-compatible roadways* designed to accommodate the shared use of the roadway by bicycles and motor vehicles.[101] Essentially, a bicycle-compatible roadway is either a roadway with low traffic volume, a roadway with moderate volume and speed and a 15-foot-wide lane width in each direction, or a roadway with high traffic volume, speed, and a paved shoulder. Bikeways may also share sidewalks with pedestrians, but this practice is recommended only where pedestrian traffic is light.

National sources recommend that separate bicycle paths should be required only when they have been specified as part of a municipality's adopted master plan. Most sources recognize that high land and construction costs make bicycle lanes and shared roadways a more feasible alternative than separate bike paths.[102]

DEDICATION AND MONEY IN LIEU OF LAND

The process of urban residential growth requires streets, sewers, water, recreational and park facilities, and open space for air and light to ensure a safe, healthy, and livable environment. The courts have held that municipalities may lawfully mandate the dedication of land by subdividers to meet a part of the burden of these capital needs generated by the subdivision.[103] Two of the principal subdivision regulation tools used to achieve these public goals and objectives are the mandatory dedication of land and the payment of "money in lieu of land." The justification for requiring a subdivider to dedicate land for capital improvements is to have new development pay the costs of the burden on municipal facilities that it has created.[104]

The more traditional forms of land dedication for streets, utilities, and sewers have been tested and accepted.[105] Increasingly, governments are seeking methods to finance the cost of facilities of a greater magnitude—such as sewage treatment plants, parks, and schools—without burdening existing community residents.[106] It is in this area of exactions that subdivision regulations are now being subjected to the greatest scrutiny because of the difficulty of the constitutional questions created by those exactions.[107]

The United States Supreme Court's decision in *Nollan v. California Coastal Commission*[108] has raised concerns about the legality of land dedication requirements. The Court held that a condition on development that required a property owner to convey a public easement had to have a substantial relationship to public health, safety, and welfare.[109] In addition, the Court held that the dedication requirement had to be proportionate to the needs created by new development.[110] The Court did not, however, choose among the various tests that state courts have fashioned for determining the validity of dedication requirements and other development exactions.[111]

The Standard Planning Enabling Act expressly authorizes communities to require dedications for improvements other than streets, utilities, and sewers.[112] Pursuant to this authority, dedication of parks and recreational areas, or money in lieu thereof, has become a common requirement in subdivision regulations and has found judicial acceptance in virtually every jurisdiction in which the requirements have been challenged.[113]

The Model Regulations, § 5.9 (1)(a) and (d), provide for the dedication of parks and recreational facilities at the ratio of three acres per 100 dwelling units, or money in lieu of land dedication.[114] The dedication requirement applies when the subdivision actually contains suitable land that is indicated on the comprehensive plan as required for a proposed park or recreational facility. Subdividers should be required to dedicate these areas or to use modern zoning techniques, such as cluster, average density, or planned unit developments. These techniques allow the developer to reduce lot sizes in return for dedicating public land or reserving open space and recreational facilities at no cost to the community. The savings resulting from these innovative zoning techniques in utility, road, sewer, curb, and sidewalk costs usually exceed the value of the land dedicated.[115] The dedication may either be to the municipality or to a private home association owned in common by residents of the subdivision.[116] The use of private home associations can substantially lessen the municipality's maintenance and annual operating costs, but at the price of losing direct control. A local ordinance may authorize the government to maintain neglected common areas and to assess the costs of maintenance against lot owners in the subdivision.[117]

When the comprehensive plan indicates a park or recreation site on land situated outside of the boundaries of the subdivision, the Model Regulations require the subdivider to pay money in lieu of actual dedication. The money in lieu of land approach is also valuable when the subdivision is small and there is insufficient land to dedicate for parks or recreational facilities, or where the land or topography is not well suited for park or recreational purposes.[118] The money in lieu of land procedure has been generally accepted in the courts, if reasonable standards are followed.[119]

Section 5.9(1)(d) of the Model Regulations sets out the method by which the money in lieu is to be computed.[120] The money is placed in a trust fund, known as a neighborhood park and recreation fund, to be used to purchase parks in the area of the subdivision when sufficient need develops.[121] The fund can also be used for the purchase of less than a fee interest in a neighboring area to obtain open space, scenic, or historical easements. If the alternative of money in lieu of land were not provided for small parcels of land, fractional portions of land unfit for suitable municipal purposes would have to be dedicated. If, on the other hand, these small subdivisions were exempted from dedication requirements, incentives would exist for large developers to evade subdivision requirements through utilization of piecemeal development of small subdivisions. This would result in a fragmentation of the development process with a serious reduction in the efficiency with which municipal services could be provided.[122] A survey of communities conducted by the American Planning Association concerning mandatory dedication and "money in lieu" requirements indicated that there are two principal formulas.[123] The most common approach is to require a fixed percentage of the total amount of land in the subdivisions—varying from 3 percent to 15 percent or more. The fixed percentage approach has several disadvantages. It imposes the same burden on all development irrespective of the development's density or whether the subdivision contains multifamily or single-family units. It is obvious that a high-density development requires a greater percentage of land to be devoted to open space and recreational uses. The critical determinant is the amount of required land per inhabitant—not per acre. Without a variable formula, it is questionable whether the land to be dedicated is in any way related to the needs generated by the subdivision for open space, park, and school sites.[124] The Model Regulations use the density-population approach, which results in a fairer distribution of dedication requirements.

A survey of the cases in the area of mandatory dedications and money in lieu of land, while not yielding any conclusive rules of law, points to the problem of the SPEA's statutory language, which fails to delineate the nature of the permitted exactions. After this threshold question of enabling authority is resolved, a constitutional issue arises as to whether the regulation so severely impacts the landowner that it constitutes an "inverse condemnation" or "taking" of the land without due process of law or just compensation.[125]

State courts have developed a variety of tests for determining the constitutional validity of development exactions. One line of cases has required a "specific and uniquely attributable" relationship between the needs expressed in the exaction and the development creating the need. This line of decisions began in Illinois with *Rosen v. Village of Downers Grove*,[126] which upheld the requirement for dedication of a school site as bearing a valid relationship to the subdivision. The next year the same court, in *Pioneer Trust and Savings Bank v. Mount Prospect*,[127] held unconstitutional a requirement of dedication for school sites. *Pioneer Trust*'s rationale was based on *Rosen* and *Ayres v. City Council*,[128] a California case, and found that schools were a part of the total community and that a unique causal relationship to the subdivision could not be shown, hence the burden could not be assessed to a particular subdivision.[129] In later decisions, the Illinois Supreme Court, while ostensibly affirming the "specifically and uniquely attributable" test, has upheld dedications and money contributions for school sites.[130] It would seem that the need for schools is a clear example of the extra needs generated by a subdivision directly related to the new school-age children who will live there. Section 5.9(2) of the Model Regulations gives the school board the opportunity to use land in the subdivision for a school site if such a location would be in accordance with the board's future plans. The developer must reserve the land for public use and the government has 12 months from the date that the developer notifies the government that it is commencing development to acquire the land.

Rhode Island has adopted the "uniquely attributable" formula, citing *Pioneer Trust* as the better rule, stating: "Fixed percentage requirements will inevitably cause inequities which will be less likely to arise under the specifically and uniquely attributable formula."[131]

Other jurisdictions have repudiated the "specifically and uniquely attributable" test and have substituted a "reasonably related" test. In New York, a statute requiring dedication for park land was upheld in the early case of *In re Lake Secor Development Co.*[132] A 1959 amendment of the Town Law added a money in lieu of land provision. The latter was struck down by the Appellate Division in *Gulest Associates v. Town of Newburgh*[133] because there was no guarantee that the trust fund would be used directly for recreational facilities for the benefit of the subdivision paying into the fund. The court also held that the need for the park must result from activity on the land on which the burden of payment falls. The *Gulest* case was overruled as a precedent by the New York Court of Appeals in *Jenad, Inc. v. Village of Scarsdale*,[134] which held that such a requirement was indeed a valid exercise of the police power and that the need for the facility should be only "reasonably related" to the subdivision activity.

In the *Jenad* case, the rules and regulations of the village gave the planning commission power to direct that, in lieu of the dedication of land, a charge or fee of $250 per lot could be collected by the village "and credited to a separate fund to be used for park, playground, and recreational purposes in such manner as may be determined by the Village Board of Trustees from time to time."[135] Subsequent decisions in New York have continued to uphold money in lieu of land regulations[136] and the "reasonable relationship" test.[137]

The high courts of most other states also have adopted the "reasonably related" test.[138] In *Associated Home Builders v. City of Walnut Creek*,[139] the California Supreme Court sustained the constitutionality of a statute authorizing money in lieu of land or mandatory dedication as a condition of plat approval and adopted the reasonably related test.

A third test, labeled the "rational nexus" test, has been promulgated by a few other jurisdictions. In *Wald Corp. v. Metropolitan Dade County*,[140] the developer refused to dedicate land for a canal system to control periodic flooding and sought to have the county ordinance requiring the dedication declared unconstitutional. In upholding the regulation as a valid exercise of police power, the court reviewed and rejected both the "reasonable relationship" test and the "specifically and uniquely attributable" rule. According to the court, the "reasonable relation" standard put a "heavy burden on the developer to show that the required dedication bears no relation to the general health, safety and welfare" and allows "virtually unbridled interference with private property."[141] The court viewed the "specifically and uniquely attributable" rule as unduly restricting local exercises of police power. Consequently, the court adopted the intermediate "rational nexus" approach. To survive attack under this standard, there must be a sufficient rational nexus between the dedication and the "intelligent planning which is designed to protect the health, safety and welfare of the citizens."[142]

The rational nexus approach looks to the benefits conferred upon the subdivision and "allows the local authorities to implement future-oriented comprehensive planning without according undue deference to legislative judgments. It requires a balancing of the prospective need of the community and the property rights of the developer."[143] The "rational nexus" test was further refined by the Supreme Court of New Hampshire in *Land/Vest Properties, Inc. v. Town of Plainfield*,[144] where the court held that a township could not condition its approval of a developer's subdivision on the developer's upgrading roads leading to, but located beyond, the subdivision. As characterized by the New Hampshire court, the "rational nexus" test does not seem to vary significantly from the "reasonably related" test. The court, analogizing to special assessments, concluded that "where offsite improvements can properly be required of a subdivider, the subdivider can be compelled 'only to bear that portion of the cost which bears a rational nexus to the needs created by, and [special] benefits conferred upon, the subdivision.'"[145] This same approach was used in a later New Hampshire case to invalidate a zoning regulation requiring, as a condition for subdivision approval, dedications of 7 ½ percent of the subdivision's acreage for playgrounds.[146]

The rationale for approving subdivision dedications and money in lieu of land for park sites has been extended to school sites in several jurisdictions. Although several cases have rejected such dedications,[147] the recent trend is to approve mandatory school site dedications, if a causal relationship can be shown between the development and the increased need for schools. The Supreme Court of Illinois has upheld both dedications and money in lieu of land in two separate decisions. In *Board of Education v. Surety Developers*,[148] the court upheld conditions imposed on a developer for subdivision approval, requiring a dedication of land for a school site, $50,000 contribution for school construction, and $200 for each home constructed.[149] While noting that 98 percent of the students in the two schools were from the defendant's development, the court cited *Pioneer Trust* and held that "the conditions imposed in this case were designed to alleviate a school problem specifically and uniquely attributable to defendant's activity."[150]

In *Krughoff v. City of Naperville*,[151] decided the next year, the Illinois Supreme Court noted the increase in student and adult population as a result of the new subdivision and perfunctorily concluded that "the required contributions of land, or money in lieu of land, were 'uniquely attributable to' and fairly proportioned to the need for new school and park facilities created by the proposed developments."[152] California has, under the "reasonably related" standard, upheld an ordinance requiring developers to pay fees or dedicate land for school purposes to relieve overcrowding as a precondition to issuance of a building permit.[153] These decisions indicate that there is a clear relationship between the need for new school facilities and the requirements of the subdivision regulations.

Some commentators have attempted to rationalize a difference between school and park exactions by asserting that dedication and money in lieu of land are appropriate only when the residents of a subdivision could be specially assessed for the cost of a similar improvement.[154] This position would prohibit exactions for general community service facilities such as schools, city halls, and police stations. Other commentators, in an often-cited article, reject this reasoning and assert that school exactions are in the nature of an excise tax. Such a tax, in view of the overriding benefit-burden theory, would allow school exactions by reason of the financial impact that a new subdivision places on the community.[155] Under either the "reasonably related" or "uniquely attributable" test, the amount of dedicated land or money in lieu of land must be kept within reasonable limits. Where the courts suspect that the land exaction is *totally* unrelated to the needs of the subdivision, or that the money collected is *unlimited* in amount so as to constitute a general tax rather than an exaction, the regulations or their application in the specific case will be stricken.[156] Likewise, when the dedication extends to areas beyond the jurisdiction of the city or county[157] or pertains to parcels not actually developed,[158] it may be invalid.

Dedication and money in lieu provisions may work well for the creation of parks and school sites, but other public services and facilities cannot be provided this way. As a result, Article 6 of the Model Regulations authorizes the payment of a comprehensive system of public facilities and services fees by the subdivider to offset the impact of its development on the community. If a local government adopts an impact fee program that includes fees for parks or schools, it must be careful to integrate land dedication and money in lieu requirements into the impact fee program.[159]

ADEQUATE PUBLIC FACILITIES OR CONCURRENCY ORDINANCES

Section 5.1(2) contains a provision commonly referred to as an "adequate public facilities" requirement or "concurrency" ordinance. The provision is drawn substantially from the Montgomery County, Maryland, adequate public facilities requirement, discussed below. An adequate public facilities ordinance (APF or APFO) requires that public facilities and services are available when needed to serve new development and are adequate to support the proposed development at adopted service level standards, or, in the alternative, that new development is conditioned on the availability and adequacy of public facilities.[160] A clear delineation of the standards by which adequacy of public facilities is judged is a critical component of an APFO. These standards (referred to as level of service (LOS) standards) are typically contained in a public facilities element of the general plan and/or in an adopted Capital Improvements Program (CIP) and are based either on existing service levels or on optimum service levels that may be achieved in the future, possibly at ultimate build-out of the community. The following language, from the Florida Local Government Comprehensive Planning Act, provides a good example of the goals of an adequate public facilities requirement.

> It is the intent of the Legislature that public facilities and services needed to support development shall be available concurrent with the impacts of such developments. In meeting this intent, public facility and service availability shall be deemed sufficient if the public facilities and services for development are phased, or the development is phased, so that the public facilities and those related services which are deemed necessary by the local government to operate the facilities necessitated by that development, are available concurrent with the impacts of the development.[161]

Rationale for an Adequate Public Facilities Requirement

Public services and facilities adequate to meet the needs generated by new development must be in place or committed to in order to ensure a community's fiscal integrity and to preserve and enhance a desirable quality of life. Therefore, a compelling interest exists in linking the availability and adequacy of public facilities to the demand for public improvements created by projected growth and new development.

The most common way of linking public improvements and land use planning is through regulatory devices, such as zoning and subdivision regulation. According to Henry Fagin, the first person to recognize the role of timing and sequencing of growth to achieve important public objectives, there are at least five "well-considered motivations" to ensure the linkage of adequate public facilities and growth.[162] These include:

- The need to economize on the costs of public facilities and services.
- The need to retain governmental control over the eventual character of development.
- The need to maintain a desirable degree of balance among the various uses of land.
- The need to achieve greater detail and specificity in development regulation
- The need to maintain a high quality of public services and facilities.[163]

Most local units of government generally find themselves reacting to development in areas of rapid growth rather than anticipating and planning for growth and development. As a result, the development process becomes excessively demand-driven and too little consideration is given to all the myriad factors critical to good planning and sound community development. This problem is diminished if a community requires that new development be responsive to adequate public facilities standards.[164] These requirements further the public health, safety, and general welfare. The key is to provide specific, ascertainable standards that are not based on arbitrary or ad hoc considerations.[165]

The provision of public services and facilities traditionally has been a public sector responsibility.[166] Encompassed within this responsibility is the authority to provide, finance, and control the timing and location of public facilities. This authority, however, must be utilized in a reasonable and nondiscriminatory manner. The principal issue in adequate public facilities cases often involves the ability and willingness of a local unit of government to provide for or to delay in providing services to influence growth.[167] Importantly, where it can be demonstrated that these requirements are part of an integrated and comprehensive system to manage and accommodate growth, legal challenges to adequate public facilities requirements are often ineffective.[168] The landmark case of *Golden v. Planning Board of the Town of Ramapo*[169] upheld the timing and sequential control of residential subdivision activity based upon the adequacy of public facilities for periods of up to 18 years as a part of a comprehensive growth management system. It was the first instance of a state high court upholding the uncompensated restriction of development timing by means of adequate public facilities requirements.

Historical Note: The Ramapo Decision

Ramapo, New York, is located in what was in the early 1970s an expanding suburban area within commuting distance of New York City. During this period, the town was faced with the typical problems of a city on the urban fringe. The community was suffering from a series of unfortunate side effects that often result from rapid growth:

- Imbalance of growth between types of uses.
- Inability to provide public services to match private development.
- Soaring tax rates on property due to inefficient provision of public services.
- Poor quality of services provided due to rapid growth.
- Land speculation, poor design, uncontrolled character and quality of private development and destruction of the natural landscape.
- Inability to implement the planning process, lack of time to develop solutions, and inadequate legal and administrative mechanisms.
- Development of negative policies concerning social, racial, and metropolitan solutions; formation of defensive incorporations and annexations; unwillingness to provide proper housing and facilities for diverse economic, racial, and ethnic groups; and irrational tax policies.[170]

The solution to these problems was to relate residential development more directly to capital investment, and to link the private development to the public's capacity to build facilities. The Ramapo approach was to coordinate comprehensive planning and capital improvements programming to make public facilities available to all areas of the community within a reasonable time frame.[171] Coupled with the public construction program was the requirement that the approval of subdivisions of lands for residential development be granted in accordance with the special permit procedures. The program worked as follows:

> To obtain a special permit, the applicant had to show that certain municipal services existed: public sanitary sewers or approved substitutes; drainage facilities; improved public parks or recreation facilities, including public schools; state, county, or town roads; and firehouses. Each facility or service was given a sliding point value and the degree of availability of each service to the particular development determined the number of points awarded. In order to obtain a special permit, a project had to have at least 15 such points. Thus, where municipal services and facilities were readily available, a project would be given a permit, but a proposed development further away would have to wait for a permit until the city services reached it, unless the developer chose to install the necessary facilities himself.[172]

The New York Court of Appeals held that, while enactment of phased controls was not specifically authorized by state enabling legislation, it was implied by the inherent power to restrict land use. The plaintiff's claim that the controls, in effect, prohibited any subdivision because one could be carried out only if the town provided services, was rejected by the court because the developer was given the option of installing facilities on its own. Subdivision was not denied, but merely conditioned upon a future and calculable event.

The significance of this case is that: it represents the first time that any court in the United States has upheld the concept of restricting development in metropolitan areas through comprehensive planning or an exercise of the zoning power without compensation. Now for the first time regions, states and the federal government, as well as municipal government, have the tool to develop a rational urban growth policy that can balance suburban developments with inner city revitalization and new community development. The recognition that timing and sequential controls, even over a period of 18 years, is a necessary concomitant of the police power to regulate urban growth finally provides us with the tool for controlling the direction of growth and the public capital investment in metropolitan areas. The necessity to use condemnation to purchase land areas in order to regulate their development is of doubtful validity under eminent domain in any event, is avoided.[173]

The *Ramapo* case was the first of a series of court decisions from states across the nation upholding the right of local governments to plan for and condition approval of development on the existence and/or provision of adequate public facilities. Cases involving consideration of the issue of the validity of adequate public facilities requirements have arisen in the context of different methods of land use control utilized in conjunction with capital facilities planning. These include the comprehensive plan, subdivision or building permit controls, or zoning. Although arising in different contexts, such ordinances have been universally upheld.

The Legal Context

A municipality must have adequate enabling authority for the adoption of a staged growth ordinance based on the adequacy of public facilities. The authority of municipalities to condition or to deny development approval on public facility or service availability is fairly well established. These include the authority of a municipality to condition development approval on the provision of facilities and services,[174] the municipality's authority to plan,[175] the power to approve subdivision plats,[176] or the power to enter into intergovernmental contracts or plans.[177] The denial of development approval based on inadequate public facilities is often tied to special exceptions,[178] rezonings,[179] site plan approvals,[180] conditional use permits,[181] and building permit approval.[182]

From a legal perspective, relying on such authority without detailed standards is risky. Ad hoc, standardless review by local governments is not favored by the courts. By not formalizing facilities standards in an ordinance or regulation, disapproval of a subdivision plat based on facilities inadequacy raises the specter of the application of varying standards to different development proposals. For example, in *Southern Co-op Development Fund v. Driggers*, a subdivision plat complying with the letter of the local government's subdivision regulations was denied without findings.[183] The District Court ruled that subdivision denial was limited to those factors contained in the subdivision regulations and remanded the application to the county commission for reconsideration. The county commission again denied the application, based on findings of fact that road, public school facilities, sewers, and public services were inadequate, and that the subdivision would constitute "urban sprawl" and "leapfrog development."[184]

The federal appeals court affirmed the entry of a summary judgment in favor of the landowners for violations of due process, ruling that the application of unauthorized adequate public facilities standards on an ad hoc basis "would permit the Commission to hold in reserve unpublished requirements capable of general application for occasional use as the Commission deems desirable."[185] The court rejected the county's arguments that the preamble to the subdivision regulations[186] and a state statute, which empowered local governments to disapprove development applications where school facilities were not available or planned concurrently with the subdivision, constituted adequate authority for the exercise of such broad discretion.

The *Driggers* decision underscores the need for a local government to explicate its standard of review in advance of development applications. The adoption of an adequate public facilities ordinance is one method to avoid the application of uneven standards to different development proposals by providing clear guidance to local decision makers. Developers are also provided notice of the standards against which their proposals will be reviewed.

Several states have enacted express enabling legislation for the adoption of concurrency requirements and adequate public facilities ordinances. Maryland authorizes the enactment of "ordinances requiring the planning, staging or provision of adequate public facilities" for cities having planning and zoning authority.[187] New Hampshire authorizes "timing incentives" and "phased development" where the city has adopted a master plan and a capital improvements plan.[188] Maryland prohibits state or local authorities from issuing building permits where water supply systems, sewage systems, or solid waste facilities would be inadequate in light of existing and approved area developments.[189] Florida has enacted a comprehensive "concurrency" requirement, which requires "that public facilities and services needed to support development . . . be available concurrent with the impact of such development."[190] "Concurrency" is measured by level of service (LOS) standards adopted for each facility in the comprehensive plan. Thus, the statute prohibits permitting decisions by local governments that would cause LOS standards to fall below those established by the comprehensive plan.[191] In 1990, Washington became the second state to require local governments to link development approval and provision of facilities.[192]

In addition to takings challenges such as that rejected in *Ramapo*, phased growth ordinances are often attacked as illegal devices designed to exclude the poor. This argument was rejected in *Ramapo*, where the court commented favorably on the town's efforts to accommodate future growth by accommodating public, low-, and moderate-income housing.[193] Similarly, a challenge based on the emerging concept of regional general welfare was raised in a California case involving an ordinance prohibiting the issuance of building permits until local school, sewage, and water supply facility standards were met.[194] In addressing the regional general welfare argument, the court distinguished cases involving traditional exclusionary zoning devices, such as large-lot zoning, which exclude low-income housing while preserving the right to build upscale units on large lots. Instead, the court found that the ordinance applied universally to all forms of housing, whether designed for upper- or lower-income persons. The case was remanded for a determination of whether the city's police power exercise adversely affected the welfare of surrounding residents.[195]

Right-to-travel challenges are almost universally rejected in challenges to APFOs. The usual basis for the rejection of right-to-travel challenges is lack of standing, where the ordinances are challenged by developers of new residential communities.[196] A California court also rejected a right-to-travel challenge to an ordinance conditioning rezonings on the availability of schools, reasoning that the conditions would merely divert residents in overcrowded areas to areas not burdened with inadequate facilities.[197]

Case Study: Montgomery County, Maryland

Montgomery County, Maryland's adequate public facilities ordinance is an example of the use of level of service (LOS) standards to regulate the pace of development.[198] The ordinance requires that facilities adequate to serve the development be currently available or scheduled in the capital improvements program. The requirements are tied to preliminary plan approval.[199] Applicants for preliminary plan approval are required to demonstrate the project's impacts on (1) roads and public transportation, (2) sewer and water service, (3) schools, (4) police stations, (5) fire houses, and (6) health clinics. The guidelines governing the adequacy of facilities are established through an annual growth policy approved by the county council. The most recent annual growth policy subjects new developments to two levels of review. "Police area review" uses average LOS standards within designated geographic "policy areas."[200] Developments are evaluated against existing levels of service within the policy area, compared to target levels of service established by the county. "Staging ceilings" are used to cap the level of growth within a given target area.[201] Where the staging ceiling has been reached by previously approved development, facilities are deemed inadequate for subsequent preliminary plan applications. Relief from the staging ceiling is provided for developers constructing public facilities themselves or taking similar measures to add capacity, for full or partial developer participation in the construction of planned improvements, or for developments that provide primary employment or needed employment in designated locations. A special ceiling allocation is set aside for affordable housing projects.

In addition to policy area review, most projects are also subjected to local area review. Local area review is used because many projects meet the average policy area LOS standards, yet overload nearby facilities. Planning board guidelines subject residential projects over 50 units or nonresidential projects generating at least 50 peak hour trips to local area review where such projects either cause nearby congestion, or are within 5 percent of the staging ceiling.[202] The planning board makes findings regarding the adequacy of the facilities, and presents these findings to the board for its consideration.[203] The board's recommendations regarding the adequacy of facilities are based on findings concerning (1) solutions to transportation problems proposed by the developer, (2) the degree of local congestion, (3) the availability of alternate routes to serve the increased traffic, (4) the availability of public transit, and (5) the degree to which increased congestion is attributable to the applicant's project.

The application of the LOS standards pursuant to Montgomery County's APFO was sustained in an unpublished trial court opinion.[204] The court sustained the reliance of the planning board on a staff report indicating that the development's impacts on nearby road congestion would "create unacceptable levels of service" in its local area review.[205]

Recently a trial court rejected a constitutional challenge to the imposition of a moratorium under the APFO, ruling that it did not constitute a taking or an improper use of the county's police powers.[206]

NOTES

1. E. YOKLEY, THE LAW OF SUBDIVISIONS 58 at 273 (2d ed. 1981); *see, e.g.,* Glennon v. Zoning Hearing Bd., 529 A.2d 1171 (Pa. Commw. 1987) (township, pursuant to police power, may set standards relating to the layout, design and grade of access streets as a condition of developing land); Total Quality, Inc. v. Scarborough, 558 A.2d 283 (Me. 1991) (upholding conditions related to traffic safety); Castle Properties Co. v. Anderson, 163 App. Div. 785, 558 N.Y.S.2d 334 (3d Dept. 1990) (planning board may impose reasonable conditions); Los Ranchos de Albuquerque v. Shiveley, 791 P.2d 466 (N.M. App. 1989) (property owner must comply with reasonable conditions); Urban v. Planning Bd., 592 A.2d 240 (N.J. 1991) (landscaping, access, safety improvements, aesthetics are all appropriate conditions).

2. Zukis v. Town of Fitzwilliam, 604 A.2d 956 (N.H. 1992) (subdivision approval can be denied on the ground that access roads are so inadequate that additional development would create an unacceptable safety hazard); Sheston Oil Co. v. Avalon Planning Bd., 520 A.2d 802 (N.J. Super. 1987) (offsite traffic flow and safety). *See* Pearson Kent Corp. v. Bear, 271 N.E.2d 218 (N.Y. 1971) (off-site roads); Just v. Marinette County, 201 N.W.2d 761 (Wis. 1972) (wetlands); Eschette v. City of New Orleans, 245 So.2d 383 (La. 1971) (drainage); Rodrigues v. State, 472 P.2d 509 (Hawaii 1970) (sewers); Frustuck v. City of Fairfax, 28 Cal. Rptr. 357 (Ct. App. 1963) (access roads); Squires Gate, Inc. v. County of Monmouth, 488 A.2d 824 (N.J. Super. 1991) (requiring widening of offsite bridge where stormwaters from the development will drain into county culverts).

3. Standard City Planning Enabling Act (SPEA) 14 (U.S. Dept. of Commerce, 1928); Haar, *In Accordance With a Comprehensive Plan,* 68 HARV. L. REV. 1154 (1955); Mandelker, *The Role of the*

Comprehensive Plan in Land Use Regulation, 74 MICH. L. REV. 900 (1976); Nelson, *The Master Plan and Subdivision Controls*, 16 ME. L. REV. 107 (1964). There are three different positions that states take on this issue: (1) *Mandatory requirement of consistency*: Baker v. City of Milwaukee, 533 P.2d 772 (Ore. 1975) (zoning ordinance not in accord with a comprehensive plan is void); Sierra Club v. Kern County Bd. of Supervisors, 179 Cal. Rptr. 261 (Cal. App. 1981); City of Gainesville v. Hope, 377 So.2d 736 (Fla. App. 1979); (2) *Inconsistency does not void but will shift burden of proof*: Udell v. Haas, 235 N.E.2d 897 (N.Y. 1968); (3) *Plan is advisory only and inconsistency is not fatal*: Toandos Peninsula Ass'n v. Jefferson County, 648 P.2d 448 (Wash. App. 1982); Wildner v. City of Winslow, 664 P.2d 1316 (Colo. App. 1983); Sasich v. City of Omaha, 347 N.W.2d 93 (Neb. 1984). A number of states have adopted comprehensive planning requirements and consistency in recent years, particularly with regard to housing elements: CAL. GOV'T CODE § 65300 et. seq.; FLA. STAT. § 163.3177(6)(f); GA. CODE ANN. § 50-8-7.1(b)(1); 30 ME. REV. STAT. ANN. § 4960-C(2)-(4); ORE. REV. STAT. § 197.015(2)(a), R.I. STAT. ANN. § 45-22.2-5-6; VT. STAT. ANN. tit. 24, § 4382(a)(10); Washington, Ch. 17, S.B. 2929, §§ 4.7(2) (applicable to metropolitan counties).

4. Pearson-Kent Corp. v. Bear, 271 N.E.2d 218 (N.Y. 1971); Smith v. Morris Township, 244 A.2d 145 (N.J. Super. Ct. App. Div. 1968); Wheeler v. City of Berkeley, 485 S.W.2d 707 (Mo. Ct. App. 1972). Denial of development approval based on inadequate offsite public facilities may be tied to any type of development approval: special exceptions (Malmar Assocs. v. Board of County Comm'rs, 272 A.2d 6 (Md. 1971)); rezonings (Freundshuh v. City of Blain, 385 N.W.2d 6 (Minn. App. 1986)); Larsen v. County of Washington, 387 N.W.2d 902 (Minn. App. 1986); Mira Dev. Co. v. City of San Diego, 252 Cal. Rptr. 825 (Cal. App. 1988); site plan approvals (Chase Manhattan Mortgage and Realty Trust v. Wacha, 402 So.2d 61 (Fla. App. 1981)); conditional use permits (International Villages v. Board of Comm'rs of Jefferson County, 585 P.2d 999 (Kan. 1978)); and building permit approval (Belle Harbor Realty Corp. v. Kerr, 364 N.Y.S.2d 160 (N.Y. 1974)); inconsistency with comprehensive plan, (Sherwood Land Co. v. Municipal Planning Comm'n, 413 S.E.2d 411 (W.Va. 1991)).

5. P. GREEN JR., PRINCIPLES AND PRACTICE OF URBAN PLANNING, LAND SUBDIVISION (1968); the

authority is well established that a local government may condition or deny development approval based on inadequate facility or service availability: implied power to provide facilities and services based on authority to regulate land use (Golden v. Planning Board of Town of Ramapo, 285 N.E.2d 291 (N.Y.); app. dismissed, 409 U.S. 1003 (1972)); the authority to plan (Norbeck Village Joint Venture v. Montgomery County Council, 254 A.2d 700 (Md. 1969)); the authority over subdivision (Wincamp Partnership v. Anne Arundel County, 458 F. Supp. 1009 (D. Md. 1978); Guiliano v. Town of Edgartown, 531 F. Supp. 1076 (D. Mass. 1982)); or the power to enter into intergovernmental contracts (Unity Ventures v. Lake County, 631 F. Supp. 181 (N.D. Ill. 1986); Dateline Builders v. Santa Rosa, 194 Cal. Rptr. 258 (1983)).

6. *See* SPEA, *supra* note 3, at 14; *see also* Appendix A for the full content of the SPEA.

7. *Id.*

8. AMERICAN LAW INSTITUTE, A MODEL LAND DEVELOPMENT CODE 2-203, "Division of Land into Parcels" (Proposed Official Draft No. 1, 1974) (ALI Code): "If a development ordinance does not permit a division of land into parcels as general development, the Land Development Agency shall grant a special development permission for the division of land into parcels if it finds that each parcel resulting from the division can reasonably be developed pursuant to the provisions of the development ordinance." As the notes to the ALI Code suggest, modern subdivision control ordinances will be contained within a comprehensive set of development regulations, not under any separate procedure for land subdivision. For further analysis of the effect of the ALI Code, see Appendix B.

9. ALI Code, *supra* note 8, at § 2-103(2); Bonner v. Upper Makefield Township, 597 A.2d 196 (Pa. Commw. 1991) (a municipality can approve a subdivision with conditions); Total Quality, Inc. v. Scarborough, 588 A.2d 283 (Me. 1991) (conditions related to traffic safety); River Vale Planning Bd. v. E&R Office Interiors, 575 A.2d 55 (N.J. Super. 1990) (conditions binding on subsequent owner upon development of site plan).

10. *Compare* the approach of performance standards described in McDougal, *Performance Standards: A Viable Alternative to Euclidean Zoning*, 47 TULANE L. REV. 255 (1973); Urban v. Planning Bd., 592 A.2d 240 (N.J. 1991) (aesthetics, access, landscaping, and safety performance standards can be appropriate basis for conditional subdivision approval).

11. *See* Comment, *Interrelationship Between Exclusionary Zoning and Exclusionary Subdivision Control*, 5 U. MICH. J.L. REF. 351 (1972) (subdivision regulations can be potentially more discriminatory than zoning regulations if they are poorly defined and therefore interpreted by highly subjective decisions of planning boards). *See also* Payne, *Title VIII and Mt. Laurel—Is Affordable Housing Fair Housing?*, 6 YALE L. & POL'Y REV. 361 (1988).

12. *See* James, *Evaluation of Local Impact Fees As a Source of Infrastructure Finance*, 11 MUN. FINANCE J. 407, 414 (1990): "Some experts argue that fees and exactions are generally shifted forward to the users or consumers of land developments: homebuyers, renters or non-residential tenants. This conclusion appears to be largely based on anecdotes and hunches. In fact, there can be no doubt that significant portions of the fees are shifted backward to landowners or (in rare instances) to developers . . . Exactions increase the supply of developable land in communities imposing them. To the extent that communities increase the supply of developable land they will reduce its price"; *see also* 26 URB. LAW. No. 3 (Summer 1994).

13. *See also* FULTON, CALIFORNIA PLANNING DEVELOPMENT REPORT, September 1990, Vol. 5, No. 9, "Studies Refute Cliches About Growth Control" (reporting on Glickfield-Levine study of 500 communities in California entitled "Evaluating Local and State Growth Management Programs: What We Can Learn From Experience," (UCLA Extension Public Policy Program). Despite the common perception that growth control cities are hostile to affordable housing, Glickfield and Levine found that cities with growth control ordinances are far more likely to also have strong policies for building low cost housing. For example, more than 60 percent of jurisdictions with at least five growth control measures also have density bonus ordinances compared with only 30 percent of jurisdictions with no growth control measures.

14. REAL ESTATE RESEARCH CORPORATION, REAL ESTATE REPORT (Vol. 17, No. 1, 1987) after a study of 43 communities has found "there is little evidence that developer exactions alone have significantly dampened development in communities where they have been imposed, nor that they have driven development elsewhere."

15. Moreover, aside from the obvious zoning practices discussed above, the impact of using the property tax for such improvements can only exacerbate the quickening taxpayer revolt

against this most regressive of taxes. *See* NATIONAL COMMISSION ON URBAN PROBLEMS (DOUGLAS COMMISSION), THE IMPACT OF THE PROPERTY TAX UPON HOUSING (Research Report No. 1, 1968); FINAL REPORT OF THE PRESIDENT'S COMMISSION ON SCHOOL FINANCE (MCELROY REPORT) (1972); Serrano v. Priest, 487 P.2d 1241 (Cal. 1971); Coons, *Symposium on Serrano v. Priest: The Death Knell to Ad Valorem Financing*, 5 URB. LAW. 83 (1973); Graham & Kravitt, *The Evolution of Equal Protection: Education, Municipal Services and Wealth*, 7 HARV. C.R.-C.L. L. REV. 103, 200 (1972). For cases analyzing the use of property taxes to finance public improvements, *see* Rodriguez v. San Antonio Independent School Dist., 337 F. Supp. 280 (S.D. Tex. 1971), *rev'd*, 411 U.S. 1 (1973).

16. Dailey v. City of Lawton, 425 F.2d 1037 (10th Cir. 1970); Southern Alameda Spanish Speaking Organizations v. City of Union City, 424 F.2d 291 (9th Cir. 1970); Kennedy Park Homes Ass'n v. City of Lackawanna, 436 F.2d 108 (2nd Cir. 1970).

17. Friedman, *Public Housing and the Poor: An Overview*, 54 CAL. L. REV. 642 (1966). *See also* O. NEWMAN, DEFENSIBLE SPACE: CRIME PREVENTION THROUGH URBAN DESIGN (1972), which makes the thesis that the elimination of amenities for low-income families in public housing actually increases rather than lessens crime and social disorder. Poor families require the same or, in some cases, greater amenities than middle- or upper-income families in order to overcome income, education, and social disabilities. *See also* Kain & Persky, *Alternatives to the Guilded Ghetto*, 14 PUB. INT. 74 (1969); M. STONE, ONE-THIRD OF A NATION: A NEW LOOK AT HOUSING AFFORDABILITY IN AMERICA (1990); White, *Using Fees and Taxes to Promote Affordable Housing*, 43 LAND USE L. & ZON. DIG. at 3 (Sept. 1991). What is needed is housing for low-income households, not low-cost housing; ADVISORY COMMISSION ON REGULATORY BARRIERS TO AFFORDABLE HOUSING, NOT IN MY BACK YARD (1991).

18. S.M. White, *Affordable Housing: Proactive & Reactive Planning Strategies*, PAS Report 441 (1992); S. M. White, *Development Fees and Exemptions For Affordable Housing: Tailoring Regulations To Achieve Multiple Public Objectives*, 6 J. LAND USE AND ENVTL. L. 25 (1990). *See* 31 U.S.C. § 6702 (1982); ADVISORY COMMISSION ON INTERGOVERNMENTAL RELATIONS, URBAN AND RURAL AMERICA: POLICIES FOR FUTURE GROWTH, Doc. A-32 (April 1968); Joint Economic Committee of Congress, Report of the Subcommittee on Urban Affairs,

Restoration of Effective Sovereignty to Solve Social Problems, (Dec. 6, 1971).

19. *See* Netter, *Legal Foundations for Municipal Affordable Housing Programs: Inclusionary Zoning, Linkage, and Housing Preservation*, 10 ZONING & PLANNING L. REP. 161 (Nov. 1987); Mallach, *The Tortured Reality of Suburban Exclusion: Zoning, Economics, and the Future of the Berenson Doctrine*, 4 PACE L. REV. 37 (1986); Freilich & Bass, *Exclusionary Zoning, Some Suggested Litigation Approaches*, 3 URB. LAW. 344 (1971); Hagman, *Urban Planning and Development, Race, Poverty, Past, Present, and Future*, 1971 UTAH L. REV. 49, 68-70; Schulman & Reilly, *The State Urban Development Corporation: New York's Innovation*, 1 URB. LAW. 129 (1969). The court in Floyd v. New York State Urban Development Corp., 300 N.E.2d 704 (N.Y. 1973) upheld as constitutional a state statute granting exemption over local zoning regulation to a state agency constructing low- and moderate-income housing. Similarly, it is not improper under state law to grant public housing, or similarly preferred public uses, a status distinct from private or nonpublic uses of the same kind. Taxpayers Ass'n v. Weymouth Township, 364 A.2d 1016 (N.J. 1976) (low-cost housing for the elderly); Fletcher v. Romney, 323 F. Supp. 189 (S.D.N.Y. 1971) (public housing); De Simone v. Greater Englewood Housing Corp. No. 1, 267 A.2d 31 (N.J. 1970) (public housing); Farrell v. Town of Ramapo, 317 N.Y.S.2d 837 (App. Div. 1970) (public housing); Abbott House v. Village of Tarrytown, 312 N.Y.S.2d 841 (App. Div. 1970) (halfway house); Cameron v. Zoning Agent of Bellingham, 260 N.E.2d 143, 146 (Mass. 1970) (public housing—"[A] town . . . reasonably concluded that the public interest requires (or makes appropriate) the allowance of public housing in specified areas of the town as a permitted use, while it imposes greater restrictions on the construction of private housing . . . the public nature of, and regulation imposed upon, public housing reasonably permits it to be placed in a separate classification for zoning purposes.") *But see* Board of Supervisors v. DeGroff Enter., 198 S.E.2d 600 (Va. 1973) (mandatory requirement of 15 percent low- and moderate-income housing is void as "socioeconomic" zoning). For analyses of the judicial treatment of group homes see Note, *Denial of Quasi-Suspect Status for the Mentally Retarded and its Effect on Exclusionary Zoning of Group Homes*, 17 U. TOLEDO L. REV. 1041 (1986); Mandelker, *Group Homes: The Supreme Court Revives the Equal Protection Clause in Land Use Cases*, in 1986 Institute

on Planning, Zoning, and Eminent Domain, Southwestern Legal Foundation, Municipal Legal Studies Center (Matthew Bender, 1986); City of Cleburne v. Cleburne Living Center, 473 U.S. 432, 105 S.Ct. 3249, 87 L.Ed.2d 313 (1985).

20. Simmons v. City of Royal Oak, 196 N.W.2d 811 (Mich. Ct. App. 1972); Kropf v. Sterling Hts., 199 N.W.2d 567 (Mich. Ct. App. 1972), *rev'd*, 215 N.W.2d 179 (Mich. 1974).

21. Massachusetts Zoning Appeals Law, MASS. GEN. LAWS ANN. ch. 40 B, §§ 20-23 (West 1979). Zoning Bd. of Appeals v. Housing Appeals Committee, 446 N.E.2d 748 (Mass. Ct. App. 1983) (purpose of the "Anti-Snob Zoning Act" is to provide expeditious relief from exclusionary zoning practices). *See* Healy, *Massachusetts Zoning Practice Under the Amended Zoning Enabling Act*, 64 MASS. L. REV. 157 (1979).

22. Board of Appeals v. Housing Appeals Committee, 294 N.E.2d 393 (Mass. 1973).

23. CONN. GEN. STAT. ANN. § 8-30(9) (Supp. 1991).

24. Southern Burlington County NAACP v. Township of Mount Laurel, 456 A.2d 390 (N.J. 1983) (Mount Laurel "II"). *See also* the Cranston-Gonzalez National Affordable Housing Act of 1990 (Pub. L. No. 101-625 [S-566], Nov. 28, 1990 (local governments are required to prepare a Comprehensive Housing Affordability Strategy (CHAS) as a condition to receiving direct financial aid from the federal government for affordable housing. The CHAS replaces the Community Development Housing Assistance Plan (HAP) and the McKinney Act Homeless Assistance Plan (CHAP)).

25. Kayden & Pollard, *Linkage Ordinances and Traditional Exactions Analysis: The Connection Between Office Development and Housing*, 50 LAW & CONTEMP. PROBS. 127 (1987); Porter, *Boston's Linkage Program: Sharing or Shackling Downtown Development?*, URB. LAND 34 (Jan. 1985); Taub, *Exactions, Linkages, and Regulatory Takings: The Developer's Perspective*, 20 URB. LAW. 515 (1988); Delaney, Gordon & Hess, *The Needs-Nexus Analysis: A Unified Test for Validating Subdivision Exactions, User Impact Fees and Linkage*, 50 LAW & CONTEMP. PROBS. 139 (1987); Connors & High, *The Expanding Circle of Exactions: From Dedication To Linkage*, 50 LAW & CONTEMP. PROBS. 69, 72 (1987).

26. Linkage addresses the need for affordable housing through either building housing on site, paying an in-lieu fee into a housing trust fund, or making equity contributions to a low-income housing project. White, *Using Fees and*

Taxes to Promote Affordable Housing, 43 LAND USE L. & ZONING DIG. at 3 (Sept. 1991); Boston, Mass., Zoning Code art. 26 (1983), *amended by* Boston, Mass., Zoning Code art. 26A and 26B (1986); San Francisco, Calif., Planning Code § 314 (1986).

27. Freilich & Morgan, *Municipal Strategies for Imposing Valid Development Exactions*, ZONING AND PLANNING L. REP., No. 11 (Dec. 1987).

28. *See* Taub, *supra* note 25, at 549; Connors & High, *supra* note 25, at 82. Linkage ordinances have been held valid by courts in Commercial Builders of Northern California v. City of Sacramento, 941 F.2d 872 (9th Cir. 1991), *cert. denied*, 112 S.Ct. 1997, 118 L.Ed.2d 593 (1992); Blue Jeans Equities West v. City and County of San Francisco, 4 Cal.Rptr.2d 114 (Cal. Ct. App. 1992), *cert. denied* 113 S.Ct. 191, 121 L.Ed.2d 135 (1992); Holmdel Builders Assn. v. Township of Holmdel, 583 A.2d 277 (N.J. 1990) (nexus established between fee amount and need for affordable housing created by new development); Bonan v. City of Boston, 496 N.E.2d 640 (Mass. 1986); *but see* Seawall Assocs. v. City of New York, 544 N.Y.S.2d (N.Y. 1989); San Telmo Assoc. v. City of Seattle, 735 P.2d 673 (Wash. 1987); Sintra v. City of Seattle (Wash. 1992) (unauthorized tax) (cases that relate to developer expenditure to maintain existing residential housing or pay a fee in lieu).

29. Bosselman & Stroud, *Mandatory Tithes: The Legality of Land Development Linkage*, 9 NOVA L.J. 381, 408 (1985); *see* Blagden Alley Ass'n v. District of Columbia Zoning Comm'n, 590 A.2d 139 (D.C. App. 1991) (approving site-specific exaction of contributions to affordable housing needs but remanding for findings on standards, criteria, and nexus); *see also* the recent decision of Dolan v. City of Tigard, 114 S.Ct. 2309 (1994).

30. An increasing number of states seem to require consistency between the community's comprehensive plan and the proposed subdivision plan, but the case law is still contradictory. *See, e.g.*, California (Selinger v. City Council, 264 Cal. Rptr. 499 (Cal. App. 1989) *cf.* Greenbaum v. City of Los Angeles, 200 Cal. Rptr. 237 (Cal. App. 1984)); Colorado (Beaver Meadows v. Board of County Comm'rs, 709 P.2d 938 (Colo. 1985)); Connecticut (Town of Lebanon v. Wood, 215 A.2d 112 (Conn. 1965) *cf.* Lordship Park Ass'n v. Board of Zoning Appeals, 75 A.2d 379 (Conn. 1950)); Florida (White v. Metropolitan Dade County, 563 So.2d 117 (Fla. Dist. Ct. App. 1990)); Maryland (Board of County Comm'rs v. Gaster, 401 A.2d 666 (Md. 1979) *cf.* Krieger v. Planning Comm'n, 167 A.2d 885 (Md. 1961)).

For more examples and further discussion of this situation, *see* KUSHNER, SUBDIVISION LAW AND GROWTH MANAGEMENT, 7.02[1] (1991). In addition to local comprehensive plans, some require consistency between the proposed subdivision and any applicable state or regional plan. *Id. See* ARIZ. REV. STAT. ANN. § 9-462.01E (1990); CAL. GOV'T CODE §§ 65567, 65860 (West 1983); FLA. STAT. ANN. § 163.3194 (West 1990); HAW. REV. STAT. § 205-16 (1985); KY. REV. STAT. § 100.213 (Michie Supp. 1990); N.J. STAT. ANN. § 40:55D-62 (West Supp. 1990); ORE. REV. STAT. § 197.010(3) (1985).

31. The importance of a comprehensive planning program in sustaining a community's legal position on dedication and other innovative land-use control techniques cannot be underestimated. *See* F. BOSSELMAN, D. CALLIES & J. BANTA, THE TAKING ISSUE, AN ANALYSIS OF THE CONSTITUTIONAL LIMITS OF LAND-USE CONTROLS, 290 (Council on Environmental Quality, 1973):

The importance of a sound factual presentation is apparent. . . . The Town of Ramapo, on the outskirts of the New York metropolitan area, successfully defended a growth-control ordinance before New York's highest court with success due to no small part to a thorough presentation of their case. In their defense they had to rebut contentions based on a number of recent cases exhibiting hostility and other sharp judicial criticism of similar controls in other communities. The town was able to present a vast array of planning data in their defense. In its statement of the facts in Golden v. Town of Ramapo, 334 N.Y.S.2d 138, 285 N.E.2d 291 (1972), the Court of Appeals pointed to the Town Master Plan, "whose preparation included a four-volume study of the existing land uses, public facilities, transportation, industry and commerce, housing needs, and projected population trends. Additional sewage district and drainage studies were undertaken which culminated in the adoption of a capital budget." 285 N.E.2d 291, 294. Thus not only could the town rely upon a large number of formal municipal actions, adoption of a master plan, a capital budget, zoning and subdivision regulations, and the like, but they could also document each with thorough and detailed planning studies. This impressive detail allowed the court to open its consideration of legal issues on the premises that: "The undisputed effect of these integrated efforts in land-use planning and development is to provide an overall program of orderly growth and adequate facilities through a sequential development policy commensurate with progressing availability and capacity of public facilities." 285 N.E.2d 291, 296. Thus, the court, at the outset of its discussion of the taking issue, termed the program reasonable, "both in its inception and its implementation." 285 N.E.2d 291, 303. *See also,* Schaffer v. New Orleans, 743 F.2d 1086 (5th Cir. 1984); Wincamp Partnership, OTC v. Anne Arundel County, 458 F. Supp. 1009 (D. Md. 1978).

Similarly, in Dolan v. City of Tigard, 114 S.Ct. 2309 (1994), the U.S. Supreme Court made the requirement of specific findings and studies an important factor in determining the validity of nexus requirements for subdivision and site plan exactions.

32. Local environmental impact statements can now be required of developers in some states to assure that development does not occur in environmentally critical areas. Woodland Hills Res. Ass'n v. City Council, 609 P.2d 1029 (Cal. 1980); Montana Wilderness Ass'n v. Board of Health, 559 P.2d 1157 (Mont. 1976); Sun Beach Real Estate Dev. Corp. v. Anderson, 469 N.Y.S.2d 964 (App. Div. 1983), *aff'd,* 468 N.E.2d 269; Buchseib/Danard, Inc. v. Skagit County, 663 P.2d 487 (Wash. 1983). *See also,* The Bowie, Maryland, Commission for Environmental Quality, Levine & Colgan, *The Role of Environmental Impact Statements in Local Government Decision Making,* 6 Urb. Law. 1 (1974). States have also required that local governments utilize environmental impact statements for subdivision activity: Oakwood Co. v. Planning Bd., 452 N.Y.S.2d 457 (App. Div. 1982); Friends of Mammoth v. Board of Supervisors, 502 P.2d 1049 (Cal. 1972); Cal. Pub. Res. Code § 21000-21177 (West 1986); Freilich, *Friends of Mammoth v. Board of Supervisors of Mono County: Local Government Inherits Environmental Protection,* 5 Urb. Law. (1973).

33. Walker & Listokin, The Subdivision and Site Plan Handbook, (Rutgers 1989); Marx v. Zoning Bd. of Appeals, 529 N.Y.S.2d 330 (App. Div., 2d Dept. 1988) ("subdivision control is aimed at protecting the community from an uneconomical development of land, and assuring persons living in the area where the subdivision is sought that there will be adequate streets, sewers, water supply and other essential services"); Cootey v. Sun Invest, Inc., 718 P.2d 1086 (Hawaii 1986) ("in order to protect the health, welfare and safety of the public at large, developers of private subdivisions are required to include certain improvements and meet certain standards relating to subdivisions").

34. *Organization of the Subdivision Ordinance* (PAS Report 116, Nov. 1958). *See generally* 5 N. Williams, American Planning Law—Land Use and The Police Power 156.04-.06 (1985). Southern Co-op. Dev. Fund v. Driggers, 696 F.2d 1347 (11th Cir.), *cert. denied,* 463 U.S. 1208 (1983); Del Mar Estates v. California Coastal Comm'n, 171 Cal. Rptr. 773 (Cal. App. 1981); City of Hollywood v. Hollywood, Inc., 432 So.2d 1332 (Fla. Dist. Ct. App. 1983).

35. *See* Apache Assoc. v. Planning Bd. of Nyack, 517 N.Y.S.2d 28 (App. Div. 2d Dept. 1987); Singer v. Davenport, 264 S.E.2d 637, 642 (W. Va. 1980); Sonn v. Planning Comm'n, 374 A.2d 159, 161 (Conn. 1976). This topic is discussed more fully in Chapter 3.

36. Cattle Properties Co. v. Anderson, 558 N.Y.S.2d 334 (App. Div, 3rd Dept., 1990) (standards must be able to be supported by substantial evidence in the record); Viscio v. Town of Guilderland Planning Bd., 525 N.Y.S.2d 439 (App. Div., 3rd. Dept., 1988) (disapproval on basis of inadequate curb cuts requires evidence in record); Parker v. Board of County Comm'rs, 603 P.2d 1098, 1100 (N.M. 1979) (citing City of Santa Fe v. Gamble-Skogmo, Inc., 389 P.2d 13, 18 (N.M. 1964)).

37. North Landers Corp. v. Planning Bd., 400 N.E.2d 273, 275 (Mass. App. Ct. 1980). *But cf.* Novak v. Planning Bd. of LaGrange, 523 N.Y.S.2d 590 (App. Div. 2d Dept. 1988); Reed v. Planning and Zoning Comm'n, 529 A.2d 1338 (Conn. App. 1987).

38. Kaufman & Gold Constr. Co. v. Planning and Zoning Comm'n, 298 S.E.2d 148, 154-55 (W. Va. 1982).

39. Sonn v. Planning Comm'n, 374 A.2d 159, 161 (Conn. 1976).

40. Castle Estates, Inc. v. Park and Planning Bd., 182 N.E.2d 540, 545 (Mass. 1962).

41. Parker v. Board of County Comm'rs, 603 P.2d 1098, 1100 (N.M. 1979).

42. Mac-Rich Realty Constr. v. Planning Bd., 341 N.E.2d 916, 919 (Mass. App. Ct. 1976).

43. Glennon v. Zoning Hearing Bd., 529 A.2d 1171 (Pa. Commw. 1987) (township, pursuant to police power, may establish standards relating to layout, design, and grade of access streets).

44. Turner v. Galgi, 176 N.Y.S.2d 680 (Sup. Ct. 1958); Fox v. Planning Bd. of Milton, 511 N.E.2d 30 (Mass. App. 1987); Curtis v. City of Ketchum, 720 P.2d 210 (Idaho 1986); Sheston Oil Co. v. Avalon, 520 A.2d 802 (N.J. Super. 1987), *cert. denied,* 526 A.2d 199. *But cf.* Reed v. Planning and Zoning Comm'n, 544 A.2d 1213 (Conn.

1983) (no authority in regulations to deny subdivision based on inadequate access). City of Lawrence Subdivision Regulations § 21-603 (1986).

45. Noncompliance with the official map, however, may not be sufficient to prevent planning board from approving the application. Nigro v. Planning Bd., 584 A.2d 1350 (N.J. 1991). Recent Florida cases disagree. *Compare* Palm Beach County v. Wright, 612 So.2d 709 (Fla. Ct. App. 1993) (county thoroughfare map designating future right-of-way unconstitutional) *with* Department of Transportation v. Weisenfeld, 617 So.2d 1071 (Fla. Ct. App. 1993) (mere filing of reservation map does not constitute a taking).

46. The design standards for streets were taken primarily from standards developed by the Metropolitan Planning Commission-Kansas City Region in its "Planning Guide No. 1." These standards were found to be comparable to those published by the American Society of Planning Officials, now known as the American Planning Association, which collected corresponding requirements from 22 subdivision regulations. American Society of Planning Officials, *Street Standards in Subdivision Regulations* (Planning Advisory Service Report No. 183, February, 1964).

47. Existing regulations will prevent the developer from naming roads after the first names of favorite relatives; e.g., "Alice Avenue," "Linda Lane," "Bobby Boulevard;" or flowers: e.g., "Camelia Crescent," "Dogwood Drive," "Azalea Alley"; and, finally, last names, "Zeckendorf Zee," "Schlammershlag Street," "Tydings Terrace." *See* American Society of Planning Officials, *Street Naming and House Numbering Systems* (Planning Advisory Service Report 13, 1950).

48. For a detailed study of these problems, *see id.*

49. Ayres v. City Council 207 P.2d 1 (Cal. 1949).

50. Brous v. Smith, 106 N.E.2d 503 (N.Y. 1952) (the developer sought building permits for houses on lots that did not have access to suitably improved roads, and the New York Court of Appeals upheld the denial of subdivision approval).

51. Zukis v. Town of Fitzwilliam, 604 A.2d 956 (N.H. 1992); Sheston Oil Co. v. Avalon Planning Bd., 520 A.2d 802 (N.J. Super. 1987); Tobin v. Radnor Township Bd. of Comm'rs, 597 A.2d 1258 (Pa. Commw. 1991); Novak v. Planning Bd., 523 N.Y.S.2d 590 (1988); Pearson-Kent Corp.

v. Bear, 271 N.E.2d 218 (N.Y. 1971); Wheeler v. City of Berkeley, 485 S.W.2d 707 (Mo. Ct. App. 1972).

52. 271 N.E.2d 218 (N.Y. 1971). *See also* Nastri v. Michael, 527 N.Y.S.2d 738 (1988). *Compare* Sowin Assoc. v. Planning and Zoning Comm'n, 580 A.2d 91 (Conn. App. 1990) (consideration of issues beyond the scope of subdivision regulations, including off-site traffic, municipal services, and land-use harmony, is inappropriate when the zone permits the proposed use); Richardson v. City of Little Rock Planning Comm'n, 747 S.W.2d 116 (Ark. 1988) (planning commission did not have authority to deny approval of preliminary plat based on considerations not stated in the subdivision ordinance).

53. Schwing v. City of Baton Rouge, 249 So.2d 304 (La. Ct. App. 1971).

54. McKain v. Toledo City Planning Comm'n, 270 N.E.2d 370 (Ohio Ct. App. 1971).

55. State *ex rel.* Noland v. St. Louis County, 478 S.W.2d 363 (Mo. 1972). *See also* Unlimited v. Kitsap County, 750 P.2d 651 (Wash. App. 1988) (dedication invalid without showing that the development will make the road necessary); Simpson v. City of N. Platte, 292 N.W.2d 297 (Neb. 1980) (dedication of future street where there is no present need constituted illegal land banking); Kokeu v. Smith, 551 So.2d 275 (Ala. 1989) (denial of subdivision based on lack of access must be "flexible" to prevent an applied taking).

56. City of Corpus Christi v. Unitarian Church of Corpus Christi, 436 S.W.2d 923 (Tex. Civ. App. 1968).

57. Selby Realty Co. v. City of San Buenaventura, 514 P.2d 111 (Cal. 1973). *See also* R.G. Dunbar v. Toledo Planning Comm'n, 367 N.E.2d 1193; Shea v. Danvers, 490 N.E.2d 806 (Mass App. 1986) (cannot make land unusable by denying all access).

58. Taquino v. City of Ocean Springs, 253 So.2d 854 (Miss. 1971). *Compare* Simpson v. City of N. Platte, 292 N.W.2d 297 (Neb. 1980) (invalid dedication requirement not cured by variance availability); American Nassau Bldg. Systems Ltd. v. Press, 533 N.Y.S.2d 316 (A.D., 2d Dept. 1988) (denial of variance improper where conclusion not supported by substantial evidence).

59. Howard County v. JJM, Inc., 301 Md. 256, 482 A.2d 908 (Md. Ct. App. 1984); *but c.f.* Woodbury Place Partners v. City of Woodbury, 492 N.W.2d 258 (Minn. App. 1992) (moratorium of all use for two years at freeway interchange pending plan upheld against *Lucas* per se taking challenge).

60. Joint Ventures, Inc. v. Department of Transportation, 563 So.2d 622 (Fla. 1990); Lackman v. Hall, 364 A.2d 1244 (Del. 1976).

61. Miles v. Planning Bd., 536 N.E.2d 328 (Mass. 1989) (when determining whether requirements for subdivision roads exceed local standards, comparison to roads built 12 years ago, roads in commercial districts, reconstruction, and state projects was not relevant). American Society of Planning Officials, *Varying Improvement Requirements in Subdivision Ordinances* 2, 8 (Planning Advisory Service Report No. 174, July 1963).

62. City of Arvada v. City and County of Denver, 663 P.2d 611 (Colo. 1983).

63. *See* Hagman, *Windfalls or Wipeouts*, 1 LAND-USE PLANNING REPORTS, No. 16 at 6 (1973).

64. "Excess facility" arrangements require more detailed planning than most municipalities are prepared to undertake. At a minimum, a drainage survey would have to provide information on the cost of all drainage basin facilities necessary when the basin has been fully utilized through land development. Any development coming in "upstream" should be required to assume the entire cost of any improvement in its immediate vicinity and its pro rata cost of any "downstream" improvements. The developer who installed off-site or excess "downstream" improvements will receive the pro rata distribution to reduce its total cost to a figure proportionate to its impact. This system has been employed in a number of states. A recent Virginia statute, VA. CODE ANN. § 15.1-466(j) (1981), provides:

(j) For payment by a subdivider or developer of land of his pro rata share of the cost of providing reasonable and necessary sewerage and drainage facilities located outside the property limits of the land owned or controlled by him but necessitated or required, at least in part, by the construction or improvement of his subdivision or development; provided, however, that no such payment shall be required until such time as the governing body or a designated department or agency thereof shall have established a general sewer and drainage improvement program for an area having related and common sewer and drainage conditions and within which the land owned or controlled by the subdivider or developer is located. Such regulations shall set forth and establish reasonable standards to determine the proportionate share of total estimated cost of ultimate sewerage and drainage facilities required adequately to serve a related and common area, when and if fully developed in accord with the adopted comprehensive plan, that shall be borne by each subdivider or developer within the area. Such share shall be limited to the proportion of such total estimated cost which the increased sewage flow and/or increased volume and velocity of storm water runoff to be actually caused by his subdivision or development bears to total estimated volume and velocity of such sewage and/or runoff from such area in its fully developed state. . . .

See also Ellis v. Larchmont Pharmacy Plaza, 506 A.2d 22 (N.J. Super. 1986) (any imposition of excess costs must be accompanied by provisions for partial reimbursement). *Compare* Long Meadow Assoc. v. Glen Cove, 567 N.Y.S.2d 287 (App. Div. 2d Dept. 1991) (agreement between municipality and developer for construction of a pumping station with costs to be recovered from neighboring subdivider, was invalid under state competitive bidding requirements).

65. The density increase resulting from a proposed subdivision of 14 homes was found not to create the necessary volume of traffic to warrant a major street improvement. State *ex rel.* Noland v. St. Louis County, 478 S.W.2d 363 (Mo. 1972). *Accord* Briarwest, Inc. v. City of Lincoln, 291 N.W.2d 730 (Neb. 1980). *See also* New Jersey Builders Ass'n v. Bernards Township, 511 A.2d 740 (N.J. 1985) (relationship between development and need for improvements must be clear, direct, and substantial); Baltica Constr. Co. v. Planning Bd. of Franklin, 537 A.2d 319 (N.J. Super. 1988); Colborne v. Corrales, 739 P.2d 972 (N.M. 1987). *See also* Squire's Gate v. County of Monmouth, 588 A.2d 824 (N.J. Super. 1991) (dedication requirement for off-site bridge widening was ultra vires).

66. The Federal Emergency Management Agency regulations concerning construction within floodplains requires federal coordination with local officials in order to control stormwater drainage and floods, 44 C.F.R. 66.1-66.5 (1987). *See also* COUNCIL ON ENVIRONMENTAL QUALITY, FOURTH ANNUAL REPORT 225 (1973).

67. *See, e.g.,* CAL. GOV'T CODE § 66483 (West 1983).

68. It may be illegal for the government to require a subdivider to acquire off-site rights-of-way. *See* Robert Mueller Assocs. v. Zoning Hearing Bd., 373 A.2d 1173 (Pa. Commw. Ct. 1977); while subdivision approval may not condition construction of offsite facilities in excess of need created by the subdivision, the subdivision can be denied based on the lack of adequate public facilities servicing the site. Beaver Meadows v. Larimer County, 709 P.2d 928 (Colo. 1985); Nollan v. California Coastal Comm'n, 483 U.S. 825 (1987).

69. El Shear v. Planning Bd., 592 A.2d 565 (N.J. Super. 1991) (it is the duty of the planning board to protect the public and future owners by requiring that a subdivision have adequate drainage facilities); Eschette v. City of New Orleans, 245 So.2d 383 (La. 1971); Frustuck v. City of Fairfax, 28 Cal. Rptr. 357 (Ct. App. 1963) (city liability for subdivision approval resulting in flooding).

70. *See, e.g.*, Maple Leaf Investors v. Department of Ecology, 565 P.2d 1162 (Wash. 1977) (upholding flood control zoning as valid exercise of police power). An early but excellent analysis of the constitutional problems involved in this area is Dunham, *Flood Control Via the Police Power*, 107 U. PA. L. REV. 1098 (1959). *See also* Note, *United States v. James: Expanding the Scope of Sovereign Immunity for Federal Flood Control Activities*, 37 CATH. U. L. REV. 219 (1987); Comment, *Ecological and Legal Aspects of Flood Plain Zoning*, 20 KAN. L. REV. 268 (1972). For the history of federal involvement in flood control, beginning in the mid-19th century, *see* 5 WATER AND WATER RIGHTS, Chap. 60 (Beck ed. 1991).

71. Responsible Citizens v. City of Asheville, 302 S.E.2d 204 (N.C. 1983); Sturdy Homes v. Redford Township, 186 N.W.2d 43 (Mich. Ct. App. 1971). *See generally* D. HAGMAN, URBAN PLANNING AND LAND DEVELOPMENT CONTROL LAW 3.13 (2d ed. 1986); *but see* Dooley v. Town of Fairfield Planning and Zoning Comm'n, 197 A.2d 770 (Conn. 1964).

72. For example, Minnesota has created a Flood Plain Management Act, MINN. STAT. ANN. §§ 104.01-104.07 (West 1987), creating a state commission with authority to coordinate state, local, and federal activities with regard to floodplains. Local ordinances and regulations must be reviewed for conformity with state goals, and a failure of local initiative can be rectified. *See, e.g.*, CONN. GEN. STAT. ANN. § 8-25(a) (West Supp. 1989); MD. ANN. CODE art. 66B, § 5.03 (1988); MONT. CODE ANN. § 76-3-504 (5) (1987). For an interesting analysis of state legislation, see COUNCIL ON ENVIRONMENTAL QUALITY, FOURTH ANNUAL REPORT 155-261 (1973), which includes a lengthy analysis of federally funded floodplain insurance that becomes available upon local adop-

tion of floodplain regulations (National Flood Insurance Program of 1968).

73. Adolph v. Federal Emergency Management Agency, 854 F.2d 732, 738, n.9 (5th Cir. 1988) (collecting cases); Maple Leaf Investors v. Department of Ecology, 565 P.2d 1162 (Wash. 1977); Pope v. City of Atlantic, 249 S.E.2d 16 (Ga. 1978); Town of Salem v. Kenosha County, 204 N.W.2d 467 (Wis. 1973); Turnpike Realty Co. v. Town of Dedham, 284 N.E.2d 891 (Mass. 1973) *cert. denied*, 409 U.S. 1108 (1973); Turner v. County of Del Norte, 101 Cal. Rptr. 93 (Ct. App. 1972); Vartelas v. Water Resources Comm'n, 153 A.2d 822 (Conn. 1959).

74. City of Austin v. Teague, 570 S.W.2d 389 (Tex. 1978); Baker v. Planning Bd. of Framingham, 228 N.E.2d 831 (Mass. 1967); Dooley v. Town Planning and Zoning Comm'n, 197 A.2d 770 (Conn. 1964). *But see* Ravalese v. Town of East Hartford, 608 F. Supp. 575 (D. Conn. 1985) (property owner did not have constitutionally protected interest in not having a portion of his property excluded from the floodplain zone); *see* Singer, *Flooding the Fifth Amendment: The National Flood Insurance Program and the Takings Clause*, 17 B.C. ENVTL. L. REV. 323 (1990).

75. Minnesota has adopted the Shorelands-Development in Municipalities Act, MINN. STAT. ANN. § 105.485 (West 1987), whereby a state commission promulgates model standards for land within specified distances of lakes, ponds, and flowage. Local plans must be in conformity or face change by the commission. *See generally* SALVESEN, WETLANDS: MITIGATING AND REGULATING DEVELOPMENT IMPACTS (Urban Land Institute 1990).

76. MacGibbon v. Zoning Bd. of Appeals 255 N.E.2d 347 (Mass. 1970).

77. Commonwealth v. John G. Grant & Sons Co., 526 N.E.2d 768 (Mass. 1988); *In re* Application of Christenson, 417 N.W.2d 607 (Minn. 1987); Juanita Bay Valley Community Ass'n v. Kirkland, 510 P.2d 1140 (Wash. Ct. App. 1973); *In re* Spring Valley Dev., 300 A.2d 736 (Me. 1973); Potomac Sand & Gravel Co. v. State, 293 A.2d 241 (Md. 1972).

78. Just v. Marinette County, 201 N.W.2d 671 (Wis. 1972). Federal regulation of wetlands is based primarily on the Clean Water Act, which prohibits the discharge of dredged or fill material into navigable waters without a permit. 33 U.S.C.A. § 1344(a). The Supreme Court has held that the act covered wetlands that are adjacent to bodies of water. If the wetland is isolated, there is some doubt that it is covered within the act. Hoffman Homes v. United States, 999 F.2d 256 (7th Cir. 1993). *See* Dickerson, *The Evolving Federal Wetland Program*, 44 S.W.L.J. 1473 (1991).

79. *See generally* Steinberg, Wetlands and Real Estate Development Handbook (Gov't Institutes, 1989); Loveladies Harbor, Inc. v. United States, 15 Cl. Ct. 381 (1988). Morris County Land Improvement Co. v. Township of Parsippany-Troy Hills, 193 A.2d 232 (N.J. 1963); *but see* Florida Rock Ind. v. United States, ___ F.3d ___ (Fed. Cir. 1994) (1994 WL 73987) (finding no taking for wetland regulation severely restricting use).

80. McDougal, *Performance Standards: A Viable Alternative to Euclidean Zoning*, 47 Tulane L. Rev. 255 (1973).

81. *See, e.g.,* State v. Lake Lawrence Public Lands Protection Ass'n, 601 P.2d 494 (Wash. 1979) (state environmental policy act provided authority to deny subdivision plat approval on environmental grounds); Inland Vale Farm Co. v. Stergianopoulos, 481 N.E.2d 547 (N.Y. 1985) (town planning board's approval of site development plan without preparation of EIS was arbitrary and capricious); Newaukum Hill Protective Ass'n v. Lewis County, 574 P.2d 1199 (Wash. 1978). Freilich, *Friends of Mammoth v. Board of Supervisors of Mono County: Local Government Inherits Environmental Protection*, 5 Urb. Law. 1 (1973).

82. 42 U.S.C.A. §§ 4331-4347 (1982).

83. *See* Greis, *The Environmental Impact Statement: A Small Step Instead of a Giant Leap*, 5 Urb. Law. 264, 272 (1973). Examples of nonfederal action held to be outside of the domain of NEPA are: (1) state toll highways, Bradford Township v. Illinois State Toll Hwy. Auth., 463 F.2d 537 (7th Cir. 1972), *cert. denied*, 409 U.S. 1047 (1972); (2) private pollution from refineries, Tanner v. Armco Steel Corp., 340 F. Supp. 532 (S.D. Tex. 1972).

84. Del. Code Ann. tit. 7 §§ 7001-7013 (1983); Mass. Gen. Laws Ann. ch. 30, §§ 61, 62 (1979); Mich. Comp. Laws Ann. §§ 691.1201-691.1207 (West 1979); Minn. Stat. Ann. §§ 116D.01-116D.07 (West 1987); Mont. Code Ann. §§ 69-6501 to 69-6598 (Supp. 1977); N.C. Gen. Stat. §§ 113A-1 to 113A-g (1983); Va. Code Ann. §§ 10-17.107 to 10-17-112 (1985); Wash. Rev. Code Ann. § 43.216.010 (1983); Wis. Stat. Ann. § 1.11 (West 1986); Me. Rev. Stat. Ann. §§ 481-488.

85. Cal. Pub. Res. Code §§ 21000-21177 (West 1994).

86. Friends of Mammoth v. Board of Supervisors, 502 P.2d 1049 (Cal. 1972).

87. Mont. Code Ann. § 75-20-211 (1994).

88. *See* Bowie, Maryland, Commission on Environmental Quality, *The Role of Environmental Impact Statements in Local Government Decision Making*, 6 Urb. Law. No. 1 (Winter 1974).

89. Carmel Valley View, Ltd. v. Maggini, 155 Cal. Rptr. 208 (Cal. App. 1979) ("[w]e have no difficulty in according priority to SEQA because the legislative declaration of purpose in that statute makes it obvious that protection of [the environment] far overshadows the rights of developers to obtain prompt action on their proposals"; Sun Beach Real Estate Dev. Corp. v. Anderson, 469 N.Y.S.2d 964 (App. Div., 2d. Dept., 1983).

90. Model Regulations § 5.6(3)(b) & (c).

91. For a detailed discussion of this topic, *see* R. Harral, Preparing for Public Waste Disposal System—Capped Sewers (University of Pittsburgh Institute of Local Government, Local Government Conference on Subdivision Control, May 1957). The standards indicated in 5.6(6) (b) are the criteria for sanitary sewer projects of the Kansas City, Missouri, Public Works Department, August 4, 1969.

92. Swanson v. Marin County Water District, 128 Cal.Rptr. 485 (Cal. App. 1976); South Cutler Bay, Inc. v. Metropolitan Dade County, 349 F. Supp. 1205 (S.D. Fla. 1972). *See also* Fairfax County, Va., Proposal for Implementing an Improved Planning and Land-Use Control System in Fairfax County, Final Report of the Task Force on Comprehensive Planning and Land-Use Control (June 11, 1973). The validity of withholding permits where water and sewer facilities are inadequate has been upheld by the courts. *See also* Tisei v. Town of Ogunquit, 491 A.2d 564 (Me. 1985) (local governments may impose moratorium based on inability to provide public services and utilities in appropriate circumstances); Bethlehem Evangelical Lutheran Church v. City of Lakewood, 626 P.2d 668 (Colo. 1981); Metropolitan Dade County v. Rosell Constr. Corp., 297 So.2d 46 (Fla. Dist. Ct. App. 1974); Kaplan v. Clear Lake City Water Auth., 794 F.2d 1059 (5th Cir. 1986) (city's refusal to provide water and sewer service to developer's property upheld in light of moratorium on services based on the need for a new sewage treatment plant); *but see* Westwood Forest Estates, Inc. v. Village of Nyack, 297 N.Y.S.2d 129 (N.Y. 1969) (identifying criteria that must be in effect to validate moratorium).

93. Marin County, California relied upon the Cal. Env. Quality Act, Cal. Pub. Res. Code

§§ 21000-21177 (West 1986) and Wilson v. Hidden Valley Municipal Water District, 63 Cal. Rptr. 889 (Ct. App. 1967) for the principle that municipal authorities may implement municipal growth policies that recognize preservation of the environment as the guiding criterion in all public decisions. For an analysis of a moratorium in Pinellas County, Florida, see STIERHEIM, POSITION STATEMENT NO. 2, RESOURCE NEEDS AND MANAGED GROWTH FOR PINELLAS COUNTY, FLORIDA (Oct. 30, 1973). *See also* Delight, Inc. v. Baltimore County, 624 F.2d 12 (4th Cir. 1980); Moviematic Indus. v. Board of County Comm'rs, 349 So.2d 667 (Fla. App. 1977).

94. Hawkins v. Town of Shaw, 461 F.2d 1171 (5th Cir. 1972) (for racially discriminatory pattern of services between white and minority areas); Ammons v. Dade City, 783 F.2d 982 (11th Cir., 1986).

95. Robinson v. City of Boulder, 547 P.2d 228 (Colo. 1976), *but* overruled in Board of County Comm'rs v. Denver Bd. of Water Comm'rs, 718 P.2d 235 (Colo. 1978); Reid v. Township of Parsippany-Troy Hills, 89 A.2d 667 (N.J. 1952); *but cf.* Crownhill Homes v. City of San Antonio, 433 S.W.2d 448 (Tex. Civ. App. 1968). *See* Lodge of Ozarks v. Branson, 796 S.W.2d 646 (Mo. App. 1990); Dateline Builders, Inc. v. City of Santa Rosa, 194 Cal. Rptr. 258 (Cal. App. 1983) (no duty if inconsistent with city and county regional plan).

96. Westwood Forest Estates, Inc. v. Village of South Nyack, 244 N.E.2d 700 (App. Div. 1969); Belle Harbor Realty Corp. v. Kerr, 364 N.Y.S.2d 160 (N.Y. 1974); Charles v. Diamond, 392 N.Y.S.2d 594 (N.Y. 1977) (10-year delay—remand to trial court to determine reasonableness).

97. Golden v. Planning Bd. of Ramapo, 285 N.E.2d 291, *appeal dismissed,* 409 U.S. 1003 (1972); Franklin County v. Leisure Properties, 430 So.2d 475 (Fla. App. 1983); Zibler v. Town of Moraga, 692 F. Supp. 1195 (N.D. Cal. 1988); Smoke Rise, Inc. v. Washington Suburban Sanitary Comm'n, 400 F. Supp. 1369 (D. Md. 1975); Freil v. Triangle Oil Co., 543 A.2d 863 (Md. App. 1988).

98. 33 U.S.C. §§ 1251-1376 (1982).

99. 33 U.S.C. § 1319.

100. 40 C.F.R. §§ 130.0-131.13. *See also* COUNCIL ON ENVIRONMENTAL QUALITY, FOURTH ANNUAL REPORT (1973).

101. *See* Pedestrian and Bikeway Regulations of City of Tigard, noted in Dolan v. City of Tigard, 854 P.2d 437 (Ore. 1993), *cert. granted,* 114 S.Ct 544, 126 L.Ed.2d 446.

102. *See* Freilich & White, *Transportation Congestion and Growth Management: Comprehensive Approaches to Resolving America's Major Quality of Life Crisis,* 24 LOY. L.A.L. REV. 915 (1991).

103. Johnston, *Constitutionality of Subdivision Control Exactions: The Quest for a Rationale,* 52 CORNELL L. REV. 871 (1967); Ferguson & Rasnic, *Judicial Limitations on Mandatory Subdivision Dedications,* 13 REAL EST. L. J. 250, 252 (1984). *See also* Middlemist v. Plymouth, 387 N.W.2d 190 (Minn. App. 1986) (reasonableness of dedication may be evidenced by showing that group of subdivisions has created need for the public use).

104. Note, *Constitutional Law—Mandatory Subdivision Exactions for Park and Recreational Purposes,* 43 MO. L. REV. 582, 583-84 (1978).

105. Pengilly v. Multnomah County, 810 F.Supp 1111 (D.Ore. 1992); *see* Note, *Land Subdivision Regulation: Its Effect and Constitutionality,* 41 ST. JOHNS L. REV. 374 (1967); Middlemist v. Plymouth, 387 N.W.2d 190 (Minn. App. 1986); Mansfield & Swett, Inc. v. Town of West Orange, 198 A. 225 (N.J. 1938); Gavin v. Baker, 59 So.2d 360 (Fla. 1952); Hudson Oil Co. v. Wichita, 396 P.2d 271 (Kan. 1964); *In re* Lake Secor Dev. Co., 252 N.Y.S. 809 (Sup. Ct. 1931), *aff'd,* 255 N.Y.S. 853 (App. Div. 1932); Mitchell v. Rancho Viejo, Inc., 736 S.W.2d 757 (Tex. Ct. Civ. App. 1987); Bethlehem Evangelical Lutheran Church v. City of Lakewood, 626 P.2d 668 (Colo. 1981) (dedication of land for street as a condition of building permit approval was upheld).

106. The government costs of a new subdivision are divided into two categories—capital and service costs. Service costs, being per capita, remain relatively stable as population increases. Capital costs increase disproportionately faster than population. This situation is due to the fact that older residents have already paid for costs of capital facilities while new residents have paid nothing. Subdivision regulations should, therefore, be used to offset this unfair burden on older residents. Heyman & Gilhool, *The Constitutionality of Imposing Increased Community Costs on New Suburban Residents Through Subdivision Exactions,* 73 YALE L.J. 1119 (1964). *See, e.g.,* Associated Homebuilders of the Greater East Bay v. City of Walnut Creek, 484 P.2d 606, *appeal dismissed,* 404 U.S. 878 (1971) (parks); Hollywood, Inc. v. Broward County, 431 So.2d 606 (Fla. Dist. Ct. App. 1983) (parks); Kahmi v. Yorktown, 547 N.E.2d 346 (N.Y. 1989) (parks); Trent Meredith, Inc. v. City of Oxnard, 170 Cal. Rptr. 685 (1981) (schools); Cimarron Corp. v. Board of County Comm'rs, 563 P.2d 946 (Colo. 1977) (schools);

Nunziato v. Planning Bd. of Edgewater, 541 A.2d 1105 (N.J. Super. 1988) (schools).

107. Heyman and Gilhool, *The Constitutionality of Imposing Increased Community Costs on New Suburban Residents Through Subdivision Exactions*, 73 YALE L.J. 1119, 1134 (1964):

"It would seem clear that the objectives of these exactions are permissible. They are intended to minimize the overcrowding of existing facilities devoted to education and recreation—activities clearly important to the general welfare of the community. Since there is value left to the property owner and since the regulation is required to obtain the objective, the newer exactions would also appear to avoid the barriers of confiscation and arbitrariness as easily as the conventional exactions.

"Discrimination and taking limitations, however, are seen to pose a unique problem. The problem is the same under both rubrics. It is whether the subdivision homebuyer, who ultimately finances such exactions, will be required to pay more than a 'fair' share for community schools, parks, and other facilities financed by the exactions. If they are forced to pay more than a fair share, the result arguably is both a taking and discriminatory. Taking occurs because there is imposed on the homebuyers costs resulting not only from their own activities but from the activities of the rest of the community. Discrimination flows because such buyers unreasonably are being isolated to pay costs attributable to other residents as well."

Many articles have been written on this subject. *See, e.g.,* Johnston, *supra* note 103); Reps & Smith, *Control of Urban Land Subdivision*, 14 SYRACUSE L. REV. 405 (1963); Strine, *The Use of Conditions in Land-Use Control*, 67 DICK. L. REV. 109 (1963); Cutler, *Legal and Illegal Methods for Controlling Community Growth on the Urban Fringe*, 1961 WIS. L. REV. 370; Shultz & Kelley, *Subdivision Improvement Requirements and Guarantees: A Primer*, 28 J. URB. & CONTEMP. L. 3 (1985); Netter & Dilworth, *Local Government Exactions from Developers*, THE PRACTICAL REAL EST. LAW. 23 (Sept. 1985); Ferguson & Rasnic, *Judicial Limitations on Mandatory Subdivision Dedications*, 13 REAL EST. LAW J. 250 (1984); Pavelko, *Subdivision Exactions: A Review of Judicial Standards*, 25 WASH. U. J. URB. AND CONTEMP. L. 269 (1983); Sheen, *Development Fees: Standards to Determine Their Reasonableness*, 1982 UTAH L. REV. 549; Delaney, Gordon & Hess, *The Needs-Nexus Analysis: A Unified Test for Validating Subdivision Exactions, User Impact Fees, and Linkage*, 50 L. & CONTEMP. PROB. 139 (1987).

108. Nollan v. California Coastal Comm'n, 483 U.S. 825 (1987).

109. The court held that the imposition of the access easement was not a valid exercise of the police power for the regulation of land use because the condition imposed does not serve a public purpose related to the permit requirements. The public purposes listed by the California Coastal Commission—to protect the public's ability to see the beach, assisting the public in overcoming "psychological" barriers to using the beach, and preventing beach congestion—were not public purposes validly related to the imposed condition. *Id.*

110. *Id.* at 3148.

111. *See infra* notes 117-137 and accompanying text.

112. *See* SPEA, *supra* note 3, at Title II, Subdivision Control, § 14; HHFA, LAND SUBDIVISION REGULATIONS 5, 6 (1952).

113. *See, e.g.,* City of College Station v. Turtle Rock Corp., 680 S.W.2d 802 (Tex. 1984); Collis v. City of Bloomington, 246 N.W.2d 19 (Minn. 1976).

114. This standard is one of the two major types of density formulas used to calculate the amount of land to be dedicated. The second standard is determined by a required percentage of land based on the density of the subdivision expressed either in terms of dwelling units per acre, size of lots in square feet, or by type of residential district. M. Brooks, *Mandatory Dedication of Land or Fees in Lieu of Land for Parks and Schools* 11 (Planning Advisory Service Report No. 266, Feb. 1971).

115. *See* J. KRASNOWIECKI, URBAN HOUSING AND RENEWAL 533 (1969).

116. *See* URBAN LAND INSTITUTE, THE HOMES ASSOCIATION HANDBOOK (Tech. Bull. No. 50, Rev. Ed. 1966).

117. *See* NEV. REV. STAT. ANN. § 278.320-.569 (1987); a transportation "utility" may be created to collect monthly maintenance and operation costs for public streets. Bloom v. City of Fort Collins, 784 P.2d 304 (Colo. 1989).

118. Several California communities have developed a "procedure" for determining whether land dedication or money in lieu of land should be utilized. *See* M. Brooks, *supra* note 114, at 25.

119. Supporting the approach, *see* Oswego Properties, Inc. v. City of Oswego, 814 P.2d 539 (Ore. App. 1991); Jenad Inc. v. Village of Scarsdale, 271 N.Y.S.2d 955, 218 N.E.2d 673 (1960) ($250 per lot charged in lieu of actual dedication); Jordan v. Village of Menomonee Falls, 137 N.W.2d 442 (Wis. 1965), appeal dismissed, 385 U.S. 4 (1966) (equalization fee justified on same grounds as actual dedication—such a fee is not a tax but rather a fee imposed on the transaction of plat approval); Billings Properties v. Yellowstone County, 394 P.2d 182 (Mont. 1964); Associated Home Builders v. City of Walnut Creek, 484 P.2d 606 (Cal.) *appeal dismissed*, 404 U.S. 878 (1971); Trent Meredith, Inc. v. City of Oxnard, 170 Cal. Rptr. 685 (Ct. App. 1981) (dedication or money in lieu of dedication for schools was not a special tax that would require voter approval under Proposition 13, nor is it an ad valorem tax imposed upon the land but "is imposed on the privilege of subdividing land" and is a proper exercise of police power); Call v. City of West Jordan, 606 P.2d 217 (Utah 1979) (ordinance requiring subdividers to dedicate seven percent of the land or the equivalent value in cash was within the general police power delegation of the State and Municipal Planning Enabling Act); Home Builders Ass'n v. City of Kansas City, 555 S.W.2d 832 (Mo. 1977) (ordinance requiring nine percent dedication or $60 per living unit in lieu thereof for parks upheld as within the city's police power); Board of Educ. v. Surety Dev., 347 N.E.2d 149 (Ill. 1975) ($200 per house built, $50,000 contribution and dedication of land for school purposes upheld under county home rule statute). In validating the approach, *see* Haugen v. Gleason, 359 P.2d 108 (Ore. 1961) (a $37.50/lot fee to be used by the county school district struck down as an unauthorized tax); Sanchez v. City of Santa Fe, 481 P.2d 401 (N.M. 1971) (money in lieu of land technique invalid because no assurance that the fees will be used to solve a problem peculiar to the land being subdivided); Enchanting Homes v. Rapanos, 143 N.W.2d 618 (Mich. Ct. App. 1966) (no statutory authority to require either dedication or money in lieu thereof); City of Montgomery v. Crossroads Land Co., 355 So.2d 363 (Ala. 1978) (without specific legislative authorization, city had no power to require money in lieu of land for public parks; state enabling statute for "open spaces" insufficient); Cimarron Corp. v. Board of County Comm'rs, 563 P.2d 946 (Colo. 1977) (regulation requiring dedication and money in lieu of land for school and park sites went beyond enabling statute because the funds were not retained by county commissioners, which the state required); Berg Dev. Co. v. Missouri City, 603 S.W.2d 273 (Tex. Civ. App. 1980) (ordinance providing for dedication or

money in lieu of land for park purposes bore no substantial relation to safety and health of the community and was thus a taking without compensation).

120. There are three major approaches currently being used to calculate the money to be paid in by the developer: (1) the assessed or fair market value of the land at a specific point in time; (2) a fixed dollar amount per lot or dwelling unit; or (3) a variable percentage of the fair market value based on the density of the subdivision. M. Brooks, *supra* note 114, at 13. The Model Regulation provision 5.9(1)(d) eliminates much of the potential conflict between the developer and the planning commission.

121. When a developer decides not to proceed with the project after paying a fee in lieu of dedication, he will be entitled to a reimbursement even if there is "no requirement that the facilities purchased with a particular contribution must be used only by the residents of the subdivision that made the contribution." Wright Dev. v. City of Mountain View, 125 Cal. Rptr. 723, 724 (Ct. App. 1976). Such a requirement cannot be imposed at final approval if the preliminary plat approval did not require the payment in lieu of parkland dedication, Joseph v. Planning Bd. of Yorktown, 529 N.Y.S.2d 17 (A.D., 2nd Dept., 1988).

122. M. Brooks, *supra* note 114.

123. *Id.* at 25.

124. Frank Ansuini, Inc. v. City of Cranston, 264 A.2d 910 (R.I. 1970) (court upheld the constitutionality of dedication provisions but ruled that a seven percent fixed percentage requirement, regardless of density, was fatally arbitrary). *See also* Dolbeare, *Mandatory Dedication of Public Sites as a Condition in the Subdivision Process in Virginia*, 9 U. RICH. L. REV. 435, 459 (1975). Dolbeare notes that fixed percentage dedications penalize subdivisions with large lots. He suggests a sliding scale based on density that would recognize "that it is the people living in the subdivision that create the needs." *Id.*; *see* Sudarsky v. City of New York, 779 F. Supp. 287 (S.D.N.Y. 1991): "The nexus between higher population density occasioned by newer development and increased use of public facilities has long been recognized as sufficient to justify the transfer of a portion of the developer's property to public use to alleviate the burden placed on public services"; *see also* State *ex. rel.* Kessler v. Shay, 820 S.W.2d 311 (Mo. App. 1991).

125. *See* F. Bosselman, D. Callies, & J. Banta, The Taking Issue, (Council on Environmental Quality 1973). *See also* Nollan v. California Coastal Comm'n, 483 U.S. 825 (1987).

126. 167 N.E.2d 230 (Ill. 1960).

127. 176 N.E.2d 799 (Ill. 1961).

128. Ayres v. City Council, 207 P.2d 1 (Cal. 1949).

129. The *Pioneer Trust* court restated the *Rosen* rule: "If the requirement is within the statutory grant of power to the municipality and if the burden cast upon the subdivision is *specifically and uniquely attributable* to his activity, then the requirement is permissible. . . ." 176 N.E.2d at 802 (emphasis added); *see also* Nunziato v. Planning Bd. of Edgewater, 541 A.2d 1105 (N.J. 1988) (New Jersey follows strict Illinois rule, particularly as to statutory authority).

130. In Board of Education v. Surety Developers, 347 N.E.2d 149 (Ill. 1976), the Illinois Supreme Court upheld the authority of a county board to require a developer to donate a parcel of land for use as school grounds, contribute $50,000 toward construction, and pay $200 for each home built. In holding that the problem was "specifically and uniquely attributable" to the development, the court noted that 98 percent of the elementary school children lived in the defendant's subdivision. *See also* Krughoff v. City of Naperville, 369 N.E.2d 892, 895 (Ill. 1977) (ordinance requiring dedication or money in lieu of land for school and park sites upheld; court carefully documented the increase in student and adult population and concluded that the requirements were "'uniquely attributable to' and fairly proportioned to the need for new school and park facilities created by the proposed developments"). At least one author has read *Krughoff* as signalling a tacit abandonment of the "specifically and uniquely attributable" rule set out in *Pioneer Trust* in favor of a more liberal test. *See* Staples, "Exaction—Mandatory Dedications and Payments in Lieu of Dedication," in 1980 Institute on Planning, Zoning and Eminent Domain 132-33.

131. Frank Ansuini, Inc. v. City of Cranston, 264 A.2d 910 (R.I. 1970); *see also* R.G. Dunbar, Inc. v. Toledo Plan Comm'n, 367 N.E.2d 1193 (Ohio Ct. App. 1976) (commission could not require developer to dedicate a 100-foot-wide road through its subdivision; the dedication was not "specifically and uniquely attributable" to the developer because it was only for the benefit of the general public).

132. 252 N.Y.S. 809 (Sup. Ct. 1931), *aff'd*, 255 N.Y.S. 853 (1932).

133. 209 N.Y.S.2d 729 (Sup. Ct. 1960), *aff'd*, 225 N.Y.S.2d 538 (1962).

134. 218 N.E.2d 673 (1966).

135. *See* Jenad Inc. v. Village of Scarsdale, 271 N.Y.S.2d 955, 956 (1960). The requirement in the Model Regulations that money in lieu of land funds be placed in a neighborhood park and recreation improvement fund to be used in the vicinity of the subdivision, Model Regulations, 5.9(1)(d), stems from the *Jenad* case. In Haugen v. Gleason, 359 P.2d 108 (Ore. 1961), a money in lieu of land provision was struck down because the funds could go to "any county or school district," and there was no requirement that the money paid by the subdivider would be expended by the county for park purposes within the vicinity or for use of the subdivision. Accordingly, the provision was declared an illegal "general" tax.

136. *See, e.g.*, Riegert Apts. Corp. v. Planning Bd., 432 N.Y.S.2d 43 (Sup. Ct. 1979) (land earlier conveyed by developer for flood control did not satisfy regulations requiring dedication or money in lieu of land for recreational purposes; town could require developer to deposit money in lieu of land as a condition for granting site approval).

137. Holmes v. Planning Bd., 433 N.Y.S.2d 587 (App. Div. 1980) (plan requiring elimination of individual drives to control traffic congestion upheld under "reasonable relationship" standard).

138. Billings Properties v. Yellowstone Co., 394 P.2d 182 (Mont. 1964) (the "reasonable needs" test had been established by the legislature in passing the statute, and the court bowed to this determination); Jordan v. Village of Menomonee Falls, 137 N.W.2d 442 (Wis.), *appeal dismissed*, 385 U.S. 4 (1965) (reasonably related test adopted both for parks and school sites); State *ex rel* Noland v. St. Louis County, 478 S.W.2d 363 (Mo. 1972) (there must be some "reasonable relationship" between the proposed activity of the landowner and the exactions of government); Lampton v. Pinaire, 610 S.W.2d 915 (Ky. Ct. App. 1981) ("so long as the taking of a portion of land [for streets], whether on the exterior or from the interior is based on the reasonably anticipated burdens to be caused by the development," there is no taking); Simpson v. City of North Platte, 292 N.W.2d 297 (Neb. 1980) (city could not require street dedication that bore no "reasonable relationship or nexus" to the use made of the property); Call v. City of West Jordan, 606 P.2d 217 (Utah 1979) (reasonable relationship adopted for dedication of flood control and/or parks and recreational facilities); Home Builders Ass'n v. City of Kansas City, 555 S.W.2d 832 (Mo. 1977) (applies "reasonably attributable" test to an ordinance requiring dedication or money in lieu of land for parks); Cimarron Corp. v. Board of County Comm'rs, 563 P.2d 946 (Colo. 1977) (statute authorizing dedication for schools and park sites only "when such are reasonably necessary to serve the proposed subdivision" and its future residents held not unreasonably vague; regulation allowing counties to require both a dedication of land and money invalid as beyond the powers granted in enabling act); Collis v. City of Bloomington, 246 N.W.2d 19 (Minn. 1976) (dedication for parks "reasonably related" to a subdivision's recreational need).

139. Associated Home Builders v. City of Walnut Creek, 484 P.2d 606 (Cal.) *appeal dismissed*, 404 U.S. 878 (1971). The decision relied upon the earlier precedent-setting case of Ayres v. City Council of Los Angeles, where the court held the dedication of land as a condition of subdivision approval not to be a taking "where it is a condition reasonably related to increased traffic and other needs of the proposed subdivision..." Ayres v. City Council, 207 P.2d 1, 8 (Cal. 1949). *See also* Scrutton v. Sacramento County, 79 Cal. Rptr. 872, 879 (Ct. App. 1969). Under the *Scrutton* decision, the California courts recognize two kinds of reasonable need: (1) the protection against the potential deleterious effects of the landowners' proposal (see *Ayres*); and (2) the community's need for facilities to meet public service demands created by the proposal. Sommers v. City of Los Angeles, 62 Cal. Rptr. 523 (Ct. App. 1967); Bringle v. Board of Supervisors, 351 P.2d 765 (Cal. 1960).

140. 338 So.2d 863 (Fla. Dist. Ct. App. 1976).
141. *Id.* at 866.
142. *Id.* at 868. The court found such a nexus to exist, noting that the subdivision was in a "glade area" and other properties would be subject to runoff from it.
143. *Id.*
144. 379 A.2d 200 (N.H. 1977).
145. *Id.* at 204, citing Longridge Builders v. Planning Bd., 245 A.2d 336, 337 (N.J. 1968). *See also* J.E.D. Assoc. v. Town of Atkinson, 432 A.2d 12 (N.H. 1981); Oakes Constr. Co. v. Iowa City, 304 N.W.2d 797 (Iowa 1981).
146. J.E.D. Assoc. v. Town of Atkinson, 432

A.2d 12 (N.H. 1981). *See also* Patentaude v. Town of Meredith, 392 A.2d 582 (N.H. 1978) (conditioning approval of subdivision on developer leaving four lots unimproved did not constitute a taking because the need for recreational space was necessitated by the subdivision).

147. *See, e.g.*, Pioneer Trust & Savings Bank v. Mount Prospect, 176 N.E.2d 799 (Ill. 1961); Cimarron Corp. v. Board of County Comm'rs, 563 P.2d 946 (Colo. 1977) (enabling statute constitutional, but regulation requiring dedication and funds for school and park sites went beyond statutory powers); *but see* St. Johns County v. Northeast Florida Bldg. Ass'n, 583 So.2d 635 (Fla. 1991) (upholding school impact fees on same rational basis test for all exactions).
148. 347 N.E.2d 149 (Ill. 1975).
149. *Id.* at 151. The developer complied with the first two conditions but later refused to pay the "per house" fee.
150. *Id.* at 154.
151. 369 N.E.2d 892 (Ill. 1977).
152. 369 N.E.2d at 895.
153. Trent Meredith, Inc. v. City of Oxnard, 170 Cal. Rptr. 685 (Ct. App. 1981). The ordinance in *Trent* was adopted pursuant to CAL. GOV'T CODE §§ 65970-65978 (West Supp. 1981) adopted in 1977 and modeled after parkland dedication that authorizes a city or county "to require a dedication of land or fees, or both, for [interim] elementary or high school classrooms and related facilities, upon a finding that these facilities would be consistent with the general plan, as a condition to the approval of the residential development." Legislative Counsel's Digest, Senate Bill No. 201, Chapter 955 (Sept. 21, 1977). *See also* Brookhill Dev. v. City of Waukesha, 299 N.W.2d 610 (Wis. Ct. App. 1980), *aff'd*, 307 N.W.2d 242 (Wis. 1981) (city may require dedication or fees in lieu of land for school sites, but only within its boundaries or its extraterritorial plat approval jurisdiction).
154. Reps and Smith, *supra* note 107, at 407-12.
155. Heyman and Gilhool, *supra* note 107, at 1140-49. *See also* Johnston, *supra* note 103, at 908-09.
156. J.E.D. Assoc. v. Town of Atkinson, 432 A.2d 12 (N.H. 1981) (seven percent dedication requirement made no consideration of specific need created by development); Simpson v. City of North Platte, 292 N.W.2d 297 (Neb. 1980) (dedication of future street where no present need constitutes an illegal "land banking" scheme); Land/Vest Properties v. Town of

Plainfield, 379 A.2d 200 (N.H. 1977) (upgrading roads outside subdivision bore no rational nexus to needs created by subdivision); State *ex rel.* Noland v. St. Louis County, 478 S.W.2d 363 (Mo. 1972) (dedication to extend major street would almost eliminate subdivision when coupled with other dedication requirements); Schwing v. City of Baton Rouge, 249 So.2d 304 (La. Ct. App. 1971) (dedication of future right-of-way having no relationship to subdivision); Haugen v. Gleason, 359 P.2d 108 (Ore. 1961) (no express limit on amount of land or money that could be demanded results in holding that ordinance is illegal general tax rather than police power regulation); recall that Nollan v. California Coastal Comm'n, 483 U.S. 825, 107 S.Ct. 3141, 97 L.Ed.2d 677 (1987) requires a higher scrutiny for regulations that constitute "physical" exactions, i.e. dedications. It has been held that "money in lieu of land" does *not* require the heightened scrutiny. Sintra, Inc. v. City of Seattle, 829 P.2d 765, 773 (n.7) (Wash. 1992) (demolition fee not physical exaction); Blue Jeans Equities West v. San Francisco, 4 Cal. Rptr. 114 (Cal. App. 1992) (linkage fees); Commercial Bldrs. v. City of Sacramento, 941 F.2d 872 (9th Cir., 1991).

157. Brookhill Dev. v. City of Waukesha, 307 N.W.2d 242 (Wis. 1981).

158. Business Health v. Johnson, 395 N.Y.S.2d 689 (App. Div. 1977) (regulation requiring dedication for parks valid, but planning board could apply "set aside" percentage only toward property actually sought to be developed, not entire acreage owned by developer).

159. Model Regulations § 6; *see generally* Freilich & Morgan, *Municipal Strategies for Imposing Valid Development Exactions: Responding to Nollan*, 10 ZONING AND PLANNING L. REP., No. 11 at 170 (Dec. 1987).

160. *See* Davidson, *Using Infrastructure Controls to Guide Development*, 8 ZONING & PLANNING L. REP. 169, 170 (1985).

161. FLA. STAT. ANN. § 163.3177(10)(h).

162. Fagin, *Regulating the Timing of Urban Development*, 20 L. & CONTEMP. PROBS. 298 (1955), reprinted in I.R. SCOTT, ED., MANAGEMENT & CONTROL OF GROWTH, 296, 298-99 (The Urban Land Institute 1975).

163. *Id.*

164. Pelham, *Adequate Public Facility Requirements: Reflections on Florida's Concurrency System for Managing Growth*, 19 FLA. ST. U.L. REV. 973 (1992); Freilich & Ragsdale, *Timing and Sequential Control—The Essential Basis for Effective Regional Planning: An Analysis of the New Directions*

for Land Use Control in the Minneapolis-St. Paul Metropolitan Region, 58 MINN. L. REV. 1011, 1054 (1974); Fagin, *supra*, at 298; Schmandt, *Municipal Control of Urban Expansion*, 29 FORD. L. REV. 637 (1961); *see also* J. NOBLE, A PROPOSED SYSTEM FOR REGULATORY LAND USE IN URBANIZING COUNTIES (1967); Joseph v. Town Bd., 24 Misc. 2d 366, 198 N.Y.S.2d 695 (Sup. Ct. 1960).

165. Freilich & Ragsdale, *supra* note 5, at 1057.

166. This raises the related issue of whether cities may refuse service or utility extensions in order to control growth. Where the utilities are operated in a proprietary capacity, some courts have disallowed the refusal of service extension to control growth, applying the rule that service refusal may be based only on a "utility-related reason." Note, *Public Utility Land Use Control on the Urban Fringe*, 63 IOWA L. REV. 889, 899 (1978); Stone, *The Prevention of Urban Sprawl Through Utility Extension Control*, 14 URBAN LAW. 357 (1982); Note, *Control of the Timing and Location of Government Utility Extensions*, 26 STAN. L. REV. 945 (1974); Robinson v. City of Boulder, 547 P.2d 228 (Colo. 1976); Delmarva Enterprises v. City of Dover, 282 A.2d 601 (Del. 1971). These cases were rejected in Dateline Builders v. City of Santa Rosa, 146 Cal. App. 3d 531, 194 Cal. Rptr. 258, 264-65 (Cal. App. 1983), which affirmed the ability of cities to refuse utility connections beyond their boundaries to prevent leapfrog development and urban sprawl. The city's ability to control service extensions was predicated on its police powers. *Id.* at 266; *see also* Board of County Comm'rs v. Denver Bd. of Water Comm'rs, 718 P.2d 235 (Colo. 1978) (overruling Robinson).

167. Wincamp Partnership OTC v. Anne Arundel County, 458 F. Supp. 1009 (1978).

168. *Id.* at 1025-27 (D. Md. 1978). Conway v. Town of Stratham, 414 A.2d 539 (N.H. 1980); Rancourt v. Town of Barnstead, 523 A.2d 55 (N.H. 1987); Beck v. Town of Raymond, 394 A.2d 847 (N.H. 1978); Sturges v. Town of Chilmark, 402 N.E.2d 1346 (Mass. 1980); Begin v. Inhabitants of Sabattus, 409 A.2d 1269 (Me. 1979); Guiliano v. Town of Edgartown, 531 F. Supp. 1076 (Mass. 1982); Associated Home Builders v. Livermore, 557 P.2d 472 (Cal. 1976); Building Industry Ass'n v. City of Camarillo, 718 P.2d 68 (Cal. 1986); Long Beach Equities v. County of Ventura, 282 Cal. Rptr. 877 (Ct. App. 1991). Basing development approvals on the adequacy of public facilities is invalidated only where the city has demonstrated no commitment to provide the facilities in good faith. Thus, the condition could amount to a de facto moratorium and a taking of private property without just compensation. *See* City National Bank of Miami v. City of Coral Springs, 475 So.2d 984, 986 (Fla. App. 1985). The absence of plans and of past efforts to maintain the public facilities could also result in the invalidation of such conditions, since the conditions are attributable to the effects of past development and not to the impacts of the new developer. Westwood Forest Estates, Inc. v. South Nyack, 23 N.Y.2d 424, 297 N.Y.S.2d 129, 244 N.E.2d 700 (1969); Kennedy Park Homes Ass'n v. City of Lackawanna, 436 F.2d 108, 114 (2d Cir. 1970).

169. Golden v. Planning Bd. of the Town of Ramapo, 30 N.Y.2d 359, 334 N.Y.S.2d 138, 295 N.E.2d 291 (1972).

170. Freilich, *Development Timing, Moratoria and Controlling Growth: A Preliminary Report*, in II R. Scott, ed., Management and Control of Growth 361, 362 (1975).

171. *See* Freilich, *Development Timing, Moratoria and Controlling Growth*, 1974 Inst. on Planning, Zoning & Eminent Domain 147, 162-64.

172. Comment, *The Ramapo Case*, 24 Zoning Digest 99 (1972).

173. Freilich, *Golden v. Town of Ramapo: Establishing a New Dimension in American Planning Law*, 4 Urb. Law. 3 (1972).

174. Golden v. Planning Bd. of the Town of Ramapo, 30 N.Y.2d 359, 334 N.Y.S.2d 138; 285 N.E.2d 291, *appeal dismissed* 409 U.S. 1003 (1972).

175. Norbeck Village Joint Venture v. Montgomery County Council, 254 Md. 50, 254 A.2d 700, 706 (1969); Smoke Rise, Inc. v. Washington Suburban Sanitary Comm'n, 400 F. Supp. 1369, 1384 (D. Md. 1975) (citing Golden v. Planning Bd., *supra*).

176. Wincamp Partnership v. Anne Arundel County, 458 F. Supp. 1009, 1030 (D. Md. 1978); Guiliano v. Town of Edgartown, 531 F. Supp. 1076 (D. Mass. 1982) (prohibition of sales exceeding 10 lots per year in any one subdivision based on inadequacy of public facilities approved); *see* Tisel v. Town of Ogunquit, 491 A.2d 564 (Me. 1985) (approving moratorium to avoid overloading public services such as police, fire, road maintenance, and waterfront protection).

177. Unity Ventures v. Lake Country, 631 F. Supp. 181 (N.D. Ill. 1986) (upholding denial of sewer service pursuant to agreement between city and county); Long Beach Equities v. County of Ventura, 282 Cal. Rptr. 877 (Ct. App. 1991).

178. Malmar Assoc. v. Board of County Comm'rs, 260 Md. 292, 272 A.2d 6, 13-14 (1971).

179. Freundshuh v. City of Blaine, 385 N.W.2d 6 (Minn. App. 1986); Larsen v. County of Washington, 387 N.W.2d 902 (Minn. App. 1986); Builders Ass'n of Santa Clara-Santa Cruz County v. Superior Court, 524 P.2d 582, 118 Cal. Rptr. 158 (1974); Mira Dev. Co. v. City of San Diego, 252 Cal. Rptr. 825 (Cal. App. 1988).

180. Chase Manhattan Mortgage and Realty Trust v. Wacha, 402 So.2d 61 (Fla. App. 1981).

181. International Villages, Inc. of America v. Board of Comm'rs, 585 P.2d 999 (Kans. 1978).

182. Belle Harbor Realty Corp. v. Kerr, 35 N.Y.2d 507, 364 N.Y.S.2d 160, 323 N.E.2d 697 (1974); *but see* City National Bank of Miami v. City of Coral Springs, 475 So.2d 984 (Fla. App. 1985).

183. 696 F.2d 1347, 1349 (11th Cir. 1983). The plaintiff was a developer of low-income housing communities. The initial plat denial was prompted by the county residents' racially motivated objections to the development.

184. 696 F.2d at 1350.

185. *Id.* at 1351-52.

186. The preamble stated that the purpose of the regulations was to promote "harmonious development of the county . . . [and] to secure adequate provision for light, air, open space, recreation, transportation, potable water, flood prevention, drainage, sewers and other sanitary facilities." *Id.* at 1351 n.7.

187. Md. Zoning and Planning Code § 10.01.

188. N.H. Rev. Stat. Ann. §§ 674:21, 674:22 (1986).

189. Md. Environment Code § 9.512(b)(1).

190. Fla. Stat. Ann. § 163.3177(10)(h) (West Supp. 1989).

191. Fla. Stat. Ann. § 163.3202(1)-(2)(g) (West Supp. 1989). Taub, *Florida's Growth Management Concurrency Doctrine—Moratorium or Impetus to Fund Needed Infrastructure?*, 15 Fla. Evnt. & Urban Issues, No. 1 at 5 (1988); DeGrove & Stroud, *New Development and Future Trends in Local Government Comprehensive Plans*, 17 Stetson L. Rev. 574, 579-81 (1988).

192. *See* Smith, *Planning for Growth, Washington Style* in State and Regional Comprehensive Planning: Implementing New Models for Growth Management (Buchsbaum ed. 1993); Freilich, Garvin & White, *Economic Development and Public Transit: Making the Most of the Washington Growth Management Act*, 16 Puget Sound L. Rev. 949 (1993).

193. 334 N.Y.S.2d at 153; *see also,* Wincamp Partnership v. Anne Arundel County, 458 F. Supp. 1009, 1027 (D. Md. 1978) (adequate public facilities ordinance valid if it serves a legitimate government interest such as the preservation of a rural environment or small-town character); South Burlington County N.A.A.C.P. v. Mt. Laurel Township, 456 A.2d 390 (N.J. 1983) (rural areas); Orgo Farms v. Colts Neck Township, 499 A.2d 565 (N.J. Super. 1985) (agricultural areas).

194. Associated Home Builders of the Greater Eastbay v. City of Livermore, 18 Cal. 3d 582, 135 Cal. Rptr. 41, 557 P.2d 473 (1976).

195. *Id.* at 610-611.

196. Wincamp Partnership v. Anne Arundel County, 458 F. Supp. 1009, 1025 (D. Md. 1978); *see also* Construction Industry Ass'n v. City of Petaluma, 522 F.2d 897 (9th Cir. 1975), *cert. denied,* 424 U.S. 934 (1976).

197. Builders Association of Santa Clara-Santa Cruz County v. Superior Court, 524 P.2d 582, 587, 118 Cal. Rptr. 158 (1974).

198. Montgomery County Code, Subdivision of Land, Ch. 50, Section 50-35(k); N. Christeller, *Wrestling with Growth in Montgomery County, Maryland,* Growth Management: Keeping on Target? 81 (1986); J. Clancy, *Montgomery County's Development Hurdles,* Growth Management: Keeping on Target? 95 (1986); The Montgomery County Blue Ribbon Committee on the Planning Process, 1985, reprinted in *Id.* at 99-104.

199. Imposing adequate public facilities requirements at a later stage in the process, such as final plat approval, would be of questionable legality because most states do not allow the imposition of additional conditions after tentative plat approval. 7 P. Rohan, Zoning and Land Use Controls 45.04[1] n.13 (1989) (citing Levin v. Livingston Township, 35 N.J. 500, 173 A.2d 391 (1961). In any event, imposing the condition on preliminary plat approval allows the local government to ensure that the conditions have been complied with on final plat review.

200. FY 90 Annual Growth Policy, Montgomery County, Maryland (July 27, 1989).

201. The staging ceiling is "the maximum amount of land development that can be accommodated by the existing and programmed public facilities serving the area 'at an assigned level of service standard.'"

202. Montgomery County Planning Department, Local Area Transportation Review Guidelines (July 14, 1988).

203. Montgomery County Code, Subdivision of Land, Ch. 50, 50-35(f).

204. Tartan Development Corp. v. Montgomery County Planning Bd., Docket Nos. 63708, 63718 (Cir. Ct. Montgomery County, 1983), discussed in Davidson, *supra* note 160, at 174.

205. Davidson, *Plan Based Land Development and Infrastructure Controls: New Directives for Growth Management,* 2 J. Land Use and Envtl. L. Rev. 151 (1986).

206. Schneider, et al. v. Montgomery County, Nos. 39760, 41353, 49950, 51370 (Cir. Ct. Montgomery County, 1991). The case was affirmed on appeal in an unreported opinion.

6

Public Facilities Impact Fees

PART I. GENERAL PROVISIONS

6.1 **Short Title.** This article of the Subdivision Regulations shall be known and cited as the [name of local government] impact fee regulations.

6.2 **Purpose.** This article is intended to assure the provision of adequate public facilities needed to serve new development within the local government by requiring each new development as a condition of approval to pay its pro rata share of the costs of such improvements. This article is intended to mitigate the adverse impacts on community facilities by providing a means of allocating the costs of needed services and facilities among new developments in proportion to the demand for such facilities created by each new development.

6.3 **Authority.** This article is adopted pursuant to [cite state statute] and/or the [municipal or county] home rule charter. The provisions of this article shall not be construed to limit the power of the of the local government to utilize other methods authorized under state law or pursuant to other local government powers to accomplish the purposes set forth herein, either in substitution or in conjunction with this article.

6.4 **Applicability.** The provisions of this article apply to all new development within the boundaries of the local government. The provisions of this article shall apply uniformly within each service area or subarea established.

6.5 **Capital Improvements Program.** Whenever the local government has adopted a capital improvements program for any category of public facility, which identifies capital improvements and that portion of the costs of such improvements that are attributable to new development, the governing body may adopt an impact fee for such public facility utilizing the procedures and subject to the standards contained in this article.

6.6 Establishment of Service Area. For each category of public facility for which an impact fee is established, the local government shall first designate the boundaries of a service area within which impact fees shall be imposed and collected. For purposes of collecting and expending impact fees, the local government shall establish as many subareas as may be necessary to assure that the expenditure of the proceeds of impact fees on those capital improvements identified in the capital improvements program directly benefits each new development that pays impact fees within the subarea.

6.7 Calculation of Impact Fees.

1. For each category of public facility for which an impact fee is established, the local government shall determine an impact fee per service unit, by dividing that portion of the total costs of capital improvements identified in the capital improvements program, which are attributable to the demand for such facility generated by new development, by the total number of service units of new development anticipated within the service area.

2. The maximum impact fee per service unit shall be established, by type of public facility, within each service area and shall be as set forth in Schedule 1, attached hereto and made a part of this article by reference.

3. The impact fee per service unit that is to be paid by each new development within a service area shall be that established by resolution of the governing body, and shall be an amount less than or equal to the maximum impact fee per service unit established in subsection (1). Impact fees that are actually to be paid shall be set forth in Schedule 2, attached hereto and made a part of this article by reference. The governing body may vary Schedule 2 impact fees per service unit among subareas within a service area for a particular category of public facility in order to achieve a valid regulatory purpose, provided that such impact fee per service unit may not exceed the maximum established under subsection (1).

4. Impact fee Schedules 1 and 2 may be amended from time to time by utilizing the procedures used to determine the fee.

6.8 Imposition of Impact Fees.

1. Impact fees shall be imposed as a condition of approval of new development as follows:

a. For a development that is submitted for approval pursuant to the local government's subdivision regulations following the effective date of this article, impact fees shall be imposed at the time of final plat approval.

b. For a development that has received final plat approval prior to the effective date of this article, and for which no replatting is necessary prior to issuance of a building permit, impact fees shall be imposed at the time of issuance of the building permit.

2. Following imposition of the impact fee for a new development pursuant to subsection (1), the amount of the impact fee per service unit for that development cannot be increased, unless the owner proposes to change the approved development by the submission of a new application for final plat approval, in which case a new impact fee per service unit may be imposed.

3. Following the lapse or expiration of approval for a new development, a new impact fee per service unit shall be imposed at the time a new application for such development is filed.

6.9 Computation and Collection of Impact Fees.

1. The impact fees due for the new development shall be collected prior to or at the time of connection to the local government's water or sanitary sewer system, for water or sanitary sewer facilities, and prior to or at the time of issuance of the building permit for all other public services and facilities, unless an agreement between the developer and the local government has been executed providing for a different time of payment.

2. Following the filing and acceptance of an application for a building permit or the request for connection to the City's water or sanitary sewer system, the local government shall compute the impact fees due for the new development in the following manner:

a. The amount of each impact fee due shall be determined by multiplying the number of service units generated by the new development by the impact fee due per service unit for the service area using schedule 2. The number of service units shall be determined by using the conversion table attached hereto and incorporated by reference herein.

b. The amount of each impact fee due shall be reduced by any allowable offsets or credits for that category of capital improvements, in the manner provided in Section 6.10.

3. If the building permit for which an impact fee has been paid has expired, and a new application is thereafter filed, the impact fees due shall be computed using schedule 2 then in effect, with credits for previous payment of fees being applied against the new fees due.

4. In its sole discretion, the local government may permit the developer or property owner, upon written application, to pay impact fees for all or a portion of single-family residential lots at the time of final plat recording for such development.

6.10 Offsets and Credits.

1. The local government shall offset the reasonable costs of any area-related facilities or other oversized facilities, pursuant to rules established in this section or pursuant to administrative guidelines and which have been dedicated to and accepted by the City on or after [set date prior to effective date of ordinance], including the costs of land, rights-of-way for roadways, or capital improvements constructed pursuant to an agreement with the local government against the amount of the impact fee due for that category of capital improvement.

2. The local government shall credit escrow fees and other charges for area-related or oversized capital facilities previously collected from a development prior to the effective date of this article against the amount of an impact fee due for that category of capital improvement, subject to guidelines established by the City.

3. All offset and credits against impact fees shall be subject to the following limitations and shall be granted based on this article and additional standards promulgated by the local government, which may be adopted as administrative guidelines:

   a. No offset shall be given for the dedication or construction of site-related facilities.

   b. No offset or credit shall exceed an amount equal to the eligible costs of the offset multiplied by a fraction, the numerator of which is the impact fee per service unit due for the new development as computed using schedule 2 and the denominator of which is the maximum impact fee per service unit for the new development as computed using schedule 1.

   c. The unit costs used to calculate the offsets shall not exceed those assumed for the capital improvements included in the capital improvements program for the category of facility for which the impact fee is imposed.

   d. No offsets shall be given for area-related facilities that are not identified within the applicable fees capital improvements program as serving new development, unless otherwise agreed to by the local government.

   e. Offsets or credits given for new developments that have received final plat approval prior to the effective date of this Chapter shall be reduced by subtracting an amount equal to the impact fees that would have been due for the number of existing service units using schedule 2 adopted hereby.

f. If an offset or credit applicable to a plat has not been exhausted within ten (10) years from the date of the acquisition of the first building permit issued after the effective date of this article or within such period as may be otherwise designated by contract, such offset or credit shall lapse.

g. In no event will the local government reimburse the property owner or developer for an offset or credit when no impact fees for the new development can be collected or for any amount exceeding the total impact fees dues of the development for that category of capital improvement, unless otherwise agreed to by the local government.

4. An applicant for new development shall apply for an offset or credit against impact fees due for the development either at the time of application for plat approval or at the time of building permit application, unless the local government agrees to a different time. The applicant shall file a petition for offsets or credits with the local government on a form provided for such purpose. The contents of the petition shall be established by administrative guidelines. The local government shall determine, in writing, the maximum value of the offset or credit that may be applied against an impact fee, which amount shall be associated with the plat for the new development.

5. The offset or credit associated with the plat shall be applied against an impact fee in the following manner:

a. For single-family residential lots in a new development that has received final plat approval such offset or credit shall be prorated among such lots and shall remain associated with such lot, to be applied at the time of filing and acceptance of an application for a building permit against impact fees due.

b. For all other types of new development, including those involving mixed uses, the offset or credit associated with the plat shall be applied to an impact fee due at the time of issuance of the first building permit or utility connection to which the offset or credit is applicable following determination of the offset or credit, and thereafter to all subsequently issued building permits or utility connections, until the offset or credit has been exhausted.

c. At its sole discretion, the local government may authorize alternative credit or offset agreements upon petition by the owner in accordance with administrative guidelines.

6.11 Establishment of Accounts.

1. The Finance Department shall establish an account to which interest is allocated for each service area or subarea for each type of capital facility for which an impact fee is imposed pursuant to this article. Each impact fee collected within such service area or subarea shall be deposited in such account.

2. Interest earned on the account into which the impact fees are deposited shall be considered funds of the account and shall be used solely for the purposes authorized in Section 6.12.

3. The Finance Department shall establish adequate financial and accounting controls to ensure that impact fees disbursed from the account are utilized solely for the purposes authorized in Section 6.12. Disbursement of funds shall be authorized at such times as are reasonably necessary to carry out the purposes and intent of this article; provided, however, that funds shall be expended within a reasonable period of time, but not to exceed ten (10) years from the date impact fees are deposited into the account.

4. The Finance Department shall maintain and keep financial records for impact fees, which shall show the source and disbursement of all fees collected in or expended from each service area or subarea. The records of the account into which impact fees are deposited shall be open for public inspection and copying during ordinary business hours.

6.12 Use of Proceeds of Impact Fee Accounts.

1. The impact fees collected for each service area or subarea pursuant to this article may be used to finance or to recoup the costs of any capital improvements identified in the applicable capital improvements program which serve new development within the service area, including but not limited to the construction contract price, surveying and engineering fees, and land acquisition costs. Impact fees may also be used to pay the principal sum and interest and other finance costs on bonds, notes, or other obligations issued by or on behalf of the local government to finance such capital improvements.

2. Impact fees collected pursuant to this ordinance shall not be used to pay for any of the following expenses:
   a. Construction, acquisition, or expansion of capital improvements or assets other than those identified in the applicable capital improvements program;
   b. Repair, operation, or maintenance of existing or new capital improvements or facilities expansions;
   c. Upgrading, expanding, or replacing existing capital improvements to serve existing development in order to meet stricter safety,

efficiency, environmental, or regulatory standards or to provide better service;

d. Administrative and operating costs.

3. In the event that a service area has been divided into subareas for purposes of collecting and expending impact fees, the local government may expend impact fees for capital improvements identified in the capital improvements plan within an immediately adjacent subarea, if the facilities serve development within the subarea from which the fees are collected and the facilities form an integral part of the facilities network utilized by such developments.

6.13 Appeals.

1. The property owner or applicant for new development may appeal the following decisions to the governing body of the local government: (1) the applicability of an impact fee to the development; (2) the amount of the impact fee due; (3) the availability or the amount of an offset or credit; (4) the application of an offset or credit against an impact fee due; or (5) the amount of a refund due, if any.

2. The burden of proof shall be on the appellant to demonstrate that the amount of the fee or the amount of the offset or credit was not calculated according to the applicable schedule of impact fees or the guidelines established for determining offsets and credits.

6.14 Refunds.

1. Any impact fee or portion thereof collected pursuant to this article, which has not been expended within the service area or eligible subareas within ten (10) years from the date of payment, shall be refunded, upon application, to the record owner of the property for which the impact fee was paid or, if the impact fee was paid by another governmental entity, to such governmental entity, together with interest calculated from the date of collection to the date of refund.

2. An impact fee collected pursuant to this Chapter shall be considered expended if the total expenditures for eligible capital improvements within the service area or eligible subareas within ten (10) years following the date of payment exceeds the total fees collected for such improvements or expansions during such period.

3. If a refund is due pursuant to subsections 1 and 2, the City shall divide the difference between the amount of expenditures and the amount of the fees collected by the total number of service units assumed within the service area for the period to determine the refund due per service unit. The refund to the record owner shall be calculated by multiplying the refund due per service unit by the number of service units for the

development for which the fee was paid, and interest due shall be calculated upon that amount.

4. If the building permit for a new development for which an impact fee has been paid has expired, and a modified or new application has not been filed within six (6) months of such expiration, the local government shall, upon written application, refund the amount of the impact fee to the applicant.

6.15 Updates to Plan and Revision of Fees.

The local government shall update the capital improvements program for impact fees every three (3) years, commencing from the date of adoption of such program, and shall recalculate the impact fees based thereon accordingly.

6.16 Impact Fee as Additional and Supplemental Regulation.

Impact fees established by this article are additional and supplemental to, and not in substitution of, any other requirements imposed by the local government on the development of land or the issuance of building permits or certificates of occupancy. Such fee is intended to be consistent with and to further the policies of local government's comprehensive land use plan, the capital improvements plan, the zoning ordinance, subdivision regulations and other policies, ordinances, and resolutions by which the local government seeks to ensure the provision of adequate public facilities in conjunction with the development of land.

6.17 Procedures for Update and Amendment.

The capital improvements program and impact fees shall be updated utilizing the procedures prescribed in [cite state enabling act or local government land use procedure].

6.18 Relief Procedures.

1. The governing body may grant a variance from any requirement of this ordinance, upon written request by a developer or owner of property subject to the ordinance, following a public hearing, and only upon finding that a strict application of such requirement would, when regarded as a whole, result in confiscation of the property.
2. The governing body may grant a waiver from any requirement of this ordinance to an applicant or class of applicants to achieve a valid regulatory objective, using criteria established in administrative guidelines.
3. If the governing body grants a variance or waiver to the amount of the impact fee due for a new development under this section, it shall cause to be appropriated from other funds the amount of the

reduction in the impact fee to the account for the service area in which the property is located.

6.19 Exemption from Ordinance.

Any building permit application which was duly accepted for filing prior to the effective date of this article and which is subsequently granted, shall be exempt from the payment of an impact fee, unless such application thereafter expires.

PART II. PARTICULAR PUBLIC FACILITIES

6.20 Public Facility [identify facility] Service Area.

1. There are hereby established [insert number of service areas or subareas] public facility service areas, each of which is designated on the map attached hereto as Exhibit ____ and which is incorporated by reference herein.
2. Public facility [identify facility] service area boundaries may be amended from time to time, or new service areas may be established, pursuant to the procedures in Section 6.17.

6.21 Public Facility Improvements Program [here identify facility].

1. The public facility [identify facility] improvements program for the local government is hereby adopted as Exhibit ____ attached hereto and incorporated by reference herein.
2. The public facility [identify facility] improvements program may be amended from time to time, pursuant to the procedures in Section 6.17.

6.22 Public Facilities [identify facility] Impact Fees.

1. The maximum impact fees for each public facility service area and subarea are hereby adopted and incorporated in Schedule 1 attached hereto and made a part hereof by reference.
2. The impact fees per service unit which are to be paid by each new development for each public facility service area and subarea are hereby adopted and incorporated in Schedule 2 attached hereto and made a part hereof by reference.
3. The impact fees per service unit for [identify facility] may be amended from time to time, pursuant to the procedures in Section 6.17.

PART III.

6.23 Housing Benefit Contribution for Nonresidential Developments.

The Governing Body hereby finds and declares that nonresidential developments such as office, commercial, retail, and institutional uses have attracted and continue to attract additional employees to the City, and there is a causal connection between such developments and the need for additional housing in the City, particularly housing affordable to persons of moderate and low income. The Governing Body further finds and declares that nonresidential developments such as office, commercial, retail, and institutional uses benefit from the availability of housing for persons employed in such developments in close proximity to such development.

1. *Application.*
    a. This Section shall apply to [specify type of nonresidential development subject to the ordinance, such as office, commercial, retail, and/or institutional] projects proposing the net addition of 50,000 or more gross square feet of space.
    b. This Section shall not apply to [list types of development not subject to the ordinance, such as nonresidential developments not specified in Section 6.23 above, residential projects, vested projects, and/or state government projects].
2. *Imposition of Housing Requirement.*
    a. The Planning Commission shall impose conditions on the approval of applications for development projects covered by this Section in order to mitigate the impact on the availability of housing, which will be caused by the employment facilitated by the proposed project. The conditions shall require that the applicant construct housing or pay an in-lieu fee to the City Controller that shall thereafter be used exclusively for the development of housing affordable to households of low or moderate income. The amount of net addition of gross square feet of space that the City anticipates is subject to this Section shall be set forth in any public notice and/or calendar item announcement of any Planning Commission hearing to review a development project subject to this Section. The Planning Commission shall use a formula to compute the housing requirement for an office development project as follows:

    Net Addition Gross Sq. Ft. Office Space x nonresidential fraction per square foot of office space representing [1] the projected net increase in space; [2] divided by the estimated "employment density factor," or square feet per worker, to calculate net addition in nonresidential employment; [3] multiplied by the percentage of workers expected to reside in the City; [4] multiplied by the percentage of workers in households; [5] divided by the average number of employees in households with employees.[1] = Housing Units

b. The final net addition of gross square feet of space subject to this Section shall be determined by the Planning Commission and a housing requirement imposed according to the above formula, and shall be set forth in the Planning Commission Resolution approving the project. The Administrative Assistant shall notify the Building and Zoning Inspector that a project is subject to this Section at the time the Planning Commission approves the project.

c. In the event that the Planning Commission takes action affecting any project subject to this Section and such action is thereafter modified, superseded, vacated, or reversed by court action, the permit application for such office development project shall be remanded to the Planning Commission to determine whether the proposed project has been changed in a manner that affects the calculation of the amount of housing required under this Section and, if so, the Planning Commission shall revise the housing requirement imposed on the permit application in compliance with this Section within sixty (60) days of such remand and notify the sponsor in writing of such revision or that a revision is not required.

d. The sponsor shall supply all information to the Planning Commission necessary to make a determination as to the applicability of this Section and the number of gross square feet of space subject to this Section.

e. Prior to the issuance by the Building and Zoning Inspector of the first certificate of occupancy for any project subject to this Section, the sponsor must notify the Administrative Assistant in writing of the manner in which it elects to provide the housing units required under Subsections (3), (4), or (5) below. In order to discharge its obligation under this Section, the sponsor of any project subject to this Section shall have the option of:

  i. Constructing housing units in the amount set forth in the above formula pursuant to Subsection (3) below;

  ii. Paying an in-lieu fee in the sum established by the formula set forth in Subsection 4 below; or

  iii. Combining the above options pursuant to Subsection 5 below.

3. *Compliance Through Construction of Housing.*

    a. If the sponsor elects to construct housing units itself or through participation in a joint venture or partnership to meet the requirements of this Section, 62 percent of those housing units constructed must be affordable to households of low or moderate income for twenty (20) years.

    b. Prior to issuance by the Building and Zoning Inspector of the first certificate of occupancy for a project subject to this Section, the sponsor shall submit to the Administrative Assistant a written proposal for a housing development project. Where the sponsor intends to construct housing units through participation in a joint venture or partnership, the sponsor must further certify to the Administrative Assistant that the sponsor has made a binding commitment, enforceable by the sponsor's joint venturer(s) or partner(s), to contribute an amount to the joint venture or partnership equivalent to or greater than the amount of the in-lieu fee that would otherwise be required under Subsection (4) and that the joint venture or partnership shall use such funds to develop the housing subject to this Section. The Administrative Assistant must determine pursuant to Part (d) of this Subsection that such housing development project complies with the requirements of this Section prior to the issuance by the Building and Zoning Inspector of the first certificate of occupancy for a project subject to this Section.

c. Within thirty (30) days after the sponsor has submitted a written housing development project plan to the Administrative Assistant, the Administrative Assistant shall notify the sponsor in writing of his or her initial determination as to whether the plan is in compliance with this Section and shall cause a public notice to be published in an official newspaper of general circulation stating that such housing development plan has been received and stating the Administrative Assistant's initial determination. Within ten (10) days after such written notification and published notice, the sponsor or any other person may request a hearing before the Planning Commission to contest such initial determination. If the Administrative Assistant receives no request for a hearing within such 10-day period, the determination of the Administrative Assistant shall become a final determination. Upon receipt of any timely request for hearing, the Administrative Assistant shall schedule a hearing before the Planning Commission within thirty (30) days. The scope of the hearing shall be limited to the compliance of the housing development plan with this Section, and shall not include a challenge to the amount of the housing requirement imposed on the project by the Planning Commission. At the hearing, the Planning Commission may either make such revisions of the Administrative Assistant's initial determination as it may deem just, or confirm the Administrative Assistant's initial determination. The Planning Commission's determination shall then become a final determination, and the Administrative Assistant shall provide written notice of the final determination to the sponsor and to any person who timely requested a hearing of the Administrative Assistant's determination. The Administrative Assistant shall also provide written notice to the Building and Zoning Inspector that the housing units to be constructed pursuant to such plan are subject to this Section.

d. In making a determination as to whether a sponsor's housing development plan complies with this Section, the Administrative Assistant and the Planning Commission shall credit to the sponsor any excess Interim Guideline credits or excess credits which the sponsor elects to apply against its housing requirement. The remaining housing units required shall be subject to the requirements of Part (a) of this Subsection.

e. The Building and Zoning Inspector shall provide notice in writing to the Administrative Assistant at least five (5) business days prior to issuance of the first certificate of occupancy for any project subject to this Section. If the Administrative Assistant notifies the Building and Zoning Inspector within the five (5) business days that the sponsor has not complied with the provisions of this Section, the Building and Zoning Inspector shall refuse any and all certificates of occupancy for the project. If the Administrative Assistant notifies the Building and Zoning Inspector that the sponsor has complied with this Section or fails to respond within five (5) business days, the Building and Zoning Inspector shall not disapprove a certificate of occupancy pursuant to this Section. Any failure of the Building and Zoning Inspector or the Administrative Assistant to give any notice under this Subsection shall not relieve a sponsor from compliance with this Section. Where a housing development plan has not been approved by the Administrative Assistant in compliance with this Section prior to the issuance by the Building and Zoning Inspector of the first certificate of occupancy for the office development project, the Administrative Assistant shall initiate lien proceedings against the office development project under Subsection 8 below.

f. Within one (1) year of the issuance of the first certificate of occupancy by the Building and Zoning Inspector for the project, the sponsor shall provide written certification to the Administrative Assistant that it has commenced construction of the housing units under this Subsection, and where the sponsor elects to construct housing through a joint venture or partnership, that the sponsor's monetary contribution to the joint venture or partnership has been paid in full or has been posted in an irrevocable letter of credit. This one-year period may be extended for a maximum of two (2) one-year periods where, based upon evidence submitted by the sponsor, the Administrative Assistant determines within one (1) year of the issuance by the Building and Zoning Inspector of the first certificate of occupancy for the project, or within a one-year extension, that (1) there is good cause for an extension or an additional extension, (2) the failure to comply with the time limits of this Subsection is beyond the sponsor's immediate control, and (3) the sponsor has made a reasonable effort to comply with this Subsection. Upon the Administrative Assistant's final determination that a sponsor has failed to commence construction of such housing within said one-year period and any extensions thereto, the Administrative Assistant shall initiate lien proceedings under Subsection 8 below. Where the Administrative Assistant initiates lien proceedings for a violation of this Subsection, the amount of the lien set forth in Subsection 8(a) shall bear interest at 10 percent per annum commencing on the date of issuance by the Building and Zoning Inspector of the first certificate of occupancy for the project.

g. Within thirty (30) days after the issuance by the Building and Zoning Inspector of any site or building permit to construct any housing units in a housing development project plan submitted to the Administrative Assistant under this Subsection, the sponsor shall identify the designated units by written notice to the Administrative Assistant, including:

    i. The commitment that such housing units will be affordable for rent or sale or households of low or moderate income for twenty (20) years; and

    ii. A statement of whether each designated unit is an owned unit or a rental unit.

Within thirty (30) days after the sponsor's identification of designated units, the Administrative Assistant shall notify the Local Government Engineer in writing identifying the intended owned units and request an appraisal of the fair market value of each designated unit which is intended to be an owned unit. Within sixty (60) days of receipt of written notice from the Administrative Assistant, an appraisal of the fair market value of each such designated unit as of the date of the appraisal applying accepted valuation methods shall be performed by a qualified appraiser and a written appraisal of each such designated unit shall be delivered to the Administrative Assistant and the sponsor.

h. The sponsor shall supply all information to the Administrative Assistant necessary to make determinations under this Subsection, including all plans and specifications for each designated unit.

     i. Within three months of the effective date of this Section, the Administrative Assistant is hereby directed to prepare and publish written guidelines by which compliance with this Subsection shall be determined.

4. *Compliance Through Payment of In-lieu Fee.*

    a. The amount of the fee that may be paid by the sponsor of an office development project in lieu of developing and providing the housing required by Subsection (3) shall be computed as follows:

Net Addition Gross Sq. Ft. Office Space x (a per-square-foot fee derived by multiplying the number of additional units derived from the formula applied in Subsection (2)(a) by the amount of subsidy needed per unit, divided by the projected increase in net nonresidential space) = Total Fee.

Such in-lieu fee shall be revised effective January 1st of each year, commencing on January 1st following the effective date of this Section, by the percentage increase or decrease of the *Building Cost Index of the Cost Indices for Twenty Cities,* published by McGraw-Hill, Inc. or its successor since January 1st of the previous year.

    b. In making a determination as to the amount of the fee to be paid, the Administrative Assistant shall credit to the sponsor any excess Interim Guideline credits or excess credits which the sponsor elects to apply against its housing requirement.

    c. Upon payment of the fee in full to the Controller and upon request of the sponsor, the Controller shall issue a certification that the fee has been paid. The sponsor shall present such certification to the Administrative Assistant prior to the issuance by the Building and Zoning Inspector of the first certificate of occupancy for the office development project. The Building and Zoning Inspector shall provide notice in writing to the Administrative Assistant at least five (5) business days prior to issuing the first certificate of occupancy for any project subject to this Section. If the Administrative Assistant notifies the Building and Zoning Inspector within such time that the sponsor has not complied with the provisions of this Section, the Building and Zoning Inspector shall deny any and all certificates of occupancy. If the Administrative Assistant notifies the Building and Zoning Inspector that the sponsor has complied with this Section or fails to respond within five (5) business days, a certificate of occupancy shall not be disapproved pursuant to this Section. Any failure of the Building and Zoning Inspector or the Administrative Assistant to give any notice under this Subsection shall not relieve a sponsor from compliance with this Section. Where a sponsor fails for any reason to pay the in-lieu fee to the

Controller in compliance with this Section prior to the Building and Zoning Inspector's issuance of the first certificate of occupancy for the project, the Administrative Assistant shall initiate lien proceedings against the project under Subsection 8 below.

5. *Compliance Through Combination of Construction or Payment of In-Lieu Fee.* The sponsor of an office development project may elect to satisfy its housing requirement by providing a partial number of the units required under Subsections 3 and 4 above and satisfying the balance of its requirement by paying an in-lieu fee in the amount of $_____ (average amount of subsidy per unit) per unit remaining. The housing units constructed must conform to all requirements of this Section, including, but not limited to, the proportion that must be affordable to households of low or moderate income as set forth in Subsection 3 above. Such in-lieu fee per unit shall be revised effective January 1st of each year concurrently with the revision of the in-lieu fee in Subsection 4. A sponsor who satisfies part of a housing requirement by applying excess credits or excess Interim Guideline credits pursuant to Subsection 6 below may satisfy all or part of the balance of the housing requirement by paying an in-lieu fee per unit as computed in this Subsection or by developing housing pursuant to Subsection 3. In such case, all of the requirements of Subsections 3 or 4 shall apply, including the requirements with respect to the timing of development of housing or payment of the in-lieu fee.

6. *Transfer of Housing Credits.* In making their determination of the number of housing units required under Subsections 3 and 4 above, the Administrative Assistant shall credit to the sponsor any housing units constructed or in-lieu fee paid in excess of that required to satisfy the housing unit requirement under this Section, which shall be denominated "excess credits." The Administrative Assistant shall permit the transfer of any excess credits received under this Section to be applied to satisfy all or part of a housing unit requirement for any other project that is subject to the provisions of this Section. Each excess credit shall be equivalent to one (1) housing unit as computed under Subsection 2 above. Excess credits may be obtained only under Subsection 10 below or if:

   a. They have been obtained after the commencement of construction of housing under Subsection 3 above, commencement of construction of housing and payment or irrevocable commitment of a sum to a joint venture or partnership under Subsection 3 above, or payment of an in-lieu fee to the Controller under Subsection 4 above, or a combination of the above under Subsection 5 above; and

b. The excess credits result from either:
   i. Abandonment of the office development project that received approval by the Planning Commission as evidenced by cancellation of the site or building permit or the site or building permit application; or
   ii. A decrease in the net addition of gross square feet of office space as a result of Planning Commission or court action taken after: (1) The amount of such net addition of gross square feet has been determined by the Planning Commission under Subsection 2; and (2) the sponsor has commenced construction of housing under Subsection 3 above, construction has commenced and the sponsor has paid or irrevocably committed a sum to a joint venture or partnership under Subsection 3 above, paid an in-lieu fee under Subsection 4 above, or a combination of the above under Subsection 5.

c. If the number of excess credits or excess Interim Guidelines credits held by a sponsor is not sufficient to satisfy the entire housing unit requirement of that sponsor's office development project subject to the provisions of this Section, then the balance of the housing unit requirement shall be satisfied in accordance with the provisions of this Section, including the requirement set forth in Subsections 3 and 5 that a percentage of the units constructed must be affordable to households of low or moderate income.

d. Excess credits and excess Interim Guideline credits may be transferred from one sponsor to another only if:
   i. The Administrative Assistant has been notified in writing of the proposed transfer of the credits;
   ii. The Administrative Assistant has determined that the transferor sponsor has obtained the credits through meeting the requirements of this Subsection; and
   iii. The transfer is made in writing, a true copy of which is provided to the Administrative Assistant.

e. The Local Government makes no warranties that any excess credits or excess Interim Guidelines credits will be marketable during the period in which this Section is in effect or thereafter. The Local Government makes no warranties that an applicant possessing excess credits or excess Interim Guidelines credits is entitled to Planning Commission approval of a project subject to this Section.

7. *Enforcement of Restriction on Housing Units Affordable to Households of Low or Moderate Income.*
   a. Prior to the filing by the Local Government Engineer of a final subdivision map or parcel map for a designated unit that is in-

tended to be an owned unit, the sponsor shall execute and deliver to the Administrative Assistant for each such unit a promissory note payable to the Local Government, secured by a deed of trust on the unit, and a grant to the Local Government or a right of first refusal to purchase the unit, which documents shall comply with and recite the following restrictions:

i. The promissory note shall be a non-interest note, due and payable at such time as the unit is sold. The note shall be canceled twenty (20) years from the date on which the first deed of trust is recorded for such unit. The amount of the promissory note shall be for $_____ plus the excess of the market value of such unit over the base price. The amount of $_____ shall be revised annually according to the formula in Subsection 5.

ii. The Local Government shall be granted a right of first refusal to purchase the unit and any improvements therein for twenty (20) years from the date on which the deed of trust is recorded for such unit. Such right shall be exercised within sixty (60) days after the Administrative Assistant is notified in writing of the intended sale of such unit by the owner. The Local Government may assign its right to purchase the unit to any person including, but not limited to, a household of low or moderate income. The Local Government's failure to exercise its right to purchase upon any sale of the unit shall not eliminate its right to purchase upon any future sale of the unit.

iii. If the unit is sold to a household other than a household of low or moderate income, the promissory note shall be due and payable to the Local Government at the time of such sale. Upon payment of the full face amount of the promissory note, the unit shall no longer be deemed a designated unit subject to this Section;

iv. If the unit is to be sold to a household of low or moderate income as determined by the Administrative Assistant, the Local Government will release the seller's note and right of first refusal and reconvey the deed of trust, in exchange for a new grant of right of first refusal from the purchaser and a promissory note from the purchaser payable to the Local Government and secured by a deed of trust on the unit, all of which shall be in full satisfaction of the seller's obligations under the former note, deed of trust, and right of first refusal, and which shall comply with and recite the terms and conditions set forth in Parts (a)(ii), (iii), (iv), (v), (vi), and (vii) of this Subsection and the following restrictions:

1. The amount of the promissory note shall be the excess of the market value of such unit over the base price, plus simple interest at 4 percent per annum; and

2. The note shall be canceled twenty (20) years from the date on which the deed of trust was recorded for such unit under Part (b)(i) of this Subsection.

v. Prior to the close of escrow of any sale of the unit to a household of low or moderate income, the seller shall provide the Administrative Assistant with a copy of the contract to purchase the unit, and the intended purchaser shall supply to the Administrative Assistant a certification identifying by full name and address each member of the purchaser's household, federal income tax returns for the previous two years for each member of such household, and verification of employment and current salary for each employed member of such household. The Administrative Assistant shall make a determination as to whether the purchaser qualifies as a low- or moderate-income household and notify the seller and the purchaser of such determination within ten (10) days of receipt of all of the above information;

vi. If the Administrative Assistant, after close of escrow of the sale to a household of purported low and moderate income, determines that such household at the time of sale knowingly misrepresented or concealed facts in order to qualify as a household of low or moderate income, the promissory note delivered to the Local Government by such household in escrow shall become immediately due and payable; and

vii. An owned unit may be rented only to a household of low or moderate income at the base rent. The violation of this restriction shall make the promissory note for such unit immediately due and payable.

b. Within thirty (30) days after the issuance by the Building and Zoning Inspector of a site or building permit to construct any designated unit that is a rental unit, the sponsor shall execute and deliver to the Administrative Assistant a promissory note payable to the Local Government and a deed of trust with the Local Government as sole beneficiary, which documents shall comply with and recite the following restrictions:

i. The promissory note shall be a non-interest note and shall be immediately due and payable at such time as any rental unit in the building or buildings covered by the deed of trust securing the note is rented to a household which is not of low or moderate income or rented at a monthly rate higher than 1/12 of the base rent. The note shall be canceled twenty (20) years from the date on which the deed of trust in favor of the Local Government is recorded for such unit.

ii. The amount of the promissory note shall be $_____ times the number of designated units covered by the promissory note and deed of trust. The amount of $_____ shall be revised annually according to the formula in Subsection 5;

iii. The deed of trust shall be on the building or buildings in which the rental unit is located; provided, however, that there shall be no more than one deed of trust required on any single building in which there is more than one designated rental unit;

iv. In the event that an owner of any rental unit intends to convert the unit to an owned unit during the 20-year period in which such unit is subject to this Section, the owner shall provide written notice of such intention to convert to the Administrative Assistant. Within sixty (60) days of such notice:

1. The Administrative Assistant shall provide written notice of the identity of the intended owned unit to the Local Government; and

2. A qualified appraiser shall appraise the market value of the unit as of the date of the appraisal and deliver a written appraisal of the unit to the Administrative Assistant and the owner. The owner shall provide the appraiser with all information necessary to render such appraisal.

   Prior to the filing by the Local Government Engineer of a final subdivision map or parcel map of the building in which the unit is located, the owner shall execute and deliver to the Administrative Assistant a promissory note, deed of trust, and grant of right of first refusal for the intended owned unit, which comply with and recite the restrictions set forth in Part 1 of this Subsection. At the time of recording of a final map or parcel map for the building in which the designated unit is located, the Local Government shall release the former promissory note and reconvey the former deed of trust in exchange for a grant of right of first refusal and a new promissory note secured by a deed of trust on each owned unit in such building. The new promissory note and right of first refusal shall have a term equivalent to the remainder of the 20-year period which commenced on the date on which the deed of trust for the unit is recorded pursuant to Part (b)(i) of this Subsection.

c. The base rent of a rental unit or of an owned unit, if it is rented, shall be increased or decreased according to any change in the median income for a family of a size equivalent to the number of persons residing in the household renting the unit. The base rent shall be adjusted for such change on the date of the commencement of a tenancy of the unit and annually thereafter.

d. Each owner of a designated unit who occupies the unit shall report in writing to the Administrative Assistant no later than August 1st of each year stating the full name and address of each of the owners of the unit, the date of purchase and the purchase price, and the names and relationship of all persons permanently residing in said unit from July 1st of the previous year through June 30th of the current year.

e. Prior to the rental of any designated unit, the prospective tenant shall provide the Administrative Assistant with a copy of any proposed written lease of the unit, a certification identifying by full name and address each member of the tenant's household, federal income tax returns for the previous two years for each member of such household, and verification of employment and current salary for each employed member of such household. Each owner of a designated rental unit shall report in writing to the Administrative Assistant on August 1st of each year identifying the unit by address, the name of the tenant or tenants of the unit since July 1st of the previous year through June 30th of the current year, and the amount of total monthly rent paid by such tenants for each month of such 12-month period. Each tenant of a designated unit shall report in writing to the Administrative Assistant on August 1st of each year by identifying the unit by address, the full names and relationship of each of the persons residing in the unit since July 1st of the previous year through June 30th of the current year, the amount of total monthly rent paid by such tenants for each month of such 12-month period, and by providing to the Administrative Assistant federal income tax returns for the previous year for each member of such household.

f. The sale of any designated unit prior to the sponsor's compliance with Parts 1 or 2 of this Subsection shall be a violation of this Section and shall constitute cause for the Administrative Assistant to initiate lien proceedings against the office development project pursuant to Subsection 8 in the sum of $_____ as revised annually for each unit sold in violation of this Section.

g. All funds paid to the City pursuant to promissory notes under this Subsection shall be deposited in the citywide Affordable Housing Fund established in Subsection 11 below.

h. Any person, including any owner, seller, purchaser, converter, landlord, or tenant of a designated unit, who violates any of the requirements of this Subsection shall be guilty of a misdemeanor. Any person convicted of a misdemeanor hereunder shall be punishable by a fine of not more than $1,000 or by imprisonment in the County Jail for a period of not more than six (6) months, or by both. Each and every violation of this Subsection, as it pertains to each unit, shall constitute a separate offense.

8. *Lien Proceedings.*

a. A sponsor's failure to comply with the requirements of Subsections 3, 4, 5, and 7 shall constitute cause for the Local Government to record a special assessment lien against the office development project in the sum of $_____ for each housing unit required under this Section. The amount of the lien per unit shall be revised annually according to the formula in Subsection 5.

b. The Administrative Assistant shall initiate proceedings to impose the special assessment lien by preparing a preliminary report notifying the sponsor of a special assessment hearing to confirm such report by the Governing Body at least ten (10) days before the date of the hearing. The report to the sponsor shall contain the sponsor's name, a description of the sponsor's office development project, a description of the parcels of real property to be encumbered as set forth in the Assessor's Map Books for the current year, a description of the alleged violation of this Section, and shall fix a time, date, and place for hearing. The Administrative Assistant shall cause this report to be mailed to each owner of record of the parcels of real property to be assessed.

c. At the hearing fixed for consideration of the report, the Governing Body shall hear the report with any objections of the owners of the parcels liable to be assessed. The Governing Body may make such revisions, corrections, or modifications of the report as it may deem just. In the event that the Governing Body is satisfied with the correctness of the report as submitted or as revised, corrected, or modified, it shall be confirmed as a final report. Any delinquent account may be removed from the report by payment in full at any time prior to confirmation of a final report. The Administrative Assistant shall cause the confirmed report to be verified in form sufficient to meet recording requirements.

d. Upon confirmation of the report by the Governing Body, the delinquent charges contained therein shall constitute a special assessment against the parcel or parcels used in the office development project. Each such assessment shall be subordinate to all existing special assessment liens previously imposed upon such parcels and paramount to all other liens except those for State, County, and municipal taxes with which it shall be upon parity. The lien shall continue until the assessment and all interest due and payable thereon are paid to the Tax Collector or the Local Government. All laws applicable to the levy, collection, and enforcement of municipal taxes shall be applicable to said special assessment.

e. The Administrative Assistant shall cause the confirmed and verified report to be recorded in the County Recorder's Office and the special assessment lien on each parcel of property described in said report shall carry additional charges for administrative expenses of $50 or 10 percent of the amount of the unpaid balance, whichever is greater, plus interest at a rate of 1½ percent per full month compounded monthly from the date of the recordation of the lien on all charges due.

f. The Administrative Assistant shall file a certified copy of each confirmed final report with the Controller and Tax Collector within ten (10) days after confirmation of the report, whereupon it shall be the duty of said officers to add the amount of said assessment to the next regular bill for taxes levied against said parcel or parcels of land for municipal purposes, and thereafter said amount shall be collected at the same time and in the same manner as City and County taxes are collected and shall be subject to the same procedure under foreclosure and sale in case of delinquency as provided for property taxes of the City and County. Except for the release of lien recording fee authorized below, all sums collected by the Tax Collector pursuant to this Section shall be held in trust by the Treasurer and deposited in the citywide Affordable Housing Fund established in Section 11 below.

g. On payment to the Tax Collector of the special assessment, the Tax Collector shall cause to be recorded a release of lien with the County Recorder, and from the sum collected pursuant to Part (a) of this Subsection, shall pay to the County Recorder a recording fee of $6.

h. Any notice required to be given to a sponsor or owner shall be sufficiently given or served upon the sponsor or owner for all purposes hereunder if personally served upon the sponsor or owner or if deposited, postage prepaid, in a post office letterbox addressed in the name of the sponsor or owner at the official address of the sponsor or owner maintained by the Tax Collector for the mailing of tax bills or, if no such address is available, to the sponsor at the address of the office development project.

9. *In-Lieu Fee Refund When Building Permit Expires Prior to Completion of Work and Commencement of Occupancy.* In the event a building permit expires prior to completion of the work on and commencement of occupancy of an office development project so that it will be necessary to obtain a new permit to carry out any development, the obligation to comply with this Section shall be cancelled, and any in-lieu fee previously paid shall be refunded. If and when the sponsor applies for a new permit, the procedures set forth in this Section regarding construction of housing or payment of the in-lieu fee shall be followed.

10. *One-Time Fee Payment.* In the event that an office development project for which housing units have been constructed or an in-lieu fee has been fully paid is demolished or converted to non-office use prior to the expiration of its estimated useful life, the City shall grant to the sponsor excess credits transferable under Subsection 6 for a portion of any housing units actually constructed, or refund to the sponsor a portion of the amount of an in-lieu fee paid. The portion of excess credits granted or the fee refunded shall be determined on a pro rata basis according to the ratio of the remaining useful life of the project at the time of demolition or conversion in relation to its total useful life. For purposes of this Section, the useful life of an office development project shall be forty (40) years.

11. *Affordable Housing Fund.* There is hereby established as a separate fund set aside for a special purpose called the "Citywide Affordable Housing Fund" (Fund). All monies contributed pursuant to Subsections or assessed pursuant to Subsection 8 shall be deposited in the Fund. All monies deposited in the Fund shall be used solely to increase the supply of housing affordable to households of low and moderate income. No portion of the Fund may be used, by way of loan or otherwise, to pay any administrative, general overhead, or similar expense of any entity. The Fund shall be administered by the Administrative Assistant who shall have the authority to prescribe rules and regulations governing the Fund which are consistent with this Section.

12. *Annual Evaluation.* Commencing one (1) year after the effective date of this Section, the Administrative Assistant shall report to the Planning Commission, the Governing Body, and the Mayor each year on the status of compliance with this Section and the efficacy of this Section in mitigating the Local Government's shortage of affordable housing available to employees working in office development projects subject to this Section. Five (5) years after the effective date of this Section, the Planning Commission shall review the formula set forth in Subsection 2 in such report, the Director shall recommend any changes

in the forecasts and other assumptions with respect to demand for or supply of housing in the Local Government that would warrant modification of such formula should the Local Government extend the duration of this Section beyond five (5) years.

13. ***Partial Invalidity and Severability.*** If any provision of this Section, or its application to any project or to any geographical area of the Local Government, is held invalid, the remainder of the Section, or the application of such provision to other projects or to any other geographical areas of the Local Government, shall not be affected thereby.

NOTES

1. *See* Housrath, *Economic Basis for Linking Jobs and Housing in San Francisco*, 54 J.Am.Planning A. 210, 212-14 (1988).

COMMENTARY ON ARTICLE 6

INTRODUCTION

The rapid unprecedented outward development of metropolitan areas has triggered a major problem for cities and counties with limited financial resources. Provision of capital facilities, the need for which has been generated by new growth, has also been hampered by a severe existing infrastructure crisis.[1] Estimates are that as many as three-quarters of American cities face debilitating problems because of inadequate resources and infrastructure.[2] More than one-half of the nation's paved roads need "immediate attention,"[3] water supply systems are deteriorating in the Northeast and Midwest,[4] and the Southwest continuously experiences water shortages.[5] Nearly $165 billion will be needed by the year 2000 to deal with sewage treatment facilities alone.[6] Courts across the nation have recognized the impact of infrastructure problems.[7]

The cost of providing new facilities should not be borne by the general fund that is required to maintain and operate the system and finance reconstruction and repair of existing deficiencies.[8] There is increasing evidence that imposing the one-time cost of capital facilities on new development is not only fairer to existing neighborhoods that have already paid for their facilities, but also lowers land costs and thus the cost of new housing itself.[8] The need to shift these costs has been greatly heightened by several factors.[10] Municipalities are increasingly reluctant to impose higher property taxes on existing neighborhoods.[11] Correspondingly, the established community often is called upon to finance capital improvements for redressing existing deficiencies and is unwilling to approve bond issues for capital improvements in newly developing areas.[12] New financing techniques are needed to meet the capital requirements and prevent deterioration of existing facilities.[13] Dwindling federal funds and the continuing need to provide services as well as maintenance of existing facilities completely exhausts a municipality's coffers, rendering it unable to meet any new demand for capital funding.[14]

A parallel constitutional and statutory development, the enactment of tax and spending limitations, has magnified the headaches of municipal officials searching for capital to satisfy demands created by new development.[15] The general impact of these limitations will be a decrease in the revenue base,[16] an increase in developed land prices,[17] and a decrease in the price of undeveloped land.[18] In those states that have enacted property tax limitation systems, there is a danger that passing the cost of new facilities on to the developer who created the need for the facilities will be treated as a "special tax" requiring voter approval.[19] At least one California court, however, views regulatory fees as valid charges imposed on developers and not special taxes.[20]

Despite such difficulties, regulatory fees have fast become an important source of financing for capital improvements for sewer and water systems,[21] roads,[22] libraries and schools,[23] public park and recreational facilities,[24] and municipal services such as police and fire protection.[25] Recent surveys indicate that the use of regulatory fees and the amount charged are on the rise, especially in the western states.[26] In California, regulatory fees may even be used city or countywide so long as they provide benefit to and the need is generated by the regulated subdivision.[27] It has been argued that regulatory fees are valid if they provide for "private" goods, such as utilities, but should be struck if they finance "public" goods, such as schools, which benefit the entire community and are properly funded only through general revenues.[28] This view, however, is not constitutionally mandated[29] and the few courts that have considered it have rejected it, holding instead that general improvements may be financed through fees so long as the need is generated by the new development.[30]

The Model Regulations provide a generic "Public Services and Facilities Impact Mitigation Fee" to cover capital improvement costs of facilities and services. The fee has been specifically tied to adoption of a Capital Improvements Program by the local governing body to ensure a coordinated and well-planned effort. Municipalities may also consider a School Impact Mitigation Fee, to be imposed at the initiative of the local school board, provided it is levied by the land use regulatory authority.

ALTERNATIVE FINANCING TECHNIQUES

Historical Perspective

Land development creates the need to expand public services and install public improvements and facilities. Although these needs have traditionally been met through general revenues, local governments have turned to alternative methods in an effort to shift the burden of development-generated infrastructure costs to the new development itself.

Local governments traditionally have had the responsibility of providing public facilities to accommodate new urban growth. Street and highway improvements, sanitary and storm sewers, water supply, parks, fire and police protection, mass transit services, schools, and other public facilities historically were paid for through the general fund or utilizing special assessments or special district ad valorem taxes. More recently, local governments have imposed off-site public facility requirements on developers through the authority of subdivision regulations. Local governments have always required that developers "dedicate" land for some public facilities.

An alternative to land dedication, where the dedicated property is not suitable for the particular facility, has been to impose a fee in lieu of land dedication, sometimes based on the market value of the land that would have been dedicated. These fees, which evolved in the 1960s and 1970s, are deposited in a fund to purchase offsite land for facilities serving the particular subdivision from which the fees are exacted. Other exactions have evolved in the late 1960s and 1970s, including impact fees and linkage fees for affordable housing. This section will analyze each of these regulatory fees and their appropriate usage.

Special Assessments

Special assessments were the earliest technique used to shift capital facility costs from the general fund and may be viewed as the precursor to subdivision exactions and impact fees. The special assessment is the traditional method of financing public facility needs of local projects, used primarily for streets, sidewalks, curbs, and sewers. Either a district or a special service area is created by the governing body or by petition of the residents, and the cost of the public facility is spread among those lands that benefit from construction of the facility in relation to the degree to which each is benefitted. Those lands benefitted by the project compose the service area or district. Each land parcel and improvement in the service area or district is then assessed its proportionate share of the cost, which may be paid immediately or spread over a number of years. If an entity chooses to spread the cost over a number of years, a lien is placed on the property to secure payment of the assessment.

Universal enabling authority exists to issue bonds to finance the cost of the improvement. The bonds are retired from the property assessments. The bonding authority provides a mechanism to construct the improvement before funds are available to pay its full cost.

The advantage of the special assessment is that, unlike other mechanisms, it can be applied retroactively upon existing development. It allows the public sector to pass the cost of improvements designed to eliminate capacity deficiencies in existing facilities on to those who benefit from the improvement, rather than the citizenry at large.[31]

The amount of special assessment charged to the land and improvements reflects the special benefit that a parcel of land enjoys as a result of the improvement.[32] Traditionally, special assessments have been viewed as an exercise of the taxing power,[33] although recent authority supports the proposition that such measures are regulatory in nature and are an exercise of the police power.[34] The key to determining the validity of a special assessment is the existence of special benefits.[35] The primary benefit must inure to the property assessed.[36] The test most often utilized by the courts is that the assessment may not exceed the amount of special benefit to the property and must have appropriate statutory authority.[37]

Facility Benefit Assessments

The City of San Diego used a unique blend of special assessment and regulatory fee, in the nature of an impact fee known as a Facilities Benefit Assessment. The FBA, created by Professor Freilich, was designed to impose charges upon property within a designated area to pay for public facilities serving the needs of those who will reside in the area.[38] The FBA was upheld by the California Court of Appeals in two far-reaching and significant decisions.[39]

In the mid-1960s, San Diego adopted and later amended its progress guide and general plan. The general plan set out growth management policies to deal with population growth, industrial development, capital facility provision, and environmental concerns. The general plan classified community planning areas as urbanized, planned urbanizing, and future urbanizing and required the development of land in the planned urbanizing areas to be consistent with the policies set out in specific community plans. Developers were required to bear the prime responsibility for providing community facilities, the need for which was generated by the new development.

The ordinance provided for the designation of an area of benefit, defined as lands receiving special benefits from the construction of public facilities projects— any public improvement "the need for which is directly or indirectly generated by development." The definition of public improvements embraced a broad spectrum of works, including water mains, utilities, sewers, drainage systems, streets and sidewalks, parks, transit and transportation, libraries, fire stations, school buildings, and police stations. Liens were authorized to be placed on land to secure the payment of the FBA.

Building permits were not to be issued for development of any FBA land within the area of benefit until the FBA on such land was paid. The FBA would be paid when the capital improvement program for the area calls for commencement of the public facilities project. FBA payments are deposited in a special dedicated fund. For failure to pay, the city may foreclose the lien. Annual adjustments of the FBA may be made by the city, reflecting increases or decreases in cost or scope of the facilities or availability of other funds for construction.

While traditional assessments are spread on a front or square foot or ad valorem basis, the FBA is apportioned among the parcels according to the number of "net equivalent dwelling units" attributable to each parcel at its highest potential development under current zoning. The formula is based on an assumed level of need for the proposed facilities generated by maximum zoned development of the assessed parcels. The formula does not consider the location of an assessed parcel vis-a-vis any particular improvement.

The FBA constitutes a vast improvement upon impact fee utilization (discussed later in this chapter) by adding both the retroactivity and lien features of special assessment to the superior methods of calculating the benefit and the fee used by impact fee methodology, but limiting the imposition of the assessment to new development and not to existing structures within the district.

Exactions

The need to ensure that development pays its required share of the cost of capital facilities has led government to adopt development requirements known as exactions. Exactions adopted through subdivision regulations include dedication, money in lieu of dedication, impact fees, linkage fees, and special facility benefit assessments.

Exactions constitute a process by which developers are required, as a condition of development approval, to dedicate sites for public or common facilities; construct and dedicate public or common facilities; purchase and donate vehicles and equipment for public or common use; make payments to defray the cost of land, facilities, vehicles, and equipment in connection with public or private off-site facilities; or otherwise provide other specifically agreed upon public amenities.

Dedications

In the first chapter, the eras of subdivision regulation are described and it is noted that, from the promulgation of the Standard Planning Enabling Act of 1928 until the 1960s, the primary purpose of subdivision regulation was to assure the provision of onsite facilities. This included the necessary dedication of onsite or perimeter land where such facilities were to be maintained and operated by the municipality.

Dedication is appropriate where the subdivision contains suitable land on-site or at the perimeter for a public facility, needed roads, drainage, sewer and water lines or onsite treatment facilities, park, school, and other facilities. Dedication has now been uniformly accepted in virtually all states, so long as the appropriate legal test is satisfied and the amount of land required to be dedicated is reasonable in relation to the need generated by the subdivision. Statutory authority must exist for authorization to require dedication of land.[40]

The federal constitutional test of validity requires that the dedication meet three important tests imposed by the Fifth and Fourteenth amendments to the U.S. Constitution.[41] The dedication must be:

1. adopted to accomplish a legitimate state purpose or goal;
2. "substantially related" to the health, safety, or general welfare of the people; and
3. reasonably related to, or in rough proportionality with, the impacts caused by the development.

Each state requires a form of the federal nexus requirement as a condition of validity of the dedication in order to pass statutory or state constitutional standards.[42] These standards vary from a very tight requirement that the need for the dedication must be caused solely by the subdivision itself, the "specifically and uniquely attributable" test,[43] to a middle ground "rational nexus" test,[44] or a liberal "reasonable relationship" standard.[45] If a dedication of an arterial road right-of-way is needed only in part for the trips generated by the subdivision itself, it would probably fail the uniquely attributable test but would pass muster on the reasonable relationship test.[46] Specific care must be taken not to use an arbitrary fixed or limited percentage but a sliding scale related to the actual needs generated.[47]

Money in Lieu of Land

Money in lieu of land is valuable particularly for park, recreation, or school sites, when the subdivision is too small and there is insufficient land to dedicate for the facility needed; where the land available is not well suited for the facility (e.g., by reason of location or topography); or where the comprehensive plan indicates a need for the facility at a different location outside the boundaries of the particular subdivision.

In drafting the regulations, the municipality must take care to assure that there is a choice by the landowner between dedication and monetary payment (where suitable land exists on site), that the money be placed in a trust fund to be actually used for park or recreation, that the park site be located near the subdivision generating the need, be spent within a reasonable time after collection, and bear a proper relationship between need and benefit.[48] The majority of courts in the United States have approved of the process, provided authority by statute or home rule power exists.[49] An ordinance provision requiring both partial dedication and partial payment of money in lieu for the same approval may not be authorized.[50]

Excise Taxes

Before proceeding with the major regulatory fee system—the impact fee—it is important to stress that communities may, if statutorily authorized, be able to utilize nonregulatory fees or excise taxes levied specifically on new construction

and new development without the restrictions of the benefit or nexus requirements of a regulatory fee. Nor need it be uniform and all inclusive of the existing
community as in an ad valorem property tax.[51] In this case the objectives are
completely reversed from regulatory exactions. The excise tax should be primarily to raise revenue and not be related to the "approval" process.[52] Similarly, you
may state the purpose of the tax as providing capital facilities, but you may not
"earmark" the funds or place them in a trust fund.[53] To avoid classification as an
invalid or non-uniform property tax, the excise tax should avoid the following
characteristics of general and property taxes:

- The tax is imposed on *every use* of property.
- The measure of the tax is based on *valuation* of property.
- Unpaid taxes are secured *by a lien.*
- The tax is levied by *reason of ownership.*
- Payment is required by a *specific date.*[54]

The excise tax has no structural limitations. Different rates may be established
for residential development and commercial-industrial development,[55] or the
tax may be limited exclusively to residential units.[56] The excise tax, like the utility
service charge (for sewer, water, drainage, transportation, and other public
utility functions) may be used for noncapital operating and maintenance costs.[57]
Many developers prefer the impact fee to the excise tax, since the former's funds
must be earmarked for capital facilities that benefit the development, while the
latter may be placed in the general fund for any public purpose.[58]

Impact Fee

Description of Impact Fee. The latest step in the continuum of land use financing
techniques is the impact fee. Functionally, it is similar to the in-lieu fee in that
both are imposed to pay for offsite capital improvements. Some courts use the
terms interchangeably.[59] Because in-lieu fees may be imposed only as an alternative to actual dedication, they must meet the same dedication requirements.

The impact fee has recently been used by many developing communities with
mixed success. Impact fees are charges levied by local governing bodies against
developers for their pro rata share of capital funding for facilities necessitated,
at least in part, by the new development. Because of their flexibility and
advantages over more traditional land use devices, such as special assessments
and dedications, impact fees offer a convenient, though sometimes controversial, alternative to more traditional funding schemes.

Impact fees have characteristics that distinguish them from both special
assessments and other exactions, allowing them to be a more flexible device for
shifting the costs of new development to the development itself. One such
characteristic is that fees may be collected when building permits or certificates
of occupancy are issued, rather than at the platting stage.[60] This results in several
advantages over traditional financing techniques for both municipalities and

developers. Funds are required only at the time the need for new services is actually generated and the new capital funding is required. Collecting impact fees when building permits are issued provides more leeway and certainty for developers trying to calculate the amount of financing needed.[61] Because the fees, in contrast to exactions, are collected nearer to the time that units are actually sold, developers need not finance and carry the fees over a long period of time.[62] Finally, because impact fees are collected at the building permit or certificate of occupancy stage, developments platted before the adoption of the impact fee ordinance are required to pay the impact fees.[63] This addresses a problem that is particularly acute in Florida, where thousands of acres have been platted but not developed.[64]

Model Regulations Section 6.9 establishes a dual timing system for the collection of impact fees to ensure that all new development pays its own way regardless of whether the construction occurs on either raw land or subdivided land. Impact fees may be imposed in the first instance at the platting stage for two reasons: (1) the use and density of development will be known at the platting stage and fees can be calculated; and (2) the payment of fees at the platting stage gives the government sufficient lead time to bring capital facilities "on line," especially in states requiring that "concurrency" or adequate public facilities be available at the time of development. Alternatively, fees may be collected at the building permit or certificate of occupancy stage in those jurisdictions in which there are substantial lands platted prior to the effective date of the impact fee ordinance. The Model Regulations permit the local government to defer the payment of fees until the building permit stage if it finds that deferral will not unreasonably delay construction of capital facilities and that imposition of the fees at the platting stage will add unnecessarily to the cost of lots or units in the subdivision. The counter argument is that the subdivider should not be required to pay fees if homes are not built in the subdivision and there is no increase in the demand for public services. Yet when the demand occurs, the government should be in a position to provide services to residents in the subdivision. Those services cannot be available immediately if fees are paid by individual lot owners when they apply for building permits. If the original subdivider is required to pay the fees, the government will have the resources with which to make services available.

Impact fees are a far more appropriate device than in-lieu fees for financing offsite public facilities not requiring land dedication, such as sewer and water facilities. Dedications of land are unnecessary when a general community facility is being constructed and the major cost of the improvement is the construction of the facility and not the land acquisition. The test for impact fees is more likely to be rational nexus or reasonable relationship rather than uniquely or specially attributable.[66]

The flexibility of impact fees results in other advantages for developing areas, such as their application to condominium, apartment, and commercial developments. This type of development creates many of the same needs as traditional housing but often avoids exactions or in-lieu fees because of the statutory nonapplicability of subdivision regulations or because of the small land area involved.[67] The impact fees for multifamily units may be simpler to administer because they are calculated at a flat rate per unit or number of bedrooms.[68]

General Validity of Impact Fees. Local governments must anticipate both constitutional and statutory challenges in devising impact fee ordinances. State courts typically focus on two primary questions in determining the validity of impact fees: (1) Did the municipality have state law authority to enact the fee ordinance?[69] and (2) Is the ordinance within limits imposed by state and federal constitutional provisions?[70]

In deciding the authority question, courts usually employ a two-step procedure.[71] First, the ordinance is classified as a regulatory measure, tax, or mixed classification (e.g., special assessment). Then the court determines whether the measure is authorized under state law.

In examining the classification, the court will focus on the nature of the improvements that can be funded from the collected revenues. If the revenues are to be spent on facilities that benefit primarily the residents or users of new development, the fee will be regarded as regulation.[72] This is determined by whether the collected funds are segregated from general revenues and are earmarked to pay, within a reasonable time frame, for specific improvements that would directly (and primarily) benefit the users of the property on which the fees were imposed.[73]

In general, if the court views the fee as primarily a revenue measure, and therefore a tax, it may be invalidated as beyond the regulating body's taxing authority. Even if authorized, it may be held in violation of constitutional or statutory uniformity and public approval requirements.

If the impact fee is characterized as primarily regulatory in nature and an exercise of the police power, broad legislative discretion will usually suffice to validate the measure as long as it does not produce considerably more revenue than is required to construct the facilities or provide the services. The "result-oriented" method that the courts use to label impact fees often precludes an in-depth analysis of the theoretical and policy reasons for the classification.[74]

Judicial deference to legislative action will generally lead to validation of the classification as a regulatory measure.[75] Stating the purposes for which the regulation is imposed in a preamble and designation of a particular fund for receipt of revenues may be necessary.[76] Regulatory conditions relating to public facility improvements may be imposed on a development complex when they are required to mitigate the direct impact of development.[77] Administrative fees may also be charged and will become an invalid tax only if revenues collected exceed the cost of administering the system.[78]

Judicial Review of Impact Fees. Once the ordinance has been classified as a regulatory measure, the court looks to state law to determine whether it is authorized under law or is ultra vires.[79]

Impact fees must meet the same tests for validity as other exactions. Courts have generally judged impact fees by a "reasonableness" test, as illustrated by the following:

> [T]o comply with the standards of reasonableness, a municipal fee . . . must not require newly developed properties to bear more than their equitable share of the capital costs in relation to the benefits conferred . . .

> [A] municipality should determine the relative burdens previously borne and yet to be borne by those properties in comparison with other properties in the municipality as a whole; the fee in question should not exceed the amount sufficient to equalize the relative burdens of newly developed and other properties.[80]

Planning and subdivision enabling statutes may impliedly grant the necessary power to local governments. Even without a specific grant of authority, municipalities have been allowed to charge impact fees as a valid exercise of the police power.[81] Authority for the adoption of impact fee ordinances can be derived from planning, zoning, and/or subdivision enabling legislation,[82] and express statutory authority generally focusing on sewer, water, drainage, and roads.[83] Other courts refer to impact fees as charges for services rendered rather than regulations under the police power. In these jurisdictions, broad statutory authority will support the measure.[84] Some decisions upholding impact fees are somewhat vague about the exact source of the authority upon which the fee rests.[85]

Over the past 10 years, many states have begun enacting specific impact fee enabling legislation.[86] There are two basic types of statutes. The first is enacted by states that have municipal or county home rule.[87] This type of statute is limited to existing home rule authority of the local governmental unit. The other type occurs in *non*-home rule states and grants limited authority to the local governmental unit to impose the impact fee.[88]

Despite the classification or type of statute enacted, there are restrictions set out in each statute limiting use of the impact fee revenue to specific public improvement projects. The statutes fall on a continuum from allowing unrestricted use to specifically limiting use to a single purpose. The most restrictive statutes are found in Illinois, Pennsylvania, and Virginia, which limit application of the statute only to road improvements.[89]

The least restrictive statutes are found in California and Vermont. These states' statutes place no limits on what can constitute a public improvement. Thus, an impact fee may be levied in these states for any project reasonably related or attributable to the development.[90]

All other states fall somewhere between these two extremes. Their statutes set out *specific categories* of public improvements for which an impact fee may be levied.

Public improvements most frequently mentioned in the various statutes are road improvements, water facility improvements, and sewer facility improvements.[91]

Eight states have legislation that authorize drainage and stormwater facility improvements.[92] Seven states provide specific authorization for parks and recreational facility improvements.[93] Four states specifically authorize fire protection facilities in the enabling legislation.[94] Three states list improvements for public education in the enabling legislation.[95] Of all the states that authorize specific facilities, West Virginia and Georgia are by far the most inclusive without being unrestricted. West Virginia's enabling statute provides for all the above mentioned improvements as well as a provision for emergency medical facilities.[96] Georgia provides for all the above mentioned improvements while also specifically authorizing library facilities.[97]

Even though the statutes authorize a range of facilities, all require that certain criteria be met in order to impose the fee. Some states have chosen to require that the fee be "specifically and uniquely attributable to" the public facility demands.[98] These criteria vary from state to state, but generally require there to be a certain connection between the fee imposed and the development needs. This requirement imposes a closer connection between the fee and the development than the language to be discussed next. Other states have used language that requires a "reasonable relationship" between the fee and the cost of the proposed facility.[99] The remainder of the states are somewhat ambiguous. This group focuses more on the amount and not so much on the relationship, thus requiring that the fee be limited to pro rata, or proportionate share, of that needed.[100]

There are particular features of each statute that merit specific mention. All states except Arizona require a capital facilities plan. Most of the states that have enacted enabling legislation require identification of any deficiencies in the municipality's existing public facilities. The states that do not require this identification include Arizona, Maine, New Jersey, and Texas. Those few states that have a grandfather clause are Arizona, Illinois, Indiana, Virginia, and Texas.[101] Some states require that service areas be set up.[102]

In general, fees collected from developers must be earmarked by being placed into a separate trust fund to ensure that the monies are expended only for the facilities necessitated by the new development.[103] In upholding a sewer connection fee, an appellate court in Oregon stressed the importance of earmarking the funds for sewers only.[104] The extent of separate earmarking required when fees are imposed for multiple improvements is unclear, but presumably, at a minimum, separate funds should be set up for each type of improvement and for each benefit area.

All states with enabling legislation have an express provision for earmarking and accounting of the collected funds.[105] This requirement usually provides that a separate, interest-bearing account be established for a single purpose.[106] Most statutes also require annual accounting for any account containing impact fee proceeds or interest therefrom.[107] It is under this statute section that a provision is made for the kind of expenditure permitted.[108] This generally is the case with states having specific statutory authority.[109]

There are two issues of timing applicable to a valid impact fee ordinance. The first concerns the point in the development approval process at which the fee is imposed. The second relates to a sufficient nexus between the time the impact fee is assessed and the time when the public facility for which it is imposed is actually constructed.

Most impact fees are imposed at the building permit stage rather than at the platting stage. This generally is the case with the states having specific statutory authority.[110] This results in several advantages to the municipality and the developer: (1) the fees become available at the same time the need for the new facilities is generated and new capital funding is required; (2) the municipality may be able to exact an impact fee from already platted land;[111] and (3) the developer benefits from collection at the latest possible point in the development approval process, the costs can be more readily passed on to the ultimate purchaser or consumer, and the developer's up-front carrying costs are minimized.

Retroactive application of fees has been allowed, based on analogy to taxes that can be imposed at any time.[112] Fees must be spent within a reasonable time of collection to ensure that the development receives a benefit from the facilities constructed. Most states have made specific provision for the time in which the collected fee must be spent. It may be as short as two or three years,[113] or as long as 10 years.[114] The most common period in the enabling statutes is five or six years.[115]

Provisions for refunds or credits should be made to avoid overpayment or double payment when a developer constructs offsite improvements that would have been funded by impact fees.[116] All but three statutes that have current statutory authority for impact fees require credits or offsets.[117] Offsets may also be granted for taxes as they are in Georgia, Illinois, Vermont, and Washington.[118]

Impact fees may be computed in a number of ways. A municipality may levy a fixed fee based on the classification of the developer,[119] or it may base the fee on a variable formula calculated on a case-by-case method.[120] Most fees are of the fixed variety and take the form of a per-unit charge, often based on the number of bedrooms or quantity of water or road capacity used, rather than a percentage of acreage or assessed valuation. Regardless of method used, the fee must relate to the cost of the additional facilities necessitated by the new development.[121] The calculation is one appropriately done in conjunction with a comprehensive plan and a capital improvements program prepared to cover a 20-year period, taking into consideration employment as well as population increase over the life of the plan. In this way, not only can the need for new facilities generated by development possible under the plan be calculated, but actual deficiencies can be identified and factored into the calculation. The states with legislation are split on prescribing specific calculation methodology. Only eight states provide for this in their legislation.[122] The remainder rely on the common law of benefit, nexus, and reasonableness set out above.

LINKAGE FEES

Dwindling federal funding for housing programs has prompted a new and innovative use of impact fees termed "linkage" and "linkage fees."[123]

Overview

Linkage may be charged to both residential and nonresidential development so long as a nexus is created between the development and the need for affordable housing.

It is well recognized that new office construction is a leading indicator of new residential construction. Commercial construction causes an increase in competition for residential units, which in turn causes "an indirect displacement of lower income units."[124] To mitigate this increase in housing demand, a number of cities have enacted linkage programs that require office developers to pay exaction fees into a housing trust fund.[125] The linkage provision included here is drawn primarily from the successful San Francisco ordinance.

Linkage programs in Boston and San Francisco have received wide publicity. The San Francisco program was formerly an administrative policy administered under the authority of the California Environmental Quality Act (CEQA).[126] Because CEQA has been amended to address only changes in the physical environment, the planning commission has relied on its discretionary authority under the municipal code to grant or deny building permits.[127] The program was codified in 1985 and is not tied to the mandatory residence element of the city's general plan.[128]

The Office of Affordable Housing Production Program requires office projects of at least 50,000 net square feet of office space to build housing or to pay an in-lieu fee into a housing trust fund.[129] The program did not originally require this housing to be affordable. Instead, the program offered credits against the developer's obligations under the program to encourage the construction of affordable housing. This system was criticized because its usage, while making the program politically defensible to developers at the outset, restrained overall housing production.[130] The present ordinance requires that 62 percent of the housing units constructed be affordable to low-income households for a period of 20 years.[131]

Boston's linkage program requires commercial projects of over 100,000 square feet to pay a "housing payment exaction" of $5 per square foot into a neighborhood housing trust fund, or to construct new housing.[132] The linkage fee is payable over a period of 12 years. Boston's program is designed to benefit only low- and moderate-income residents and is administered by the city's redevelopment agency. Linkage payments are required as a condition of rezoning or other discretionary development approvals. Because of the strength of Boston's office and commercial market in the 1980s before the recession, more than $45 million, including the construction or rehabilitation of 2,000 housing units, has been generated by the program.[133]

Preservation of Existing Housing Supply

Linkage programs have enjoyed increasingly greater success in the courts, particularly in fighting the most common challenge, that the linkage payment is an unauthorized tax.

Related to linkage fee regulation are programs to preserve the existing housing supply. These have been more controversial and have run into few successful takings challenges. Housing preservation and single-room occupancy[134] (SRO) unit programs generally require a permit to demolish or convert existing low-income housing.[135] As a condition of conversion or demolition, housing preservation ordinances require the developer to construct or rehabilitate housing units elsewhere or to pay an in-lieu fee into a housing trust fund. These programs are ordinarily enacted pursuant to the city's general police powers rather than its zoning powers.[136]

In *Terminal Plaza Corporation v. City and County of San Francisco*,[137] San Francisco's SRO program was upheld both as a valid substantive due process exercise of the city's general police powers and as a program that did not constitute a taking of private property without just compensation. The SRO ordinance required that developers converting single-room occupancy buildings to commercial uses construct an equivalent amount of housing or pay a fee into the city's housing trust fund. The California Court of Appeal ruled that the fee was not a "special tax" because it was not a general revenue-raising device and it was not compulsory, but rather an exaction on the voluntary privilege of land development.[138] The court also rejected substantive due process challenges on the grounds that the ordinance was rationally related to the legitimate state interest of preserving low-income housing and that no fundamental right to cease doing business was implicated.[139] Noting previous decisions dealing with rent control ordinances, the court was impressed with the fact that the developer was free to withhold units from the market and to sell or convert the property.[140]

A takings challenge was also rejected on the grounds that the owners were not deprived of all reasonable use of their property. Again, the court noted that landowners were allowed to sell or convert their property, adding that the ordinance permitted landowners to continue using the property as low-rent housing.[141] The mere "restriction upon more economic uses of [the landowner's] property" was insufficient to rise to the level of a taking.[142]

The Washington Supreme Court invalidated an ordinance requiring that developers demolishing and converting low-income housing to other uses construct additional housing or make a payment into the city's housing trust fund.[143] Seattle's ordinance required a housing demolition license, which could be granted only if the developer provided relocation assistance and replaced a percentage of the demolished units with "other suitable housing."[144] The ordinance permitted the payment of an in-lieu fee into the city's housing replacement fund as an alternative to housing construction. The court ruled that the ordinance imposed a tax categorized as "in kind or in money" since it was designed to accomplish public benefits and not to regulate land.[145] As an aside, the court also hinted that the ordinance might preclude the developers from deriving any profitable use of their property, this constituting a taking.[146] The case was decided against Seattle, however, on the basis that it constituted an unauthorized tax.

The *San Telmo* decision must be considered against the unique feature of Washington's land use enabling legislation. Unlike most states, Washington at the time had an "anti-impact fee" statute expressly precluding the imposition by a city of "any tax, fee, or charge, either direct or indirect . . . on the development, subdivision, classification, or reclassification of land."[147] This feature allowed the *San Telmo* court to invalidate Seattle's SRO program with little discussion, and limits the applicability of the decision to other jurisdictions.

A more pervasive decision was handed down by New York's highest court, which ruled New York City's housing preservation ordinance an unconstitutional physical and regulatory taking.[148] New York had imposed a moratorium on the conversion of SRO dwelling units to other uses. Conversion or demolition could proceed only where the owner purchased an exemption from the moratorium upon the payment of a $45,000 per unit fee or the replacement of an equal number of units. A rehabilitation and anti-warehousing provision imposed an affirmative obligation on SRO owners to rehabilitate existing SRO units and to lease them to bona fide tenants.

New York's highest court ruled that this requirement constituted a regulatory taking by imposing a communitywide burden on discrete property owners, and found that the ordinance constituted a physical taking by limiting the owner's right to exclude others from the property. The court was particularly concerned with the rehabilitation and anti-warehousing provision. The "forced occupation by strangers" amounted to a physical invasion of the property and deprived the owners of their fundamental property right to exclude strangers.[149] This affirmative obligation was imposed regardless of the landowner's decision to convert or to destroy the unit.[150] Thus, the court expressly affirmed the city's power to prohibit the demolition of SRO units and to require their rehabilitation. However, the court ruled that compensation must be paid where the regulation imposed a communitywide burden on discrete property owners, depriving them of their right to possess, use, or dispose of their properties.[151]

The court was also unimpressed with the relationship or nexus between the regulation and the goals it purported to advance. The ordinance was directed primarily at the alleviation of homelessness. To refute the asserted nexus between the goals and the regulations, the court cited a study by the city asserting that the ordinance would scarcely advance the resolution of the homeless problem and the fact that the units were not earmarked for homeless persons.[152] By contrast, many linkage programs are directed not only to homeless persons, but to a broader range of low- and moderate-income persons.[153]

Thus, the effect of the *Seawall Associates* decision might not be as devastating as it appears on first glance. The court was particularly taken by the affirmative obligations imposed by the ordinance absent a decision to convert SRO units and the lack of a close relationship between the regulation and the goal of providing shelter for the homeless. These problems are not applicable to most linkage programs, which apply only to voluntary decisions to develop or convert and which are related to a broader set of community goals. However, the language of the decision regarding deprivation is particularly broad. Thus, compensation may be required where laudable goals such as affordable housing production are determined to be a general community responsibility and not closely related to the development activity or generated by it.

Legal Authority for Linkage Related to New Development

Nexus Requirements. Courts are increasingly willing to support the direct concept of linkage so long as the local government has established a nexus between the fee amount and the need for affordable housing created by new development.[154]

Courts have also approved the site-specific exaction of contributions to affordable housing needs so long as adequate standards are contained in the state or local enabling ordinances.[155]

Regional general welfare cases requiring cities and counties to provide their "fair share" of regional housing needs can be used as authority for linkage fee programs.[156]

The "Good Faith" Requirement. The use of inclusionary zoning or linkage programs essentially ties development approval to the adequacy of available affordable housing to accommodate growth. Where local governments tie the rate of growth to carrying capacity standards, several important constitutional principles apply.

The use of carrying capacity standards cannot be used to mask ulterior exclusionary motives. The denial of development approval on an ad hoc basis, premised on the inadequacy of public facilities, can be invalidated where used as an artifice to exclude low- or moderate-income persons from a jurisdiction.[157]

Other resources must be applied to remedy existing housing deficiencies. Where local governments condition development approval on the adequacy of public facilities, good faith attempts to remedy existing housing deficiencies through other funding sources must be shown.[158] As a corollary, where jurisdictions are making real and substantial attempts to remedy public facility or housing deficiencies and to accommodate new growth through the planning process, courts will assume their good faith.[159]

Development Excise Taxes

Because the level of judicial scrutiny for exactions has been refined by *Nollan v. California Coastal Commission*, 107 S.Ct. 3141 (1987), some local governments have turned to development excise taxes for added flexibility for housing funds.[160]

FEDERAL CONSTITUTIONAL REQUIREMENT: REGULATORY TAKINGS

There are three types of regulatory takings which are recognized: physical, title, and economic. A physical invasion of property is typically referred to as a "possessory" or "trespassory" taking. Closely akin to the physical take is a "title" take, where the government acquires incidents of ownership or title to the property or an exaction in lieu of the dedication of land. The third type, an "economic" taking, occurs when governmental action interferes with the property owner's viable economic interests in the property.

Physical Takings

If the government physically invades land, the regulation will generally be held to be a taking unless such acquisition secured private benefit to the landowner, abated burdens imposed on the public by private development, or was a "temporary deprivation," in which case the balancing test is applied.[161]

In *Loretto v. Teleprompter Manhattan CATV Corp.*,[162] the Supreme Court announced a *per se* rule requiring that an enactment that authorizes a "permanent physical occupation" of a landowner's property constitutes a taking regardless of the nature of the governmental interest involved.

Title Takings: The "Rough Proportionality" Requirement After Dolan

Closely akin to physical invasion of property is the situation where the imposition of a regulation results in governmental acquisition of title to the property. This presents the greatest risk to governing bodies that impose conditions or exactions on development application approvals. The most recent case in this area is *Dolan v. City of Tigard*, decided in 1994.

The Court's holding in *Dolan v. City of Tigard*,[163] as well as the accompanying discussion in the Court's opinion, address many of the issues raised when the imposition of a regulation results in governmental acquisition of title to private property. Although *Dolan* answers some questions, it also raises many others. As a result, *Dolan* will certainly generate much new discussion about the legal implications of imposing permit-conditioned exactions, as well as the effects this case (together with *Lucas* and *Nollan*) will have on the takings equation as a whole.[164]

In *Dolan*, the property owners sought a building permit to demolish a 9,700-square foot building and construct a replacement 17,600-square foot building for an electric and plumbing supply business on 1.67 acres of land in Tigard's downtown central business district. The property lies within an "action area" overlay zone, which allowed the city to attach conditions to the Dolans' development at the building permit stage in order to accommodate projected transportation and public facility needs.

Pursuant to the requirements of Oregon's comprehensive land use management program, the City of Tigard codified its comprehensive plan in a Community Development Code (CDC). The CDC required the Dolans and all others located in the Central Business District to comply with a 15 percent open space requirement. Tigard granted the Dolans' application, but required them to dedicate a 15-foot easement strip that was within the 100-year floodplain for a storm drainage system. The City of Tigard also required an eight-foot easement strip for construction of a pedestrian and bicycle pathway as a condition of the permit. The exactions amounted to approximately 10 percent of the Dolans' total property.

The Tigard Planning Commission's final order for the permit based the two easement conditions on the Comprehensive Master Drainage Plan and the Pedestrian/Bicycle Pathway Plan, which created a "reasonable relationship" between the Dolans' developmental impacts and the need for increased drainage and alternative means of transportation, respectively.[165] The commission specifically found that "[i]t is reasonable to assume that customers and employees of the future uses of this site *could* utilize a pedestrian/bicycle pathway adjacent to this development for their transportation and recreational needs."[166] As to the anticipated increase in stormwater runoff, the commission concluded that "the requirement of dedication of the floodplain area on the site is related to the applicant's plan to intensify development of the site."[167]

The Oregon Supreme Court upheld the district court's finding that Tigard's exaction did not create a taking of the Dolans' property.[168] The Oregon court accepted the planning commission's conclusions that the bicycle path requirement was reasonably related to the Dolans' business expansion and anticipated increase in traffic, and that the drainage system reasonably related to the increased impervious surface of a larger parking lot. The Oregon court rejected the Dolans' argument that *Nollan v. California Coastal Commission*[169] abandoned the "reasonably related" test (substituting an "essential nexus" requirement) for the connection between the city's condition for permit approval and the needs created by the new development. Despite accepting *Nollan* as representing only the reasonable nexus requirement, however, the Oregon court concluded that there was an "essential nexus" between the Dolans' developmental needs and the bike path and drainage system dedications.[170]

Following the analysis established in *Nollan*, the U.S. Supreme Court first asked whether an "essential nexus" existed between the "legitimate state interest" and the permit condition exacted by the city.[171] In *Nollan*, a public easement was demanded across the Nollans' beachfront property in exchange for a permit to demolish a bungalow on the property and replace it with a three-bedroom house. The easement was required to connect two public beaches on either side of the Nollan property, and the purported legitimate state interest was to diminish blockage of the ocean view from the roadway on the landward side of the property, which would be caused by a larger house on the property. Justice Rehnquist summarized *Nollan*'s holding that the required lateral easement was unconstitutional by stating: "The Coastal Commission's regulatory authority was set completely adrift from its constitutional moorings when it claimed that a nexus existed between visual access to the ocean and a permit condition requiring lateral public access along the Nollans' beachfront lot."[172]

The absence of any nexus left the coastal commission in the position of "trying to obtain an easement through gimmickry, which converted a valid regulation of land use into 'an out-and-out plan of extortion.'"[173] It is thus clear that "essential nexus" in this sense is related to a "public purpose" requirement and in no way is related to the second causal requirement of reasonable relationship or rough proportionality.[174]

The essential nexus that was absent in *Nollan*, however, was found to be plainly evident in *Dolan*, as "no such gimmicks are associated with the permit conditions" which were imposed upon the Dolans' request to enlarge their hardware store.[175] The prevention of flooding along the creek abutting the Dolans' property, and the reduction in traffic congestion in the Central Business District qualified as "legitimate public purposes."[176] There was a nexus between preventing flooding along the creek and limiting development within the creek's 100-year floodplain; there was likewise a nexus between the city's attempt to reduce traffic congestion and the city's bicycle path as an alternate means of transportation.

Since the first test of the essential nexus requirement was not satisfied in *Nollan*, there was no occasion to address the second test of the degree of connection required between the impact of the beachfront development and the coastal commission's required dedication. The second issue in *Dolan*, however, was "whether the degree of the exactions demanded by the city's permit conditions bear the required relationship to the projected impact of petitioner's proposed development."[177] The Court turned to state court decisions to determine the degree of connection that is constitutionally sufficient to justify the city's conditions. In what is certainly destined to be oft-quoted and controversial language, Justice Rehnquist held:

> We think the "reasonable relationship" test adopted by a majority of the state courts is closer to the federal constitutional norm than either of those previously discussed. But we do not adopt it as such, partly because the term "reasonable relationship" seems confusingly similar to the term "rational basis" which describes the minimal level of scrutiny under the Equal Protection Clause of the Fourteenth Amendment. We think a term such as "rough proportionality" best encapsulates what we hold to be the requirement of the Fifth Amendment. No precise mathematical calculation is required, but the city must make some sort of individualized determination that the required dedication is related both in nature and extent to the impact of the proposed development.[178]

Although approval of the reasonable relationship nexus does seem to confirm a trend, rather than signal a sharp departure from established takings jurisprudence,[179] many issues are raised by this decision and the new "rough proportionality" requirement language. The most troubling aspects of *Dolan* are the several questions presented in Justice Stevens's and Justice Souter's dissents.

1. Where does the "rough proportionality" language come from?

Justice Stevens points out that, "Not one of the state cases cited by the Court announces anything akin to a 'rough proportionality' requirement."[180] The footnote following Justice Rehnquist's "rough proportionality" holding does not provide a single citation or authority for the new language, and appears to be only a response to Justice Stevens's concerns that the burden will now be placed on the city to justify the exactions.[181]

Creating the phrase "rough proportionality" may simply be the Court's way of distinguishing this nexus requirement from the multitude of phrases that exist to test and qualify constitutional relationships in a variety of contexts. Justice Rehnquist's stated reason for adopting the rough proportionality test is, in part, because the reasonable relationship test is too close to the "rational basis" test used in minimal scrutiny for Equal Protection analysis.[182] This new "rough proportionality" language also may be a product of the Court's emphasis on elevating the Fifth Amendment rights of property owners to an equal footing with other guarantees conferred through the Bill of Rights.[183] In attempting to distinguish the nexus requirement established in *Dolan* from the already cluttered landscape of constitutional requirements, however, the Court may simply be muddying the water a bit further by failing to define the new term and its applicability.[184]

Dolan illustrates the often convoluted reasoning and labeling of academics, practitioners, and the courts. The "reasonable relationship" test has traditionally been the label for the "expansive" or "liberal" test.[185] However, the *Dolan* Court describes the expansive test as one in which only "very generalized statements as to the necessary connection" are required.[186] The "rational nexus" test has traditionally been considered the "middle ground" test,[187] but the *Dolan* Court instead calls this the "reasonable relationship" test,[188] and adopts this standard under the new label of "rough proportionality."[189] In an interesting conflict with the text of Justice Rehnquist's opinion, the syllabus of the *Dolan* opinion, which is presumably approved by the author of the majority opinion, claims that the required nexus "is essentially the 'reasonable relationship' test adopted by the majority of the state courts."[190]

In addition, although the opinion first establishes the new rough proportionality test, as an alternative to the previously labeled reasonable relationship test, Justice Rehnquist missed the opportunity to use this new test (or substituted label) after he applied the test to the facts of the Dolans' challenge: "We conclude that the findings upon which the city relies do not show the required *reasonable relationship* between the floodplain easement and the petitioner's proposed new building."[191]

Verbal semantics notwithstanding, the rough proportionality requirement is not a novelty introduced by *Dolan*. The majority of state development exactions cases address whether the dedication or fee requirement is excessive. This determination is reached by evaluating the exaction under proportionality standards, which consider the nature and amount of the exaction in relation to both the impacts generated by the development project and the benefit derived from the exaction.[192]

A court will consider a variety of factors to test the reasonableness of an exaction, particularly an impact fee. These include: (1) spatial factors, or the distance between the improvement and the development paying the fee or dedicating the land; (2) temporal factors, or the time elapsing between imposition of the exaction and construction of the improvement; (3) amount of the fee in relation to the actual costs necessitated by improvements; (4) the need, or relationship between the burden created by the development and the increased facility needs; (5) the benefit, or ability of the improvements constructed to satisfy the facility needs resulting from the development; and (6) earmarking, which in the case of an impact fee is the assurance that fee revenues are restricted in use solely to fund the type of facility for which the fees were collected.[193]

2. What does the "reasonable relationship" or "rough proportionality" standard now require?

Although rough proportionality seems to be merely a replacement phrase for reasonable relationship, as derived from the cited state cases, Justice Stevens suggests that there are now heightened burdens that must be met to satisfy the nexus requirement. As Justice Stevens reads the opinion, to establish a valid permit-conditioned exaction, it must be shown that: (1) there is an "essential nexus" present which satisfies *Nollan*; (2) the city has demonstrated "rough proportionality" between the harm caused by the new land use and the benefit obtained by the condition; and (3) the city has established the constitutionality of its conditions by making an "individual determination" that the conditions satisfy the proportionality requirement.[194]

The third requirement of an individualized determination was initially labeled the most controversial aspect of *Dolan*,[195] but it does not signify a substantial departure from the previously established doctrine that the landowner has the burden of proving the unconstitutionality of the city's actions in the context of an administrative decision that affects property.[196] The burden of establishing an individualized determination in *Dolan* arises from the manner in which this case is distinguished from previous cases, such as *Euclid v. Ambler Realty*[197] and *Pennsylvania Coal Co. v. Mahon*.[198] First, those cases were *legislative* determinations which classified an entire area, whereas in *Dolan* the city made an *adjudicative decision* to condition the building permit on a specific parcel.[199] Second, the conditions imposed were not mere limitations on the manner in which the property may be used, but were a requirement that the Dolans *deed* part of their property to the city.[200]

Instead of requiring an individualized determination conducted by the city in each case where the nature and extent of the relationship between the conditions and the impacts are questioned, Justice Stevens's dissent argues that this burden should be required only when "the developer establishes that a concededly germane condition is so grossly disproportionate to the proposed development's adverse effects that it manifests motives other than land use regulation on the part of the city."[201] This criticism, however, does not seem to be a quarrel with the added "individualized determination" requirement so much as an agreement with Justice Souter's dissent, when he argues that the nexus analysis in *Dolan* need not proceed beyond the essential nexus test established in *Nollan*. Justice Souter would limit the analysis in this case to what *Nollan* required, and skip any discussion of proportionality, "because of the lack of any rational connection at all between exaction of a *public recreational area* and the governmental interest in providing for the effect of increased water runoff. That is merely an application of *Nollan*'s nexus analysis."[202]

Justice Stevens begins his criticism of the majority's new rough proportionality requirement by arguing that, "The state cases the Court consults . . . either fail to support or decidedly undermine the Court's conclusion in key respects. First, although discussion of the state cases permeates the Court's analysis of the appropriate test to apply in this case, the test on which the Court settles is not naturally derived from those courts' decisions."[203] Justice Stevens agrees with Justice Rehnquist's application of the initial essential nexus requirement of *Nollan*, but strongly disputes both the new rough proportionality and individualized determination requirements, and the authority cited for these requirements: "For the most part . . . those cases that invalidated municipal ordinances did so on state law or unspecified grounds roughly equivalent to *Nollan's* 'essential nexus' requirement."[204]

This analysis reinforces Justice Souter's admonition that *Dolan* requires no further consideration than *Nollan* received; and that there is no essential nexus between the burdens created by increased stormwater runoff and traffic flow and the imposition of a recreational greenway as part of approving the Dolans' development permit. Nevertheless, the state cases cited by the majority in support of the intermediate rough proportionality test are indeed revealing.

The first case cited by Justice Rehnquist in support of the reasonable relationship/rough proportionality test is *Simpson v. City of North Platte*,[205] from the Supreme Court of Nebraska. In *Simpson*, landowners applied for a development permit from the City of North Platte to build a restaurant on a parcel of land situated on the northeast side of two streets that intersected into a "T". The City of North Platte had an ordinance that read, "no building or structure shall be erected or enlarged . . . unless half of the street adjacent to such lot has been dedicated to its comprehensive plan width."[206]

The city denied the Simpsons' building permit because they refused to dedicate a 40-foot strip of their property to the city as a condition of approving the permit. This dedication would have allowed the city to extend one street through their property, thereby transforming the "T" into a bisecting intersection according to the city's comprehensive plan.[207]

The issue presented in *Simpson* was whether the city's dedication requirement had some reasonable relationship or nexus to the proposed commercial use of the property, or whether the requirement was merely being used as an excuse for taking property because the landowner happened to be asking the city for a permit.[208] In finding that there was no nexus, the court stated:

> The evidence introduced at the time of trial established that, although the comprehensive plan indicated a proposed extension of Leota Street east of the intersection of existing Leota Street and Jeffers Street, no project was immediately contemplated whereby the street would be constructed nor is there any evidence regarding what the particular project would involve.[209]

In support of its conclusion, the *Simpson* court cited the New Jersey Appeals Court case of *181 Incorporated v. Salem City Planning Board*,[210] which held that "for the *nexus* to apply, thus making a compulsory dedication constitutionally valid, the *nexus* must be rational. This means it must be substantial, demonstrably clear and present."[211]

This analysis in *Simpson* is more akin to the *Nollan* essential nexus requirement than the reasonable relationship test or new rough proportionality test for which it is cited by Justice Rehnquist in *Dolan*. The connection to *Nollan* rather than *Dolan* is reinforced when the *Simpson* court adds that its decision is best understood by considering that "if the Simpsons were simply asking for a building permit in order to add one more foot to the kitchen of his home located on property in North Platte, he would be required to dedicate 40 feet of his land for street purposes without compensation."[212]

Other cases cited by the majority do support the general reasonableness test that *Dolan* establishes, despite Justice Stevens's insistence to the contrary. One case, *Jordan v. Village of Menominee Falls*[213] from the Wisconsin Supreme Court, not only supports the reasonable relationship test, but also may represent the new rough proportionality test established in *Dolan* without expressly labeling it as such. Following a discussion which recognized *Pioneer Trust & Savings Bank v. Village of Mt. Prospect*[214] as establishing the restrictive "specific and uniquely attributable" test,[215] the *Jordan* court wrote:

> We deem this to be an acceptable statement of the yard stick to be applied, provided the words "specific and uniquely attributable to this activity" are not so restrictively applied as to cast an unreasonable burden of proof upon the municipality which has enacted the ordinance under attack.[216]

Following *Jordan*, various states have applied some form of the reasonableness test, while acknowledging that *Jordan* established the "Wisconsin modification" of the specific and uniquely attributable test.[217] As a result, *Jordan* probably falls somewhere between the restrictive and the intermediate tests, as does *Dolan*. This allows a court to apply a reasonableness nexus test, examining a variety of different factors, while at the same time applying a heightened burden on the city imposing the exaction, similar to the "individualized determination" requirement set forth in *Dolan*.[218]

Following *Dolan*, it may be preferable to analyze the nexus requirement in terms of an overall "spectrum of connectedness," and resist the tendency to pigeonhole an exaction, such as that required of the Dolans, into a rigid nexus requirement of "reasonable relationship" or "rough proportionality." This conclusion is supported by Justice Rehnquist's apparent hesitation to adopt a precise "reasonable relationship" test by tentatively stating, "*We think a term such as 'rough proportionality' best encapsulates*" the Fifth Amendment requirement.[219] Future decisions relying on *Dolan* would do well to avoid reading the *Dolan* test as establishing a rigid requirement, but instead interpret the circumstances of a dedication in terms of a general reasonableness standard,[220] and applying heightened scrutiny to a dedication that is required as the result of an adjudicative or administrative determination.[221] Whether *Dolan* will be applied to all non-taking cases of mandatory exactions will now be addressed.

3. Will Dolan be applied to all exaction cases?

There exists a fairly compelling basis to narrowly interpret *Dolan* and limit its application to exaction cases in which the property owner is required to dedicate land as a condition of permit approval. As with *Nollan*, this dedication can be classified as a "title" take and not a purely economic take.[222] The *Dolan* opinion emphasizes that the City of Tigard required the Dolans not only to leave open space for the increased quantity and rate of stormwater flow, but required that they deed a portion of their property for the city's greenway system in connection with this burden.[223]

The majority found that this requirement injured the Dolans' ability to exclude others from their property, a right which is "one of the most essential sticks in the bundle of rights that are commonly characterized as property."[224] Land is opened for use to the public, which destroys one of the key elements of ownership. Justice Stevens is particularly troubled with this aspect of the opinion, pointing out that the Court traditionally considers the character of the entire economic transaction rather than focusing on the "power to exclude" as maintaining any special significance.[225] The Stevens analysis, however, seems to apply to a situation in which the developer is required to dedicate either a percentage of the entire parcel or an equivalent value in cash to finance local improvements. Two differences apply to the Dolans' situation, upon which Justice Rehnquist comments. First, the City of Tigard imposed a "permanent recreational easement" which "eviscerated" the Dolans' ability to control the time and manner in which the public could be excluded, even though the Dolans' development was to occur on commercial property, a fact that inherently limits the ability to exclude the public to begin with.[226] Second, whereas developers are often given the option of paying the cash equivalent as an alternative to dedicating land, the Dolans had no such option. As such, Justice Stevens's arguments based upon the balancing that traditionally occurs with an economic take does not apply, as this is a title take.[227]

This analysis reinforces the concept that *Dolan* will, or should be, limited to land dedications, as opposed to cash equivalent or other types of exactions. Several courts have in fact held that *Nollan's* nexus requirement does not apply to monetary exactions, or "linkage" fees. In *Sintra, Inc. v. City of Seattle*,[228] *Blue Jeans Equities West v. City and County of San Francisco*,[229] and *Commercial Builders v. City of Sacramento*,[230] the courts uniformly agreed that heightened scrutiny is applicable only to physical exactions.

This issue may be determined by *Ehrlich v. Culver City*.[231] The Supreme Court accepted *Ehrlich* on certiorari, vacated the decision, and has remanded to the appeals court in light of the *Dolan* decision. In *Ehrlich*, a developer closed a private tennis club which was a financial failure, and applied to the city for changes in the land use restrictions to permit the construction of 30 deluxe townhouses valued at $10 million. The city initially denied the application but later granted it subject to certain conditions, including payment of a $280,000 fee to mitigate the impact of the land use change, and a $33,220 fee in lieu of a requirement that art be placed on the new development.[232]

The trial court found the mitigation fee invalid as an attempt to shift the cost of a public benefit to a private entity, with no reasonable relationship existing between the project and the need for tennis courts.[233] The trial court refused to invalidate the art fee, finding it a valid exercise of the police power similar to open space or landscaping requirements.[234]

The California Court of Appeal first addressed the mitigation fee under the *Nollan* two-part test: (1) the government agency could have denied the request without the denial constituting a taking, and (2) the condition imposed substantially furthers the government goal furthered by the denial.[235] The court easily dispatched the first prong, finding that a denial of the developer's request would not have effected a compensable taking.[236] As to the second prong, the court distinguished between two types of conditions. If the condition constitutes a physical taking, the condition must substantially advance the governmental purpose, and is subject to heightened scrutiny.[237] If the condition is a monetary exaction, the condition need be only rationally related to the governmental purpose.[238] As this development condition was a mitigation fee, the easier standard was applied, and the court found that the mitigation fee was directly related to the original denial of the development application, satisfying *Nollan*. The court added that the mitigation fee was imposed to compensate the city for the benefit conferred on the developer and for the burden on the community that resulted from the loss of recreational facilities.[239]

Secondly, the court addressed the in-lieu art fee. A city ordinance required that certain development projects participate in the Art in Public Places Program. Developers could choose among several alternatives, including placement of art on the project, donating art work to the city, or paying a fee in lieu of placing art on the property. The appeals court agreed with the trial court that requiring art to be placed on new developments is within the city's police powers,[240] which was a requirement similar to requiring scenic zoning,[241] landmark preservation,[242] and residential zoning.[243]

As this case is reviewed upon remand, it is entirely plausible that the appeals court will conclude that *Dolan* applies only to dedications of land, and the original decision was therefore correct with regard to the mitigation fee and in-lieu art fee. The *Dolan* land dedication was invalidated based on the property owner's right to exclude the public.[244] Charging a fee as a condition of development is a non-title take, and does not raise the specter of the property owner's right to exclude the public.

On the other hand, an alternate outcome has been suggested. The "doctrine of unconstitutional conditions" was invoked by the *Dolan* Court to apply a heightened scrutiny upon the City of Tigard's dedication.[245] This doctrine states that "the government may not require a person to give up a constitutional right . . . in exchange for a discretionary benefit conferred by the government where the property sought has little or no relationship to the benefit."[246] As Merriam and Lyman suggest, if the Court is willing to apply this doctrine to a takings claim, the jurisprudential question then becomes whether there are other sticks in the bundle of property rights, besides the right to exclude, that are "essential" enough to trigger the unconstitutional conditions doctrinal analysis.[247] If so, *Dolan* may apply to *Ehrlich* at a conceptual level, and "property rightists may continue their assault on land use law by invoking unconstitutional conditions to protect other sticks in the bundle of property rights."[248]

The California appeals court is unlikely to reverse itself, however, after rethinking the problem with *Dolan* in mind. Future decisions that consider the application of the unconstitutional conditions doctrine should resist the temptation to insert other constitutional rights into the doctrine, in place of the right to exclude, and thereby expand *Dolan* to situations where a title take has not occurred.

It may be a stretch, however, to assume that the courts will be so willing to apply this general doctrine when it was previously invoked only for First Amendment cases. It is more likely that *Dolan* will have less of an impact on the ability of a municipality to impose conditions than was predicted before the decision was handed down. It appears that there are numerous ways in which a *legislative* body can circumvent the limitations that *Dolan* applies to exactions. This relates to the dual issue of what category of take is applicable and what happens to the burden of proof. The shift of the burden of proof to the municipality that the Court imposed in *Dolan* is applied only when the condition is rendered administratively. Hence, the remedy the Court imposes may be avoided by simply using legislatively determined floating zones and PUDs, instead of conditional use permits.

Title Takings After *Dolan*

Dolan will have the greatest impact on those cities that do not plan. As has been suggested,[249] the City of Tigard now has two clear options to avoid a title taking: (1) deny the permit altogether, which the Court stated was clearly still an option, or (2) develop a "rough proportionality" between the dedication required of Florence Dolan's property and the burden imposed by the new hardware store. Similarly situated municipalities that choose the latter option will benefit from basic planning techniques.

The key to assuring the validity of exactions will now be in structuring each exaction to comport with the demands imposed by the alteration of the property in question. Always an alternative to the land dedication is the impact fee.[250] When the fee is properly calculated, the revenue collected can be used to purchase interests in land necessary to ameliorate the developer's new burdens, as well as construct facilities required to mitigate the new impacts. The additional costs of acquiring new property rights-of-way or easements can be included in a capital improvements plan for impact fees and thereby distribute the costs over all developments that contribute to the need. This is a solution that cities such as Tigard should contemplate for future growth management, including credits for developers actually dedicating and paying the impact fee.

Economic Takings

The third type of regulatory taking, an "economic" taking, occurs when governmental action interferes with the property owner's viable economic interest in the property. At one end of the economic taking scale is the situation where a landowner has been deprived of all permanent economic use or value of the property. This is a per se taking according to *Lucas v. South Carolina Coastal Council*:[251] "When the owner of real property has been called upon to sacrifice all economically beneficial uses in the name of a common good, that is, to leave his property economically idle, he has suffered a taking."[252]

Where the government has not deprived the owner of all use or value of the property, however, the courts have developed a two-tier inquiry to determine if a taking has occurred: (1) the purpose of the regulation must be a legitimate state interest and the means chosen must substantially advance the intended purpose, and (2) the court will determine if there is a reasonable beneficial use remaining for the property when viewed as a whole.[253]

The first inquiry concerns the legitimacy of the governmental action. Under "legitimacy analysis," the court examines two distinct questions: (1) whether the purpose of the regulatory action is a "legitimate state interest"; and (2) whether the means used to achieve the objective "substantially advances" the intended purpose.[254] If the regulatory action passes muster under legitimacy review, it is only then that the court must undertake the second inquiry into the economic impact of the regulation on the property owner.[255] Under "impact review," the court examines whether there is a reasonable beneficial use remaining for the property when taken as a whole.

The scope of legitimate state interest is extremely broad, and the governmental action is entitled to a *presumption* that it legitimately advances the public interest.[256] Local governmental police powers will be given the widest latitude under both substantive due process and equal protection tests, including broad land use regulatory approaches of slum clearance, growth management, and historic preservation.[257] Conversely, the role of the courts in reviewing exercises of police power is "an extremely narrow one."[258] In *Hawaii Housing Authority v. Midkiff*,[259] the U.S. Supreme Court held that the police power may extend to any *conceivable* public purpose, coterminous with the power of eminent domain. "[T]he Court has made clear that it will not substitute its judgment for a legislature's judgment as to what constitutes a public use 'unless the use be palpably without reasonable foundation.'"[260]

The second tier level of inquiry—economic impact—will be reached after the regulation passes muster under the legitimacy review. Under impact review, the court examines whether there is permanent beneficial value remaining for the property, when viewed as a whole.[261] As indicated, this level of review will be circumscribed unless the property owner has ripened the controversy by submitting a development application and by pursuing administrative remedies at the local level.[262]

Authority

Most decisions concerning impact fees are somewhat vague regarding the statutory authority for the fees.[263] One basis of authority is the home rule power for cities and counties that exists in some states.[264] Home rule or charter cities may enact impact fees pursuant to their charters.[265] Other possible sources of authority are planning statutes or subdivision control statutes.[266] State statutes authorizing local governments to provide public services and to set charges for public services also may be bases for impact fees.[267] Statutory cities may even possess the authority to enact fees under a state law authorizing local governments to enact all laws necessary to protect public health, safety, and welfare.[268] In California, cities may enact impact "taxes" under licensing taxing statutes.[269] The resulting confusion and strained reasoning to find statutory authority highlights the need for state legislatures to adopt specific impact fee authorization to clarify the fee's status as a tax or regulation and to prescribe procedural requirements for the adoption of fees.[270]

The basic question is whether the fee reflects the cost of expansion attributable to new development.[271] Some courts simply judge impact fees by the same "specifically and uniquely attributable" standard they apply to subdivision exactions.[272] These restrictive standards for validity, however, are not appropriate for evaluating schemes for financing communitywide improvements that will benefit all new development.[273] Recent decisions have judged impact fees by a "reasonableness" test. In *Dunedin*, for instance, the court recognized the difficulty of matching the "costs of expansion" and the timing of certain capital expenditures and held that "perfection is not the standard" of the city's duty to establish the nexus between the impact fee and reasonably anticipated costs of expansion.[274]

In Utah, the court has adopted a "reasonableness" test for impact fees:

> To comply with the standard of reasonableness, a municipal fee . . . must not require newly developed properties to bear more than their equitable share of the capital costs in relation to benefits conferred. . . . [A] municipality should determine the relative burdens previously borne and yet to be borne by those properties in comparison with other properties in the municipality as a whole; the fee in question should not exceed the amount sufficient to equalize the relative burdens of newly developed and other properties.[275]

In addition, the Utah Supreme Court has enumerated not less than eight factors to be used in determining whether the fee meets the test of reasonableness.[276] That court has also emphasized the need for "flexibility" to deal realistically with impact fees since they are "not susceptible [to] . . . exact measurement."[277]

Although the "criteria for validity is not mathematical precision, but reasonableness,"[278] if the fees are excessively above the costs of new facilities or services necessitated by new development, the fee will be seen as a revenue measure and an invalid tax. Perhaps one way to assure that fees for new facilities are reasonably related to needs created by the development is to set up benefit districts for those facilities that serve a limited geographical area.[279]

The methods used for the computation of impact fees vary widely. One of the simplest is the use of a fixed fee based on the land use and the size of the proposed development. Residential projects are assessed on a per unit basis[280] or according to the number of bedrooms,[281] while commercial developments pay according to floor area.[282] Other more complex formulas take into account factors such as the actual cost of the infrastructure required by the new development[283] and the available capacity of existing facilities.[284] Because of its flexibility, the formula approach has the advantage of more accurately reflecting the real costs of development. A distinct disadvantage, however, is the increasing complexity of such procedures, resulting in higher costs of administration and potential administrative problems.[285]

Municipalities need a certain amount of flexibility to deal realistically with impact fees.[286] The difficulty in calculating construction costs[287] mandates a system of fee calculation that can be adjusted for inflation and other unforeseen events. The Model Regulations provide for an adjustment in the level of fees in Section 6.17. Properties that have already paid the fee would not be subject to later adjustments, whether they be fee increases or decreases.

Additional flexibility has been provided by the Model Regulations to allow the local planning commission to accept other kinds of consideration in lieu of a fee. This provision allows a municipality a certain amount of latitude in the preapplication negotiation process. An example of how this could be used involves a developer who owns a parcel of prime land adjacent to a city hall or other public facility. Government acquisition of the parcel would be highly advantageous to the city. The city could negotiate for that piece of property in lieu of assessment of an impact fee against the new development. Of course, a court might be persuaded that conveyance of the land is unrelated to any demands created by new development.

In general, fees collected from developers must be earmarked and placed into a separate trust fund to ensure that the monies are expended only for those facilities necessitated by the new development. The *Dunedin* court, although approving of impact fees in principle,[288] invalidated the fees in that case because they were not sufficiently earmarked:

> [Imposition of an impact fee] is permissible where expansion is reasonably required, if use of the money collected is limited to meeting the costs of expansion. . . . If the ordinance in the present case had so restricted use of the fees which it required to be collected, there would be little question as to its validity.[289]

Other Florida decisions invalidating impact fees have turned, at least in part, on a lack of sufficient earmarking.[290] In upholding a sewer connection fee, an appellate court in Oregon stressed the importance of earmarking to ensure that the funds were not diverted to general public uses.[291] In California, however, such earmarking is not required since funds from impact "taxes" may be spent like general revenue except to the extent that revenues must be used for the purposes specified in the local ordinance.[292] The extent of separate earmarking required for each benefit district is unclear, but presumably, at a minimum, separate accounts should be set up for each type of fee (water, sewer, school) and for each benefit zone. Admittedly, this system may be too complex for many local governments to manage effectively.

The Model Regulations have addressed the issue of earmarking in Section 6.11 by requiring that separate capital facilities project accounts be established for specific public facilities projects fees collected, and that any funds not used within five years of collection be returned to the party designated at the time of payment. The funds revert to a general fund only in the event that their return is not possible.

There are two issues of timing that must be considered when drafting a valid impact fee ordinance. The first concerns the point in the development process at which the fee is imposed. Second, there should not be an unreasonably long period of time between payment of the fee and construction of the improvement.

When considering the first issue, it should be noted that most impact fees are imposed at the building permit stage.[293] In Utah, fees may be imposed as a condition of connection to municipal services and as a condition of final subdivision plat approval. In *Banberry Development Corp. v. South Jordan City*, the Utah Supreme Court reasoned that the imposition of water connection and park improvement fees at these points was reasonable because:

> [W]hen the subdivision is connected to the city's water and sewer systems, the city must be prepared to perform its services on demand, and from that fact the subdividers derive immediate benefit. The provision of standby capacity to a subdivision requires the commitment of substantial capital. The city does not have to wait until someone turns on a tap or flushes a toilet before it requires participation in the cost of providing its service.[294]

In California, however, it may be that the payment of fees or impact taxes cannot be a condition of final plat approval;[295] but instead, the fees or taxes may be collected at the time of issuance of a certificate of occupancy[296] or building permit.[297] Under the revenue-producing approach, the California courts have held that these are "reasonable time[s] for payment of . . . validly imposed license tax[es] and not an [improper] attempt to regulate [mere] steps in the conduct of the business."[298] There may be other factors in determining when to collect the impact fee. For instance, fees imposed at an early stage provide the city with capital in advance and allow a longer lead time when constructing facilities.[299]

On the other hand, fees collected at later stages, in addition to capturing revenue from pre-platted properties, provide a clearer determination of exact land use and building size.[300]

The second timing issue, the time period between the collection of fees and when the developer receives the benefit of some improvement, has not been extensively litigated. Courts have held that local governments may not require a developer to reserve land for future road construction, and it is arguable that fees should be imposed only for immediate service expansion.[301] With regard to facilities construction, a court would certainly impose a standard of reasonableness when determining how soon developers paying fees must receive the benefit of the new facility.[302] The Model has addressed the issue by requiring that the funds must be used for the designated capital improvement within five years of collection.

Impact fees have been challenged on the basis that they are discriminatory and violate equal protection because different types of developments are charged varying amounts of money and existing development is not charged at all. In jurisdictions where impact fees are upheld in principle, courts usually reject these arguments if the classification has any reasonable basis whatever. For instance, in *Associated Home Builders v. City of Newark*,[303] the home builders association argued that substantially higher charges for residential construction than for commercial and industrial facilities violated the guarantees of equal protection. The California court upheld the fees, noting that their use had not "reached the point of confiscation or prohibition."[304] A mere showing of "discrimination" is not sufficient "to overthrow the ordinance if the classification is reasonable."[305] In another California case, discriminatory rates charged to residential developers as opposed to contractors were upheld as reasonable.[306]

Most courts uphold impact fees only if the charges against new developments are limited to the portion of costs the development creates.[307] The Utah Supreme Court articulated the rule in somewhat different terms, sustaining impact fees so long as they do not "require newly developed properties to bear more than their equitable share of the capital costs in relation to *benefits conferred*."[308] In other jurisdictions, where the fee bears no relationship to the costs created, the ordinance violates equal protection in that it places "a disproportionate and unfair burden on new households."[309]

Impact fees may result in a situation comparable to double taxation. For example, if a developer is charged through impact fees for a park improvement that serves a new subdivision, it would be paying twice if it were forced to pay, through ad valorem taxation debt service on bonds, for those same parks.[310] Although impact fees are often challenged on the grounds that they result in double charging, courts usually avoid the issue since the charges are normally less than the proportionate system cost.[311] Nevertheless, one solution to this problem would be to compute the fee in such a way as to include a credit for that part of the ad valorem tax that represents the debt service on the bonds used to finance the facility for which the fee is charged.[312]

NOTES

1. "How to Solve the Nation's infrastructure Problem: Hearings Before the House Comm. on Public Works and Transp.," 99th Cong., 2nd Sess. (1984):

"In an era of competition for limited public resources, it had become expedient for public officials to delay, to eliminate expenditures for maintenance, and allocate these funds to other, more immediate needs. . . . With virtually every level of government facing either major revenue shortfalls or significant unmet needs, the temptation to further postpone addressing this situation is great. It is time to measure the need, to understand that investment in our capital stock must be a priority to help keep our economy competitive and sustain our quality of life, to support the efforts of state and local governments to mobilize and finance infrastructure programs and to define what the role of the federal government in this national effort should be."

See also, Fragile Foundations: A Report on America's Public Works, prepared for the Joint Economic Committee of the United States Congress (1988); U.S. Dep't of Transportation, *Moving America*, 5, 24 (Feb. 1990).

2. Bollinger, *What's Happening: Rebuilding America's Infrastructure Through the CDBG Program*, 10 CUR. MUN. PROBS. 20 (1983).

3. "Our Nation's Infrastructure: Hearings Before the Joint Economic Commission," 99th Cong., 1st Sess. 872 (1984) (report of the National Infrastructure Study):

The total national infrastructure gap between revenues and needs through the year 2000 is over $400 billion. It stems from many different kinds of problems in the various states and regions. . . . The single most dominant need across the country is for investment in highways and bridges. . . . The total highway network is aging. The needs facing state and local governments are growing, as evidenced by the fact that more than one-half of the nation's two million miles of paved roads require immediate attention and over one-third of the interstate highway system is in need of repair. As a result, the projected highway and bridge needs through the year 2000 approach $720 billion. Even though

federal and state gas tax levies have been increased in recent years, the projected shortfall is estimated at $265 billion.

Hard Choices, Summary Report of the National Infrastructure Study Prepared for the Joint Economic Committee of the United States Congress (Feb. 1984).

4. *Id.* at 872.

5. *Id.* at 872.

6. *Id.* at 874.

7. *See, e.g.*, Pleasant Ridge Ass'n v. Town of Burlington, 506 N.E.2d 1152, 1157 (Mass. 1987) (infrastructure problems are a "reasonable and consistent" justification for zoning decisions); Lampton v. Pinaire, 610 S.W.2d 915, 919 (Ky. Ct. App. 1980) ("most local governments barely have funds for necessary [infrastructure] maintenance purposes, much less for original construction purposes").

8. Nancy S. Rutledge, *Public Infrastructure As a National Concern*, 11 URB., STATE AND LOCAL L. NEWSL., No.1 (Fall 1987, American Bar Association). Ms. Rutledge, executive director of the National Council on Public Works Improvement, discusses the second report issued by the National Council. The National Council, established by Congress in late 1984 to provide an objective and comprehensive overview of the nation's infrastructure, was mandated to provide a series of reports to the President and Congress on such questions as the age and condition of public works, finance methods, maintenance needs, the capacity of public works to sustain the economy, and the criteria and procedures needed to properly assess the nation's public works at all levels of government. The council's first report was released in September 1986. It explored the definition of needs and provided a brief review of key issues. The second report was issued as a nine-volume set, each dealing with a major category of public works. In one of the major policy considerations of the Council's Final Report: How should public works be financed?, the Report recommended that new growth pay for the full cost of capital facilities the need for which it generates through the following policies and techniques: (1) increased reliance on the "beneficiary pays prin-

ciple" to finance public works at all levels of government; (2) promote developer financing of new infrastructure investments. *Id.* at 18. For a general discussion of local government budget problems, *see* Kenneth J. Drexler, *The Four Causes of the State and Local Budget Crisis and Proposed Solutions*, 26 URB. LAW. 563 (1994).

9. Professor Hagman argued that impact fees and required dedications do not add to the cost of housing. Rather, it is the landowner who pays. He postulated that:

Property sells based on what it can be used for, and if it is necessary to infrastructure that property in order for the developer to make usable, the infrastructure costs will capitalize into a lower value for the land. Note that as a developer, I don't care whether the infrastructure is in or is not in. I will either pay, say, $500,000 for land and incur $500,000 infrastructure costs, or $1,000,000 for otherwise identical infrastructured land.

Id. at 26. Basing his analysis on the law of supply and demand, he contended that these increased costs will not be added onto the price of housing since to do so would require a "substantial shift up the demand curve." *See also* Chapter 5, *supra*, regarding the effect of development fees on affordable housing costs; James, in *Evaluation of Local Impact Fees As a Source of Infrastructure Finance*, 11 MUN. FINANCE J. 407, 414 states: "Some experts argue that fees and exactions are generally shifted forward to the users or consumers off land developments: homebuyers, renters, or non-residential tenants. This conclusion appears to be largely based on anecdotes and hunches. In fact there can be no doubt that significant portions of the fees are shifted backwards to landowners (or in rare instances to developers) [citing S. Weitz 'Impact Fees: There Is No Free Lunch,' 50 PLANNING 12-14 (1988)]." *See also* Arthur C. Nelson, *Development Impact Fees: The Next Generation*, 26 URB. LAW. 541 (1994). *But see* SEIDEL, HOUSING COSTS AND GOVERNMENT REGULATIONS: CONFRONTING THE REGULATORY MAZE (Rutgers Univ. Center for Urban Policy Research, 1979).

10. Juergensmeyer & Blake, *Impact Fees: An Answer to Local Governments' Capital Funding Dilemma*, 9 FLA. ST. U. L. REV. 414 to 419 (1981); Connors & High, *The Expanding Circle of Exactions: From Dedication to Linkage*, 50 LAW & CONTEMP. PROBS. 69, 70 (1987). Exactions in general have also been justified based on the receipt of benefits. *See* Hagman, *Landowner-Developer Provision of Communal Goods Through Benefit-*

Based and Harm Avoidance 'Payments' (BHAPS), 5 ZONING & PLANNING L. REP. 17 (1982) (hereinafter Hagman I). *See also* Jacobsen & Redding, *Impact Taxes: Making Development Pay Its Way*, 55 N.C.L. REV. 407 (1977), where the authors reason that, absent such charges, the developer enjoys a windfall where the community at large finances development generated costs. This unearned increment theory is further discussed in WIND-FALLS FOR WIPEOUTS (D. Hagman & D. Misczynski eds. 1978). Other cases have justified exactions on the privilege theory (developer may be asked to provide for needs created based on the "privilege" of developing), though this theory has been somewhat discredited. *See* Shultz & Kelley, *Subdivision Improvement Requirements & Guarantees: A Primer*, 28 J. URB. & CONTEMP. L. 1, 31 (1985); D. HAGMAN, URBAN PLANNING & LAND DEVELOPMENT CONTROL LAW 136 (1975).

11. The shifting of costs for new facilities generated by new development to the development itself rather than to existing built-up areas is fully endorsed by the courts. J.W. Jones Cos. v. City of San Diego, 203 Cal. Rptr. 580 (Ct. App. 1984). "Developed property within the area of benefit is presently served with public facilities . . . consistent with general plan policies, undeveloped property is required to bear the burden of paying for public facilities the need for which is generated by their development. . . . There is no discriminatory classification." If the motive to shift costs from the general fund to new development is actually to exclude lower income or minorities from the community the result then might lead to a successful judicial challenge. In Heisey v. Elizabethtown Commonwealth Area School District, 445 A.2d 1344 (Pa. Commw. 1982) the court invalidated a one percent tax imposed by a school district on the privilege of obtaining a building permit in part because it "create[d] another obstacle against citizens moving into developable communities." *Id.* at 1347. Despite the lack of "conscious exclusionary" intent, the effect of the tax violated the state's "judicial policy against housing exclusion . . . strongly stated as a matter of substantive due process. . . . Thus . . . the result is the same as in communities where present residents might knowingly take steps to raise the gangplank of entry because they are already aboard." *Id.*

Other courts view attacks based on exclusionary effects as a matter of legislative, rather than judicial, concern. The court in Home Builders & Contractors Ass'n v. Board of County Comm'rs, 446 So.2d 140 (Fla. Ct. App. 1983) refused to adjudicate the "wisdom or fairness" of Palm Beach County's "Fairshare" ordinance for new road construction. In a footnote, the court commented on a $1,110 fee which West Palm Beach charged a couple for capital expansion of a sewer system:

It takes little imagination to realize that if this form of public finance flourishes, and if government continues to expand its functions and services as it has in the past, society will soon reach a point where "impact fees" for roads, parks, sewerage, and other forms of government services, will make it financially impossible to build any new homes at all, regardless of the fact that fees may be reasonably related to the costs of expansion. There is merit to the Plaintiffs' concern on this point, but it is a concern that goes to the wisdom or fairness of the ordinance and not to its legality.

See also New Jersey Builders Ass'n v. Bernards Township, 528 A.2d 555 (N.J. 1987):

The variety of governmental devices used to impose public facility costs on new development reflect a policy choice that higher taxes for existing residents are less desirable than higher development costs for builders, and higher acquisition costs for new residents. An obvious concern is that the disproportionate or excessive use of development exactions could discourage new development or inflate housing prices to an extent that excludes large segments of the population from the available market. *See generally* Nicholas, *Impact Exactions: Economic Theory, Practice, and Incidence,* LAW & CONTEMP. PROBS., Winter 1987 at 85 (arguing for more restricted use of developer exactions). *Id.* at 560.

In the seminal article in the field, Heyman & Gilhool, *The Constitutionality of Imposing Increased Community Costs on New Suburban Residents Through Subdivision Exactions,* 73 YALE L.J. 1119 (1964), the authors frankly admit that subdivision exactions and impact fees may add to the cost of housing, resulting in the exclusion of low income and non-white populations from suburban neighborhoods. They point out, however, that income level exclusion from suburbs has already occurred to some extent, and that "modest additional price increments are inconsequential." *See also* New Jersey Builders Ass'n v. Bernards Township, 528 A.2d 555 (N.J. 1987):

The variety of governmental devices used to impose public facility costs on new development reflect a policy choice that higher taxes for existing residents are less desirable than higher development costs for builders, and higher ac-

quisition costs for new residents. An obvious concern is that the disproportionate or excessive use of development exactions could discourage new development or inflate housing prices to an extent that excludes large segments of the population from the available market. *See generally* Nicholas, *Impact Exactions: Economic Theory, Practice, and Incidence,* LAW & CONTEMP. PROBS., Winter 1987 at 85 (arguing for more restricted use of developer exactions).

12. Bauman & Ethier, *Development Exactions and Impact Fees: A Survey of American Practices,* 50 LAW & CONTEMP. PROBS. 51-52 (1987). In FINANCING REGIONAL INFRASTRUCTURE, Robert A. Lamb of L.F. Rothschild, Inc. states: "At the local level, costs will have to be absorbed by a combination of user fees and user-oriented charges, along with indirect broad-based excise or sales tax." *Id.* at 20. Stating that there is already pressure on the property tax as the basis for raising revenues, Lamb expects to see a continuing process of utilizing nonproperty tax sources to secure the financing of basic projects. "[A]dditional creation of special revenue funds, developed by some combination of user fees, excise taxes and assessments is inevitable." *Id.* at 21. 11 URB., STATE AND LOCAL GOV'T NEWSL. 20-21 (Fall 1987, American Bar Association).

13. The National Council on Public Works Improvement discusses at length the basic goal "to make efficient use of existing facilities as a partial substitute for major expansions in capital funds." *Id.* fn. 8 at 18.

14. Currier, "Legal and Practical Problems Associated with Drafting Impact Fee Ordinances," 1986 Institute on Planning, Zoning, & Eminent Domain 273, 274.

15. *See, e.g.,* Cal. Const. art. XIIIA (West Supp. 1987). Proposition 13 set the property tax rate in the state at one percent of the property's value. For property acquired before the proposition took effect, the value is defined as the 1975-76 assessment. The tax cannot increase faster than two percent a year, under the proposition. For property bought after 1978, the value is essentially the purchase price. A homeowner in the case of Nordlinger v. Hahn, 112 S.Ct. 2326 (1992), Stephanie Nordlinger, found that her $1,700 annual tax bill was as much as five times higher than those for similar houses on her street. She presented evidence that her tax was the same as that paid by the owner of a $2.1 million house on the beach at Malibu. In upholding Proposition 13, the U.S. Supreme Court, by an 8-1 vote, found that the tax limitation was unfair but not palpably arbitrary under the U.S. Constitution. Other states have passed legislation limiting tax increases: MASS. GEN. LAWS ANN. ch. 5a App., § 1-5 and § 11-12 (West 1984); MICH. CONST. art. IX, § 25-26 (1983); MO. CONST. art. 10, § 18 and § 22 (1987); ORE. CONST. art. XI, § 11 (1985); TEX. CONST. art. 8, § 21 (Supp. 1987); art. VII, § 2 (Supp. 1987). *See generally* Freilich & Perry, *Effect on Growth, Housing and Development Mix*, in TAX AND EXPENDITURE LIMITATIONS: HOW TO IMPLEMENT AND LIVE WITH THEM (J. Rose ed. 1982); Hagman I, *supra* note 9, at 20.

16. Bacon, *Paying for Public Facilities After Proposition 13*, 8 CURRENT MUN. PROBS. 444, 454 (1982).

17. Rose, *Speculations on the Effect on Land Use in New Jersey*, in TAX AND EXPENDITURE LIMITATIONS: HOW TO IMPLEMENT AND LIVE WITH THEM 111, 115 (J. Rose ed. 1982).

18. Strauss, Mikels, & Hagman, *Effect of Propositions 13 and 4 on Land Use and Development*, in TAX AND EXPENDITURE LIMITATIONS: HOW TO IMPLEMENT AND LIVE WITH THEM 43, 44 (J. Rose ed. 1982).

19. Under CAL. CONST. art XIIIA, § 4 (West Supp. 1987), "special taxes" may be imposed by cities, counties, and special districts only upon approval by two-thirds of the electorate. For a discussion of these problems surrounding Proposition 13 in the context of special assessments, *see* Marc N. Melnick, *New Avenues for Special Assessment Financing*, 25 URB. LAW. 539, 545 (1993).

20. In Trent Meredith, Inc. v. City of Oxnard, 170 Cal. Rptr. 685 (Ct.App. 1981), the court rejected a broad definition of "special tax" under art. 13A, § 4 and held that fees imposed under CAL. GOV'T CODE § 65970 (West 1978) for school facilities were regulatory fees rather than special taxes. Even if the fees were taxes, they were not ad valorem taxes because they were "not imposed on the land in the subdivision as such but . . . on the privilege of subdividing land. . . ." 170 Cal. Rptr. at 689. In rejecting the "special tax" label for subdivision exactions, the court extended the analogy of special assessments. *See* J.W. Jones Cos. v. City of San Diego, 203 Cal. Rptr. (Cal. App. 1984); *see also* 62 Op. Cal. Att'y Gen. 712 (Nov. 1, 1979) (exaction imposed upon subdivider, requiring him to build improvements which would benefit subdivided land, was in the nature of a special assessment, not a "special tax"); Fresno v. Malmstrom, 156 Cal. Rptr. 777 (Cal.App. 1979) (special assessments imposed on specially benefitted property owners were not "special taxes" under art. XIIIA, §

4); Huntington Park Redevelopment Agency v. Martin, 695 P.2d 220 (Cal. 1985) (a tax increment financing system used by an urban redevelopment agency is not a special tax).

Where the nexus between the exaction and benefit is not as close, however, the exaction may require voter approval. *See* 62 Op. Cal. Att'y Gen. 673 (in-lieu fee is a "special tax" which requires voter approval when imposed as a condition for issuance of a building permit for the purpose of providing low and moderate housing). The *Trent* court, however, undercut the validity of this opinion by specifically rejecting its broad definition of special taxes. 170 Cal. Rptr. 688-89; *see also* Commercial Builders v. City of Sacramento, 941 F.2d 872 (9th Cir. 1991) (upholding "linkage" fees for low and moderate income housing as valid regulatory fees). *See also* Commercial Builders v. City of Sacramento, 941 F.2d 873 (9th Cir. 1991) (upholding linkage fees for low- and moderate-income housing as valid regulatory fees).

21. Contractors & Builders Ass'n v. City of Dunedin, 329 So.2d 314 (Fla. 1976), *cert. denied*, 444 U.S. 867 (1979). *See* Susan P. Schoettle & David G. Richardson, *Nontraditional Uses of the Utility Concept to Fund Public Facilities*, 25 URB. LAW. 519 (1993).

22. Home Builders & Contractors Ass'n v. Board of County Comm'rs, 446 So.2d 140 (Fla. Dist. Ct. App. 1983), *appeal dismissed*, 469 U.S. 976 (1984).

23. Trent Meredith, 170 Cal. Rptr. 685, *supra* at note 20.

24. Hollywood, Inc. v. Broward County, 431 So.2d 606 (Fla. Dist. Ct. App. 1983).

25. *See generally* J. JUERGENSMEYER & J. WADLEY, FLORIDA LAND USE RESTRICTION 17.02 (1976).

26. Bauman & Ethier, *supra* note 12, at 62. One survey, conducted by the authors in 1985, involved responses from 220 communities in 46 states, and indicated that 45.4 percent used impact fees. In a 1986 update of the survey, 21 percent of the respondent communities reported imposition of tougher exaction and impact fees, or that such action was under consideration. *Id.* at 63. A national telephone survey of 493 homebuilders conducted in 1986 by Builder Magazine indicated similar results. *Id.* at 63-64.

27. Westfield-Palos Verdes Co. v. City of Rancho Palos Verdes, 141 Cal. Rptr. 36 (Ct. App. 1977) (proceeds could be used "to provide open space, improve the quality of life and ecology of the city . . . to fight pollution and contamination of the air, water and land . . . develop, improve, and expand public parks, public services, police and fire protection, public utilities, water, and the treatment and disposal of sanitary sewage . ... [The] city may act ... to accomplish any of the foregoing purposes *for the benefit of the whole,* or any portion, of the City of Rancho Palos Verdes") (emphasis supplied). *See also* Associated Home Builders v. City of Newark, 95 Cal. Rptr. 648 (Ct. App. 1971); Jacobsen & Redding, *supra* note 10, at 408, 416-18. *But see* Town of Longboat Key v. Lands End, Ltd., 433 So.2d 574 (Fla. Dist. Ct. App. 1983) (impact fee invalid because there was no guarantee that the fees collected would be used to mitigate the impact they were collected to address); Lafferty v. Payson City, 642 P.2d 376 (Utah 1982) (impact fees deposited in city's general fund are an invalid tax).

28. *See* Reps & Smith, *Control of Urban Land Subdivision,* 14 SYRACUSE L. REV. 405, 409-10 (1963).

29. *See* Juergensmeyer & Blake, *supra* note 10, at 425; Hagman I, *supra* note 9, at 22.

30. Associated Home Builders v. City of Walnut Creek, 484 P.2d 606, (Cal.), *appeal dismissed,* 404 U.S. 878 (1971). *See also* Call v. City of West Jordan, 606 P.2d 217 (Utah 1979); Hollywood, Inc. v. Broward County, 431 So.2d 606 (Fla. Dist. Ct. App. 1983). *See generally* Heyman & Gilhool, *The Constitutionality of Imposing Increased Community Costs on New Suburban Residents Through Subdivision Exactions,* 73 YALE L. J. 1119, 1136-41 (1964), which refuted, point by point, the Reps & Smith position, *supra* note 28, at 409-410, that community facilities should be financed only through general revenues. Thus, *see* St. Johns County v. Northeast Florida Builders Assoc., Inc. 583 So.2d 635 (Fla. 1991) (countywide school impact fees are valid).

31. *See* Melnick, *supra* note 19; Joe Stevens, *The Ever-Expanding Use of Special Benefit Assessments,* 25 URB. LAW. 567 (1993). This ability may not, however, be exercised by two entities at once. *See* City of Boise v. Bench Sewer Dist., 773 P.2d 642 (Idaho 1989) (city not allowed to impose connection fee in area governed by sewer district board).

32. Theoretically, this is the basis for special assessments. Determining exact benefits is oftentimes difficult. In Weitz v. Davis, 424 P.2d 168 (Ariz. 1967), the court held that methods of allocation which attempt to proportion the assessment to the benefit conferred should not be struck down "merely because they fail to attain the unattainable." Assessments are generally apportioned according to a standardized sys-

tem which assesses the benefit conferred upon a number of alternative bases:

a. the number of lineal feet of the parcel fronting on the improvement;

b. the number of total square feet of the parcel;

c. the number of square feet in any improvement on the parcel which is benefitted by the improvement;

d. ad valorem; or

e. any other method which is designed to reasonably reflect the degree to which the land is benefitted by the improvement.

See J.W. Jones Cos. v. City of San Diego, 175 Cal. App. 3d 745, 203 Cal. Rptr. 580, 587 (1984) where the court upheld a Facility Benefit Assessment (FBA), akin to a special assessment, under which a lien was placed on undeveloped property within an area of benefit to vary in the future for public facilities to be installed in the future. The FBA was apportioned among the parcels according to the number of "net equivalent dwelling units" attributable to each parcel at its highest potential development under current zoning."

33. *See* 14 E. McQUILLIN, MUNICIPAL CORPORATIONS § 38.01 (1970 and Supp. 1987).

34. Morrison v. Morey, 48 S.W. 629 (Mo. 1898) (levee district special assessment as an exercise of the police power); E. McQuillin, *supra* note 33, at § 338.01, n. 18; County of Fresno v. Malmstrom, 156 Cal. Rptr. 777, 783 (Ct. App. 1979) ("a special assessment is charged to real property to pay for benefits that property has received from a local improvement and, strictly speaking, is not a tax at all").

35. *See, e.g.,* Soncoff v. City of Inkster, 177 N.W.2d 243 (Mich. App. 1970); City Council v. South, 194 Cal. Rptr. 110 (Ct.App. 1983). *See also* W. VALENTE, LOCAL GOVERNMENT LAW, CASES AND MATERIALS 611 (2d ed. 1980). However, if the special assessment is viewed as a police power measure, mere benefit rather than special benefits may be sufficient for validity. Berkvam v. Glendale, 255 N.W.2d 521 (Wis. 1977) (police power and taxation methods for special assessments allowed under statutory scheme; under the former, city need only show that properties assessed were "benefitted").

36. The assessment must be levied in proportion to the special benefit received by landowner. When a special district is formed to include property which is not and cannot be benefitted directly or indirectly there is an abuse of power and an act of confiscation.

Myles Salt Co. v. Board of Comm'rs of Iberia & St. Mary Drainage Dist., 239 U.S. 478, 36 S.Ct. 204 (1916); *see also* Village of Norwood v. Baker, 172 U.S. 269, 279 (1898) (a local government takes private property without just compensation when, through a special assessment on land, it compels a landowner to pay for a public improvement in an amount "in substantial excess of the special benefit accruing to him"); *but see* Furey v. City of Sacramento, 780 F.2d 1448 (9th Cir. 1986) (no taking under U.S. Constitution when *consenting* landowners initiated sewer assessment at their own expense and subsequent government action under police power restricts the landowners' ability to make use of the improvements).

37. E. McQuillin, *supra* note 33, at § 38.124. *See, e.g.,* Beaumont Investors v. Beaumont-Cherry Valley Water Dist., 211 Cal. Rptr. 567 (Ct.App. 1985).

38. Smith, *From Subdivision Improvement Requirements to Community Benefit Assessments and Linkage Payments: A Brief History of Land Development Exactions*, 50 LAW & CONTEMP. PROBS. 5, 6 (1987).

39. In J.W. Jones Co. v. City of San Diego, 157 Cal. App. 3d 745, 203 Cal. Rptr. 580 (1984), the Court of Appeals held that the FBA is not a tax. The FBA is a special assessment on property benefitted by the public facilities levied to pay for the cost of the facility. The special assessment is a compulsory charge to recoup those costs levied under the police power. The spread of the assessment based upon the use of undeveloped property as presently contemplated by the community plan and zoning is reasonable and implements the policies of the general plan. Exemption of developed property from the lien of an assessment does not deny the equal protection of the law. The ordinance was held to be a valid exercise of the police power of San Diego, a charter city.

40. Billings Properties v. Yellowstone County, 144 Mont. 25, 394 P.2d 182 (1964) (presumption of validity where express enabling act); Beaver Meadows v. Board of County Comm'rs, 709 P.2d 928 (Colo. 1985) (PUD approval can require developer to provide parks, roads, and drainage or payment in lieu); Wald Corp. v. Metropolitan Dade County, 338 So.2d 863 (Fla.App. 1976); Lampton v. Pinaire, 610 S.W.2d 915 (Ky. App. 1980); Associated Home Builders v. City of Walnut Creek, 484 P.2d 606 (Cal. 1971); *but see* Arrowhead Dev. Co. v. Livingston County Rd. Comm'n, 413 Mich. 505, 322 N.W.2d 702

(1982) (county road commission exceeded its statutory authority in conditioning plat approval upon developer's agreement to pay off-site county road improvement; and Admiral Dev. Corp. v. City of Maitland, 267 So.2d 860 (Fla. Dist. Ct. App. 1972) (no express authority for five percent parkland dedication). Regardless of which formula is used, there must be an express limit on the amount of land to be dedicated in relation to the site. Hargen v. Gleason , 359 P.2d 108 (Ore. 1961).

41. Nollan v. California Coastal Comm'n, 483 U.S. 825, 107 S.Ct. 3141, 97 L.Ed. 2d 677 (1987) (the key to the validity of the dedication is the rational nexus between the dedication and the need created by the landowner); Dolan v. City of Tigard, 114 S.Ct. 2309 (1994) (municipality must demonstrate "rough proportionality" between impact caused by land use development and exaction imposed as a condition of issuing building permit); Freilich and Morgan, *Municipal Strategies For Imposing Valid Development Exactions: Responding to Nollan*, 10 ZONING AND PLANNING L. REP. No. 11 at 170 (1987).

42. Dolan v. City of Tigard, 114 S.Ct. 2309 (1994), detailed *infra*, provides a review of state-imposed nexus tests and denominates the "reasonable relationship" test as that which is required of development dedications. Must be related to the needs of the subdivision. State ex rel. Noland v. St. Louis County, 478 S.W.2d 363 (Mo. 1971) (dedication to extend major street would almost eliminate subdivision when coupled with other dedication requirements and was invalid); Haugen v. Gleason, 226 Ore. 99, 359 P.2d 108 (1961); Schwing v. City of Baton Rouge, 249 So.2d 304 (La. Ct. App. 1971) (dedication of future right-of-way bearing no relationship to subdivision constituted unreasonable exercise of police power); and Simpson v. City of North Platte, 206 Neb. 240, 292 N.W.2d 292, 297 (1980) (dedication of future street where no present need constitutes an illegal "land banking" scheme). *See, infra*, page 15.

43. Specifically and Uniquely Attributable (most restrictive standard). This standard is very difficult to meet because the need for communitywide facilities by definition cannot be attributed to a single development project. This test has been applied in only three states: Illinois, New Jersey, and Rhode Island. Pioneer Trust and Sav. Bank v. Village of Mount Prospect, 22 Ill. 2d 375, 175 N.E.2d 799 (1961) (burden cast upon subdivider must be directly attributable to his activity) (no longer followed by

Illinois courts). The Illinois Supreme Court has affirmed the "specifically and uniquely attributable test" in school site cases for dedications and contribution of funds. Board of Educ. v. Surety Dev., Inc., 347 N.E.2d 149 (Ill. 1976) (the Illinois Supreme Court upheld the authority of a county board to require a developer to donate a parcel of land for use as school grounds, contribute $50,000 toward construction, and pay $200 for each home built). Krughoff v. City of Naperville, 369 N.E.2d 892 (Ill. 1977) (ordinance requiring dedication or money in lieu of land for school and park sites upheld; court carefully documented the increase in student and adult population and concluded that the requirements were "uniquely attributable to" and fairly proportioned to the need for a new school and park facility created by the proposed development; the New Jersey Supreme Court in New Jersey Builders Ass'n v. Bernards Township, 528 A.2d 555 (N.J. 1987) adopted a similar strict necessity statute purportedly to conform to an amendment of the subdivision statute.

44. Rational Nexus (moderate standard). This test, as applied, was adopted by Dolan v. City of Tigard, 114 S.Ct. 2309 (1994), but was labeled the "reasonable relationship" test by Justice Rehnquist. Adopted in New Hampshire, Land/Vest Properties, Inc. v. Town of Plainfield, 379 A.2d 200 (N.H. 1981); J.E.D. Associates, Inc. v. Town of Atkinson, 432 A.2d 12 (N.H. 1981); Wald Corp. v. Metropolitan Dade County, 338 So.2d 863 (Fla. App. 1976). Dual nexus requirement: (1) there must be proportionality between the need for new capital facilities generated by the development and the amount of the fees; (2) there must be a reasonable connection between the funds collected and the benefits accruing to the development. *See* Home Builders & Contractors Ass'n v. Board of County Comm'rs, 446 So.2d 140 (Fla. Dist. Ct. App. 1983), *cert. denied*, 451 So.2d 848, *appeal dismissed*, 409 U.S. 976 (1984).

45. Reasonable Relationship Test (liberal standard). Ayres v. City Council of Los Angeles, 34 Cal.2d 31, 207 P.2d 1 (1949) (upheld dedication requirement which contemplated future as well as immediate city needs); Associated Homebuilders v. Walnut Creek, 4 Cal.3d 633, 94 Cal. Rptr. 630, 484 P.2d 606 (1971) (exaction justified even though the public at large is benefitted as well as the residents of the subdivision); Lampton v. Pinaire, 610 S.W.2d 915 (Ky. App. 1980); Simpson v. City of North Platte, 292 N.W.2d 297 (Neb. 1980); Home Builders Assoc. v. Kansas City, 555 S.W.2d 832 (Mo. 1977).

46. Honey Springs Homeowners Ass'n v. Board of Supervisors, 157 Cal. App.3d 1122, 203 Cal. Rptr. 886 (1984) (developer's proposal of low-density, clustered developments accompanied by dedication of surrounding lands to open space and restricted by local growth management plans to preserve rural character of surrounding lands was a practical response to competing state interests of preserving open space and guaranteeing adequate housing for its residents through orderly development); City of Mobile v. Waldon, 429 So.2d 945 (Ala. 1983) (city's regulations requiring dedication of property for service roads or marginal access roads where such subdivision abuts a major street were well within powers granted to municipalities under statute); County Builders, Inc. v. Lower Providence Township, 5 Pa. Commw. 1, 287 A.2d 849 (1972) (in view of township requirement of dedication of a 50-foot-wide right-of-way, board of supervisors of township properly refused to approve subdivision application prior to receipt of adequate assurance of such a dedication in form of a deed or a formal offer of dedication); Town of Seabrook v. Tra-Sea Corp., 119 N.H. 937, 410 A.2d 240 (1979) (a planning board may condition its subdivision approval upon dedication of a road providing access to individual lots within a proposed subdivision); Unlimited v. Kitsap County, 750 P.2d 651 (Wash. Ct. App. 1988) (dedication of strip of property across plaintiff's land was not reasonably related to public purpose and resulted in unconstitutional taking); Batch v. Town of Chapel Hill, 376 S.E.2d 22 (N.C. Ct. App. 1989) (required dedication for water and sewer lines resulted in denial of due process and taking; additionally, town lacked regulatory power given that North Carolina adheres to Dillon's Rule); Board of Supervisors v. Rowe, 216 Va. 128, 216 S.E.2d 199 (1975) (dedication of road right-of-way as precondition to subdivision approval constitutes a taking); East Neck Estates, Ltd v. Luchsinger, 61 Misc. 2d 619, 305 N.Y.S.2d 922 (N.Y. Sup. 1969) (where subdivider paid $208,000 for tract, and where dedication of shore frontage as park would decrease value of tract by over $90,000, requirement that such frontage be so dedicated would be confiscatory); *but see*, Bayswater Realty and Capital Corp. v. Town of Lewisboro, 560 N.Y.S.2d 623 (1990) (a planning board may impose a recreation fee only if (1) it determines that the town needs additional recreational space because of the new development; and (2) a fee is necessary because the plat does not contain sufficient suitable area to meet the need).

47. Frank Ansuini, Inc. v. City of Cranston, 107 R.I. 63, 264 A.2d 910 (1970) (upheld the constitutionality of dedication provisions but ruled that a seven percent fixed percentage requirement, regardless of density, was fatally arbitrary); Haugen v. Gleason, 236 Ore. 99, 359 P.2d 108 (1961) (no express limit on amount of land or money which could be demanded resulted in holding that ordinance is illegal general tax rather than valid police power regulation); *see also* Dolbeare, *Mandatory Dedication of Public Sites in Virginia*, 9 U. Rich. L.Rev. 435, 459 (1975) (suggesting sliding scale).

48. *See* City of College Station v. Turtle Rock Corp., 680 S.W.2d 802 (Tex. 1984) (an ordinance requiring park land dedication or money in lieu thereof as a condition of subdivision plat approval was not unconstitutionally arbitrary or unreasonable on its face. The court distinguished prior Texas decisions finding that similar park land dedication ordinances constituted an unconstitutional taking of private property without just compensation). The College Station ordinance was distinguishable because the property owner, rather than the regulator, made the dedication versus monetary payment election, required that the land or money be used for a neighborhood park, required that the park be located near the subdivision generating the need, and placed limits on the time during which the funds could be expended. The court emphasized that both need and benefit must be considered in determining the validity of such an ordinance. *See also* Jenad, Inc. v. Village of Scarsdale, 218 N.E.2d 673 (N.Y. 1966); Trent Meredith, Inc. v. City of Oxnard, 170 Cal. Rptr. 685 (Ct. App. 1981); Call v. City of West Jordan, 606 P.2d 217 (Utah 1979); Weingarten v. Town of Lewisboro 542 N.Y.S.2d 1012, *aff'd* 559 N.Y.S.2d 807 (App. Div. 1990); *see* Brooks, *Mandatory Dedication or Fees in Lieu of Land for Parks and Schools*, Planning Advisory Service Report No. 266 (Feb. 1971).

49. Call v. City of West Jordan, 606 P.2d 217 (Utah 1979) (ordinance requiring subdividers to dedicate 7 percent of the land or the equivalent value in cash for parks was within the general police power delegation of the State and Municipal Planning Enabling Act); Hirsch v. City of Mountain View, 64 Cal. App. 3d 425, 134 Cal. Rptr. 519 (1976) (prior statute authorizing city by ordinance to require payment of fees for park or recreational purposes as condition to approval of final subdivision map, but limiting "subdivision" to division of land into five or more parcels, did not preempt field of control of land development and did not preclude charter city from imposing park or recreation fee as condition for approval of map creating less than five parcels). *See also*, Codding Enters. v. City of Merced, 42 Cal. App. 3d 375, 116 Cal. Rptr. 730 (1974); Collis v. City of Bloomington, 310 Minn. 5, 246 N.W.2d 19 (1976) (dedication of 10 percent of subdivision property for parks and playgrounds or contribution of equivalent amount in cash, was within scope of enabling legislation, and was not, on its face, a taking of property without just compensation); Kessler v. Town of Shelter Island Planning Bd., 40 App. Div. 2d 10-05, 338 N.Y.S.2d 778 (1972) (a town planning board may require as a condition of approval a payment to the town of an amount set by town board which shall be available for use by town for neighborhood park, playground, or recreation purposes); *but see*, Enchanting Homes, Inc. v. Rapanos, 4 Mich.App. 109, 143 N.W.2d 618 (1966) (no statutory authority to require money in lieu of land); City of Montgomery v. Crossroads Land Co., 355 So.2d 363 (Ala. 1978) (without specific legislative authority, city had no power to require money in lieu of land for public parks; state enabling statutes for "open spaces" insufficient).

50. As used in statute authorizing dedication of areas for parks or schools in subdivision plats, or "in lieu" thereof payment of sum of money, phrase "in lieu" meant "instead of" or "in the place of." The statute therefore did not permit counties to require combination of land and money. Cimarron Corp. v. Board of County Comm'rs, 563 P.2d 946 (Colo. 1977).

51. Morgan & Leitner, *Financing Public Facilities With Development Excise Taxes: An Alternative to Exactions and Impact Fees*, 11 Zoning & Planning L. Rep. 17-22 (March 1988).

52. Eastern Diversified Properties v. Montgomery County, 570 A.2d 850 (Md. St. App. 1990); American National Building & Loan Ass'n v. City of Baltimore, 224 A.2d 883 (Md. 1966).

53. Westfield-Palos Verdes Co. v. City of Rancho Palos Verdes, 73 Cal. App. 2d 678 (Ct. App. 1977).

54. *See* Cherry Hill Farm v. City of Cherry Hills, 670 P.2d 779 (Colo. 1983); Bloom v. City of Fort Collins, 784 P.2d 304 (Colo. 1990) (differentiating taxes, exactions, and utility charges).

55. Associated Homebuilders, Inc. v. City of Newark, 95 Cal. Rptr. 648 (Cal. 1971).

56. City of Mesa v. Homebuilders Association of Central Arizona, Inc., 523 P.2d 57 (Ariz. 1974).

57. Bloom v. City of Fort Collins, 784 P.2d 304 (Colo. 1994).

58. Morgan & Leitner, *supra* note 51, at 17-22.

59. Robert Freilich & Stephen Chinn, *Finetuning the Takings Equation: Applying It to Development Exactions, Parts I & II,* 40 LAND USE L. & ZONING DIG. Nos. 2 and 3 (1988); one commentator noted that "[I]n lieu payments are currently being assimilated into the impact fee concept. Both are fees used to fund schools, parks and other facilities located outside the subdivision." Juergensmeyer & Blake, *supra* note 8, at 418 n. 19. *See also* Currier, *supra* note 11, at 274.

60. J. Juergensmeyer and J. Wadley, *supra* note 23, at 17.01; D. Callies & R. Freilich, *Financing of Capital Facilities Generated by New Development,* in CASES AND MATERIALS ON LAND USE 181 (West 1994).

61. "The exaction system has grown up under a practice involving a highly elastic ruler; the process is often quite informal and open to negotiation. Some developers may consider this flexibility as tantamount to extortion." Jacobsen & Redding, *supra* note 8, at 411.

62. *Id.* One author states that the cost of impact fees imposed late in the development process is more likely to be passed on to the buyer. Nicholas, *Impact Exactions: Economic Theory, Practice, and Incidence,* 50 LAW & CONTEMP. PROB. 85, 97 (1987). *See* City of Key West v. R.L.J.S. Corp., 537 So.2d 641 (Fla. App. 1989) (authorized collection of impact fees at the certificate of occupancy stage and overruled claim of vested right arising upon issuance of building permit without requiring fees).

63. *See, e.g.,* Fontana Unified School Dist. v. City of Rialto, 219 Cal. Rptr. 254 (Ct. App. 1985) (fees imposed for school facilities as a condition of building permit issuance were held to be valid, although the plat was approved more than four years prior to enactment of the ordinance authorizing the fees); Key West v. R.J.L.S. Corp., 537 So.2d 641 (Fla. Dist. Ct. App. 1989); Fairmont Township v. Beardmore, 431 N.W.2d 292 (N.D. 1989) (solid waste water fee imposed even though ordinance establishing fee was adopted after permit application but prior to issuance; *but see,* Coppell v. General Homes, 763 S.W.2d 448 (Tex. Ct. App. 1988) (retroactive application of fees not allowed in absence of specific enabling authority).

64. *See generally* Juergensmeyer & Blake, *supra* note 8, at 420, 434-38; Schnidman & Baker, *Planning for Platted Lands: Land Use Remedies for Lot Sale Subdivisions,* 11 FLA. ST. U. L.REV. 505 (1983). One commentator has advocated the collection of development fees for off-site improvements later in the development process, in order to minimize the burden placed on the developer. Nicholas, *supra* note 41, at 97.

65. *See generally Symposium: The Local Government Capital Improvements Financing Game: Who Plays, Who Pays, and Who Stays,* 25 URB. LAW. 479 (1993); Juergensmeyer & Blake, *supra* note 10, at 420. *See also* James, *Evaluation of Impact Fees as a Source of Infrastructure Finance,* 11 MUN. FIN. J. 407 (1990).

66. Contractors & Builders Ass'n v. City of Dunedin, 329 So.2d 314 (Fla. 1976), *cert. denied,* 444 U.S. 867 (1979) (city need show only a rational nexus between the fee charged and the need created by the new subdivision); Russ Bldg. Partnership v. San Francisco, 737 P.2d 359 (Cal. 1987) (reasonable relationship). Some courts inexplicably provide greater flexibility for money in lieu of land. Call v. City of West Jordan, 606 P.2d 219 (Utah 1979).

67. Juergensmeyer & Blake, *supra* note 8, at 420; D. Callies & R. Freilich, *supra* note 39. *See* CAL. GOV'T CODE § 66477 (West Supp. 1987) (statute authorizing money in lieu of land or mandatory dedication as a condition to approval of a subdivision map specifically excluded condominium projects until amended in 1984).

68. *See, e.g.,* Westfield-Palos Verdes Co. v. City of Rancho Palos Verdes, 141 Cal. Rptr. 36 (Ct. App. 1977) ($500 per bedroom with a maximum of $1,000 per new dwelling unit).

69. Martin L. Leitner & Susan P. Schoettle, *A Survey of State Impact Fee Enabling Legislation,* 25 URB. LAW. 491 (1993); *see also* T. Morgan, J. Duncan & B. McClendon, *Drafting Impact Fee Ordinance Part 1: A Legal Foundation,* PAS MEMO (Oct. 1986). *See* M. Leitner & E. Strauss, *Elements of a Municipal Impact Fee Ordinance, with Commentary,* 54 J. AM. PLANNING A. 225, 227 (Spring 1988).

70. T. Morgan, E. Strauss, & M. Leitner, *State Impact Fee Legislation,* 40 LAND USE L. 3 (Jan. 1988).

71. *Id.;* T. Morgan, J. Duncan & B. McClendon, *supra* note 69.

72. Even if the exaction or impact fee is primarily regulatory it may not be able to withstand the tests for reasonable relationship or special benefit if the revenues are utilized throughout the city. Town of Longboat Key v.

Lands End, Ltd., 433 So.2d 574 (Fla. Ct. App. 1983); Santa Clara County Contractors & Homebuilders Ass'n v. City of Santa Clara, 232 Cal. App. 2d 564, 43 Cal. Rptr. 86 (1965).

73. Home Builders and Contractors Ass'n of Palm Beach County, Inc. v. Board of County Comm'rs of Palm Beach County, 446 So.2d 140 (Fla. App. 1983); Hillis Homes, Inc. v. Snohomish County, 650 P.2d 193 (Wash. 1982).

74. Banberry Dev. Corp. v. South Jordon City, 631 P.2d 899 (Utah 1981).

75. Coulter v. City of Rawlings, 662 P.2d 888 (Wyo. 1983); Hollywood, Inc. v. Broward County, 431 So.2d 606 (Fla. Dist. Ct. App. 1983).

76. S & P Enters., Inc. v. City of Memphis, 672 S.W.2d 213 (Tenn App. 1983) (taxes are distinguished from fees by the objectives for which they are imposed. If imposition is primarily for the purpose of raising revenue it is a tax—but if for the purpose of regulating some activity under the police power of the government it is a regulatory fee); Teeter v. Clark County, 704 P.2d 1171 (Wash. 1985).

77. Southwick, Inc. v. City of Lacy, 795 P.2d 712 (Wash. App. 1990), but not when its major purpose is to shift costs from the public to the development, San Telmo Assoc. v. City of Seattle, 735 P.2d 673 (Wash. 1987).

78. Merrelli v. City of St. Clair Shoes, 96 N.W.2d 14 (Mich. 1959).

79. Albany Area Builders Ass'n v. Town of Guilderland, 546 N.E.2d 920 (N.Y. 1989), *aff'd*, 534 N.Y.S.2d 791 (1988). New Jersey Builders Ass'n v. Mayor and Township Committee of Bernards Township, 528 A.2d 555 (N.J. 1987); Middlesex Boston St. Railway v. Board of Alderman, 359 N.E.2d 1279 (Mass. 1977); Coronado Dev. Co. v. City of McPherson, 368 P.2d 51 (Kan. 1962) (pre-home rule statute); Aunt Hack Estates, Inc. v. Planning Comm'n of Danbury, 273 A.2d 880 (Conn. 1970).

80. Banberry Dev. Corp. v. South Jordan City, 631 P.2d 899, 903 (Utah 1981). *See also*, Contractors & Builders Ass'n v. City of Dunedin, 329 So.2d 314 (Fla. 1976) *cert. denied*, 444 U.S. 867 (1979). In *Dunedin*, the court recognized the difficulty of matching the "costs of expansion" and timing certain capital expenditures and held that "perfection is not the standard" of the city's duty to establish the nexus between the impact fee and reasonably anticipated costs of development. 329 So.2d at 320. Citing *Dunedin*, the Washington Supreme Court stated that the fact that the connection charge necessarily imposes some burden on new customers does not make it an invalid

tax. Hillis Homes v. Public Util. Dist. No. 1, 105 Wash. 2d 288, 714 P.2d 1163 (1986).

81. *See, e.g.,* Coulter v. City of Rawlins, 662 P.2d 888 (Wyo. 1983); and Hollywood, Inc. v. Broward County, 431 So.2d 606 (Fla. Dist. Ct. App. 1983). *See also* Home Builders and Contractors Ass'n of Palm Beach County v. Board of County Comm'rs, 446 So.2d 140 (Fla. Dist. Ct. App. 1983) and Contractors and Builders' Ass'n v. City of Dunedin, 329 So.2d 314 (Fla. 1976), *cert. denied* 444 U.S. 867 (1979).

82. Divan Builders, Inc. v. Planning Bd., 66 N.J. 582, 334 A.2d 30 (1975).

83. *See, e.g.,* Senate Bill 336, 1987 Texas Session Laws, Ch. 956, p. 6519; Ariz. Rev. Stat. § 9.463.05; Cal. Gov't Code 66477, §§ 65970, 66483, 66484, and 66484.5; N.J. Stat. Ann. § 40:55 D-42; state constitutions; Amherst Builders v. City of Amherst, 61 Ohio St. 2d 345, 402 N.E.2d 1181 (1980) and home rule authority, Associated Home Builders, Inc. v. City of Walnut Creek, 4 Cal. 3d 633, 484 Cal. Rptr. 580 (1984).

84. *See* Banberry Dev. Corp. v. South Jordan City, 631 P.2d 899 (Utah 1981); Call v. City of West Jordan, 606 P.2d 217 (Utah 1979); Home Builders Ass'n v. Provo City, 28 Utah 2d 402, 503 P.2d 451, 452 (1972). *But see* City of Miami Beach v. Jacobs, 315 So.2d 227 (Fla. App. 1975) ("fire line charges" bore no relation to use).

85. *See* City of Mesa v. Home Building Association, 111 Ariz. 29, 523 P.2d 57 (1974) (Mesa's charter implies power to enact residential development tax).

86. Leitner & Schoettle, *supra* note 69, at 493. *See also, e.g.,* Tex. Loc. Gov't Code § 395.074 (Vernon 1990); Vt. Stat. Ann. tit. 24, § 5200 (1991 Supp.); Ariz. Rev. Stat. Ann. § 9-463.05 (1989); Ore. Rev. Stat. § 223.313 (1989); Me. Rev. Stat. Ann. ch. 104, § 4345 (1989); Ga. Code Ann. § 36-17-12 (1990); Cal. Gov't Code § 66000 (1990); N.J. Stat. Ann. § 40:55D-42 (1990); Va. Code Ann. § 15.1-498.1 (1990); Wash. Rev. Code § 39.92.900 (1989); Cal. Gov't Code § 66000 (West 1992); Ill. Rev. Stat. ch. 121, para. 5-91 (1991); Ind. Stat. Ann. § 36-7-4-1300 (Supp. 1991); Pa. Stat. Ann. tit. 53, § 10501-A (Supp. 1991); Nev. Rev. Stat. § 278B.010 (1991); W.Va. Code Ann. § 7-20-1 (Supp. 1991).

87. The home rule states that have enacted statutes limiting the home rule authority are: California: Cal. Gov't Code § 66000, *et seq.* (West Cum. Supp. 1992); Illinois: Ill. Ann. Stat. Ch. 121, para. 5-901, *et seq.* (West Cum. Supp. 1991); and Maine: Me. Rev. Stat. Ann. tit. 30, § 4301, *et seq.* (West Cum. Supp. 1991).

88. The non-home rule states that have granted limited authority to the local government to impose impact fees are: Arizona: ARIZ. REV. STAT. ANN. § 9-463.05 (West 1990) (deals with city authority) and ARIZ. REV. STAT. ANN. § 1102(A) (West Cum. Supp. 1991) (deals with county authority); Georgia: GA. CODE ANN. § 36-71-1 *et seq.* (Michie 1992); Indiana: IND. CODE. ANN. § 36-7-4-1300 *et seq.* (Burns Cum. Supp. 1991); Nevada: NEV. REV. STAT. § 278B.010 *et seq.* (1991); New Jersey: N.J. STAT. ANN. § 40:55D-42 (West Cum. Supp. 1991); Oregon: ORE. REV. STAT. § 223.297 (1991); Pennsylvania: PA. STAT. ANN. tit. 53, § 10501-A *et seq.* (Cum. Supp. 1991); Texas: TEX. LOC. GOV'T CODE ANN. § 394.032 *et seq.* (1993); Vermont: VT. STAT. ANN. tit. 24, § 5200 *et seq.* (1992); Virginia: VA. CODE ANN. § 15.1-498.2 (Michie 1989); Washington: WASH. REV. CODE ANN. § 82.02.050 *et seq.*, § 39.92.010 *et seq.*, § 36.73.120 *et seq.* (1990); West Virginia: W.VA. CODE § 7-20-1 *et seq.* (Cum. Supp. 1991).

89. *See* ILL. ANN. STAT. ch. 121, para. 5-906(1) (West Cum. Supp. 1991); PA. STAT. ANN. tit. 53, § 10502-A (Cum. Supp. 1991); VA. CODE ANN. § 15.1-498.2 (Michie 1989).

90. *See* CAL. GOV'T CODE § 66.02(c)(8) (West Cum. Supp. 1992); VT. STAT. ANN. tit. 24, § 5201(2) (1990).

91. Arizona: ARIZ. REV. STAT. § 11-1104(14) (West 1990) (deals with county authority); Indiana: IND. CODE ANN. § 36-7-4-1308 (Burns Cum. Supp. 1991); Georgia: GA. CODE ANN. § 36-71-2(16) (Michie 1992); Oregon: ORE. REV. STAT. § 223.299 (1991); Maine: ME. REV. STAT. ANN. tit. 30 § 4354(1)(A); Nevada: NEV. REV. STAT. § 786B.020(1)-(5) (1991); New Jersey: N.J. STAT. ANN. § 40:55D-42 (West Cum. Supp. 1991); Texas: TEX. LOC. GOV'T CODE ANN. § 395.001 (1993); West Virginia: W.VA. CODE § 7-20-3(a) (Cum Supp. 1991).

92. These states include: Arizona: ARIZ. REV. STAT. § 11-1104(14) (West 1990) (dealing with county authority); Georgia: GA. CODE ANN. § 36-71-2(16) (Michie 1992); Indiana: IND. CODE ANN. § 36-7-4-1308 (Burns Cum. Supp. 1991); Oregon: ORE. REV. STAT. § 223.299 (1991); Nevada: NEV. REV. STAT. § 786B-020(1)-(5) (1991); New Jersey: N.J. STAT. ANN. § 40:55D-42 (West Cum. Supp. 1991); Texas: TEX. LOC. GOV'T CODE ANN. § 395.001 (1993); West Virginia: W.VA. CODE § 7-20-3(a) (Cum Supp. 1991).

93. These states include: Arizona: ARIZ. REV. STAT. § 11-1104(14) (West 1990) (dealing with county authority); Georgia: GA. CODE ANN. § 36-71-2(16) (Michie 1992); Indiana: IND. CODE ANN.

§ 36-7-4-1308 (Burns Cum. Supp. 1991); Oregon: ORE. REV. STAT. § 223.299 (1991); Maine: ME. REV. STAT. ANN. tit. 30 § 4354(1)(A) (West Cum. Supp. 1991); Washington: WASH. REV. CODE ANN. §§ 88.03.120 (1990); West Virginia: W.VA. CODE § 7-20-3(a) (Cum. Supp. 1991).

94. These states include: Georgia: GA. CODE ANN. § 36-71-2(16) (Michie 1992); Maine: ME. REV. STAT. ANN. tit. 30 § 4354(1)(A) (West Cum. Supp. 1991); Washington: WASH. REV. CODE ANN. § 82.03.120 (1990); West Virginia: W.VA. CODE § 7-20-3(a) (Cum Supp. 1991).

95. These states include: Georgia: GA. CODE ANN. § 36-71-2(16) (Michie 1992); Washington: WASH. REV. CODE ANN. § 82.03.120 (1990); West Virginia: W.VA. CODE § 7-20-3(a) (Cum Supp. 1991).

96. *See* W.VA. CODE § 7-2-3(a) (Cum. Supp. 1991).

97. *See* GA. CODE ANN. § 36-71-2(16) (Michie 1992).

98. *See* ILL. ANN. STAT. ch. 121, para. 5-904 (West Cum. Supp. 1991); *see also* NEV. REV. STAT. 278B.160(1) (1991) (providing that the "need for capital improvement must be necessitated by and attributable to the new development"); PA. STAT. ANN. tit. 53, § 10502-A (Cum. Supp. 1991) (providing that capital improvements must be "necessitated by and attributable to the new development"); TEX. LOC. GOV'T CODE ANN. § 395.001(4) (1993) (requiring that the capital improvements be "necessitated by and attributable to" the new development).

99. *See* ARIZ. REV. STAT. § 9-463.05(B)(4) (West 1990) (statute granting authority to cities); ARIZ. REV. STAT. § 11-1105(B)(1) (West 1990) (statute granting authority to counties); CAL. GOV'T CODE § 66.000(6) (West Cum. Supp. 1992); ME. REV. STAT. ANN. tit. 30, § 4354(2)(A) (West Cum. Supp. 1991).

100. *See* GA. CODE ANN. § 36-71-1(b)(1) (Michie 1992); N.J. STAT. ANN. § 40.55D-42 (West Cum. Supp. 1991) (only a "pro rata share" of the costs must be borne by developers); ORE. REV. STAT. § 223.304(1) (1991) (measures the fee by an equitable share standard); VT. STAT. ANN. tit. 24, § 5201(3) (1990) ("any portion of project costs that will benefit or are attributable to" is the pertinent language); WASH. REV. CODE ANN. § 82.02.050 (1990); W.VA. CODE § 7-20-4 (Cum. Supp. 1991).

101. *See* ARIZ. REV. STAT. § 9-463.05(c) (West 1990) (statute authorizing cities); ILL. ANN. STAT. Ch. 121, para. 5-918(b) (Cum. Supp. 1991); IND. CODE ANN. § 36-7-4-1317(d) (Burns Cum. Supp. 1991); VA. CODE ANN. § 15.1-491.6 (Michie 1989); TEX. LOC. GOV'T CODE ANN. § 395.016 (1993).

102. *See* GA. CODE ANN. § 36-71-4(6) (Michie 1992); ILL. ANN. STAT. ch. 121, para. 5-903 (West Cum. Supp. 1991; IND. CODE ANN. § 36-7-4-1315 (Burns Sum Supp. 1991); NEV. REV. STAT. § 278B.100 (1991); PA. STAT. ANN. tit. 53, § 10504-A(b) (Cum. Supp. 1991); TEX. LOC. GOV'T CODE ANN. § 395.001 (1993); VA. CODE ANN. § 15.1-491.3(1) (Michie 1989); WASH. REV. CODE ANN. § 82.02.060(6) (1990); W.VA. CODE § 7-20-8(a) (Cum. Supp. 1991).

103. *See* Contractors & Building Ass'n v. City of Dunedin, *supra*; Broward County v. Janis Dev. Corp., 311 So.2d 371 (Fla. Dist. Ct. App. 1975).

104. *See* Hayes v. City of Albany, 7 Ore. App. 277, 490 P.2d 1018 (1971).

105. *See* ARIZ. REV. STAT. ANN. § 9.463.05(c) (West 1990) (city authorization statute); ARIZ. REV. STAT. § 11-1105(A)(3)(d)-(e) (West 1990) (county authorization statute); CAL. GOV'T CODE § 66006(a)-(d) (West Cum. Supp. 1992); GA. CODE ANN. § 36-71-8 (Michie 1992); ILL. ANN. STAT. ch. 121 para. 5-913 (West Cum. Supp. 1991); IND. CODE ANN. § 36-7-4-1329 (Burns Cum. Supp. 1991); ME. REV. STAT. ANN. tit. 30, § 4354(2)(B)-(C) (West Cum. Supp. 1991); NEV. REV. STAT. § 278B.210(2)-(4) (1991); ORE. REV. STAT. § 223.307 (1991); PA. STAT. ANN. tit. 53, § 10505-A(d) (Cum. Supp. 1991); TEX. LOC. GOV'T CODE ANN. § 395.024 (1993); VT. STAT. ANN. tit. 24, § 5203(e) (1990); VA. CODE ANN. § 15.1-498.9 (Michie 1989); WASH. REV. CODE ANN. § 83.02.070 (1990); W.VA. CODE § 7-20-6(a)(2) (Cum. Supp. 1991).

106. *See,* e.g., ILL. ANN. STAT. ch. 121, para. 5-913 (West Cum. Supp. 1991).

107. *See, e.g.,* CAL. GOV'T CODE 6606(a)-(d) (West Cum. Supp. 1992).

108. *See* WASH. REV. CODE ANN. § 82.02.070 (1990).

109. *See* CAL. GOV'T CODE § 6607(a) (West Cum. Supp. 1992); GA. CODE ANN. § 36-71-4(d) (Michie 1992); ILL. ANN. STAT. ch. 121, para. 5-911 (West Cum. Supp. 1991); NEV. REV. STAT. § 278B.230(3) (1991); ORE. REV. STAT. § 223.299(4)(a) (1991); PA. STAT. ANN. tit. 53 § 10505-A(c) (Cum. Supp. 1991); TEX. LOC. GOV'T CODE § 395.016 (1993); *cf.* VA. CODE ANN. § 15.1-498.6 (Michie 1989); VT. STAT. ANN. tit. 24, § 5204(b) (1990) (phasing does not require time for imposition specifically but allows imposition at time of building permit or certification of occupancy).

110. *See* CAL. GOV'T CODE § 6607(a) (West Cum. Supp. 1992); GA. CODE ANN. § 36-71-4(d) (Michie 1992); ILL. ANN. STAT. ch. 121, para. 5-911 (West Cum. Supp. 1991); IND. CODE ANN. § 36-7-

4-1322 (Burns Cum. Supp. 1991); NEV. REV. STAT. § 278B.230(3) (1991); ORE. REV. STAT. § 223.299(4)(a) (1991); PA. STAT. ANN. tit. 53, § 10505-A(c) (Cum. Supp. 1991); TEX. LOCAL GOV'T CODE § 395.016 (1993); *cf.* VA. CODE ANN. § 15.1-498.6 (Michie 1989); VT. STAT. ANN. tit. 24, § 5204(b) (1990) (phasing does not require time for imposition specifically but allows imposition at time of building permit or certificate of occupancy).

111. *See* Fontana Unified School District v. City of Rialto, 219 Cal. Rptr. 254, 173 Cal. App. 3d 725 (1985) (school facilities).

112. *See* Key West v. R.L.J.S. Corp., 537 So.2d 641 (Fla. Dist. Ct. App. 1989); Fairmont Township v. Beardmore, 431 N.W.2d 292 (N.D. 1988) (solid waste fee imposed on applicant even though ordinance establishing fee was adopted after permit application). *Compare* Coppell v. General Homes, 763 S.W.2d 448 (Tex. Ct. App. 1988) (retroactive imposition of fees not allowed in absence of specific enabling authority).

113. *See* ME. REV. STAT. ANN. tit. 30, § 4354 (West Cum. Supp. 1991) (two-year limit); PA. STAT. ANN. tit. 53, § 10505-A(g)(2) (Cum. Supp. 1991) (three-year limit).

114. *See* TEX. LOC. GOV'T CODE § 395.024 (1993).

115. *See* GA. CODE ANN. § 36-71-91(1) (Michie 1992) (six-year limit before money must be spent); CAL. GOV'T CODE § 66.001(d) (West Cum. Supp. 1992) (limited to five years at which point the money must have been spent or an additional showing by the governmental unit that a reasonable relationship still exists); ILL. ANN. STAT. ch. 121, para. 5-916 (West Cum. Supp. 1992) (six-year limit); NEV. REV. STAT. § 278B.260(1)(a)-(b) (1991) (five-year limit); VT. STAT. ANN. tit. 24, § 5203(a)(1) (1990) (six-year limit); VA. CODE ANN. § 15.1-491.10 (Michie 1989) (five-year limit); WASH. REV. CODE ANN. § 82.02.070 (1990) (six-year limit); W.VA. CODE § 7-20-8(e) (Cum. Supp. 1991) (six-year limit).

116. *But see* Village Square No. 1 v. Crow-Frederick Retail Ltd. Partnership, 551 A.2d 471 (Md. Ct. Spec. App. 1989) (developer not allowed to force city to collect funds from other landowners to reimburse developer for constructed improvements based on finding that ordinance failed to provide adequate due process to potentially liable landowners).

117. *See* ARIZ. REV. STAT. ANN. § 11-1106(D) (West Cum. Supp. 1991) (county authorizing statute); GA. CODE ANN. 36-71-7 (Michie 1992); ILL. ANN. STAT. ch. 121, para. 5-906(b)-(c) (West Cum. Supp. 1991); IND. CODE. ANN. § 36-7-4-

1335(b), (c) (Burns Cum. Supp. 1991); Nev. Rev. Stat. § 278B.249 (19910: Ore. Rev. Stat. § 223.304(3) (1991); Pa. Stat. Ann. tit. 53, § 10505-A(f) (Cum. Supp. 19910: Tex. Loc. Gov't Code § 395.023 (1993); Vt. Stat. Ann. tit. 24, § 5203(C)(3) (1990); Va. Code Ann. § 15.1-498.7 (Michie 1989); Wash. Rev. Code Ann. § 82.02.060(3) (1990); W.Va. Code § 7-20-5 (Cum. Supp. 1991).

118. *See* Ga. Code Ann. § 36-71-7 (Michie 1992); Ill. Ann. Stat. ch. 121, para. 5-906(b)-(c) (West Cum. Supp. 1991); Vt. Stat. Ann. tit. 24, § 5203(c)(3) (1990); and Wash. Rev. Code Ann. § 82.02.060(3) (1990).

119. *See* City of Mesa v. Home Builders Ass'n, *supra.*

120. *See* Home Builders & Contractors Ass'n v. City of Dunedin, *supra.*

121. *See* Meglino v. Township Comm. of Eagleswood, 103 N.J. 144, 510 A.2d 1134 (1986) (a municipality may recover capital costs through utility charges); Warrenville Plaza, Inc. v. Warren Township Sewerage Auth., 553 A.2d 874 (N.J. Super. Ct. App. Div. 1989) (as long as authority's methodology was not wholly arbitrary and was reasonably related to objectives of enabling legislation, fees were acceptable and mathematical precision was not required). *But see* Longmont Retirement Res. v. City of Longmont, 767 P.2d 777 (Colo. App. 1988) (court refused to apply city imposed park and sewer fee to individual units in retirement complex because central kitchen defeated definition of family residential unit). Cameron & Cameron v. Planning Bd., 593 A.2d 1250 (N.J. App. 1991) (under New Jersey statute, landowners are required to pay for on-site improvements and only a proportionate share of off-site improvements).

122. *See* Ga. Code Ann. § 36-71-3(a) (Michie 1992); Ill. Ann. Stat. ch. 121, para. 5-906(b)-(c) (West Cum. Supp. 1991); Ind. Code Ann. § 36-7-4-1320 (Burns Cum. Supp. 1991); Nev. Rev. Stat. § 278B.230(1) (1991); Pa. Stat. Ann. tit. 53, § 10505-A(a) (Cum. Supp. 1991); Tex. Loc. Gov't Code Ann. § 395.015 (1993); Vt. Stat. Ann. tit. 24, § 5203(b) (1990); Va. Code Ann. § 15.1-498.6 (Michie 1989).

123. Linkage addresses the need for affordable housing by requiring developers of office buildings (San Francisco) or other commercial, retail or institutional development (Boston) to build housing, to pay an in-lieu fee into a housing trust fund, or to make equity contributions to a low-income housing project. White, *Using Fees and Taxes to Promote Afford-* *able Housing*, 43 Land Use L. & Zoning Dig., no. 9, at 3 (Sept. 1991). The linkage concept is similar to impact fees, dedication and money-in-lieu of land for parks and recreation; the rational nexus standard (Nollan, *infra*) justified requiring the provider of the jobs to pay for the facilities the need for which is generated by the employment. Local governments must be careful, however, to comply with the constitutional standards of nexus and proportionality established by Nollan v. California Coastal Comm'n, 483 U.S. 825, 107 S.Ct. 3141, 97 L.Ed.2d 677 (1987), Dolan v. City of Tigard, 114 S.Ct. 2309 (1994), and other state court decisions. *See* Freilich & Morgan, *Municipal Strategies for Imposing Valid Development Exactions: Responding to Nollan*, 10 Zoning & Planning L. Rep. 169, 172 (Dec. 1987); Freilich & Chinn, *supra* note 59.

124. Tegeler, *Developer Payments and Downtown Housing Trust Funds*, Clearinghouse Rev. (Nov. 1984), at 678, 692.

125. Alterman, *Evaluating Linkage, and Beyond*, 34 J. Urb. & Contemp. L. 3 (1988), reprinted in abridged form at 41 Land Use L. & Zoning Dig., no. 6, at 3 (June 1989); Porter & Lassar, *The Latest on Linkage*, Urb. Land (Dec. 1988), at 7; Newman & Feola, *Housing Incentives: A National Perspective*, 21 Urb. Law. 307 (1989); *Symposium-Linkage Programs*, 54 J. Am. Planning A. 197-224 (Spring 1988); Porter, *The Office-Linkage Issue*, Urb. Land (Sept. 1985) at 16.

126. Diamond, *The San Francisco Office/Housing Program: Social Policy Underwritten by Private Enterprise*, 7 Harvard Envtl. L. Rev. 449, 463 (1983).

127. *Id.* at 463-64.

128. San Francisco Planning Code 313(b) (Sept. 1988).

129. *Id.* at 313(c), (d).

130. Goetz, *Office-Housing Linkage in San Francisco*, 55 J. Am. Planning A. 66, 72 (Winter 1989).

131. San Francisco Planning Code 313(3)(1).

132. Newman & Feola, *supra*, at 341; Porter, *The Latest on Linkage*, Urb. Land (Dec. 1988), at 8-9.

133. Porter, *supra*, at 8; the Boston linkage program has been sustained in the courts. A trial court decision that invalidated the program as an unauthorized and illegal tax (Bonan v. General Hospital Corp., Suffolk Supt. Ct. no. 76438 (March 31, 1986) was vacated by the Massachusetts Supreme Judicial Court on standing and procedural grounds; Bonan v. City of Boston, 496 N.E.2d 640 (1986).

134. A single-room occupancy unit generally consists of a small living unit with shared living room, kitchen, and bathroom facilities.

135. Netter, *Legal Foundations for Municipal Affordable Housing Programs: Inclusionary Zoning, Linkage, and Housing Preservation*, 10 ZONING & PLANNING L. REP. 161, 162-63 (Nov. 1987).

136. *Id.* at 162.

137. 223 Cal. Rptr. 379, 177 Cal. App. 3d 892 (Cal. 1986).

138. *Id.* at 387.

139. 223 Cal. Rptr. at 388-389; *see also* Pennell v. City of San Jose, 485 U.S. 1 (1988) where the Court upheld rent control ordinances fixing the maximum rent against substantive due process allegations.

140. 223 Cal. Rptr. at 389.

141. *Id.* at 390-91; *see also* the U.S. Supreme Court decision in Yee v. City of Escondido, 112 S.Ct. 1522 (1992) in which the court upheld against a "physical" taking challenge a mobile home rent control ordinance that prohibited the owner from dispossessing the tenant as long as the property was devoted to mobile home park use.

142. *Id.* at 391.

143. San Telmo Assoc. v. City of Seattle, 735 P.2d 673 (Wash. 1987).

144. 735 P.2d at 673-74.

145. *Id.* at 674-75 (citing Hillis Homes v. Snohomish County, 97 Wash. 2d 804, 650 P.2d 193 (1982).

146. This "hint" resulted in subsequent findings that the ordinance did constitute a taking of the developer's property, *see* Sintra, Inc. v. City of Seattle, 829 P.2d 765, 771 (Wash. 1992) (where the regulation destroys one or more of the fundamental attributes of property ownership—the right to possess, to exclude others, and to dispose of property); *see also* companion holding in Robinson v. City of Seattle, 830 P.2d 318 (Wash. 1992).

147. WASH. REV. CODE ANN. § 82.02.020, the legislature has subsequently authorized the use of impact fees for the state's major coastal counties (and cities) in the Growth Management Act, 36.70A WASH. REV. STAT. (1990). *See also* Morgan, Strauss & Leitner, *State Impact Fee Legislation*, 40 LAND USE L. & ZONING DIG. 3, 5 (Jan. 1988).

148. Seawall Associates v. City of New York, 544 N.Y.S.2d 542 (Ct. App. N.Y. 1989).

149. *Id.* at 548.

150. *Id.; compare* Terminal Plaza, *supra*, where the ordinance applied only where the landowner voluntarily decided to overt or to destroy the units. 223 Cal. Rptr. at 387, 398; *see also* Yee v. City of Escondido, *supra*, where the "physical" taking rule will not apply if the property has the option of withdrawing the property from the market.

151. 544 N.Y.S.2d at 552-53.

152. *Id.* at 549.

153. *See* San Francisco Planning Code 313(a)(ii), (12) (Sept. 1988).

154. Commercial Builders of Northern California v. City of Sacramento, 941 F.2d 872 (9th Cir. 1991); Holmdel Builders Ass'n v. Township of Holmdel, 121 N.J. 550, 583 A.2d 277 (1990); *see also* Bonan v. General Hospital Corp., 398 Mass. 315, 496 N.E.2d 640 (1986), vacating No.76438 (Mass. Super. Ct. March 31, 1986); (linkage fee invalidated at trial court level, decision vacated on procedural grounds).

155. Blagden Alley Ass'n v. District of Columbia Zoning Comm'n, 590 A.2d 139 (D.C. App. 1991) (approving practice of offsite housing exactions but remanding for findings); Nunziato v. Planning Bd., 225 N.J. Super. 124, 541, A.2d 1105 (1988) (invalidating $500 per dwelling unit contribution to affordable housing program exacted as a condition of variance approval); Alexander's Dep't Stores of New Jersey v. Borough of Paramus, 243 N.J. Super. 157, 578 A.2d 1241 (1990) (rejecting neighboring landowner's challenge to affordable housing contribution on standing grounds).

156. Holmdel Builders Ass'n v. Township of Holmdel, 121 N.J. 550, 583 A.2d 277 (1990); *see also* In re Egg Harbor Assocs., 94 N.J. 358, 464 A.2d 1115 (1983).

157. Dailey v. City of Lawton, 296 F. Supp. 266 (W.D. Okla. 1969), *aff'd*, 425 F.2d 1037 (10th Cir. 1970) (denial of multifamily zoning for low-income housing sponsor based on inadequacy of public facilities invalid and discriminatory); Urban League of Essex County v. Mahwah Township, 207 N.J. Super. 169, 504 A.2d 66, 79-81 (1984); Kennedy Park Homes Ass'n v. City of Lackawanna, 436 F.2d 108, 114 (2d Cir. 1970), *cert. denied*, 401 U.S. 1010 (1971) (moratorium on rezoning and subdivision approvals due to asserted lack off sewer capacity invalidated where there was evidence of racial discrimination and lack of effort to resolve existing facility deficiencies).

158. Stoney-Brook Development Corp. v. Town of Fremont, 474 A.2d 561 (N.H. 1984); Conway v. Town of Stratham, 414 A.2d 539 (N.H. 1980); Westwood Forest Estates, Inc. v. Village of South Nyack, 244 N.E.2d 700 (N.Y.

1969), Q.C. Constr. v. Gallo, 649 F. Supp. 1331 (D. R.I. 1986); Associated Homebuilders, Inc. v. City of Livermore, 557 A.2d 473 (Cal. 1976) (J. Mosk, dissenting).

159. *See, e.g.,* Golden v. Planning Bd. of Town of Ramapo, 30 N.Y.2d 359, 334 N.Y.S.2d 138, 285 N.E.2d 291, *appeal dismissed,* 409 U.S. 1003 (1972); Smoke Rise, Inc. v. Washington Suburban Sanitary Comm'n, 400 F. Supp. 1369 (D. Md. 1975); Beck v. Town of Raymond, 394 A.2d 847 (N.H. 1978); Rancourt v. Town of Barnstead, 523 A.2d 55 (N.H. 1986); Westwood Forest Estates, Inc. v. Village of South Nyack, 244 N.E.2d 700 (N.Y. 1969); Belle Harbor Realty v. Kerr, 323 N.E.2d 697 (N.Y. 1974).

160. *See* White, *supra* (discussing Boulder, Colorado housing excise tax). *Cf.* 1990 Washington Laws, Ch. 17, S.H.B. 2929, 36 (to be codified at Wash. Rev. Code § 82.46.010) (authorizing excise tax on real estate transfers of 0.25 percent or a supplemental tax of 1.5 percent of the selling price in order to finance capital improvements designated in a comprehensive plan and housing relocation assistance for tenants displaced from the change in use or conversion of residential developments).

161. Griggs v. Allegheny, 369 U.S. 84 (1962); Hodel v. Irving, 481 U.S. 704 (1987).

162. 458 U.S. 419 (1982).

163. 114 S. Ct. 2309 (1994).

164. *See* Robert H. Freilich & Elizabeth A. Garvin, *Takings After Lucas: Growth Management, Planning, and Regulatory Implementation Will Work Better Than Before,* 22 Stetson L. Rev. 409, 411 (1993); Robert H. Freilich, *Solving the "Taking" Equation: Making the Whole Equal the Sum of Its Parts,* 15 Urb. Law. 447 (1983). *see also* Freilich and Chinn, *supra* note 59; Robert H. Freilich and Richard G. Carlisle, *The U.S. Supreme Court Blockbusters of 1986-1987: Analyzing the Inverse Condemnation and Regulatory Taking Cases,* in Institute on Planning, Zoning, and Eminent Domain § 9 (1988).

165. 854 P.2d at 539-40.

166. Dolan, 114 S.Ct. at 2314 (emphasis added).

167. *Id.*

168. 854 P.2d 437, 444 (Ore. 1993).

169. 483 U.S. 825 (1987). *see also* Robert H. Freilich and Terry D. Morgan, *Municipal Strategies for Imposing Valid Development Exactions: Responding to Nollan,* Zoning & Planning L. Rep., Dec. 1987, at 169.

170. 845 P.2d at 443-44.

171. Dolan, 114 S.Ct. at 2317.

172. *Id.*

173. *Id.* (quoting Nollan, 483 U.S. at 837).

174. Freilich and Chinn, *supra* note 59.

175. 114 S.Ct. at 2317.

176. *Id.* at 2318.

177. *Id.* (citing Nollan, 483 U.S. at 834).

178. Dolan, 114 S.Ct. at 2319-20.

179. *See* Linda Greenhouse, "High Court Limits the Public Power on Private Land," New York Times, June 25, 1994, at 1, 8. Initial reaction to the decision was that the reasonable relationship test alone was "fair," but the additional requirements of an individualized determination and the burden of proof being placed on the city was "troubling." *Id.* at 8.

180. Dolan, 114 S.Ct. at 2323 (Stevens, J., dissenting).

181. Justice Stevens's complaint that *Dolan* is more properly based on substantive due process grounds is answered by Justice Rehnquist in footnote 5 where he cites to previous Supreme Court decisions which hold that the Fourteenth Amendment makes the Takings Clause of the Fifth Amendment applicable to the States. *See* Penn Central Transp. Co. v. New York City, 438 U.S. 104 (1978); Nollan, 483 U.S. at 827. This point, however, works to the advantage of cities, since a more expansive reading of substantive due process to incorporate "rough proportionality" would be far more detrimental. *See* Yee v. City of Escondido, 112 S.Ct. 1522 (1992) (which rejected a physical or title taking test for mobile home rent controls and used a rational nexus substantive due process test for economic legislation). Footnote 8 following the "rough proportionality" holding is similarly a response to Justice Stevens's argument that the majority incorrectly places the burden of proof on the city to justify the exaction. Justice Rehnquist responds that since the City of Tigard made an *adjudicative* decision regarding the Dolans' property, the burden is properly on the city when the property owner challenges the exaction. For further discussion *see infra,* notes 40-47, and accompanying text.

182. Dolan, 114 S.Ct. at 2319.

183. "[S]imply denominating a governmental measure as a 'business regulation' does not immunize it from constitutional challenge on the grounds that it violates a provision of the Bill of Rights. . . . We see no reason why the Takings Clause of the Fifth Amendment, as much a part of the Bill of Rights as the First Amendment or Fourth Amendment, should be relegated to the status of a poor relation in these comparable

circumstances." 114 S.Ct. at 2320. This comment was apparently prompted by Justice Stevens's concerns that elevating the "right to exclude," as merely one strand in a property owner's larger bundle of rights, is particularly inappropriate in light of the fact that the Dolans are developing commercial property which has traditionally carried a strong presumption of constitutional validity. *See* 114 S.Ct. at 2325 (Stevens, J., dissenting).

184. Does *Dolan* apply to takings, or to substantive due process as a reading of the remand in Ehrlich v. Culver City, 19 Cal. Rptr. 2d 468 (Cal. Ct. App. 1993), *cert. granted* and judgment *vacated* by 114 S.Ct. 2731 (1994), might suggest? *See* discussion *infra.*

185. Jenad, Inc. v. Village of Scarsdale, 218 N.E.2d 673 (N.Y. 1966).

186. Dolan, 114 S.Ct. at 2318.

187. Wald Corp. v. Metropolitan Dade County, 338 So.2d 863 (Fla. App. 1976); Longboat Key v. Land's End, Ltd., 433 So.2d 574 (Fla. App. Ct. 1983). In *Wald*, the "rational nexus" test was specifically adopted as a middle ground test in response to the two extremes already used: the reasonable relationship requirement as the expansive test placed a "heavy burden on the developer" which allowed "virtually unbridled interference with public property," 338 So.2d at 866, while the specific and uniquely attributable test was found to be unduly restrictive on local police power.

188. Dolan, 114 S.Ct. at 2319.

189. *Id.*

190. Syllabus of Dolan v. City of Tigard, __ U.S. __, 114 S. Ct. 2309 (1994).

191. Dolan, 114 S.Ct. at 2321.

192. *See* Kushner, *Property and Mysticism: The Legality of Exactions as A Condition for Public Development in the Time of the Rehnquist Court*, 8 J. LAND USE & ENV'TL L.53 (1992), and Bierman & Ethier, *Development Exactions and Impact Fees: A Survey of American Practices*, 50 L. & CONTEMP. PROBS. 51 (1987).

193. *See* Martin L. Leitner, *Introduction: The Gameboard and Rules of the Game*, 25 URB. LAW. 481 (1993); Martin L. Leitner & Susan P. Schoettle, *A Survey of State Impact Fee Enabling Legislation*, 25 URB. LAW. 491 (1993); and Delaney, *The Needs-Nexus Analysis: A Unified Test for Validating Exactions, User Fees, Impact Fees and Linkage*, 50 L. & CONTEMP. PROBS. 139 (1987).

194. *Id.* (Stevens, J., dissenting). Justice Stevens's dissent disputes the majority's new requirements primarily on the basis that the state court cases cited as establishing the reasonable relationship test are actually grounding their holdings on something closer to *Nollan's* essential nexus. A review of those state cases, *infra*, shows that they are not consistent in the level of scrutiny applied through what they all label a "reasonableness" test, but rather demonstrate a spectrum of nexus requirements. *See also* Delaney, *supra* note 38.

195. The New York Times labels *Dolan* as a classic "ideological split," and its initial reaction states that "the most important part of the decision today lay in the Court's directions for applying the new test. The Justices gave the city the burden of justifying its restrictions, a distinct and unexpected shift from current law under which the landowner seeking to challenge a land use restriction has the burden of proving that the regulation would remove all or substantially all economic value from the property." Greenhouse, *supra* note 24, at 1. This comment, however, does not seem to take into consideration the *adjudicative*, as opposed to *legislative*, nature of the City of Tigard's actions.

196. Many will differ with this conclusion. "This shift in allocating the burden of proof is truly revolutionary, upsetting constitutional doctrine firmly established since at least 1938, when the Court dropped another famous footnote." *See* United States v. Carolene Products, Co., 304 U.S. 778, 783 n. 4 (1938). Dwight H. Merriam & R. Jeffrey Lyman, *Dealing With Dolan, Practically and Jurisprudentially*, ZONING & PLANNING L. RPT., Sept. 1994, at 57, 60. However, these authors are viewing the Court's holding with regard to the burden of proof in the context of elevating the Takings Clause to the level of "the nuclear family of preferred constitutional rights . . ." *Id.* When placed in the perspective of an adjudicative or administrative decision that was made by the City of Tigard, the Court's required burden on the city does not seem so revolutionary. As the Oregon Supreme Court said in the case of Fasano v. Board of County Comm'rs of Washington County, 507 P.2d 23 (Ore. 1973), "[b]ecause the action of the commission in this instance is an exercise of judicial authority, the burden of proof should be placed, as is usual in judicial proceedings, upon the one seeking change. The more drastic the change, the greater will be the burden of showing that it is in conformance with the comprehensive plan . . ."

197. 272 U.S. 365 (1926).

198. 260 U.S. 393 (1922).

199. An analogy to the state court case of Fulling v. Palumbo, 233 N.E.2d 272 (N.Y. 1967), may also provide an explanation or justification as to why the Court was willing to shift the burden to the municipality in the instance of an administrative decision. Although not cited by the court or considered by any commentary to the *Dolan* decision, Fulling v. Palumbo is enlightening for its willingness to shift the burden of proof to the municipality in the case of an administrative variance. In the context of determining the as applied constitutionality of a zoning ordinance which restricted lot sizes, the New York Court of Appeals indicated that the initial burden is placed on the landowner where the case is adjudicative (i.e. a variance). If the landowner is able to show "severe financial harm," then the burden shifts to the municipality to prove that its ordinance supports the public health, safety, and general welfare. Without such a showing, a court should be willing to provide relief to property owners who would suffer a severe financial loss. The burden then finally shifts back to the landowners to demonstrate that a "taking" has occurred. "To state the matter more precisely: until it is demonstrated that some legitimate purpose will be served by restricting the use of petitioner's property, he has sufficient standing to challenge the ordinance. Once it is demonstrated that some legitimate public interest will be served, [the property owner then] must demonstrate that the hardship caused is such as to deprive him of any use of his property to which it is reasonably adapted . . . ." *Id.* at 274.

200. *Dolan* reinforces Professor Freilich's classifications that exist for takings challenges as described above: physical, economic, and title takes. As part of the condition for development, the Dolans were required to deed 10 percent of their land to the City of Tigard. The Court's analysis of this exaction as a dedication may limit *Dolan* to title take situations. For further discussion of these categories, *see* Freilich and Garvin, *supra* note 164, at 409, 411. For a discussion on the limited applications of *Dolan*, *see infra*.

201. Dolan, 114 S.Ct. at 2325 (Stevens, J., dissenting).

202. *Id.* at 2330 (Souter, J., dissenting) (emphasis added).

203. *Id.* at 2323 (Stevens, J., dissenting).

204. *Id.* (Stevens, J., dissenting).

205. 292 N.W.2d 297 (Neb. 1980).

206. *Id.* at 299.

207. The North Platte comprehensive plan contained a proposal to extend the street in question through the Simpsons' property. The court pointed out that the city had not yet acted on this proposal nor acquired any of the real estate to expand this street. Consequently, the court viewed the permit condition as a method of completing the comprehensive plan without purchasing the property through appropriate means. *Id.* at 300.

208. *Id.* at 301. The court used the language of "reasonable relationship" in posing the issue, but cited to a case which required a "rational" nexus. Again the confusion arises between the labels that may attach to the variety of nexus requirements and the interpretation of those tests upon application. *See supra*, notes 30-38, and accompanying text.

209. *Id.*

210. 336 A.2d 501 (N.J. Super. 1975).

211. *Id.* at 506. This language again points to the confusion that the "rational basis" test is the intermediate nexus requirement for some courts.

212. 292 N.W.2d at 301.

213. 137 N.W.2d 442 (Wis. 1966).

214. 176 N.E.2d 799 (Ill. 1961).

215. *Id.* at 802. *Dolan* cites *Pioneer Trust* as the first state court case to establish this restrictive test. 114 S.Ct. at 2319. The specific and uniquely attributable test was later affirmed by the Illinois Supreme Court in school site cases which required dedications and contributions of funds. *See* Board of Educ. v. Surety Dev., Inc., 347 N.E.2d 149 (Ill. 1976) (county board had authority to require developer to donate a parcel of land for use as school grounds, contribute $50,000 toward construction, and pay $200 for each home built), and Krughoff v. City of Naperville, 369 N.E.2d 892 (Ill. 1977) (ordinance requiring dedication or money in lieu of land for school and park sites upheld as uniquely attributable to the need for new facilities, after documentation of student and adult population increases). *See also* Billings Properties, Inc. v. Yellowstone County, 394 P.2d 182 (Mont. 1964). Ironically, *Pioneer Trust* cited Ayres v. City of Los Angeles, 207 P.2d 1 (1957) as support for the "specifically and uniquely attributable" test. In a subsequent decision, the California Supreme Court criticized Illinois—stating that its decision in Ayres was a rational relationship test and that California was capable of describing its own judicial standards without Illinois's help. Associated Homebuilders v. City of Walnut Creek, 484 P.2d 606 (Cal. 1972).

216. 137 N.W.2d at 447.

217. Collis v. City of Bloomington, 246 N.W.2d 19 (Minn. 1976), provides a thorough discussion of those state cases establishing some form of the reasonableness test, and categorizes *Jordan* as the Wisconsin modification of *Pioneer Trust*. Various subdivision dedications were upheld, based on an application of a reasonable relationship test, in Jenad, Inc. v. Village of Scarsdale, 218 N.E.2d 673 (N.Y. 1966); Aunt Hack Ridge Estates, Inc. v. Planning Comm'n of Danbury, 273 A.2d 880 (Conn. 1970); and Associated Home Builders of the Greater East Bay, Inc. v. City of Walnut Creek, 484 P.2d 606, *appeal dismissed*, 404 U.S. 878 (1971).

218. City of College Station v. Turtle Rock Corp., 680 S.W.2d 802 (Tex. 1984), is also cited by Justice Rehnquist in support of the new rough proportionality requirement. Turtle Rock applies a discussion of "reasonable connection" analysis to a challenge of parkland dedications, or money in lieu thereof, as a condition of subdivision plat approval. While the dedication was approved, the Texas Supreme Court warned that "'There is . . . no one test and no single sentence rule. . . . The need to adjust the conflicts between private ownership of property and the public's interests in a very old one which has produced no single solution.' . . . The cases provide examples of numerous factors that have proven useful in resolving particular police power questions, but ultimately a fact-sensitive test of reasonableness is required." 680 S.W.2d at 804 (citing City of Austin v. Teague, 570 S.W.2d 389, 392 (Tex. 1978)). This also appears to be sound advice following *Dolan*, given the Court's tentative nature in establishing the new rough proportionality test.

219. 114 S.Ct. at 2319 (emphasis added).

220. "A reasonable portion is construed to mean that portion of land which the evidence reasonably establishes the municipality will need to acquire for the purposes stated as a result of approval of the subdivision. This is, of necessity, a facts-and-circumstances test, but it is the only kind of test that will consider the myriad of factors which may bear on a municipality's needs for certain kinds of facilities and the relationship of a particular subdivision to those needs." Collis, 246 N.W.2d at 26.

221. The adjudicative nature of the City of Tigard's exaction, which attached to the Dolans' permit, distinguishes *Dolan* from those cases cited in support of the rough proportionality holding such as *Simpson* or *Turtle Rock*. Dolan,

114 S.Ct. at 2316-17.

222. *See* Freilich and Garvin, *supra* note 200, at 415.

223. Dolan, 114 S.Ct. at 2320.

224. *Id.* (citing Kaiser Aetna v. United States, 444 U.S. 164, 176 (1979)).

225. *Id.* at 2324 (Stevens, J., dissenting).

226. *Id.* at 2320. Justice Stevens points out that based on Pruneyard Shopping Center v. Robins, 447 U.S. 74 (1980), infringements on the right to exclude others does not rise to the level of a taking unless it unreasonably impairs the value of the property. However, Justice Rehnquist counters by pointing out that while the expressive activity in *Pruneyard* may be restricted by reasonable time, place, and manner regulations, it is a different matter when the city imposes a permanent easement on property which destroys completely the right to exclude. This damage would indeed go far beyond what natural limitations exist upon the right to exclude based on the fact that the Dolans' improvements were proposed for commercial property.

227. Justice Stevens attacks the "fledgling test of rough proportionality " by pointing out that the state cases cited as support for this test routinely consider what the developer receives as a benefit of the city's permit approval. Dolan, 114 S.Ct. at 2324. However, Justice Rehnquist appears to have cited to these cases more for the reasonable relationship nexus test than the factual similarities. This is important because the cited cases, such as Collis v. Bloomington, 246 N.W.2d 19 (Minn. 1976), and College Station v. Turtle Rock Corp., 680 S.W.2d 802 (Tex. 1984), are discussing the appropriate nexus in the context of dedications required pursuant to approval of subdivision plats, where fees in lieu of the dedication are an element of the equation. It is therefore appropriate to apply a balancing-type test and consider what the developer receives in return for exacting the dedication. However, the Dolans' circumstances did not provide the Court with the balancing option that was present in these cases.

228. 829 P.2d 765 (Wash. 1992) (demolition fee for low income housing not subject to *Nollan* nexus because exaction was not physical).

229. 4 Cal. Rptr. 2d 114 (Cal. Ct. App. 1992), *cert. denied*, 113 S.Ct. 191 (1992) (*Nollan* held not applicable to a transit impact fee).

230. 941 F.2d 872 (9th Cir. 1991), *cert. denied*, 112 S.Ct. 1997 (1992) (commercial building permit conditioned on paying a fee to housing trust fund to build lower income housing not subject to higher scrutiny).

231. 19 Cal. Rptr. 2d 468 (Cal. Ct. App. 1993), *cert. granted* and *judgment vacated* by 114 S.Ct. 2731 (1994).

232. *Id.* at 471-72.

233. *Id.* at 472.

234. *Id.* at 480.

235. *Id.* at 474 (citing Nollan v. California Coastal Comm'n, 483 U.S. 825 (1987)).

236. The court found that the developer was not deprived of all economically beneficial use of his property, a profitable recreational facility could be operated on the property despite the developer's previous failure, and the land use regulations which the developer sought to change were present when the developer purchased the property. Ehrlich, 19 Cal. Rptr. 2d at 475.

237. *Id.* at 475 (citing Blue Jeans Equities West v. City and County of San Francisco, 4 Cal. Rptr. 114 (Cal. App. Ct. 1992)).

238. *Id.* (citing Commercial Builders v. Sacramento, 941 F.2d 872, 875 (9th Cir. 1991)).

239. The Court decided it was irrelevant that the developer was being forced to pay a mitigation fee for the public impact of the loss of tennis courts and recreational facilities, despite the fact that the facility being destroyed was entirely a privately owned facility. "The City had a legitimate need for community recreational facilities whether public or private, and both the land use restriction and the mitigation fee served that same need." Ehrlich, 19 Cal. Rptr. 2d at 476.

240. *Id.* at 481.

241. Agins v. City of Tiburon, 447 U.S. 255 (1980).

242. Penn Cent. Transp. Co. v. New York City, 438 U.S. 104 (1978).

243. Euclid v. Ambler Realty Co., 272 U.S. 365 (1926).

244. *See* Dolan, regarding discussion of right to exclude.

245. Dolan, 114 S.Ct. at 2317.

246. *Id.* (citing Perry v. Sindermann, 408 U.S. 593 (1972), and Pickering v. Board of Ed. of Township High School Dist., 391 U.S. 563 (1968)).

247. Merriam & Lyman, *supra* note 196, at 63.

248. *Id.*

249. *Id.* at 63-64.

250. *See* Freilich & Chinn, *supra* note 164, at 5.

251. 112 S.Ct. 2886 (1992).

252. 112 S.Ct. at 2895.

253. Freilich & Chinn, *supra* note 164.

254. *Id.; see generally* LAND USE LITIGATION, ch. 4.

255. Freilich & Morgan, *supra* note 2, at 170.

256. *See* Pace Resources, Inc. v. Shrewsbury Township, 808 F.2d 1023 (3rd Cir. 1987).

257. The Court has moved to the broadest form of legitimate public purpose as the standard used for substantive due process review of police power regulation; the test for which is symmetrical to the legitimacy prong of the taking test. *See* Hawaii Hous. Auth. v. Midkiff, 467 U.S. 229 (1984); Berman v. Parker, 348 U.S. 26 (1954); *see also* D. CALLIES, R. FREILICH & T. ROBERTS, CASES & MATERIALS ON LAND USE 311 (1994) (discussing public purpose in the context of due process); E.A. Boyle, *The Status of Public Use Requirement: Post Midkiff*, 30 WASH. U.J. URB. & CONTEMP. L. 115 (1986); Department of Transp., 532 So.2d 1267 (Fla. 1988). In PFZ Properties v. Rodriguez, 928 F.2d 28 (1st Cir. 1992), the Supreme Court dismissed a land use action, involving substantive due process issues, as improvidently granted based upon its sweeping limitation of review of local government police power when challenged on substantive due process grounds. *See also* Collins v. Harker Heights, 112 S.Ct. 1061 (1992). The Court in Collins held that governmental action or omission must be "properly characterized as arbitrary, or conscience-shocking" to rise to the level of a violation of substantive due process. *Id.* at 1070. "[T]he Court has always been reluctant to expand the concept of substantive due process because guideposts for responsible decision-making in this uncharted area are scarce and open-ended. The doctrine of judicial self-restraint requires us to exercise the utmost care whenever we are asked to break new ground in this field." *Id.* at 1068 (citation omitted). *See also* Sierra Lake Reserve v. City of Rocklin, 938 F.2d 951 (9th Cir. 1991) (holding that in order to establish substantive due process, claim must prove government action was clearly arbitrary and unreasonable, having no substantial relation to public health, safety, morals, or general welfare); Christian Gospel Church v. San Francisco, 896 F.2d 1221 (9th Cir. 1990) (discussing the invidious and irrational test); Weimer v. Amen, 870 F.2d 1400 (8th Cir. 1989) (holding that substantive due process violations are not viable in federal court simply from violations of state law; the conduct in question must shock the conscience of the court or offend judicial notions of fairness); Coniston Corp. v. Village of Hoffman Estates, 844 F.2d 461 (7th Cir. 1988) (finding that a violation of state law is not a denial of due process without something more); Lemke v. Cass County, 846 F.2d 469 (8th Cir. 1987) (holding that a decision must be so irrational as to bear no relationship whatsoever to the merits of the pending matter); Pace Resources, Inc. v. Shrewsbury Township, 808 F.2d 1023 (3rd Cir. 1987) (stating that decision below must be more than arbitrary or capricious—it must be invidious or irrational); ABN 151st St. Partners v. City of New York, 724 F. Supp. 1142 (S.D.N.Y. 1989) (finding a legislative scheme unconstitutional only for lack of foundation in "any thought or consideration whatsoever"); SECTION 1983: SWORD AND SHIELD (R. Freilich & R. Carlisle eds. 1983).

258. Berman v. Parker, 348 U.S. 26, 32 (1954).

259. 467 U.S. 229 (1984).

260. *Id.* at 241 (citing United States v. Gettysburg Elec. Railway Co., 160 U.S. 668, 680 (1896)).

261. R. Freilich et al., *Supreme Court Review: The New Conservative Paradigm Impacts State and Local Government*, 23 URB. LAW. 499, 608 (1991).

262. *Id.*

263. Impact fees are commonly invalidated for lack of statutory authority. *See, e.g.*, City of Montgomery v. Crossroads Land Co., 355 So.2d 363 (Ala. 1978); Kamhi v. Planning Bd. of Yorktown, 452 N.E.2d 1193 (N.Y. 1983); Briar West, Inc. v. City of Lincoln, 291 N.W.2d 730 (Neb. 1980); Middlesex Boston St. Railway v. Board of Alderman, 359 N.E.2d 1279 (Mass. 1977).

264. Contractors and Builder's Ass'n v. City of Dunedin, 329 So.2d 314, 319-20 (Fla. 1976), *cert. denied*, 444 U.S. 867 (1979) (distinguishing several other states decisions where the city did not have home rule powers); J.W. Jones Cos. v. City of San Diego, 203 Cal. Rptr. 580 (Ct. App. 1984); Associated Home Builders v. City of Walnut Creek, 484 P.2d 606 (Cal.), *appeal dismissed*, 404 U.S. 878 (1971).

265. *See* City of Mesa v. Home Builders Ass'n, 523 P.2d 57 (Ariz. 1974) (Mesa's charter implied the power to enact residential development tax); Home Builders Ass'n v. Provo City, 503 P.2d 451 (Utah 1972) (sewer connection charge statute).

266. Call v. City of West Jordan, 606 P.2d 217, 219 (Utah 1980) (fees for flood control and parks were authorized by state enabling statutes regulating the use and subdivision of land).

267. Dunedin, 329 So.2d 314; Loup-Miller Constr. Co. v. City and County of Denver, 676 P.2d 1170 (Colo. 1984) (en banc).

268. 3 C. SANDS & M. LIBONTI, LOCAL GOVERNMENT LAW 13.06, at 13-29 (1982) ("The trend of decision is to give effect to general welfare and similar broad grants of power subject only to the limitations of reasonableness and constitutionality").

269. Associated Home Builders v. City of Newark, 95 Cal. Rptr. 645 (Ct. App. 1971); Westfield-Palos Verdes Co. v. City of Rancho Palos Verdes, 141 Cal. Rptr. 36 (Ct. App. 1977).

270. Juergensmeyer & Blake, *supra* note 10, at 444.

271. Connors & Meacham, "Paying the Piper: What Can Local Governments Require as a Condition of Development Approval," 1985 Inst. on Planning, Zoning, & Eminent Domain 2.02 [a][d]; Callies et al., *supra* note 257, at 385. *See also* Meglino v. Township Committee of Eagleswood, 510 A.2d 1144 (N.J. 1986).

272. Princeton Research Lands, Inc. v. Planning Bd. of Princeton Township, 271 A.2d 719 (N.J. Super 1970); Apartment Ass'n of Los Angeles County, Inc. v. City of Los Angeles, 141 Cal. Rptr. 794 (Ct. App. 1977); Waterbury Dev. Co. v. Witten, 387 N.E.2d 1380 (Ohio App. 1977); McLain Western No. 1 v. San Diego County, 194 Cal. Rptr. 594 (Ct. App. 1983). *See* Juergensmeyer & Blake, *supra* note 10, at 427-33 for a discussion of the historical development of the "specifically and uniquely attributable" test and a proposed "rational nexus" test for impact fees.

273. It has been suggested that the reason for application of this restrictive test to impact fees was the "judicial suspicion that payment requirements for extra development capital expenditures were in reality a tax." Juergensmeyer & Blake, *supra* note 10, at 428-29. The "reasonableness" test is more consistent with the exercise of the police power and the presumption of validity for legislative acts. The "specifically and uniquely attributable" test does not take both the needs generated and the benefits received into consideration as the "reasonableness" standard does. *Id.* at 431-32.

274. Contractors and Builder's Ass'n v. City of Dunedin, 329 So.2d 314, 320, n. 10 (Fla. 1976), *cert. denied*, 444 U.S. 867 (1979). The *Dunedin* court also spoke in terms of what would be "just and equitable." *Id.* at 320. *See also id.* at 318, no. 5, where the court answers the petitioner's contention that the "utility revenues constitute taxes, to the extent such revenues are expended for purposes unrelated to the utility" by stating that "nothing prohibits a municipality's 'making a modest return of its utility operation or certain portions thereof, providing the rate is not un-reasonable.'" (citation omitted). *Accord* Land/Vest Properties, Inc. v. Town of Plainfield, 379 A.2d 200 (N.H. 1977); Wald Corp. v. Metropolitan Dade County, 338 So.2d 863 (Fla. Dist. Ct. App. 1976).

275. Banberry Dev. Corp. v. South Jordan City, 631 P.2d 899, 903 (Utah 1981). *See* M. Leitner and E. Strauss, *Elements of a Municipal Impact Fee Ordinance, With Commentary*, 54 J. AM. PLANNING A. 225, 226 (Spring 1988).

276. The court listed these factors to be considered: (1) the cost of existing capital facilities; (2) the manner of financing existing capital facilities (such as user charges, special assessments, bonded indebtedness, general taxes, or federal grants); (3) the relative extent to which the newly developed properties and the other properties in the municipality have already contributed to the cost of existing capital facilities (by such means as user charges, special assessments, or payments from the proceeds of general taxes); (4) the relative extent to which the newly developed properties and the other properties in the municipality will contribute to the cost of existing capital facilities in the future; (5) the extent to which the newly developed properties are entitled to a credit because the municipality is requiring their developers or owners (by contractual arrangement or otherwise) to provide common facilities (inside or outside the proposed development) that have been provided by the municipality and financed through general taxation or other means (apart from user charges) in other parts of the municipality; (6) extraordinary costs, if any, in servicing the newly developed properties; and (7) fair comparisons of amounts paid at different times. *Id.* at 904 (citations omitted). *See also* Home Builders Ass'n v. Provo City, 503 P.2d 451 (Utah 1972).

277. Banberry, 631 P.2d at 904. In this same vein, the court noted: "Precise mathematical equality 'is neither feasible nor constitutionally vital.'" *Id.*

278. Home Builders & Contractors Ass'n v. Board of County Comm'rs, 446 So.2d 140, 143 (Fla. 1983), *appeal dismissed*, 469 U.S. 976 (1984).

279. *See, e.g.*, J.W. Jones Cos. v. City of San Diego, 203 Cal. Rptr. 580 (Ct. App. 1984); J. Frank, *Considerations in the Design of Fiscal Impact Fees*, Jan. 1982, pp. 17-18 (unpublished manuscript submitted to Florida State University). *See also* M. Leitner & E. Strauss, *supra* note 275, at 227.

280. *See, e.g.*, City of Mesa v. Home Builders Ass'n, 523 P.2d 57 (Ariz. 1974) (residential development tax of $150 charged for each new dwelling unit, mobile home, or trailer space).

281. Juergensmeyer & Blake, *supra* note 10, at 419.

282. Jacobsen & Redding, *supra* note 10, at 408. Westfield-Palos Verdes Co. v. City of Rancho Palos Verdes, 141 Cal. Rptr. 36, 40 (Ct. App. 1977) ("environmental excise tax" was $500 per bedroom with a $1,000 maximum per dwelling unit for residential construction and 30 cents per square foot of gross building area for new industrial and commercial buildings).

283. In Home Builders, 446 So.2d 140, the Palm Beach County ordinance which was being challenged set out a complex formula for computing road impact fees:

A. Residential:

$$\text{Fee} = \frac{\text{External trips divided by 2*}}{\text{capacity}}$$

x Cost to construct 1 lane for 1/2 mile

* given a 50/50 directional split

(a) "External Trips" is the number of trips generated by the land development activity (the trip generation rate).

(b) The "directional split" assumed for each set of trips for the land development activity is 50/50, the most conservative estimate possible.

(c) "Capacity" is the capacity of the roadway system in the year 2000.

(d) "Construction Costs" are assumed to be $300,000 per lane mile, and $150,000 per 1/2 land mile.

(e) The average trip length assumed is one mile for residential land development activity and 1/2 mile for non-residential land development activity.

(f) The ordinance assumes capacity of the system will be 6,000 vehicles per day per lane.

The Collier County, Florida, Ordinance 78-36 (July 18, 1978) (quoted in Juergensmeyer & Blake, *supra* note 10, at 7.21) is another example of a computational approach:

The amount of fee to be paid shall be calculated according to the following formulae and shall be an amount equal to the sum of the educational facilities and acreage costs necessary to support the pupils generated by each new dwelling unit, less the estimated percentage of State Aid received for capital outlay.

a. Acreage cost per dwelling unit shall be calculated: (a x b x c x h) + (e x b x c x f) + (g x b x c x H) = x.

b. Construction costs per dwelling unit shall be calculated: b x j = w.

c. Percentage of State Aid shall be determined by the estimates provided in the Five Year School Plan Survey conducted by the Florida Department of Education - y.

d. Total fee owed shall be calculated as the construction costs plus acreage cost less State Aid = (1 - y) (x + w).

e. In the above formulae, the letters used are given the following significance: "a" represents the percentage of school age children in grades kindergarten - 5. "b" represents the average school age children per household. "c" represents the existing raw land prices per acre. "d" represents the number of acres required per elementary school site divided by the number of pupils per middle school. "e" represents the percentage of school age children in grades 6-8. "f" represents the number of acres required per middle school site divided by the number of pupils per middle school. "g" represents the percentage of school age children in grades 9-12. "h" represents the number of acres required per secondary school site divided by the number of pupils per secondary school. "j" represents the current cost of facilities per pupil (excluding land costs). "w" represents the construction cost per dwelling expressed in dollars. "x" represents the acreage cost per dwelling expressed in dollars. "y" represents the percentage of State Aid available.

284. *See, e.g.*, Banberry Dev. Corp. v. South Jordan City, 631 P.2d 899, 904 (Utah 1981) ("the courts must concede municipalities the flexibility necessary to deal realistically with questions not susceptible of exact measurement").

285. By way of illustration, the Palm Beach "Fair Share Ordinance" formula for road impact fees required the amount to be determined by the costs of road construction and the number of trips generated by different types of land use, with the established fees subject to annual review. Home Builders, 446 So.2d at 142.

286. Banberry, 631 P.2d at 904.

287. Miller v. City of Port Angeles, 691 P.2d 229, 234 (Wash. Ct. App. 1984) ("construction costs can rarely be known precisely in the planning stages . . .").

288. "In principle . . . we see nothing wrong with transferring to the new user of a municipally owned water or sewer system a fair share

of the costs new use of the system involves." Dunedin, 329 So.2d at 317-18.

289. *Id.* at 320-21. In particularly strong language, the court, when invalidating the ordinance, chastised the drafters:

The failure to include necessary restrictions on the use of the fund is bound to result in confusion, at best. City personnel may come and go before the fund is exhausted, yet there is nothing in writing to guide their use of those moneys, although certain uses, even within the water and sewer systems, would undercut the legal basis for the fund's existence. There is no justification for such casual handling of public moneys and we therefore hold that the ordinance is defective for failure to spell out necessary restrictions on the use of fees it authorized to be collected.

Id. at 321. Earmarking is not required, however, when a private utility charges "impact-type" fees. Christian and Missionary Alliance Found., Inc. v. Florida Cities Water Co., 386 So.2d 543 (Fla. 1980).

290. The court in Broward County v. Janis Dev. Corp., 311 So.2d 371, 375 (Fla. Dist. Ct. App. 1975), in ruling an impact fee as an invalid tax, stated: "[T]he fee here is simply an exaction of money to be put in trust for roads . . . . There are no other requirements. There are no specifics provided in the ordinance as to where and when these monies are to be expended for roads . . ." *Accord* Village of Royal Palm Beach v. Home Builders & Contractors Ass'n, 386 So.2d 1304 (Fla. Dist. Ct. App. 1980).

291. Hayes v. City of Albany, 490 P.2d 1018, 1020 (Ore. Ct. App. 1971). *Accord* Heinrich v. City of Moline, 375 N.E.2d 572 (Ill. App. Ct. 1978).

292. The California court in Associated Home Builders v. City of Newark, 95 Cal. Rptr. 648 (Ct. App. 1971) did not place any restrictions on how the bedroom tax revenues had to be spent. Since these business license taxes are considered general revenues rather than subdivision exactions which must be spent to benefit the subdivision, presumably no impact "taxes" need to be earmarked in California.

293. Juergensmeyer & Blake, *supra* note 10, at 419. *See* Leitner & Strauss, *supra* note 275, at 226-27.

294. 631 P.2d 899, 902 (Utah 1981).

295. *See supra* notes discussing California impact fees.

296. Westfield-Palos Verdes Co. v. City of Rancho Palos Verdes, 141 Cal. Rptr. 36, 44 (Ct.

App. 1977) ("while the environmental excise tax here is collected at the time of the issuance of the certificate of occupancy, it represents a choice of a reasonable time for collection of a tax fixed by the number of bedrooms").

297. Associated Home Builders v. City of Newark, 95 Cal. Rptr. 648 (Ct. App. 1971).

298. Westfield-Palos Verdes, 141 Cal. Rptr. at 44.

299. Frank, *supra* note 279, at 7.

300. *Id.* Section 6.8(1) of the Model provides that fees may be paid at either the building permit stage or platting stage.

301. Lackman v. Hall, 364 A.2d 1244 (Del. 1976); Ventures in Property I v. City of Wichita, 594 P.2d 671 (Ks. 1979); Howard v. JJM, Inc., 482 A.2d 908 (Md. 1984).

302. The court in Associated Home Builders v. City of Walnut Creek, 484 P.2d 606, 614 (Cal.), *appeal dismissed*, 404 U.S. 878 (1971), held that a city ordinance requiring land dedication for parks which specify that improvements would be made as the area developed was not unreasonable.

303. 95 Cal. Rptr. 648 (Ct. App. 1971).

304. *Id.* at 649. *Accord* J.W. Jones Cos. v. City of San Diego, 203 Cal. Rptr. 580 (Ct. App. 1984).

305. *Id.* The fact that new residents, as opposed to new industry, create relatively greater needs for police and fire protection and increased street use "affords an adequate basis for the classification." *Id.*

306. "[T]here are significant differences both in business function and in scope of development which justify the developer-contractor classification. That is, a developer normally plans an entire subdivision and then mass produces the homes within a somewhat expansive tract . . . the contractor usually custom designs homes pursuant to individual contracts with the owners. Given such distinctions, the fact that the burden of the license tax may be borne unequally among the different classifications is of no constitutional significance." Westfield-Palos Verdes Co. v. City of Rancho Palos Verdes, 141 Cal. Rptr. 36, 43 (Ct. App. 1977).

307. *See, e.g.,* Home Builders & Contractors Ass'n v. Board of County Comm'rs, 446 So.2d 140, 151 (Fla. Dist. Ct. App. 1983), *appeal dismissed*, 469 U.S. 976 (1984) (charges against new developers are reasonable "because only the new developers have created the necessity for new road construction"); Contractors & Builder's Ass'n v. City of Dunedin, 329 So.2d 314, 321 (Fla. 1976), *cert. denied*, 444 U.S. 867 (1979) ("The cost of new facilities should be borne by new users to the extent new use requires new facilities, but only to that extent"). *See generally,* Jacobsen & Redding, *supra* note 10, at 409-10.

308. Banberry Dev. Corp. v. South Jordan City, 631 P.2d 889, 903 (Utah 1981). This phraseology, at first glance, seems to indicate a more liberal position since "benefits conferred" is a broader concept than "costs created." The *Banberry* court, however, in listing several factors to be considered when determining the equitable share of costs to be borne by newly developed properties, concentrated primarily on relative costs rather than benefits. *See supra* note 108, where factors are listed.

309. Weber Basin Home Builders Ass'n v. Roy City, 487 P.2d 866, 888-89 (Utah 1971) (city had the authority to raise fees for the increasing costs of city government and services, but "in that connection, the new residents are entitled to be treated equally and on the same basis as the old residents"; city made no allegation that charges were necessary to improve their water and sewer systems because of the construction of new homes).

310. Likewise, in Lafferty v. Payson City, 642 P.2d 376 (Utah 1982), the court recognized that it was necessary, in determining the validity of the impact fee, to examine the method of financing for the existing system: "This is necessary . . . to assure that a property owner involved in a new home development is not required to buy into the capital value of existing municipal services and then pay for some portion of the same capital value *a second time* by indebtedness used to construct them originally." *Id.* at 379. The fees in *Lafferty* were invalidated since they did not meet the equitable allocation required by Banberry.

311. *Id.* at 10. *Accord* City of Mesa v. Home Builders Ass'n, 523 P.2d 57 (Ariz. 1974).

312. M. Leitner & E. Strauss, *supra* note 275, at 230-31. The *Banberry* court's list of factors by which to judge the reasonableness of a fee includes the extent to which newly developed properties are entitled to a credit because the developer has already contributed to facilities through general taxation or by other means. 631 P.2d at 904.

Land Readjustment

7.1 Resubdivision of Land.

1. *Procedure for Resubdivision.* Whenever a developer desires to resubdivide an already approved final subdivision plat, the developer shall first obtain approval for the resubdivision by the same procedures prescribed for the subdivision of land.

2. *Resubdivision.* Resubdivision includes:

   a. Any change in any street layout or any other public improvement;
   b. Any change in any lot line;
   c. Any change in the amount of land reserved for public use or the common use of lot owners;
   d. Any change in any easements shown on the approved plat.

3. *Waiver.* Whenever the Planning Commission, in its sole discretion, makes a finding on the record that the purposes of these regulations may be served by permitting resubdivision by the procedure established in this Section 7.1(3), the Planning Commission may waive the requirement of Section 7.1(1). The Planning Commission, after an application for resubdivision that includes an express request for waiver, shall publish notice of the application in a local newspaper of general circulation and shall provide personal notice to property owners in the subdivision. The notice shall include:

   a. The name and legal description of the subdivision affected by the application;
   b. The proposed changes in the final subdivision plat;
   c. The place and time at which the application and any accompanying documents may be reviewed by the public;
   d. The place and time at which written comments on the proposed resubdivision may be submitted by the public; and

e. The place and time of the public meeting at which the Planning Commission will consider whether to approve, conditionally approve, or disapprove the proposed resubdivision.

No sooner than thirty (30) days and no later than forty-five (45) days after notice is published, the Planning Commission shall consider the application for resubdivision at a public meeting and shall approve, conditionally approve, or disapprove the application.

4. *Procedure for Subdivisions When Future Resubdivision is Indicated.* Whenever land is subdivided and the subdivision plat shows one or more lots containing more than one (1) acre of land and there is reason to believe that such lots eventually will be resubdivided, the Planning Commission may require that the applicant allow for the future opening of streets and the ultimate extension of adjacent streets. Easements providing for the future opening and extension of streets may be made a requirement of plat approval.

7.2   Plat Vacation.

1. *Owner Initiated Plat Vacation.* The owner or owners of lots in any approved subdivision, including the developer, may petition the Planning Commission to vacate the plat with respect to their properties. The petition shall be filed in triplicate on forms provided by the Planning Commission and one (1) copy shall be referred to the governing body by the Planning Commission.

    a. *Notice and Hearing.* The Planning Commission shall publish notice in a land newspaper of general circulation and provide personal notice of the petition for vacation to all owners of property within the affected subdivision and shall state in the notice the time and place for a public hearing on the vacation petition. The public hearing shall be no sooner than thirty (30) and no later than forty-five (45) days after the published and personal notice.

    b. *Criteria.* The Planning Commission shall approve the petition for vacation on such terms and conditions as are reasonable to protect public health, safety, and welfare; but in no event may the Planning Commission approve a petition for vacation if it will materially injure the rights of any nonconsenting property owner or any public rights in public improvements unless expressly agreed to by the governing body.

    c. *Recordation of Revised Plat.* Upon approval of any petition for vacation, the Planning Commission shall direct the petitioners to prepare a Revised Final Subdivision Plat in accordance with these regulations. The Revised Final Subdivision Plat may be recorded only after having been signed by the Chairman of the Planning Commission and the Local Government Attorney.

d. *Developer Initiated Vacation.* When the developer of the subdivision, or its successor, owns all of the lots in the subdivision, the developer or successor may petition for vacation of the subdivision plat and the petition may be approved, conditionally approved, or disapproved at a regular public meeting of the Planning Commission subject to the criteria in Section 7.2(1)(b). The petition shall be made in triplicate on forms provided by the Planning Commission at least thirty (30) days prior to a regular Planning Commission public meeting and the Commission shall refer one (1) copy of the petition to the governing body. Regardless of the Planning Commission's action on the petition, the developer or its successor will have no right to a refund of any monies, fees, or charges paid to the municipality nor to the return of any property or consideration dedicated or delivered to the municipality except as may have previously been agreed to by the Planning Commission, the governing body, and the developer.

2. *Government Initiated Plat Vacation.*

   a. *General Conditions.* The Planning Commission, on its motion, may vacate the plat of an approved subdivision when:

      i. No lots within the approved subdivision have been sold within five (5) years from the date that the plat was signed by the Chairman of the Planning Commission;

      ii. The developer has breached a subdivision improvement agreement and the municipality is unable to obtain funds with which to complete construction of public improvements, except that the vacation shall apply only to lots owned by the developer or its successor;

      iii. The plat has been of record for more than five (5) years and the Planning Commission determines that the further sale of lots within the subdivision presents a threat to public health, safety and welfare, except that the vacation shall apply only to lots owned by the developer or its successor.

   b. *Procedure.* Upon any motion of the Planning Commission to vacate the plat of any previously approved subdivision, in whole or in part, the Commission shall publish notice in a newspaper of general circulation and provide personal notice to all property owners within the subdivision and shall also provide notice to the governing body. The notice shall state the time and place for a public hearing on the motion to vacate the subdivision plat. The public hearing shall be no sooner than thirty (30) and no later than forty-five (45) days from the date of the published and personal notice. The Planning Commission shall approve the resolution effecting the vacation only if the criteria in Section 7.2(1)(b) are satisfied.

c. *Recordation of Notice.* If the Planning Commission adopts a resolution vacating a plat in whole, it shall record a copy of the resolution in the Clerk and Recorder's Office of _____ (county in which municipality is located). If the Planning Commission adopts a resolution vacating a plat in part, it shall record a copy of the resolution as described above and cause a Revised Final Subdivision Plat to be recorded which shows that portion of the original subdivision plat that has been vacated and that portion that has not been vacated.

COMMENTARY ON ARTICLE 7

Land use controls have traditionally been prospective in nature, focusing on the regulation of unplatted, raw land. Such regulation has not always addressed adequately the problems that arise when an already recorded subdivision is either partially developed or not developed at all, and no longer meets current regulatory standards. This situation has occurred most often when property was "prematurely subdivided"; that is, when land was platted long before there was a need or a market for development at that location.

Land often has been platted before local governments adopted substantive subdivision controls. The subdivider was able to plat the property without incurring substantial capital costs and before the government realized the need for stringent controls.[1] The land sometimes has remained entirely under the ownership of the subdivider or subdivider's successor, but just as often has been sold on a lot-by-lot basis to individual owners.[2] Development of the land in accordance with current regulations could require cooperation from numerous absentee landowners and costly public improvements.

The problem of premature subdivision is particularly acute in some Sunbelt states and vacation areas—such as Florida, Colorado, and California—where there are large areas of premature subdivisions.[3] Resolution of this problem calls for some degree of retroactive application of police power controls, which could be grounds for a constitutional attack.[4]

The drafting of specific land readjustment provisions in Article 7 of the Model Regulations is an attempt to bring already platted lands within the scope of subdivision control. The subdivision process is required for any change in a lot line, street layout, common or public use of designated land, or easement. Article 7 additionally provides for both publicly and privately initiated plat vacation. A local government is thereby given the tools to avoid the development of poorly designed subdivisions that would result in environmental degradation and excessive fiscal pressure on the government to provide facilities to widely scattered development.

RESUBDIVISION

The Model Regulations require that changes in the physical layout of a plat go through the entire regulatory approval process as would a new subdivision of land.[5] This assures that the development complies with current regulatory standards and pays its fair share of service and infrastructure costs. The provisions of Article 7 complement the policies of Sections 1.5 and 2.2(145), wherein the inclusive definition of "subdivision" was designed to prevent circumvention of subdivision controls. Resubdivision through the full subdivision approval process also assures that all due process requirements are met and that all affected property owners have an ample opportunity to be heard on any proposed resubdivision. Even where the rights of third persons are not involved, a developer should not be permitted unilaterally to modify the subdivision previously approved by the government.

The planning commission is additionally given the discretion in section 7.1(3) of the Model Regulations to waive the requirement of the full approval process for resubdivision. The commission may approve a resubdivision after one public hearing with statutory notice provided that this resubdivision will not violate the intent of the subdivision regulations.[6] This provision gives the government the flexibility to expedite minor plat revisions while assuring the satisfaction of due process considerations.

Resubdivision could also be used in a cooperative effort by individual lot owners in a premature subdivision who want to develop all or a portion of the platted property. Land could be pooled and then reassembled and redesigned to comply with current regulations and planning requirements. Such cooperation has grown into a system of large-scale urban redevelopment in other countries, most notably Japan.[7] Resubdivision could also, of course, be used by the original developer who still owns all or a major portion of the subdivision.

PLAT VACATION

Publicly and privately initiated plat vacations have become an increasingly popular public response to the problems of undeveloped "paper subdivisions," as development pressures mount in fast-growing areas. Several states have statutes that permit local governments or property owners to vacate all or part of a subdivision plat.[8] The Model Regulations, in section 7.2, adopt plat vacation as a valuable method for accomplishing land readjustment. Without express authorization for plat vacation, a local government must decide if implied authority or home rule powers permit local plat vacation ordinances.

Plat vacation is a legal process by which the government approves the elimination of a plat, in whole or in part. The vacation may apply to subdivided lots as well as roads, alleys, and other areas shown on the plat. Government-initiated plat vacation must be preceded by notice and an opportunity for affected property owners to be heard.[9] Although existing state statutes do not specify the grounds on which the government may approve a vacation, they often require that the government consider whether any person will suffer material injury as a result.[10] The Model Regulations provide that plat vacation initiated by a property owner cannot be allowed if it will materially injure the rights of any nonconsenting property owner.

Once the full or partial vacation is approved, the government should record a statement of the vacation. The original plat should be endorsed with a statement that it has been fully or partially vacated and include a reference to the book and page at which the statement of vacation can be found. When necessary, a revised plat should be recorded.[11] The Model Regulations have been drafted to include these provisions.

The plat vacation technique can be an effective tool for dealing with premature subdivisions when the property affected by the vacation is owned by the original developer or a successor, including a foreclosing lender. The effect of the vacation should be to eliminate subdivided lots that make up the portion of the plat that has been vacated and any roads shown on the plat unless those roads are specifically excluded from the vacation. Any subsequent sale of a portion of the affected property would require a current subdivision approval at that time.

When a premature subdivision is sold into multiple ownership, the effect of plat vacation is less clear. Although plat vacation statutes contemplate that several owners of platted property may seek to have a plat vacated as to their properties, the statutes do not indicate the effect of the vacation. If the only legal description for the affected parcels is with reference to the plat, these parcels will no longer have a legal identity unless deeds are recorded including metes and bounds descriptions or a replatting occurs. Clearly, the government may not eliminate property lines and assemble individually owned parcels without the consent of the owners of those parcels. Thus, it is doubtful that the local government may vacate a plat when lots are in individual ownership unless lot owners agree to a reassemblage.[12]

The intent of the Model Regulations is to allow vacation of lots in separate ownership only on initiation by the property owner or owners, and only if the property rights of any non-consenting property owner are not materially injured.[13] Government-initiated plat vacation is permitted only in regard to lots still owned by the developer or his successor in interest. In this manner the Model Regulations avoid interfering with property rights of individual lot owners. As discussed below under "Land Readjustment," local governments may want to consider the adoption of incentive-type and compulsory land readjustment schemes.

The primary benefit of plat vacation is to eliminate those lots still owned by the developer and to reassemble the land into one parcel. In some premature subdivisions, the original developer or developer's successor owns a substantial portion of the subdivided lots. If, however, even one lot in a premature subdivision has been sold, there may be legal problems with vacating that portion of the platted property owned by the developer. First, lot purchasers acquire a property interest in their own lot and an interest in all areas that are shown on the plat for public use.[14] Often, a recorded declaration of covenants, conditions, and restrictions will grant lot owners express easements in roads shown on the plat. Thus, it is arguable that government-initiated plat vacation will constitute a taking of property if it interferes with any of these rights.[15] Second, express or implied restrictions on the use of property often exist with platted property. These restrictions may be express within the declaration of covenants, conditions, and restrictions or they may be implied under theories of implied reciprocal negative easements or promissory or equitable estoppel.[16] The effect is that lot owners may have a right to enjoin any alteration in the use of property shown on the subdivision plat at the time they acquired their lots.

If the government vacates that portion of a plat still owned by the developer, but the developer can use the property only for residential purposes due to restrictive covenants on the property, the developer may claim that the plat vacation violates due process or constitutes a taking of property. Assuming that the government permits resubdivision under contemporary standards, the developer's constitutional objections should fail. They also should fail because the developer may be said to have created its own hardship by imposing the restrictions in the first instance.

LAND READJUSTMENT

Plat vacation and resubdivision can be used on an individual, small-scale basis, or both could be integrated into a large-scale solution to the problems of premature subdivision. Such a solution, known as "land readjustment," has been used in other countries[17] and has been studied in the United States.[18] The California legislature, for example, as a result of ever-increasing pressures to develop land to meet the needs of the increasing population, has considered land readjustment legislation.[19] Because this is a recent innovation in American land use control systems, the Model Regulations do not incorporate express provisions for the type of land readjustment done in other countries.[20]

Land readjustment refers to a process by which subdivided lands are readjusted to produce a more appropriate land development scheme. Such techniques are necessary when subdivided lands have been sold into multiple ownership and the government cannot simply vacate the plat of inappropriately subdivided lands. The typical land readjustment project involves the replatting of land, the construction or improvement of infrastructure, and, in some instances, the rezoning of land to permit more intense uses. In Japan, land readjustment has been used to turn areas of small agricultural plots into urban serviced land for residential and commercial development.[21] In Germany, the technique is used to redevelop urban areas.[22]

In a land readjustment program, property owners contribute their individual parcels to a land readjustment association or similar entity that has the responsibility for replatting the land. As part of the replatting process, a portion of each parcel is taken for open space, public rights-of-way, and for cost-equivalent land. Cost-equivalent land is land that the association sells to recoup the costs of project execution, including the cost of constructing infrastructure. The result of the project usually is that individual owners receive smaller but more valuable parcels of land in return for their contributions. In some cases, when the project involves the construction of some residential, commercial, or mixed-use development, the owners will take an equity position in the project.[23]

Few people know that our nation's capital was actually the result of a land readjustment effort engineered by George Washington.[24] Since that time, however, only a few jurisdictions have had experience with land readjustment projects. These experiences range from replatting simulations[25] to completed replattings through negotiations between the local government and the developer of a premature subdivision.[26]

In some ways, land readjustment is little more than a resubdivision of land that could be accomplished under the typical set of subdivision regulations. For example, when the land readjustment project consists only of owners who have voluntarily entered into the project, these owners may act through an association or trustee to obtain resubdivision and rezoning. The association or trustee may then try to sell the reassembled land to a developer or, in rare cases, may actually attempt to redevelop the land itself. The voluntary land readjustment process is commonly referred to as neighborhood lot pooling.[27] Property owners or a redeveloper may be encouraged to undertake a land readjustment project through incentive zoning schemes that permit greater density of development when parcels are aggregated.[28]

When owners are not all willing to participate in a resubdivision process, a land readjustment program may be necessary. Land readjustment programs are either of the mandatory participation type or the condemnation type. The first type requires that all property owners in the land readjustment area participate in the specific project. This is true even though owners will have their individual parcels taken from them and receive a reconfigured parcel in return (or an interest in a development project). This procedure raises obvious concerns about the taking of property in violation of state and federal constitutions. Under the condemnation technique, property owners who do not want to participate in the project may sell their interests to the land readjustment association under threat of condemnation. This implies that the association, which is most likely a private association or corporation, must be able to use the power of eminent domain or be able to have the government use the power for the benefit of the land readjustment association.[29]

One problem that local governments may face when considering the adoption of land readjustment techniques is how to determine which land readjustment projects should be approved. The lure of profits may encourage many property owners to join in a land readjustment project. Yet, it may not be consistent with the local comprehensive plan to have numerous areas in the jurisdiction replatted and redeveloped. The best approach for the government is to coordinate land readjustment programs with the comprehensive plan, including any plans for urban redevelopment, and with the government's capital improvements program.

Strategic capital facilities decision making can provide the improvement in market conditions in an area appropriate for redevelopment that may be necessary to make a land readjustment project work. This is true because land readjustment cannot work unless there will be a real market for the reconfigured land that will provide an adequate rate of return to property owners who participate in a land readjustment project. The strategic decision to place a government facility, such as a convention center, can stimulate the market for property around the center and thereby provide the incentive that private owners may need to participate in a land readjustment project.

Local governments around the United States should carefully study the use of land readjustment techniques. Many of these governments could probably adopt such programs under their home rule powers. In other jurisdictions, state legislation should be sought to authorize local adoption of land readjustment programs. This privatization of urban redevelopment may be necessary to assist financially strapped governments with their redevelopment activities.

NOTES

1. *See* Stroud, *Environmental Problems Associated With Large Recreational Subdivision*, 35 Prof. Geographer 303, 304 (1983) (emphasis added): "Several important variables appear to influence the location of these large scale land development operations. The most important are availability of large tracts of relatively inexpensive land, accessibility, nearness to urban centers, *and absence of local and regional land use plans and regulations that might hamper land development operations.*" Stroud continues: "The absence of governmental regulations may be the single most important determinant in site selection." *Id.* at 307.

2. M. Shultz & J. Groy, The Premature Subdivision of Land in Colorado: A Survey With A Commentary (Lincoln Institute of Land Policy, 1986).

3. *See generally* Schnidman & Baker, *Planning for Platted Lands: Land Use Remedies for Lot Sale Subdivisions*, 11 Fla. St. U. L. Rev. 505 (1983). *See also* Shultz & Groy, *The Failure of Subdivision Control in the Western United States: A Blueprint for Local Government Action*, 1988 Utah L. Rev. 569, 581-82.

4. *See, e.g.,* Usery v. Turner Elkhorn Mining Co., 428 U.S. 1 (1976) (holding that law that is retroactive in operation does not necessarily violate due process clause of Fourteenth Amendment).

5. Model Regulations, § 7.1(1).

6. Model Regulations, § 7.1(3).

7. Nishiyama, *Kukaku-Seiri (Land Readjustment): A Japanese Land Development Technique,* 1 Land Assembly & Dev. 1, 1 (Spring 1987).

8. *See* Va. Code Ann. §§ 15.1-481--15.1-485 (1981 & Supp. 1988) (in Virginia, a plat can be vacated before or after the sale of any lots therein, by an action initiated by the landowners, by the local government or by "any interested party," with an appeal process for landowners "irreparably damaged"). *See also* Alaska Stat. § 40.15.140-.180 (1987); Cal. Gov't Code §§ 66499.11-.20 and .21-.29 (West 1983); Idaho Code §§ 50-1306 (A), 50-1317 and 50-1321 (1980); Mont. Code Ann. §§ 7-5-2501 and 7-5-2502 (1985); Utah Code Ann. §§ 57-5-5.5 to 57-5-8 (1986 & Supp. 1987); Wyo. Stat. §§ 34-12-106 to 34-12-111 (1977). The majority of these statutes recognize the right of owners of lots in a subdivision to vacate only that portion of the plat applicable to them. California, Oregon, Virginia, and Utah permit the local government, under appropriate conditions, to vacate all or part of subdivision plat. Cal. Gov't Code § 66499.12 (West 1983); Ore. Rev. Stat. §§ 92.040 and 92.234 (1985); Va. Code Ann. §§ 15.1-481(2), 15.1-482(b) (1981 & Supp. 1988); Utah Code Ann. § 57-5-7.1 (Supp. 1987). *See also* Schnidman & Baker, *supra* note 3, at 566-69 (discussing government mandated deplatting).

In California, plat vacation is referred to as "reversions to acreage." Reversion to acreage is only one of five methods for reconfiguring platted lands under California law. Other methods include merger and resubdivision, Cal. Gov't Code § 66499.20 1/2 (West 1983); merger of contiguous parcels under common ownership, *id.* § 66499.20 3/4; exclusions from a plat (partial vacation), *id.* § 66499.21-.29; and government initiated merger of parcels, *id.* § 66451.10-.21 (West 1987). Florida, plagued with thousands of acres of undeveloped premature subdivisions, repealed legislation that had allowed a local government to vacate a plat which had been recorded for more than five years and which had less than 10 percent of its lots individually sold, with a finding that such action promoted the general welfare and complied with the comprehensive plan. The repeal came after an adverse court decision. Maselli v. Orange County,

488 So.2d 904 (Fla. Dist. Ct. App. 1986) (court interpretation of statutory language rendered the regulation useless). Washington State repealed its plat vacation provisions in 1987 (formerly Wash. Rev. Code §§ 58.11.010-.050 and 58.12.010-.140 (1961)).

9. *See, e.g.,* Utah Code Ann. § 57-5-7.5 (1987) (requiring published notice and mailed notice to all owners of record of land contained in the entire plat). *But see* Nev. Rev. Stat. §§ 270.160 and 270.170 (1985) (allowing vacation following published notice only and permitting a person claiming material injury to commence an action setting aside the vacation). The Model Regulations require published and personal notice for both privately and publicly initiated vacations.

10. *See, e.g.,* Utah Code Ann. § 57-5-8 (1987) (government may vacate, alter, or amend plat or portion of plat if "it is satisfied that neither the public nor any person will be materially injured" by the government action and that "there is good cause" for the action). *Compare* N.M. Stat. Ann. § 47-6-7 (1982), providing that the planning authority "shall determine whether or not the vacation will adversely affect the interests of persons on contiguous land or within the subdivision being vacated." *But see* Va. Code Ann. §§ 15.1-481(2) and 15.1-482(b) (1981 & Supp. 1988), wherein any findings of irreparable damage to the property owner must be made by appeal to the circuit court.

11. *See, e.g.,* N.M. Stat. Ann. § 47-6-7(C) (1982) (concerning recordation of notice of vacation).

12. *See, e.g.,* Ore. Rev. Stat. § 92.225(2)(e) (1985), which prohibits government-initiated vacation when one or more lots in a subdivision have been sold. The Oregon law considers such subdivisions to be "developed." If the effect of a plat vacation is to eliminate the basis for the legal description of individual lots, but lot owners continue to own those areas shown on the plat that will need to be redescribed if those areas are conveyed, the government may legally vacate the plat unless there is some claim of vested rights. Presumably, those areas will carry a metes and bounds description when conveyed following the full or partial plat vacation unless a new plat is recorded. These conveyances of individual areas in whole will not require subdivision approval. The owner of contiguous lots in a vacated subdivision will own the area covered by those lots but will no longer own individual lots. If that owner attempts to convey a portion of the area covered by the lots, the owner probably will need to obtain subdivision approval. California law permits the government to vacate a plat where lots have been sold if "[n]one of the improvements required to be made have been made within two years from the date the final or parcel map was filed for record, or within the time allowed by agreement for completion of the improvements." CAL. GOV'T CODE § 66499.16(b)(2) (West 1983). The only other basis for government-initiated plat vacation is if "all owners of an interest in the real property within the subdivision have consented to reversion" or if "[n]o lots shown on the final or parcel map have been sold within five years from the date such map was filed for record." *Id.* § 66499.16(b)(1) and (3). *See also* Schnidman & Baker, *supra* note 3, at 505, 573: "[D]eplatting may deprive the lot owner of the essence of his purchase—a distinct lot whose existence is in part traceable to a governmental act and whose acquisition, rather than use, was accompanied by a financial detriment." The authors continue: "[A] challenge by a lot owner to deplatting is much more likely to prevail, though direct authority for this proposition is slim."

13. See Model Regulations, § 7.2 (1)(b). The Virginia Code, on the other hand, has no criteria for government approval of plat vacations and provides that a government-initiated plat vacation that irreparably damages the owner of any lot shown on that plat may be nullified by the circuit court if an appeal is taken within 30 days of the adoption of such vacation ordinance. VA. CODE ANN. §§ 15.1-481(2) and 15-1-482(b) (1981 & Supp. 1988).

14. *See* 6 P. ROHAN, HOME OWNER ASSOCIATIONS AND PLANNED UNIT DEVELOPMENTS--LAW AND PRACTICE 4.02 [1]-[3] (1982).

15. *See* D. HAGMAN & J. JUERGENSMEYER, URBAN PLANNING AND LAND DEVELOPMENT CONTROL LAW 19.8 (2d ed. 1986). The authors state that "[t]he majority rule is that compensation is due [when the government interferes with rights derived from restrictive covenants] on the theory that an equitable servitude is a property right, analogous to an easement, loss of which must be paid for by the condemning authority. Other courts hold that equitable servitudes are merely contractual rights cognizable in equity and do not constitute sufficient property interests to be paid for when taken." *Id.* at 584 (footnotes omitted). *Following* First English Evangelical Lutheran Church v. County of Los Angeles, 107 S.Ct. 2378, 2386 (1987) (land-use regulations may constitute a taking of property for which compensation must be paid). Furthermore, the Court recently has stressed that it will take property rights seriously and not treat the taking of a property interest as a mere regulation on the use of property. *See* Nollan v. California Coastal Comm'n, 107 S.Ct. 3141, 3145 (1987).

16. *See* Sanborn v. McLean, 206 N.W. 496 (Mich. 1925) (dealing with implied reciprocal negative easements); Burgess v. Putnam, 464 S.W.2d 698 (Tex. Civ. App. 1971) (dealing with promissory estoppel); Crane-Berkley Corp. v. Lavis, 263 N.Y.S. 556 (App. Div. 1933) (discussing estoppel principles). For a general discussion of restrictive covenants, *see* Stoebuck, *Running Covenants: An Analytical Primer*, 52 WASH. L. REV. 861 (1977).

17. For example, around the turn of the century in Germany, an early form of land readjustment resulted from land ownership patterns incompatible with the rapid urbanization and industrialization of that country. Kuppers, Nishiyama, & Nakamura, *Selected European Land Readjustment Experiences*, in LAND READJUSTMENT: THE JAPANESE SYSTEM 33 (1986).

18. *Id.* at 3.

19. Bergeson & Glickfeld, *The Evolution of Land Readjustment Law in California: Solving a Hidden Land Use Problem*, 1 LAND ASSEMBLY & DEV. 45, 45-46 (1987).

20. *See* Schnidman, *Land Readjustment: An Alternative to Development Exactions*, in PRIVATE SUPPLY OF PUBLIC SERVICES 250 (R. Alterman, ed., 1988).

21. *See* Shultz and Schnidman, *The Potential Application of Land Readjustment in the United States*, 22 URB. LAW. 224, 224-27 (1990).

22. *See id.* at 231-32.

23. *See, e.g.*, Northrop, *The Farmer's Market District*, URB. LAND 19 (1984) (discussing commercial redevelopment in Dallas).

24. *See* J. REPS, MONUMENTAL WASHINGTON (1967); H. CAEMMERER, THE NATIONAL CAPITAL (1932).

25. *See* Schnidman, *Resolving Platted Lands Problems: The Florida Experience*, 1 LAND ASS. & DEV. J. 27, 33-38 (1987).

26. *See* Nelson, *More Lessons from Negotiated Replatting in Oregon*, 3 PLATTED LANDS PRESS 6 (March 1986).

27. *See* Johnson, *Neighborhood Pooling—An Overview*, 3 PLATTED LANDS PRESS 1 (February 1986); B. BERNS & Y. CHANDLER, NEIGHBORHOOD BUYOUTS: BALANCING CONFLICTING INTERESTS (1986).

28. Freilich, *Inducing Replatting Through Performance Zoning*, 2 PLATTED LANDS PRESS 5 (Jan. 1985) (discussing performance zoning ordinance

adopted in Miami Beach to encourage private redevelopment).

29. *Compare* Mo. Rev. Stat. § 353.130 (1986) (permitting private urban redevelopment corporations to exercise the government's power of eminent domain). The Missouri Supreme Court upheld this private use of the eminent domain power in Annbar Assocs. v. West Side Redevelopment Corp., 397 S.W.2d 635 (Mo. 1965), *appeal dismissed,* 385 U.S. 5 (1966). *See generally* Shultz and Sapp, *Urban Redevelopment and the Elimination of Blight: A Case Study of Missouri's Chapter 353,* 37 J. Urb. & Contemp. L. 3 (1990).

8

Specifications for Documents to be Submitted

8.1   Sketch Plat.

Sketch plats submitted to the Planning Commission, prepared in pen or pencil, shall be drawn to a convenient scale of not more than one hundred (100) feet to an inch and shall show the following information:

1. *Name.*
   a. Name of subdivision if property is within an existing subdivision.
   b. Proposed name if not within a previously platted subdivision. The proposed name shall not duplicate the name of any plat previously recorded.
   c. Name of property if no subdivision name has been chosen. (This is commonly the name by which the property is locally known.)
2. *Ownership.*
   a. Name and address, including telephone number, of legal owner or agent of property, and citation of last instrument conveying title to each parcel of property involved in the proposed subdivision, giving grantor, grantee, date, and land records reference.
   b. Citation of any existing legal rights-of-way or easements affecting the property.
   c. Existing covenants on the property, if any.
   d. Name and address, including telephone number, of the professional person(s) responsible for subdivision design, for the design of public improvements, and for surveys.
3. *Description.* Location of property by government lot, section, township, range and county, graphic scale, north arrow, and date.

a. Location of property lines, existing easements, burial grounds, railroad rights-of-way, watercourses, and existing wooded areas or trees eight (8) inches or more in diameter, measured four (4) feet above ground level; location, width, and names of all existing or platted streets or other public ways within or immediately adjacent to the tract; names of adjoining property owners from the latest assessment rolls within five hundred (500) feet of any perimeter boundary of the subdivision.

b. Location, sizes, elevations, and slopes of existing sewers, water mains, culverts, and other underground structures within the tract and immediately adjacent thereto; existing permanent building and utility poles on or immediately adjacent to the site and utility rights-of-way.

c. Approximate topography, at the same scale as the sketch plat.

d. The approximate location and widths of proposed streets.

e. Preliminary proposals for connection with existing water supply and sanitary sewage systems, or alternative means of providing water supply and sanitary waste treatment and disposal; preliminary provisions for collecting and discharging surface water drainage.

f. The approximate location, dimensions, and areas of all proposed or existing lots.

g. The approximate location, dimensions, and area of all parcels of land proposed to be set aside for park or playground use or other public use, or for the use of property owners in the proposed subdivision.

h. The location of temporary stakes to enable the Planning Commission to find and appraise features of the sketch plat in the field.

i. Whenever the sketch plat covers only a part of an applicant's contiguous holdings, the applicant shall submit, at the scale of no more than two hundred (200) feet to the inch, a sketch in pen or pencil of the proposed subdivision area, together with its proposed street system, and an indication of the probable future street system, and an indication of the probable future street and drainage system of the remaining portion of the tract.

j. A vicinity map showing streets and other general development of the surrounding area. The sketch plat shall show all school and improvement district lines with the zones properly designated.

8.2 Preliminary Plat.

1. *General.* The preliminary plat shall be prepared by a licensed land surveyor at a convenient scale not more than one (1) inch equals one

hundred (100) feet, may be prepared in pen or pencil, and the sheets shall be numbered in sequence if more than one (1) sheet is used and shall be of such size as is acceptable for filing in the office of the Recorder of Deeds, but shall not be thirty-four by forty-four (34 x 44) inches or larger. The map prepared for the preliminary plat may also be used for the final subdivision plat and, therefore, should be drawn on tracing cloth or reproducible mylar. Preparation in pencil will make required changes and additions easier.

2. *Features.* The preliminary plat shall show the following:

   a. The location of property with respect to surrounding property and streets, the names of all adjoining property owners of record, or the names of adjoining developments; the names of adjoining streets.

   b. The location and dimensions of all boundary lines of the property to be expressed in feet and decimals of a foot.

   c. The location of existing streets, easements, water bodies, streams, and other pertinent features such as swamps, railroads, buildings, parks, cemeteries, drainage ditches, and bridges, as determined by the Planning Commission.

   d. The location and width of all existing and proposed streets and easements, alleys, and other public ways, and easement and proposed street rights-of-way and building set-back lines.

   e. The locations, dimensions, and areas of all proposed or existing lots.

   f. The location and dimensions of all property proposed to be set aside for park or playground use, or other public or private reservation, with designation of the purpose of those set asides, and conditions, if any, of the dedication or reservation.

   g. The name and address of the owner or owners of land to be subdivided, the name and address of the subdivider if other than the owner, and the name of the land surveyor.

   h. The date of the map, approximate true north point, scale, and title of the subdivision.

   i. Sufficient data acceptable to the Local Government Engineer to determine readily the location, bearing, and length of all lines, and to reproduce such lines upon the ground; the location of all proposed monuments.

   j. Names of the subdivision and all new streets as approved by the Planning Commission.

   k. Indication of the use of any lot (single-family, two-family, multi-family, townhouse) and all uses other than residential proposed by the subdivider.

l. Blocks shall be consecutively numbered or lettered in alphabetical order. The blocks in numbered additions to subdivisions bearing the same name shall be numbered or lettered consecutively throughout the several additions.

m. All lots in each block shall be consecutively numbered. Outlots shall be lettered in alphabetical order. If blocks are numbered or lettered, outlots shall be lettered in alphabetical order within each block.

n. All information required on sketch plat should also be shown on the preliminary plat, and the following notation shall also be shown:

    i. Explanation of drainage easements, if any.

    ii. Explanation of site easements, if any.

    iii. Explanation of reservations, if any.

    iv. Endorsement of owner, as follows:

_____

Owner   *Date*

o. Form for endorsements by Commission Chairman as follows: Approved by Resolution of the Planning Commission.

_____

Chairman   *Date*

p. The lack of information under any item specified herein, or improper information supplied by the applicant, shall be cause for disapproval of a preliminary plat.

8.3 Construction Plans.

1. *General.* Construction plans shall be prepared for all required improvements. Plans shall be drawn at a scale of no more than one (1) inch equals fifty (50) feet, and map sheets shall be of the same size as the preliminary plat. The following shall be shown:

a. Profiles showing existing and proposed elevations along center lines of all roads. Where a proposed road intersects an existing road or roads, the elevation along the center line of the existing road or roads within one hundred (100) feet of the intersection, shall be shown. Approximate radii of all curves, lengths of tangents, and central angles on all streets shall be shown.

b. The Planning Commission may require, where steep slopes exist, that cross-sections of all proposed streets at one-hundred-foot (100-foot) stations be shown at five (5) points as follows: On a line at right angles to the center line of the street, and said elevation points shall be at the center line of the street, each property line, and points twenty-five (25) feet inside each property line.

c. Plans and profiles showing the locations and typical cross-section of street pavements including curbs and gutters, sidewalks, drainage easements, servitudes, rights-of-way, manholes, and catch basins; the locations of street trees, street lighting standards, and street signs; the location, size, and invert elevations of existing and proposed sanitary sewers, stormwater drains, and fire hydrants, showing connection to any existing or proposed utility systems; and exact location and size of all water, gas, or other underground utilities or structures.

d. Location, size, elevation, and other appropriate descriptions of any existing facilities or utilities, including, but not limited to, existing streets, sewers, drains, water mains, easements, water bodies, streams, and other pertinent features such as swamps, railroads, buildings, features noted on the Official Map or Master Plan, at the point of connection to proposed facilities and utilities within the subdivision, and each tree with a diameter of eight (8) inches or more, measured twelve (12) inches above ground level. The water elevations of adjoining lakes or streams at the date of the survey, and the approximate high- and low-water elevations of such lakes or streams. All elevations shall be referred to the U.S.G.S. datum plane. If the subdivision borders a lake, river, or stream, the distances and bearings of a meander line established not less than twenty (20) feet back from the ordinary high-water mark of such waterways.

e. Topography at the same scale as the sketch plat with a contour interval of two (2) feet, referred to sea-level datum. The datum provided shall be latest applicable U.S. Coast and Geodetic Survey datum and should be so noted on the plat.

f. All specifications and references required by the local government's construction standards and specifications, including a site-grading plan for the entire subdivision.

g. Notation of approval as follows:

_____

Owner   *Date*

_____

Planning Commission Chairman   *Date*

h. Title, name, address, and signature of professional engineer and surveyor, and date revision dates.

8.4   Final Subdivision Plat.

1. *General.* The final subdivision plat shall be presented in india ink on tracing cloth or reproducible mylar at the same scale and contain the same information, except for any changes or additions required by resolution of the Planning Commission, as shown on the preliminary plat. The preliminary plat may be used as the final subdivision plat if it meets these requirements and is revised in accordance with the Planning Commission's resolution. All revision dates must be shown as well as the following:

   a. Notation of any self-imposed restrictions, and locations of any building lines proposed to be established in this manner, if required by the Planning Commission in accordance with these regulations.

   b. Endorsement of the local government Health Department.

   c. Endorsement on the plat by every person having a security interest in the subdivision property that they are subordinating their liens to all covenants, servitudes, and easements imposed on the property.

   d. Lots numbered as approved by the Local Government Assessor.

   e. All monuments erected, corners, and other points established in the field in their proper places. The material of which the monuments, corners, or other points are made shall be noted at the representation thereof or by legend, except that lot corners need not be shown. The legend for metal monuments shall indicate the kind of metal, the diameter, length, and weight per lineal foot of the monuments.

2. *Preparation.* The final subdivision plat shall be prepared by a land surveyor licensed by the state.

COMMENTARY ON ARTICLE 8

The subdivision approval process contains numerous detailed steps.[1] The level of sophistication of the subdivision regulations may be reflected in the developer's submission requirements. The developer generally is required to show, in varying degrees of detail, the ownership and financial matters relating to the property, topography and other geological factors, construction and engineering plans, and the relationship of the plat to surrounding properties and municipal facilities.

To eliminate uncertainties surrounding submission requirements, Article 8 sets out in specific terms the forms and plans that the subdivision applicant must present to the government. The submission requirements, along with the companion forms in Appendix C, will provide the developer with reasonably sufficient standards for compliance with local application procedures. These standards should assist a city in defending against judicial challenges to subdivision regulations based on their vagueness.[2]

The strategy involved in the establishment of a three-stage approval process requires that the degree of complexity and specificity of the submission requirements increase as the developer moves through the approval process. This process is intended to prevent the premature expenditure of time and money. Although subdivision regulation is a relatively complex process, it should not become a trap for the unwary. At sketch plat approval, temporary staking of the property is required so that the commission or its staff can make a field trip to the subdivision site. A vicinity map also is essential to show surrounding lands, including the owner's other contiguous holdings, thereby preventing inappropriate subdivision or evasion of the subdivision regulations.

At the preliminary plat approval stage, a licensed surveyor is required to make all plans to assure accuracy. The preliminary plat indicates blocks and lots, names, streets, and all details required for final subdivision approval. A detailed set of construction plans for engineering and environmental features also is required. A contour interval of two feet is required for topographic maps, together with a site-grading plan for the entire subdivision. Construction plans must be prepared by a professional engineer. The final subdivision plat must indicate all features of the preliminary plat along with those additions and changes required by the planning commission. Health department endorsement and assessor approval of lots and monuments also are required.

The forms contained in Appendix C are designed to be complementary to the submission requirements. These forms include applications and checklists for each stage of approval, planning commission resolutions approving the plat, offers of irrevocable dedication, and a sample subdivision improvement agreement and security (letter of credit). The checklists in Appendix C will ensure that all steps required by the regulations have been completed, and that all appropriate fees and documentation have been submitted.

NOTES

1. Sonn v. Planning Comm'n, 374 A.2d 159 (Conn. 1976); 5 N. Williams, American Land Planning Law § 5.05 (1985).

2. Commonwealth Properties v. Washington County, 582 P.2d 1384 (Ore. Ct. App. 1978). *See generally* 5 N. Williams, *supra* note 1, at § 156.11.

APPENDIX A
A STANDARD CITY PLANNING ENABLING ACT

Title II—Subdivision Control*

---

*Title II of the SPEA has been reprinted from the AMERICAN LAW INSTITUTE, A MODEL LAND DEVELOPMENT CODE, Tentative Draft No. 1, at 224,244-253 (1968). The entire act, including Title I—Municipal Planning and Planning Commissions, Title III—Buildings in Mapped Streets, Title IV—Regional Planning and Planning Commissions, and Title V—Miscellaneous Provisions, can be found at 222 to 271 of Tentative Draft No. 1. Due to the extreme length, only the portion of the act relating to subdivision controls has been reproduced here.

For an analysis of the provisions of the AMERICAN LAW INSTITUTE, A MODEL LAND DEVELOPMENT CODE, Proposed Official Draft No. 1, Article II (1974) dealing with subdivision control, see Appendix B herein.

For an analysis of the statutes of the various states with respect to subdivision control, see generally, ANDERSON & ROSWEIG, PLANNING ZONING & SUBDIVISION: A SUMMARY OF STATUTORY LAW IN THE FIFTY STATES 228 (New York State Federation of Official Planning Organizations, 1966).

Section 12. Subdivision Jurisdiction[1]—The territorial jurisdiction of any municipal planning commission over the subdivision of land shall include all land located in the municipality and all land lying within five miles[2] of the corporate limits of the municipality and not located in any other municipality, except that, in the case of any such nonmunicipal land lying within five miles of more than one municipality having a planning commission, the jurisdiction[3] of each such municipal planning commission shall terminate at a boundary line equidistant from the respective corporate limits of such municipalities.[4]

Section 13. Scope of Control of Subdivisions.— Whenever a planning commission shall have adopted a major street plan[5] of the territory within its subdivision jurisdiction or part thereof, and shall have filed a certified copy of such plan in the office of the county recorder of the county in which such territory or part is located, then no plat of a subdivision of land within such territory or part shall be filed or recorded[6] until it shall have been approved by such planning commission and such approval entered in writing on the plat by the chairman or secretary of the commission.

Section 14. Subdivision Regulations—Before exercising the powers[7] referred to in Section 13, the planning commission shall adopt regulations[8] governing the subdivision of land within its jurisdiction. Such regulations may provide for the proper arrangement of streets[9] in relation to other existing or planned streets and to the master plan, for adequate and convenient open spaces for traffic, utilities, access of fire-fighting apparatus, recreation, light and air, and for the avoidance of congestion of population, including minimum width and area of lots.[10]

Such regulations may include provisions as to the extent to which streets and other ways shall be graded and improved and to which water and sewer and other utility mains, piping, or other facilities shall be installed as a condition precedent to the approval of the plat.[11] The regulations or practice of the commission may provide for a tentative approval[12] of the plat previous to such installation: but any such tentative approval shall be revocable and shall not be entered on the plat. In lieu of the completion of such improvements and utilities prior to the final approval of the plat, the commission may accept a bond[13] with surety to secure to the municipality the actual construction and installation of such improvements or utilities at a time and according to specifications fixed by or in accordance with the regulations of the commission.[14] The municipality is hereby granted the power to enforce such bond by all appropriate legal and equitable remedies.

All such regulations shall be published as provided by law for the publication of ordinances, and, before adoption, a public hearing shall be held thereon. A copy thereof shall be certified by the commission to the recorders of the counties in which the municipality and territory are located.

Section 15. Procedure,[15] Legal Effect of Approval of Plat—The planning commission shall approve or disapprove a plat within 30 days[16] after the submission thereof to it; otherwise such plat shall be deemed to have been approved, and a certificate to that effect shall be issued by the commission on demand: *Provided, however,* that the applicant for the commission's approval may waive this requirement and consent to an extension of such period. The ground of disapproval[17] of any plat shall be stated upon the records of the commission. Any plat submitted to the commission shall contain the name and address of a person to whom notice[18] of a hearing shall be sent; and no plat be acted on by the commission without affording a hearing thereof. Notice shall be sent to the said address by registered mail of the time and place of such hearing, not less than five days before the date fixed therefor. Similar notice shall be mailed to the owners of land immediately adjoining[19] the platted land, as their names appear upon the plats in the county auditor's office and their addresses appear in the directory of the municipality or on the tax records of the municipality or county. Every plat approved by the commission shall, by virtue of such approval, be deemed to be an amendment of or an addition to or a detail of the municipal plan and a part thereof. Approval of a plat shall not be deemed to constitute or effect an acceptance by the public of any street or other open space shown upon the plat. The planning commission may, from time to time, recommend to council amendments of the zoning ordinance or map or additions thereto to conform to the commission's recommendations for the zoning regulation of the territory comprised within approved subdivisions.[20] The commission shall have the power to agree with the applicant upon use, height, area, or bulk requirements[21] or restrictions governing buildings and premises within the subdivision, provided such requirements or restrictions do not authorize the violation of the then effective zoning ordinance of the municipality. Such requirements or restrictions shall be stated upon the plat prior to the approval and recording thereof and shall have the same force of law and be enforceable in the same manner and with the same sanctions and penalties and subject to the same power of amendment or repeal as though set out as a part of the zoning ordinance or map of the municipality.

Section 16. Penalties for Transferring Lots in Unapproved Subdivisions—Whoever, being the owner or agent of the owner of any land located within a subdivision, transfers or sells[22] or agrees to sell or negotiates to sell any land by reference to or exhibition of or by other use of a plat[23] of a subdivision, before such plat has been approved by the planning commission and recorded or filed in the office of the appropriate county recorder, shall forfeit and pay a penalty of $100 for each lot or parcel so transferred or sold by agreed or negotiated to be sold; and the description of such lot or parcel by metes and bounds[24] in the instrument of transfer or other document used in the process of selling or transferring shall not exempt the transaction from such penalties or from the remedies herein provided. The municipal corporation may enjoin such transfer or sale or agreement by action for injunction brought in any court of equity jurisdiction or may recover the said penalty by a civil action[25] in any court of competent jurisdiction.

Section 17. County Recorder's Duties—A county recorder[26] who files or records a plat of a subdivision without the approval of the planning commission as required by law shall be deemed guilty of a misdemeanor and shall be fined not less than $100 nor more than $500.

Section 18. Improvements in Unapproved Streets—The municipality shall not accept, lay out, open, improve, grade, pave, curb, or light any street, or lay or authorize[27] water mains or sewers or connections to be laid in any street, within any portion of territory for which the planning commission shall have adopted[28] a major street plan, unless such street (a) shall have been accepted or opened as or shall otherwise have received the legal status of a public street prior to the adoption of such plan, or unless such street (b) corresponds with a street shown on the official master plan or with a street on a subdivision plat approved by the planning commission or with a street on a street plat[29] made by and adopted by the commission. Council may, however, accept any street not shown on or not corresponding with a street on the official master plan or on an approved subdivision plat or an approved street plat, provided the ordinance or other measure accepting such street be first submitted to the municipal planning commission for its approval and, if approved by the commission, be enacted or passed by not less than a majority of the entire membership of council or, if disapproved by the commission, be enacted or passed by not less than two-thirds of the entire membership of council. A street approved by the planning commission upon submission by council, or a street accepted by a two-thirds vote after disapproval by the planning commission, shall thereupon have the status of an approved street as fully as though it had been originally shown on the official master plan or on a subdivision plat approved by the commission or had been originally platted by the commission.[30]

Section 19. Erection of Buildings—From and after the time when a planning commission shall have adopted a major street plan of the territory within its subdivision jurisdiction or part thereof, no building shall be erected[31] on any lot within such territory or part, nor shall a building permit be issued therefor unless the street giving access to the lot upon which such building is proposed to be placed (a) shall have been accepted or opened as or shall otherwise have received the legal status of a public street prior to that time, or unless such street (b) corresponds with a street shown on the official master plan or with a street on a subdivision plat approved by the planning commission or with a street on a street plat[32] made by and adopted by the commission or with a street accepted by council, after submission to the planning commission, by the favorable vote required in Section 18 of this act. Any building erected in violation of this section shall be deemed an unlawful structure, and the building inspector or other appropriate official[33] may cause it to be vacated and have it removed.

Section 20. Status of Existing Platting Statutes[34]—From and after the time when a planning commission shall have control over subdivisions as provided in Section 13 of this act, the jurisdiction of the planning commission over plats shall be exclusive within the territory under its jurisdiction, and all statutory control over plats or subdivisions of land granted by other statutes shall insofar as in harmony with the provisions of this act be deemed transferred to the planning commission of such municipality, and, insofar as inconsistent with the provisions of this act, are hereby repealed.

NOTES

1. *Subdivision jurisdiction*: The municipality is not the only agency that is locating streets and other public open spaces. On the contrary, except in the case of major thoroughfares, most of the highways are located by private agencies; namely, the subdividers of land. Obviously, the way the subdivider locates the streets and his lots determines, to as great an extent as any other factor, the adequacy and economy of the city's highway system, the density of population, the flow of traffic, the open spaces for light, air, health, and recreation. After the subdivider has sold his lots and people have built houses, it becomes almost inescapable that the public will accept, sooner or later, the streets and lots as laid out by the subdivider. Therefore, the subdivider has it in his power to dislocate or destroy the city plan, and the community must needs exercise this control at a time when the control can be made effective; namely, at the time of the subdividing or platting of the land.

Provisions of this title provide an effective control in a way that will work no hardship on the legitimate subdivider but, on the contrary, will be a help to him. In the actual workings of such a system of control, the planning commission and the subdivider usually cooperate to produce a result that will be beneficial to the community nd subdivider alike. The statute will bring the subdivider and the commission into conference with each other, and the final result will usually be amicably reached. The commission will seldom have to impose its judgment over the hostile position of the subdivider, but these are the very cases in which the control is most essential.

Obviously, this control of subdivisions, within the reasonable limits and subject to the fair and reasonable procedure set out in the act, needs to be comprehensive, for any dislocation of the city plan is a progressive evil which spreads and may ultimately break down the whole plan.

2. *Five miles*: As has been pointed out in note 34, intelligent city planning of a municipality must take into consideration conditions which exist in the surrounding territory. For a number of years, in many states, control has been given to the municipality over the subdivision of property in the territory within a certain zone outside the city limits. This zone varies in different states. In some it is a three-

mile zone, in others five miles; in others less, in others more.

Three miles has been the usual distance, but the automobile is rapidly making that too small. No uniform figure will quite fit all municipalities, since, naturally, the larger municipalities have larger urban fringes than the smaller ones. It would not be difficult to include a provision for varying distances according to the size of the municipality.

The reason why control of platting in this territory should be given to the planning commission of the municipality in question is obvious, for practically all of this territory will ultimately become a part of that municipality or at least seriously affect the development of the municipality. Even though it may never come within the corporate limits, it will in all essential respects be a part of the municipality. Ultimately the control of property in territory outside the corporate limits of municipalities should be handled in relation to regional planning and regional organization. When and where regional planning is well developed, control in such territory by an adjacent city may very wisely be discontinued. In the meantime, however, pending the development of regional plans and regional control, control by the central municipality is necessary in many cases if that city is to insured against the ill effects of badly planned developments near its borders. There is ample precedent for such control, as, for instance, in Ohio there has been control of plats within the three-mile limits of municipalities for the past 16 years. From the legal point of view, there is no difficulty in exercising such control if the legislature gives the power.

3. *Jurisdiction*: The statute itself must necessarily define the jurisdiction of each planning commission. Compulsory joint action by two or more planning commissions would create many practical difficulties, many delays in dealing with subdividers, and might result in decisions which represent enforced compromises rather than intelligent solutions. Voluntary cooperation by two or more municipalities for the regulation of the platting of territory which is tributary to all of them is always advisable and requires no statutory authority.

4. *Municipalities*: In using the text of this section, care should be taken to keep in mind the definition of "municipality" and "municipal" which may have been adopted for Section 1 of the act. For instance, if, under the definition set forth in Section 1, there is no nonmunicipal territory in the state, then, of course, changes will need to made in Section 12 to correspond with this situation. In each state, care should be exercised that the phraseology of Section 12, taken in connection with that adopted for Section 1, will carry out the legislative intention regarding the scope of subdivision control by each planning commission.

5. *Major street plan*: The planning commission is empowered to exercise its control of subdivisions only after it shall have developed at least a major street plan of the territory to be controlled. Until that phase of its plan has been reached, platting should continue under the existing form of control or lack of control, for the imposition of requirements which might turn out to have little or no relation to the ultimate principles of control would be unfair to the subdivider's plan. This limitation, of course, does not involve the necessity of the commission having completed all the other features of the comprehensive plan, but merely that a main thoroughfare plan shall have been adopted.

6. *Filed or recorded*: In each state using this act, it would be well to mention here the office at which the plat is required to be recorded. The word "filed" or the word "recorded," or both, should be used, according to the individual practice of the different states.

7. *Before exercising the powers*: Before acquiring jurisdiction over plats, the planning commission is required to adopt general regulations laying down the principles and rules governing the subdivision of land within its jurisdiction. Any other arrangement would be unfair to subdividers and might easily give rise to arbitrary or capricious regulation.

8. *Regulations*: Platting control, like all other control of private property or conduct, should be applied according to general rules and regulations, so as thereby to reduce the field of arbitrary discretion on the part of the planning commissions, so far as this is practicable to do by means of general rules and regulations. These general rules and regulations should be prepared, discussed, adopted, and promulgated like other laws or ordinances governing private conduct, so that the subdivider, in the preparation of his surveys and plats, may have a general indication of the standards to which he is expected to conform. Such platting regulations have been adopted by many planning commis-

sions throughout the country, and models and precedents are available.

9. *Arrangement of streets*: To ensure that streets or rights-of-way, whether dedicated as public streets or not, shall fit into each other and the ultimate street plan of the city and coordinate with that plan, is one of the primary purposes of giving control of land subdivision to planning commissions. The regulations which the commission is empowered to adopt with regard to platting should be primarily concerned with this end. The commission should, however, not be limited to this purpose of street coordination and should be empowered to take into account the supply of adequate open spaces for traffic, for utilities, for access of fire-fighting apparatus, for recreation, for light and air, for healthful population density, and for other public benefits.

10. *Width and area of lots*: One of the fundamental purposes of platting regulations, in addition to insuring a proper street plan, is also to insure that property shall not be subdivided into narrow lots which will bring in their train a host of evils, notably congestion of population, as well as an unsatisfactory type of housing development. Most platting regulations in force in the different states, therefore, include provisions as to the width, area, and arrangement of building lots, generally setting a minimum width below which lots cannot be platted.

Planning commissions should have the power to cooperate and agree with the subdivider upon restrictions as to height, area, and even use of buildings, so long as these do not authorize violation of the zoning ordinance. In other words, the planning commission and the subdivider may cooperate to bring about development of the territory of the subdivision in accordance with high standards of health and convenience. The commission is peculiarly well fitted for this, because it is, in most places, the maker of the original zone plan and passes upon all changes in that plan and, consequently, is well qualified to mutually adjust the standards of subdivisions and the general standards of the zone plan. These building restrictions, however, are so unmistakably legislative in their nature and so integrally related to the zoning ordinance that the planning commission should not have the power to impose those building restrictions upon the subdivider.

11. *Plat*: Properly speaking, this is not a planning matter, as it is not a matter of location and extent, but rather a matter of construction. Both to protect persons who buy the lots and to assure that the materials and locations of the improvements and utilities will conform to the proper standards, as well as to protect the city from the incurring of costs which should be borne by the original subdivider, this time of the approval of the plat is the best one at which to require these features. This includes not only the paving, but also such items as sidewalks, curbs, gutters, and service connections to various utility mains placed in the streets.

12. *Tentative approval*: It is manifestly fair to the subdivider that before he be put to the expense of paving, installing utilities, or other work connected with the development, he receive a reasonable degree of assurance that the plan of the subdivision will meet with the approval of the planning commission and that it will ultimately receive official approval. This is accomplished by the practice of a tentative approval, which tentative approval, in all but the most exceptional cases, will be later followed by the formal and final approval.

13. *May accept a bond*: In most cases, the subdivider will desire to proceed with the sale of some of the lots before carrying out the paving and other improvements throughout the whole subdivision, and if the plat of the whole subdivision is one which meets with the approval of the commission, there is no reason why the subdivider should be required to build all the streets and utilities throughout the subdivision, provided he secure to the city that the improvements will be carried out at the appropriate time.

14. *Commission*: Possibly the director of public works, city manager, or other administrative official in charge of street and utility work would be more appropriate officials than the planning commission for determining the time within which and the specifications according to which the improvements or utilities should be constructed. For the sake of simplicity, this power has, in the text of the act, been left with the planning commission, but those states which prefer to place these determinations within the jurisdiction of one of the administrative departments can easily vary at the text in this particular.

15. *Court review*: In some statutes, provision is expressly made for court review of the action of the planning commission on plats. There is a difference of opinion as to the necessity or advisability of such provision. The right of court review to test the legality of genuineness of the action of the planning commission always exists without express statutory provisions therefor. The only type of appeal to a court for which express provisions would be required would not be a review of the legality of the planning commission's disapproval of the plat, but rather a complete rehearing and redetermination by a court of the same administrative questions as were before the commission. In other words, a court review provision would be necessary only if the problem to be placed before the court be not one of law but be whether or not the plat should be approved as a matter of good city planning and platting. The courts, with less experience or technical knowledge in this field, are, as a rule, not qualified for as intelligent a decision on such administrative problems as are the planning commissions themselves. It seems a mistake to have administrative problems decided by tribunals less qualified to pass on these questions than the administrative board from whom the appeal is made. If court review be desired, the following draft of a section, to be modified to suit local practice, may be useful.

Section 15A. Court review: Any person aggrieved by any decision of the planning board concerning a plat or subdivision may present to a court of record a petition, duly verified, setting forth that such decision is illegal in whole or in part, specifying the grounds of the illegality. Such petition shall be presented to the court within 30 days after the filing of the decision in the office of the commission. Upon the presentation of such petition, the court may allow certiorari order directed to the planning commission to review such decision and shall prescribe therein the time within which return thereto shall be made and served upon the petitioner's attorney, which shall not be less than 10 days and may be extended by the court. The allowance of the order shall stay proceedings upon the decision appealed from. The planning commission shall not be required to return the original papers acted upon by it, but it shall be sufficient to return certified or sworn copies thereof, or of such portions thereof as may be called for by such order. The return shall concisely set forth such other facts as may be pertinent and material to show the grounds of the decision appealed from and shall be verified. If, upon the hearing, it shall appear to the court that testimony is necessary for the proper disposition of the matter, it may take evidence or appoint a referee to take such evidence as it may direct and report the same to the court with his findings of fact and conclusions of law, which shall constitute a part of the proceedings upon which the determination of the court shall be made. The court may reverse or affirm, wholly or partly, or may modify the decision brought up for review. Costs shall not be allowed against the municipality, unless it shall appear to the court that the planning commission acted with gross negligence or in bad faith or with malice in making the decision appealed from.

16. *Within 30 days*: In all fairness, the subdivider should not be subjected to unreasonable delay, and, consequently, this time limit is imposed upon the planning commission. Naturally, the planning commission will have to gather considerable information upon which to base its decision and in most cases will desire to consult with the city engineer and other city departments. In actual practice there will usually be back-and-forth discussions and negotiations between the subdivider and the planning commission, and this 30-day requirement will be waived by mutual consent where longer time is found necessary to reach an agreement.

17. *Disapproval*: The object of this requirement is to compel, so far as practicable, the planning commission's control over subdivisions to be exercised in accordance with general standards and principles and thus reduce the dangers of arbitrary action. The requirement that the ground of disapproval be expressed on the records of the commission has the further advantage that in case of a contest in court there will be official record of the reasons for and the justifications for the commission's decision.

18. *Notice*: In order to satisfy the requirement of due process of law, it is important that the subdivider should have proper notice of the action by the commission.

19. *Owner of land adjoining*: Obviously, owners of adjoining land have an interest in the layout of the subdivision, and it is, therefore, good practice to send them this notice required by the text of the act. Such notice, however, is not required by any principles of constitutional law; and if this provision for notifying of adjoining landowners be deemed too difficult or productive of unnecessary delay or trouble, it may be omitted without danger of impairing the legality of the procedure.

20. *Subdivisions*: As stated in a previous note, the power to make zoning regulations should be reposed exclusively in council. However, in the course of its work of passing upon subdivisions, the commission will frequently see the need of changes in the zoning regulations or changes in the zoning map. This sentence is inserted in the act for the purpose of pointing out to the commission its duty to bring the advisability of such changes to the attention of the council.

21. *Use, height, area, or bulk requirements*: As has been pointed out in a previous note, while the commission should not have the power to impose height, area, bulk, and use restrictions, cases will arise in which, in the course of negotiations between the subdivider and the commission, the subdivider will himself offer to impose certain building restrictions, and the commission's final approval of the plat will be based upon the assurance that such restrictions will be placed upon the land and carried out. This portion of the text of the act enables such agreements to be carried out by giving the agreed restrictions the force of law.

22. *Sells*: The act does not invalidate or attempt to invalidate the sale itself. This is by virtue of certain legal considerations, and especially on account of the practical consideration of the inadvisability of affecting titles or creating uncertainties as to title.

23. *Of a plat*: This section is limited to those transfers or sales of land in connection with which a plat or diagram of some kind is used. In the absence of such a penalty, irresponsible dealers are apt to use an unapproved or disapproved plat for facilitating sales by metes and bounds in a manner calculated to deceive innocent purchasers, and to create de facto subdivisions and streets that are serious misfits in the city plan, and bring needless expense and complications upon the municipality.

24. *By metes and bounds*: An effort is sometimes made by subdividers to evade those requirements by describing the property by metes and bounds. Therefore, this provision.

25. *Action*: The punishment for violation of this provision is a civil penalty of $100 for each offense, to be sued for and recovered in a civil action.

26. *County recorder*: The title of this public official will vary in different states, but the term here used is sufficiently descriptive to be understood.

27. *Authorize*: As the promoter of the subdivision usually or often needs a permit of some kind from the city before he can carry out is project, this prohibition will indirectly force him to submit his plat to the planning commission; which is, of course, the main object that this section of the act has in mind.

28. *Adopted a major street plan*: For reasons which have been stated in note 66, there cannot be any reasonable and intelligent control of subdivisions until the commission shall have made and adopted at least a major street plan of the territory in which the subdivision lies. Consequently, all sanctions behind this control, such as those provided in Section 18, should not go into effect until the city planning commission's accomplishments have reached at least this stage of a major street plan.

29. *Street plat*: The term "street plat" refers to the type of plat made by the commission and approved by a council provided for in Section 21.

30. *Commission*: This final and ultimate power granted to council to accept a street by a two-thirds vote, even in the face of the disapproval of the planning commission, is in line with and consistent with analogous provisions in other parts of the statute, such as the provision in Section 9 which permits council to overrule the planning commission on questions or the location of public buildings, works, and utilities. The theory of this has been discussed at some length in note 47. Council should be required, on all problems which relate themselves to planning, to submit the proposal to the planning commission; but, consistently with fundamental principles of democracy, the ultimate and final power of decision should rest with council. The requirement of a vote greater than an ordinary majority is fully consistent with these principles, as is evidenced by similar requirements in the case of a veto by the mayor or the chief executive or similar requirements governing the issuance of bonds.

A practical effect of the provisions of Section 18 is to abolish the common law or implied acceptance of future streets. Any state which has on its statute books express provisions inconsistent with these provisions of Section 18 should incorporate in the act an express repeal of such inconsistent provisions.

31. *Shall be erected*: This prohibition of buildings on unapproved streets may seem drastic, but experience has shown the necessity for such provision. The city plan cannot be protected in its integrity unless the control of subdivisions be substantially complete and effective. There is both danger to the city plan and an unfairness to those subdividers who do submit their plats if other subdividers succeed in escaping from this supervision. Every responsible method of forcing all subdivisions to be submitted to the commission should be taken. There is nothing unreasonable about this requirement. If neither the approval of the planning commission nor of two-thirds of council be obtainable, that certainly indicates that there is something wrong about the proposed street location.

There might be difficulty in enforcing this section in municipalities which do not have any system of building permits. Where there is provision in the statute or ordinance for appeals from refusals of building permits, such provision should apply to cases arising under this section.

32. See footnote 90.

33. *Official*: Instead of relying upon a blanket phrase, such as "other appropriate officials," it would be well for each state to designate by official title such official, or officials, as is or are appropriate to this function.

34. *Status of existing platting statutes*: Many states, at the time of enacting a general city planning act, may have on the statute books provisions for control of plats. The intention of this section is that, from the time that the planning commission puts itself in position to become the platting authority, the entire platting control should be transferred to that commission, and any existing statutory provisions which would stand in the way of such a transfer should be repealed. Up to that time, however, the existing platting statutes would remain in force and effect.

APPENDIX B
THE ALI MODEL LAND DEVELOPMENT CODE

[A cautionary note should be added at this point that the Model Land Development Code is only a model and that to date no state has adopted its provisions with respect to local government land use regulation. A few states have adopted certain statutes similar to the code with respect to state land use planning regulations. This appendix, therefore, should be consulted only if your state has adopted this code.]

Focusing on land use regulation and present and future development, the American Law Institute's *Model Land Development Code* embodies both zoning and subdivision controls within the same framework.[1] The implementation of the code is designed to be centralized in the local government of a community, with the state or region's planning interests being limited to development affecting a wider based community.[2] The adoption of the code by a state would repeal many of the separate enabling statutes including those modeled after the Standard Zoning Enabling Act (SZEA) and the Standard Planning Enabling Act (SPEA). Therefore the adoption of the code by a state would have a decisive impact on previously adopted local subdivision regulations. Far from becoming obsolete, the proposed Model Subdivision Regulations, with certain modifications, can be adopted to meet the requirements of the code and provide the local standards which will be essential guidelines to future development, in accordance with code provisions.

Two categories of alteration are necessary. First, key revision in nomenclature is required so that the traditional language used in the Model Subdivision Regulations conform to the new terminology of the code. The code assigns some new terms to old concepts to differentiate the requirements and scope of its provisions. Secondly, the procedural aspects of the Model Subdivision Regulations must be changed to meet the code's specifications. The planner and lawyer is advised that the ALI Code is still an enabling act, and local ordinances and regulations are required to implement zoning or subdivision regulations. Emphasizing the process rather than substantive standards, the code allows each local government to determine its own standards for development while relying on the structure of the code's procedural standards to prevent an abuse of constitutional rights. As a result of provisions for the regulation of subdivision into the code, certain important standards are supplied.[3] However, to assist in the adoption of the Model Subdivision Regulations at the local level which will comply with the code, a step-by-step analysis of the major code sections applicable to subdivisions follows.

Article I. General Provisions

Each state delegates to its political subdivisions under Section 1-102(1) all power available to a local government to "plan or otherwise encourage, regulate, or undertake the development of land" within its jurisdiction. Section 1.2 of the Subdivision Regulations should be revised to correspond with the state's granting of regulatory power.

Section 1-202 sets out the most important definition under the code—the meaning of "development." The scope of the code's authority encompasses all development, including "the division of land into two or more parcels" and "the making of any material change in the use or appearance of any structure or land." Subdivision as defined in the Model Regulations [6.2—Words and Terms Defined] clearly comes within the code's definitional latitude. Not only is the act of subdividing itself within the code's delegation development authority to localities, but planning of utility and sewerage systems and the laying out of streets is also included. To determine if the statutory meaning of development has been exceeded, Sections 1-202(2) and 1-202(3) are provided as guidelines.[4] The code stresses the physical development of land, giving limited recognition to social and economic factors affecting a local community's environment.[5]

Article II. Power to Regulate Development

If a local government decides to regulate its land development, a "development ordinance" is passed by the governing body. This development ordinance must be complied with when any development is undertaken or if a development permit is sought [2-101(1)]. The code sets out two primary types of development permissions which may be provided for in the ordinance: (1) a general development permit granting use as a right upon compliance with the terms of the ordinance; and (2) a special development permit granted only after an exercise of discretion by the administrative agency in accordance with the criteria of the code and any additional criteria contained in the ordinance [2-101(2)]. With regard to subdivision, the code states that if the development ordinance does not expressly provide for subdivision as of right,[6] it will come under the jurisdiction of the ordinance and require a special development permit. [2-201(1)(b)]. This special development permit shall be issued in accordance with Section 2-203 of the code, stipulating that each parcel resulting from the division must be found to be reasonably suitable for development under the general or special development provisions of the development ordinance. The Model Subdivision Regulations can either be adopted by the legislature of the local government in the form of special development provisions or adopted as regulations by the Land Development Agency, a body established to act on permit applications (2-102), as the criteria for their discretionary action in the granting of special development permits. This new agency, the Land Development Agency, constitutes a single administrative body replacing the former separate Planning Commission, Zoning Board of Adjustment, Architectural Review Board, or other administrative local agencies.

The decision as to who will adopt the subdivision regulations depends on whether the local government intends to retain the regulating power given to it by the state or whether the local government intends to retain the regulating power given to it by the state or whether it desires to delegate this power to the administrative body. (2-301) The Land Development Agency can be the local governing body or any committee, commission, board, or officer of the local government as determined by the legislature. Whatever the final structure evolving, the term Land Development Agency should be substituted for Planning Commission through the Model Subdivision Regulations (1.2—Authority).

Another type of special development permit pertaining to subdivision may be authorized in the development ordinance—a special permit for community service facilities. (2-206). For facilities to fall within the scope of this section, it must be shown that they comprise one of the services specified in the ordinance and that the proposed location is essential in order to provide such community services. If a special development permit for community services is authorized, dedication provisions in the Model Regulations may serve as the required standards. See the Model Regulations (4-4—Drainage and Storm Sewers, 4.5—Water Facilities, 4.6—Sewerage Facilities, 4.8—Utilities).

Before discussing procedure, it should be helpful to understand and coordinate the terminology used in the code with traditional usage. The special development permit corresponds to Final Plat Approval (2.4); Sketch Plat Approval (2.2) and Preliminary Plat Approval (2.3) are interim steps utilized to insure more efficient final proceedings. An "order" issued by the Land Development Agency is either approval, conditional approval, or denial of the developer's application.

Article II of the Model Subdivision Regulations specifies a procedure for subdivision application and approval. This process can be incorporated into the internal workings of the Land Development Agency either by prescription of the legislature or by authorized regulation of the Land Development Agency itself [2-301(2)].

The Land Development Agency exercises discretion upon the issuance of a special development permit and, where an exercise of discretion is involved, the code requires that notice be given and a public hearing be held [2-201(3)]. The hearing and notice are analogous to the public hearing provided for prior to preliminary and final plat approval in the Model Subdivision Regulations [2.4(4)]. Detailed formal hearing provisions are set out in the code (2-304). Notice of a public hearing is to be published in a newspaper of general circulation as well as given individually to designated parties. Such parties under the Model Subdivision Regulations are property owners "immediately adjacent extending one hundred (100) feet therefrom, or of that directly opposite thereto one hundred (100) feet therefrom, or of that directly opposite thereto extending one hundred (100) feet from the street frontage of such opposite property owners as are correct within the knowledge of the applicant as shown on the latest tax assessment roll." These notice provisions should be expanded to cover all property owners within five hundred (500) feet of the parcel on which development is proposed. Under Section 2-307 of the code, a neighborhood organization, an entity that has filed a request to receive notices of hearings [2-304(2)(d)], or any other designated person, agency, or organization, as required by the code is also entitled to notices of hearings.

The receipt of notice does not automatically create a right to be a formal party at the hearing. In order to be a party, a person or organization must show a significant interest in the subject matter of the hearing [2-304(5)]. The code, consequently, is more restrictive concerning participation in the hearing than the Model Subdivision Regulations which require only that the person heard be "interested."

Precise guidelines for conducting the hearings confirm the intent of the code to emphasize the "judicial" nature of the proceedings.[7] Therefore, the Model Subdivision Regulations should be revised to require that all testimony be under oath, [2-304(6)], that subpoena power be vested in the presiding officer[8] to compel the attendance of witnesses and the production of relevant papers requested by any party [2-304(6)], that a full record of the hearing be taken and kept, that every party have the opportunity to present evidence, argument, and cross-examination on all relevant issues [2-304(7)], and that a transcript be made by the Agency and be available on request [2-304(8)].

A local legislature may delegate to the Land Development Agency not only the powers authorized by the code, but other powers delegated by the local government [2-302(1)]. It may allow the Agency to establish rules prescribing supplementary criteria for the granting of development permits as long as these additional criteria remain consistent with the ordinance and code [2-302(3)]. The code recognizes that some states have intentionally made planning commissions independent so as to prevent political interests from dominating development. Hence, for states adhering to this philosophy, the code directs that an independently formed agency may adopt rules including the adoption or amendment of an ordinance required by the code [2-302(4)]. If the Agency does engage in this rule-making power, it must publish notice and comply with the legislative hearing requirements [2-303(2)].[9] According to the Model Subdivision Regulations, the Planning Commission may amend such provision and must hold public hearings prior to amendment (1.9). A close check must be made to assure that the Land Development Agency and the Planning Commission have corresponding authority.

Upon issuance of a development permit, the Land Development Agency must give notice to the developer and all parties to the hearing [2-306(1)(a)]. In addition, the permit grant is to be published in a newspaper of general circulation so that anyone challenging the grant under Article 9 of the code will have notification. Notice will also be given to neighborhood organizations (2-307) and other groups or parties showing a "significant interest in the subject matter" upon payment of reasonable fees [2-306(1)(c)]. An open public record must also be kept of all dates when notices were given.

If a developer's application for a development permit is denied in the Agency's order, the order is final for a year. After the year has passed, a new application can be submitted [2-306(3)]. By eliminating amendments after denial, the possibility for collusion between Agency personnel and the developer is reduced. Sketch Plat Approval, Preliminary Plat Approval, and Administrative Assistant's duties created in Article II of the Model Subdivision Regulations were purposely supplied to cope with this situation. Interim critiquing, as well as written reasons for the denial, should sufficiently acquaint the developer with the inadequacies of his application.

Changes in the development ordinance or applicable rule before a permit has been granted but after the application has been submitted must be complied with (2-309). This is in accord with established judicial precedent upholding the right of a municipality to deny administratively a building permit where the use would conflict with a proposed change in a zoning ordinance after public hearings have been held or general notice given. Absent a vested right, the municipality may either deny a permit or in fact revoke an existing permit.[10] The code in Section 2-309(1)(c) allows a court or the agency to ameliorate this situation "in the interests of justice," which would allow for the granting of permits where, for example, an agency delays the granting of a development permit intentionally to bring it within the bounds of a proposed amendment.[11] Once a development permit (final plat approval) has been granted, the developer has a right to complete subdivision development in accordance with the permit, but this right is qualified and may be lost [2-309(2)].

Dedication and money in lieu of land are basic elements regarding regulation of subdivision. The Model Subdivision Regulations, Article 5, provide for both, based upon precise formulas. Under Section 2-103(3) of the code, the Land Development Agency may not condition a permit.

> ...[on] payment or conveyance by the developer of any money, land, or other property, except the payment of reasonable fees for the filing of applications for development permits,[12] unless the development ordinance authorizes the Land Development Agency to condition a special development permit on (a) provision by the developer of streets, other rights-of-way, utilities, parks, and other open space, but with required provision must be of a quality and quantity no more than reasonably necessary for the proposed development; or (b) payment of an equivalent amount of money into a fund for the provision of streets, other rights-of-way, utilities, parks, or other open space if the Land Development Agency finds that the provision thereof under paragraph (a) is not feasible. . . .

It is imperative that the ordinance include the power of the Agency to condition approval on dedication requirements.[13]

Article III. Land Development Plans and Powers of Planning Governments
The code speaks in terms of a Land Development Plan (3-101) which would be the equivalent of the master or comprehensive plan under the SPEA and the Model Subdivision Regulations. Such a plan "may" adopt a statement setting forth its objectives, policies, and standards to guide public and private development of land which will be referred to as a Land Development Plan. Certain powers are granted to the local government conditioned on the adoption of a Land Development Plan by the local legislature.[14] Guidelines for the preparation of the Plan are stated in Section 3-102 with follow-up material in Section 3-104. The policy and purposes identified in the Model Regulations (1.4[1]-[2]) should be examined, but generally they conform to those in the code.[15] Provisions for the use of comprehensive studies and surveys as the Land Development Plan's foundation are contained in the code (3-103) and, when pertaining to subdivision, in the Model Regulations (1.4). By preparing the Plan from the perspective of problem solving as opposed to creating an ideal, the code, though regulating physical development, recognizes social and economic considerations through these current statistics.

The basic criticism of the Plan provisions of the Model Land Development Code focuses on the fact that a Plan is not required for basic Euclidean zoning but is mandatory if certain devices such as dedication of land, official map, flexible zoning are to be used. Just as the courts have begun to adopt the requirement that zoning reflect a comprehensive plan which can be influenced by state and regional policies,[16] the Model Land Development Code proposes to abolish the requirement of comprehensive planning except for "flexible" zoning devices such as floating zones, planned unit development, and cluster zoning, a prospect which exclusionary zoners may accept with glee, forsaking the "frills" for the standard large-lot zoning envelope.[17]

Section 2-211 allows a local government which has adopted a Land Development Plan to authorize the Land Development Agency to designate specially planned areas in which development will be permitted only in compliance with a plan of development for the entire area designated. In Section 2-11(3), the code specifies that the precise plan may include (a) the location and characteristics of streets, other rights-of-way and utilities; (b) the dimensions and grading of parcels and dimensions and siting of structures; (c) the location and characteristics of permissible types of development; and (d) any other planning matters which contribute to the development as a whole. All of these factors are important to the subdivider and should be evaluated in relation to the Subdivision Regulations. Under 2-211(5) a subdivider may submit his own plan to the Land Development

Agency with a written request for the adoption or amendment to the precise plan in accordance with the proposed plan.

A planning government is authorized by Section 3-201 to reserve areas for public uses. This "official map" is an extension of the SPEA's official map for the erection of buildings and determination of streets. Fitting easily into the kinds of public uses named by the code—streets, proposed schools, airports, public buildings (3-201(2))—the streets and Public Uses sections of the Model Subdivision Regulations provide for similar reservation of future land. At this point a caveat should be mentioned. Just as the zoning requirement contained in the Standard Zoning Enabling Act that zoning "be in accordance with a comprehensive Plan" has never been interpreted to require that a comprehensive plan precede adoption of a zoning ordinance,[18] a comprehensive plan need not precede subdivision regulations.[19] Indeed, the Model Land Development Code proposes to regulate all development, yet does not require a plan before implementation of controls but stipulates only that if a plan is adopted, certain special allowances will follow.[20]

NOTES

1. AMERICAN LAW INSTITUTE (ALI), A MODEL LAND DEVELOPMENT CODE, Proposed Official Draft No. 1 (1974) (hereinafter cited as ALI MODEL CODE).

2. ALI MODEL CODE, Articles 7 and 8, Tentative Draft No. 3 (1971).

3. The SPEA included minimum standards, but the code has not denoted any standards.

4. ALI MODEL CODE, Tentative Draft No. 2, Note at 15 (1970).

5. For a substantial criticism of this aspect of the code, *see* HAGMAN, URBAN PLANNING AND LAND DEVELOPMENT CONTROL LAW, 73 (1971): "This feature of the code is not particularly new. In fact, it falls short of expressing the view of modern planning which attempts to emphasize the unity of physical, social, and economic planning."

6. If subdivision regulation is expressly stated as constituting general development, restrictions can be imposed only if they are specified in the ordinance and the ordinance indicates the type of development (subdivision) to which they are to be applied [2-102(3)].

7. ALI MODEL CODE, Proposed Official Draft No. 1 at 94 (1974).

8. To make these hearings a viable and efficient process, the code supplies the Land Development Agency with the power to appoint a presiding officer from outside the agency, for example, from a pool of hearing examiners, or from the agency's staff [2-304(4)], Note at 93.

9. Legislative hearings require notice to be published in a newspaper of general circulation four weeks prior to the hearing and must contain material on the substance of the hearing, name of the officer of the agency where additional information is available, and give the time, place, and method of presentation. The agency must accept written recommendations and comments but may provide for oral testimony at its discretion (2-305).

10. A.J. Aberman, Inc. v. City of New Kensington, 377 Pa. 520, 105 A.2d 586 (1954); Beverly Bldg. Corp. v. Lower Merion Township, 409 Pa. 417, 187 A.2d 567 (1963); Gold v. Building Committee of Warren Borough, 334 Pa. 10, 5 A.2d 367 (1939); A.N. "Ab" Young Zoning Case, 360 Pa. 429, 61 A.2d 839 (1948); Chicago Title & Trust Co. v. Village of Palatine, 22 Ill. App. 2d 264, 268, 160 N.E.2d 697 (1959); Russian Hill Imp. Ass'n v. Board of Permit Appeals, 66 Cal. 2d 34, 56 Cal. Rptr. 672, 680-681, 423 P.2d 824 (1967). For a comprehensive review of the law in this area, *see* Freilich, *Interim Development Controls, Essential Tools for Implementing Flexible Planning and Zoning*, 49 J. OF URB. L. 65 (1971).

11. This is already established law in many jurisdictions under the SPEA or SZEA; *See* Dato v. Village of Vernon Hills, 91 Ill. App. 2d 111, 233 N.E. 2d 48 (1968); Krekeler v. St. Louis County Bd. of Zoning Adjustment, 422 S.W.2d 265 (Mo. 1967); Dubow v. Ross, 254 App. Div. 706, 3 N.Y.S. 2d 862 (1938); Shapiro v. Zoning Bd. of Adjustment, 377 Pa. 621, 105 A.2d 299 (1954); Udell v. Haas, 21 N.Y. 2d 463, 235 N.E.2d 847 (1968).

12. Fees that come under the exception in the code would encompass Sketch Plat Fees of $10.00 per lot (2.2[2][e]), Preliminary Plat Fees of $10.00 per lot (2.3[1][A]), Final Subdivision Plat application fees of $15.00 per lot, $20.00 for the Final Subdivision Plat reproduction of plans (2.4[1][a]), Inspection Fees (2.4[5]), $50.00 fee for street signs shown in construction plans (2.4[1][j], 4.3[1][g], and inspection of improvements equaling two percent of the amount of the performance bond or estimated cost of required improvements (3.2[1]).

13. The interpretation of the phrase "other open space" [2-103(3)(a)(b)] should specifically identify school sites in the ordinance if they are intended to be included. Section 4.9(2), Other Public Uses, does include school sites.

14. Section 3-101, Note at 143-4. Curiously, a Land Development Plan may not be reviewed by any court as to compliance with this code on the ground that the contents or purposes are not consistent with this code [3-101(3)]. *See infra* note 16 for differences under present judicial precedent.

15. Specifically, the purpose "to set forth the desired sequence, patterns, and characteristics of future development and its probable economic and social consequences" [3-102(3)] ac-knowledges the growing necessity of controlling growth in urban areas presently unable to cope adequately with increasing population. This is contained in the purposes of the Model Regulations. *See* Golden v. Planning Bd. of the Town of Ramapo, 30 N.Y.2d 359 (1972), *appeal dismissed* 409 U.S. 1003 (1972); *See also* Freilich, *Golden v. Planning Board of the Town of Ramapo, Establishing a New Dimension in American Planning Law,* 4 URB. LAW. No. 3, ix (1972); and Freilich, *Growth Controls,* 24 ZONING DIGEST 99 at 72 (1973).

16. Udell v. Haas, 21 N.Y.2d 463, 469 (1969); citing with approval Haar, *In Accordance with a Comprehensive Plan,* 68 HARV. L. REV. 1154 (1955) and rejecting the long-standing concept that zoning can be a "rational process" in itself. Kozesnik v. Township of Montgomery, 24 N.J. 154, 166, 131 A.2d 1 (1957).

17. For severe criticism of this draft proposal, *see* Shulman, The American Law Institute's Model State, Planning and Zoning Statutes, paper presented at 1968 ASPO National Planning and Zoning Conference, San Francisco.

18. Haar, *supra* note 16, at 1154.

19. Nelson, *The Master Plan and Subdivision Control,* 16 ME. L. REV. 107 (1964).

20. *See* Freilich and Seidel, *Recent Trends in Housing Law, Prologue to the 70's,* 2 URB. LAW. 1 (1970). For a comprehensive analysis of the ALI Model Land Development Code, *see* AMERICAN BAR ASSOCIATION, SECTION OF LOCAL GOVERNMENT LAW, 1973 COMMITTEE REPORTS, A MODEL LAND DEVELOPMENT CODE: SYNOPSIS AND COMMENT, 418 *et seq.*; and *Special Section—The ALI Model Land Development Code: Comments and Criticism,* 1971 LAND USE CONTROLS ANNUAL 1-116 (ASPO 1972).

The following forms are keyed to the Model Subdivision Regulations. They were compiled from several jurisdictions presently utilizing the Model Regulations and have been legally tested. In order to meet the political subdivision's specific requirements, the governing legislation should be consulted and the proper jurisdictional term for the words "local government" should be substituted wherever appropriate. With the conforming alterations, these forms will provide the important vehicle necessary to successfully carry out the objectives of the Model Subdivision Regulations.

FORM 1. APPLICATION FOR SKETCH PLAT APPROVAL
(To be filed in duplicate)

Date_____

1. Name of Subdivision _____

2. Name of Applicant_____ Phone _____

   Address _____
          (STREET NO. AND NAME)   (POST OFFICE)   (STATE)   (ZIP CODE)

3. Name of Local Agent _____

   Address _____
          (STREET NO. AND NAME)   (POST OFFICE)   (STATE)   (ZIP CODE)

4. Owner of Record _____ Phone _____

   Address _____
          (STREET NO. AND NAME)   (POST OFFICE)   (STATE)   (ZIP CODE)

5. Engineer _____ Phone _____

   Address _____
          (STREET NO. AND NAME)   (POST OFFICE)   (STATE)   (ZIP CODE)

6. Land Surveyor _____ Phone _____

   Address _____
          (STREET NO. AND NAME)   (POST OFFICE)   (STATE)   (ZIP CODE)

7. Attorney _____ Phone _____

   Address _____
          (STREET NO. AND NAME)   (POST OFFICE)   (STATE)   (ZIP CODE)

8. Subdivision Location: on the _____ side of _____

   _____feet _____ of _____
              (DIRECTION)   (STREET)

9. Postal Delivery Area_____ School District _____

10. Total Acreage _____ Zone_____ Number of Lots _____

    Fee Required at $_____ per Lot _____

11. Tax Map Designation: Section_____ Lots _____

12. Is any open space being offered as part of this subdivision application?

    _____

    If so, what amount? _____

13. Has the Board of Zoning Adjustment (Board of Zoning Appeals) granted any variance, exception, or special permit concerning this property?

    _____

    If so, list Case No. and Name _____

14. Is any variance from the Subdivision Regulations requested? _____

    If so, describe _____

15. Proposed Classification of Subdivision _____
    (Major or Minor)

16. Does the application involve a flexible zoning application? _____

    If so, describe _____

17. Attach seven (7) copies of Sketch Plat.

    The applicant hereby consents to the provisions of § 3.5(4) of the subdivision regulations providing that the decision of the Planning Commission shall be made within thirty (30) days after the close of the public hearing on final plat approval.

List all contiguous holdings in the same ownership (as defined in the Subdivision Regulations).

    Section _____ Lot(s) _____

Attached hereto is an affidavit of ownership indicating the dates the respective holdings of land were acquired, together with the book and page of each conveyance into the present owner as recorded in the _____ County _____ Office. This affidavit shall indicate the legal owner of the
(Clerk or Recorder of Deeds)

property, the contract owner of the property, and the date the contract of sale was executed. IN THE EVENT OF CORPORATE OWNERSHIP: A list of all directors, officers, and stockholders of each corporation owning more than five percent (5%) of any class of stock must be attached.

STATE OF_____)

COUNTY OF_____) SS:

I, _____ hereby depose and say that all of the above statements and the statements contained in the papers submitted here-with are true.

_____

Mailing Address_____
                              (STREET)

_____
(CITY)   (STATE)   (ZIP CODE)

Subscribed and sworn to before me this day of _____

_____
(CITY)   (STATE)   (ZIP CODE)

MY COMMISSION EXPIRES:

FORM 2. SKETCH PLAT CHECKLIST
(For Local Government Use Only)

Subdivision _____

_____ 1. Two copies of application   _____ 2. Received check for $ _____
(_____ lots at $ _____)

_____ 3. Seven copies of Plat (At scale of 1" = 100' or less) showing the following information:

_____ 4. Legal Description (Lot, Section, Township, City, Village, County)

_____ 5. Name of Proposed Subdivision _____ 6. Graphics Scale

_____ 7. North Arrow   _____ 8. Date

_____ 9. Property Owners Name and Address

_____ 10. Covenants, Liens and Encumbrances

_____ 11. Conveyance (Book and Page) to Owner

_____ 12. Name and Address of licensed professional engineer, surveyor preparing the Sketch Plat, Attorney.

_____ 13. Location of Property Lines   _____ 14. Existing Easements

_____ 15. Burial Grounds   _____ 16. Railroad Rights-of-Way

_____ 17. Water Courses   _____ 18. Existing Wooded Areas

_____ 19. Trees eight inches (8") or more in diameter, measured four feet (4') above ground level.

_____ 20. Location, width, and names of all existing or platted streets or other public ways within or immediately adjacent to tract.

_____ 21. Names of adjoining property owners from the latest County, City, or Township assessment rolls within five hundred feet (500') of any perimeter boundary of the subdivision.

_____ 22. Location, sizes, elevations and slopes of existing sewers, water mains, culverts, and other underground structures within the tract and immediately adjacent thereto.

_____ 23. Existing permanent buildings.

_____ 24. Utility poles on or immediately adjacent to the site and utility right-of-way.

_____ 25. Approximate Topography, at the same scale as the Sketch Plat.

_____ 26. The approximate location and widths of proposed streets.

_____ 27. Preliminary proposals for connection with existing water supply and sanitary sewerage systems, preliminary provisions for collecting and discharging surface water drainage.

_____ 28. The approximate location, dimensions and areas of all proposed or existing lots.

_____ 29. The approximate location, dimensions, and areas of all parcels of land proposed to be set aside for park or playground use or other public use or for the use of property owners in the proposed subdivision.

_____ 30. The location of temporary stakes to enable the Planning Commission to find and appraise features of the sketch plat in the field.

_____ 31. Whenever the sketch plat covers only a part of an applicant's contiguous holdings, the applicant shall submit, at the scale of no more than two hundred feet (200') to the inch, a sketch in pen or pencil of the proposed subdivision area, together with its proposed street systems and an indication of the probable future street and drainage system for the remaining portion of the tract.

_____ 32. A vicinity map showing streets and other general developments of the surrounding area at a scale of 1" = 100'; the sketch plat shall show all school and improvement district lines and zoning district lines with the zones properly designated.

_____ 33. Has applicant or agent discussed sketch plat with Administrative Assistant to Planning Commission prior to filing?

Date of Conference _____

With Whom _____

_____ 34. Submitted to Community Design Review Committee on _____

_____

_____ 35. Referred to the following officials, agencies, and municipalities:

      Official, Agency or Local Government   Date

      _____   _____

      _____   _____

      _____   _____

      _____   _____

      _____   _____

_____ 36. Reports (or protests) from Officials, Agencies and Local Governments received:

      Official, Agency or Local Government   Date

      _____   _____

      _____   _____

      _____   _____

      _____   _____

      _____   _____

_____ 37. Date sketch plat referred to Planning Commission _____

_____ 38. Date of Planning Commission Field Trip _____

_____ 39. Date of Planning Commission Meeting on Sketch Plat _____

———— 40. Date of Approval of Sketch Plat ——————————————————

———— 41. Conditions and Remarks by Planning Commission ——————————

——————————————————————————————————

——————————————————————————————————

——————————————————————————————————

FORM 3. APPLICATION FOR
PRELIMINARY PLAT APPROVAL
(To be filed in duplicate)

Date _____

Major _____

1. Name of Subdivision _____ Minor_____

2. Name of Applicant _____ Phone _____

   Address _____
          (STREET NO. AND NAME)   (POST OFFICE)   (STATE)   (ZIP CODE)

3. Name of Local Agent _____ Phone _____

   Address _____
          (STREET NO. AND NAME)   (POST OFFICE)   (STATE)   (ZIP CODE)

4. Owner of Record _____ Phone _____

   Address _____
          (STREET NO. AND NAME)   (POST OFFICE)   (STATE)   (ZIP CODE)

5. Engineer _____ Phone _____

   Address _____
          (STREET NO. AND NAME)   (POST OFFICE)   (STATE)   (ZIP CODE)

6. Land Surveyor_____ Phone _____

   Address _____
          (STREET NO. AND NAME)   (POST OFFICE)   (STATE)   (ZIP CODE)

7. Attorney_____ Phone _____

   Address _____
          (STREET NO. AND NAME)   (POST OFFICE)   (STATE)   (ZIP CODE)

8. Subdivision Location: on the _____ side of _____

   _____ feet _____ of _____
             (DIRECTION)   (STREET)

9. Postal Delivery Area_____ School District _____

10. Total Acreage _____ Zone _____ Number of Lots _____

11. Tax Map Designation: Section _____ Lot(s) _____

12. Has the Zoning Board of Appeals (Board of Zoning Adjustment) granted variance, exception, or special permit concerning this property? _____

    If so, list Case No. and Name _____

13. Date of sketch plat approval _____

14. Have any changes been made since this plat was last before the Board?

    _____ If so, describe _____

15. List all land proposed to be subdivided _____

    _____

    _____

16. Owners of land 100 feet adjacent or opposite _____

    _____

    _____

17. Attach ten (10) copies of proposed preliminary plat.

18. Attach three (3) copies of construction plans.

19. List all contiguous holdings in the same ownership: _____

    Section _____ Lot(s) _____

    The applicant hereby consents to the provisions of § 3.5(4) of the subdivision regulations providing that the decision of the Planning Commission shall be made within thirty (30) days after the close of the public hearing on final plat approval.

    Attached hereto is an affidavit of ownership indicating the dates the respective holdings of land were acquired, together with the book and page of each conveyance into the present owner as recorded in the County Recorder of Deeds (County Clerk's) office. This affidavit shall indicate the legal ownership of the property, the contract owner of the property, and the date the contract of sale was executed.

N THE EVENT OF CORPORATE OWNERSHIP: A list of all directors, officers, stockholders of each corporation owning more than five percent (5%) of any class of stock must be attached.

STATE OF_____)

COUNTY OF_____) SS:

I, _____ hereby depose and say that all of the above statements and the statements contained in the papers submitted herewith are true.

_____

Mailing Address_____

(STREET)

_____

(CITY)   (STATE)   (ZIP CODE)

Subscribed and sworn to before me this day of _____

_____

(CITY)   (STATE)   (ZIP CODE)

MY COMMISSION EXPIRES:

FORM 4. PRELIMINARY PLAT CHECKLIST

_____ 1. Two copies of application   _____ 2. Received check for $ _____
(_____ lots at $ _____)

_____ 3. Ten copies of plat (at a scale of not more than 1" = 100').

_____ 4. Location of property with respect to surrounding property and streets.

_____ 5. Names of all adjoining property owners, or names of adjoining developers.

_____ 6. Names of adjoining streets.

_____ 7. Location and dimensions of all boundary lines of the property in feet and decimals of a foot.

_____ 8. Location of existing streets.

_____ 9. Location of existing easements.

_____ 10. Location of existing waterbodies, streams, and other pertinent features such as swamps, railroads, buildings, parks, cemeteries, drainage ditches, bridges, etc.

_____ 11. Locations, dimensions, and areas of all proposed or existing lots.

_____ 12. Location and dimensions of all property proposed to be set aside for park or playground use, or other public or private reservation, with designation of the purpose thereof, and conditions, if any, of the dedication or reservation.

_____ 13. Date of plat.   _____ 14. Approximate true north point.

_____ 15. Scale of plat.   _____ 16. Title of subdivision.

_____ 17. Data from which the location, bearing, and length of all lines can be determined and reproduced on the ground.

_____ 18. Location of all proposed monuments.

_____ 19. Names of new streets as approved by the Planning Commission.

_____ 20. Indication of the use of any lot and all uses other than residential.

_____ 21. Blocks consecutively numbered or lettered.

_____ 22. Lots in each block consecutively numbered.

_____ 23. Explanation of drainage easements.

_____ 24. Explanation of site easements.

_____ 25. Explanation of shade tree easements.

_____ 26. Explanation of reservations.

_____ 27. All information shown on sketch plat.

_____ 28. Endorsement of owner.

_____ 29. Construction plans (at a scale of not more than 1" = 50')

     _____ A. Profiles showing existing and proposed evaluations along center lines of all roads. Where a proposed road intersects an existing road or roads, the elevation along the center line of the existing road or roads within one hundred (100) feet of the intersection, shall be shown.

     _____ B. Approximate radii of all curves, lengths of tangents, and central angles on all streets.

     _____ C. If required, where steep slopes exist, cross-sections of all proposed streets at one-hundred foot stations shown at five (5) points as follows: On a line at right angles to the center line of the street, and said elevation points shall be at the center line of the street, each property line, and points twenty-five (25) feet inside each property line.

     _____ D. Plans and profiles showing the locations and typical cross-section of street pavements including curbs and gutters, sidewalks, drainage easements, servitudes, rights-of-way, manholes, and catch basins.

     _____ E. Locations of street trees.

     _____ F. Location of street lighting standards.

_____ G. Location of street signs.

_____ H. Location, size, and invert elevations of existing and proposed sanitary sewers, stormwater drains, and fire hydrants, showing connection to any existing and proposed utility systems.

_____ I. Location and size of all water, gas, or other underground utilities or structures.

_____ J. Location, size, elevation, and other appropriate description of any existing facilities or utilities including, but not limited to, existing streets, sewers, drains, water mains, easements, water bodies, streams and other pertinent features such as swamps, railroads, buildings, features noted on the Official Map (Major Street Plan) or Master (Comprehensive) Plan, and each tree with a diameter of eight (8) inches or more measured twelve (12) inches above ground level, at the point of connection to proposed facilities and utilities within the subdivision.

_____ K. Water elevations of adjoining lakes or streams at date of survey and approximate high and low water elevations referred to the U.S.G.S. datum plane.

_____ L. If the subdivision borders a lake, river, or stream, the distances and bearings of a meander line established not less than twenty (20) feet back from the ordinary high water mark of such waterways.

_____ M. Topography at the same scale as sketch plat with contour interval of two feet.

_____ N. Other specifications and references required by the local government construction standards and specifications, including a site-grading plan for the entire subdivision.

_____ O. Title, name, address and signature of professional engineer and surveyor.

_____ P. Date, including revision dates.

_____ Q. Notation of approval.

FORM 5. APPLICATION FOR FINAL PLAT APPROVAL
(To be filed in duplicate)

Date _____

Major _____

1. Name of Subdivision _____ Minor _____

2. Name of Applicant _____ Phone _____

   Address _____
   (Street No. and Name)   (Post Office)   (State)   (Zip Code)

3. Name of Local Agent _____ Phone _____

   Address _____
   (Street No. and Name)   (Post Office)   (State)   (Zip Code)

4. Owner of Record _____ Phone _____

   Address _____
   (Street No. and Name)   (Post Office)   (State)   (Zip Code)

5. Engineer _____ Phone _____

   Address _____
   (Street No. and Name)   (Post Office)   (State)   (Zip Code)

6. Land Surveyor_____ Phone _____

   Address _____
   (Street No. and Name)   (Post Office)   (State)   (Zip Code)

7. Attorney_____ Phone _____

   Address _____
   (Street No. and Name)   (Post Office)   (State)   (Zip Code)

8. Subdivision Location: on the _____ side of _____

   _____ feet _____ of _____
                  (Direction)   (Street)

9. Postal Delivery Area_____ School District _____

10. Total Acreage _____ Zone _____ Number of Lots _____

11. Tax Map Designation: Section _____ Lot(s) _____

12. Has the Zoning Board of Appeals (Board of Zoning Adjustment) granted variance, exception, or special permit concerning this property? _____

    If so, list Case No. and Name _____

13. Date of sketch plat approval _____

14. Date of preliminary plat approval _____

15. Have any changes been made since this plat was last before the Commission? _____

    List all contiguous holdings in the same ownership:

    Section _____ Lot(s) _____

Attached hereto is an affidavit of ownership indicating the dates the respective holdings of land were acquired, together with the book and page of each conveyance into the present owner as recorded in the County Recorder of Deeds (County Clerk) Office. This affidavit shall indicate the legal owner of the property, the contract owner of the property, and the date the Contract of Sale was executed. IN THE EVENT OF CORPORATE OWNERSHIP: A list of all directors, officers, and stockholders of each corporation owning more than five percent (5%) of any class of stock must be attached.

The applicant hereby consents to the provisions of § 3.5(4) of the subdivision regulations providing that the decision of the Planning Commission shall be made within thirty (30) days after the close of the public hearing on final plat approval.

STATE OF_____)

COUNTY OF_____) SS:

I, _____ hereby depose and say that all of the above statements and the statements contained in the papers submitted herewith are true.

_____

Mailing Address_____
(STREET)

_____
(CITY)   (STATE)   (ZIP CODE)

Subscribed and sworn to before me this day of _____

_____
(CITY)   (STATE)   (ZIP CODE)

MY COMMISSION EXPIRES:

FORM 6. CHECKLIST FOR FILING OF
FINAL SUBDIVISION PLAT

Major _____

Plat Name_____ Minor _____

Location _____

Owner _____

_____

1. Date of Final Approval _____

    Date(s) of Reapproval _____

2. Bonds:
    Public Improvement _____

    Sewer _____

    Other_____

    Other_____

    (Bond Resolutions Provided On _____)

3. Fees: (To Planning Board)
    A. Money in lieu of land _____

    B. Shade Tree Deposit _____

    C. Two percent (2%) Inspection Fee_____

    D. Money In Lieu of Public Improvement _____

    E. Recorder of Deeds (County Clerk) (For Filing of Plat) _____

    F. Street Signs _____

    G. Other _____

    H. Other_____

4. Linen:
   Received _____
   Checked:

   _____ a. Signature Block

   _____ b. Owner's Signature

   _____ c. Tax Lot Designations

   _____ d. Seal(s)

   _____ e. _____

   _____ f. _____

   _____ g. _____

   _____ h. _____

5. Instruments Necessary for Public Improvements (Checked by Local Government Engineer)
   (a) Off-Site (Easements, Servitudes, Agreements, Deeds)

   1. _____

   2. _____

   3. _____

   4. _____

   (b) Streets

   1. _____

   2. _____

   3. _____

   4. _____

(c) Road Widening (City, County, Town, State, Village)

1. _____

2. _____

3. _____

4. _____

(d) On-Site Drainage (Easements)

1. _____

2. _____

3. _____

4. _____

(e) Sewer Line (Easements)

1. _____

2. _____
                         (Purpose)

(f) Reserved Lands

1. _____

2. _____

(g) Other Right-of-Way

1. _____

2. _____

(h) Conformity to Engineering Report

1. _____

(Instruments checked above to be recorded immediately)

APPROVED FOR FILING: _____
LOCAL GOVERNMENT ENGINEER

6. Administrative Assistant to Planning Commission

   1.   List of Stockholders   _____

   2.   Performance Bonds   _____

   3.   (a)   Off-Site Instruments   _____

         (b)   Title Report*   _____
         (c)   Releases of any existing
               mortgages   _____

         (d)   Check for recording   _____

   4.   (a)   On-Site Instruments   _____

         (b)   Agreement of Dedication _____

         (c)   Title Report*   _____
         (d)   Releases of any existing
               mortgages   _____

         (e)   Check for Recording
               (Agreement and Releases) _____

   5.   Water Supply Distribution
        Formation (Special District) _____

   6.   Sanitary Sewer Formation
        (Special District)   _____

               Instruments Received   _____
                                   ADMINISTRATIVE ASSISTANT

               Instruments Approved _____
                                   LOCAL GOVERNMENT ATTORNEY

*Can be included in one title report.

        Filed _____
        Book _____
        Page _____

FORM 7. RESOLUTION OF PLANNING COMMISSION APPROVING FINAL SUBDIVISION PLAT

Name of Plat _____

Name of Owner _____

PLANNING COMMISSION

_____

_____
ADDRESS

The following is an extract from the minutes of the meeting of the _____

_____ Planning Commission held _____ .

1. That roads, sidewalks, curbs, drainage systems, storm drains, catch basins, rights-of-way, easements, open spaces, park and recreation sites, and other improvements and installations, etc., be constructed as set forth on such approved final plat, including the construction of all off-site improvements and drainage systems.

2. That all of the aforesaid improvements and installations be constructed in accordance with local government specifications. That in addition to the improvements and installations set forth on the approved final plat, all stipulations and undertakings appearing in the minutes of the Planning Commission, together with the Agreement offering irrevocable dedication of such improvements which the owner or developer has agreed to, are incorporated in this Resolution by reference, as well as all Agreements, regulations, rules, resolutions and orders of the local government.

3. That said _____ as owners of the above plat, execute and file with the Clerk a performance bond in the amount of $ _____ sufficient to cover the full cost of said improvements as estimated by the Commission or other appropriate local government officials or agencies, which performance bond shall be issued by a Bonding or Surety Company to be approved by the Governing Body and shall also be approved by such Governing Body as to form sufficiency and manner of execution. Said performance bond shall run for a term of _____ ( ) years (not exceeding _____ ( ) years), provided, however, that the terms of such performance bond may be extended by the Planning Commission with the consent of the parties

thereto as provided by law, for a period not to exceed one (1) additional year. The bond shall also provide, among other things, that in the event that any required improvements have not been installed and deeded to the municipality free and clear of all encumbrances as provided by this Resolution, with the terms of such performance bond, the Governing Body may thereupon declare said performance bond to be in default and collect the sum remaining payable thereunder and apply said sum towards obtaining free and clear title to said improvements, including payment of all liens and encumbrances on the property and all costs and expenses, including legal fees, incurred by the local government in acquiring free and clear title, and install such improvements as are covered by such performance bond commensurate with the extent of building development that has taken place in the subdivision but not exceeding in cost, the amount of such proceeds.

4. That the final plat will not be signed by the Chairman of the Planning commission until the submission and approval of the required bond by the Governing Body of the local government.

5. That said bond will not be released or reduced until the public improvements are approved as built by the office of the local government engineer and all improvements, roads, rights-of-way, easements, open spaces, park and recreation sites, including off-site improvements, and land have been deeded to and accepted by the local government, in accordance with the procedure for dedication of improvements adopted by the Governing Body and after approval of the Planning Commission, after public hearing as provided for by law, subject to approval by the Governing Body.

6. This Resolution expires on _____

STATE OF_____)

COUNTY OF_____) SS:

I,_____ , Administrative Assistant to the Planning Commission of the Local Government, hereby certify that I have compared the foregoing copy of an extract from the minutes of the _____ Planning Commission held_____ , with the original now in my office, and find the same to be a true and correct transcript therefrom.

IN TESTIMONY WHEREOF, I have hereunder subscribed my name and affixed the seal of said municipality this _____ day of _____, 19___.

_____
ADMINISTRATIVE ASSISTANT
PLANNING COMMISSION

FORM 8. OFFER OF IRREVOCABLE DEDICATION

AGREEMENT made this _____ day of _____, 19___, by and between _____

_____, a _____, having its office and place of business at

_____ , hereinafter designated as Developer, and the local gov-

ernment having its principal office at _____ , hereinafter
designated as the local government;

WHEREAS, the Planning Commission of _____ is in the

process of approving a subdivision plat entitled _____ ,

dated _____ , made by _____ ; and

WHEREAS, said map designates certain public improvements consisting of

_____

_____

to be dedicated to the local government free and clear of all encumbrances and
liens, pursuant to the regulations and requirements of the local government; and

WHEREAS, the developer, simultaneously herewith shall post a performance bond with the municipality for the construction, maintenance, and
dedication of said improvements; and

WHEREAS, the developer is desirous of offering for dedication the said
improvements and land to the local government more particularly described in
Schedule _____ attached hereto; and

WHEREAS, the developer has delivered deeds of conveyance to the Local
Government for the said land and improvements as described herein;

NOW, THEREFORE, in consideration of the sum of $1.00 lawful money of
the United States paid by the local government to the developer and other good
and valuable consideration, it is mutually
AGREED as follows:

1. The developer herewith delivers to the local government deeds of
conveyance for the premises described in Schedule _____ attached hereto, said
delivery being a formal offer of dedication to the local government to be held by
the local government until the acceptance or rejection of such offer of dedication
by the Governing Body.

2. The developer agrees that said formal offer of dedication is irrevocable
and can be accepted by the local government at any time.

3. The developer agrees to complete the construction and maintenance of the land and improvements pursuant to the performance bond and the requirements of the Planning Commission of the local government and any ordinances, regulations, requirements, covenants, and agreements that may be imposed by the local government with respect thereto and upon acceptance by the local government of the offer of dedication shall within thirty (30) days after written notice from the local government of the said acceptance of the offer of dedication, shall furnish to the local government a title insurance policy issued by a licensed title insurance company authorized to do business in the State of _____ in a minimum amount of $_____, certifying that the premises are free and clear of all liens and encumbrances and shall furnish to the local government a check for all necessary fees and taxes to record the deeds heretofore delivered.

4. That this irrevocable offer of dedication shall run with the land and shall be binding on all assigns, grantees, successors, or heirs of the developer.

(SEAL)

ATTEST: LOCAL GOVERNMENT

_____   By _____
COUNTY CLERK (RECORDER OF DEEDS)

SSTATE OF_____)

COUNTY OF_____) SS:

On the _____ day of _____, 19___, before me personally came _____, to me known, who being by me duly sworn, did depose and say that he is the individual described in and who executed the foregoing instrument, and he duly acknowledged to be that he executed the same.

STATE OF_____)

COUNTY OF_____) SS:

On the _____ day of _____, 19___, before me personally came _____, to me known, who being by me duly sworn, did depose and say that he resides at _____, that he is the _____ of _____, the corporation described in and which executed the foregoing instrument; that he knows the seal of said corporation; that the seal affixed to said instrument is the seal of said corporation and was affixed thereto by order of the Board of Directors of said corporation and that he signed his name thereto by like order.

_____

STATE OF_____)

COUNTY OF_____) SS:

On the _____ day of _____, 19__, before me personally came _____, to me known, who being by me duly sworn, did depose and say that he resides at _____, that he is the _____ of _____, the corporation described in and which executed the foregoing instrument; that he knows the seal of said corporation; that the seal affixed to said instrument is the seal of said corporation and was affixed thereto by order of the Board of Directors of said corporation and that he signed his name thereto by like order.

_____

FORM 9. PERFORMANCE BOND
(To be required in this form only)

KNOW ALL MEN BY THESE PRESENTS, That We, _____

_____, as Principals, _____,

and the _____ INSURANCE COMPANY, a

Corporation authorized to do business in the State of_____, having an

office and place of business at_____,

as Surety, are held and firmly bound unto the municipality, as Obligee, in the

sum of DOLLARS ($_____) lawful money of the United States, for the
payment whereof to the Obligee, the Principal and the Surety bind themselves,
their heirs, executors, administrators, successors, and assigns, jointly and sever-
ally, firmly to these presents:

SIGNED, SEALED AND DATED, this _____ day of _____, 19____.

WHEREAS, application was made to the Obligee for approval of a subdivision
shown on plat entitled "_____

_____

_____

_____"

filed with the Administrative Assistant to the Planning Commission of _____
_____ on _____, 19____, said final plat was approved upon
certain conditions, one of which is that a performance bond in the amount of
($_____), to be filed with the _____ Clerk to guarantee
certain improvements in said subdivision;

NOW, THEREFORE, THE CONDITION OF THIS OBLIGATION is such
that if the above named Principal shall within two (2) years from the date
hereof (time may be extended for one year only by the Planning Commission
of _____ with the consent of the parties) will and truly make and
perform the required improvements and construction of public improvements
in said subdivision in accordance with the local government specifications and

the Resolution of _____, 19____, then this obligation to be void; otherwise to remain in full force and effect.

It is hereby understood and agreed that in the event that any required improvements have not been installed as provided by said Resolution, within the term of this Performance Bond, the Governing Body may thereupon declare this bond to be in default and collect the sum remaining payable thereunder and upon receipt of the proceeds thereof, the local government shall install such improvements as are covered by this bond and commensurate with the extent of building development that has taken place in the subdivision but not exceeding the amount of such proceeds.

_____
PRINCIPAL

_____
PRINCIPAL

_____ INSURANCE COMPANY

By_____
ATTORNEY-IN-FACT

BOND NO._____

FORM 10. ACKNOWLEDGMENTS

COPARTNERSHIP

STATE OF_____)

COUNTY OF_____) SS:

On this _____ day of _____, 19____, before me personally appeared _____, to me known and known to me to be one of the firm of _____, described in and who executed the foregoing instrument, and he thereupon acknowledged to me that he executed the same as and for the act and deed of said firm.

_____

CORPORATE

STATE OF_____)

COUNTY OF_____) SS:

On this _____ day of _____, 19____, before me personally appeared _____, to me known, who, being by me first duly sworn, did depose and say that he resides in _____; that he is the _____ of _____, the corporation described in and which executed the foregoing instrument; that he knows the corporate seal of said corporation; that the corporate seal affixed to said instrument is such corporate seal; that it was so affixed by order and authority of the Board of Directors of said corporation, and that he signed his name thereto by like order and authority.

_____

INDIVIDUAL

STATE OF_____)

COUNTY OF_____) SS:

On this _____ day of _____, 19____, before me personally appeared _____, to me known and known to me to be the individual described in and who executed the foregoing instrument and _____ acknowledged to me that _____ executed the same.

_____